THE MORAL
OBLIGATION
TO BE
INTELLIGENT

Edited and with an Introduction by

LEON WIESELTIER

FARRAR • STRAUS • GIROUX

New York

THE MORAL
OBLIGATION
TO BE
INTELLIGENT

Selected Essays

LIONEL
TRILLING

Farrar, Straus and Giroux
19 Union Square West, New York 10003

Copyright © 2000 by the Estate of Lionel Trilling
Introduction copyright © 2000 by Leon Wieseltier

Published in 2000 by Farrar, Straus and Giroux
First paperback edition, 2001

Library of Congress Cataloging-in-Publication Data
Trilling, Lionel, 1905–1975.
    The moral obligation to be intelligent : selected essays / by Lionel Trilling ; edited and
with an introduction by Leon Wieseltier. — 1st ed.
        p.   cm.
    Includes bibliographical references (p.   ) and index.
    ISBN 0-374-52799-7 (pbk.)
    I. Wieseltier, Leon. II. Title.

PS3539.R56 M6 2000
812´.52—dc21

                                                                                99-087875

Designed by Jonathan D. Lippincott

In memory of
Diana Trilling

Contents

Contents

Introduction

by Leon Wieseltier

In 1971 Lionel Trilling gave a talk at Purdue University on the subject of his work as a critic. He spoke autobiographically, which was not his custom. His notes for the occasion dwell at length on his experience as an undergraduate at Columbia College in the 1920s. "The great word in the college was INTELLIGENCE," he wrote. "An eminent teacher of ours, John Erskine, provided a kind of slogan by the title he gave to an essay of his which, chiefly through its title, gained a kind of fame: THE MORAL OBLIGATION TO BE INTELLIGENT."

Trilling must have startled his audience when he submitted that as a young man "I did not count myself among those who were intelligent." Instead "I was intuitive; and I rather prided myself on a quality that went by the name of subtlety." He did not aspire to intelligence, he explained, because it was not a quality that was required of a novelist, and he aspired to be a novelist, a calling that required "only a quick eye for behavior and motive and a feeling heart." In Trilling's criticism, certainly, there is no trace of this depleted conception of the novel. In 1947 he gave his own demonstration of the utility of "intelligence" for the writer of fiction in his novel *The Middle of the Journey*, which shrewdly examined the fideist mentality of American Communism and recorded the disfigurements that ideology visits upon experience. (It included a portrait of Whittaker

Chambers as George Eliot might have drawn him.) It is hard to imagine a waking moment in Trilling's life in which he was not consecrated to the intellect and to its cause. He had almost no higher term of approbation than to call something or someone "exigent" and "strenuous." But youth is unexigent and unstrenuous. In any event, Trilling's early indifference to intellectuality did not last long. (As he later remarked fondly about Elliot Cohen, "he never played the game of being young.") And so he recalled that he was soon "seduced into bucking to be intelligent by the assumption which was prepotent in Columbia College—that intelligence was connected with literature, that it was advanced by literature."

It must be said that Trilling's professor did not always live up to his own maxim. John Erskine's works included the novels *Galahad: Enough of His Life to Explain His Reputation* and *Penelope's Man: The Homing Instinct*, and a particularly witless essay in misogyny called *The Influence of Women—And Its Cure*. (It concludes with a coarse colloquium among Socrates, Diogenes, Herodotus, Pericles, Casanova, and André Chénier.) But still Erskine earned a place in the history of the humanities in America. A scholar of the English literature of the Renaissance, he created the General Honors course at Columbia, the immersion in great books that eventually transformed undergraduate education in America. "We were assigned nothing else but the great books themselves," Trilling recalled in his seminar at Purdue, "confronting them as best we could without the mediation of ancillary works." The excitement of a canon, of *this* canon: there was a time when there was such an excitement, though Trilling typically animadverted that the course "was not exigent enough." In 1961, in *Partisan Review*, he complained famously of the complacence, the "delighted glibness," with which his own students at Columbia experienced, and thereby betrayed, their collision with the literary monuments of modernity. (Trilling was appointed an instructor in the English department at Columbia in 1931, and a few years later he completed the dissertation on Matthew Arnold that became his first book in 1939. Also in 1939, Nicholas Murray Butler, the president of the university, invoked his "summer powers" to appoint Trilling an assistant professor of English and the first Jew in the department to become a member of the Columbia faculty. Trilling taught at Columbia until his death in 1975. In a life without external incident, he became an authority on internal incident.)

"The Moral Obligation to Be Intelligent" had appeared in *The Hibbert Journal* in 1914. "The disposition to consider intelligence a peril," Erskine began, "is an old Anglo-Saxon inheritance." The grounds of this hoary demotion of the mind were moral, religious, and emotional—this "assumption that a choice must be made between goodness and intelligence; that stupidity is first cousin to moral conduct, and cleverness the first step into mischief; that reason and God are not on good terms with each other; that the heart and the mind are rival buckets in the well of truth, inexorably balanced—full mind, starved heart—stout heart, weak head." The aim of Erskine's manifesto was to end "the peculiar warfare between character and intellect." Conscience, in his account, originated not in the English tradition, but in the German tradition; and not in the mind, but in the will. Yet it was in America that the party of the intellect was formed. Americans, Erskine proclaimed, were "confederated in a Greek love of knowledge, in a Greek assurance that sin and misery are the fruit of ignorance." Americans momentously understood that "if you want to get out of prison, what you need is the key to the lock [and] if you cannot get that, have courage and steadfastness." Social and economic problems were not problems of will, they were problems of mind.

Erskine's essay was not immune, clearly, to the racialist idiosyncracies of its time, and its survey of anti-intellectualism in English literature (in the English novel especially) was sorely inadequate. Its construction of mental life in America was somewhat imbued with the new enthusiasm for expertise, with the technocratic inflection of the intellectual vocation. Yet finally Erskine extolled intelligence for more than its utility. Shifting rather fitfully from the pragmatic mood to the transcendental mood, he finished his essay with the vatic announcement that "we really seek intelligence not for the answers it may suggest to the problems of life, but because we believe it is life,—not for the aid in making the will of God prevail, but because we believe it is the will of God. We love it, as we love virtue, for its own sake, and we believe it is only virtue's other and more precise name."

This is an exalted jumble, and there is much in it from which Trilling would have recoiled—its supernaturalism in particular, though he allowed that there are sublimities of character and understanding that may not be competently captured by an exclusively naturalistic vocabulary. (Of Eliot's supernaturalism, Trilling wrote, "I have spoken of it with respect because it suggests elements which a rational and naturalistic philosophy, to be adequate, must encompass.") And Trilling emphatically believed that "the problems of life" must indeed be brought before the mind, though not for the purpose of eliciting anything so simple and so heart-ening as "answers." The elements of Erskine's creed to which Trilling must have kindled, and to which he hewed in all his criticism, were its avowal of the intrinsic worth of the mind, and its affiliation of the mental with the moral. The influence of the teacher upon the student is unmistakable, for example, in a withering commentary on Dreiser that Trilling wrote in 1946: "But with us it is always too late for mind, yet never too late for honest stupidity; always a little too late for understanding, never too late for righteous, bewildered wrath; always too late for thought, never too late for naïve moralizing."

Trilling never encountered a good reason to postpone thinking, though he lived in an age when such reasons were regularly and popularly advanced, in the forms of totalistic philosophies and totalistic politics. He was one of the most formidable critics of totalism that his dogmatic and pitiless century produced. Trilling was a distinguished enemy of his time. There was never just one thing, in his work: no single lock, no single key. He was mentally indefatigable; there was order in his writing, but there was no repose. This made Trilling an exceedingly unmoralistic moralist. His interest in virtue included also an interest in a doubting regard of the prevailing notions of virtue. He exemplified the intellectual vocation not least by his impiety about it. He bore down on people like himself—on the infamous "we" in his essays—almost to the point of provincialism. But this was the cheerless and thankless virtue of the true intellectual: to disquiet his own side, to "unmask the unmaskers," to "dissent from the orthodoxies of dissent."

The intellectual life, if it is genuine, is a life of strain. The business of the intellectual is the stringency business. Those were Trilling's onerous instructions. A half century later, it is impossible to read the golden pref-ace to *The Liberal Imagination*, the influential collection of essays that he published in 1950—"it has for some time seemed to me that a criticism which has at heart the interests of liberalism might find its most useful work not in confirming liberalism in its sense of general rightness but rather in putting under some degree of pressure the liberal ideas and as-sumptions of the present time"—and not to feel the sting. There is a last-ing profit in Trilling's sting. In his polemic against the undiscomfited progessivism of the 1930s and 1940s lies a lesson about the relationship of honesty to love. He deplored ease more than he deplored error. He prized fearlessness more than he prized happiness.

Innocence bored him; purity he refused to credit; sanctity was more than he wished to grasp. His gospel was complexity—or as he put it, "variousness, possibility, complexity, and difficulty." This was not a theory or a method. It was a cast of mind and a pedagogical scruple. In Trilling's hands, nuance was an instrument of clarification, not an instrument of equivocation. This made his work exhilarating and exasperating.

He was always warning about appearances, and worrying that a life without illusions was itself an illusion. Trilling cherished the modern novel for its worldliness, for its ability to provide an accurate picture of the problem of reality and appearance in modern life. The subject of the novel was society, or complication. A multiplicity of classes had engendered a multiplicity of meanings, Trilling contended, so that certainty was no longer possible, and appearances, in the form of manners, acquired a new prestige as a condition of knowledge; and of these appearances the novel was made. Since the novel was social, it was epistemological. It was the art that was born when the settled sense of reality died.

Trilling's criticism was a long search for the sense of reality, and a long tribute to it. "When, generations from now, the historian of our time undertakes to describe the assumptions of our culture, he will surely discover that the word 'reality' is of central importance in his understanding of us." Trilling deeply resented the obscurantist uses of realism in American culture, "the chronic American belief that there exists an opposition between reality and mind and that one must enlist oneself in the party of reality." But he was not quite a party man, philosophically or politically. He inhabited an essentially inharmonious world. He was enough of an idealist not to mistake reality for mind, but not so much of an idealist that he mistook mind for reality. He was, instead, a scholar of the relation.

Trilling took the sense of reality to be one of the most precious attainments of the mind, and also one of the most unlikely. "Let us not deceive ourselves," he declared at the end of an introduction to *Anna Karenina* in 1951. "To comprehend unconditioned spirit is not so very hard, but there is no knowledge rarer than the understanding of spirit as it exists in the inescapable conditions which the actual and the trivial make for it." Trilling ardently defended William Dean Howells for devoting many chapters of a novel to its hero's hunt for an apartment. In this way, he argued, the writer had acknowledged "the actuality of the conditioned, the literality of matter." And "to lose this is to lose not a material fact but a spiritual one, for it is a fact of spirit that it must exist in a world which requires it to engage in so dispiriting an occupation as hunting for a house." Trilling was not a materialist, but he was not an escapist. The objective of his work as a critic was a lucid apprehension of the thick tangle of freedom and necessity. He had no doubt that the tangle was final, that the poles of existence would never part.

But lucidity—the mixture of clarity and courage that Camus in particular promoted into a new stoical ideal—was not all that Trilling meant by "mind." When he spoke of mind, he was speaking of reason. To be sure, he might not have been delighted by the characterization of his point of regard as rationalism. The career of rationalism in modern culture did not exactly dazzle him. "To be rational, to be reasonable, is a good thing, but when we say of a thinker that he is committed to rationalism, we mean to convey a perjorative judgement. It expresses our sense that he conceives of the universe and man in a simplistic way, and often it suggests that his thought proceeds on the assumption that there is a close analogy to be drawn between man and a machine." The modern misadventures of reason were many: the reason of the utilitarians and their liberal heirs had desiccated the spirit, but the Reason of the Hegelians and their totalitarian heirs had killed it. Historically, reason had often behaved like the enemy of imagination and the enemy of decency. It had given absolution to middlebrows and murderers.

And the enemies of reason repelled Trilling as completely as some of reason's friends. His later writings in particular were a sustained assault upon "the contemporary ideology of irrationalism," a rubric of intellectual irresponsibility under which he included the sins of "intuition, inspiration, revelation; the annihilation of selfhood—perhaps through contemplation, but also through ecstasy and the various forms of intoxication; violence; madness"; in a word, the sins of immediacy. In 1972, in *Sincerity and Authenticity,* he traced the history of "the disintegrated consciousness" from Diderot and Hegel to Marcuse and Laing. Trilling inquired frequently and penetratingly into the non-ethical or anti-ethical energies in modern literature. He acknowledged the vitality of what he famously called "the adversary culture," and he was himself the most forceful (and the most wry) adversary of the adversary culture.

The important point is that Trilling's fascination with unreason followed strictly from his commitment to reason. In this respect he belonged to the most superb line of modern rationalism, to the sturdy, disabused company of Freud and Mann (who once remarked, against

Nietzsche, that the world is never suffering from a surfeit of reason) and Isaiah Berlin. These were the rationalists with night vision. When Trilling cautioned that "we must be aware of the dangers which lie in our most generous wishes," when he detected traces of evil in the good and traces of good in the evil, he was practicing this night vision. These rationalists trained reason's gaze upon its contrary, and they held fast to the study of disorder until reason no longer flinched.

They rejected the day vision, the flinching rationalism, of the Enlightenment, for which the rational was the real, or at least all the real that reason would consent to recognize. Instead they preached rationalism *after* romanticism. For the rational is plainly not the real; and before the reality of the irrational, reason's scorn will not suffice. These rationalists demanded of reason what Milton demanded of virtue, that it not be a youngling in the contemplation of evil. (The greatest of the rationalists with night vision was Primo Levi, who actually lived the night.) Trilling, too, was undeceived about the immunity of the world to mind; but it was this sobering knowledge of the world's punishing way with human purposes—Trilling called this knowledge "moral realism"—that gave to mind its muscle and its magnanimity, its power to withstand its own weakness and not be put to flight by what it could not master.

In a review of *The Liberal Imagination* that R. P. Blackmur later collected among his "essays in solicitude and critique," he patronizingly described Trilling as "an administrator of the affairs of the mind" and as "a liberal humanist in hard straits," as if there were no glory in liberal humanism and the straits were not hard. Trilling "has cut down on tykish impulses and wild insights," Blackmur observed, more in critique than in solicitude. "The trouble is that his masters, Arnold and Freud, both extremists in thought, make him think too much." To the charge of thinking too much, Trilling would have gladly pleaded guilty; but he would have demanded to know how it was possible to think too much about problems whose solutions can be discovered only by means of reflection.

He understood, of course, that not all of life's problems are of that kind. In the notes for his autobiographical lecture, he reminisced about "the rational life" of the 1930s and 1940s: "Every aspect of existence was touched by ideas, or the simulacra of ideas. Not only politics, but child-rearing, the sexual life, the life of the psyche, the innermost part of existence was subject to ideation." The mordancy of his reminiscence is evident. The "ideation" of which Trilling speaks in this passage is a little comic, almost a deformation. And many of the "New York intellectu-als"—Trilling's colleagues in the great mid-century metropolitan experi-ment in balancing the claims of Marxism and modernism, Europe and America, alienation and solidarity, justice and beauty—were in this way deformed. In their delegitimation of Stalinism and in their divorce of the criticism of literature from the criticism of politics, they made themselves genuinely indispensable to the intellectual history of their country; but they often exaggerated the transparency of the world to their minds, and in their worship of "ideas" they often failed to observe the difference be-tween an idea and an opinion. Trilling was not noisy in the New York manner. For this reason, he wrote the most lasting prose of any of the New Yorkers. His writing is precious not least for its patience. The im-perturbability of his style was the consequence of a pained and permanent sense of the opacity of life. The dialectical toil of his essays was Trilling's way of walking diligently before what he could not promptly and cleverly understand.

About one thing, then, Blackmur was right. Trilling was indeed an ex-tremist in thought, or an extremist for thought. This marked his limita-tion as a critic of literature. He was singularly unstimulated by form and by the machinery of beauty. (He wrote about Keats as if Keats, too, was an intellectual.) He did not read to be ravished. He was exercised more by "the moral imagination" than by the imagination. And he grew increas-ingly suspicious of art. (He became especially absorbed, in his later years, by Rousseau's letter to d'Alembert.) In works of literature Trilling found mainly the records of concepts and sentiments and values. "For our time the most effective agent of the moral imagination has been the novel of the last two hundred years. It was never, either aesthetically or morally, a perfect form and its faults and failures can quickly be enumerated. But its greatness and its practical usefulness lay in its unremitting work of involv-ing the reader himself in the moral life, inviting him to put his own mo-tives under examination, suggesting that reality is not as his conventional education has led him to see it . . ." In this regard, Trilling was a very un-literary literary critic. His conception of his critical duty was less profes-sional and less playful—and bigger. The novels and the poems that he pondered were documents for a moral history of his culture. Finally he was a historian of morality working with literary materials, and the ex-quisiteness of the result is most perfectly on display in the great essay on *The Princess Casamassima.*

So there is indeed nothing tykish or wild here. There is instead a climate of philosophy and deferred felicity, of renunciation and unceasing examination. There are ironies, but not shabby ones. And art, too, falls under the moral obligation to be intelligent. At the time of his death, Trilling was working on an essay about Jane Austen. He was a little baffled by the apparent revival of the writer's reputation among his students—the uprisings at Columbia and elsewhere in 1968 were still fresh in memory—and he dared to hope that "in reading about the conduct of other people as presented by a writer highly endowed with moral imagination and in consenting to see this conduct as relevant to their own, they had undertaken an activity which humanism holds precious, in that it redeems the individual from moral torpor." Trilling left the essay unfinished, though it is clear from the fragment that remains that the piece was conceived as an admonition against aesthetic ideals of life. His partisan devotion to the critical intellect, to the dignity of dialectic, was the subject of the very last sentence that he wrote: "It is, I think, open to us to believe that our alternations of view on this matter of life seeking to approximate art are not a mere display of cultural indecisiveness but, rather, that they constitute a dialectic, with all the dignity that inheres in that word . . ." And still inheres in it, if Lionel Trilling's teaching still lives.

Some years ago I remarked to Diana Trilling that the unavailability of Lionel Trilling's essays was a scandal, and she invited me to do something about it. The present volume is the grateful result of her invitation. I have included " 'That Smile of Parmenides Made Me Think,' " the essay on Santayana, because Lionel once expressed his wish to Diana that it appear in any anthology of his essays, but all the other choices were my own. Almost all of them were obvious. The essays appear in the order of their original publication. Daniel Aaron, Jennifer Bradley, Lissy Katz, Adam Kirsch, Brian Phillips, Elisabeth Sifton, Derek Walcott, and James Wood have my thanks.

THE MORAL

OBLIGATION

TO BE

INTELLIGENT

The America of John Dos Passos

1938

U.S.A. is far more impressive than even its three impressive parts — *The 42nd Parallel*, *1919*, *The Big Money* — might have led one to expect. It stands as the important American novel of the decade, on the whole more satisfying than anything else we have. It lacks any touch of eccentricity; it is startlingly normal; at the risk of seeming paradoxical one might say that it is exciting because of its quality of cliché: here are comprised the judgments about modern American life that many of us have been living on for years.

Yet too much must not be claimed for this book. Today we are inclined to make literature too important, to estimate the writer's function at an impossibly high rate, to believe that he can encompass and resolve all the contradictions, and to demand that he should. We forget that, by reason of his human nature, he is likely to win the intense perception of a single truth at the cost of a relative blindness to other truths. We expect a single man to give us all the answers and produce the "synthesis." And then when the writer, hailed for giving us much, is discovered to have given us less than everything, we turn from him in a reaction of disappointment: he has given us nothing. A great deal has been claimed for Dos Passos and it is important, now that U.S.A. is completed, to mark off the boundaries of its enterprise and see what it does not do so that we may know what it does do.

One thing *U.S.A.* does not do is originate; it confirms but does not advance and it summarizes but does not suggest. There is no accent or tone of feeling that one is tempted to make one's own and carry further in one's own way. No writer, I think, will go to school to Dos Passos, and readers, however much they may admire him, will not stand in the relation to him in which they stand, say, to Stendhal or Henry James or even E. M. Forster. Dos Passos's plan is greater than its result in feeling; his book *tells* more than it *is*. Yet what it tells, and tells with accuracy, subtlety, and skill, is enormously important and no one else has yet told it half so well.

Nor is *U.S.A.* as all-embracing as its admirers claim. True, Dos Passos not only represents a great national scene but embodies, as I have said, the cultural tradition of the intellectual Left. But he does not encompass—does not pretend to encompass in this book—all of either. Despite his title, he is consciously selective of his America and he is, as I shall try to show, consciously corrective of the cultural tradition from which he stems.

Briefly and crudely, this cultural tradition may be said to consist of the following beliefs, which are not so much formulations of theory or principles of action as they are emotional tendencies: that the collective aspects of life may be distinguished from the individual aspects; that the collective aspects are basically important and are good; that the individual aspects are, or should be, of small interest and that they contain a destructive principle; that the fate of the individual is determined by social forces; that the social forces now dominant are evil; that there is a conflict between the dominant social forces and other, better, rising forces; that it is certain or very likely that the rising forces will overcome the now dominant ones. *U.S.A.* conforms to some but not to all of these assumptions. The lack of any protagonists in the trilogy, the equal attention given to many people, have generally been taken to represent Dos Passos's recognition of the importance of the collective idea. The book's historical apparatus indicates the author's belief in social determination. And there can be no slightest doubt of Dos Passos's attitude to the dominant forces of our time: he hates them.

But Dos Passos modifies the tradition in three important respects. Despite the collective elements of his trilogy, he puts a peculiar importance upon the individual. Again, he avoids propounding any sharp conflict between the dominant forces of evil and the rising forces of good; more specifically, he does not write of a class struggle, nor is he much concerned with the notion of class in the political sense. Finally, he is not at all assured of the eventual triumph of good; he pins no faith on any force or party—indeed he is almost alone of the novelists of the Left (Silone is the only other one that comes to mind) in saying that the creeds and idealisms of the Left may bring corruption quite as well as the greeds and cynicisms of the established order; he has refused to cry "Allons! the road lies before us," and, in short, his novel issues in despair.—And it is this despair of Dos Passos's book which has made his two ablest critics, Malcolm Cowley and T. K. Whipple, seriously temper their admiration. Mr. Cowley says: "They [the novels comprising *U.S.A.*] give us an extraordinarily diversified picture of contemporary life, but they fail to include at least one side of it—the will to struggle ahead, the comradeship in struggle, the consciousness of new men and new forces continually rising." And Mr. Whipple: "Dos Passos has reduced what ought to be a tale of full-bodied conflicts to an epic of disintegration."

These critics are saying that Dos Passos has not truly observed the political situation. Whether he has or not, whether his despair is objectively justifiable, cannot, with the best political will in the world, be settled on paper. We hope he has seen incorrectly; he himself must hope so. But there is also an implicit meaning in the objections which, if the writers themselves did not intend it, many readers will derive, and if not from Mr. Whipple and Mr. Cowley then from the book itself: that the emotion in which *U.S.A.* issues is negative to the point of being politically harmful.

But to discover a political negativism in the despair of *U.S.A.* is to subscribe to a naïve conception of human emotion and of the literary experience. It is to assert that the despair of a literary work must inevitably engender despair in the reader. Actually, of course, it need do nothing of the sort. To rework the old Aristotelean insight, it may bring about a catharsis of an already existing despair. But more important: the word "despair" all by itself (or any other such general word or phrase) can never characterize the emotion the artist is dealing with. There are many kinds of despair and what is really important is what goes along with the general emotion denoted by the word. Despair with its wits about it is very different from despair that is stupid; despair that is an abandonment of illusion is very different from despair which generates tender new cynicisms. The "heartbreak" of *Heartbreak House*, for example, is the beginning of new courage and I can think of no more useful *political* job for the literary man today than, by the representation of despair, to cauterize the exposed soft tissue of too-easy hope.

Even more than the despair, what has disturbed the radical admirers of Dos Passos's work is his appearance of indifference to the idea of the class struggle. Mr. Whipple correctly points out that the characters of *U.S.A.* are all "midway people in somewhat ambiguous positions." Thus, there are no bankers or industrialists (except incidentally) but only J. Ward Morehouse, their servant; there are no factory workers (except, again, incidentally), no farmers, but only itinerant workers, individualistic mechanics, actresses, interior decorators.

This, surely, is a limitation in a book that has had claimed for it that it is a complete national picture. But when we say limitation we may mean just that or we may mean falsification, and I do not think that Dos Passos has falsified. The idea of class is not simple but complex. Socially it is extremely difficult to determine. It cannot be determined, for instance, by asking individuals to what class they belong; nor is it easy to convince them that they belong to one class or another. We may, to be sure, demonstrate the idea of class at income-extremes or function-extremes, but when we leave these we must fall back upon the criterion of "interest"—by which we must mean *real* interest ("real will" in the Rousseauian sense) and not what people say or think they want. Even the criterion of action will not determine completely the class to which people belong. Class, then, is a useful but often undetermined category of political and social thought. The political leader and the political theorist will make use of it in ways different from those of the novelist. For the former the important thing is people's perception that they are of one class or another and their resultant action. For the latter the interesting and suggestive things are likely to be the moral paradoxes that result from the conflict between real and apparent interest. And the "midway people" of Dos Passos represent this moral-paradoxical aspect of class. They are a great fact in American life. It is they who show the symptoms of cultural change. Their movement from social group to social group—from class to class, if you will—makes for the uncertainty of their moral codes, their confusion, their indecision. Almost more than the people of fixed class, they are at the mercy of the social stream because their interests cannot be clear to them and give them direction. If Dos Passos has omitted the class struggle, as Mr. Whipple and Mr. Cowley complain, it is only the external class struggle he has left out; within his characters the class struggle is going on constantly.

This, perhaps, is another way of saying that Dos Passos is primarily concerned with morality, with personal morality. The national, collective, social elements of his trilogy should be seen not as a bid for completeness but rather as a great setting, brilliantly delineated, for his moral interest. In his novels, as in actual life, "conditions" supply the opportunity for personal moral action. But if Dos Passos is a social historian, as he is so frequently said to be, he is that in order to be a more complete moralist. It is of the greatest significance that for him the barometer of social breakdown is not suffering through economic deprivation but always moral degeneration through moral choice.

This must be said in the face of Mr. Whipple's description of Dos Passos's people as "devoid of will or purpose, helplessly impelled hither and yon by the circumstances of the moment. They have no strength of resistance. They are weak at the very core of personality, the power to choose." These, it would seem, are scarcely the characters with which the moralist can best work. But here we must judge not only by the moral equipment of the characters (and it is not at all certain that Mr. Whipple's description is correct: choice of action is seldom made as the result of Socratic dialectic) but by the novelist's idea of morality—the nature of his judgments and his estimate of the power of circumstance.

Dos Passos's morality is concerned not so much with the utility of an action as with the quality of the person who performs it. *What* his people do is not so important as *how* they do it, or what they become by doing it. We despise J. Ward Morehouse not so much for his creation of the labor-relations board, his support of the war, his advertising of patent-medicines, though these are despicable enough; we despise him rather for the words he uses as he does these things, for his self-deception, the tone and style he generates. We despise G. H. Barrow, the labor-faker, not because he betrays labor; we despise him because he is mealy-mouthed and talks about "the art of living" when he means concupiscence. But we do not despise the palpable fraud, Doc Bingham, because, though he lies to everyone else, he does not lie to himself.

The moral assumption on which Dos Passos seems to work was expressed by John Dewey some thirty years ago; there are certain moral situations, Dewey says, where we cannot decide between the ends; we are forced to make our moral choice in terms of our preference for one kind of character or another: "What sort of an agent, of a person shall he be? This is the question finally at stake in any genuinely moral situation: What shall the agent *be*? What sort of character shall he assume? On its face, the question is what he shall *do*, shall he act for this or that end. But the incompatibility of the ends forces the issue back into the questions of the kind of selfhood, of agency, involved in the respective ends." One can imagine that this method of moral decision does not have meaning for all times and cultures. Although dilemmas exist in every age, we do not find Antigone settling her struggle between family and state by a reference to the kind of character she wants to be, nor Orestes settling his in that way; and so with the medieval dilemma of wife vs. friend, or the family oath of vengeance vs. the feudal oath of allegiance. But for our age with its intense self-consciousness and its uncertain moral codes, the reference to the quality of personality does have meaning, and the greater the social flux the more frequent will be the interest in qualities of character rather than in the rightness of the end.

The modern novel, with its devices for investigating the quality of character, is the aesthetic form almost specifically called forth to exercise this modern way of judgment. The novelist goes where the law cannot go; he tells the truth where the formulations of even the subtlest ethical theorist cannot. He turns the moral values inside out to question the worth of the deed by looking not at its actual outcome but at its tone and style. He is subversive of dominant morality and under his influence we learn to praise what dominant morality condemns; he reminds us that benevolence may be aggression, that the highest idealism may corrupt. Finally, he gives us the models or the examples by which, half-unconsciously, we make our own moral selves.

Dos Passos does not primarily concern himself with the burly sinners who inherit the earth. His people are those who sin against themselves and for him the wages of sin is death—of the spirit. The whole Dos Passos morality and the typical Dos Passos fate are expressed in Burns's quatrain:

I waive the quantum o' the sin,
The hazard of concealing;
But, och! it hardens a' within
And petrifies the feeling!

In the trilogy physical death sometimes follows upon this petrifaction of the feeling but only as its completion. Only two people die without petrifying, Joe Williams and Daughter, who kept in their inarticulate way a spark of innocence, generosity, and protest. Idealism does not prevent the consequences of sinning against oneself, and Mary French with her devotion to the working class and the Communist Party, with her courage and "sacrifice" is quite as dead as Richard Savage who inherits Morehouse's mantle, and she is almost as much to blame.

It is this element of blame, of responsibility, that exempts Dos Passos from Malcolm Cowley's charge of being in some part committed to the morality of what Cowley calls the Art Novel—the story of the Poet and the World, the Poet always sensitive and right, the World always crass and wrong. An important element of Dos Passos's moral conception is that, although the World does sin against his characters, the characters themselves are very often as wrong as the world. There is no need to enter the theological purlieus to estimate how much responsibility Dos Passos puts upon them and whether this is the right amount. Clearly, however, he holds people like Savage, Fainy McCreary, and Eveline Hutchins accountable in some important part for their own fates and their own ignobility.

The morality of Dos Passos, then, is a romantic morality. Perhaps this is calling it a bad name; people say they have got tired of a morality concerned with individuals "saving" themselves and "realizing" themselves. Conceivably only Dos Passos's aggressive contemporaneity has kept them from seeing how very similar is his morality to, say, Browning's—the moment to be snatched, the crucial choice to be made, and if it is made on the wrong (the safe) side, the loss of human quality, so that instead of a man we have a Success and instead of two lovers a Statue and a Bust in the public square. But too insistent a cry against the importance of the individual quality is a sick cry—as sick as the cry of "Something to live for" as a motivation of political choice. Among members of a party, the considerations of solidarity, discipline, and expedience are claimed to replace all others and moral judgment is left to history; among liberals, the idea of social determination, on no good ground, appears tacitly to exclude the moral concern: witness the nearly complete conspiracy of silence or misinterpretation that greeted Silone's *Bread and Wine*, which said not a great deal more than that personal and moral—and eventually political—problems were not settled by membership in a revolutionary party. It is not at all certain that it is political wisdom to ignore what so much concerns the novelist. In the long run is not the political choice fundamentally a choice of personal quality?

Hemingway and His Critics

1939

Between *The Fifth Column*, the play which makes the occasion for this large volume, and *The First Forty-Nine Stories*, which make its bulk and its virtue, there is a difference of essence. For the play is the work of Hemingway the "man" and the stories are by Hemingway the "artist." This is a distinction which seldom enough means anything in criticism, but now and then an author gives us, as Hemingway gives us, writing of two such different kinds that there is a certain amount of validity and at any rate a convenience in making it. Once made, the distinction can better be elaborated than defined or defended. Hemingway the "artist" is conscious, Hemingway the "man" is self-conscious; the "artist" has a kind of innocence, the "man" a kind of naïvety; the "artist" is disinterested, the "man" has a dull personal ax to grind; the "artist" has a perfect medium and tells the truth even if it be only *his* truth, but the "man" fumbles at communication and falsifies. As Edmund Wilson said in his "Letter to the Russians about Hemingway," which is the best estimate of our author that I know:

> . . . something frightful seems to happen to Hemingway as soon as he begins to write in the first person. In his fiction, the conflicting elements of his personality, the emotional situations which obsess him, are externalized and objectified; and the result is an art which

is severe, intense, and deeply serious. But as soon as he talks in his own person, he seems to lose all his capacity for self-criticism and is likely to become fatuous or maudlin.

Mr. Wilson had in mind such specifically autobiographical and polemical works as *Green Hills of Africa* (and obviously he was not referring to the technical use of the first person in fictional narrative) but since the writing of the "Letter" in 1935, we may observe of Hemingway that the "man" has encroached upon the "artist" in his fiction. In *To Have and Have Not* and now in *The Fifth Column* the "first person" dominates and is the source of the failure of both works.

Of course it might be perfectly just to set down these failures simply to a lapse of Hemingway's talent. But there is, I think, something else to be said. For as one compares the high virtues of Hemingway's stories with the weakness of his latest novel and his first play, although one is perfectly aware of all that must be charged against the author himself, what forces itself into consideration is the cultural atmosphere which has helped to bring about the recent falling off. In so far as we can ever blame a critical tradition for a writer's failures, we must, I believe, blame American criticism for the illegitimate emergence of Hemingway the "man" and the resultant inferiority of his two recent major works.

It is certainly true that criticism of one kind or another has played an unusually important part in Hemingway's career. Perhaps no American talent has so publicly developed as Hemingway's: more than any writer of our time he has been under glass, watched, checked up on, predicted, suspected, warned. One part of his audience took from him new styles of writing, of love-making, of very being; this was the simpler part, but its infatuate imitation was of course a kind of criticism. But another section of his audience responded negatively, pointing out that the texture of Hemingway's work was made up of cruelty, religion, anti-intellectualism, even of basic fascism, and looked upon him as the active proponent of evil. Neither part of such an audience could fail to make its impression upon a writer. The knowledge that he had set a fashion and become a legend may have been gratifying but surely it was also burdensome and depressing, and must have offered no small temptation. Yet perhaps more difficult for Hemingway to support with equanimity, and, from our point of view, much more important, was the constant accusation that he had attacked good human values. For upon Hemingway were turned all the fine social feelings of the now passing decade, all the noble sentiments, all the desperate optimism, all the extreme rationalism, all the contempt of irony and indirection—all the attitudes which, in the full tide of the liberal-radical movement, became dominant in our thought about literature. There was demanded of him earnestness and pity, social consciousness, as it was called, something "positive" and "constructive" and literal. For is not life a simple thing and is not the writer a villain or a counter-revolutionary who does not see it so?

As if under the pressure of this critical tradition, which persisted in mistaking the "artist" for the "man," Hemingway seems to have undertaken to vindicate the "man" by showing that he, too, could muster the required "social" feelings in the required social way. At any rate, he now brought the "man" with all his contradictions and conflicts into his fiction. But "his ideas about life"—I quote Edmund Wilson again—

> or rather his sense of what happens and the way it happens, is in his stories sunk deep below the surface and is not conveyed by argument or preaching but by directly transmitted emotion: it is turned into something as hard as crystal and as disturbing as a great lyric. When he expounds this sense of life, however, in his own character of Ernest Hemingway, the Old Master of Key West, he has a way of sounding silly.

If, however, the failures of Hemingway "in his own character" were apparent to the practitioners of this critical tradition, they did not want Hemingway's virtues—the something "hard" and "disturbing." Indeed, they were in a critical tradition that did not want artists at all; it wanted "men," recruits, and its apologists were delighted to enlist Hemingway in his own character, with all his confusions and naïvety, simply because Hemingway had now declared himself on the right side.

And so when *To Have and Have Not* appeared, one critic of the Left, grappling with the patent fact that the "artist" had failed, yet determined to defend the "man" who was his new ally, had no recourse save to explain that in this case failure was triumph because artistic fumbling was the mark of Hemingway's attempt to come to grips with the problems of modern life which were as yet too great for his art to encompass. Similarly, another critic of the Left, faced with the aesthetic inferiority of Hemingway's first play, takes refuge in praising the personal vindication which the "man" has made by "taking sides against fascism." In other words, the "man" has been a sad case and long in need of regeneration; the looseness of thought and emotion, the easy and uninteresting idealism of the social feelings to which Hemingway now gives such sudden and literal expression, are seen as the grateful signs of a personal reformation.

But the disinterested reader does not have to look very deep to see that Hemingway's social feelings, whatever they may yet become, are now the occasion for indulgence in the "man." His two recent failures are failures not only in form but in feeling; one looks at *To Have and Have Not* and *The Fifth Column*, one looks at their brag, and their disconcerting forcing of the emotions, at their downright priggishness, and then one looks at the criticism which, as I conceive it, made these failures possible by demanding them and which now accepts them so gladly, and one is tempted to reverse the whole liberal-radical assumption about literature. One almost wishes to say to an author like Hemingway, "You have no duty, no responsibility. Literature, in a political sense, is not in the least important. Wherever the sword is drawn it is mightier than the pen. Whatever you can do as a man, you can win no wars as an artist."

Very obviously this would not be the whole truth, yet saying it might counteract the crude and literal theory of art to which, in varying measure, we have all been training ourselves for a decade. We have conceived the artist to be a man perpetually on the spot, who must always report to us his precise moral and political latitude and longitude. Not that for a moment we would consider shaping our own political ideas by his; but we who of course turn for political guidance to newspapers, theorists, or historians, create the fiction that thousands—not, to be sure, ourselves— are waiting on the influence of the creative artist, and we stand by to see if he is leading us as he properly should. We consider then that we have exalted the importance of art, and perhaps we have. But in doing so we have quite forgotten how complex and subtle art is and, if it is to be "used," how very difficult it is to use it.

One feels that Hemingway would never have thrown himself into his new and inferior work if the necessity had not been put upon him to justify himself before this magisterial conception of literature. Devoted to literalness, the critical tradition of the Left took Hemingway's symbols for his intention, saw in his stories only cruelty or violence or a calculated indifference, and turned upon him a barrage of high-mindedness—that liberal-radical high-mindedness that is increasingly taking the place of thought among the "progressive professional and middle-class forces" and that now, under the name of "good will," shuts out half the world. Had it seen what was actually in Hemingway's work, it would not have forced him out of his idiom of the artist and into the idiom of the man which he speaks with difficulty and without truth.

For what should have been always obvious is that Hemingway is a writer who, when he writes as an "artist," is passionately and aggressively concerned with truth and even with social truth. And with this in mind, one might begin the consideration of his virtues with a glance at Woodrow Wilson. Hemingway has said that all modern American writing comes from the prose of Huckleberry Finn's voyage down the Mississippi, and certainly his own starts there. But Huck's prose is a sort of moral symbol. It is the antithesis to the Widow Douglas—to the pious, the respectable, the morally plausible. It is the prose of the free man seeing the world as it really is. And Woodrow Wilson was, we might say, Hemingway's Widow Douglas. To the sensitive men who went to war it was not, perhaps, death and destruction that made the disorganizing shock. It was perhaps rather that death and destruction went on at the instance and to the accompaniment of the fine grave words, of which Woodrow Wilson's speeches were the finest and gravest. Here was the issue of liberal theory; here in the bloated or piecemeal corpse was the outcome of the words of humanitarianism and ideals; this was the work of presumably careful men of good will, learned men, polite men. The world was a newspaper world, a state-paper world, a memorial-speech world. Words were trundled smoothly o'er the tongue—Coleridge had said it long ago—

> Like mere abstractions, empty sounds to which
> We join no feeling and attach no form
> As if the soldier died without a wound . . .
> Passed off to Heaven, translated and not killed.

Everyone in that time had feelings, as they called them; just as everyone has "feelings" now. And it seems to me that what Hemingway wanted first to do was to get rid of the "feelings," the comfortable liberal humanitarian feelings, and to replace them with the truth.

Not cynicism, I think, not despair, as so often is said, but this admirable desire shaped his famous style and his notorious set of admirations and contempts. The trick of understatement or tangential statement sprang from this desire. Men had made so many utterances in such fine language that it had become time to shut up. Hemingway's people, as everyone knows, are afraid of words and ashamed of them and the line from his stories which has become famous is the one that begins "Won't you please," goes on through its innumerable "pleases," and ends, "stop talking." Not only slain men but slain words made up the mortality of the war.

Another manifestation of the same desire in Hemingway was his devotion to the ideal of technique as an end in itself. A great deal can go down in the tumble but one of the things that stands best is a cleanly done job. As John Peale Bishop says in his admirable essay on Hemingway (which yet, I feel, contributes to the general misapprehension by asserting the evanescence of Hemingway's "compassion"), professional pride is one of the last things to go. Hemingway became a devotee of his own skill and he exploited the ideal of skill in his characters. His admired men always do a good job; and the proper handling of a rod, a gun, an *espada*, or a pen is a thing, so Hemingway seems always to be saying, which can be understood when speech cannot.

This does not mean that Hemingway attacks mind itself, a charge which has often been brought against him. It is perhaps safe to say that whenever he seems to be making such an attack, it is not so much *reason* as it is *rationalization* that he resists; "mind" appears simply as the complex of false feelings. And against "mind" in this sense he sets up what he believes to be the primal emotions, among others pain and death, met not with the mind but with techniques and courage. "Mind" he sees as a kind of castrating knife, cutting off people's courage and proper self-love, making them "reasonable," which is to say dull and false. There is no need to point out how erroneous his view would have been were it really mind that was in question, but in the long romantic tradition of the attitude it never really *is* mind that is in question but rather a dull overlay of mechanical negative proper feeling, or a falseness of feeling which people believe to be reasonableness and reasonable virtue. And when we think how quickly "mind" capitulates in a crisis, how quickly, for example, it accommodated itself to the war and served it and glorified it, revulsion from it and a turning to the life of action—reduced, to be sure, to athleticism: but skillful physical effort is perhaps something intellectuals too quickly dismiss as a form of activity—can be the better understood. We can understand, too, the insistence on courage, even on courage deliberately observed in its purity: that is, when it is at the service of the most sordid desires, as in "Fifty Grand."

This, then, was Hemingway's vision of the world. Was it a complete vision? Of course it was not. Was it a useful vision? That depended. If it was true, it was useful—if we knew how to use it. But the use of literature is not easy. In our hearts most of us are Platonists in the matter of art and we feel that we become directly infected by what we read; or at any rate we want to be Platonists, and we carry on a certain conviction from our Tom Swift days that literature provides chiefly a means of identification and emulation. The Platonist view is not wholly to be dismissed; we *do* in a degree become directly infected by art; but the position is too simple. And we are further Platonistic in our feeling that literature must be religious: we want our attitudes formulated by the tribal bard. This, of course, gives to literature a very important function. But it forgets that literature has never "solved" anything, though it may perhaps provide part of the data for eventual solutions.

With this attitude we asked, Can Hemingway's people speak only with difficulty? and we answered, Then it surely means that he thinks people should not speak. Does he find in courage the first of virtues? Then it surely means that we should be nothing but courageous. Is he concerned with the idea of death and of violence? Then it must mean that to him these are good things.

In short, we looked for an emotional leader. We did not conceive Hemingway to be saying, Come, let us look at the world together. We supposed him to be saying, Come, it is your moral duty to be as my characters are. We took the easiest and simplest way of using the artist and decided that he was not the "man" for us. That he was a man and a Prophet we were certain; and equally certain that he was not the "man" we would want to be or the Prophet who could lead us. That, as artist, he was not concerned with being a "man" did not occur to us. We had, in other words, quite overlooked the whole process of art, overlooked style and tone, symbol and implication, overlooked the obliqueness and complication with which the artist may criticize life, and assumed that what Hemingway saw or what he put into his stories he wanted to have exist in the actual world.

In short, the criticism of Hemingway came down to a kind of moral-political lecture, based on the assumption that art is—or should be—the exact equivalent of life. The writer would have to be strong indeed who could remain unmoved by the moral pressure that was exerted upon Hemingway. He put away the significant reticences of the artist, opened his heart like "a man," and the flat literalness, the fine, fruity social idealism, of the latest novel and the play are the result.

The Fifth Column is difficult to speak of. Summary is always likely to be a critical treachery, but after consulting the summaries of those who admire the work and regard it as a notable event, it seems fair to say that it is the story of a tender-tough American hero with the horrors, who does counterespionage in Madrid, though everybody thinks he is just a playboy, who fears that he will no longer do his work well if he continues his liaison with an American girl chiefly remarkable for her legs and her obtuseness; and so sacrifices love and bourgeois pleasure for the sake of duty. Hemingway as a playwright gives up his tools of suggestion and tone and tells a literal story—an adventure story of the Spanish war, at best the story of the regeneration of an American Scarlet Pimpernel of not very good intelligence.

It is this work which has been received with the greatest satisfaction by a large and important cultural group as the fulfillment and vindication of Hemingway's career, as a fine document of the Spanish struggle, and as a political event of significance, "a sign of the times," as one reviewer called it. To me it seems none of these things. It does not vindicate Hemingway's career because that career in its essential parts needs no vindication; and it does not fulfill Hemingway's career because that career has been in the service of exact if limited emotional truth and this play is in the service of fine feelings. Nor can I believe that the Spanish war is represented in any good sense by a play whose symbols are so sentimentally personal* and whose dramatic tension is so weak; and it seems to me that there is something even vulgar in making Spain serve as a kind of mental

---

*In fairness to Hemingway the disclaimer of an important intention which he makes in his Preface should be cited. Some people, he says, have objected that his play does not present "the nobility and dignity of the cause of the Spanish people. It does not attempt to. It will take many plays and novels to do that, and the best ones will be written after the war is over." And he goes on: "This is only a play about counterespionage in Madrid. It has the defects of having been written in wartime, and if it has a moral it is that people who work for certain organizations have very little time for home life." I do not think that this exempts the play from severe judgment by those who dislike it, just as I think that those who admire it have a right to see in it, as they do, a "sign of the times."

hospital for disorganized foreigners who, out of a kind of self-contempt, turn to the "ideal of the Spanish people." Nor, finally, can I think that Hemingway's statement of an antifascist position is of great political importance or of more than neutral virtue. It is hard to believe that the declaration of antifascism is nowadays any more a mark of sufficient grace in a writer than a declaration against disease would be in a physician or a declaration against accidents would be in a locomotive engineer. The admirable intention in itself is not enough and criticism begins and does not end when the intention is declared.

But I believe that judgments so simple as these will be accepted with more and more difficulty. The "progressive professional and middle-class forces" are framing a new culture, based on the old liberal-radical culture but designed now to hide the new anomaly by which they live their intellectual and emotional lives. For they must believe, it seems, that imperialist arms advance proletarian revolution, that oppression by the right people brings liberty. Like Hemingway's latest hero, they show one front to the world and another to themselves, know that within they are true proletarian men while they wrap themselves in Early American togas; they are enthralled by their own good will; they are people of fine feelings and they dare not think lest the therapeutic charm vanish. This is not a political essay and I am not here concerned with the political consequences of these things, bad though they be and worse though they will be, but only with the cultural consequences. For to prevent the anomaly from appearing in its genuine difficulty, emotion—of a very limited kind—has been apotheosized and thought has been made almost a kind of treachery; the reviewer of *The Fifth Column* to whom I have already referred cites as a virtue Hemingway's "unintellectual" partisanship of the Spanish cause. The piety of "good will" has become enough and fascism is conceived not as a force which complicates the world but as a force which simplifies the world—and so it does for any number of people of good will (of a good will not to be doubted, I should say) for whom the existence of an absolute theological evil makes nonexistent any other evil.

It is this group that has made Hemingway its cultural hero and for reasons that need not be canvassed very far. Now that Hemingway has become what this group would call "affirmative" he has become insufficient; but insufficiency is the very thing this group desires. When Hemingway was in "negation" his themes of courage, loyalty, tenderness, and silence, tangentially used, suggested much; but now that they are used literally and directly they say far less than the situation demands. His stories showed a great effort of comprehension and they demand a considerable effort from their readers, that effort in which lies whatever teaching powers there are in art; but now he is not making an effort to understand but to accept, which may indeed be the effort of the honest political man but not of the honest artist.

An attempt has been made to settle the problem of the artist's relation to politics by loudly making the requirement that he give up his base individuality and rescue humanity and his own soul by becoming the mouthpiece of a party, a movement, or a philosophy. That requirement has demonstrably failed as a solution of the problem; the problem, however, still remains. It may be, of course, that politics itself will settle the problem for us; it may be that in our tragic time art worthy of the name cannot be produced and that we must live with the banalities of *The Fifth Column* or even with less. However, if the problem will be allowed to exist at all, it will not be solved in theory and on paper but in practice. And we have, after all, the practice of the past to guide us, at least with a few tentative notions. We can learn to stop pressing the writer with the demand for contemporaneity when we remember the simple fact that writers have always written directly to and about the troubles of their own time and for and about their contemporaries, some in ways to us more obvious than others but all responding inevitably to what was happening around them. We can learn too that the relation of an artist to his culture, whether that culture be national or the culture of a relatively small recusant group, is a complex and even a contradictory relation: the artist must accept his culture and be accepted by it, but also—so it seems—he must be its critic, correcting and even rejecting it according to his personal insight; his strength seems to come from the tension of this ambivalent situation and we must learn to welcome the ambivalence. Finally, and simplest of all, we can learn not to expect a political, certainly not an immediately political, effect from a work of art; and in removing from art a burden of messianic responsibility which it never has discharged and cannot discharge we may leave it free to do whatever it actually can do.

T. S. Eliot's Politics

1940

It is a century ago this year that John Stuart Mill angered his Benthamite friends by his now famous essay on Coleridge in which, writing sympathetically of a religious and conservative philosopher, he avowed his intention to modify the rigid materialism of utilitarian thought. Mill did not speak out for Coleridge for what are sometimes called "romantic" reasons—that is, because he thought transcendentalism was warmer and more glowing than utilitarianism. He did think so, but the reason he urged attention to Coleridge was that he thought Coleridge's ability "to see further into the complexities of the human feelings and intellect" offered something practical to add to Bentham's too "short and easy" political analysis. And he told his radical friends that they should make their prayer this one: " 'Lord, enlighten thou our enemies' . . . sharpen their wits, give acuteness to their perceptions and consecutiveness and clearness to their reasoning powers: we are in danger from their folly, not from their wisdom."

The book of Coleridge's which Mill mentioned most often was the volume usually referred to as *Church and State*; its full title is *On the Constitution of the Church and State, According to the Idea of Each*, and it is from this work that T. S. Eliot's newest essay, "The Idea of a Christian Society," takes not only its special meaning of the word "idea" but also its whole inspiration. Mr. Eliot has always said that a connection with the past, more or less consciously maintained, is necessary for intellectual and artistic virtue. For reasons which scarcely need exploration he himself has found his own most useful affinity with the seventeenth century and the thirteenth. Yet for all his enmity to Romanticism, his own true place in politics and religion is in the Romantic line of the nineteenth century. He continues the tradition of Coleridge and, after Coleridge, of Newman, Carlyle, Ruskin, and Matthew Arnold—the men who, in the days of Reform, stood out, on something better than reasons of interest, against the philosophical assumptions of materialistic Liberalism. Their very language, if we except Carlyle's, is commemorated in his prose, and to their thought this book is the tragic coda.

A century has not seen the establishment of this line of thought, but then neither has that same century seen the establishment, though it has surely seen the dominance, of the thought it opposed. What we see at the moment is the philosophy of materialism—of the Right, the Left, and the Center—at war with itself. In that war many of our old notions have become inadequate and many of our old alliances inoperative. We all of us, from our own feelings, can understand Mr. Eliot when, in giving up *The Criterion* after his long editorship, he spoke of a "depression of spirits so different from any other experience of fifty years as to be a new emotion." But a really new emotion implies a modification of all other existing emotions and it requires a whole new world of intellect to accommodate it. Certainly the old world of those who read what I am now writing cannot give it room. Indeed, can we say that that old intellectual world of ours any longer exists? Disordered as it always was, it seems now almost to have vanished.

I am far from thinking that Mr. Eliot supplies a new world, yet in this troubled time when we are bound to think of eventual reconstructions, I should like to recommend to the attention of readers probably hostile to religion Mr. Eliot's religious politics. I say no more than *recommend to the attention*: I certainly do not recommend Mr. Eliot's ideas to the allegiance. But here we are, a very small group and quite obscure; our possibility of action is suspended by events; perhaps we have never been more than vocal and perhaps soon we can hope to be no more than thoughtful; our relations with the future are dark and dubious. There is, indeed, only one connection with the future of which we can be to any extent sure: our pledge to the critical intellect. Of the critical intellect a critic has said that "it must be patient and know how to wait; and flexible and know how to attach itself to things and how to withdraw from them." Perhaps Mr. Eliot's long if recalcitrant discipleship to Matthew Arnold gives me some justification for quoting Arnold once again: of criticism he said that "it must be apt to study and praise elements that for the fulness of spiritual perfection are wanted, even though they belong to a power which in the practical sphere may be maleficent." It is with this sentence in mind that I urge the importance of Mr. Eliot's book.

In the imagination of the Left Mr. Eliot has always figured with excessive simplicity. His story was supposed to be nothing more than this: that from the horrible realities of the Waste Land he escaped into the arms of Anglo-Catholic theology. This account may or may not be adequate; but as we review the ten years in which Marxism flourished among the intellectuals and then decayed, we can scarcely believe that this story, if true, is the worst that could be told of a man in our time. Whatever is censurable in it depends on the blind power of that weary word "escape" and on our attitude to theology. For theology I certainly do not make a stand, but when Mr. Eliot is accused of "faith," of the "surrender" of his intellect to "authority," it is hard to see, when the accusers are Marxist intellectuals, how their own action was always so very different. If we have the right to measure the personal and moral value of convictions by the disinterested intellectual effort through which they are arrived at, we might find that Mr. Eliot's conversion was notably more honorable than that of many who impugned his decision.

Mr. Eliot's book is a small one, it is not overtly dramatic and it does not have an air of "power." To readers of a different persuasion it cannot offer a solution that will seem more comprehensive or more practicable than their own; it can only serve them by questioning their assumptions. Its point of departure is simple, even obvious. Mr. Eliot, believing that a nation's political philosophy is not to be found in the conscious formulation of its ideal aims but, rather, in "the sub-stratum of collective temperament, ways of behaviour and unconscious values" which go to make up the formulation, is unable to find, what most people so easily find, a polar difference between the political philosophy of the Western democracies and that of the totalitarian states. He does not say they are the same; their forms differ and their qualities differ. Yet the difference seems to him not one of principle but of degree; and when he considers how democracy is forced to defend itself from totalitarianism by adopting the totalitarian forms, he cannot think that the differences are dependent on more than time. To be maintained, the differences must be more than temporal, they must be principled, and Mr. Eliot cannot believe that the principles to be put in opposition to the totalitarian principles can be those of liberalism and democracy. Liberalism is a necessary negative element in politics but no more than that; as for democracy, Mr. Eliot says that it is so praised by everyone that its mention makes him think of the Merovingian Emperors and look around for the Mayor of the Palace.

But because totalitarianism is what he calls "pagan," the only possible opposing principle Mr. Eliot can find is that of Christianity. He cannot yet account England—the England which responded as it did to the events of September 1938—a pagan state, though he cannot call it actually a Christian one; it has a culture "which is mainly negative, but which, so far as it is positive, is still Christian." But because the situation no longer permits a negative culture, the choice will have to be made "between the formation of a new Christian culture and the acceptance of a pagan one."

More than once in the brief course of his book we hear from Mr. Eliot that he is not interested in Christianity as revivalism and he quotes a "distinguished theologian" to the effect that the great mistake made about Christianity is to suppose it primarily a religion and emotional when in truth it is primarily dogma and intellectual. We are not, then, to be concerned with Christianity as pietistic feeling but with Christianity as a precise view of man and the world, which implies a social form. But as we prepare to hear the Idea* of a Christian society we have surely the right to ask the proposer what, in his opinion, caused the failure of such previous Christian societies as may be said to have existed. We have, too, the right to ask him what it is in the nature of Christianity which brought it to the condition in which men and nations, trained in a wholly Christian culture, felt constrained to discover the inadequacy of the dogmas which are now expected to save the world. He might perhaps answer that Christianity is right but not all-powerful and that there are human impulses with which it cannot easily deal. Or if, like Mr. Eliot, he admits a dialectical-materialistic interpretation of the past but not of the future, he might find a material cause which explains the past failure without limiting the future hope. Well, we must not put inadequate answers into Mr.

*"By an idea I mean . . . that conception of a thing . . . which is given by the knowledge of its ultimate aim."—Coleridge.

Eliot's mouth, but it is indeed hard to imagine the answer that will satisfy our historical skepticism, a skepticism which is aroused, too, by Mr. Eliot's unexpressed sense that there was once a past whose political virtues are worthy and possible of recapture.

So much for our premissed objections. They are certainly not diminished by the particular recommendations which Mr. Eliot goes on to make. He projects a society which will exist in three aspects—what he calls the Christian State, the Christian Community, and the Community of Christians. This more or less Platonic triad exists, as we cannot help observing, on a rather minimal Christianity. For of the heads of his Christian State Mr. Eliot demands no more than that they be educated to think in Christian categories; for the rest, the criterion of their value is to be the same to which statesmen have always submitted—not devoutness but effectiveness. "They may," Mr. Eliot says, "frequently perform un-Christian acts; they must never attempt to defend their actions on un-Christian principles." The State, we are told, is Christian only negatively and is no more than the reflection of the Christian society which it governs. Yet this society itself is not permeated by a very intense Christianity. The mass of its citizens make up the Christian Community and their behavior is to be "largely unconscious"—for, because "their capacity for *thinking* about the objects of faith is small, their Christianity may be almost wholly realised in behaviour: both in their customary and periodic religious observances and in a traditional code of behaviour towards their neighbours."

What is left, then, to give the positive Christian tone to the Christian Society is what Mr. Eliot calls the Community of Christians, a group reminiscent of Coleridge's "clerisy" but more exclusively an elite, constituted of those clerics and laymen who consciously live the Christian life and who have notable intellectual or spiritual gifts. It is they who, by their "identity of belief and aspiration, their background of a common system of education and a common culture" will collectively form "the conscious mind and conscience of the nation." They are not to constitute a caste and so are to be loosely joined together rather than organized, and Mr. Eliot compares them in their possible wide effectiveness with the segregated intellectuals who now write only for each other.

Of the specifically and immediately practical, Mr. Eliot says little beyond submitting his Christian Society to judgment according to its success in carrying out the reforms projected by Christian sociologists. The natural end of such a society is man's "virtue and well-being in community"; this is "acknowledged for all" but "for those who have eyes to see it" there is also the supernatural end of beatitude. Culturally such a society is to be pluralistic—perhaps in a limited sense of that word, though we are told that the Community of Christians will include minds indifferent or even hostile to Christianity. There is a certain faith in the good effect of smaller units of social organization than we now have; production for use is spoken of as natural and moral; the abolition of classes is mentioned as not an impossibility.

This, it is clear, is not a social vision likely to heighten anyone's ardor, but perhaps this is not wholly a fault when we remember that neither is it likely to engender despair by raising unrealizable expectations. Of its obvious inadequacies, some may be said to arise from certain deficiencies of Mr. Eliot's temperament where it joins with certain aspects of strict and theological Anglicanism, giving us such things as the cold ignorance of what people are really like, or a confusion of morality with snobbery or conformity, or even with a rather fierce Puritanism. More important than these, however, are the inadequacies which come from an insufficient view—insufficient even when we consider the self-imposed limitations of the work—of the relation of social forms to power and of power to wealth. Without a specific consideration of this problem even a religious politics—and even the most theoretical treatment of such a politics— must seem evasive.

Yet when we have recognized all the inadequacies of Mr. Eliot's conception there still remains a theoretical interest which in the long run has, I think, its own practical value, and this lies in the assumption upon which Mr. Eliot's society is based. Mr. Eliot has not written his apologia and has not, so far as I know, made a systematic statement of belief; but I think a sentence in his essay on Pascal makes clear what the grounds of his belief are. Mr. Eliot is talking about the "unbeliever's" inability to understand the way the "intelligent believer" comes to his faith; the unbeliever, he says, "does not consider that if certain emotional states, certain developments of character and what in the highest sense can be called 'saintliness' are inherently and by inspection known to be good, then the satisfactory explanation of the world must be an explanation which will admit the 'reality' of these values." This sentence, which could not have been carelessly written, indicates that Mr. Eliot is perhaps closer than he would admit to the pragmatic theology of Matthew Arnold which he so much disdains. But the exact nature of Mr. Eliot's theology is not for the moment important. What touches our problem of a whole new intellectual world and what I should like to take hold of, not only for itself but for what it indicates beyond itself, is the morality with which Mr. Eliot is concerned. "I am inclined," he said some time ago, "to approach public affairs from the point of view of the moralist," and over and over again he has insisted that to think of politics and economics as independent of morality is impossible: impossible in an ethical sense—the political and economic theorist *should not* so consider them; and impossible in a practical sense—the theorist *cannot* construct his theories except on the ground (often unexpressed) of moral assumptions. "I feel no confidence in any scheme for putting the world in order," Mr. Eliot said, "until the proposer has answered satisfactorily the question: What is the good life?"

Everybody, of course, approves of morality. Even Leon Trotsky, who was suspicious of the morality of all moralists, spoke well of it. But, like Trotsky, most people think of morality in a somewhat ambiguous fashion: it is something to be cultivated after the particular revolution they want is accomplished, but just now it is only in the way; or they think of it as whatever helps to bring the revolution about. But Mr. Eliot thinks of morality as absolute and not as a means but an end; and, what is more, he believes that it is at every moment a present end and not one indefinitely postponable. He does not mean merely social good and the doing of it (though this enters, too) and he does not mean anything which is to be judged only from a utilitarian point of view. He means something which is personal in a way we have forgotten and which, in a way we have denied, connects personal action with the order of the universe. When he says that he is a moralist in politics he means most importantly that politics is to be judged by what it does for the moral perfection, rather than for the physical easement, of man. For the earthly good of man—the localizing adjective is important for Mr. Eliot—is moral perfection; what advances this is politically good, what hinders it is politically bad.

Now I do not think, with Mr. Eliot, that morality is absolute but I do believe that his way of considering morality has certain political advantages over Trotsky's way or the Marxist way in general. If one thing more than another marks the culture of radicalism in recent years it is that a consideration of means has taken a priority over the consideration of ends—or perhaps, to avoid the chances of a means-and-ends misunderstanding, we might rather say that immediate ends have become more important than ultimate ends. The radical intellectual of today differs from his political ancestor of even twenty-five years ago in the interest he finds in the immediate method as against the ultimate purpose. And if we take a longer period we find an even greater difference. The preparatory days of revolution—I mean the days from Montaigne to Rousseau and Diderot—were the days in which men projected a great character for man. The social imagination, when it was fresher, gave the worlds of the future a quality which our projected worlds can no longer have. The French Revolution was advanced on the warmest considerations of personality—one thinks of Montaigne's Montaigne, of Rousseau's Rousseau and his Émile, of Diderot's d'Alembert and his Rameau's nephew. And it is incidentally significant that, after this time, in every nation touched by the Revolution, the novel should have taken on its intense life. For what so animated the novel of the nineteenth century was the passionate—the "revolutionary"—interest in what man should be. It was, that is, a moral interest, and the world had the sense of a future moral revolution. Nowadays the novel, and especially in the hands of the radical intellectuals, has become enfeebled and mechanical: its decline coincides with the increasing indifference to the question, What should man become?

The heightened tempo of events will go far toward explaining the change—the speed with which calamity approached, our sense of the ship sinking and our no doubt natural giving to survival the precedence over the quality of the life that was to be preserved. Much of the change can be laid to the account of Marx, for it was Marx, with his claim to a science of society, with his concept of materialistic and dialectical causation, who, for his adherents, made the new emphasis seem unavoidable. Considerations of morality Marx largely scorned; he begins in morality, in the great historical and descriptive chapters of *Capital*, but he does not continue in it, perhaps because he is led to believe that the order of the world is going to establish morality. He speaks often of human dignity, but just what human dignity is he does not tell us, nor has any adequate Marxist philosopher or poet told us: it is not a subject which comes within the scope of their science.

Yet not merely upon the tempo of events nor upon Marx himself can we lay the indifference to morality and to aims. It must fall on something of which Marx was indeed a part and of which the tempo is of course a part but of which each of us is also a part: on the total imagination of our time. It is the characteristic of this imagination so to conceive the human quality that it diminishes with ever-increasing speed before the exigencies of means.

Lenin gave us the cue when, at the end of *The State and Revolution*, he told us that we might well postpone the problem of what man is to become until such time as he might become anything he chose. One understands how such a thing gets said; but one understands, too, that saying it does not make possible a suspension of choice: it is a choice already made and the making of it was what gave certain people the right to wonder whether the ethics and culture of Communism were anything else than the extension of the ethics and culture of the bourgeois business world. For many years the hero of our moral myth was the Worker-and-Peasant who smiled from the covers of *Soviet Russia Today*, simple, industrious, literate—and grateful. Whether or not people like him actually existed is hard to say; one suspects not and hopes not; but he was what his leaders and the radical intellectuals were glad to propagate as a moral ideal; that probably factitious Worker was the moral maximum which the preoccupation with immediate ends could accommodate.

The diminished ideal which was represented by that Worker is what Mr. Eliot would perhaps call, in his way, a heresy. But from another point of view it is also a practical, a political, error. It is the error which lies hidden in materialist and rationalist psychology. Against it a certain part of the nineteenth century was always protesting. Wordsworth was one of the first to make the protest when he discarded the Godwinian view of the mind, advanced a psychology of his own and from it derived a politics. No doubt his politics was, in the end, reactionary enough; but it became reactionary for this reason as much as any other: that it was in protest against the view of man shared alike by Liberal manufacturing Whig and radical philosopher, the view that man was very simple and individually of small worth in the cosmic or political scheme. It was because of this view that Wordsworth deserted the Revolution; and it was to supply what the Revolution lacked or, in some part, denied, that he wrote his best poetry.

What the philosophy of the Revolution lacked or denied it is difficult to find a name for. Sometimes it gets called mysticism, but it is not mysticism and Wordsworth is not a mystic. Sometimes, as if by a kind of compromise, it gets called "mystery," but that, though perhaps closer, is certainly not close enough. What is meant negatively is that man cannot be comprehended in a formula; what is meant positively is the sense of

complication and possibility, of surprise, intensification, variety, unfold-
ment, worth. These are things whose more or less abstract expressions we
recognize in the arts; in our inability to admit them in social matters lies a
great significance. Our inability to give this quality a name, our embarrassment, even, when we speak of it, marks a failure in our thought. But
Wordsworth was able to speak of this quality and he involved it integrally
with morality and all the qualities of mind which morality suggests. Eventually he made morality absolute and admittedly he engaged it with all
sorts of unsound and even dangerous notions. But, as he conceived the
quality, it was a protection against the belief that man could be made into
a means and it was an affirmation that every man was an end.

It is a tragic irony that the diminution of the moral possibility, with all
that the moral possibility implies of free will and individual value, should
spring, as it does, from the notion of the perfectibility of man.* The *ultimate man* has become the end for which all temporal men are the means.
Such a notion is part of the notion of progress in general, a belief shared
by the bourgeois and the Marxist, that the direction of the world is that
of a never-ceasing improvement. So far as Marxism goes, this idea seems
to have a discrepancy with the Marxist dialectic, for it depends on a standard of judgment which, if not an absolute, is so close to an absolute as to
be indistinguishable from it—the judgment of direction, the certainty of
what "higher" signifies and what "better" signifies. One has only to hear a
Marxist defend (as many a Marxist will) the belief that through the ages
even art shows a definable progress and improvement to understand how
untenable the notion is in any of its usual statements. And the progress
which is held to be observable in art is held to be no less observable in human relations.

---

*I leave it to some novelist to explore the more subtle results of the confused denial of the moral
possibility as it appears in the personal lives of radical intellectuals. They have used the denial, of
course, to explain the conduct of men less equipped than themselves for thought; they have declared that the mass of men are not to be held morally responsible for their own deeds and that
only history and environment are accountable. I think no one can reject this generous assumption. But questions must arise concerning what method we are to use in the judgment of men
who are our equals in moral and intellectual training. And the same question about a method of
judgment must arise about oneself, for in actual practice we do not easily tolerate people who are
content to ascribe their personal—I do not mean their practical—failures to circumstance alone.
That novelists have not dealt with this problem seems to me to bear out what I said about the
failure of the novel in the hands of the radical intellectual. Two exceptions must be noted: Mal-
raux's *Man's Fate* and Silone's *Bread and Wine*.

And from the notion of progress has grown that contempt for the past and that worship of the future which so characteristically marks the radical thought of our time. The past is seen as a series of necessary failures which perhaps have their value as, in the dialectical way, they contribute to what comes after. The past has been a failure: the present—what can it matter in the light of the perfecting future? And from—or with—a sense of the past as failure, and of the present as nothing better than a willing tributary to the future, comes the sense of the wrongness of the human quality at any given moment. For, while they have always violently reprobated any such notion as Original Sin and by and large have held the belief that, by nature, man is good, most radical philosophies have contradicted themselves by implying that man, in his quality, in his kind, will be wholly changed by socialism in fine ways that we cannot predict: man will be good not as some men have been, but good in new and unspecified fashions. At the bottom of at least popular Marxism there has always been a kind of disgust with humanity as it is and a perfect faith in humanity as it is to be.

Mr. Eliot, as I have said in passing, has his own disgust; his later criticism has shown his pained surprise at any manifestation of life that is not canonically correct. But at least Mr. Eliot's feelings are appropriate to the universe he assumes, and at least he is aware of them and makes provision for them. Of his universe Mr. Eliot predicates two things: a divine ordination and an absolute morality. From these two assumptions spring two practical conclusions which are worthy of note. The first is that the life of man involves a dual allegiance, one to the Universal Church which represents the divinely ordained universe and one to the nation and the National Church which represents temporal necessities; and the commitment of the National Church to an absolute morality makes, within the nation itself, a dualism, for the National Church, in its function, may be in disagreement with the national state. This dualism constitutes, Mr. Eliot believes, a barrier against monistic solutions of political problems such as statism or racism, and the tensions it creates are, for him, the distinguishing mark of a Christian society. The second thing implied by Mr. Eliot's assumptions is that there exists a moral goal never to be reached and a political ideal never to be realized. The world, we are told, will never be left wholly without glory, but all earthly societies are sordidly inadequate beside the ideal. This moral Platonism puts, of course, a check upon the hopes of man and restricts the possibility of "progress" yet its tragic presuppositions have this good result: that they bar any such notion as that of a *final* conflict and prevent us from envisaging any such ultimate moral victory as will permit the "withering away of the state"; they make us admit that the conflict is everlasting and in doing so they permit us to exercise a kind of charity by which we may value the humanity of the present equally with that of the future.

We say that our assumptions arise from our needs and must suit our intentions, and so they must; and perhaps in relatively recent times intelligent men of religion have been more honest in admitting the necessary assumptive elements in thought than have the radical philosophers with their tendency to hold all assumption illegitimate. Mr. Eliot shares this honesty and his thought benefits from it and our thought may benefit from the virtues his thought has. But if our assumptions spring from our needs, it is nevertheless still true that the validity of our needs and the relations between our intentions and our needs may be logically and empirically tested. So tested, Mr. Eliot's polity will not, I think, stand. If, for example, he believes that there is an historical instance or a practical likelihood of a church effectively providing the "tensions" he speaks of, he is, I think, deceiving himself. I think, indeed, that, whatever his intentions, the ecclesiastical instrument upon which he relies is, in "the practical sphere," bound to be maleficent. If I have tried to say that the assumptions of materialism have largely failed us, it was surely not to conclude that the assumptions of supernaturalism can aid us. Based as it is on supernatural assumptions, Mr. Eliot's politics is no doubt thoroughly vulnerable. But I have spoken of it with respect because it suggests elements which a rational and naturalistic philosophy, to be adequate, must encompass.

The Immortality Ode

1941

I

Criticism, we know, must always be concerned with the poem itself. But a poem does not always exist only in itself; sometimes it has a very lively existence in its false or partial appearances. These simulacra of the actual poem must be taken into account by criticism; and sometimes, in its effort to come at the poem as it really is, criticism does well to allow the simulacra to dictate at least its opening moves. In speaking about Wordsworth's "Ode: Intimations of Immortality from Recollections of Early Childhood," I should like to begin by considering an interpretation of the poem which is commonly made.* According to this interpretation—I choose for its brevity Dean Sperry's statement of a view which is held by many other admirable critics—the Ode is "Wordsworth's conscious farewell to his art, a dirge sung over his departing powers."

How did this interpretation—erroneous, as I believe—come into being? The Ode may indeed be quoted to substantiate it, but I do not think it has been drawn directly from the poem itself. To be sure, the Ode is not wholly perspicuous. Wordsworth himself seems to have thought it difficult, for in the Fenwick notes he speaks of the need for competence and attention in the reader. The difficulty does not lie in the diction, which is

---

*The text of the poem is given at the end of this essay.

simple, or even in the syntax, which is sometimes obscure, but rather in certain contradictory statements which the poem makes, and in the ambiguity of some of its crucial words. Yet the erroneous interpretation I am dealing with does not arise from any intrinsic difficulty of the poem itself but rather from certain extraneous and unexpressed assumptions which some of its readers make about the nature of the mind.

Nowadays it is not difficult for us to understand that such tacit assumptions about the mental processes are likely to lie hidden beneath what we say about poetry. Usually, despite our general awareness of their existence, it requires great effort to bring these assumptions explicitly into consciousness. But in speaking of Wordsworth one of the commonest of our unexpressed ideas comes so close to the surface of our thought that it needs only to be grasped and named. I refer to the belief that poetry is made by means of a particular poetic faculty, a faculty which may be isolated and defined.

It is this belief, based wholly upon assumption, which underlies all the speculations of the critics who attempt to provide us with explanations of Wordsworth's poetic decline by attributing it to one or another of the events of his life. In effect any such explanation is a way of *defining* Wordsworth's poetic faculty: what the biographical critics are telling us is that Wordsworth wrote great poetry by means of a faculty which depended upon his relations with Annette Vallon, or by means of a faculty which operated only so long as he admired the French Revolution, or by means of a faculty which flourished by virtue of a particular pitch of youthful sense-perception, or by virtue of a certain attitude toward Jeffrey's criticism, or by virtue of a certain relation with Coleridge.

Now no one can reasonably object to the idea of mental determination in general, and I certainly do not intend to make out that poetry is an unconditioned activity. Still, this particular notion of mental determination which implies that Wordsworth's genius failed when it was deprived of some single emotional circumstance is so much too simple and so much too mechanical that I think we must inevitably reject it. Certainly what we know of poetry does not allow us to refer the making of it to any single faculty. Nothing less than the whole mind, the whole man, will suffice for its origin. And such was Wordsworth's own view of the matter.

There is another unsubstantiated assumption at work in the common biographical interpretation of the Ode. This is the belief that a natural and inevitable warfare exists between the poetic faculty and the faculty by which we conceive or comprehend general ideas. Wordsworth himself did not believe in this antagonism—indeed, he held an almost contrary view—but Coleridge thought that philosophy had encroached upon and destroyed his own powers, and the critics who speculate on Wordsworth's artistic fate seem to prefer Coleridge's psychology to Wordsworth's own. Observing in the Ode a contrast drawn between something called "the visionary gleam" and something called "the philosophic mind," they leap to the conclusion that the Ode is Wordsworth's conscious farewell to his art, a dirge sung over departing powers.

I am so far from agreeing with this conclusion that I believe the Ode is not only not a dirge sung over departing powers but actually a dedication to new powers. Wordsworth did not, to be sure, realize his hopes for these new powers, but that is quite another matter.

2

As with many poems, it is hard to understand any part of the Ode until we first understand the whole of it. I will therefore say at once what I think the poem is chiefly about. It is a poem about growing; some say it is a poem about growing old, but I believe it is about growing up. It is incidentally a poem about optics and then, inevitably, about epistemology, it is concerned with ways of seeing and then with ways of knowing. Ultimately it is concerned with ways of acting, for, as usual with Wordsworth, knowledge implies liberty and power. In only a limited sense is the Ode a poem about immortality.

Both formally and in the history of its composition the poem is divided into two main parts. The first part, consisting of four stanzas, states an optical phenomenon and asks a question about it. The second part, consisting of seven stanzas, answers that question and is itself divided into two parts, of which the first is despairing, the second hopeful. Some time separates the composition of the question from that of the answer; the evidence most recently adduced by Professor de Selincourt seems to indicate that the interval was two years.

The question which the first part asks is this:

Whither is fled the visionary gleam?
Where is it now, the glory and the dream?

All the first part leads to this question, but although it moves in only one direction it takes its way through more than one mood. There are at least three moods before the climax of the question is reached.

The first stanza makes a relatively simple statement. "There was a time" when all common things seemed clothed in "celestial light," when they had "the glory and the freshness of a dream." In a poem ostensibly about immortality we ought perhaps to pause over the word "celestial," but the present elaborate title was not given to the poem until much later, and conceivably at the time of the writing of the first part the idea of immortality was not in Wordsworth's mind at all. Celestial light probably means only something different from ordinary, earthly, scientific light; it is a light of the mind, shining even in darkness—"by night or day"—and it is perhaps similar to the light which is praised in the invocation to the third book of *Paradise Lost*.

The second stanza goes on to develop this first mood, speaking of the ordinary, physical kind of vision and suggesting further the meaning of "celestial." We must remark that in this stanza Wordsworth is so far from observing a diminution of his physical senses that he explicitly affirms their strength. He is at pains to tell us how vividly he sees the rainbow, the rose, the moon, the stars, the water, and the sunshine. I emphasize this because some of those who find the Ode a dirge over the poetic power maintain that the poetic power failed with the failure of Wordsworth's senses. It is true that Wordsworth, who lived to be eighty, was said in middle life to look much older than his years. Still, thirty-two, his age at the time of writing the first part of the Ode, is an extravagantly early age for a dramatic failure of the senses. We might observe here, as others have observed elsewhere, that Wordsworth never did have the special and perhaps modern sensibility of his sister or of Coleridge, who were so aware of exquisite particularities. His finest passages are moral, emotional, subjective; whatever visual intensity they have comes from his response to the object, not from his close observation of it.

And in the second stanza Wordsworth not only confirms his senses but also confirms his ability to perceive beauty. He tells us how he responds to the loveliness of the rose and of the stars reflected in the water. He can deal, in the way of Fancy, with the delight of the moon when there are no competing stars in the sky. He can see in Nature certain moral propensities. He speaks of the sunshine as a "glorious birth." But here he pauses to draw distinctions from that fascinating word "glory": despite his perception of the sunshine as a glorious birth, he knows "That there hath past away a glory from the earth."

Now, with the third stanza, the poem begins to complicate itself. It is *while* Wordsworth is aware of the "optical" change in himself, the loss of the "glory," that there comes to him "a thought of grief." I emphasize the word "while" to suggest that we must understand that for some time he had been conscious of the "optical" change *without* feeling grief. The grief, then, would seem to be coincidental with but not necessarily caused by the change. And the grief is not of long duration for we learn that

> A timely utterance gave that thought relief,
> And I again am strong.

It would be not only interesting but also useful to know what that "timely utterance" was, and I shall hazard a guess; but first I should like to follow the development of the Ode a little further, pausing only to remark that the reference to the timely utterance seems to imply that, although the grief is not of long duration, still we are not dealing with the internal experiences of a moment, or of a morning's walk, but of a time sufficient to allow for development and change of mood; that is, the dramatic time of the poem is not exactly equivalent to the emotional time.

Stanza IV goes on to tell us that the poet, after gaining relief from the timely utterance, whatever that was, felt himself quite in harmony with the joy of Nature in spring. The tone of this stanza is ecstatic, and in a way that some readers find strained and unpleasant and even of doubtful sincerity. Twice there is a halting repetition of words to express a kind of painful intensity of response: "I feel—I feel it all," and "I hear, I hear, with joy I hear!" Wordsworth sees, hears, feels—and with that "joy" which both he and Coleridge felt to be so necessary to the poet. But despite the response, despite the joy, the ecstasy changes to sadness in a wonderful modulation which quite justifies the antecedent shrillness of affirmation:

> —But there's a Tree, of many, one,
> A single Field which I have looked upon,
> Both of them speak of something that is gone:

The Pansy at my feet
Doth the same tale repeat.

And what they utter is the terrible question:

Whither is fled the visionary gleam?
Where is it now, the glory and the dream?

3

Now, the interpretation which makes the Ode a dirge over departing powers and a conscious farewell to art takes it for granted that the visionary gleam, the glory and the dream, are Wordsworth's names for the power by which he made poetry. This interpretation gives to the Ode a place in Wordsworth's life exactly analogous to the place that "Dejection: An Ode" has in Coleridge's life. It is well known how intimately the two poems are connected; the circumstances of their composition make them symbiotic. Coleridge in his poem most certainly does say that his poetic powers are gone or going: he is very explicit, and the language he uses is very close to Wordsworth's own. He tells us that upon "the inanimate cold world" there must issue from the soul "a light, a glory, a fair luminous cloud," and that this glory *is* Joy, which he himself no longer possesses. But Coleridge's poem, although it responds to the first part of Wordsworth's, is not a recapitulation of it. On the contrary, Coleridge is precisely contrasting his situation with Wordsworth's. As Professor de Selincourt says in his comments on the first version of "Dejection," this contrast "was the root idea" of Coleridge's ode.* In April of 1802 Wordsworth was five months away from his marriage to Mary Hutchison, on the point of establishing his life in a felicity and order which became his genius, while Coleridge was at the nadir of despair over his own unhappy marriage and his hopeless love for Sara, the sister of Wordsworth's fiancée. And the difference between the situations of the two friends stands in Coleridge's mind for the difference in the states of health of their respective poetic powers.

*Ernest de Selincourt, *Wordsworthian and Other Studies*, Oxford, 1947.

Coleridge explicitly ascribes the decay of his poetic power to his unhappiness, which worked him harm in two ways—by forcing him to escape from the life of emotion to find refuge in intellectual abstraction and by destroying the Joy which, issuing as "a light, a glory, a fair luminous cloud," so irradiated the world as to make it a fit object of the shaping power of imagination. But Wordsworth tells us something quite different about himself. He tells us that he has strength, that he has Joy, but still he has not the glory. In short, we have no reason to assume that, when he asks the question at the end of the fourth stanza, he means, "Where has my creative power gone?" Wordsworth tells us how he made poetry; he says he made it out of the experience of his senses as worked upon by his contemplative intellect, but he nowhere tells us that he made poetry out of visionary gleams, out of glories, or out of dreams.

To be sure, he writes very often about gleams. The word "gleam" is a favorite one with him, and a glance at the Lane Cooper concordance will confirm our impression that Wordsworth, whenever he has a moment of insight or happiness, talks about it in the language of light. His great poems are about moments of enlightenment, in which the metaphoric and the literal meaning of the word are at one—he uses "glory" in the abstract modern sense, but always with an awareness of the old concrete iconographic sense of a visible nimbus.* But this momentary and special light is the subject matter of his poetry, not the power of making it. The moments are moments of understanding, but Wordsworth does not say that they make writing poetry any easier. Indeed, in lines 59–131 of the first book of *The Prelude* he expressly says that the moments of clarity are by no means always matched by poetic creativity.

As for dreams and poetry, there is some doubt about the meaning that Wordsworth gave to the word "dream" used as a metaphor. In "Expostulation and Reply" he seems to say that dreaming—"dream my time away"—is a good thing, but he is ironically using his interlocutor's depreciatory word, and he really does not mean "dream" at all. In the Peele Castle verses, which have so close a connection with the Immortality Ode, he speaks of the "poet's dream" and makes it synonymous with "gleam," with "the light that never was, on sea or land," and with the

---

*We recall that in *The Varieties of Religious Experience* William James speaks of the "hallucinatory or pseudo-hallucinatory luminous phenomena, *photisms*, to use the term of the psychologists," the "floods of light and glory," which characterize so many moments of revelation. James mentions one person who, experiencing the light, was uncertain of its externality.

"consecration." But the beauty of the famous lines often makes us forget to connect them with what follows, for Wordsworth says that gleam, light, consecration, and dream would have made an "illusion," or, in the 1807 version, a "delusion." Professor Beatty reminds us that in the 1820 version Wordsworth destroyed the beauty of the lines in order to make his intention quite clear. He wrote:

> and add a gleam
> Of lustre known to neither sea nor land.
> But borrowed from the youthful Poet's Dream.

That is, according to the terms of Wordsworth's conception of the three ages of man, the youthful Poet was, as he had a right to be, in the service of Fancy and therefore saw the sea as calm. But Wordsworth himself can now no longer see in the way of Fancy; he has, he says, "submitted to a new control." This seems to be at once a loss and a gain. The loss: "A power is gone which nothing can restore." The gain: "A deep distress hath humanized my Soul"; this is gain because happiness without "humaniza-tion" "is to be pitied, for 'tis surely blind"; to be "housed in a dream" is to be "at distance from the kind" (i.e. mankind). In the "Letter to Mathetes" he speaks of the Fancy as "dreaming"; and the Fancy is, we know, a lower form of intellect in Wordsworth's hierarchy, and peculiar to youth.

But although, as we see, Wordsworth uses the word "dream" to mean illusion, we must remember that he thought illusions might be very use-ful. They often led him to proper attitudes and allowed him to deal suc-cessfully with reality. In *The Prelude* he tells us how his reading of fiction made him able to look at the disfigured face of the drowned man without too much horror; how a kind of superstitious conviction of his own pow-ers was useful to him; how, indeed, many of the most critical moments of his boyhood education were moments of significant illusion; and in *The Excursion* he is quite explicit about the salutary effects of superstition. But he was interested in dreams not for their own sake but for the sake of re-ality. Dreams may *perhaps* be associated with poetry, but reality *certainly* is; and reality for Wordsworth comes fullest with Imagination, the faculty of maturity. The loss of the "dream" may be painful, but it does not nec-essarily mean the end of poetry.

4

And now for a moment I should like to turn back to the "timely utterance," because I think an understanding of it will help get rid of the idea that Wordsworth was saying farewell to poetry. Professor Garrod believes that this "utterance" was "My heart leaps up when I behold," which was written the day before the Ode was begun. Certainly this poem is most intimately related to the Ode—its theme, the legacy left by the child to the man, is a dominant theme of the Ode, and Wordsworth used its last lines as the Ode's epigraph. But I should like to suggest that the "utterance" was something else. In line 43 Wordsworth says, "Oh evil day! if I were sullen," and the word "sullen" leaps out at us as a striking and carefully chosen word. Now there is one poem in which Wordsworth says that he was sullen; it is "Resolution and Independence."

We know that Wordsworth was working on the first part of the Ode on 27 March, the day after the composition of the rainbow poem. On 17 June he added a little to the Ode, but what he added we do not know. Between these two dates Wordsworth and Dorothy had paid their visit to Coleridge, who was sojourning at Keswick; during this visit Coleridge, on 4 April, had written "Dejection: An Ode," very probably after he had read what was already in existence of the Immortality Ode. Coleridge's mental state was very bad—still, not so bad as to keep him from writing a great poem—and the Wordsworths were much distressed. A month later, on 3 May, Wordsworth began to compose "The Leech-Gatherer," later known as "Resolution and Independence." It is this poem that is, I think, the timely utterance.*

"Resolution and Independence" is a poem about the fate of poets. It is also a poem about sullenness, in the sense that the people in the Fifth Circle are said by Dante to be sullen: " 'Sullen were we in the sweet air, that is gladdened by the sun, carrying lazy smoke within our hearts; now lie sullen here in the black mire!' This hymn they gurgle in their throats, for

---

*I follow Professor Garrod in assuming that the "utterance" was a poem, but of course it may have been a letter or a spoken word. And if indeed the "utterance" does refer to "Resolution and Independence," it may not refer to the poem itself—as Jacques Barzun has suggested to me, it may refer to what the Leech-gatherer in the poem says to the poet, for certainly it is what the old man "utters" that gives the poet "relief."

they cannot speak it in full words"*—that is, they cannot now have relief by timely utterance, as they would not on earth. And "sullenness" I take to be the creation of difficulties where none exist, the working of a self-injuring imagination such as a modern mental physician would be quick to recognize as a neurotic symptom. Wordsworth's poem is about a sudden unmotivated anxiety after a mood of great exaltation. He speaks of this reversal of feeling as something experienced by himself before and known to all. In this mood he is the prey of "fears and fancies," of "dim sadness" and "blind thoughts." These feelings have reference to two imagined catastrophes. One of them—natural enough in a man under the stress of approaching marriage, for Wordsworth was to be married in October—is economic destitution. He reproaches himself for his past indifference to the means of getting a living and thinks of what may follow from this carefree life: "solitude, pain of heart, distress, and poverty." His black thoughts are led to the fate of poets "in their misery dead," among them Chatterton and Burns. The second specific fear is of mental distress:

> We Poets in our youth begin in gladness;
> But thereof come in the end despondency and madness.

Coleridge, we must suppose, was in his thoughts after the depressing Keswick meeting, but he is of course thinking chiefly of himself. It will be remembered how the poem ends, how with some difficulty of utterance the poet brings himself to speak with an incredibly old leech-gatherer, and, taking heart from the man's resolution and independence, becomes again "strong."

This great poem is not to be given a crucial meaning in Wordsworth's life. It makes use of a mood to which everyone, certainly every creative person, is now and again a victim. It seems to me more likely that it, rather than the rainbow poem, is the timely utterance of which the Ode speaks because in it, and not in the rainbow poem, a sullen feeling occurs and is relieved. But whether or not it is actually the timely utterance, it is an autobiographical and deeply felt poem written at the time the Ode was being written and seeming to have an emotional connection with the first

---

*The Carlyle-Wicksteed translation. Dante's word is "*tristi*"; in "Resolution and Independence" Wordsworth speaks of "dim sadness." I mention Dante's sinners simply to elucidate the emotion that Wordsworth speaks of, not to suggest an influence.

part of the Ode. (The meeting with the old man had taken place two years earlier and it is of some significance that it should have come to mind as the subject of a poem at just this time.) It is a very precise and hard-headed account of a mood of great fear and it deals in a very explicit way with the dangers that beset the poetic life. But although Wordsworth urges himself on to think of all the bad things that can possibly happen to a poet, and mentions solitude, pain of heart, distress and poverty, cold, pain and labor, all fleshly ills, and then even madness, he never says that a poet stands in danger of losing his talent. It seems reasonable to suppose that if Wordsworth were actually saying farewell to his talent in the Ode, there would be some hint of an endangered or vanishing talent in "Resolution and Independence." But there is none; at the end of the poem Wordsworth is resolute in poetry.

Must we not, then, look with considerable skepticism at such interpretations of the Ode as suppose without question that the "gleam," the "glory," and the "dream" constitute the power of making poetry?—especially when we remember that at a time still three years distant Wordsworth in *The Prelude* will speak of himself as becoming a "*creative* soul" (Book XII, line 207; the italics are Wordsworth's own) despite the fact that, as he says (Book XIII, line 281), he "sees by glimpses now."

5

The second half of the Ode is divided into two large movements, each of which gives an answer to the question with which the first part ends. The two answers seem to contradict each other. The first issues in despair, the second in hope; the first uses a language strikingly supernatural, the second is entirely naturalistic. The two parts even differ in the statement of fact, for the first says that the gleam is gone, whereas the second says that it is not gone, but only transmuted. It is necessary to understand this contradiction, but it is not necessary to resolve it, for from the circuit between its two poles comes much of the power of the poem.

The first of the two answers (stanzas V–VIII) tells us where the visionary gleam has gone by telling us where it came from. It is a remnant of a preexistence in which we enjoyed a way of seeing and knowing now almost wholly gone from us. We come into the world, not with minds that are merely *tabulae rasae*, but with a kind of attendant light, the vestige of an existence otherwise obliterated from our memories. In infancy and childhood the recollection is relatively strong, but it fades as we move forward into earthly life. Maturity, with its habits and its cares and its increase of distance from our celestial origin, wears away the light of recollection. Nothing could be more poignantly sad than the conclusion of this part with the heavy sonority of its last line as Wordsworth addresses the child in whom the glory still lives:

> Full soon thy Soul shall have her earthly freight,
> And custom lie upon thee with a weight,
> Heavy as frost, and deep almost as life!

Between this movement of despair and the following movement of hope there is no clear connection save that of contradiction. But between the question itself and the movement of hope there is an explicit verbal link, for the question is: "Whither has *fled* the visionary gleam?" and the movement of hope answers that "nature yet remembers/What was so *fugitive*."

The second movement of the second part of the Ode tells us again what has happened to the visionary gleam: it has not wholly fled, for it is remembered. This possession of childhood has been passed on as a legacy to the child's heir, the adult man; for the mind, as the rainbow epigraph also says, is one and continuous, and what was so intense a light in childhood becomes "the fountain-light of all our day" and a "master-light of all our seeing," that is, of our adult day and our mature seeing. The child's recollection of his heavenly home exists in the recollection of the adult.

But what exactly is this fountain-light, this master-light? I am sure that when we understand what it is we shall see that the glory that Wordsworth means is very different from Coleridge's glory, which is Joy. Wordsworth says that what he holds in memory as the guiding heritage of childhood is exactly not the Joy of childhood. It is not "delight," not "liberty," not even "hope"—not for these, he says, "I raise/The song of thanks and praise." For what then does he raise the song? For this particular experience of childhood:

> . . . those obstinate questionings
> Of sense and outward things,

Fallings from us, vanishings;
Blank misgivings of a Creature
Moving about in worlds not realized.

He mentions other reasons for gratitude, but here for the moment I should like to halt the enumeration.

We are told, then, that light and glory consist, at least in part, of "questionings," "fallings from us," "vanishings," and "blank misgivings" in a world not yet *made real*, for surely Wordsworth uses the word "realized" in its most literal sense. In his note on the poem he has this to say of the experience he refers to:

> . . . I was often unable to think of external things as having external existence, and I communed with all that I saw as something not apart from, but inherent in, my own material nature. Many times while going to school have I grasped at a wall or tree to recall myself from this abyss of idealism to the reality. At this time I was afraid of such processes.

He remarks that the experience is not peculiar to himself, which is of course true, and he says that it was connected in his thoughts with a potency of spirit which made him believe that he could never die.

The precise and naturalistic way in which Wordsworth talks of this experience of his childhood must cast doubt on Professor Garrod's statement that Wordsworth believed quite literally in the notion of preexistence, with which the "vanishings" experience is connected. Wordsworth is very careful to delimit the extent of his belief; he says that it is "too shadowy a notion to be recommended to faith" as an evidence of immortality. He says that he is using the idea to illuminate another idea—using it, as he says, "for my purpose" and "as a poet." It has as much validity for him as any "popular" religious idea might have, that is to say, a kind of suggestive validity. We may regard pre-existence as being for Wordsworth a very serious conceit, vested with relative belief, intended to give a high value to the natural experience of the "vanishings."*

---

*In his *Studies in the Poetry of Henry Vaughan*, a Cambridge University dissertation, Andrew Chiappe makes a similar judgement of the quality and degree of belief in the idea of pre-existence in the poetry of Vaughan and Traherne.

The naturalistic tone of Wordsworth's note suggests that we shall be doing no violence to the experience of the "vanishings" if we consider it scientifically. In a well-known essay, "Stages in the Development of the Sense of Reality," the distinguished psychoanalyst Ferenczi speaks of the child's reluctance to distinguish between himself and the world and of the slow growth of objectivity which differentiates the self from external things. And Freud himself, dealing with the "oceanic" sensation of "being at one with the universe," which a literary friend had supposed to be the source of all religious emotions, conjectures that it is a vestige of the infant's state of feeling before he has learned to distinguish between the stimuli of his own sensations and those of the world outside. In *Civilization and Its Discontents* he writes:

> Originally the ego includes everything, later it detaches from itself the outside world. The ego-feeling we are aware of now is thus only a shrunken vestige of a more extensive feeling—a feeling which embraced the universe and expressed an inseparable connexion of the ego with the external world. If we may suppose that this primary ego-feeling has been preserved in the minds of many people—to a greater or lesser extent—it would co-exist like a sort of counterpart with the narrower and more sharply outlined ego-feeling of maturity, and the ideational content belonging to it would be precisely the notion of limitless extension and oneness with the universe—the same feeling as that described by my friend as "oceanic."

This has its clear relation to Wordsworth's "worlds not realized." Wordsworth, like Freud, was preoccupied by the idea of reality, and, again like Freud, he knew that the child's way of apprehension was but a stage which, in the course of nature, would give way to another. If we understand that Wordsworth is speaking of a period common to the development of everyone, we are helped to see that we cannot identify the vision of that period with his peculiar poetic power.

But in addition to the experience of the "vanishings" there is another experience for which Wordsworth is grateful to his childhood and which, I believe, goes with the "vanishings" to make up the "master-light," the "fountain-light." I am not referring to the

High instincts before which our mortal Nature
Did tremble like a guilty Thing surprised,

but rather to what Wordsworth calls "those first affections."

I am inclined to think that with this phrase Wordsworth refers to a later stage in the child's development which, like the earlier stage in which the external world is included within the ego, leaves vestiges in the developing mind. This is the period described in a well-known passage in Book II of *The Prelude*, in which the child learns about the world in his mother's arms:

> Blest the infant Babe,
> (For with my best conjecture I would trace
> Our Being's earthly progress), blest the Babe,
> Nursed in his Mother's arms, who sinks to sleep,
> Rocked on his Mother's breast; who with his soul
> Drinks in the feelings of his Mother's eye!
> For him, in one dear Presence, there exists
> A virtue which irradiates and exalts
> Objects through widest intercourse of sense.
> No outcast he, bewildered and depressed;
> Along his infant veins are interfused
> The gravitation and the filial bond
> Of nature that connect him with the world.
> Is there a flower, to which he points with hand
> Too weak to gather it, already love
> Drawn from love's purest earthly fount for him
> Hath beautified that flower; already shades
> Of pity cast from inward tenderness
> Do fall around him upon aught that bears
> Unsightly marks of violence or harm.
> Emphatically such a Being lives.
> Frail creature as he is, helpless as frail,
> An inmate of this active universe:
> For feeling has to him imparted power
> That through the growing faculties of sense,
> Doth like an agent of the one great Mind
> Create, creator and receiver both,

Working but in alliance with the works
Which it beholds. — Such, verily, is the first
Poetic* spirit of our human life,
By uniform control of after years,
In most, abated or suppressed; in some,
Through every change of growth and of decay
Pre-eminent till death.

The child, this passage says, does not perceive things merely as objects; he first sees them, because maternal love is a condition of his perception, as objects-and-judgements, as valued objects. He does not learn about a flower, but about the pretty-flower, the flower that-I-want-and-that-mother-will-get-for-me; he does not learn about the bird and a broken wing but about the poor-bird-whose-wing-was-broken. The safety, warmth, and good feeling of his mother's conscious benevolence is a circumstance of his first learning. He sees, in short, with "glory"; not only is he himself not in "utter nakedness" as the Ode puts it, but the objects he sees are not in utter nakedness. The passage from *The Prelude* says in naturalistic language what stanza v of the Ode expresses by a theistical metaphor. Both the *Prelude* passage and the Ode distinguish a state of exile from a state of security and comfort, of at-homeness; there is (as the *Prelude* passage puts it) a "filial bond," or (as in stanza x of the Ode) a "primal sympathy," which keeps man from being an "outcast . . . bewildered and depressed."

The Ode and *The Prelude* differ about the source of this primal sympathy or filial bond. The Ode makes heavenly pre-existence the source, *The Prelude* finds the source in maternal affection. But the psychologists tell us that notions of heavenly pre-existence figure commonly as representations of physical prenatality—the womb is the environment which is perfectly adapted to its inmate and compared to it all other conditions of life may well seem like "exile" to the (very literal) "outcast."† Even the secu-

---

*The use here of the word "poetic" is either metaphorical and general, or it is entirely literal, that is, it refers to the root-meaning of the word, which is "to make"—Wordsworth has in mind the creative nature of right human perception and not merely poetry.

†"Before born babe bliss had. Within womb won he worship. Whatever in that one case done commodiously done was."—James Joyce, *Ulysses*. The myth of Eden is also interpreted as figuring either childhood or the womb—see below, p. 51, on Wordsworth's statement of the connection of the notion of pre-existence with Adam's fall.

rity of the mother's arms, although it is an effort to re-create for the child the old environment, is but a diminished comfort. And if we think of the experience of which Wordsworth is speaking, the "vanishings," as the child's recollection of a condition in which it was very nearly true that he and his environment were one, it will not seem surprising that Wordsworth should compound the two experiences and figure them in the single metaphor of the glorious heavenly pre-existence.*

I have tried to be as naturalistic as possible in speaking of Wordsworth's childhood experiences and the more-or-less Platonic notion they suggested to him. I believe that naturalism is in order here, for what we must now see is that Wordsworth is talking about something common to us all, the development of the sense of reality. To have once had the visionary gleam of the perfect union of the self and the universe is essential to and definitive of our human nature, and it is in that sense connected with the making of poetry. But the visionary gleam is not in itself the poetry-making power, and its diminution is right and inevitable.

That there should be ambivalence in Wordsworth's response to this diminution is quite natural, and the two answers, that of stanzas v–viii and that of stanzas ix–xi, comprise both the resistance to and the acceptance of growth. Inevitably we resist change and turn back with passionate nostalgia to the stage we are leaving. Still, we fulfill ourselves by choosing what is painful and difficult and necessary, and we develop by moving toward death. In short, organic development is a hard paradox which Wordsworth is stating in the discrepant answers of the second part of the Ode. And it seems to me that those critics who made the Ode refer to some particular and unique experience of Wordsworth's and who make it relate only to poetical powers have forgotten their own lives and in consequence conceive the Ode to be a lesser thing than it really is, for it is not about poetry, it is about life. And having made this error, they are inevitably led to misinterpret the meaning of the "philosophic mind" and also to deny that Wordsworth's ambivalence is sincere. No doubt it

---

*Readers of Ferenczi's remarkable study *Thalassa*, a discussion, admittedly speculative but wonderfully fascinating, of unconscious racial memories of the ocean as the ultimate source of life, will not be able to resist giving an added meaning to Wordsworth's lines about the "immortal sea/ Which brought us hither" and of the unborn children who "Sport upon the shore." The recollection of Samuel Butler's delightful fantasy of the Unborn and his theory of unconscious memory will also serve to enrich our reading of the Ode by suggesting the continuing force of the Platonic myth.

would not be a sincere ambivalence if Wordsworth were really saying farewell to poetry, it would merely be an attempt at self-consolation. But he is not saying farewell to poetry, he is saying farewell to Eden, and his ambivalence is much what Adam's was, and Milton's, and for the same reasons.*

To speak naturalistically of the quasi-mystical experiences of his childhood does not in the least bring into question the value which Wordsworth attached to them, for, despite its dominating theistical metaphor, the Ode is largely naturalistic in its intention. We can begin to see what that intention is by understanding the force of the word "imperial" in stanza VI. This stanza is the second of the four stanzas in which Wordsworth states and develops the theme of the reminiscence of the light of heaven and its gradual evanescence through the maturing years. In stanza V we are told that the infant inhabits it; the Boy beholds it, seeing it "in his joy"; the Youth is still attended by it; "the Man perceives it die away, And fade into the light of common day." Stanza VI speaks briefly of the efforts made by earthly life to bring about the natural, and inevitable, amnesia:

> Earth fills her lap with pleasures of her own;
> Yearnings she hath in her own natural kind,
> And, even with something of a Mother's mind,
>   And no unworthy aim,
>   The homely Nurse doth all she can
> To make her Foster-child, her Inmate Man,
>   Forget the glories he hath known.
> And that imperial palace whence he came.

"Imperial" suggests grandeur, dignity, and splendour, everything that stands in opposition to what, in *The Excursion*, Wordsworth was to call

---

*Milton provides a possible gloss to several difficult points in the poem. In stanza VIII, the Child is addressed as "thou Eye among the blind," and to the Eye are applied the epithets "deaf and silent"; Coleridge objected to these epithets as irrational, but his objection may be met by citing the brilliant precedent of "blind mouths" of "Lycidas." Again, Coleridge's question of the propriety of making a master *brood* over a slave is in part answered by the sonnet "On His Being Arrived at the Age of Twenty-three," in which Milton expresses his security in his development as it shall take place in his "great Task-master's eye." Between this sonnet and the Ode there are other significant correspondence of thought and of phrase, as there also are in the sonnet "On His Blindness."

"littleness." And "littleness" is the result of having wrong notions about the nature of man and his connection with the universe; its outcome is "deadness." The melancholy and despair of the Solitary in *The Excursion* are the signs of the deadness which resulted from his having conceived of man as something less than imperial. Wordsworth's idea of splendid power is his protest against all views of the mind that would limit and debase it. By conceiving, as he does, an intimate connection between mind and universe, by seeing the universe fitted to the mind and the mind to the universe, he bestows upon man a dignity which cannot be derived from looking at him in the actualities of common life, from seeing him engaged in business, in morality and politics.

Yet here we must credit Wordsworth with the double vision. Man must be conceived of as "imperial," but he must also be seen as he actually is in the field of life. The earth is not an environment in which the celestial or imperial qualities can easily exist. Wordsworth, who spoke of the notion of imperial pre-existence as being adumbrated by Adam's fall, uses the words "earth" and "earthly" in the common quasi-religious sense to refer to the things of this world. He does not make Earth synonymous with Nature, for although Man may be the true child of Nature, he is the "Foster-child" of Earth. But it is to be observed that the foster mother is a kindly one, that her disposition is at least quasi-maternal, that her aims are at least not unworthy; she is, in short, the foster mother who figures so often in the legend of the Hero, whose real and unknown parents are noble or divine.*

Wordsworth, in short, is looking at man in a double way, seeing man both in his ideal nature and in his earthly activity. The two views do not so much contradict as supplement each other. If in stanzas v–vii Wordsworth tells us that we live by decrease, in stanzas ix–xi he tells us of the everlasting connection of the diminished person with his own ideal personality. The child hands on to the hampered adult the imperial nature, the "primal sympathy/Which having been must ever be," the mind fitted to the universe, the universe to the mind. The sympathy is not so pure and intense in maturity as in childhood, but only because another relation grows up beside the relation of man to Nature—the relation of

---

*Carlyle makes elaborate play with this idea in his account of Teufelsdröckh, and see the essay on *The Princess Casamassima* in this volume, p. 149. The fantasy that their parents are really foster parents is a common one with children, and it is to be associated with the various forms of the belief that the world is not real.

man to his fellows in the moral world of difficulty and pain. Given Wordsworth's epistemology the new relation is bound to change the very aspect of Nature itself: the clouds will take a sober coloring from an eye that hath kept watch o'er man's mortality, but a sober color is a color still.

There is sorrow in the Ode, the inevitable sorrow of giving up an old habit of vision for a new one. In shifting the center of his interest from Nature to man in the field of morality Wordsworth is fulfilling his own conception of the three ages of man which Professor Beatty has expounded so well. The shift in interest he called the coming of "the philosophic mind," but the word "philosophic" does not have here either of two of its meanings in common usage—it does not mean abstract and it does not mean apathetic. Wordsworth is not saying, and it is sentimental and unimaginative of us to say, that he has become less a feeling man and less a poet. He is only saying that he has become less a youth. Indeed, the Ode is so little a farewell to art, so little a dirge sung over departing powers, that it is actually the very opposite—it is a welcome of new powers and a dedication to a new poetic subject. For if sensitivity and responsiveness be among the poetic powers, what else is Wordsworth saying at the end of the poem except that he has a greater sensitivity and responsiveness than ever before? The "philosophic mind" has not decreased but, on the contrary, increased the power to feel.

> The clouds that gather round the setting sun
> Do take a sober colouring from an eye
> That hath kept watch o'er man's mortality;
> Another race hath been and other palms are won.
> Thanks to the human heart by which we live,
> Thanks to its tenderness, its joys, and fears,
> To me the meanest flower that blows can give
> Thoughts that do often lie too deep for tears.

The meanest flower is significant now not only because, like the small celandine, it speaks of age, suffering, and death, but because to a man who is aware of man's mortality the world becomes significant and precious. The knowledge of man's mortality—this must be carefully noted in a poem presumably about immortality—now replaces the "glory" as the agency which makes things significant and precious. We are back again at optics, which we have never really left, and the Ode in a very honest fashion has come full circle.

The new poetic powers of sensitivity and responsiveness are new not so much in degree as in kind; they would therefore seem to require a new poetic subject matter for their exercise. And the very definition of the new powers seems to imply what the new subject matter must be—thoughts that lie too deep for tears are ideally the thoughts which are brought to mind by tragedy. It would be an extravagant but not an absurd reading of the Ode that found it to be Wordsworth's farewell to the characteristic mode of his poetry, the mode that Keats called the "egotistical sublime" and a dedication to the mode of tragedy. But the tragic mode could not be Wordsworth's. He did not have the "negative capability" which Keats believed to be the source of Shakespeare's power, the gift of being able to be "content with half-knowledge," to give up the "irritable reaching after fact and reason," to remain "in uncertainties, mysteries, doubts." In this he was at one with all the poets of the Romantic movement and after—negative capability was impossible for them to come by and tragedy was not for them. But although Wordsworth did not realize the new kind of art which seems implied by his sense of new powers, yet his bold declaration that he had acquired a new way of feeling makes it impossible for us to go on saying that the Ode was his "conscious farewell to his art, a dirge sung over his departing powers."

Still, was there not, after the composition of the Ode, a great falling off in his genius which we are drawn to connect with the crucial changes the Ode records? That there was a falling off is certain, although we must observe that it was not so sharp as is commonly held and also that it did not occur immediately or even soon after the composition of the first four stanzas with their statement that the visionary gleam had gone; on the contrary, some of the most striking of Wordsworth's verse was written at this time. It must be remembered, too, that another statement of the loss of the visionary gleam, that made in "Tintern Abbey," had been followed by all the superb production of the "great decade"—an objection which is sometimes dealt with by saying that Wordsworth wrote his best work from his near memories of the gleam, and that, as he grew older and moved farther from it, his recollection dimmed and thus he lost his power: it is an explanation which suggests that mechanical and simple notions of the mind and of the poetic process are all too tempting to those who speculate on Wordsworth's decline. Given the fact of the great power, the desire to explain its relative deterioration will no doubt always be irresistible. But we must be aware, in any attempt to make this explanation, that an account of why Wordsworth ceased to write great poetry must at the same time be an account of how he once did write great poetry. And this latter account, in our present state of knowledge, we cannot begin to furnish.

ODE: INTIMATIONS OF IMMORTALITY FROM RECOLLECTIONS OF EARLY CHILDHOOD
BY WILLIAM WORDSWORTH

> The Child is father of the Man;
> And I could wish my days to be
> Bound each to each by natural piety.

I

There was a time when meadow, grove, and stream
The earth, and every common sight,
　　　　To me did seem
　　　Apparelled in celestial light,
The glory and the freshness of a dream.
It is not now as it hath been of yore;—
　　　Turn wheresoe'er I may,
　　　　By night or day,
The things which I have seen I now can see no more.

II

　　The Rainbow comes and goes,
　　And lovely is the Rose,

The Moon doth with delight
Look round her when the heavens are bare,
   Waters on a starry night
   Are beautiful and fair;
  The sunshine is a glorious birth;
  But yet I know, where'er I go,
That there hath past away a glory from the earth.

III

Now, while the birds thus sing a joyous song,
   And while the young lambs bound
     As to the tabor's sound,
To me alone there came a thought of grief:
A timely utterance gave that thought relief,
     And I again am strong:
The cataracts blow their trumpets from the steep:
No more shall grief of mine the season wrong;
I hear the Echoes through the mountains throng,
The Winds come to me from the fields of sleep,
     And all the earth is gay:
      Land and sea
    Give themselves up to jollity,
     And with the heart of May
   Doth every Beast keep holiday;—
     Thou Child of Joy,
Shout round me, let me hear thy shouts, thou happy Shepherd boy!

IV

Ye blessèd Creatures, I have heard the call
   Ye to each other make; I see
The heavens laugh with you in your jubilee;
   My heart is at your festival,

My head hath its coronal,
The fulness of your bliss, I feel—I feel it all.
    Oh evil day! if I were sullen
    While Earth herself is adorning,
      This sweet May-morning,
    And the Children are culling
      On every side,
    In a thousand valleys far and wide,
    Fresh flowers; while the sun shines warm,
And the Babe leaps up on his Mother's arm:—
    I hear, I hear, with joy I hear!
    —But there's a Tree, of many, one,
A single Field which I have looked upon,
Both of them speak of something that is gone:
    The Pansy at my feet
    Doth the same tale repeat:
Whither is fled the visionary gleam?
Where is it now, the glory and the dream?

V

Our birth is but a sleep and a forgetting:
The Soul that rises with us, our life's Star,
    Hath had elsewhere its setting,
      And cometh from afar:
    Not in entire forgetfulness,
    And not in utter nakedness,
But trailing clouds of glory do we come
    From God, who is our home:
Heaven lies about us in our infancy!
Shades of the prison-house begin to close
    Upon the growing Boy,
But He beholds the light, and whence it flows,
    He sees it in his joy;
The Youth, who daily farther from the east

Must travel, still is Nature's Priest,
And by the vision splendid
Is on his way attended;
At length the Man perceives it die away,
And fade into the light of common day.

VI

Earth fills her lap with pleasures of her own;
Yearnings she hath in her own natural kind,
And, even with something of a Mother's mind,
    And no unworthy aim,
    The homely Nurse doth all she can
To make her Foster-child, her Inmate Man,
    Forget the glories he hath known,
And that imperial palace whence he came.

VII

Behold the Child among his new-born blisses,
A six years' Darling of a pigmy size!
See, where 'mid work of his own hand he lies,
Fretted by sallies of his mother's kisses,
With light upon him from his father's eyes!
See, at his feet, some little plan or chart,
Some fragment from his dream of human life,
Shaped by himself with newly-learned art;
    A wedding or a festival,
    A mourning or a funeral;
    And this hath now his heart,
    And unto this he frames his song:
    Then will he fit his tongue
To dialogues of business, love, or strife;

But it will not be long
    Ere this be thrown aside,
    And with new Joy and pride
The little Acorn cons another part;
Filling from time to time his 'humorous stage'
With all the Persons, down to palsied Age,
That Life brings with her in her equipage;
    As if his whole vocation
    Were endless imitation.

VIII

Thou, whose exterior semblance doth belie
    Thy Soul's immensity;
Thou best Philosopher, who yet dost keep
Thy heritage, thou Eye among the blind,
That, deaf and silent, read'st the eternal deep,
Haunted for ever by the eternal mind,—
    Mighty Prophet! Seer blest!
    On whom those truths do rest.
Which we are toiling all our lives to find,
In darkness lost, the darkness of the grave;
Thou, over whom thy Immortality
Broods like the Day, a Master o'er a Slave,
A Presence which is not to be put by;
Thou little Child, yet glorious in the might
Of heaven-born freedom on thy being's height,
Why with such earnest pains dost thou provoke
The years to bring the inevitable yoke,
Thus blindly with thy blessedness at strife?
Full soon thy Soul shall have her earthly freight,
And custom lie upon thee with a weight,
Heavy as frost, and deep almost as life!

IX

O joy! that in our embers
Is something that doth live,
That nature yet remembers
What was so fugitive!
The thought of our past years in me doth breed
Perpetual benediction: not indeed
For that which is most worthy to be blest;
Delight and liberty, the simple creed
Of Childhood, whether busy or at rest,
With new-fledged hope still fluttering in his breast:—
    Not for these I raise
    The song of thanks and praise;
    But for those obstinate questionings
    Of sense and outward things,
    Fallings from us, vanishings;
    Blank misgivings of a Creature
Moving about in worlds not realized,
High instincts before which our mortal Nature
Did tremble like a guilty Thing surprised:
    But for those first affections,
    Those shadowy recollections,
  Which, be they what they may,
Are yet the fountain-light of all our day,
Are yet a master-light of all our seeing;
  Uphold us, cherish, and have power to make
Our noisy years seem moments in the being
Of the eternal Silence: truths that wake,
    To perish never:
Which neither listlessness, nor mad endeavour
    Nor Man nor Boy,
Nor all that is at enmity with joy,
Can utterly abolish or destroy.
    Hence in a season of calm weather
    Though inland far we be,
Our Souls have sight of that immortal sea
    Which brought us hither,

Can in a moment travel thither,
And see the Children sport upon the shore,
And hear the mighty waters rolling evermore.

X

Then sing, ye Birds, sing, sing a joyous song!
    And let the young Lambs bound
    As to the tabor's sound!
We in thought will join your throng,
    Ye that pipe and ye that play,
    Ye that through your hearts to-day
    Feel the gladness of the May!
What though the radiance which was once so bright
Be now for ever taken from my sight,
  Though nothing can bring back the hour
Of splendour in the grass, of glory in the flower;
    We will grieve not, rather find
    Strength in what remains behind;
    In the primal sympathy
    Which having been must ever be;
    In the soothing thoughts that spring
    Out of human suffering;
    In the faith that looks through death,
In years that bring the philosophic mind.

XI

And O, ye Fountains, Meadows, Hills, and Groves,
Forebode not any severing of our loves!
Yet in my heart of hearts I feel your might;
I only have relinquished one delight
To live beneath your more habitual sway.
I love the Brooks which down their channels fret,

Even more than when I tripped lightly as they;
The innocent brightness of a new-born Day
     Is lovely yet;
The Clouds that gather round the setting sun
Do take a sober colouring from an eye
That hath kept watch o'er man's mortality;
Another race hath been, and other palms are won.
   Thanks to the human heart by which we live,
   Thanks to its tenderness, its joys, and fears.
   To me the meanest flower that blows can give
Thoughts that do often lie too deep for tears.

Kipling

1943

Kipling belongs irrevocably to our past, and although the renewed critical attention he has lately been given by Edmund Wilson and T. S. Eliot is friendlier and more interesting than any he has received for a long time, it is less likely to make us revise our opinions than to revive our memories of him. But these memories, when revived, will be strong, for if Kipling belongs to our past, he belongs there very firmly, fixed deep in childhood feeling. And especially for liberals of a certain age he must always be an interesting figure, for he had an effect upon us in that obscure and important part of our minds where literary feeling and political attitude meet, an effect so much the greater because it was so early experienced; and then for many of us our rejection of him was our first literary-political decision.

My own relation with Kipling was intense and I believe typical. It began, properly enough, with *The Jungle Book*. This was my first independently chosen and avidly read book, my first literary discovery, all the more wonderful because I had come upon it in an adult "set," one of the ten green volumes of the Century Edition that used to be found in many homes. (The "set" has become unfashionable and that is a blow to the literary education of the young, who, once they had been lured to an author, used to remain loyal to him until they had read him by the yard.)

The satisfactions of *The Jungle Book* were large and numerous. I suppose a boy's vestigial animal totemism was pleased; there were the marvellous but credible abilities of Mowgli; there were the deadly enmities and grandiose revenges, strangely and tragically real. And it was a world peopled by wonderful parents, not only Mother Wolf and Father Wolf, but also—the fathers were far more numerous than the mothers—Bagheera the panther, Baloo the bear, Hathi the elephant, and the dreadful but decent Kaa the python, a whole council of strength and wisdom which was as benign as it was dangerous, and no doubt much of the delight came from discovering the benignity of this feral world. And then there was the fascination of the Pack and its Law. It is not too much to say that a boy had thus his first introduction to a generalized notion of society. It was a notion charged with feeling—the Law was mysterious, firm, certain, noble, in every way admirable beyond any rule of home or school.

Mixed up with this feeling about the Pack and the Law, and perfectly expressing it, was the effect of Kipling's gnomic language, both in prose and in verse, for you could not entirely skip the verse that turned up in the prose, and so you were led to trust yourself to the *Barrack Room Ballads* at a time when you would trust no other poetry. That gnomic quality of Kipling's, that knowing allusiveness which later came to seem merely vulgar, was, when first experienced, a delightful thing. By understanding Kipling's ellipses and allusions you partook of what was Kipling's own special delight, the joy of being "in." Max Beerbohm has satirized Kipling's yearning to be admitted to any professional arcanum, his fawning admiration of the man in uniform, the man with the know-how and the technical slang. It is the emotion of a boy—he lusts for the exclusive circle, for the sect with the password, and he profoundly admires the technical, secret-laden adults who run the world, the overalled people, majestic in their occupation, superb in their preoccupation, the dour engineer and the thoughtful plumber. To this emotion, developed not much beyond a boy's, Kipling was addicted all his life, and eventually it made him silly and a bore. But a boy reading Kipling was bound to find all this sense of arcanum very pertinent; as, for example, it expressed itself in *Plain Tales from the Hills*, it seemed the very essence of adult life. Kipling himself was not much more than a boy when he wrote these remarkable stories—remarkable because, no matter how one judges them, one never forgets the least of them—and he saw the adult world as full of rites of initiation, of closed doors and listeners behind them, councils, boudoir conferences, conspiracies, innuendoes, and special knowledge. It was very baffling, and certainly as an introduction to literature it went counter to all our present educational theory, according to which a child should not be baffled at all but should read only about what he knows of from experience; but one worked it out by a sort of algebra, one discovered the meaning of the unknowns through the knowns, and just as one got without definition an adequate knowledge of what a *sais* was, or a *dâk*-bungalow, and what the significance of *pukka* was, so one penetrated to what went on between the Gadsbys and to why Mrs. Hauksbee was supposed to be charming and Mrs. Reiver not. Kipling's superior cryptic tone was in effect an invitation to understand all this—it suggested first that the secret was being kept not only from oneself but from everyone else and then it suggested that the secret was not so much being kept as revealed, if one but guessed hard enough. And this elaborate manner was an invitation to be "in" not only on life but on literature; to follow its hints with a sense of success was to become an initiate of literature, a Past Master, a snob of the esoteric Mystery of the Word.

"Craft" and "craftily" were words that Kipling loved (no doubt they were connected with his deep Masonic attachment), and when he used them he intended all their several meanings at once—shrewdness, a special technique, a special *secret* technique communicated by some master of it, and the bond that one user of the technique would naturally have with another. This feeling about the Craft, the Mystery, grew on Kipling and colored his politics and even his cosmological ideas quite for the worse, but to a boy it suggested the virtue of disinterested professional commitment. If one ever fell in love with the cult of art, it was not because one had been proselytized by some intelligent Frenchman, but because one had absorbed Kipling's creedal utterances about the virtues of craft and had read *The Light that Failed* literally to pieces.

These things we must be sure to put into balance when we make up our account with Kipling—these and a few more. To a middle-class boy he gave a literary sanction for the admiration of the illiterate and shiftless parts of humanity. He was the first to suggest what may be called the anthropological view, the perception that another man's idea of virtue and honor may be different from one's own but quite to be respected. We must remember this when we condemn his mindless imperialism. Indians naturally have no patience whatever with Kipling and they condemn even his best book, *Kim*, saying that even here, where his devotion to the Indian life is most fully expressed, he falsely represents the Indians. Perhaps this is so, yet the dominant emotions of *Kim* are love and respect for the aspects of Indian life that the ethos of the West does not usually regard even with leniency. *Kim* established the value of things a boy was not likely to find approved anywhere else—the rank, greasy, over-rich things, the life that was valuable outside the notions of orderliness, success, and gentility. It suggested not only a multitude of different ways of life but even different modes of thought. Thus, whatever one might come to feel personally about religion, a reading of *Kim* could not fail to establish religion's factual reality, not as a piety, which was the apparent extent of its existence in the West, but as something at the very root of life; in *Kim* one saw the myth in the making before one's very eyes and understood how and why it was made, and this, when later one had the intellectual good luck to remember it, had more to say about history and culture than anything in one's mere experience. *Kim*, like *The Jungle Book*, is full of wonderful fathers, all dedicated men in their different ways, each representing a different possibility of existence; and the charm of each is the greater because the boy need not commit himself to one alone but, like Kim himself, may follow Ali into the shrewdness and sensuality of the bazaars, and be initiated by Colonel Strickland into the cold glamour of the Reason of State, and yet also make himself the son of the Lama, the very priest of contemplation and peace.

And then a boy in a large New York high school could find a blessed release from the school's offensive pieties about "service" and "character" in the scornful individualism of *Stalky & Co*. But it was with *Stalky & Co*. that the spell was broken, and significantly enough by H. G. Wells. In his *Outline of History* Wells connected the doings of Stalky, McTurk, and Beetle with British imperialism, and he characterized both in a way that made one see how much callousness, arrogance, and brutality one had been willing to accept. From then on the disenchantment grew. Exactly because Kipling was so involved with one's boyhood, one was quick to give him up in one's adolescence. The Wellsian liberalism took hold, and Shaw offered a new romance of wit and intellect. The new movements in literature came in to make Kipling seem inconsequential and puerile, to require that he be dismissed as official and, as one used to say, intending something aesthetic and emotional rather than political, "bourgeois." He ceased to be the hero of life and literature and became the villain, although even then a natural gratitude kept green the memory of the pleasure he had given.

But the world has changed a great deal since the days when that antagonism between Kipling and enlightenment was at its early intensity, and many intellectual and political things have shifted from their old assigned places. The liberalism of Wells and Shaw long ago lost its ascendancy, and indeed in its later developments it showed what could never in the early days have been foreseen, an actual affinity with certain elements of Kipling's own constellation of ideas. And now when, in the essay which serves as the introduction to his selection of Kipling's verse, Mr. Eliot speaks of "the fascination of exploring a mind so different from my own," we surprise ourselves—as perhaps Mr. Eliot intended that we should—by seeing that the similarities between the two minds are no less striking than the differences. Time surely has done its usual but always dramatic work of eroding our clear notions of cultural antagonisms when Kipling can be thought of as in any way akin to Eliot. Yet as Mr. Eliot speaks of the public intention and the music-hall tradition of Kipling's verse, anyone who has heard a record of Mr. Eliot reading *The Waste Land* will be struck by how much that poem is publicly intended, shaped less for the study than for the platform or the pulpit, by how much the full dialect rendition of the cockney passages suggests that it was even shaped for the music hall, by how explicit the poet's use of his voice makes the music we are so likely to think of as internal and secretive. Then it is significant that among the dominant themes of both Kipling and Eliot are those of despair and the fear of nameless psychological horror. Politically they share an excessive reliance on administration and authority. They have the same sense of being beset and betrayed by the ignoble mob; Kipling invented and elaborated the image of the Pict, the dark little hating man, "too little to love or to hate," who, if left alone, "can drag down the state"; and this figure plays its well-known part in Mr. Eliot's poetry, being for both poets the stimulus to the pathos of xenophobia.

Mr. Eliot's literary apologia for Kipling consists of asking us to judge him not as a deficient writer of poetry but as an admirable writer of verse. Upon this there follow definitions of a certain ingenuity, but the distinction between poetry and verse does not really advance beyond the old inadequate one—I believe that Mr. Eliot himself has specifically rejected it—which Matthew Arnold put forward in writing about Dryden and Pope. I cannot see the usefulness of the distinction; I can even see critical danger in it; and when Mr. Eliot says that Kipling's verse sometimes becomes poetry, it seems to me that verse, in Mr. Eliot's present sense, is merely a word used to denote poetry of a particular kind, in which certain intensities are rather low. Nowadays, it is true, we are not enough aware of the pleasures of poetry of low intensity, by which, in our modern way, we are likely to mean poetry in which the processes of thought are not, by means of elliptical or tangential metaphor and an indirect syntax, advertised as being under high pressure; Crabbe, Cowper, and Scott are rejected because they are not Donne or Hopkins or Mr. Eliot himself, or even poets of far less consequence than these; and no doubt Chaucer would be depreciated on the same grounds, if we were at all aware of him these days. I should have welcomed Mr. Eliot's speaking out in a general way in support of the admirable, and, I think, necessary, tradition of poetry of low intensity. But by making it different in kind from poetry of high intensity and by giving it a particular name which can only be of invidious import, he has cut us off still more sharply from its virtues.

Kipling, then, must be taken as a poet. Taken so, he will scarcely rank very high, although much must be said in his praise. In two evenings, or even in a single very long one, you can read through the bulky Inclusive Edition of his verse, on which Mr. Eliot's selection is based, and be neither wearied, in part because you will not have been involved, nor uninterested, because Kipling was a man of great gifts. You will have moments of admiration, sometimes of unwilling admiration, and even wish that Mr. Eliot had included certain poems in his selection that he has left out. You will be frequently irritated by the truculence and sometimes amused by its unconsciousness—who but Kipling would write a brag about English understatement? Carlyle roaring the virtues of Silence is nothing to it—but when you have done you will be less inclined to condemn than to pity: the constant iteration of the bravado will have been illuminated by a few poems that touch on the fear and horror which Mr. Wilson speaks of at length and which Mr. Eliot refers to; you feel that the walls of wrath and the ramparts of empire are being erected against the mind's threat to itself. This is a real thing, whether we call it good or bad, and its force of reality seems to grow rather than diminish in memory, seems to be greater after one's actual reading is behind one; the quality of this reality is that which we assign to primitive and elemental things, and, judge it as we will, we dare not be indifferent or superior to it.

In speaking of Kipling's politics, Mr. Eliot contents himself with denying that Kipling was a fascist; a tory, he says, is a very different thing; a tory considers fascism the last debasement of democracy. But this, I think, is not quite ingenuous of Mr. Eliot. A tory, to be sure, is not a fascist and Kipling is not properly to be called a fascist, but neither is his political temperament to be adequately described merely by reference to a tradition which is honoured by Dr. Johnson, Burke, and Walter Scott. Kipling is not like these men; he is not generous, and, although he makes much to-do about manliness, he is not manly; and he has none of the *mind* of the few great tories. His toryism often had in it a lower-middle-class snarl of defeated gentility, and it is this, rather than his love of authority and force, that might suggest an affinity with fascism. His imperialism is reprehensible not because it *is* imperialism but because it is a puny and mindless imperialism. In short, Kipling is unloved and unlovable not by reason of his beliefs but by reason of the temperament that gave them literary expression.

I have said that the old antagonism between liberalism and Kipling is now abated by time and events, yet it is still worth saying, and it is not extravagant to say, that Kipling was one of liberalism's major intellectual misfortunes. John Stuart Mill, when he urged all liberals to study the conservative Coleridge, said that we should pray to have enemies who make us worthy of ourselves. Kipling was an enemy who had the opposite effect. He tempted liberals to be content with easy victories of right feeling and with moral self-congratulation. For example, the strength of toryism at its best lies in its descent from a solid administrative tradition, while the weakness of liberalism, arising from its history of reliance upon legislation, is likely to be a fogginess about administration (or, when the fog clears away a little, a fancy and absolute notion of administration such as Wells and Shaw gave way to). Kipling's sympathy was always with the administrator and he is always suspicious of the legislator. This is foolish, but it is not the most reprehensible error in the world, and it is a prejudice which, in the hands of an intelligent man, say a man like Walter Bagehot or like Fitzjames Stephen, might make clear to the man of principled theory, to the liberal, what the difficulties not merely of government but of *governing* really are. And that is what Kipling set out to do, but he so charged his demonstration with hatred and contempt, with rancour and caste feeling, he so emptied the honorable tory tradition of its intellectual content, that he simply could not be listened to or believed, he could only be reacted against. His extravagance sprang from his hatred of the liberal intellectual—he was, we must remember, the aggressor in the quarrel— and the liberal intellectual responded by hating everything that Kipling loved, even when it had its element of virtue and enlightenment.

We must make no mistake about it—Kipling was an honest man and he loved the national virtues. But I suppose no man ever did more harm to the national virtues than Kipling did. He mixed them up with a swagger and swank, with bullying, ruthlessness, and self-righteousness, and he set them up as necessarily antagonistic to intellect. He made them stink in the nostrils of youth. I remember that in my own undergraduate days we used specifically to exclude physical courage from among the virtues; we were exaggerating the point of a joke of Shaw's and reacting from Kipling. And up to the war I had a yearly struggle with undergraduates over Wordsworth's poem "The Character of the Happy Warrior," which is, I suppose, the respectable father of the profligate "If."* It seemed too moral and "manly," the students said, and once when I remarked that John Wordsworth had apparently been just such a man as his brother had described, and told them about his dutiful and courageous death at sea, they said flatly that they were not impressed. This was not what most of them really thought, but the idea of courage and duty had been steeped for them in the Kipling vat and they rejected the idea with the color. In England this response seems to have gone even further.† And when the war came, the interesting and touching phenomenon of the cult of Richard Hillary, which Arthur Koestler has described, was the effort of the English young men to find the national virtues without the Kipling color, to know and resist their enemies without self-glorification.

In our day the idea of the nation has become doubtful and debilitated all over the world, or at least wherever it is not being enforced by ruthless governments or wherever it is not being nourished by immediate danger or the tyranny of other nations. Men more and more think it best to postulate their loyalty either to their class, or to the idea of a social organiza-

---

*The war over, the struggle is on again.
†George Orwell's essay on Kipling in *Dickens, Dali and Others* deals bluntly and fairly with the implications of easy "liberal" and "aesthetic" contempt for *everything* Kipling stood for.

tion more comprehensive than that of the nation, or to a cultural ideal or a spiritual fatherland. Yet in the attack which has been made on the national idea, there are, one suspects, certain motives that are not expressed, motives that have less to do with reason and order than with the modern impulse to say that politics is not really a proper human activity at all; the reluctance to give loyalty to any social organization which falls short of some ideal organization of the future may imply a disgust not so much with the merely national life as with the civic life itself. And on the positive side too something is still to be said for nations, the case against them is not yet closed. Of course in literature nothing ever is said; every avowal of national pride or love or faith rings false and serves but to reinforce the tendency of rejection, as the example of the response to Kipling shows. Yet Kipling himself, on one occasion, dealt successfully with the national theme and in doing so implied the reason for the general failure—the "Recessional" hymn is a remarkable and perhaps a great national poem; its import of humility and fear at the moment of national success suggests that the idea of the nation, although no doubt a limited one, is still profound enough to require that it be treated with a certain measure of seriousness and truth-telling. But the occasion is exceptional with Kipling, who by utterances that are characteristic of him did more than any other writer of our time to bring the national idea into discredit.

Reality in America

1940–46

It is possible to say of V. L. Parrington that with his *Main Currents in American Thought* he has had an influence on our conception of American culture which is not equalled by that of any other writer of the last two decades. His ideas are now the accepted ones wherever the college course in American literature is given by a teacher who conceives himself to be opposed to the genteel and the academic and in alliance with the vigorous and the actual. And whenever the liberal historian of America finds occasion to take account of the national literature, as nowadays he feels it proper to do, it is Parrington who is his standard and guide. Parrington's ideas are the more firmly established because they do not have to be imposed—the teacher or the critic who presents them is likely to find that his task is merely to make articulate for his audience what it has always believed, for Parrington formulated in a classic way the suppositions about our culture which are held by the American middle class so far as that class is at all liberal in its social thought and so far as it begins to understand that literature has anything to do with society.

Parrington was not a great mind; he was not a precise thinker or, except when measured by the low eminences that were about him, an impressive one. Separate Parrington from his informing idea of the economic and social determination of thought and what is left is a simple intelligence, notable for its generosity and enthusiasm but certainly not for its accuracy or originality. Take him even with his idea and he is, once its direction is established, rather too predictable to be continuously interesting; and, indeed, what we dignify with the name of economic and social determinism amounts in his use of it to not much more than the demonstration that most writers incline to stick to their own social class. But his best virtue was real and important—he had what we like to think of as the saving salt of the American mind, the lively sense of the practical, workaday world, of the welter of ordinary undistinguished things and people, of the tangible, quirky, unrefined elements of life. He knew what so many literary historians do not know, that emotions and ideas are the sparks that fly when the mind meets difficulties.

Yet he had after all but a limited sense of what constitutes a difficulty. Whenever he was confronted with a work of art that was complex, personal and not literal, that was not, as it were, a public document, Parrington was at a loss. Difficulties that were complicated by personality or that were expressed in the language of successful art did not seem quite real to him and he was inclined to treat them as aberrations, which is one way of saying what everybody admits, that the weakest part of Parrington's talent was his aesthetic judgment. His admirers and disciples like to imply that his errors of aesthetic judgment are merely lapses of taste, but this is not so. Despite such mistakes as his notorious praise of Cabell, to whom in a remarkable passage he compares Melville, Parrington's taste was by no means bad. His errors are the errors of understanding which arise from his assumptions about the nature of reality.

Parrington does not often deal with abstract philosophical ideas, but whenever he approaches a work of art we are made aware of the metaphysics on which his aesthetics is based. There exists, he believes, a thing called "reality"; it is one and immutable, it is wholly external, it is irreducible. Men's minds may waver, but reality is always reliable, always the same, always easily to be known. And the artist's relation to reality he conceives as a simple one. Reality being fixed and given, the artist has but to let it pass through him, he is the lens in the first diagram of an elementary book on optics: Fig. 1, Reality; Fig. 2, Artist; Fig. 1', Work of Art. Figures 1 and 1' are normally in virtual correspondence with each other. Sometimes the artist spoils this ideal relation by "turning away from" reality. This results in certain fantastic works, unreal and ultimately useless.

It does not occur to Parrington that there is any other relation possible between the artist and reality than this passage of reality through the transparent artist; he meets evidence of imagination and creativeness with a settled hostility the expression of which suggests that he regards them as the natural enemies of democracy.

In this view of things, reality, although it is always reliable, is always rather sober-sided, even grim. Parrington, a genial and enthusiastic man, can understand how the generosity of man's hopes and desires may leap beyond reality; he admires will in the degree that he suspects mind. To an excess of desire and energy which blinds a man to the limitations of reality he can indeed be very tender. This is one of the many meanings he gives to "romance" or "romanticism," and in spite of himself it appeals to something in his own nature. The praise of Cabell is Parrington's response not only to Cabell's elegance—for Parrington loved elegance—but also to Cabell's insistence on the part which a beneficent self-deception may and even should play in the disappointing fact-bound life of man, particularly in the private and erotic part of his life.*

The second volume of *Main Currents* is called *The Romantic Revolution in America* and it is natural to expect that the word romantic should appear in it frequently. So it does, more frequently than one can count, and seldom with the same meaning, seldom with the sense that the word, although scandalously vague as it has been used by the literary historians, is still full of complicated but not wholly pointless ideas, that it involves many contrary but definable things; all too often Parrington uses the word "romantic" with the word "romance" close at hand, meaning *a* romance, in the sense that *Graustark* or *Treasure Island* is a romance, as though it signified chiefly a gay disregard of the limitations of everyday fact. Romance is refusing to heed the counsels of experience (p. iii); it is ebullience (p. iv); it is utopianism (p. iv); it is individualism (p. vi); it is self-deception (p. 59)—"romantic faith . . . in the beneficent processes of trade and industry" (as held, we inevitably ask, by the romantic Adam Smith?); it is the love of the picturesque (p. 49); it is the dislike of innovation (p. 50) but also the love of change (p. iv); it is the sentimental (p. 192); it is patriotism, and then it is cheap (p. 235). It may be used to

---

*See, for example, how Parrington accounts for the "idealizing mind"—Melville's—by the discrepancy between "a wife in her morning kimono" and "the Helen of his dreams." Vol. ii, p. 259.

denote what is not classical, but chiefly it means that which ignores reality (pp. ix, 136, 143, 147, and *passim*); it is not critical (pp. 225, 235), although in speaking of Cooper and Melville, Parrington admits that criticism can sometimes spring from romanticism.

Whenever a man with whose ideas he disagrees wins from Parrington a reluctant measure of respect, the word romantic is likely to appear. He does not admire Henry Clay, yet something in Clay is not to be despised—his romanticism, although Clay's romanticism is made equivalent with his inability to "come to grips with reality." Romanticism is thus, in most of its significations, the venial sin of *Main Currents*; like carnal passion in the *Inferno*, it evokes not blame but tender sorrow. But it can also be the great and saving virtue which Parrington recognizes. It is ascribed to the transcendental reformers he so much admires; it is said to mark two of his most cherished heroes, Jefferson and Emerson: "they were both romantics and their idealism was only a different expression of a common spirit." Parrington held, we may say, at least two different views of romanticism which suggest two different views of reality. Sometimes he speaks of reality in an honorific way, meaning the substantial stuff of life, the ineluctable facts with which the mind must cope, but sometimes he speaks of it pejoratively and means the world of established social forms; and he speaks of realism in two ways: sometimes as the power of dealing intelligently with fact, sometimes as a cold and conservative resistance to idealism.

Just as for Parrington there is a saving grace and a venial sin, there is also a deadly sin, and this is turning away from reality, not in the excess of generous feeling but in what he believes to be a deficiency of feeling, as with Hawthorne, or out of what amounts to sinful pride, as with Henry James. He tells us that there was too much realism in Hawthorne to allow him to give his faith to the transcendental reformers: "he was too much of a realist to change fashions in creeds"; "he remained cold to the revolutionary criticism that was eager to pull down the old temples to make room for nobler." It is this cold realism, keeping Hawthorne apart from his enthusiastic contemporaries, that alienates Parrington's sympathy—

Eager souls, mystics and revolutionaries, may propose to refashion the world in accordance with their dreams; but evil remains, and so long as it lurks in the secret places of the heart, utopia is only the shadow of a dream. And so while the Concord thinkers were proclaiming man to be the indubitable child of God, Hawthorne was critically examining the question of evil as it appeared in the light of his own experience. It was the central fascinating problem of his intellectual life, and in pursuit of a solution he probed curiously into the hidden, furtive recesses of the soul.

Parrington's disapproval of the enterprise is unmistakable.

Now we might wonder whether Hawthorne's questioning of the naïve and often eccentric faiths of the transcendental reformers was not, on the face of it, a public service. But Parrington implies that it contributes nothing to democracy, and even that it stands in the way of the realization of democracy. If democracy depends wholly on a fighting faith, I suppose he is right. Yet society is after all something that exists at the moment as well as in the future, and if one man wants to probe curiously into the hidden furtive recesses of the contemporary soul, a broad democracy and especially one devoted to reality should allow him to do so without despising him. If what Hawthorne did was certainly nothing to build a party on, we ought perhaps to forgive him when we remember that he was only one man and that the future of mankind did not depend upon him alone. But this very fact serves only to irritate Parrington; he is put out by Hawthorne's loneliness and believes that part of Hawthorne's insufficiency as a writer comes from his failure to get around and meet people. Hawthorne could not, he tells us, establish contact with the "Yankee reality," and was scarcely aware of the "substantial world of Puritan reality that Samuel Sewall knew."

To turn from reality might mean to turn to romance, but Parrington tells us that Hawthorne was romantic "only in a narrow and very special sense." He was not interested in the world of, as it were, practical romance, in the Salem of the clipper ships; from this he turned away to create "a romance of ethics." This is not an illuminating phrase but it is a catching one, and it might be taken to mean that Hawthorne was in the tradition of, say, Shakespeare; but we quickly learn that, no, Hawthorne had entered a barren field, for although he himself lived in the present and had all the future to mold, he preferred to find many of his subjects in the past. We learn, too, that his romance of ethics is not admirable because it requires the hard, fine pressing of ideas, and we are told that "a romantic uninterested in adventure and afraid of sex is likely to become somewhat gravelled for matter." In short, Hawthorne's mind was a thin one, and Parrington puts in evidence his use of allegory and symbol and the very severity and precision of his art to prove that he suffered from a sadly limited intellect, for so much fancy and so much art could scarcely be needed unless the writer were trying to exploit to the utmost the few poor ideas that he had.

Hawthorne, then, was "forever dealing with shadows, and he knew that he was dealing with shadows." Perhaps so, but shadows are also part of reality and one would not want a world without shadows, it would not even be a "real" world. But we must get beyond Parrington's metaphor. The fact is that Hawthorne was dealing beautifully with realities, with substantial things. The man who could raise those brilliant and serious doubts about the nature and possibility of moral perfection, the man who could keep himself aloof from the "Yankee reality" and who could dissent from the orthodoxies of dissent and tell us so much about the nature of moral zeal, is of course dealing exactly with reality.

Parrington's characteristic weakness as a historian is suggested by his title, for the culture of a nation is not truly figured in the image of the current. A culture is not a flow, nor even a confluence; the form of its existence is struggle, or at least debate—it is nothing if not a dialectic. And in any culture there are likely to be certain artists who contain a large part of the dialectic within themselves, their meaning and power lying in their contradictions; they contain within themselves, it may be said, the very essence of the culture, and the sign of this is that they do not submit to serve the ends of any one ideological group or tendency. It is a significant circumstance of American culture, and one which is susceptible of explanation, that an unusually large proportion of its notable writers of the nineteenth century were such repositories of the dialectic of their times— they contained both the yes and the no of their culture, and by that token they were prophetic of the future. Parrington said that he had not set up shop as a literary critic; but if a literary critic is simply a reader who has the ability to understand literature and to convey to others what he understands, it is not exactly a matter of free choice whether or not a cultural historian shall be a literary critic, nor is it open to him to let his virtuous political and social opinions do duty for percipience. To throw out Poe because he cannot be conveniently fitted into a theory of American culture, to speak of him as a biological sport and as a mind apart from the main current, to find his gloom to be merely personal and eccentric, "only the atrabilious wretchedness of a dipsomaniac," as Hawthorne's was "no more than the sceptical questioning of life by a nature that knew no fierce storms," to judge Melville's response to American life to be less noble than that of Bryant or of Greeley, to speak of Henry James as an escapist, as an artist similar to Whistler, a man characteristically afraid of stress—this is not merely to be mistaken in aesthetic judgment; rather it is to examine without attention and from the point of view of a limited and essentially arrogant conception of reality the documents which are in some respects the most suggestive testimony to what America was and is, and of course to get no answer from them.

Parrington lies twenty years behind us, and in the intervening time there has developed a body of opinion which is aware of his inadequacies and of the inadequacies of his coadjutors and disciples, who make up what might be called the literary academicism of liberalism. Yet Parrington still stands at the center of American thought about American culture because, as I say, he expresses the chronic American belief that there exists an opposition between reality and mind and that one must enlist oneself in the party of reality.

2

This belief in the incompatibility of mind and reality is exemplified by the doctrinaire indulgence which liberal intellectuals have always displayed toward Theodore Dreiser, an indulgence which becomes the worthier of remark when it is contrasted with the liberal severity toward Henry James. Dreiser and James: with that juxtaposition we are immediately at the dark and bloody crossroads where literature and politics meet. One does not go there gladly, but nowadays it is not exactly a matter of free choice whether one does or does not go. As for the particular juxtaposition itself, it is inevitable and it has at the present moment far more significance than the juxtaposition which once used to be made between James and Whitman. It is not hard to contrive factitious oppositions between James and Whitman, but the real difference between them is the difference between the moral mind, with its awareness of tragedy, irony, and multitudinous distinctions, and the transcendental mind, with its passionate sense of the oneness of multiplicity. James and Whitman are unlike not in quality but in kind, and in their very opposition they serve to complement each other. But the difference between James and Dreiser is not of kind, for both men addressed themselves to virtually the same social and moral fact. The difference here is one of quality, and perhaps nothing is more typical of American liberalism than the way it has responded to the respective qualities of the two men.

Few critics, I suppose, no matter what their political disposition, have ever been wholly blind to James's great gifts, or even to the grandiose moral intention of these gifts. And few critics have ever been wholly blind to Dreiser's great faults. But by liberal critics James is traditionally put to the ultimate question: of what use, of what actual political use, are his gifts and their intention? Granted that James was devoted to an extraordinary moral perceptiveness, granted, too, that moral perceptiveness has something to do with politics and the social life; of what possible practical value in our world of impending disaster can James's work be? And James's style, his characters, his subjects, and even his own social origin and the manner of his personal life are adduced to show that his work cannot endure the question. To James no quarter is given by American criticism in its political and liberal aspect. But in the same degree that liberal criticism is moved by political considerations to treat James with severity, it treats Dreiser with the most sympathetic indulgence. Dreiser's literary faults, it gives us to understand, are essentially social and political virtues. It was Parrington who established the formula for the liberal criticism of Dreiser by calling him a "peasant": when Dreiser thinks stupidly, it is because he has the slow stubbornness of a peasant; when he writes badly, it is because he is impatient of the sterile literary gentility of the bourgeoisie. It is as if wit, and flexibility of mind, and perception, and knowledge were to be equated with aristocracy and political reaction, while dullness and stupidity must naturally suggest a virtuous democracy, as in the old plays.

The liberal judgment of Dreiser and James goes back to politics, goes back to the cultural assumptions that make politics. We are still haunted by a kind of political fear of the intellect which Tocqueville observed in us more than a century ago. American intellectuals, when they are being consciously American or political, are remarkably quick to suggest that an art which is marked by perception and knowledge, although all very well in its way, can never get us through gross dangers and difficulties. And their misgivings become the more intense when intellect works in art as it ideally should, when its processes are vivacious and interesting and brilliant. It is then that we like to confront it with the gross dangers and difficulties and to challenge it to save us at once from disaster. When intellect in art is awkward or dull we do not put it to the test of ultimate or immediate practicality. No liberal critic asks the question of Dreiser whether *his* moral preoccupations are going to be useful in confronting the disasters that threaten us. And it is a judgment on the proper nature of mind, rather than any actual political meaning that might be drawn from the works of the two men, which accounts for the unequal justice they have received from the progressive critics. If it could be conclusively demonstrated—by, say, documents in James's handwriting—that James explicitly intended his books to be understood as pleas for cooperatives, labor unions, better housing, and more equitable taxation, the American critic in his liberal and progressive character would still be worried by James because his work shows so many of the electric qualities of mind. And if something like the opposite were proved of Dreiser, it would be brushed aside—as his doctrinaire anti-Semitism has in fact been brushed aside—because his books have the awkwardness, the chaos, the heaviness which we associate with "reality." In the American metaphysic reality is always material reality, hard, resistant, unformed, impenetrable, and unpleasant. And that mind is alone felt to be trustworthy which most resembles this reality by most nearly reproducing the sensations it affords.

In *The Rise of American Civilization*, Professor Beard uses a significant phrase when, in the course of an ironic account of James's career, he implies that we have the clue to the irrelevance of that career when we know that James was "a whole generation removed from the odours of the shop." Of a piece with this, and in itself even more significant, is the comment which Granville Hicks makes in *The Great Tradition* when he deals with James's stories about artists and remarks that such artists as James portrays, so concerned for their art and their integrity in art, do not really exist: "After all, who has ever known such artists? Where are the Hugh Verekers, the Mark Ambients, the Neil Paradays, the Overts, the Limberts, Dencombes, Delavoys?" This question, as Mr. Hicks admits, had occurred to James himself, but what answer had James given to it? "If the life about us for the last thirty years refused warrant for these examples," he said in the preface to volume XII of the New York edition, then so much the worse for that life. . . . There are decencies that in the name of the general self-respect we must take for granted, there's a rudimentary intellectual honour to which we must, in the interest of civilization, at least pretend.

And to this Mr. Hicks, shocked beyond argument, makes this reply, which would be astonishing had we not heard it before: "But this is the purest romanticism, this writing about what ought to be rather than what is!"

The "odours of the shop" are real, and to those who breathe them they guarantee a sense of vitality from which James is debarred. The idea of intellectual honor is not real, and to that chimera James was devoted. He betrayed the reality of what is in the interests of what ought to be. Dare we trust him? The question, we remember, is asked by men who themselves have elaborate transactions with what ought to be. Professor Beard spoke in the name of a growing, developing, and improving America. Mr. Hicks, when he wrote *The Great Tradition*, was in general sympathy with a nominally radical movement. But James's own transaction with what ought to be is suspect because it is carried on through what I have called the electric qualities of mind, through a complex and rapid imagination and with a kind of authoritative immediacy. Mr. Hicks knows that Dreiser is "clumsy" and "stupid" and "bewildered" and "crude in his statement of materialistic monism"; he knows that Dreiser in his personal life—which is in point because James's personal life is always supposed to be so much in point—was not quite emancipated from "his boyhood longing for crass material success," showing "again and again a desire for the ostentatious luxury of the successful business man." But Dreiser is to be accepted and forgiven because his faults are the sad, lovable, honorable faults of reality itself, or of America itself—huge, inchoate, struggling toward expression, caught between the dream of raw power and the dream of morality.

> The liability in what Santayana called the genteel tradition was due to its being the product of mind apart from experience. Dreiser gave us the stuff of our common experience, not as it was hoped to be by any idealizing theorist, but as it actually was in its crudity.

The author of this statement certainly cannot be accused of any lack of feeling for mind as Henry James represents it; nor can Mr. Matthiessen be thought of as a follower of Parrington—indeed, in the preface to *American Renaissance* he has framed one of the sharpest and most cogent criticisms of Parrington's method. Yet Mr. Matthiessen, writing in *The New York Times Book Review* about Dreiser's posthumous novel, *The Bulwark*, accepts the liberal cliché which opposes crude experience to mind and establishes Dreiser's value by implying that the mind which Dreiser's crude experience is presumed to confront and refute is the mind of gentility.

This implied amalgamation of mind with gentility is the rationale of the long indulgence of Dreiser, which is extended even to the style of his prose. Everyone is aware that Dreiser's prose style is full of roughness and ungainliness, and the critics who admire Dreiser tell us it does not matter. Of course it does not matter. No reader with a right sense of style would suppose that it does matter, and he might even find it a virtue. But it has been taken for granted that the ungainliness of Dreiser's style is the only possible objection to be made to it, and that whoever finds in it any fault at all wants a prettified genteel style (and is objecting to the ungainliness of reality itself). For instance, Edwin Berry Burgum, in a leaflet on Dreiser put out by the Book Find Club, tells us that Dreiser was one of those who used—or, as Mr. Burgum says, utilized—"the diction of the Middle West, pretty much as it was spoken, rich in colloquialism and frank in the simplicity and directness of the pioneer tradition," and that this diction took the place of "the literary English, formal and bookish, of New England provincialism that was closer to the aristocratic spirit of the mother country than to the tang of everyday life in the new West." This is mere fantasy. Hawthorne, Thoreau, and Emerson were for the most part remarkably colloquial—they wrote, that is, much as they spoke, their prose was specifically American in quality and, except for occasional lapses, quite direct and simple. It is Dreiser who lacks the sense of colloquial diction—that of the Middle West or any other. If we are to talk of bookishness, it is Dreiser who is bookish; he is precisely literary in the bad sense; he is full of flowers of rhetoric and shines with paste gems; at hundreds of points his diction is not only genteel but fancy. It is he who speaks of "a scene more distingué than this," or of a woman "artistic in form and feature," or of a man who although "strong, reserved, aggressive, with an air of wealth and experience, was *soi-disant* and not particularly eager to stay at home." Colloquialism held no real charm for him and his natural tendency is always toward the "fine."

Moralists come and go; religionists fulminate and declare the pronouncements of God as to this; but Aphrodite still reigns. Embowered in the festal depths of the spring, set above her altars of porphyry, chalcedony, ivory and gold, see her smile the smile that is at once the texture and essence of delight, the glory and despair of the world! Dream on, oh Buddha, asleep on your lotus leaf, of an undisturbed Nirvana! Sweat, oh Jesus, your last agonizing drops over an unregenerate world! In the forests of Pan still ring the cries of the worshippers of Aphrodite! From her altars the incense of adoration ever rises! And see, the new red grapes dripping where votive hands new-press them!

Charles Jackson, the novelist, telling us in the same leaflet that Dreiser's style does not matter, remarks on how much still comes to us when we have lost by translation the stylistic brilliance of Thomas Mann or the Russians or Balzac. He is in part right. And he is right, too, when he says that a certain kind of conscious, supervised artistry is not appropriate to the novel of large dimensions. Yet the fact is that the great novelists have usually written very good prose, and what comes through even a bad translation is exactly the power of mind that made the well-hung sentence of the original text. In literature style is so little the mere clothing of thought—need it be insisted on at this late date?—that we may say that from the earth of the novelist's prose spring his characters, his ideas, and even his story itself.*

---

*The latest defense of Dreiser's style, that in the chapter on Dreiser in the *Literary History of the United States*, is worth noting: "Forgetful of the integrity and power of Dreiser's whole work, many critics have been distracted into a condemnation of his style. He was, like Twain and Whitman, an organic artist; he wrote what he knew—what he was. His many colloquialisms were part of the coinage of his time, and his sentimental and romantic passages were written in the language of the educational system and the popular literature of his formative years. In his style, as in his material, he was a child of his time, of his class. Self-educated, a type or model of the artist of plebeian origin in America, his language, like his subject matter, is not marked by internal inconsistencies." No doubt Dreiser was an organic artist in the sense that he wrote what he knew and what he was, but so, I suppose, is every artist; the question for criticism comes down to *what* he knew and *what* he was. That he was a child of his time and class is also true, but this can be said of everyone without exception; the question for criticism is how he transcended the imposed limitations of his time and class. As for the defense made on the ground of his particular class, it can only be said that liberal thought has come to a strange pass when it assumes that a plebeian origin is accountable for a writer's faults through all his intellectual life.

To the extent that Dreiser's style is defensible, his thought is also defensible. That is, when he thinks like a novelist, he is worth following—when by means of his rough and ungainly but no doubt cumulatively effective style he creates rough, ungainly, but effective characters and events. But when he thinks like, as we say, a philosopher, he is likely to be not only foolish but vulgar. He thinks as the modern crowd thinks when it decides to think: religion and morality are nonsense, "religionists" and moralists are fakes, tradition is a fraud, what is man but matter and impulses, mysterious "chemisms," what value has life anyway?

> What, cooking, eating, coition, job holding, growing, aging, losing, winning, in so changeful and passing a scene as this, important? Bunk! It is some form of titillating illusion with about as much import to the superior forces that bring it all about as the functions and gyrations of a fly. No more. And maybe less.

Thus Dreiser at sixty. And yet there is for him always the vulgarly saving suspicion that maybe, when all is said and done, there is Something Behind It All. It is much to the point of his intellectual vulgarity that Dreiser's anti-Semitism was not merely a social prejudice but an idea, a way of dealing with difficulties.

No one, I suppose, has ever represented Dreiser as a masterly intellect. It is even commonplace to say that his ideas are inconsistent or inadequate. But once that admission has been made, his ideas are hustled out of sight while his "reality" and great brooding pity are spoken of. (His pity is to be questioned: pity is to be judged by kind, not amount, and Dreiser's pity—*Jennie Gerhardt* provides the only exception—is either destructive of its object or it is self-pity.) Why has no liberal critic ever brought Dreiser's ideas to the bar of political practicality, asking what use is to be made of Dreiser's dim, awkward speculation, of his self-justification, of his lust for "beauty" and "sex" and "living" and "life itself," and of the showy nihilism which always seems to him so grand a gesture in the direction of profundity? We live, understandably enough, with the sense of urgency; our clock, like Baudelaire's, has had the hands removed and bears the legend, "It is later than you think." But with us it is always a little too late for mind, yet never too late for honest stupidity; always a little too late for understanding, never too late for righteous, bewildered wrath; always too late for thought, never too late for naïve moralizing. We seem to like to condemn our finest but not our worst qualities by pitting them against the exigency of time.

But sometimes time is not quite so exigent as to justify all our own exigency, and in the case of Dreiser time has allowed his deficiencies to reach their logical, and fatal, conclusion. In *The Bulwark* Dreiser's characteristic ideas come full circle, and the simple, didactic life history of Solon Barnes, a Quaker business man, affirms a simple Christian faith, and a kind of practical mysticism, and the virtues of self-abnegation and self-restraint, and the belief in and submission to the hidden purposes of higher powers, those "superior forces that bring it all about"—once, in Dreiser's opinion, so brutally indifferent, now somehow benign. This is not the first occasion on which Dreiser has shown a tenderness toward religion and a responsiveness to mysticism. *Jennie Gerhardt* and the figure of the Reverend Duncan McMillan in *An American Tragedy* are forecasts of the avowals of *The Bulwark*, and Dreiser's lively interest in power of any sort led him to take account of the power implicit in the cruder forms of mystical performance. Yet these rifts in his nearly monolithic materialism cannot quite prepare us for the blank pietism of *The Bulwark*, not after we have remembered how salient in Dreiser's work has been the long surly rage against the "religionists" and the "moralists," the men who have presumed to believe that life can be given any law at all and who have dared to suppose that will or mind or faith can shape the savage and beautiful entity that Dreiser liked to call "life itself." Now for Dreiser the law may indeed be given, and it is wholly simple—the safe conduct of the personal life requires only that we follow the Inner Light according to the regimen of the Society of Friends, or according to some other godly rule. And now the smiling Aphrodite set above her altars of porphyry, chalcedony, ivory, and gold is quite forgotten, and we are told that the sad joy of cosmic acceptance goes hand in hand with sexual abstinence.

Dreiser's mood of "acceptance" in the last years of his life is not, as a personal experience, to be submitted to the tests of intellectual validity. It consists of a sensation of cosmic understanding, of an overarching sense of unity with the world in its apparent evil as well as in its obvious good. It is no more to be quarrelled with, or reasoned with, than love itself—indeed, it is a kind of love, not so much of the world as of oneself in the world. Perhaps it is either the cessation of desire or the perfect balance of desires. It is what used often to be meant by "peace," and up through the nineteenth century a good many people understood its meaning. If it was Dreiser's own emotion at the end of his life, who would not be happy that he had achieved it? I am not even sure that our civilization would not be the better for more of us knowing and desiring this emotion of grave felicity. Yet granting the personal validity of the emotion, Dreiser's exposition of it fails, and is, moreover, offensive. Mr. Matthiessen has warned us of the attack that will be made on the doctrine of *The Bulwark* by "those who believe that any renewal of Christianity marks a new 'failure of nerve.' " But Dreiser's religious avowal is not a failure of nerve—it is a failure of mind and heart. We have only to set his book beside any work in which mind and heart are made to serve religion to know this at once. Ivan Karamazov's giving back his ticket of admission to the "harmony" of the universe suggests that *The Bulwark* is not morally adequate, for we dare not, as its hero does, blandly "accept" the suffering of others; and the Book of Job tells us that it does not include enough in its exploration of the problem of evil, and is not stern enough. I have said that Dreiser's religious affirmation was offensive; the offense lies in the vulgar ease of its formulation, as well as in the comfortable untroubled way in which Dreiser moved from nihilism to pietism.*

The Bulwark is the fruit of Dreiser's old age, but if we speak of it as a failure of thought and feeling, we cannot suppose that with age Dreiser weakened in mind and heart. The weakness was always there. And in a sense it is not Dreiser who failed but a whole way of dealing with ideas, a way in which we have all been in some degree involved. Our liberal, progressive culture tolerated Dreiser's vulgar materialism with its huge negation, its simple cry of "Bunk!", feeling that perhaps it was not quite intellectually adequate but certainly very *strong*, certainly very *real*. And now, almost as a natural consequence, it has been given, and is not unwilling to take, Dreiser's pietistic religion in all its inadequacy.

Dreiser, of course, was firmer than the intellectual culture that accepted him. He *meant* his ideas, at least so far as a man can mean ideas who is incapable of following them to their consequences. But we, when

---

*This ease and comfortableness seem to mark contemporary religious conversions. Religion nowadays has the appearance of what the ideal modern house has been called, "a machine for living," and seemingly one makes up one's mind to acquire and use it not with spiritual struggle but only with a growing sense of its practicability and convenience. Compare *The Seven Storey Mountain*, which Monsignor Sheen calls "a twentieth-century form of the *Confessions* of Saint Augustine," with the old, the as it were original, *Confessions* of Saint Augustine.

it came to his ideas, talked about his great brooding pity and shrugged the ideas off. We are still doing it. Robert Elias, the biographer of Dreiser, tells us that "it is part of the logic of [Dreiser's] life that he should have completed *The Bulwark* at the same time that he joined the Communists." Just what kind of logic this is we learn from Mr. Elias's further statement:

> When he supported left-wing movements and finally, last year, joined the Communist Party, he did so not because he had examined the details of the party line and found them satisfactory, but because he agreed with a general programme that represented a means for establishing his cherished goal of greater equality among men.

Whether or not Dreiser was following the logic of his own life, he was certainly following the logic of the liberal criticism that accepted him so undiscriminatingly as one of the great, significant expressions of its spirit. This is the liberal criticism, in the direct line of Parrington, which establishes the social responsibility of the writer and then goes on to say that, apart from his duty of resembling reality as much as possible, he is not really responsible for anything, not even for his ideas. The scope of reality being what it is, ideas are held to be mere "details," and, what is more, to be details which, if attended to, have the effect of diminishing reality. But ideals are different from ideas; in the liberal criticism which descends from Parrington ideals consort happily with reality and they urge us to deal impatiently with ideas—a "cherished goal" forbids that we stop to consider how we reach it, or if we may not destroy it in trying to reach it the wrong way.

Art and Neurosis

1945–47

The question of the mental health of the artist has engaged the attention of our culture since the beginning of the Romantic Movement. Before that time it was commonly said that the poet was "mad," but this was only a manner of speaking, a way of saying that the mind of the poet worked in different fashion from the mind of the philosopher; it had no real reference to the mental hygiene of the man who was the poet. But in the early nineteenth century, with the development of a more elaborate psychology and a stricter and more literal view of mental and emotional normality, the statement was more strictly and literally intended. So much so, indeed, that Charles Lamb, who knew something about madness at close quarters and a great deal about art, undertook to refute in his brilliant essay "On the Sanity of True Genius," the idea that the exercise of the imagination was a kind of insanity. And some eighty years later, the idea having yet further entrenched itself, Bernard Shaw felt called upon to argue the sanity of art, but his cogency was of no more avail than Lamb's. In recent years the connection between art and mental illness has been formulated not only by those who are openly or covertly hostile to art, but also and more significantly by those who are most intensely partisan to it. The latter willingly and even eagerly accept the idea that the artist is mentally ill and go on to make his illness a condition of his power to tell the truth.

This conception of artistic genius is indeed one of the characteristic notions of our culture. I should like to bring it into question. To do so is to bring also into question certain early ideas of Freud's and certain conclusions which literary laymen have drawn from the whole tendency of the Freudian psychology. From the very start it was recognized that psychoanalysis was likely to have important things to say about art and artists. Freud himself thought so, yet when he first addressed himself to the subject he said many clumsy and misleading things. I have elsewhere and at length tried to separate the useful from the useless and even dangerous statements about art that Freud has made.* To put it briefly here, Freud had some illuminating and even beautiful insights into certain particular works of art which made complex use of the element of myth. Then, without specifically undertaking to do so, his *Beyond the Pleasure Principle* offers a brilliant and comprehensive explanation of our interest in tragedy. And what is of course most important of all—it is a point to which I shall return—Freud, by the whole tendency of his psychology, establishes the *naturalness* of artistic thought. Indeed, it is possible to say of Freud that he ultimately did more for our understanding of art than any other writer since Aristotle; and this being so, it can only be surprising that in his early work he should have made the error of treating the artist as a neurotic who escapes from reality by means of "substitute gratifications."

As Freud went forward he insisted less on this simple formulation. Certainly it did not have its original force with him when, at his seventieth birthday celebration, he disclaimed the right to be called the discoverer of the unconscious, saying that whatever he may have done for the systematic understanding of the unconscious, the credit for its discovery properly belonged to the literary masters. And psychoanalysis has inherited from him a tenderness for art which is real although sometimes clumsy, and nowadays most psychoanalysts of any personal sensitivity are embarrassed by occasions which seem to lead them to reduce art to a formula of mental illness. Nevertheless Freud's early belief in the essential neuroticism of the artist found an all too fertile ground—found, we might say, the very ground from which it first sprang, for, when he spoke

*In "Freud and Literature," *The Liberal Imagination*.

of the artist as a neurotic, Freud was adopting one of the popular beliefs of his age. Most readers will see this belief as the expression of the industrial rationalization and the bourgeois philistinism of the nineteenth century. In this they are partly right. The nineteenth century established the basic virtue of "getting up at eight, shaving close at a quarter-past, breakfasting at nine, going to the City at ten, coming home at half-past five, and dining at seven." The Messrs. Podsnap who instituted this scheduled morality inevitably decreed that the arts must celebrate it and nothing else. "Nothing else to be permitted to these . . . vagrants the Arts, on pain of excommunication. Nothing else To Be—anywhere!" We observe that the virtuous day ends with dinner—bed and sleep are naturally not part of the Reality that Is, and nothing must be set forth which will, as Mr. Podsnap put it, bring a Blush to the Cheek of a Young Person.

The excommunication of the arts, when it was found necessary, took the form of pronouncing the artist mentally degenerate, a device which eventually found its theorist in Max Nordau. In the history of the arts this is new. The poet was always known to belong to a touchy tribe—*genus irritabile* was a tag anyone would know—and ever since Plato the process of the inspired imagination, as we have said, was thought to be a special one of some interest, which the similitude of madness made somewhat intelligible. But this is not quite to say that the poet was the victim of actual mental aberration. The eighteenth century did not find the poet to be less than other men, and certainly the Renaissance did not. If he was a professional, there might be condescension to his social status, but in a time which deplored all professionalism whatever, this was simply a way of asserting the high value of poetry, which ought not to be compromised by trade. And a certain good nature marked even the snubbing of the professional. At any rate, no one was likely to identify the poet with the weakling. Indeed, the Renaissance ideal held poetry to be, like arms or music, one of the signs of manly competence.

The change from this view of things cannot be blamed wholly on the bourgeois or philistine public. Some of the "blame" must rest with the poets themselves. The Romantic poets were as proud of their art as the vaunting poets of the sixteenth century, but one of them talked with an angel in a tree and insisted that Hell was better than Heaven and sexuality holier than chastity; another told the world that he wanted to lie down like a tired child and weep away this life of care; another asked so foolish a question as "Why did I laugh tonight?"; and yet another explained that he had written one of his best poems in a drugged sleep. The public took them all at their word—they were not as other men. Zola, in the interests of science, submitted himself to examination by fifteen psychiatrists and agreed with their conclusion that his genius had its source in the neurotic elements of his temperament. Baudelaire, Rimbaud, Verlaine found virtue and strength in their physical and mental illness and pain. W. H. Auden addresses his "wound" in the cherishing language of a lover, thanking it for the gift of insight it has bestowed. "Knowing you," he says, "has made me understand." And Edmund Wilson, in his striking phrase "the wound and the bow," has formulated for our time the idea of the characteristic sickness of the artist, which he represents by the figure of Philoctetes, the Greek warrior who was forced to live in isolation because of the disgusting odor of a suppurating wound and who yet had to be sought out by his countrymen because they had need of the magically unerring bow he possessed.

The myth of the sick artist, we may suppose, has established itself because it is of advantage to the various groups who have one or another relation with art. To the artist himself the myth gives some of the ancient powers and privileges of the idiot and the fool, half-prophetic creatures, or of the mutilated priest. That the artist's neurosis may be but a mask is suggested by Thomas Mann's pleasure in representing his untried youth as "sick" but his successful maturity as senatorially robust. By means of his belief in his own sickness, the artist may the more easily fulfill his chosen, and assigned, function of putting himself into connection with the forces of spirituality and morality; the artist sees as insane the "normal" and "healthy" ways of established society, while aberration and illness appear as spiritual and moral health if only because they controvert the ways of respectable society.

Then too, the myth has its advantage for the philistine—a double advantage. On the one hand, the belief in the artist's neuroticism allows the philistine to shut his ears to what the artist says. But on the other hand it allows him to listen. For we must not make the common mistake—the contemporary philistine does want to listen, at the same time that he wants to shut his ears. By supposing that the artist has an interesting but not always reliable relation to reality, he is able to contain (in the military sense) what the artist tells him. If he did not want to listen at all, he would say "insane"; with "neurotic," which hedges, he listens when he chooses.

And in addition to its advantage to the artist and to the philistine, we must take into account the usefulness of the myth to a third group, the group of "sensitive" people who, although not artists, are not philistines either. These people form a group by virtue of their passive impatience with philistinism, and also by virtue of their awareness of their own emotional pain and uncertainty. To these people the myth of the sick artist is the institutional sanction of their situation; they seek to approximate or acquire the character of the artist sometimes by planning to work or even attempting to work as the artist does, always by making a connection between their own powers of mind and their consciousness of "difference" and neurotic illness.

The early attempts of psychoanalysis to deal with art went on the assumption that, because the artist was neurotic, the content of his work was also neurotic, which is to say that it did not stand in a correct relation to reality. But nowadays, as I have said, psychoanalysis is not likely to be so simple in its transactions with art. A good example of the psychoanalytical development in this respect is Dr. Saul Rosenzweig's well-known essay "The Ghost of Henry James."* This is an admirable piece of work, marked by accuracy in the reporting of the literary fact and by respect for the value of the literary object. Although Dr. Rosenzweig explores the element of neurosis in James's life and work, he nowhere suggests that this element in any way lessens James's value as an artist or moralist. In effect he says that neurosis is a way of dealing with reality which, in real life, is uncomfortable and uneconomical, but that this judgment of neurosis in life cannot mechanically be transferred to works of art upon which neurosis has had its influence. He nowhere implies that a work of art in whose genesis a neurotic element may be found is for that reason irrelevant or in any way diminished in value. Indeed, the manner of his treatment suggests, what is of course the case, that every neurosis deals with a real emotional situation of the most intensely meaningful kind.

Yet as Dr. Rosenzweig brings his essay to its close, he makes use of the current assumption about the causal connection between the psychic illness of the artist and his power. His investigation of James, he says, "reveals the aptness of the Philoctetes pattern." He accepts the idea of "the sacrificial roots of literary power" and speaks of "the unhappy sources of

*First published in *Character and Personality*, December 1943, and reprinted in *Partisan Review*, Fall 1944.

James's genius." "The broader application of the inherent pattern," he says, "is familiar to readers of Edmund Wilson's recent volume *The Wound and the Bow*. . . . Reviewing the experience and work of several well-known literary masters, Wilson discloses the sacrificial roots of their power on the model of the Greek legend. In the case of Henry James, the present account . . . provides a similar insight into the unhappy sources of his genius. . . ."

This comes as a surprise. Nothing in Dr. Rosenzweig's theory requires it. For his theory asserts no more than that Henry James, predisposed by temperament and family situation to certain mental and emotional qualities, was in his youth injured in a way which he believed to be sexual; that he unconsciously invited the injury in the wish to identify himself with his father, who himself had been similarly injured—"castrated": a leg had been amputated—and under strikingly similar circumstances; this resulted for the younger Henry James in a certain pattern of life and in a preoccupation in his work with certain themes which more or less obscurely symbolize his sexual situation. For this I think Dr. Rosenzweig makes a sound case. Yet I submit that this is not the same thing as disclosing the roots of James's power or discovering the sources of his genius. The essay which gives Edmund Wilson's book its title and cohering principle does not explicitly say that the roots of power are sacrificial and that the source of genius is unhappy. Where it is explicit, it states only that "genius and disease, like strength and mutilation, may be inextricably bound up together," which of course, on its face, says no more than that personality is integral and not made up of detachable parts; and from this there is no doubt to be drawn the important practical and moral implication that we cannot judge or dismiss a man's genius and strength because of our awareness of his disease or mutilation. The Philoctetes legend in itself does not suggest anything beyond this. It does not suggest that the wound is the price of the bow, or that without the wound the bow may not be possessed or drawn. Yet Dr. Rosenzweig has accurately summarized the force and, I think, the intention of Mr. Wilson's whole book; its several studies do seem to say that effectiveness in the arts does depend on sickness.

An examination of this prevalent idea might well begin with the observation of how pervasive and deeply rooted is the notion that power may be gained by suffering. Even at relatively high stages of culture the mind seems to take easily to the primitive belief that pain and sacrifice are connected with strength. Primitive beliefs must be treated with respectful alertness to their possible truth and also with the suspicion of their being magical and irrational, and it is worth noting on both sides of the question, and in the light of what we have said about the ambiguous relation of the neurosis to reality, that the whole economy of the neurosis is based exactly on this idea of the *quid pro quo* of sacrificial pain: the neurotic person unconsciously subscribes to a system whereby he gives up some pleasure or power, or inflicts pain on himself in order to secure some other power or some other pleasure.

In the ingrained popular conception of the relation between suffering and power there are actually two distinct although related ideas. One is that there exists in the individual a fund of power which has outlets through various organs or faculties, and that if its outlet through one organ or faculty be prevented, it will flow to increase the force or sensitivity of another. Thus it is popularly believed that the sense of touch is intensified in the blind not so much by the will of the blind person to adapt himself to the necessities of his situation as, rather, by a sort of mechanical redistribution of power. And this idea would seem to explain, if not the origin of the ancient mutilation of priests, then at least a common understanding of their sexual sacrifice.

The other idea is that a person may be taught by, or proved by, the endurance of pain. There will easily come to mind the ritual suffering that is inflicted at the tribal initiation of youths into full manhood or at the admission of the apprentice into the company of journeyman adepts. This idea in sophisticated form found its way into high religion at least as early as Aeschylus, who held that man achieves knowledge of God through suffering, and it was from the beginning an important element of Christian thought. In the nineteenth century the Christianized notion of the didactic suffering of the artist went along with the idea of his mental degeneration and even served as a sort of countermyth to it. Its doctrine was that the artist, a man of strength and health, experienced and suffered, and thus learned both the facts of life and his artistic craft. "I am the man, I suffered, I was there," ran his boast, and he derived his authority from the knowledge gained through suffering.

There can be no doubt that both these ideas represent a measure of truth about mental and emotional power. The idea of didactic suffering expresses a valuation of experience and of steadfastness. The idea of natural compensation for the sacrifice of some faculty also says something that can be rationally defended: one cannot be and do everything and the wholehearted absorption in any enterprise, art for example, means that we must give up other possibilities, even parts of ourselves. And there is even a certain validity to the belief that the individual has a fund of undifferentiated energy which presses the harder upon what outlets are available to it when it has been deprived of the normal number.

Then, in further defense of the belief that artistic power is connected with neurosis, we can say that there is no doubt that what we call mental illness may be the source of psychic knowledge. Some neurotic people, because they are more apprehensive than normal people, are able to see more of certain parts of reality and to see them with more intensity. And many neurotic or psychotic patients are in certain respects in closer touch with the actualities of the unconscious than are normal people. Further, the expression of a neurotic or psychotic conception of reality is likely to be more intense than a normal one.

Yet when we have said all this, it is still wrong, I believe, to find the root of the artist's power and the source of his genius in neurosis. To the idea that literary power and genius spring from pain and neurotic sacrifice there are two major objections. The first has to do with the assumed uniqueness of the artist as a subject of psychoanalytical explanation. The second has to do with the true meaning of power and genius.

One reason why writers are considered to be more available than other people to psychoanalytical explanation is that they tell us what is going on inside them. Even when they do not make an actual diagnosis of their malaises or describe "symptoms," we must bear it in mind that it is their profession to deal with fantasy in some form or other. It is in the nature of the writer's job that he exhibit his unconscious. He may disguise it in various ways, but disguise is not concealment. Indeed, it may be said that the more a writer takes pains with his work to remove it from the personal and subjective, the more—and not the less—he will express his true unconscious, although not what passes with most for the unconscious.

Further, the writer is likely to be a great hand at personal letters, diaries, and autobiographies: indeed, almost the only good autobiographies are those of writers. The writer is more aware of what happens to him or goes on in him and often finds it necessary or useful to be articulate about his inner states, and prides himself on telling the truth. Thus, only a man as devoted to the truth of the emotions as Henry James was would have informed the world, despite his characteristic reticence, of an accident so intimate as his. We must not of course suppose that a writer's statements about his intimate life are equivalent to true statements about his unconscious, which, by definition, he doesn't consciously know; but they may be useful clues to the nature of an entity about which we can make statements of more or less cogency, although never statements of certainty; or they at least give us what is surely related to a knowledge of his unconscious—that is, an insight into his personality.*

But while the validity of dealing with the writer's intellectual life in psychoanalytical terms is taken for granted, the psychoanalytical explanation of the intellectual life of scientists is generally speaking not countenanced. The old myth of the mad scientist, with the exception of an occasional mad psychiatrist, no longer exists. The social position of science requires that it should cease, which leads us to remark that those partisans of art who insist on explaining artistic genius by means of psychic imbalance are in effect capitulating to the dominant mores which hold that the members of the respectable professions are, however dull they may be, free from neurosis. Scientists, to continue with them as the best example of the respectable professions, do not usually give us the clues to their personalities which writers habitually give. But no one who has ever lived observantly among scientists will claim that they are without an unconscious or even that they are free from neurosis. How often, indeed, it is apparent that the devotion to science, if it cannot be called a neurotic manifestation, at least can be understood as going very cozily with neurotic elements in the temperament, such as, for example, a marked compulsiveness. Of scientists as a group we can say that they are less concerned with the manifestations of personality, their own or others', than are writers as a group. But this relative indifference is scarcely a sign of normality—indeed, if we choose to regard it with the same sort of eye with which the characteristics of writers are regarded, we might say

---

*I am by no means in agreement with the statements of Dr. Edmund Bergler about "the" psychology of the writer, but I think that Dr. Bergler has done good service in warning us against taking at their face value a writer's statements about himself, the more especially when they are "frank." Thus, to take Dr. Bergler's notable example, it is usual for biographers to accept Stendhal's statements about his open sexual feelings for his mother when he was a little boy, feelings which went with an intense hatred of his father. But Dr. Bergler believes that Stendhal unconsciously used his consciousness of his love of his mother and of his hatred of his father to mask an unconscious love of his father, which frightened him. ("Psychoanalysis of Writers and of Literary Productivity," in *Psychoanalysis and the Social Sciences*, vol. 1.)

the indifference to matters of personality is in itself a suspicious evasion.

It is the basic assumption of psychoanalysis that the acts of *every* person are influenced by the forces of the unconscious. Scientists, bankers, lawyers, or surgeons, by reason of the traditions of their professions, practice concealment and conformity; but it is difficult to believe that an investigation according to psychoanalytical principles would fail to show that the strains and imbalances of their psyches are not of the same frequency as those of writers, and of similar kind. I do not mean that everybody has the same troubles and identical psyches, but only that there is no special category for writers.*

If this is so, and if we still want to relate the writer's power to his neurosis, we must be willing to relate all intellectual power to neurosis. We must find the roots of Newton's power in his emotional extravagances, and the roots of Darwin's power in his sorely neurotic temperament, and the roots of Pascal's mathematical genius in the impulses which drove him to extreme religious masochism—I choose but the classic examples. If we make the neurosis-power equivalence at all, we must make it in every field of endeavor. Logician, economist, botanist, physicist, theologian—no profession may be so respectable or so remote or so rational as to be exempt from the psychological interpretation.†

*Dr. Bergler believes that there is a particular neurosis of writers, based on an oral masochism which makes them the enemy of the respectable world, courting poverty and persecution. But a later development of Dr. Bergler's theory of oral masochism makes it *the* basic neurosis, not only of writers but of everyone who is neurotic.

†In his interesting essay "Writers and Madness" (*Partisan Review*, January–February 1947), William Barrett his taken issue with this point and has insisted that a clear distinction is to be made between the relation that exists between the scientist and his work and the relation that exists between the artist and his work. The difference, as I understand it, is in the claims of the ego. The artist's ego makes a claim upon the world which is personal in a way that the scientist's is not, for the scientist, although he does indeed want prestige and thus "responds to one of the deepest urges of his ego, it is only that his prestige may come to attend his person through the public world of other men; and it is not in the end his own being that is exhibited or his own voice that is heard in the learned report to the Academy." Actually, however, as is suggested by the sense which mathematicians have of the *style* of mathematical thought, the creation of the abstract thinker is as deeply involved as the artist's—see *An Essay on the Psychology of Invention in the Mathematical Field* by Jacques Hadamard, 1945—and he quite as much as the artist seeks to impose *himself*, to *express* himself. I am of course not maintaining that the processes of scientific thought are the same as those of artistic thought, or even that the scientist's creation is involved with his total personality *in the same way* that the artist's is—I am maintaining only that the scientist's creation is as *deeply* implicated with his total personality as is the artist's.

This point of view seems to be supported by Freud's monograph on Leonardo. One of the problems that Freud sets himself is to discover why an artist of the highest endowment should

Further, not only power but also failure or limitation must be accounted for by the theory of neurosis, and not merely failure or limitation in life but even failure or limitation in art. Thus it is often said that the warp of Dostoyevsky's mind accounts for the brilliance of his psychological insights. But it is never said that the same warp of Dostoyevsky's mind also accounted for his deficiency in insight. Freud, who greatly admired Dostoyevsky, although he did not like him, observed that "his insight was entirely restricted to the workings of the abnormal psyche. Consider his astounding helplessness before the phenomenon of love; he really only understands either crude, instinctive desire or masochistic submission or love from pity."* This, we must note, is not merely Freud's comment on the extent of the province which Dostoyevsky chose for his own, but on his failure to understand what, given the province of his choice, he might be expected to understand.

And since neurosis can account not only for intellectual success and for failure or limitation but also for mediocrity, we have most of society involved in neurosis. To this I have no objection—I think most of society is indeed involved in neurosis. But with neurosis accounting for so much, it cannot be made exclusively to account for one man's literary power.

We have now to consider what is meant by genius when its source is identified as the sacrifice and pain of neurosis.

In the case of Henry James, the reference to the neurosis of his personal life does indeed tell us something about the latent intention of his work and thus about the reason for some large part of its interest for us. But if genius and its source are what we are dealing with, we must observe that the reference to neurosis tells us nothing about James's passion, energy, and devotion, nothing about his architectonic skill, nothing about the other themes that were important to him which are not connected with his unconscious concern with castration. We cannot, that is,

---

have devoted himself more and more to scientific investigation, with the result that he was unable to complete his artistic enterprises. The particular reasons for this that Freud assigns need not be gone into here; all that I wish to suggest is that Freud understands these reasons to be the working out of an inner conflict, the attempt to deal with the difficulties that have their roots in the most primitive situations. Leonardo's scientific investigations were as necessary and "compelled" and they constituted as much of a claim on the whole personality as anything the artist undertakes; and so far from being carried out for the sake of public prestige, they were largely private and personal, and were thought by the public of his time to be something very like insanity.

*From a letter quoted in Theodor Reik, *From Thirty Years With Freud*, p. 175.

make the writer's inner life exactly equivalent to his power of expressing it. Let us grant for the sake of argument that the literary genius, as distinguished from other men, is the victim of a "mutilation" and that his fantasies are neurotic.* It does not then follow as the inevitable next step that his ability to express these fantasies and to impress us with them is neurotic, for that ability is what we mean by his genius. Anyone might be injured as Henry James was, and even respond within himself to the injury as James is said to have done, and yet not have his literary power.

The reference to the artist's neurosis tells us something about the material on which the artist exercises his powers, and even something about his reasons for bringing his powers into play, but it does not tell us anything about the source of his power, it makes no causal connection between them and the neurosis. And if we look into the matter, we see that there is in fact no causal connection between them. For, still granting that the poet is uniquely neurotic, what is surely not neurotic, what indeed suggests nothing but health, is his power of using his neuroticism. He shapes his fantasies, he gives them social form and reference. Charles Lamb's way of putting this cannot be improved. Lamb is denying that genius is allied to insanity; for "insanity" the modern reader may substitute "neurosis." "The ground of the mistake," he says,

> is, that men, finding in the raptures of the higher poetry a condition of exaltation, to which they have no parallel in their own experience, besides the spurious resemblance of it in dreams and fevers, impute a state of dreaminess and fever to the poet. But the true poet dreams being awake. He is not possessed by his subject but has dominion over it. . . . Where he seems most to recede from humanity, he will be found the truest to it. From beyond the scope of nature if he summon possible existences, he subjugates them to the law of her consistency. He is beautifully loyal to that sovereign directress, when he appears most to betray and desert her. . . .

---

*I am using the word *fantasy*, unless modified, in a neutral sense. A fantasy, in this sense, may be distinguished from the representation of something that actually exists, but it is not opposed to "reality" and not an "escape" from reality. Thus the idea of a rational society, or the image of a good house to be built, as well as the story of something that could never really happen, is a fantasy. There may be neurotic or non-neurotic fantasies.

Herein the great and the little wits are differenced; that if the latter wander ever so little from nature or natural existence, they lose themselves and their readers. . . . They do not create, which implies shaping and consistency. Their imaginations are not active—for to be active is to call something into act and form—but passive as men in sick dreams.

The activity of the artist, we must remember, may be approximated by many who are themselves not artists. Thus, the expressions of many schizophrenic people have the intense appearance of creativity and an inescapable interest and significance. But they are not works of art, and although Van Gogh may have been schizophrenic he was in addition an artist. Again, as I have already suggested, it is not uncommon in our society for certain kinds of neurotic people to imitate the artist in his life and even in his ideals and ambitions. They follow the artist in everything except successful performance. It was, I think, Otto Rank who called such people half-artists and confirmed the diagnosis of their neuroticism at the same time that he differentiated them from true artists.

Nothing is so characteristic of the artist as his power of shaping his work, of subjugating his raw material, however aberrant it be from what we call normality, to the consistency of nature. It would be impossible to deny that whatever disease or mutilation the artist may suffer is an element of his production which has its effect on every part of it, but disease and mutilation are available to us all—life provides them with prodigal generosity. What marks the artist is his power to shape the material of pain we all have.

At this point, with our recognition of life's abundant provision of pain, we are at the very heart of our matter, which is the meaning we may assign to neurosis and the relation we are to suppose it to have with normality. Here Freud himself can be of help, although it must be admitted that what he tells us may at first seem somewhat contradictory and confusing.

Freud's study of Leonardo da Vinci is an attempt to understand why Leonardo was unable to pursue his artistic enterprises, feeling compelled instead to advance his scientific investigations. The cause of this Freud traces back to certain childhood experiences not different in kind from the experiences which Dr. Rosenzweig adduces to account for certain elements in the work of Henry James. And when he has completed his study Freud makes this *caveat*:

> Let us expressly emphasize that we have never considered Leonardo as a neurotic. . . . We no longer believe that health and disease, normal and nervous, are sharply distinguished from each other. We know today that neurotic symptoms are substitutive formations for certain repressive acts which must result in the course of our development from the child to the cultural man, that we all produce such substitutive formations, and that only the amount, intensity, and distribution of these substitutive formations justify the practical conception of illness. . . .

The statement becomes the more striking when we remember that in the course of his study Freud has had occasion to observe that Leonardo was both homosexual and sexually inactive. I am not sure that the statement that Leonardo was not a neurotic is one that Freud would have made at every point in the later development of psychoanalysis, yet it is in conformity with his continuing notion of the genesis of culture. And the *practical*, the quantitative or economic, conception of illness he insists on in a passage in the *Introductory Lectures*. "The neurotic symptoms," he says,

> . . . are activities which are detrimental, or at least useless, to life as a whole; the person concerned frequently complains of them as obnoxious to him or they involve suffering and distress for him. The principal injury they inflict lies in the expense of energy they entail, and, besides this, in the energy needed to combat them. Where the symptoms are extensively developed, these two kinds of effort may exact such a price that the person suffers a very serious impoverishment in available mental energy which consequently disables him for all the important tasks of life. This result depends principally upon the amount of energy taken up in this way; therefore you will see that 'illness' is essentially a practical conception. But if you look at the matter from a theoretical point of view and ignore this question of degree, you can very well see that we are all ill, i.e., neurotic; for the conditions required for symptom-formation are demonstrable also in normal persons.

We are all ill: the statement is grandiose, and its implications—the implications, that is, of understanding the totality of human nature in the terms of disease—are vast. These implications have never been properly met (although I believe that a few theologians have responded to them), but this is not the place to attempt to meet them. I have brought forward Freud's statement of the essential sickness of the psyche only because it stands as the refutation of what is implied by the literary use of the theory of neurosis to account for genius. For if we are all ill, and if, as I have said, neurosis can account for everything, for failure and mediocrity—"a very serious impoverishment of available mental energy"—as well as for genius, it cannot uniquely account for genius.

This, however, is not to say that there is no connection between neurosis and genius, which would be tantamount, as we see, to saying that there is no connection between human nature and genius. But the connection lies wholly in a particular and special relation which the artist has to neurosis.

In order to understand what this particular and special connection is we must have clearly in mind what neurosis is. The current literary conception of neurosis as a *wound* is quite misleading. It inevitably suggests passivity, whereas, if we follow Freud, we must understand a neurosis to be an *activity*, an activity with a purpose, and a particular kind of activity, a *conflict*. This is not to say that there are no abnormal mental states which are not conflicts. There are; the struggle between elements of the unconscious may never be instituted in the first place, or it may be called off. As Freud says in a passage which follows close upon the one I last quoted, "If regressions do not call forth a prohibition on the part of the ego, no neurosis results; the libido succeeds in obtaining a real, although not a normal, satisfaction. But if the ego . . . is not in agreement with these regressions, conflict ensues." And in his essay on Dostoyevsky Freud says that "there are no neurotic complete masochists," by which he means that the ego which gives way completely to masochism (or to any other pathological excess) has passed beyond neurosis; the conflict has ceased, but at the cost of the defeat of the ego, and now some other name than that of neurosis must be given to the condition of the person who thus takes himself beyond the pain of the neurotic conflict. To understand this is to become aware of the curious complacency with which literary men regard mental disease. The psyche of the neurotic is not equally complacent; it regards with the greatest fear the chaotic and destructive forces it contains, and it struggles fiercely to keep them at bay.*

We come then to a remarkable paradox: we are all ill, but we are ill in the service of health, or ill in the service of life, or, at the very least, ill in the service of life-in-culture. The form of the mind's dynamics is that of the neurosis, which is to be understood as the ego's struggle against being overcome by the forces with which it coexists, and the strategy of this conflict requires that the ego shall incur pain and make sacrifices of itself, at the same time seeing to it that its pain and sacrifice be as small as they may.

But this is characteristic of all minds: no mind is exempt except those which refuse the conflict or withdraw from it; and we ask wherein the mind of the artist is unique. If he is not unique in neurosis, is he then unique in the significance and intensity of his neurosis? I do not believe that we shall go more than a little way toward a definition of artistic genius by answering this question affirmatively. A neurotic conflict cannot ever be either meaningless or merely personal; it must be understood as exemplifying cultural forces of great moment, and this is true of any neurotic conflict at all. To be sure, some neuroses may be more interesting than others, perhaps because they are fiercer or more inclusive; and no doubt the writer who makes a claim upon our interest is a man who by reason of the energy and significance of the forces in struggle within him provides us with the largest representation of the culture in which we, with him, are involved; his neurosis may thus be thought of as having a connection of concomitance with his literary powers. As Freud says in the Dostoyevsky essay, "the neurosis . . . comes into being all the more readily the richer the complexity which has to be controlled by his ego." Yet

---

*In the article to which I referred in the note on p. 96, William Barrett says that he prefers the old-fashioned term "madness" to "neurosis." But it is not quite for him to choose—the words do not differ in fashion but in meaning. Most literary people, when they speak of mental illness, refer to neurosis. Perhaps one reason for this is that the neurosis is the most benign of the mental ills. Another reason is surely that psychoanalytical literature deals chiefly with the neurosis, and its symptomatology and therapy have become familiar; psychoanalysis has far less to say about psychosis, for which it can offer far less therapeutic hope. Further, the neurosis is easily put into a causal connection with the social maladjustments of our time. Other forms of mental illness of a more severe and degenerative kind are not so widely recognized by the literary person and are often assimilated to neurosis with a resulting confusion. In the present essay I deal only with the conception of neurosis, but this should not be taken to imply that I believe that other pathological mental conditions, including actual madness, do not have relevance to the general matter of the discussion.

even the rich complexity which his ego is doomed to control is not the
definition of the artist's genius, for we can by no means say that the artist
is pre-eminent in the rich complexity of elements in conflict within him.
The slightest acquaintance with the clinical literature of psychoanalysis
will suggest that a rich complexity of struggling elements is no uncommon possession. And that same literature will also make it abundantly
clear that the devices of art—the most extreme devices of poetry, for example—are not particular to the mind of the artist but are characteristic
of mind itself.

But the artist is indeed unique in one respect, in the respect of his relation to his neurosis. He is what he is by virtue of his successful objecti-
fication of his neurosis, by his shaping it and making it available to others
in a way which has its effect upon their own egos in struggle. His genius,
that is, may be defined in terms of his faculties of perception, representation, and realization, and in these terms alone. It can no more be defined
in terms of neurosis than can his power of walking and talking, or his sexuality. The use to which he puts his power, or the manner and style of his
power, may be discussed with reference to his particular neurosis, and so
may such matters as the untimely diminution or cessation of its exercise.
But its essence is irreducible. It is, as we say, a gift.

We are all ill: but even a universal sickness implies an idea of health.
Of the artist we must say that whatever elements of neurosis he has in
common with his fellow mortals, the one part of him that is healthy, by
any conceivable definition of health, is that which gives him the power to
conceive, to plan, to work, and to bring his work to a conclusion. And if
we are all ill, we are ill by a universal accident, not by a universal necessity,
by a fault in the economy of our powers, not by the nature of the powers
themselves. The Philoctetes myth, when it is used to imply a causal connection between the fantasy of castration and artistic power, tells us no
more about the source of artistic power than we learn about the source of
sexuality when the fantasy of castration is adduced, for the fear of castration may explain why a man is moved to extravagant exploits of sexuality,
but we do not say that his sexual power itself derives from his fear of castration; and further the same fantasy may also explain impotence or homosexuality. The Philoctetes story, which has so established itself among
us as explaining the source of the artist's power, is not really an explanatory myth at all; it is a moral myth having reference to our proper behavior in the circumstances of the universal accident. In its juxtaposition of

the wound and the bow, it tells us that we must be aware that weakness does not preclude strength nor strength weakness. It is therefore not irrelevant to the artist, but when we use it we will do well to keep in mind the other myths of the arts, recalling what Pan and Dionysius suggest of the relation of art to physiology and superabundance, remembering that to Apollo were attributed the bow and the lyre, two strengths together, and that he was given the lyre by its inventor, the baby Hermes—that miraculous infant who, the day he was born, left his cradle to do mischief: and the first thing he met with was a tortoise, which he greeted politely before scooping it from its shell, and, thought and deed being one with him, he contrived the instrument to which he sang "the glorious tale of his own begetting." These were gods, and very early ones, but their myths tell us something about the nature and source of art even in our grim, late human present.

Manners, Morals, and the Novel

1947

The invitation that was made to me to address you this evening was couched in somewhat uncertain terms. Time, place, and cordiality were perfectly clear, but when it came to the subject our hosts were not able to specify just what they wanted me to talk about. They wanted me to consider literature in its relation to manners—by which, as they relied on me to understand, they did not really mean *manners*. They did not mean, that is, the rules of personal intercourse in our culture; and yet such rules were by no means irrelevant to what they did mean. Nor did they quite mean manners in the sense of *mores*, customs, although, again, these did bear upon the subject they had in mind.

I understood them perfectly, as I would not have understood them had they been more definite. For they were talking about a nearly indefinable subject.

Somewhere below all the explicit statements that a people makes through its art, religion, architecture, legislation, there is a dim mental region of intention of which it is very difficult to become aware. We now and then get a strong sense of its existence when we deal with the past, not by reason of its presence in the past but by reason of its absence. As we read the great formulated monuments of the past, we notice that we are reading them without the accompaniment of something that always goes along with the formulated monuments of the present. The voice of multifarious intention and activity is stilled, all the buzz of implication which always surrounds us in the present, coming to us from what never gets fully stated, coming in the tone of greetings and the tone of quarrels, in slang and humor and popular songs, in the way children play, in the gesture the waiter makes when he puts down the plate, in the nature of the very food we prefer.

Some of the charm of the past consists of the quiet—the great distracting buzz of implication has stopped and we are left only with what has been fully phrased and precisely stated. And part of the melancholy of the past comes from our knowledge that the huge, unrecorded hum of implication was once there and left no trace—we feel that because it is evanescent it is especially human. We feel, too, that the truth of the great preserved monuments of the past does not fully appear without it. From letters and diaries, from the remote, unconscious corners of the great works themselves, we try to guess what the sound of the multifarious implication was and what it meant.

Or when we read the conclusions that are drawn about our own culture by some gifted foreign critic—or by some stupid native one—who is equipped only with a knowledge of our books, when we try in vain to say what is wrong, when in despair we say that he has read the books "out of context," then we are aware of the matter I have been asked to speak about tonight.

What I understand by manners, then, is a culture's hum and buzz of implication. I mean the whole evanescent context in which its explicit statements are made. It is that part of a culture which is made up of half-uttered or unuttered or unutterable expressions of value. They are hinted at by small actions, sometimes by the arts of dress or decoration, sometimes by tone, gesture, emphasis, or rhythm, sometimes by the words that are used with a special frequency or a special meaning. They are the things that for good or bad draw the people of a culture together and that separate them from the people of another culture. They make the part of a culture which is not art, or religion, or morals, or politics, and yet it relates to all these highly formulated departments of culture. It is modified by them; it modifies them; it is generated by them; it generates them. In this part of culture assumption rules, which is often so much stronger than reason.

The right way to begin to deal with such a subject is to gather together as much of its detail as we possibly can. Only by doing so will we become fully aware of what the gifted foreign critic or the stupid native one is not aware of, that in any complex culture there is not a single system of manners but a conflicting variety of manners, and that one of the jobs of a culture is the adjustment of this conflict.

But the nature of our present occasion does not permit this accumulation of detail and so I shall instead try to drive toward a generalization and an hypothesis which, however wrong they turn out to be, may at least permit us to circumscribe the subject. I shall try to generalize the subject of American manners by talking about the attitude of Americans toward the subject of manners itself. And since in a complex culture there are, as I say, many different systems of manners and since I cannot talk about them all, I shall select the manners and the attitude toward manners of the literate, reading, responsible middle class of people who are ourselves. I specify that they be reading people because I shall draw my conclusions from the novels they read. The hypothesis I propose is that our attitude toward manners is the expression of a particular conception of reality.

All literature tends to be concerned with the question of reality—I mean quite simply the old opposition between reality and appearance, between what really is and what merely seems. "Don't you *see?*" is the question we want to shout at Oedipus as he stands before us and before fate in the pride of his rationalism. And at the end of *Oedipus Rex* he demonstrates in a particularly direct way that he now sees what he did not see before. "Don't you *see?*" we want to shout again at Lear and Gloucester, the two deceived, self-deceiving fathers: blindness again, resistance to the clear claims of reality, the seduction by mere appearance. The same with Othello—reality is right under your stupid nose, how *dare* you be such a gull? So with Molière's Orgon—my good man, my honest citizen, merely *look* at Tartuffe and you will know what's what. So with Milton's Eve— "Woman, watch out! Don't you see—anyone can see—that's a *snake!*"

The problem of reality is central, and in a special way, to the great forefather of the novel, the great book of Cervantes, whose four-hundredth birthday was celebrated in 1947. There are two movements of thought in *Don Quixote*, two different and opposed notions of reality. One is the movement which leads toward saying that the world of ordinary practicality is reality in its fullness. It is the reality of the present moment in all its powerful immediacy of hunger, cold, and pain, making the past and the future, and all ideas, of no account. When the conceptual, the ideal, and the fanciful come into conflict with this, bringing their notions of the past and the future, then disaster results. For one thing, the ordinary proper ways of life are upset—the chained prisoners are understood to be good men and are released, the whore is taken for a lady. There is general confusion. As for the ideal, the conceptual, the fanciful, or romantic—whatever you want to call it—it fares even worse: it is shown to be ridiculous.

Thus one movement of the novel. But Cervantes changed horses in midstream and found that he was riding Rosinante. Perhaps at first not quite consciously—although the new view is latent in the old from the very beginning—Cervantes begins to show that the world of tangible reality is not the real reality after all. The real reality is rather the wildly conceiving, the madly fantasying mind of the Don: people change, practical reality changes, when they come into its presence.

In any genre it may happen that the first great example contains the whole potentiality of the genre. It has been said that all philosophy is a footnote to Plato. It can be said that all prose fiction is a variation on the theme of *Don Quixote*. Cervantes sets for the novel the problem of appearance and reality: the shifting and conflict of social classes becomes the field of the problem of knowledge, of how we know and of how reliable our knowledge is, which at that very moment of history is vexing the philosophers and scientists. And the poverty of the Don suggests that the novel is born with the appearance of money as a social element—money, the great solvent of the solid fabric of the old society, the great generator of illusion. Or, which is to say much the same thing, the novel is born in response to snobbery.

Snobbery is not the same thing as pride of class. Pride of class may not please us but we must at least grant that it reflects a social function. A man who exhibited class pride—in the day when it was possible to do so—may have been puffed up about what he *was*, but this ultimately depended on what he *did*. Thus, aristocratic pride was based ultimately on the ability to fight and administer. No pride is without fault, but pride of class may be thought of as today we think of pride of profession, toward which we are likely to be lenient.

Snobbery is pride in status without pride in function. And it is an uneasy pride of status. It always asks, "Do I belong—do I really belong? And does he belong? And if I am observed talking to him, will it make me seem to belong or not to belong?" It is the peculiar vice not of aristocratic societies which have their own appropriate vices, but of bourgeois democratic societies. For us the legendary strongholds of snobbery are the Hollywood studios, where two thousand dollars a week dare not talk to three hundred dollars a week for fear he be taken for nothing more than fifteen hundred dollars a week. The dominant emotions of snobbery are uneasiness, self-consciousness, self-defensiveness, the sense that one is not quite real but can in some way acquire reality.

Money is the medium that, for good or bad, makes for a fluent society. It does not make for an equal society but for one in which there is a constant shifting of classes, a frequent change in the personnel of the dominant class. In a shifting society great emphasis is put on appearance—I am using the word now in the common meaning, as when people say that "a good appearance is very important in getting a job." To appear to be established is one of the ways of becoming established. The old notion of the solid merchant who owns far more than he shows increasingly gives way to the ideal of signalizing status by appearance, by showing more than you have: status in a democratic society is presumed to come not with power but with the tokens of power. Hence the development of what Tocqueville saw as a mark of democratic culture, what he called the "hypocrisy of luxury"—instead of the well-made peasant article and the well-made middle-class article, we have the effort of all articles to appear as the articles of the very wealthy.

And a shifting society is bound to generate an interest in appearance in the philosophical sense. When Shakespeare lightly touched on the matter that so largely preoccupies the novelist—that is, the movement from one class to another—and created Malvolio, he immediately involved the question of social standing with the problem of appearance and reality. Malvolio's daydreams of bettering his position present themselves to him as reality, and in revenge his enemies conspire to convince him that he is literally mad and that the world is not as he sees it. The predicament of the characters in *A Midsummer Night's Dream* and of Christopher Sly seems to imply that the meeting of social extremes and the establishment of a person of low class in the privileges of a high class always suggested to Shakespeare's mind some radical instability of the senses and the reason.

The characteristic work of the novel is to record the illusion that snobbery generates and to try to penetrate to the truth which, as the novel assumes, lies hidden beneath all the false appearances. Money, snobbery, the ideal of status, these become in themselves the objects of fantasy, the support of the fantasies of love, freedom, charm, power, as in *Madame Bovary*, whose heroine is the sister, at a three-centuries remove, of Don Quixote. The greatness of *Great Expectations* begins in its title: modern society bases itself on great expectations which, if ever they are realized, are found to exist by reason of a sordid, hidden reality. The real thing is not the gentility of Pip's life but the hulks and the murder and the rats and decay in the cellarage of the novel.

An English writer, recognizing the novel's central concern with snobbery, recently cried out half-ironically against it.

Who cares whether Pamela finally exasperates Mr B. into marriage, whether Mr Elton is more or less moderately genteel, whether it is sinful for Pendennis nearly to kiss the porter's daughter, whether young men from Boston can ever be as truly refined as middle-aged women in Paris, whether the District Officer's fiancée ought to see so much of Dr Aziz, whether Lady Chatterley ought to be made love to by the gamekeeper, even if he was an officer during the war? Who cares?

The novel, of course, tells us much more about life than this. It tells us about the look and feel of things, how things are done and what things are worth and what they cost and what the odds are. If the English novel in its special concern with class does not, as the same writer says, explore the deeper layers of personality, then the French novel in exploring these layers must start and end in class, and the Russian novel, exploring the ultimate possibilities of spirit, does the same—every situation in Dostoyevsky, no matter how spiritual, starts with a point of social pride and a certain number of rubles. The great novelists knew that manners indicate the largest intentions of men's souls as well as the smallest and they are perpetually concerned to catch the meaning of every dim implicit hint.

The novel, then, is a perpetual quest for reality, the field of its research being always the social world, the material of its analysis being always manners as the indication of the direction of man's soul. When we understand this we can understand the pride of profession that moved D. H. Lawrence to say, "Being a novelist, I consider myself superior to the saint, the scientist, the philosopher and the poet. The novel is the one bright book of life."

Now the novel as I have described it has never really established itself in America. Not that we have not had very great novels but that the novel in America diverges from its classic intention, which, as I have said, is the investigation of the problem of reality beginning in the social field. The fact is that American writers of genius have not turned their minds to society. Poe and Melville were quite apart from it; the reality they sought was only tangential to society. Hawthorne was acute when he insisted that he did not write novels but romances—he thus expressed his awareness of the lack of social texture in his work. Howells never fulfilled himself because, although he saw the social subject clearly, he would never take it with full seriousness. In America in the nineteenth century, Henry James was alone in knowing that to scale the moral and aesthetic heights in the novel one had to use the ladder of social observation.

There is a famous passage in James's life of Hawthorne in which James enumerates the things which are lacking to give the American novel the thick social texture of the English novel—no state; barely a specific national name; no sovereign; no court; no aristocracy; no church; no clergy; no army; no diplomatic service; no country gentlemen; no palaces; no castles; no manors; no old country houses; no parsonages; no thatched cottages; no ivied ruins; no cathedrals; no great universities; no public schools; no political society; no sporting class—no Epsom, no Ascot! That is, no sufficiency of means for the display of a variety of manners, no opportunity for the novelist to do his job of searching out reality, not enough complication of appearances to make the job interesting. Another great American novelist of very different temperament had said much the same thing decades before: James Fenimore Cooper found that American manners were too simple and dull to nourish the novelist.

This is cogent but it does not explain the condition of the American novel at the present moment. For life in America has increasingly thickened since the nineteenth century. It has not, to be sure, thickened so much as to permit our undergraduates to understand the characters of Balzac, to understand, that is, life in a crowded country where the competitive pressures are great, forcing intense passions to express themselves fiercely and yet within the limitations set by a strong and complicated tradition of manners. Still, life here has become more complex and more pressing. And even so we do not have the novel that touches significantly on society, on manners. Whatever the virtues of Dreiser may be, he could not report the social fact with the kind of accuracy it needs. Sinclair Lewis is shrewd, but no one, however charmed with him as a social satirist, can believe that he does more than a limited job of social understanding. John Dos Passos sees much, sees it often in the great way of Flaubert, but can never use social fact as more than either backdrop or "condition." Of our novelists today perhaps only William Faulkner deals with society as the field of tragic reality and he has the disadvantage of being limited to a provincial scene.

It would seem that Americans have a kind of resistance to looking closely at society. They appear to believe that to touch accurately on the matter of class, to take full note of snobbery, is somehow to demean themselves. It is as if we felt that one cannot touch pitch without being defiled—which, of course, may possibly be the case. Americans will not deny that we have classes and snobbery, but they seem to hold it to be indelicate to take precise cognizance of these phenomena. Consider that Henry James is, among a large part of our reading public, still held to be at fault for noticing society as much as he did. Consider the conversation that has, for some interesting reason, become a part of our literary folklore. Scott Fitzgerald said to Ernest Hemingway, "The very rich are different from us." Hemingway replied, "Yes, they have more money." I have seen the exchange quoted many times and always with the intention of suggesting that Fitzgerald was infatuated by wealth and had received a salutary rebuke from his democratic friend. But the truth is that after a certain point quantity of money does indeed change into quality of personality: in an important sense the very rich *are* different from us. So are the very powerful, the very gifted, the very poor. Fitzgerald was right, and almost for that remark alone he must surely have been received in Balzac's bosom in the heaven of novelists.

It is of course by no means true that the American reading class has no interest in society. Its interest fails only before society as it used to be represented by the novel. And if we look at the commercially successful serious novels of the last decade, we see that almost all of them have been written from an intense social awareness—it might be said that our present definition of a serious book is one which holds before us some image of society to consider and condemn. What is the situation of the dispossessed Oklahoma farmer and whose fault is it, what situation the Jew finds himself in, what it means to be a Negro, how one gets a bell for Adano, what is the advertising business really like, what it means to be insane and how society takes care of you or fails to do so—these are the matters which are believed to be most fertile for the novelist, and certainly they are the subjects most favored by our reading class.

The public is probably not deceived about the quality of most of these books. If the question of quality is brought up, the answer is likely to be: no, they are not great, they are not imaginative, they are not "literature." But there is an unexpressed addendum: and perhaps they are all the better for not being imaginative, for not being literature—they are not literature, they are reality, and *in a time like this* what we need is reality in large doses.

When, generations from now, the historian of our times undertakes to describe the assumptions of our culture, he will surely discover that the word "reality" is of central importance in his understanding of us. He will observe that for some of our philosophers the meaning of the word was a good deal in doubt, but that for our political writers, for many of our literary critics, and for most of our reading public, the word did not open discussion but, rather, closed it. Reality, as conceived by us, is whatever is external and hard, gross, unpleasant. Involved in its meaning is the idea of power conceived in a particular way. Some time ago I had occasion to remark how, in the critical estimates of Theodore Dreiser, it is always being said that Dreiser has many faults but that it cannot be denied that he has great power. No one ever says "a kind of power." Power is assumed to be always "brute" power, crude, ugly, and undiscriminating, the way an elephant appears to be. It is seldom understood to be the way an elephant actually is, precise and discriminating; or the way electricity is, swift and absolute and scarcely embodied.

The word "reality" is an honorific word and the future historian will naturally try to discover our notion of its pejorative opposite, appearance, mere appearance. He will find it in our feeling about the internal; whenever we detect evidences of style and thought we suspect that reality is being a little betrayed, that "mere subjectivity" is creeping in. There follows from this our feeling about complication, modulation, personal idiosyncrasy, and about social forms, both the great and the small.

Having gone so far, our historian is then likely to discover a puzzling contradiction. For we claim that the great advantage of reality is its hard, bedrock, concrete quality, yet everything we say about it tends toward the abstract and it almost seems that what we want to find in reality is abstraction itself. Thus we believe that one of the unpleasant bedrock facts is social class, but we become extremely impatient if ever we are told that social class is indeed so real that it produces actual differences of personality. The very people who talk most about class and its evils think that Fitzgerald was bedazzled and Hemingway right. Or again, it might be observed that in the degree that we speak in praise of the "individual" we have contrived that our literature should have no individuals in it—no people, that is, who are shaped by our liking for the interesting and memorable and special and precious.

Here, then, is our generalization: that in proportion as we have committed ourselves to our particular idea of reality we have lost our interest in manners. For the novel this is a definitive condition because it is inescapably true that in the novel manners make men. It does not matter in what sense the word manners is taken—it is equally true of the sense which so much interested Proust or of the sense which interested Dickens or, indeed, of the sense which interested Homer. The Duchesse de Guermantes unable to delay departure for the dinner party to receive properly from her friend Swann the news that he is dying but able to delay to change the black slippers her husband objects to; Mr. Pickwick and Sam Weller; Priam and Achilles—they exist by reason of their observed manners.

So true is this, indeed, so creative is the novelist's awareness of manners, that we may say that it is a function of his love. It is some sort of love that Fielding has for Squire Western that allows him to note the great, gross details which bring the insensitive sentient man into existence for us. If that is true, we are forced to certain conclusions about our literature and about the particular definition of reality which has shaped it. The reality we admire tells us that the observation of manners is trivial and even malicious, that there are things much more important for the novel to consider. As a consequence our social sympathies have indeed broadened, but in proportion as they have done so we have lost something of our power of love, for our novels can never create characters who truly exist. We make public demands for love, for we know that broad social feeling should be infused with warmth, and we receive a kind of public product which we try to believe is not cold potatoes. The reviewers of Helen Howe's novel of a few years ago, *We Happy Few*, thought that its satiric first part, an excellent comment on the manners of a small but significant segment of society, was ill-natured and unsatisfactory, but they approved the second part, which is the record of the heroine's self-accusing effort to come into communication with the great soul of America. Yet it should have been clear that the satire had its source in a kind of affection, in a real community of feeling, and told the truth, while the second part, said to be so "warm," was mere abstraction, one more example of our public idea of ourselves and our national life. John Steinbeck is generally praised both for his reality and his warmheartedness, but in *The Wayward Bus* the lower-class characters receive a doctrinaire affection in proportion to the suffering and sexuality which define their existence, while the ill-observed middle-class characters are made to submit not only to moral judgment but to the withdrawal of all fellow-feeling, being mocked for their very misfortunes and almost for their susceptibility to death. Only a little thought or even less feeling is required to perceive that the basis of his creation is the coldest response to abstract ideas.

Two novelists of the older sort had a prevision of our present situation. In Henry James's *The Princess Casamassima* there is a scene in which the heroine is told about the existence of a conspiratorial group of revolutionaries pledged to the destruction of all existing society. She has for some time been drawn by a desire for social responsibility; she has wanted to help "the people," she has longed to discover just such a group as she now hears about, and she exclaims in joy, "Then it's real, it's solid!" We are intended to hear the Princess's glad cry with the knowledge that she is a woman who despises herself, "that in the darkest hour of her life she sold herself for a title and a fortune. She regards her doing so as such a terrible piece of frivolity that she can never for the rest of her days be serious enough to make up for it." She seeks out poverty, suffering, sacrifice, and death because she believes that these things alone are real: she comes to believe that art is contemptible; she withdraws her awareness and love from the one person of her acquaintance who most deserves them, and she increasingly scorns whatever suggests variety and modulation, and is more and more dissatisfied with the humanity of the present in her longing for the more perfect humanity of the future. It is one of the great points that the novel makes that with each passionate step that she takes toward what she calls the real, the solid, she in fact moves further away from the life-giving reality.

In E. M. Forster's *The Longest Journey* there is a young man named Stephen Wonham who, although a gentleman born, has been carelessly brought up and has no real notion of the responsibilities of his class. He has a friend, a country laborer, a shepherd, and on two occasions he outrages the feelings of certain intelligent, liberal, democratic people in the book by his treatment of this friend. Once, when the shepherd reneges on a bargain, Stephen quarrels with him and knocks him down; and in the matter of the loan of a few shillings he insists that the money be paid back to the last farthing. The intelligent, liberal, democratic people know that this is not the way to act to the poor. But Stephen cannot think of the shepherd as the poor now, although he is a country laborer, as an object of research by J. L. and Barbara Hammond; he is rather a reciprocating subject in a relationship of affection—as we say, a friend—and therefore liable to anger and required to pay his debts. But this view is held to be deficient in intelligence, liberalism, and democracy.

In these two incidents we have the premonition of our present cultural and social situation, the passionate self-reproachful addiction to a "strong" reality which must limit its purview to maintain its strength, the replacement by abstraction of natural, direct human feeling. It is worth noting, by the way, how clear is the line by which the two novels descend from *Don Quixote*—how their young heroes come into life with large preconceived ideas and are knocked about in consequence; how both are concerned with the problem of appearance and reality, *The Longest Journey* quite explicitly, *The Princess Casamassima* by indirection; how both evoke the question of the nature of reality by contriving a meeting and conflict of diverse social classes and take scrupulous note of the differences of manners. Both have as their leading characters people who are specifically and passionately concerned with social injustice and both agree in saying that to act against social injustice is right and noble but that to choose to act so does not settle all moral problems but on the contrary generates new ones of an especially difficult sort.

I have elsewhere given the name of moral realism to the perception of the dangers of the moral life itself. Perhaps at no other time has the enterprise of moral realism ever been so much needed, for at no other time have so many people committed themselves to moral righteousness. We have the books that point out the bad conditions, that praise us for taking progressive attitudes. We have no books that raise questions in our minds not only about conditions but about ourselves, that lead us to refine our motives and ask what might lie behind our good impulses.

There is nothing so very terrible in discovering that something does lie behind. Nor does it need a Freud to make the discovery. Here is a publicity release sent out by one of our oldest and most respectable publishing houses. Under the heading "What Makes Books Sell?" it reads,

> Blank & Company reports that the current interest in horror stories has attracted a great number of readers to John Dash's novel . . . because of its depiction of Nazi brutality. Critics and readers alike have commented on the stark realism of Dash's handling of the torture scenes in the book. The publishers originally envisaged a woman's market because of the love story and now find men reading the book because of the other angle.

This does not suggest a more than usual depravity in the male reader, for "the other angle" has always had a fascination, no doubt a bad one, even for those who would not themselves commit or actually witness an act of torture. I cite the extreme example only to suggest that something may indeed lie behind our sober intelligent interest in moral politics. In this instance the pleasure in the cruelty is protected and licensed by moral indignation. In other instances moral indignation, which has been said to be the favorite emotion of the middle class, may be in itself an exquisite pleasure. To understand this does not invalidate moral indignation but only sets up the conditions on which it ought to be entertained, only says when it is legitimate and when not.

But, the answer comes, however important it may be for moral realism to raise questions in our minds about our motives, is it not at best a matter of secondary importance? Is it not of the first importance that we be given a direct and immediate report on the reality that is daily being brought to dreadful birth? The novels that have done this have effected much practical good, bringing to consciousness the latent feelings of many people, making it harder for them to be unaware or indifferent, creating an atmosphere in which injustice finds it harder to thrive. To speak of moral realism is all very well. But it is an elaborate, even fancy, phrase and it is to be suspected of having the intention of sophisticating the simple reality that is easily to be conceived. Life presses us so hard, time is so short, the suffering of the world is so huge, simple, unendurable—anything that complicates our moral fervor in dealing with reality as we immediately see it and wish to dive headlong upon it must be regarded with some impatience.

True enough: and therefore any defense of what I have called moral realism must be made not in the name of some highflown fineness of feeling but in the name of simple social practicality. And there is indeed a simple social fact to which moral realism has a simple practical relevance, but it is a fact very difficult for us nowadays to perceive. It is that the moral passions are even more willful and imperious and impatient than the self-seeking passions. All history is at one in telling us that their tendency is to be not only liberating but also restrictive.

It is probable that at this time we are about to make great changes in our social system. The world is ripe for such changes and if they are not made in the direction of greater social liberty, the direction forward, they will almost of necessity be made in the direction backward, of a terrible social niggardliness. We all know which of those directions we want. But it is not enough to want it, not even enough to work for it—we must want it and work for it with intelligence. Which means that we must be aware of the dangers which lie in our most generous wishes. Some paradox of our natures leads us, when once we have made our fellow men the objects of our enlightened interest, to go on to make them the objects of our pity, then of our wisdom, ultimately of our coercion. It is to prevent this corruption, the most ironic and tragic that man knows, that we stand in need of the moral realism which is the product of the free play of the moral imagination.

For our time the most effective agent of the moral imagination has been the novel of the last two hundred years. It was never, either aesthetically or morally, a perfect form and its faults and failures can quickly be enumerated. But its greatness and its practical usefulness lay in its unremitting work of involving the reader himself in the moral life, inviting him to put his own motives under examination, suggesting that reality is not as his conventional education has led him to see it. It taught us, as no other genre ever did, the extent of human variety and the value of this variety. It was the literary form to which the emotions of understanding and forgiveness were indigenous, as if by the definition of the form itself. At the moment its impulse does not seem strong, for there never was a time when the virtues of its greatness were so likely to be thought of as weaknesses. Yet there never was a time when its particular activity was so much needed, was of so much practical, political, and social use—so much so that if its impulse does not respond to the need, we shall have reason to be sad not only over a waning form of art but also over our waning freedom.

The Kinsey Report

1948

By virtue of its intrinsic nature and also because of its dramatic reception, the Kinsey Report, as it has come to be called, is an event of great importance in our culture. It is an event which is significant in two separate ways, as symptom and as therapy. The therapy lies in the large permissive effect the Report is likely to have, the long way it goes toward establishing the *community* of sexuality. The symptomatic significance lies in the fact that the Report was felt to be needed at all, that the community of sexuality requires now to be established in explicit quantitative terms. Nothing shows more clearly the extent to which modern society had atomized itself than the isolation in sexual ignorance which exists among us. We have censured the folk knowledge of the most primal things and have systematically dried up the social affections which might naturally seek to enlighten and release. Many cultures, the most primitive and the most complex, have entertained sexual fears of an irrational sort, but probably our culture is unique in strictly isolating the individual in the fears that society has devised. Now, having become somewhat aware of what we have perpetrated at great cost and with little gain, we must assure ourselves by statistical science that the solitude is imaginary. The Report will surprise one part of the population with some facts and another part with other facts, but really all that it says to society as a whole is that there is an almost universal involvement in the sexual life and therefore much variety of conduct. This was taken for granted in any comedy that Aristophanes put on the stage.

There is a further diagnostic significance to be found in the fact that our society makes this effort of self-enlightenment through the agency of science. Sexual conduct is inextricably involved with morality, and hitherto it has been dealt with by those representatives of our cultural imagination which are, by their nature and tradition, committed to morality—it has been dealt with by religion, social philosophy, and literature. But now science seems to be the only one of our institutions which has the authority to speak decisively on the matter. Nothing in the Report is more suggestive in a large cultural way than the insistent claims it makes for its strictly scientific nature, its pledge of indifference to all questions of morality at the same time that it patently intends a moral effect. Nor will any science do for the job—it must be a science as simple and materialistic as the subject can possibly permit. It must be a science of statistics and not of ideas. The way for the Report was prepared by Freud, but Freud, in all the years of his activity, never had the currency or authority with the public that the Report has achieved in a matter of weeks.

The scientific nature of the Report must be taken in conjunction with the manner of its publication. The Report says of itself that it is only a "preliminary survey," a work intended to be the first step in a larger research; that it is nothing more than an "accumulation of scientific facts," a collection of "objective data," a "report on what people do, which raises no question of what they should do," and it is fitted out with a full complement of charts, tables, and discussions of scientific method. A work conceived and executed in this way is usually presented only to an audience of professional scientists; and the publishers of the Report, a medical house, pay their ritual respects to the old tradition which held that not all medical or quasi-medical knowledge was to be made easily available to the general lay reader, or at least not until it had been subjected to professional debate; they tell us in a foreword for what limited professional audience the book was primarily intended—physicians, biologists, and social scientists and "teachers, social workers, personnel officers, law enforcement groups, and others concerned with the direction of human behavior." And yet the book has been so successfully publicized that for many weeks it was a national bestseller.

This way of bringing out a technical work of science is a cultural phenomenon that ought not to pass without some question. The public which receives this technical report, this merely preliminary survey, this accumulation of data, has never, even on its upper educational levels, been properly instructed in the most elementary principles of scientific thought. With this public, science is authority. It has been trained to accept heedlessly "what science says," which it conceives to be a unitary utterance. To this public nothing is more valuable, more precisely "scientific," and more finally convincing than raw data without conclusions; no disclaimer of conclusiveness can mean anything to it—it has learned that the disclaimer is simply the hallmark of the scientific attitude, science's way of saying "thy unworthy servant."

So that if the Report were really, as it claims to be, only an accumulation of objective data, there would be some question of the cultural wisdom of dropping it in a lump on the general public. But in point of fact it is full of assumptions and conclusions; it makes very positive statements on highly debatable matters and it editorializes very freely. This preliminary survey gives some very conclusive suggestions to a public that is quick to obey what science says, no matter how contradictory science may be, which is most contradictory indeed. This is the public that, on scientific advice, ate spinach in one generation and avoided it in the next, that in one decade trained its babies to rigid Watsonian schedules and believed that affection corrupted the infant character, only to learn in the next decade that rigid discipline was harmful and that cuddling was as scientific as induction.

Then there is the question of whether the Report does not do harm by encouraging people in their commitment to mechanical attitudes toward life. The tendency to divorce sex from the other manifestations of life is already a strong one. This truly absorbing study of sex in charts and tables, in data and quantities, may have the effect of strengthening the tendency still more with people who are by no means trained to invert the process of abstraction and to put the fact back into the general life from which it has been taken. And the likely mechanical implications of a statistical study are in this case supported by certain fully formulated attitudes which the authors strongly hold despite their protestations that they are scientific to the point of holding no attitudes whatever.

These, I believe, are valid objections to the book's indiscriminate circulation. And yet I also believe that there is something good about the manner of publication, something honest and right. Every complex soci-

ety has its agencies which are "concerned with the direction of human behaviour," but we today are developing a new element in that old activity,
the element of scientific knowledge. Whatever the Report claims for itself, the social sciences in general no longer pretend that they can merely
describe what people do; they now have the clear consciousness of their
power to manipulate and adjust. First for industry and then for government, sociology has shown its instrumental nature. A government which
makes use of social knowledge still suggests benignity; and in an age that
daily brings the proliferation of government by police methods it may
suggest the very spirit of rational liberalism. Yet at least one sociologist
has expressed the fear that sociology may become the instrument of a
bland tyranny—it is the same fear that Dostoyevsky gave immortal expression to in "The Grand Inquisitor." And indeed there is something repulsive in the idea of men being studied for their own good. The
paradigm of what repels us is to be found in the common situation of the
child who is *understood* by its parents, hemmed in, anticipated and lov-
ingly circumscribed, thoroughly taped, finding it easier and easier to conform internally and in the future to the parents' own interpretation of the
external acts of the past, and so, yielding to understanding as never to coercion, does not develop the mystery and wildness of spirit which it is still
our grace to believe is the mark of full humanness. The act of understanding becomes an act of control.

If, then, we are to live under the aspect of sociology, let us at least all
be sociologists together—let us broadcast what every sociologist knows,
and let us all have a share in observing one another, including the sociologists. The general indiscriminate publication of the Report makes sociology a little less the study of many men by a few men and a little more
man's study of himself. There is something right in turning loose the Report on the American public—it turns the American public loose on the
Report. It is right that the Report should be sold in stores that never before sold books and bought by people who never before bought books,
and passed from hand to hand and talked about and also snickered at and
giggled over and generally submitted to humor: American popular culture has surely been made the richer by the Report's gift of a new folk
hero—he already is clearly the hero of the Report—the "scholarly and
skilled lawyer" who for thirty years has had an orgasmic frequency of
thirty times a week.

As for the objection to the involvement of sex with science, it may be said that if science, through the Report, serves in any way to free the physical and even the "mechanical" aspects of sex, it may by that much have acted to free the emotions it might seem to deny. And perhaps only science could effectively undertake the task of freeing sexuality from science itself. Nothing so much as science has reinforced the moralistic or religious prohibitions in regard to sexuality. At some point in the history of Europe, some time in the Reformation, masturbation ceased to be thought of as merely a sexual sin which could be dealt with like any other sexual sin, and, perhaps by analogy with the venereal diseases with which the sexual mind of Europe was obsessed, came to be thought of as the specific cause of mental and physical disease, of madness and decay.* The prudery of Victorian England went forward with scientific hygiene; and both in Europe and in America the sexual mind was haunted by the idea of *degeneration*, apparently by analogy with the second law of thermodynamics—here is enlightened liberal opinion in 1896: "The effects of venereal disease have been treated at length, but the amount of vitality burned out through lust has never been and, perhaps, never can be adequately measured."† The very word "sex," which we now utter so casually, came into use for scientific reasons, to replace "love," which had once been indiscriminately used but was now to be saved for ideal purposes, and "lust," which came to seem both too pejorative and too human: "sex" implied scientific neutrality, then vague devaluation, for the word which neutralizes the mind of the observer also neuterizes the men and women who are being observed. Perhaps the Report is the superfetation of neutrality and objectivity which, in the dialectic of culture, was needed before sex could be free of their cold dominion.

Certainly it is a great merit of the Report that it brings to mind the earliest and best commerce between sex and science—the best thing about the Report is the quality that makes us remember Lucretius. The dialectic of culture has its jokes, and *alma Venus* having once been called to preside protectively over science, the situation is now reversed. The Venus of the Report does not, like the Venus of *De rerum natura*, shine in the light of the heavenly signs, nor does the earth put forth flowers for her. She is rather fusty and hole-in-the-corner and no doubt it does not

---

*See Abram Kardiner, *The Psychological Frontiers of Society*, p. 32 and the footnote on p. 441.
†Article on "Degeneration" in *The Encyclopedia of Social Reform*.

help her charm to speak of her in terms of mean frequencies of 3.2. No *putti* attend her: although Dr. Gregg in his Preface refers to sex as the reproductive instinct, there is scarcely any further indication in the book that sex has any connection with propagation. Yet clearly all things still follow where she leads, and somewhere in the authors' assumptions is buried the genial belief that still without her "nothing comes forth into the shining borders of light, nothing joyous and lovely is made." Her pandemic quality is still here—it is one of the great points of the Report how much of every kind of desire there is, how early it begins, how late it lasts. Her well-known jealousy is not abated, and prodigality is still her characteristic virtue: the Report assures us that those who respond to her earliest continue to do so longest. The Lucretian flocks and herds are here, too. Professor Kinsey is a zoologist and he properly keeps us always in mind of our animal kinship, even though he draws some very illogical conclusions from it; and those who are honest will have to admit that their old repulsion by the idea of human-animal contacts is somewhat abated by the chapter on this subject, which is, oddly, the only chapter in the book which hints that sex may be touched with tenderness. This large, recognizing, Lucretian sweep of the Report is the best thing about it and it makes up for much that is deficient and confused in its ideas.

But the Report is something more than a public and symbolic act of cultural revision in which, while the Heavenly Twins brood benignly over the scene in the form of the National Research Council and the Rockefeller Foundation, Professor Kinsey and his coadjutors drag forth into the light all the hidden actualities of sex so that they may lose their dark power and become domesticated among us. It is also an early example of science undertaking to deal head-on with a uniquely difficult matter that has traditionally been involved in valuation and morality. We must ask the question very seriously: how does science conduct itself in such an enterprise?

Certainly it does not conduct itself the way it says it does. I have already suggested that the Report overrates its own objectivity. The authors, who are enthusiastically committed to their method and to their principles, make the mistake of believing that, being scientists, they do not deal in assumptions, preferences, and conclusions. Nothing comes more easily to their pens than the criticism of the subjectivity of earlier writers on sex, yet their own subjectivity is sometimes extreme. In the nature of the enterprise, a degree of subjectivity was inevitable. Intellectual safety would then seem to lie not only in increasing the number of mechanical checks or in more rigorously examining those assumptions which had been brought to conscious formulation, but also in straightforwardly admitting that subjectivity was bound to appear and inviting the reader to be on the watch for it. This would not have guaranteed an absolute objectivity, but it would have made for a higher degree of relative objectivity. It would have done a thing even more important—it would have taught the readers of the Report something about the scientific processes to which they submit their thought.

The first failure of objectivity occurs in the title of the Report, *Sexual Behavior in the Human Male.* That the behavior which is studied is not that of the human male but only that of certain North American males has no doubt been generally observed and does not need further comment.* But the intention of the word "behavior" requires notice. By "behavior" the Report means behavioristic behavior, only that behavior which is physical. "To a large degree the present study has been confined to securing a record of the individual's overt sexual experiences." This limitation is perhaps forced on the authors by considerations of method, because it will yield simpler data and more manageable statistics, but it is also a limitation which suits their notion of human nature and its effect is to be seen throughout the book.

The Report, then, is a study of sexual behavior in so far as it can be quantitatively measured. This is certainly very useful. But, as we might fear, the sexuality that is measured is taken to be the definition of sexuality itself. The authors are certainly not without interest in what they call attitudes, but they believe that attitudes are best shown by "overt sexual experiences." We want to know, of course, what they mean by an experience and we want to know by what principles of evidence they draw their conclusions about attitudes.

We are led to see that their whole conception of a sexual experience is totally comprised by the physical act and that their principles of evidence are entirely quantitative and cannot carry them beyond the conclusion that the more the merrier. Quality is not integral to what they mean by

---

*The statistical method of the report lies, necessarily, outside my purview. Nor am I able to assess with any confidence the validity of the interviewing methods that were employed.

experience. As I have suggested, the Report is partisan with sex, it wants people to have a good sexuality. But by good it means nothing else but frequent.

It seems safe to assume that daily orgasm would be within the capacity of the average male and that the more than daily rates which have been observed for some primate species could be matched by a large portion of the human population if sexual activity were unrestricted.

The Report never suggests that a sexual experience is anything but the discharge of specifically sexual tension and therefore seems to conclude that frequency is always the sign of a robust sexuality. Yet masturbation in children may be and often is the expression not of sexuality only but of anxiety. In the same way, adult intercourse may be the expression of anxiety; its frequency may not be so much robust as compulsive.

The Report is by no means unaware of the psychic conditions of sexuality, yet it uses the concept almost always under the influence of its quantitative assumption. In a summary passage (p. 159) it describes the different intensities of orgasm and the various degrees of satisfaction, but disclaims any intention of taking these variations into account in its record of behavior. The Report holds out the hope to respectable males that they might be as frequent in performance as underworld characters if they were as unrestrained as this group. But before the respectable males aspire to this unwonted freedom they had better ascertain in how far the underworld characters are ridden by anxiety and in how far their sexuality is to be correlated with other ways of dealing with anxiety, such as dope, and in how far it is actually enjoyable. The Report's own data suggest that there may be no direct connection between on the one hand lack of restraint and frequency and on the other hand psychic health; they tell us of men in the lower social levels who in their sexual careers have intercourse with many hundreds of girls but who despise their sexual partners and cannot endure relations with the same girl more than once.

But the Report, as we shall see, is most resistant to the possibility of making any connection between the sexual life and the psychic structure. This strongly formulated attitude of the Report is based on the assumption that the whole actuality of sex is anatomical and physiological; the emotions are dealt with very much as if they were a "superstructure."

The subject's awareness of the erotic situation is summed up by this statement that he is "emotionally" aroused; but the material sources of the emotional disturbance are rarely recognized, either by laymen or scientists, both of whom are inclined to think in terms of passion, or natural drive, or a libido, which partakes of the mystic* more than it does of solid anatomy and physiologic function.

Now there is of course a clear instrumental advantage in being able to talk about psychic or emotional phenomena in terms of physiology, but to make a disjunction between the two descriptions of the same event, to make the anatomical and physiological description the "source" of the emotional and then to consider it as the more real of the two, is simply to commit not only the Reductive Fallacy but also what William James called the Psychologist's Fallacy. It must bring under suspicion any subsequent generalization which the Report makes about the nature of sexuality.†

The emphasis on the anatomical and physiological nature of sexuality is connected with the Report's strong reliance on animal behavior as a norm. The italics in the following quotation are mine.

For those who like the term, it is clear that there is a sexual drive which cannot be set aside for any large portion of the population, by any sort of social convention. *For those who prefer to think in sim-*

---

*We must observe how the scientific scorn of the "mystic" quite abates when the "mystic" suits the scientist's purpose. The Report is explaining why the interviews were not checked by means of narcosynthesis, lie-detectors, etc.: "In any such study which needs to secure quantities of data from human subjects, there is no way except to win their voluntary cooperation through the establishment of that intangible thing known as rapport." This intangible thing is established by looking the respondent squarely in the eye. It might be asked why a thing which is intangible but real enough to assure scientific accuracy should not be real enough to be considered as having an effect in sexual behavior.

†The implications of the Reductive Fallacy may be seen by paraphrasing the sentence I have quoted in which Professor Kinsey commits it: "Professor Kinsey's awareness of the intellectual situation is summed up by his statement that he 'has had an idea' or 'has come to a conclusion'; but the material sources of his intellectual disturbances are rarely recognized, either by laymen or scientists, both of whom are inclined to think in terms of 'thought' or 'intellection' or 'cognition,' which partakes of the mystic more than it does of solid anatomy or physiologic function." The Psychologist's Fallacy is what James calls "the confusion of his own standpoint with that of the mental fact about which he is making a report." "Another variety of the Psychologist's Fallacy is the assumption that the mental fact studied must be conscious of itself as the psychologist is conscious of it." *Principles of Psychology*, vol. I, pp. 196–97.

pler terms of action and reaction, it is a picture of an animal who, however civilized or cultured, continues to respond to the constantly present sexual stimuli, albeit with some social and physical restraints.

The Report obviously finds the second formulation to be superior to the first, and implies with a touch of irony that those who prefer it are on firmer ground.

Now there are several advantages in keeping in mind our own animal nature and our family connection with the other animals. The advantages are instrumental, moral, and poetic—I use the last word for want of a better to suggest the mere pleasure in finding kinship with some animals. But perhaps no idea is more difficult to use with precision than this one. In the Report it is used to establish a dominating principle of judgment, which is the Natural. As a concept of judgment this is notoriously deceptive and has been belabored for generations, but the Report knows nothing of its dangerous reputation and uses it with the naïvest confidence. And although the Report directs the harshest language toward the idea of the Normal, saying that it has stood in the way of any true scientific knowledge of sex, it is itself by no means averse to letting the idea of the Natural develop quietly into the idea of the Normal. The Report has in mind both a physical normality—as suggested by its belief that under optimal conditions men should be able to achieve the orgasmic frequency of the primates—and a moral normality, the acceptability, on the authority of animal behavior, of certain usually taboo practices.

It is inevitable that the concept of the Natural should haunt any discussion of sex. It is inevitable that it should make trouble, but most of all for a scientific discussion that bars judgments of value. Thus, in order to show that homosexuality is not a neurotic manifestation, as the Freudians say it is, the Report adduces the homosexual behavior of rats. But the argument *de animalibus* must surely stand by its ability to be inverted and extended. Thus, in having lost sexual periodicity, has the human animal lost naturalness? Again, the female mink, as we learn from the Report itself, fiercely resists intercourse and must be actually coerced into submission. Is it she who is unnatural or is her defense of her chastity to be taken as a comment on the females, animal or human, who willingly submit or who merely play at escape? Professor Kinsey is like no one so much as Sir Percival in Malory, who, seeing a lion and a serpent in battle with each other, decided to help the lion, "for he was the more natural beast of the two."

This awkwardness in the handling of ideas is characteristic of the Report. It is ill at ease with any idea that is in the least complex and it often tries to get rid of such an idea in favor of another that has the appearance of not going beyond the statement of physical fact. We see this especially in the handling of certain Freudian ideas. The Report acknowledges its debt to Freud with the generosity of spirit that marks it in other connections and it often makes use of Freudian concepts in a very direct and sensible way. Yet nothing could be clumsier than its handling of Freud's idea of pregenital generalized infantile sexuality. Because the Report can show, what is interesting and significant, that infants are capable of actual orgasm, although without ejaculation, it concludes that infantile sexuality is not generalized but specifically genital. But actually it has long been known, though the fact of orgasm had not been established, that infants can respond erotically to direct genital stimulation, and this knowledge does not contradict the Freudian idea that there is a stage in infant development in which sexuality is generalized throughout the body rather than specifically centred in the genital area; the fact of infant orgasm must be interpreted in conjunction with other and more complex manifestations of infant sexuality.*

The Report, we may say, has an extravagant fear of all ideas that do not seem to it to be, as it were, immediately dictated by simple physical fact. Another way of saying this is that the Report is resistant to any idea that seems to refer to a specifically human situation. An example is the position it takes on the matter of male potency. The folk feeling, where it is formulated on the question, and certainly where it is formulated by women, holds that male potency is not to be measured, as the Report measures it, merely by frequency, but by the ability to withhold orgasm long enough to bring the woman to climax. This is also the psychoanalytic view, which holds further that the inability to sustain intercourse is the result of unconscious fear or resentment. This view is very strongly resisted by the Report. The denial is based on mammalian behavior—"in many species" (but not in all?) ejaculation follows almost immediately

---

*The Report also handles the idea of sublimation in a very clumsy way. It does not represent accurately what the Freudian theory of sublimation is. For this, however, there is some excuse in the change of emphasis and even in meaning in Freud's use of the word.

upon intromission; in chimpanzees ejaculation occurs in ten to twenty seconds. The Report therefore concludes that the human male who ejaculates immediately upon intromission "is quite normal [here the word becomes suddenly permissible] among mammals and usual among his own species." Indeed, the Report finds it odd that the term "impotent" should be applied to such rapid responses.

> It would be difficult to find another situation in which an individual who was quick and intense in his responses was labelled anything but superior, and that in most instances is exactly what the rapidly ejaculating male probably is, however inconvenient and unfortunate his qualities may be from the standpoint of the wife in the relationship.

But by such reasoning the human male who is quick and intense in his leap to the lifeboat is natural and superior, however inconvenient and unfortunate his speed and intensity may be to the wife he leaves standing on the deck, as is also the man who makes a snap judgment, who bites his dentist's finger, who kicks the child who annoys him, who bolts his—or another's—food, who is incontinent of his feces. Surely the problem of the natural in the human was solved four centuries ago by Rabelais, and in the simplest naturalistic terms; and it is sad to have the issue all confused again by the naïvety of men of science. Rabelais's solution lay in the simple perception of the *natural* ability and tendency of man to grow in the direction of organization and control. The young Gargantua in his natural infancy had all the quick and intense responses just enumerated; had his teachers confused the traits of his natural infancy with those of his natural manhood, he would not have been the more natural but the less; he would have been a monster.

In considering the Report as a major cultural document, we must not underestimate the significance of its petulant protest against the inconvenience to the male of the unjust demand that is made upon him. This protest is tantamount to saying that sexuality is not to be involved in specifically human situations or to be connected with desirable aims that are conceived of in specifically human terms. We may leave out of account any ideal reasons which would lead a man to solve the human situation of the discrepancy—arising from conditions of biology or of culture or of both—between his own orgasmic speed and that of his mate, and we can consider only that it might be hedonistically desirable for him to do so, for advantages presumably accrue to him in the woman's accessibility and responsiveness. Advantages of this kind, however, are precisely the matters of quality in experience that the Report ignores.*

And its attitude on the question of male potency is but one example of the Report's insistence on drawing sexuality apart from the general human context. It is striking how small a role woman plays in *Sexual Behavior in the Human Male*. We learn nothing about the connection of sex and reproduction; the connection, from the sexual point of view, is certainly not constant yet it is of great interest. The pregnancy or possibility of pregnancy of his mate has a considerable effect, sometimes one way, sometimes the other, on the sexual behavior of the male; yet in the index under "Pregnancy" there is but a single entry—"fear of." Again, the contraceptive devices which "Pregnancy, fear of," requires have a notable influence on male sexuality; but the index lists only "Contraception, techniques." Or again, menstruation has an elaborate mythos which men take very seriously; but the two indexed passages which refer to menstruation give no information about its relation to sexual conduct.

Then too the Report explicitly and stubbornly resists the idea that sexual behavior is involved with the whole of the individual's character. In this it is strangely inconsistent. In the conclusion of its chapter on masturbation, after saying that masturbation does no physical harm and, if there are no conflicts over it, no mental harm, it goes on to raise the question of the effect of adult masturbation on "the ultimate personality of the individual." With a certain confusion of cause and effect which we need not dwell on, it says:

> It is now clear that masturbation is relied upon by the upper [social] level primarily because it has insufficient outlet through heterosexual coitus. This is, to a degree, an escape from reality, and the effect upon the ultimate personality of the individual is something that needs consideration.

---

*It is hard not to make a connection between the Report's strong stand against any delay in the male orgasm and its equally strong insistence that there is no difference for the woman between a clitoral and vaginal orgasm, a view which surely needs more investigation before it is as flatly put as the Report puts it. The conjunction of the two ideas suggests the desirability of a sexuality which uses a minimum of sexual apparatus.

The question is of course a real one, yet the Report strenuously refuses to extend the principle of it to any other sexual activity. It summarily rejects the conclusions of psychoanalysis which make the sexual conduct an important clue to, even the crux of, character. It finds the psychoanalytical view unacceptable for two reasons: (1) The psychiatric practitioner misconceives the relation between sexual aberrancy and psychic illness because only those sexually aberrant people who are ill seek out the practitioner, who therefore never learns about the large incidence of mental health among the sexually aberrant. (2) The emotional illness which sends the sexually aberrant person to find psychiatric help is the result of no flaw in the psyche itself that is connected with the aberrancy but is the result only of the fear of social disapproval of his sexual conduct. And the Report instances the many men who are well adjusted socially and who yet break, among them, all the sexual taboos.

The quality of the argument which the Report here advances is as significant as the wrong conclusions it reaches. "It is not possible," the Report says,

> to insist that any departure from the sexual mores, or any participation in socially taboo activities, always, or even usually, involves a neurosis or psychosis, for the case histories abundantly demonstrate that most individuals who engage in taboo activities make satisfactory social adjustments.

In this context either "neuroses and psychoses" are too loosely used to stand for all psychic maladjustment, or "social adjustment" is too loosely used to stand for emotional peace and psychic stability. When the Report goes on to cite the "socially and intellectually significant persons," the "successful scientists, educators, physicians," etc., who have among them "accepted the whole range of the so-called abnormalities," we must keep in mind that very intense emotional disturbance, known only to the sufferer, can go along with the efficient discharge of social duties, and that the psychoanalyst could counter with as long a list of distinguished and efficient people who do consult him.

Then, only an interest in attacking straw men could have led the Report to insist that psychoanalysis is wrong in saying that *any* departure from sexual mores, or *any* participation in sexually taboo activities, involves a neurosis or a psychosis, for psychoanalysis holds nothing like this view. It is just at this point that distinctions are needed of a sort which the Report seems not to want to make. For example: the Report comes out in a bold and simple way for the naturalness and normality and therefore for the desirability of mouth-genital contacts in heterosexual lovemaking. This is a form of sexual expression which is officially taboo enough, yet no psychoanalyst would say that its practice indicated a neurosis or psychosis. But a psychoanalyst would say that a person who disliked or was unable to practice any other form of sexual contact thereby gave evidence of a neurotic strain in his psychic constitution. His social adjustment, in the rather crude terms which the Report conceives of it, might not be impaired, but certainly the chances are that his psychic life would show signs of disturbance, not from the practice itself but from the psychic needs which made him insist on it. It is not the breaking of the taboo but the emotional circumstance of the breaking of the taboo that is significant.

The Report handles in the same oversimplified way and with the same confusing use of absolute concepts the sexual aberrancy which is, I suppose, the most complex and the most important in our cultural life, homosexuality. It rejects the view that homosexuality is innate and that "no modification of it may be expected." But then it goes on also to reject the view that homosexuality provides evidence of a "psychopathic personality." "Psychopathic personality" is a very strong term which perhaps few analysts would wish to use in this connection. Perhaps even the term "neurotic" would be extreme in a discussion which, in the manner of the Report, takes "social adjustment," as indicated by status, to be the limit of its analysis of character. But this does not leave the discussion where the Report seems to want to leave it—at the idea that homosexuality is to be accepted as a form of sexuality like another and that it is as "natural" as heterosexuality, a judgment to which the Report is led in part because of the surprisingly large incidence of homosexuality it finds in the population. Nor does the practice of "an increasing proportion of the most skilled psychiatrists who make no attempt to redirect behavior, but who devote their attention to helping an individual accept himself" imply what the Report seems to want it to, that these psychiatrists have thereby judged homosexuality to be an unexceptionable form of sexuality; it is rather that, in many cases, they are able to effect no change in the psychic disposition and therefore do the sensible and humane next best thing. Their opinion of the etiology of homosexuality as lying in some warp—as our culture judges it—of the psychic structure has not, I believe, changed. And I think that they would say that the condition that produced the homosexuality also produces other character traits on which judgment could be passed. This judgment need by no means be totally adverse; as passed upon individuals it need not be adverse at all; but there can be no doubt that a society in which homosexuality was dominant or even accepted would be different in nature and quality from one in which it was censured.

That the Report refuses to hold this view of homosexuality, or any other view of at least equivalent complexity, leads us to take into account the motives that animate the work, and when we do, we see how very characteristically *American* a document the Report is. In speaking of its motives, I have in mind chiefly its impulse toward acceptance and liberation, its broad and generous desire for others that they be not harshly judged. Much in the Report is to be understood as having been dictated by a recoil from the crude and often brutal rejection which society has made of the persons it calls sexually aberrant. The Report has the intention of habituating its readers to sexuality in all its manifestations; it wants to establish, as it were, a democratic pluralism of sexuality. And this good impulse toward acceptance and liberation is not unique with the Report but very often shows itself in those parts of our intellectual life which are more or less official and institutionalized. It is, for example, far more established in the universities than most of us with our habits of criticism of America, particularly of American universities, will easily admit; and it is to a considerable extent an established attitude with the foundations that support intellectual projects.

That this generosity of mind is much to be admired goes without saying. But when we have given it all the credit it deserves as a sign of something good and enlarging in American life, we cannot help observing that it is often associated with an almost intentional intellectual weakness. It goes with a nearly conscious aversion from making intellectual distinctions, almost as if out of the belief that an intellectual distinction must inevitably lead to a social discrimination or exclusion. We might say that those who most explicitly assert and wish to practice the democratic virtues have taken it as their assumption that all social facts—with the exception of exclusion and economic hardship—must be *accepted*, not merely in the scientific sense but also in the social sense, in the sense, that is, that no judgment must be passed on them, that any conclusion drawn from them which perceives values and consequences will turn out to be "undemocratic."

The Report has it in mind to raise questions about the official restrictive attitudes toward sexual behavior, including those attitudes that are formulated on the statute books of most states. To this end it accumulates facts with the intention of showing that standards of judgment of sexual conduct as they now exist do not have real reference to the actual sexual behavior of the population. So far, so good. But then it goes on to imply that there can be only one standard for the judgment of sexual behavior— that is, sexual behavior as it actually exists; which is to say that sexual behavior is not to be judged at all, except, presumably, in so far as it causes pain to others. (But from its attitude to the "inconvenience" of the "wife in the relationship," we must presume that not all pain is to be reckoned with.) Actually the Report does not stick to its own standard of judgment; it is, as I have shown, sometimes very willing to judge among behaviors. But the preponderant weight of its argument is that a fact is a physical fact, to be considered only in its physical aspect and apart from any idea or ideal that might make it a social fact, as having no ascertainable personal or cultural meaning and no possible consequences—as being, indeed, not available to social interpretation at all. In short, the Report by its primitive conception of the nature of fact quite negates the importance and even the existence of sexuality as a social fact. That is why, although it is possible to say of the Report that it brings light, it is necessary to say of it that it spreads confusion.

Huckleberry Finn

1948

In 1876 Mark Twain published *The Adventures of Tom Sawyer* and in the same year began what he called "another boys' book." He set little store by the new venture and said that he had undertaken it "more to be at work than anything else." His heart was not in it—"I like it only tolerably well as far as I have got," he said, "and may possibly pigeonhole or burn the MS when it is done." He pigeonholed it long before it was done and for as much as four years. In 1880 he took it out and carried it forward a little, only to abandon it again. He had a theory of unconscious composition and believed that a book must write itself; the book which he referred to as "Huck Finn's Autobiography" refused to do the job of its own creation and he would not coerce it.

But then in the summer of 1887 Mark Twain was possessed by a charge of literary energy which, as he wrote to Howells, was more intense than any he had experienced for many years. He worked all day and every day, and periodically he so fatigued himself that he had to recruit his strength by a day or two of smoking and reading in bed. It is impossible not to suppose that this great creative drive was connected with—was perhaps the direct result of—the visit to the Mississippi he had made earlier in the year, the trip which forms the matter of the second part of *Life on the Mississippi*. His boyhood and youth on the river he so profoundly loved had been at once the happiest and most significant part of Mark Twain's life; his return to it in middle age stirred memories which revived and refreshed the idea of *Huckleberry Finn*. Now at last the book was not only ready but eager to write itself. But it was not to receive much conscious help from its author. He was always full of second-rate literary schemes and now, in the early weeks of the summer, with *Huckleberry Finn* waiting to complete itself, he turned his hot energy upon several of these sorry projects, the completion of which gave him as much sense of satisfying productivity as did his eventual absorption in *Huckleberry Finn*.

When at last *Huckleberry Finn* was completed and published and widely loved, Mark Twain became somewhat aware of what he had accomplished with the book that had been begun as journeywork and depreciated, postponed, threatened with destruction. It is his masterpiece, and perhaps he learned to know that. But he could scarcely have estimated it for what it is, one of the world's great books and one of the central documents of American culture.

Wherein does its greatness lie? Primarily in its power of telling the truth. An awareness of this quality as it exists in *Tom Sawyer* once led Mark Twain to say of the earlier work that "it is *not* a boys' book at all. It will be read only by adults. It is written only for adults." But this was only a manner of speaking, Mark Twain's way of asserting, with a discernible touch of irritation, the degree of truth he had achieved. It does not represent his usual view either of boys' books or of boys. No one, as he well knew, sets a higher value on truth than a boy. Truth is the whole of a boy's conscious demand upon the world of adults. He is likely to believe that the adult world is in a conspiracy to lie to him, and it is this belief, by no means unfounded, that arouses Tom and Huck and all boys to their moral sensitivity, their everlasting concern with justice, which they call fairness. At the same time it often makes them skillful and profound liars in their own defense, yet they do not tell the ultimate lie of adults: they do not lie to themselves. That is why Mark Twain felt that it was impossible to carry Tom Sawyer beyond boyhood—in maturity "he would lie just like all the other one-horse men of literature and the reader would conceive a hearty contempt for him."

Certainly one element in the greatness of *Huckleberry Finn*, as also in the lesser greatness of *Tom Sawyer*, is that it succeeds first as a boys' book. One can read it at ten and then annually ever after, and each year find that it is as fresh as the year before, that it has changed only in becoming somewhat larger. To read it young is like planting a tree young—each year adds a new growth ring of meaning, and the book is as little likely as the tree to become dull. So, we may imagine, an Athenian boy grew up together with the *Odyssey*. There are few other books which we can know so young and love so long.

The truth of *Huckleberry Finn* is of a different kind from that of *Tom Sawyer*. It is a more intense truth, fiercer and more complex. *Tom Sawyer* has the truth of honesty—what it says about things and feelings is never false and always both adequate and beautiful. *Huckleberry Finn* has this kind of truth, too, but it has also the truth of moral passion; it deals directly with the virtue and depravity of man's heart.

Perhaps the best clue to the greatness of *Huckleberry Finn* has been given to us by a writer who is as different from Mark Twain as it is possible for one Missourian to be from another. T. S. Eliot's poem "The Dry Salvages," the third of his *Four Quartets*, begins with a meditation on the Mississippi, which Mr. Eliot knew in his St. Louis boyhood:

> I do not know much about gods; but I think that the river
> Is a strong brown god . . .

And the meditation goes on to speak of the god as

>   almost forgotten
> By the dwellers in cities—ever, however, implacable,
> Keeping his seasons and rages, destroyer, reminder of
> What men choose to forget. Unhonoured, unpropitiated
> By worshippers of the machine, but waiting, watching and waiting.

Huckleberry Finn is a great book because it is about a god—about, that is, a power which seems to have a mind and will of its own, and which to men of moral imagination appears to embody a great moral idea.

Huck himself is the servant of the river-god, and he comes very close to being aware of the divine nature of the being he serves. The world he inhabits is perfectly equipped to accommodate a deity, for it is full of presences and meanings which it conveys by natural signs and also by preternatural omens and taboos: to look at the moon over the left shoulder, to shake the tablecloth after sundown, to handle a snakeskin, are ways of offending the obscure and prevalent spirits. Huck is at odds, on moral and aesthetic grounds, with the only form of established religion he knows, and his very intense moral life may be said to derive almost wholly from his love of the river. He lives in a perpetual adoration of the Mississippi's power and charm. Huck, of course, always expresses himself better than he can know, but nothing draws upon his gift of speech like his response to his deity. After every sally into the social life of the shore, he returns to the river with relief and thanksgiving; and at each return, regular and explicit as a chorus in a Greek tragedy, there is a hymn of praise to the god's beauty, mystery, and strength, and to his noble grandeur in contrast with the pettiness of men.

Generally the god is benign, a being of long sunny days and spacious nights. But, like any god, he is also dangerous and deceptive. He generates fogs which bewilder, and contrives echoes and false distances which confuse. His sand bars can ground and his hidden snags can mortally wound a great steamboat. He can cut away the solid earth from under a man's feet and take his house with it. The sense of the danger of the river is what saves the book from any touch of the sentimentality and moral ineptitude of most works which contrast the life of nature with the life of society.

The river itself is only divine; it is not ethical and good. But its nature seems to foster the goodness of those who love it and try to fit themselves to its ways. And we must observe that we cannot make—that Mark Twain does not make—an absolute opposition between the river and human society. To Huck much of the charm of the river life is human: it is the raft and the wigwam and Jim. He has not run away from Miss Watson and the Widow Douglas and his brutal father to a completely individualistic liberty, for in Jim he finds his true father, very much as Stephen Dedalus in James Joyce's *Ulysses* finds his true father in Leopold Bloom.* The boy and the Negro slave form a family, a primitive community—and it is a community of saints.

Huck's intense and even complex moral quality may possibly not appear on a first reading, for one may be caught and convinced by his own estimate of himself, by his brags about his lazy hedonism, his avowed

---

*In Joyce's *Finnegans Wake* both Mark Twain and Huckleberry Finn appear frequently. The theme of rivers is, of course, dominant in the book; and Huck's name suits Joyce's purpose, for Finn is one of the many names of his hero. Mark Twain's love of and gift for the spoken language make another reason for Joyce's interest in him.

preference for being alone, his dislike of civilization. The fact is, of course, that he is involved in civilization up to his ears. His escape from society is but his way of reaching what society ideally dreams of for itself. Responsibility is the very essence of his character, and it is perhaps to the point that the original of Huck, a boyhood companion of Mark Twain's named Tom Blenkenship, did, like Huck, "light out for the Territory," only to become a justice of the peace in Montana, "a good citizen and greatly respected."

Huck does indeed have all the capacities for simple happiness he says he has, but circumstances and his own moral nature make him the least carefree of boys—he is always "in a sweat" over the predicament of someone else. He has a great sense of the sadness of human life, and although he likes to be alone, the words "lonely" and "loneliness" are frequent with him. The note of his special sensibility is struck early in the story:

Well, when Tom and me got to the edge of the hilltop we looked away down into the village and could see three or four lights twinkling where there were sick folks, maybe; and the stars over us was sparkling ever so fine; and down by the village was the river, a whole mile broad, and awful still and grand.

The identification of the lights as the lamps of sick-watches defines Huck's character.

His sympathy is quick and immediate. When the circus audience laughs at the supposedly drunken man who tries to ride the horse, Huck is only miserable: "It wasn't funny to me . . .; I was all of a tremble to see his danger." When he imprisons the intending murderers on the wrecked steamboat, his first thought is of how to get someone to rescue them, for he considers "how dreadful it was, even for murderers, to be in such a fix. I says to myself, there ain't no telling but I might come to be a murderer myself yet, and then how would I like it." But his sympathy is never sentimental. When at last he knows that the murderers are beyond help, he has no inclination to false pathos. "I felt a little bit heavy-hearted about the gang, but not much, for I reckoned that if they could stand it I could." His will is genuinely good and he has no need to torture himself with guilty second thoughts.

Not the least remarkable thing about Huck's feeling for people is that his tenderness goes along with the assumption that his fellow men are likely to be dangerous and wicked. He travels incognito, never telling the truth about himself and never twice telling the same lie, for he trusts no one and the lie comforts him even when it is not necessary. He instinctively knows that the best way to keep a party of men away from Jim on the raft is to beg them to come aboard to help his family stricken with smallpox. And if he had not already had the knowledge of human weakness and stupidity and cowardice, he would soon have acquired it, for all his encounters forcibly teach it to him—the insensate feud of the Graingerfords and Shepherdsons, the invasion of the raft by the Duke and the King, the murder of Boggs, the lynching party, and the speech of Colonel Sherburn. Yet his profound and bitter knowledge of human depravity never prevents him from being a friend to man.

No personal pride interferes with his well-doing. He knows what status is and on the whole he respects it—he is really a very *respectable* person and inclines to like "quality folks"—but he himself is unaffected by it. He himself has never had status, he has always been the lowest of the low, and the considerable fortune he had acquired in *The Adventures of Tom Sawyer* is never real to him. When the Duke suggests that Huck and Jim render him the personal service that accords with his rank, Huck's only comment is, "Well, that was easy so we done it." He is injured in every possible way by the Duke and the King, used and exploited and manipulated, yet when he hears that they are in danger from a mob, his natural impulse is to warn them. And when he fails of his purpose and the two men are tarred and feathered and ridden on a rail, his only thought is, "Well, it made me sick to see it; and I was sorry for them poor pitiful rascals, it seemed like I couldn't ever feel any hardness against them any more in the world."

And if Huck and Jim on the raft do indeed make a community of saints, it is because they do not have an ounce of pride between them. Yet this is not perfectly true, for the one disagreement they ever have is over a matter of pride. It is on the occasion when Jim and Huck have been separated by the fog. Jim has mourned Huck as dead, and then, exhausted, has fallen asleep. When he awakes and finds that Huck has returned, he is overjoyed; but Huck convinces him that he has only dreamed the incident, that there has been no fog, no separation, no chase, no reunion, and then allows him to make an elaborate "interpretation" of the dream he now believes he has had. Then the joke is sprung, and in the growing light of the dawn Huck points to the debris of leaves on the raft and the broken oar.

Jim looked at the trash, and then looked at me, and back at the trash again. He had got the dream fixed so strong in his head that he couldn't seem to shake it loose and get the fact back into its place again right away. But when he did get the thing straightened around he looked at me steady without ever smiling, and says:

'What do dey stan' for? I'se gwyne to tell you. When I got all wore out wid work, en wid de callin' for you, en went to sleep, my heart wuz mos' broke bekase you wuz los', en I didn't k'yer no mo' what became er me en de raf'? En when I wake up en fine you back agin, all safe en soun', de tears come, en I could a got down on my knees en kiss yo' foot, I's so thankful. En all you wuz thinkin' 'bout wuz how you could make a fool uv ole Jim wid a lie. Dat truck dah is *trash*; en trash is what people is dat puts dirt on de head er dey fren's en makes 'em ashamed.'

Then he got up slow and walked to the wigwam, and went in there without saying anything but that.

The pride of human affection has been touched, one of the few prides that has any true dignity. And at its utterance, Huck's one last dim vestige of pride of status, his sense of his position as a white man, wholly vanishes: "It was fifteen minutes before I could work myself up to go and humble myself to a nigger; but I done it, and I warn't sorry for it afterwards either."

This incident is the beginning of the moral testing and development which a character so morally sensitive as Huck's must inevitably undergo. And it becomes an heroic character when, on the urging of affection, Huck discards the moral code he has always taken for granted and resolves to help Jim in his escape from slavery. The intensity of his struggle over the act suggests how deeply he is involved in the society which he rejects. The satiric brilliance of the episode lies, of course, in Huck's solving his problem not by doing "right" but by doing "wrong." He has only to consult his conscience, the conscience of a Southern boy in the middle of the last century, to know that he ought to return Jim to slavery. And as

soon as he makes the decision according to conscience and decides to inform on Jim, he has all the warmly gratifying emotions of conscious
virtue.

> Why, it was astonishing, the way I felt as light as a feather right
> straight off, and my troubles all gone. . . . I felt good and all
> washed clean of sin for the first time I had ever felt so in my life,
> and I knowed I could pray now.

And when at last he finds that he cannot endure his decision but must
sacrifice the comforts of the pure heart and help Jim in his escape, it is not
because he has acquired any new ideas about slavery—he believes that he
detests Abolitionists; he himself answers when he is asked if the explosion
of a steamboat boiler had hurt anyone, "No'm, killed a nigger," and of
course finds nothing wrong in the responsive comment, "Well, it's lucky
because sometimes people do get hurt." Ideas and ideals can be of no help
to him in his moral crisis. He no more condemns slavery than Tristram
and Lancelot condemn marriage; he is as consciously *wicked* as any illicit
lover of romance and he consents to be damned for a personal devotion,
never questioning the justice of the punishment he has incurred.

Huckleberry Finn was once barred from certain libraries and schools
for its alleged subversion of morality. The authorities had in mind the
book's endemic lying, the petty thefts, the denigrations of respectability
and religion, the bad language, and the bad grammar. We smile at that excessive care, yet in point of fact *Huckleberry Finn* is indeed a subversive
book—no one who reads thoughtfully the dialectic of Huck's great moral
crisis will ever again be wholly able to accept without some question and
some irony the assumptions of the respectable morality by which he lives,
nor will ever again be certain that what he considers the clear dictates of
moral reason are not merely the engrained customary beliefs of his time
and place.

We are not likely to miss in *Huckleberry Finn* the subtle, implicit moral
meaning of the great river. But we are likely to understand these moral
implications as having to do only with personal and individual conduct.
And since the sum of individual pettiness is on the whole pretty constant,
we are likely to think of the book as applicable to mankind in general and
at all times and in all places, and we praise it by calling it "universal." And
so it is; but like many books to which that large adjective applies, it is also

local and particular. It has a particular moral reference to the United States in the period after the Civil War. It was then when, in Mr. Eliot's phrase, the river was forgotten, and precisely by the "dwellers in cities," by the "worshippers of the machine."

The Civil War and the development of the railroads ended the great days when the river was the central artery of the nation. No contrast could be more moving than that between the hot, turbulent energy of the river life of the first part of *Life on the Mississippi* and the melancholy reminiscence of the second part. And the war that brought the end of the rich Mississippi days also marked a change in the quality of life in America which, to many men, consisted of a deterioration of American moral values. It is of course a human habit to look back on the past and to find it a better and more innocent time than the present. Yet in this instance there seems to be an objective basis for the judgment. We cannot disregard the testimony of men so diverse as Henry Adams, Walt Whitman, William Dean Howells, and Mark Twain himself, to mention but a few of the many who were in agreement on this point. All spoke of something that had gone out of American life after the war, some simplicity, some innocence, some peace. None of them was under any illusion about the amount of ordinary human wickedness that existed in the old days, and Mark Twain certainly was not. The difference was in the public attitude, in the things that were now accepted and made respectable in the national ideal. It was, they all felt, connected with new emotions about money. As Mark Twain said, where formerly "the people had desired money," now they "fall down and worship it." The new gospel was, "Get money. Get it quickly. Get it in abundance. Get it in prodigious abundance. Get it dishonestly if you can, honestly if you must."*

With the end of the Civil War capitalism had established itself. The relaxing influence of the frontier was coming to an end. Americans increasingly became "dwellers in cities" and "worshippers of the machine." Mark Twain himself became a notable part of this new dispensation. No one worshipped the machine more than he did, or thought he did—he ruined himself by his devotion to the Paige typesetting machine, by which he hoped to make a fortune even greater than he had made by his writing, and he sang the praises of the machine age in *A Connecticut Yankee in King Arthur's Court*. He associated intimately with the dominant figures

---

*Mark Twain in Eruption, edited by Bernard De Voto, p. 77.

of American business enterprise. Yet at the same time he hated the new way of life and kept bitter memoranda of his scorn, commenting on the low morality or the bad taste of the men who were shaping the ideal and directing the destiny of the nation.

Mark Twain said of *Tom Sawyer* that it "is simply a hymn, put into prose form to give it a wordly air." He might have said the same, and with even more reason, of *Huckleberry Finn*, which is a hymn to an older America forever gone, an America which had its great national faults, which was full of violence and even of cruelty, but which still maintained its sense of reality, for it was not yet enthralled by money, the father of ultimate illusion and lies. Against the money-god stands the river-god, whose comments are silent—sunlight, space, uncrowded time, stillness, and danger. It was quickly forgotten once its practical usefulness had passed, but, as Mr. Eliot's poem says, "The river is within us. . . ."

In form and style *Huckleberry Finn* is an almost perfect work. Only one mistake has ever been charged against it, that it concludes with Tom Sawyer's elaborate, too elaborate, game of Jim's escape. Certainly this episode is too long—in the original draft it was much longer—and certainly it is a falling off, as almost anything would have to be, from the incidents of the river. Yet it has a certain formal aptness—like, say, that of the Turkish initiation which brings Molière's *Le Bourgeois Gentilhomme* to its close. It is a rather mechanical development of an idea, and yet some device is needed to permit Huck to return to his anonymity, to give up the role of hero, to fall into the background which he prefers, for he is modest in all things and could not well endure the attention and glamour which attend a hero at a book's end. For this purpose nothing could serve better than the mind of Tom Sawyer with its literary furnishings, its conscious romantic desire for experience and the hero's part, and its ingenious schematization of life to achieve that aim.

The form of the book is based on the simplest of all novel-forms, the so-called picaresque novel, or novel of the road, which strings its incidents on the line of the hero's travels. But, as Pascal says, "rivers are roads that move," and the movement of the road in its own mysterious life transmutes the primitive simplicity of the form: the road itself is the greatest character in this novel of the road, and the hero's departures from the river and his returns to it compose a subtle and significant pattern. The linear simplicity of the picaresque novel is further modified by the story's having a clear dramatic organization: it has a beginning, a middle, and an end, and a mounting suspense of interest.

As for the style of the book, it is not less than definitive in American literature. The prose of *Huckleberry Finn* established for written prose the virtues of American colloquial speech. This has nothing to do with pronunciation or grammar. It has something to do with ease and freedom in the use of language. Most of all it has to do with the structure of the sentence, which is simple, direct, and fluent, maintaining the rhythm of the word-groups of speech and the intonations of the speaking voice.

In the matter of language American literature had a special problem. The young nation was inclined to think that the mark of the truly literary product was a grandiosity and elegance not to be found in the common speech. It therefore encouraged a greater breach between its vernacular and its literary language than, say, English literature of the same period ever allowed. This accounts for the hollow ring one now and then hears even in the work of our best writers in the first half of the last century. English writers of equal stature would never have made the lapses into rhetorical excess that are common in Cooper and Poe and that are to be found even in Melville and Hawthorne.

Yet at the same time that the language of ambitious literature was high and thus always in danger of falseness, the American reader was keenly interested in the actualities of daily speech. No literature, indeed, was ever so taken up with matters of speech as ours was. "Dialect," which attracted even our serious writers, was the accepted common ground of our popular humorous writing. Nothing in social life seemed so remarkable as the different forms which speech could take—the brogue of the immigrant Irish or the mispronunciation of the German, the "affectation" of the English, the reputed precision of the Bostonian, the legendary twang of the Yankee farmer, and the drawl of the Pike County man. Mark Twain, of course, was in the tradition of humor that exploited this interest, and no one could play with it nearly so well. Although today the carefully spelled-out dialects of nineteenth-century American humor are likely to seem dull enough, the subtle variations of speech in *Huckleberry Finn*, of which Mark Twain was justly proud, are still part of the liveliness and flavor of the book.

Out of his knowledge of the actual speech of America Mark Twain forged a classic prose. The adjective may seem a strange one, yet it is apt.

Forget the misspellings and the faults of grammar, and the prose will be seen to move with the greatest simplicity, directness, lucidity, and grace. These qualities are by no means accidental. Mark Twain, who read widely, was passionately interested in the problems of style; the mark of the strictest literary sensibility is everywhere to be found in the prose of *Huckleberry Finn*.

It is this prose that Ernest Hemingway had chiefly in mind when he said that "all modern American literature comes from one book by Mark Twain called *Huckleberry Finn*." Hemingway's own prose stems from it directly and consciously; so does the prose of the two modern writers who most influenced Hemingway's early style, Gertrude Stein and Sherwood Anderson (although neither of them could maintain the robust purity of their model); so, too, does the best of William Faulkner's prose, which, like Mark Twain's own, reinforces the colloquial tradition with the literary tradition. Indeed, it may be said that almost every contemporary American writer who deals conscientiously with the problems and possibilities of prose must feel, directly or indirectly, the influence of Mark Twain. He is the master of the style that escapes the fixity of the printed page, that sounds in our ears with the immediacy of the heard voice, the very voice of unpretentious truth.

The Princess Casamassima

1948

I

In 1888, on the second of January, which in any year is likely to be a sad day, Henry James wrote to his friend William Dean Howells that his reputation had been dreadfully injured by his last two novels. The desire for his productions, he said, had been reduced to zero, editors no longer asked for his work, they even seemed ashamed to publish the stories they had already bought. But James was never without courage. "However, I don't despair," he wrote, "for I think I am now really in better form than I ever have been in my life and I propose yet to do many things." And then, no doubt with the irony all writers use when they dare to speak of future recognition, but also, surely, with the necessary faith, he concludes the matter: "Very likely too, some day, all my buried prose will kick off its various tombstones at once."

And so it happened. The "some day" has arrived and we have been hearing the clatter of marble as James's buried prose kicks off its monuments in a general resurrection. On all sides James is being given the serious and joyous interest he longed for in his lifetime.

One element of our interest must be the question of how some of James's prose ever came to be buried at all. It is not hard to understand why certain of James's books did not catch the contemporary fancy. But the two books on which James placed the blame for his diminishing popularity were *The Bostonians* and *The Princess Casamassima*, and of all James's novels these are the two which are most likely to make an immediate appeal to the reader of today. That they should not have delighted their contemporary public, but on the contrary should have turned it against James, makes a lively problem in the history of taste.*

In the masterpieces of his late years James became a difficult writer. This is the fact and nothing is gained for James by denying it. He himself knew that these late works were difficult; he wished them to be dealt with as if they were difficult. When a young man from Texas—it was Mr. Stark Young—inquired indirectly of James how he should go about reading his novels, James did not feel that this diffidence was provincial but happily drew up lists which would lead the admirable young man from the easy to the hard. But the hostility with which *The Bostonians* and *The Princess Casamassima* were received cannot be explained by any difficulty of either manner or intention, for in these books there is none. The prose, although personally characteristic, is perfectly in the tradition of the nineteenth-century novel. It is warm, fluent, and on the whole rather less elaborate and virtuoso than Dickens's prose. The motives of the characters are clear and direct—certainly they are far from the elaborate punctilio of the late masterpieces. And the charge that is sometimes made against the later work, that it exists in a social vacuum, clearly does not pertain here. In these novels James is at the point in his career at which society, in the largest and even the grossest sense, is offering itself to his mind with great force. He understands society as crowds and police, as a field of justice and injustice, reform and revolution. The social texture of his work is grainy and knotted with practicality and detail. And more: his social observation is of a kind that we must find startlingly prescient when we consider that it was made some sixty years ago.

It is just this prescience, of course, that explains the resistance of

*Whoever wishes to know what the courage of the artist must sometimes be could do no better than to read the British reviews of *The Bostonians* and *The Princess Casamassima*. In a single year James brought out two major works; he thought they were his best to date and expected great things of them; he was told by the reviewers that they were not really novels at all; he was scorned and sneered at and condescended to and dismissed. In adjacent columns the ephemeral novels of the day were treated with gentle respect. The American press rivaled the British in the vehemence with which it condemned *The Bostonians*, but it was more tolerant of *The Princess Casamassima*.

James's contemporaries. What James saw he saw truly, but it was not what the readers of his time were themselves equipped to see. That we now are able to share his vision required the passage of six decades and the events which brought them to climax. Henry James in the 1880s understood what we have painfully learned from our grim glossary of wars and concentration camps, after having seen the state and human nature laid open to our horrified inspection. "But I have the imagination of disaster—and see life as ferocious and sinister": James wrote this to A. C. Benson in 1896, and what so bland a young man as Benson made of the statement, what anyone then was likely to make of it, is hard to guess. But nowadays we know that such an imagination is one of the keys to truth.

It was, then, "the imagination of disaster" that cut James off from his contemporaries and it is what recommends him to us now. We know something about the profound disturbance of the sexual life which seems to go along with hypertrophy of the will and how this excess of will seems to be a response to certain maladjustments in society and to direct itself back upon them; D. H. Lawrence taught us much about this, but Lawrence himself never attempted a more daring conjunction of the sexual and the political life than Henry James succeeds with in *The Bostonians*. We know much about misery and downtroddenness and of what happens when strong and gifted personalities are put at a hopeless disadvantage, and about the possibilities of extreme violence, and about the sense of guilt and unreality which may come to members of the upper classes and the strange complex efforts they make to find innocence and reality, and about the conflict between the claims of art and of social duty—these are among the themes which make the pattern of *The Princess Casamassima*. It is a novel which has at its very center the assumption that Europe has reached the full of its ripeness and is passing over into rottenness, that the peculiarly beautiful light it gives forth is in part the reflection of a glorious past and in part the phosphorescence of a present decay, that it may meet its end by violence and that this is not wholly unjust, although never before has the old sinful continent made so proud and pathetic an assault upon our affections.

2

The Princess Casamassima belongs to a great line of novels which runs through the nineteenth century as, one might say, the very backbone of its fiction. These novels, which are defined as a group by the character and circumstance of their heroes, include Stendhal's *The Red and the Black*, Balzac's *Père Goriot* and *Lost Illusions*, Dickens's *Great Expectations*, Flaubert's *Sentimental Education*; only a very slight extension of the definition is needed to allow the inclusion of Tolstoy's *War and Peace* and Dostoyevsky's *The Idiot*.

The defining hero may be known as the Young Man from the Provinces. He need not come from the provinces in literal fact, his social class may constitute his province. But a provincial birth and rearing suggest the simplicity and the high hopes he begins with—he starts with a great demand upon life and a great wonder about its complexity and promise. He may be of good family but he must be poor. He is intelligent, or at least aware, but not at all shrewd in worldly matters. He must have acquired a certain amount of education, should have learned something about life from books, although not the truth.

The hero of *The Princess Casamassima* conforms very exactly to type. The province from which Hyacinth Robinson comes is a city slum. "He sprang up at me out of the London pavement," says James in the preface to the novel in the New York edition. In 1883, the first year of his long residence in England, James was in the habit of prowling the streets, and they yielded him the image

> of some individual sensitive nature or fine mind, some small obscure creature whose education should have been almost wholly derived from them, capable of profiting by all the civilization, all the accumulation to which they testify, yet condemned to see things only from outside—in mere quickened consideration, mere wistfulness and envy and despair.

Thus equipped with poverty, pride, and intelligence, the Young Man from the Provinces stands outside life and seeks to enter. This modern hero is connected with the tales of the folk. Usually his motive is the legendary one of setting out to seek his fortune, which is what the folktale says when it means that the hero is seeking himself. He is really the third and youngest son of the woodcutter, the one to whom all our sympathies go, the gentle and misunderstood one, the bravest of all. He is likely to be in some doubt about his parentage; his father the woodcutter is not really his father. Our hero has, whether he says so or not, the common belief of children that there is some mystery about his birth; his real parents, if the truth were known, are of great and even royal estate. Julien Sorel of *The Red and the Black* is the third and youngest son of an actual woodcutter, but he is the spiritual son of Napoleon. In our day the hero of *The Great Gatsby* is not really the son of Mr. Gatz; he is said to have sprung "from his Platonic conception of himself," to be, indeed, "the son of God." And James's Hyacinth Robinson, although fostered by a poor dressmaker and a shabby fiddler, has an English lord for his real father.

It is the fate of the Young Man to move from an obscure position into one of considerable eminence in Paris or London or St. Petersburg, to touch the life of the rulers of the earth. His situation is as chancy as that of any questing knight of medieval romance. He is confronted by situations whose meanings are dark to him, in which his choice seems always decisive. He understands everything to be a "test." Parsifal at the castle of the Fisher King is not more uncertain about the right thing to do than the Young Man from the Provinces picking his perilous way through the irrationalities of the society into which he has been transported. That the Young Man be introduced into great houses and involved with large affairs is essential to his story, which must not be confused with the cognate story of the Sensitive Young Man. The provincial hero must indeed be sensitive, and in proportion to the brassiness of the world; he may even be an artist; but it is not his part merely to be puzzled and hurt; he is not the hero of *The Way of All Flesh* or *Of Human Bondage* or *Mooncalf*. Unlike the merely sensitive hero, he is concerned to know how the political and social world are run and enjoyed; he wants a share of power and pleasure and in consequence he takes real risks, often of his life. The "swarming facts" that James tells us Hyacinth is to confront are "freedom and ease, knowledge and power, money, opportunity, and satiety."

The story of the Young Man from the Provinces is thus a strange one, for it has its roots both in legend and in the very heart of the modern actuality. From it we have learned most of what we know about modern society, about class and its strange rituals, about power and influence and about money, the hard fluent fact in which modern society has its being. Yet through the massed social fact there runs the thread of legendary romance, even of downright magic. We note, for example, that it seems necessary for the novelist to deal in transformation. Some great and powerful hand must reach down into the world of seemingly chanceless routine and pick up the hero and set him down in his complex and dangerous fate. Pip meets Magwitch on the marsh, a felon-godfather; Pierre Bezukhov unexpectedly inherits the fortune that permits this uncouth young man to make his tour of Russian society; powerful unseen forces play around the proud head of Julien Sorel to make possible his astonishing upward career; Rastignac, simply by being one of the boarders at the Maison Vauquer which also shelters the great Vautrin, moves to the very center of Parisian intrigue; James Gatz rows out to a millionaire's yacht, a boy in dungarees, and becomes Jay Gatsby, an Oxford man, a military hero.

Such transformations represent, with only slight exaggeration, the literal fact that was to be observed every day. From the late years of the eighteenth century through the early years of the twentieth the social structure of the West was peculiarly fitted—one might say designed—for changes in fortune that were magical and romantic. The upper-class ethos was strong enough to make it remarkable that a young man should cross the borders, yet weak enough to permit the crossing in exceptional cases. A shiftless boy from Geneva, a starveling and a lackey, becomes the admiration of the French aristocracy and is permitted by Europe to manipulate its assumptions in every department of life: Jean-Jacques Rousseau is the father of all the Young Men from the Provinces, including the one from Corsica.

The Young Man's story represents an actuality, yet we may be sure that James took special delight in its ineluctable legendary element. James was certainly the least primitive of artists, yet he was always aware of his connection with the primitive. He set great store by the illusion of probability and verisimilitude, but he knew that he dealt always with illusion; he was proud of the devices of his magic. Like any primitive story-teller, he wished to hold the reader against his will, to *enchant*, as we say. He loved what he called "the story as story"; he delighted to work, by means of the unusual, the extravagant, the melodramatic, and the supernatural, upon what he called "the blessed faculty of wonder"; and he understood primitive story to be the root of the modern novelist's art. F. O. Matthiessen speaks of the fairy-tale quality of *The Wings of the Dove*; so sophisticated a work as *The Ambassadors* can be read as one of those tales in which the hero finds that nothing is what it seems and that the only guide through the world must be the goodness of his heart.

Like any great artist of story, like Shakespeare or Balzac or Dickens or Dostoyevsky, James crowds probability rather closer than we nowadays like. It is not that he gives us unlikely events but that he sometimes thickens the number of interesting events beyond our ordinary expectation. If this, in James or in any story-teller, leads to a straining of our sense of verisimilitude, there is always the defense to be made that the special job of literature is, as Marianne Moore puts it, the creation of "imaginary gardens with real toads in them." The reader who detects that the garden is imaginary should not be led by his discovery to a wrong view of the reality of the toads. In settling questions of reality and truth in fiction, it must be remembered that, although the novel in certain of its forms resembles the accumulative and classificatory sciences, which are the sciences most people are most at home with, in certain other of its forms the novel approximates the sciences of experiment. And an experiment is very like an imaginary garden which is laid out for the express purpose of supporting a real toad of fact. The apparatus of the researcher's bench is not nature itself but an artificial and extravagant contrivance, much like a novelist's plot, which is devised to force or foster a fact into being. This seems to have been James's own view of the part that is played in his novels by what he calls "romance." He seems to have had an analogy with experiment very clearly in mind when he tells us that romance is "experience liberated, so to speak; experience disengaged, disembroiled, disencumbered, exempt from the conditions that usually attach to it." Again and again he speaks of the contrivance of a novel in ways which will make it seem like illegitimate flummery to the reader who is committed only to the premises of the naturalistic novel, but which the intelligent scientist will understand perfectly.

Certainly *The Princess Casamassima* would seem to need some such defense as this, for it takes us, we are likely to feel, very far along the road to romance, some will think to the very point of impossibility. It asks us to accept a poor young man whose birth is darkly secret, his father being a dissipated but authentic English lord, his mother a French courtesan-seamstress who murders the father; a beautiful American-Italian princess who descends in the social scale to help "the people"; a general mingling of the very poor with persons of exalted birth; and then a dim mysterious leader of revolution, never seen by the reader, the machinations of an underground group of conspirators, an oath taken to carry out an assassination at some unspecified future day, the day arriving, the hour of the killing set, the instructions and the pistol given.

Confronted by paraphernalia like this, even those who admire the book are likely to agree with Rebecca West when, in her exuberant little study of James, she tells us that it is "able" and "meticulous" but at the same time "distraught" and "wild," that the "loveliness" in it comes from a transmutation of its "perversities"; she speaks of it as a "mad dream" and teases its vast unlikelihood, finding it one of the big jokes in literature that it was James, who so prided himself on his lack of naïvety, who should have brought back to fiction the high implausibility of the old novels which relied for their effects on dark and stormy nights, Hindu servants, mysterious strangers, and bloody swords wiped on richly embroidered handkerchiefs.

Miss West was writing in 1916, when the English naturalistic novel, with its low view of possibility, was in full pride. Our notion of political possibility was still to be changed by a small group of quarrelsome conspiratorial intellectuals taking over the control of Russia. Even a loyal Fabian at that time could consider it one of the perversities of *The Princess Casamassima* that two of its lower-class characters should say of a third that he had the potentiality of becoming Prime Minister of England; today Paul Muniment sits in the Cabinet and is on the way to Downing Street. In the 1930s the book was much admired by those who read it in the light of knowledge of our own radical movements; it then used to be said that although James had dreamed up an impossible revolutionary group he had nonetheless managed to derive from it some notable insights into the temper of radicalism; these admirers grasped the toad of fact and felt that it was all the more remarkably there because the garden is so patently imaginary.

Yet an understanding of James's use of "romance"—and there is "romance" in Hyacinth's story—must not preclude our understanding of the striking literary accuracy of *The Princess Casamassima*. James himself helped to throw us off the scent when in his preface to the novel he told us that he made no research into Hyacinth's subterranean politics. He justified this by saying that the value I wished most to render and the effect I wished most to produce were precisely those of our not knowing, of society's not knowing, but only guessing and suspecting and trying to ignore, what "goes on" irreconcilably, subversively, beneath the vast smug surface.

And he concludes the preface with the most beautifully arrogant and truest thing a novelist ever said about his craft:

What it all came back to was, no doubt, something like *this* wisdom—that if you haven't, for fiction, the root of the matter in you, haven't the sense of life and the penetrating imagination, you are a fool in the very presence of the revealed and assured; but that if you *are* so armed, you are not really helpless, not without your resource, even before mysteries abysmal.

If, to learn about the radical movement of his time, James really did no more than consult his penetrating imagination—which no doubt was nourished like any other on conversation and the daily newspaper—then we must say that in no other novelist did the root of the matter go so deep and so wide. For the truth is that there is not a political event of *The Princess Casamassima*, not a detail of oath or mystery or danger, which is not confirmed by multitudinous records.

3

We are inclined to flatter our own troubles with the belief that the late nineteenth century was a peaceful time. But James knew its actual violence. England was, to be sure, rather less violent than the Continent, but the history of England in the 1880s was one of profound social unrest often intensified to disorder. In March of 1886, the year in which *The Princess Casamassima* appeared in book form, James wrote to his brother William of a riot in his street, of ladies' carriages being stopped and the "occupants hustled, rifled, slapped, and kissed." He does not think that the rioters were unemployed working men, more likely that they were "the great army of roughs and thieves." But he says that there is "immense destitution" and that "everyone is getting poorer—from causes which, I fear, will continue." In the same year he wrote to Charles Eliot Norton that the state of the British upper class seems to be "in many ways very much the same rotten and *collapsible* one of the French aristocracy before the revolution."

James envisaged revolution, and not merely as a convenience for his fiction. But he imagined a kind of revolution with which we are no longer familiar. It was not a Marxian revolution. There is no upsurge of an angry proletariat led by a disciplined party which plans to head a new strong state. Such a revolution has its conservative aspect—it seeks to save certain elements of bourgeois culture for its own use, for example, science and the means of production and even some social agencies. The revolutionary theory of *The Princess Casamassima* has little in common with this. There is no organized mass movement; there is no disciplined party but only a strong conspiratorial center. There are no plans for taking over the state and almost no ideas about the society of the future. The conspiratorial center plans only for destruction, chiefly personal terrorism. But James is not naïvely representing a radical Graustark; he is giving a very accurate account of anarchism.

In 1872, at its meeing in The Hague, the First International voted the expulsion of the anarchists. Karl Marx had at last won his long battle with Bakunin. From that point on, "scientific socialism" was to dominate revolutionary thought. Anarchism ceased to be a main current of political theory. But anarchism continued as a force to be reckoned with, especially in the Latin countries, and it produced a revolutionary type of great courage and sometimes of appealing interest. Even in decline the theory and action of anarchism dominated the imagination of Europe.

It is not possible here to give a discriminating account of anarchism in all its aspects; to distinguish between the mutation which verges on nihilism and that which is called Communist-anarchism, or between its representatives, Sergei Nechayev, who had the character of a police spy, and Kropotkin or the late Carlo Tresca, who were known for their personal sweetness; or to resolve the contradiction between the violence of its theory and action and the gentle world toward which these are directed. It will have to be enough to say that anarchism holds that the natural goodness of man is absolute and that society corrupts it, and that the guide to anarchist action is the desire to destroy society in general and not merely a particular social form.

When, therefore, Hyacinth Robinson is torn between his desire for social justice and his fear lest the civilization of Europe be destroyed, he is dealing reasonably with anarchist belief. "The unchaining of what is today called the evil passions and the destruction of what is called public order" was the consummation of Bakunin's aim which he defended by saying that "the desire for destruction is at the same time a creative desire." It was not only the state but all social forms that were to be demolished according to the doctrine of amorphism; any social form held the seeds of the state's rebirth and must therefore be extirpated. Intellectual disciplines were social forms like any other. At least in its early days anarchism expressed hostility toward science. Toward the arts the hostility was less, for the early leaders were often trained in the humanities and their inspiration was largely literary; in the 1890s there was a strong alliance between the French artists and the anarchist groups. But in the logic of the situation art was bound to come under the anarchist fire. Art is inevitably associated with civil peace and social order and indeed with the ruling classes. Then too, any large intense movement of moral-political action is likely to be jealous of art and to feel that it is in competition with the full awareness of human suffering. Bakunin on several occasions spoke of it as of no account when the cause of human happiness was considered. Lenin expressed something of the same sort when, after having listened with delight to a sonata by Beethoven, he said that he could not listen to music too often.

> It affects your nerves, makes you want to say stupid, nice things, and stroke the heads of people who could create such beauty while living in this vile hell. And you mustn't stroke anyone's head—you might get your hand bitten off.

And similarly the Princess of James's novel feels that her taste is but the evidence of her immoral aristocratic existence and that art is a frivolous distraction from revolution.

The nature of the radicals in *The Princess Casamassima* may, to the modern reader, seem a distortion of fact. The people who meet at the Sun and Moon to mutter their wrongs over their beer are not revolutionists and scarcely radicals; most of them are nothing more than dull malcontents. Yet they represent with complete accuracy the political development of a large part of the working class of England at the beginning of the 1880s. The first great movement of English trade unionism had created an aristocracy of labor largely cut off from the mass of the workers, and the next great movement had not yet begun; the political expression of men such as met at the Sun and Moon was likely to be as fumbling as James represents it.

James has chosen the occupations of these men with great discrimination. There are no factory workers among them; at that time anarchism did not attract factory workers so much as the members of the skilled and relatively sedentary trades: tailors, shoemakers, weavers, cabinetmakers, and ornamental-metal workers. Hyacinth's craft of bookbinding was no doubt chosen because James knew something about it and because, being at once a fine and a mechanic art, it perfectly suited Hyacinth's fate, but it is to the point that bookbinders were largely drawn to anarchism.

When Paul Muniment tells Hyacinth that the club of the Sun and Moon is a "place you have always overestimated," he speaks with the authority of one who has connections more momentous. The anarchists, although of course they wished to influence the masses and could on occasion move them to concerted action, did not greatly value democratic or quasi-democratic mass organizations. Bakunin believed that "for the international organization of all Europe one hundred revolutionists, strongly and seriously bound together, are sufficient." The typical anarchist organization was hierarchical and secret. When in 1867 Bakunin drew up plans of organization, he instituted three "orders": a public group to be known as the International Alliance of Social Democracy; then above this and not known to it the Order of National Brothers; above this and not known to it the Order of International Brothers, very few in number. James's Muniment, we may suppose, is a National Brother.

For the indoctrination of his compact body of revolutionists, Bakunin, in collaboration with the amazing Sergei Nechayev, compiled *The Revolutionary Catechism*. This *vade mecum* might be taken as a guidebook to *The Princess Casamassima*. It instructs the revolutionist that he may be called to live in the great world and to penetrate into any class of society: the aristocracy, the church, the army, the diplomatic corps. It tells how one goes about compromising the wealthy in order to command their wealth, just as the Princess is compromised. There are instructions on how to deal with people who, like James's Captain Sholto, are drawn to the movement by questionable motives; on how little one is to trust the women of the upper classes who may be seeking sensation or salvation—the Princess calls it reality—through revolutionary action. It is a ruthless little book: eventually Bakunin himself complains that nothing— no private letter, no wife, no daughter—is safe from the conspiratorial zeal of his coauthor Nechayev.

The situation in which Hyacinth involves himself, his pledge to commit an assassination upon demand of the secret leadership, is not the extreme fancy of a cloistered novelist, but a classic anarchist situation. Anarchism could arouse mass action, as in the riots at Lyon in 1882, but typically it showed its power by acts of terror committed by courageous individuals glad to make personal war against society. Bakunin canonized for anarchism the Russian bandit Stenka Razin; Balzac's Vautrin and Stendhal's Valbayre (of *Lamiel*) are prototypes of anarchist heroes. Always ethical as well as instrumental in its theory, anarchism conceived assassination not only as a way of advertising its doctrine and weakening the enemy's morale, but also as punishment or revenge or warning. Of the many assassinations or attempts at assassination that fill the annals of the late years of the century, not all were anarchist, but those that were not were influenced by anarchist example. In 1878 there were two attempts on the life of the Kaiser, one on the King of Spain, one on the King of Italy; in 1880 another attempt on the King of Spain; in 1881 Alexander II of Russia was killed after many attempts; in 1882 the Phoenix Park murders were committed, Lord Frederick Cavendish, Secretary for Ireland, and Undersecretary Thomas Burke being killed by extreme Irish nationalists; in 1883 there were several dynamite conspiracies in Great Britain and in 1885 there was an explosion in the House of Commons; in 1883 there was an anarchist plot to blow up, all at once, the Emperor Wilhelm, the Crown Prince, Bismarck, and Moltke. These are but a few of the terroristic events of which James would have been aware in the years just before he began *The Princess Casamassima*, and later years brought many more.

Anarchism never established itself very firmly in England as it did in Russia, France, and Italy. In these countries it penetrated to the upper classes. The actions of the Princess are not unique for an aristocrat of her time, nor is she fabricating when she speaks of her acquaintance with revolutionists of a kind more advanced than Hyacinth is likely to know. In

Italy she would have met on terms of social equality such notable anarchists as Count Carlo Cafiero and the physician Enrico Malatesta, who was the son of a wealthy family. Kropotkin was a descendant of the Ruriks and, as the novels of James's friend Turgenev testify, extreme radicalism was not uncommon among the Russian aristocracy. In France in the eighties and still more markedly in the nineties there were artistic, intellectual, and even aristocratic groups which were closely involved with the anarchists.

The great revolutionary of *The Princess Casamassima* is Hoffendahl, whom we never see although we feel his real existence. Hoffendahl is, in the effect he has upon others, not unlike what is told of Bakunin himself in his greatest days, when he could enthrall with his passion even those who could not understand the language he spoke in. But it is possible that James also had the famous Johann Most in mind. Most figured in the London press in 1881 when he was tried because his newspaper, *Freiheit*, exulted in the assassination of the Tsar. He was found guilty of libel and inciting to murder and sentenced to sixteen months at hard labor. The jury that convicted him recommended mercy on the ground that he was a foreigner and "might be suffering violent wrong." The jury was right—Most had suffered in the prisons of Germany after a bitter youth. It is not clear whether he, like James's Hoffendahl, had had occasion to stand firm under police torture, but there can be no doubt of his capacity to do so. After having served his jail sentence, he emigrated to America, and it has been said of him that terrorist activities in this country centered about him. He was implicated in the Haymarket Affair and imprisoned for having incited the assassin of President McKinley; Emma Goldman and Alexander Berkman were his disciples, and they speak of him in language such as Hyacinth uses of Hoffendahl. It is worth nothing that Most was a bookbinder by trade.

In short, when we consider the solid accuracy of James's political detail at every point, we find that we must give up the notion that James could move only in the thin air of moral abstraction. A writer has said of *The Princess Casamassima* that it is "a capital example of James's impotence in matters sociological." The very opposite is so. Quite apart from its moral and aesthetic authority, *The Princess Casamassima* is a brilliantly precise representation of social actuality.

4

In his preface to *The Princess* in the New York edition, James tells us of a certain autobiographical element that went into the creation of Hyacinth Robinson. "To find his possible adventures interesting," James says, "I had only to conceive his watching the same public show, the same innumerable appearances I had myself watched and of watching very much as I had watched."

This, at first glance, does not suggest a very intense connection between author and hero. But at least it assures us that at some point the novel is touched by the author's fantasy about himself. It is one of the necessities of successful modern story that the author shall have somewhere entrusted his personal fantasy to the tale; but it may be taken as very nearly a rule that the more the author disguises the personal nature of his fantasy, the greater its force will be. Perhaps he is best off if he is not wholly aware that he is writing about himself at all: his fantasy, like an actual dream, is powerful in the degree that its "meaning" is hidden.

If Hyacinth does indeed express James's personal fantasy, we are led to believe that the fantasy has reference to a familial situation. James puts an insistent emphasis upon his hero's small stature. Hyacinth's mere size is decisive in the story. It exempts him from certain adult situations; for example, where Paul Muniment overcomes the class barrier to treat the Princess as a woman, taking so full an account of her sexual existence and his own that we expect him to make a demand upon her, Hyacinth is detached from the sexual possibility and disclaims it. The intention is not to show him as unmanly but as too young to make the claims of maturity; he is the child of the book, always the very youngest person. And this child-man lives in a novel full of parental figures. Hyacinth has no less than three sets of parents: Lord Frederick and Florentine, Miss Pynsent and Mr. Vetch, Eustache Poupin and Madame Poupin, and this is not to mention the French-revolutionary grandfather and the arch-conspirator Hoffendahl; and even Millicent Henning appears, for one memorable Sunday, in a maternal role. The decisive parental pair are, of course, the actual parents, Lord Frederick and Florentine, who represent—some will feel too schematically—the forces which are in conflict in Hyacinth. Undertaking to kill the Duke as a step in the destruction of the ruling class, Hyacinth is in effect plotting the murder of his own father; and one reason that he comes to loathe the pledged deed is his belief that, by repeating poor Florentine's action, he will be bringing his mother to life in all her pitiful shame.

It is as a child that Hyacinth dies; that is, he dies of the withdrawal of love. James contrives with consummate skill the lonely circumstance of Hyacinth's death. Nothing can equal for delicacy of ironic pathos the incidents of the last part of the book, in which Hyacinth, who has his own death warrant in his pocket, the letter ordering the assassination, looks to his adult friends for a reason of love which will explain why he does not have to serve it on himself, or how, if he must serve it, he can believe in the value of his deed. But the grown-up people have occupations from which he is excluded and they cannot believe in his seriousness. Paul Muniment and the Princess push him aside, not unkindly, only condescendingly, only as one tells a nice boy that there are certain things he cannot understand, such things as power and love and justification.

The adult world last represents itself to Hyacinth in the great scene of lust in the department store. To make its point the crueller, James has previously contrived for Hyacinth a wonderful Sunday of church and park with Millicent Henning*; Millicent enfolds Hyacinth in an undemanding, protective love that is not fine or delicate but for that reason so much the more useful; but when in his last hunt for connection Hyacinth seeks out Millicent in her shop, he sees her standing "still as a lay-figure" under Captain Sholto's gaze, exhibiting "the long grand lines" of her body under pretense of "modelling" a dress. And as Hyacinth sees the Captain's eyes "travel up and down the front of Millicent's person," he knows that he has been betrayed.

So much manipulation of the theme of parent and child, so much interest in lost protective love, suggests that the connection of Hyacinth and his author may be more intense than at first appears. And there is one consideration that reinforces the guess that this fantasy of a child and his family has a particular and very personal relation to James in his own fam-

*The reviewer for *The Athenaeum* remarked it as "an odd feature of the book that nearly all the action, or nearly all of which the date is indicated, takes place on Sundays." The observation was worth making, for it suggests how certain elements of the book's atmosphere are achieved: what better setting for loneliness and doubt than Sunday in a great city? And since the action of the book must depend on the working schedule of the working-class characters, who, moreover, live at considerable distance from one another, what more natural than that they should meet on Sundays? But the reviewer thinks that "possibly a London week-day suggests a life too strenuous to be lived by the aimless beings whom Mr. James depicts." The "aimless beings" note was one that was struck by most of the more-or-less liberal reviewers.

ily situation. The matter which is at issue in *The Princess Casamassima*, the dispute between art and moral action, the controversy between the glorious unregenerate past and the regenerate future, was not of merely general interest to Henry James, nor, indeed, to any of the notable members of the James family. Ralph Barton Perry in his *Thought and Character of William James* finds the question so real and troubling in William's life that he devotes a chapter to it. William, to whom the antithesis often represented itself as between Europe-art and America-action, settled in favor of America and action. Henry settled, it would seem, the other way—certainly in favor of art. But whether Henry's option necessarily involved, as William believed, a decision in favor of the past, a love of the past for, as people like to say, the past's sake, may be thought of as the essential matter of dispute between William and Henry.

The dispute was at the very heart of their relationship. They had the matter out over the years. But in the having-out William was the aggressor, and it is impossible to suppose that his statement of the case did not cause Henry pain. William came to suspect that the preoccupation with art was very close to immorality. He was perhaps not so wrong as the clichés in defense of art would make him out to be; his real error lay in his not knowing what art, as a thing to contemplate or as a thing to make, implied for his brother. His suspicion extended to Henry's work. He was by no means without sympathy for it, but he thought that Henry's great gifts were being put at the service of the finicking and refined; he was impatient of what was not robust in the same way he was. Henry, we may be sure, would never have wanted a diminution of the brotherly frankness that could tell him that *The Bostonians* might have been very fine if it had been only a hundred pages long; but the remark and others of similar sort could only have left his heart a little sore.

When, then, we find Henry James creating for his Hyacinth a situation in which he must choose between political action and the fruits of the creative spirit of Europe, we cannot but see that he has placed at the center of his novel a matter whose interest is of the most personal kind. Its personal, its familial, nature is emphasized by Alice James's share in the dispute, for she and William were at one against their brother in aggressively holding a low view of England, and William's activism finds a loud and even shrill echo in Alice, whose passionate radicalism was, as Henry said of her, "her most distinguishing feature." But far more important is the father's relation to the family difference. The authority of the elder Henry James could be fairly claimed by both his sons, for he was brilliantly contradictory on the moral status of art. If William could come to think of art as constituting a principle which was antagonistic to the principle of life, his father had said so before him. And Henry could find abundant support for his own position in his father's frequent use of the artist as one who, because he seeks to create and not to possess, most closely approximates in mankind the attributes of divinity.

The Princess Casamassima may, then, be thought of as an intensely autobiographical book, not in the sense of being the author's personal record but in the sense of being his personal act. For we may imagine that James, beautifully in control of his novel, dominant in it as almost no decent person can be in a family situation, is continuing the old dispute on his own terms and even taking a revenge. Our imagination of the "revenge" does not require that we attribute a debasing malice to James— quite to the contrary, indeed, for the revenge is gentle and innocent and noble. It consists, this revenge, only in arranging things in such a way that Paul Muniment and the Princess shall stand for James's brother and sister and then so to contrive events to show that, at the very moment when this brilliant pair think they are closest to the conspiratorial arcanum, the real thing, the true center, they are in actual fact furthest from it.* Paul and the Princess believe themselves to be in the confidence of *Them*, the People Higher Up, the International Brothers, or whatever, when really they are held in suspicion in these very quarters. They conde-

*When I say that Paul and the Princess "stand for" William and Alice, I do not mean that they are portraits of William and Alice. It is true that in the conditioning context of the novel Paul suggests certain equivalences with William James: in his brisk masculinity, his intelligence, his downright common sense and practicality, most of all his relation to Hyacinth. What we may most legitimately guess to be a representation is the *ratio* of the characters—Paul: Hyacinth :: William : Henry. The Princess has Alice's radical ideas; she is called "the most remarkable woman in Europe," which in effect is what Henry James said Alice would have been if the full exercise of her will and intellect had not been checked by her illness. But such equivalence is not portraiture and the novel is not a family *roman à clef*. And yet the matter of portraiture cannot be so easily settled, for it has been noticed by those who are acquainted with the life and character of Alice James that there are many points of similarity between her and Rosy Muniment. Their opinions are, to be sure, at opposite poles, for Rosy is a staunch Tory and a dreadful snob, but the very patness of the opposition may reasonably be thought significant. In mind and pride of mind, in outspokenness, in will and the license given to will by illness, there is similarity between the sister of Paul and the sister of William and Henry. There is no reason why anyone interested in Henry James should not be aware of this, provided that it not be taken as the negation of Henry's expressed love for Alice and William—provided, too, that it be taken as an aspect of his particular moral imagination, a matter which is discussed later.

scend to Hyacinth for his frivolous concern with art, but Hyacinth, unknown to them, has received his letter of fatal commission; he has the
death warrant in his pocket, another's and his own; despite his having
given clear signs of lukewarmness to the cause, he is trusted by the secret
powers where his friends are not. In his last days Hyacinth has become
aware of his desire no longer to bind books but to write them: the novel
can be thought of as Henry James's demonstrative message, to the world
in general, to his brother and sister in particular, that the artist quite as
much as any man of action carries his ultimate commitment and his death
warrant in his pocket. "Life's nothing," Henry James wrote to a young
friend, "—unless heroic and sacrificial."

James even goes so far as to imply that the man of art may be close to
the secret center of things when the man of action is quite apart from it.
Yet Hyacinth cannot carry out the orders of the people who trust him.
Nor of course can he betray them—the pistol which, in the book's last dry
words, "would certainly have served much better for the Duke," Hyacinth
turns upon himself. A vulgar and facile progressivism can find this to be a
proof of James's "impotence in matters sociological"—"the problem remains unsolved." Yet it would seem that a true knowledge of society com-
prehends the reality of the social forces it presumes to study and is aware
of contradictions and consequences; it knows that sometimes society offers an opposition of motives in which the antagonists are in such a balance of authority and appeal that a man who so wholly perceives them as
to embody them in his very being cannot choose between them and is
therefore destroyed. This is known as tragedy.

5

We must not misunderstand the nature of Hyacinth's tragic fate. Hyacinth dies sacrificially, but not as a sacrificial lamb, wholly innocent; he
dies as a human hero who has incurred a certain amount of guilt.

The possibility of misunderstanding Hyacinth's situation arises from
our modern belief that the artist is one of the types of social innocence.
Our competitive, acquisitive society ritualistically condemns what it practices—with us money gives status, yet we consider a high regard for
money a debasing thing and we set a large value on disinterested activity.

Hence our cult of the scientist and the physician, who are presumed to be free of the acquisitive impulses. The middle class, so far as it is liberal, admires from varying distances the motives and even the aims of revolutionists: it cannot imagine that revolutionists have anything to "gain" as the middle class itself understands gain. And although sometimes our culture says that the artist is a subversive idler, it is nowadays just as likely to say that he is to be admired for his innocence, for his activity is conceived as having no end beyond itself except possibly some benign social purpose, such as "teaching people to understand each other."

But James did not see art as, in this sense, innocent. We touch again on autobiography, for on this point there is a significant connection between James's own life and Hyacinth's.

In Chapter 15 of *A Small Boy and Others*, his first autobiographic volume, James tells how he was initiated into a knowledge of style in the Galerie d'Apollon of the Louvre. As James represents the event, the varieties of style in that gallery assailed him so intensely that their impact quite transcended aesthetic experience. For they seemed to speak to him not visually at all but in some "complicated sound" and as a "deafening chorus"; they gave him what he calls "a general sense of glory." About this sense of glory he is quite explicit. "The glory meant ever so many things at once, not only beauty and art and supreme design, but history and fame and power, the world in fine raised to the richest and noblest expression."

Hazlitt said that "the language of poetry naturally falls in with the language of power," and goes on to develop an elaborate comparison between the processes of the imagination and the processes of autocratic rule. He is not merely indulging in a flight of fancy or a fashion of speaking; no stauncher radical democrat ever lived than Hazlitt and no greater lover of imaginative literature, yet he believed that poetry has an affinity with political power in its autocratic and aristocratic form and that it is not a friend of the democratic virtues. We are likely not to want to agree with Hazlitt; we prefer to speak of art as if it lived in a white bungalow with a garden, had a wife and two children, and were harmless and quiet and cooperative. But James is of Hazlitt's opinion; his first great revelation of art came as an analogy with the triumphs of the world; art spoke to him of the imperious will, with the music of an army with banners. Perhaps it is to the point that James's final act of imagination, as he lay dying, was to call his secretary and give her as his last dictation what purported to be an autobiographical memoir by Napoleon Bonaparte.

But so great an aggression must carry some retribution with it, and as James goes on with the episode of the Galerie d'Apollon, he speaks of the experience as having the effect not only of a "love-philtre" but also of a "fear-philtre." Aggression brings guilt and then fear. And James concludes the episode with the account of a nightmare in which the Galerie figures; he calls it "the most appalling and yet most admirable" nightmare of his life. He dreamed that he was defending himself from an intruder, trying to keep the door shut against a terrible invading form; then suddenly there came "the great thought that I, in my appalled state, was more appalling than the awful agent, creature or presence"; whereupon he opened the door and, surpassing the invader for "straight aggression and dire intention," pursued him down a long corridor in a great storm of lightning and thunder; the corridor was seen to be the Galerie d'Apollon. We do not have to presume very far to find the meaning in the dream, for James gives us all that we might want; he tells us that the dream was important to him, that, having experienced art as "history and fame and power," his arrogation seemed a guilty one and represented itself as great fear which he overcame by an inspiration of straight aggression and dire intention and triumphed in the very place where he had had his imperious fantasy. An admirable nightmare indeed. One needs to be a genius to counterattack nightmare; perhaps this is the definition of genius.

When James came to compose Hyacinth's momentous letter from Venice, the implications of the analog of art with power had developed and become clearer and more objective. Hyacinth has had his experience of the glories of Europe, and when he writes to the Princess his view of human misery is matched by a view of the world "raised to the richest and noblest expression." He understands no less clearly than before "the despotisms, the cruelties, the exclusions, the monopolies and the rapacities of the past." But now he recognizes that "the fabric of civilization as we know it" is inextricably bound up with this injustice; the monuments of art and learning and taste have been reared upon coercive power. Yet never before has he had the full vision of what the human spirit can accomplish to make the world "less impracticable and life more tolerable." He finds that he is ready to fight for art—and what art suggests of glorious life—against the low and even hostile estimate which his revolutionary friends have made of it, and this involves of course some reconciliation with established coercive power.

It is easy enough, by certain assumptions, to condemn Hyacinth and even to call him names. But first we must see what his position really means and what heroism there is in it. Hyacinth recognizes what very few people wish to admit, that civilization has a price, and a high one. Civilizations differ from one another as much in what they give up as in what they acquire; but all civilizations are alike in that they renounce something for something else. We do right to protest this in any given case that comes under our notice and we do right to get as much as possible for as little as possible; but we can never get everything for nothing. Nor, indeed, do we really imagine that we can. Thus, to stay within the present context, every known theory of popular revolution gives up the vision of the world "raised to the richest and noblest expression." To achieve the ideal of widespread security, popular revolutionary theory condemns the ideal of adventurous experience. It tries to avoid doing this explicitly and it even, although seldom convincingly, denies that it does it at all. But all the instincts or necessities of radical democracy are against the superbness and arbitrariness which often mark great spirits. It is sometimes said in the interests of an ideal or abstract completeness that the choice need not be made, that security can be imagined to go with richness and nobility of expression. But we have not seen it in the past and nobody really strives to imagine it in the future. Hyacinth's choice is made under the pressure of the counter-choice made by Paul and the Princess; their "general rectification" implies a civilization from which the idea of life raised to the richest and noblest expression will quite vanish.

There have been critics who said that Hyacinth is a snob and the surrogate of James's snobbery. But if Hyacinth is a snob, he is of the company of Rabelais, Shakespeare, Scott, Dickens, Balzac, and Lawrence, men who saw the lordliness and establishment of the aristocrat and the gentleman as the proper condition for the spirit of man, and who, most of them, demanded it for themselves, as poor Hyacinth never does, for "it was not so much that he wished to enjoy as that he wished to know; his desire was not to be pampered but to be initiated." His snobbery is no other than that of John Stuart Mill when he discovered that a grand and spacious room could have so enlarging an effect upon his mind; when Hyacinth at Medley had his first experience of a great old house, he admired nothing so much as the ability of a thing to grow old without loss

but rather with gain of dignity and interest; "the spectacle of long duration unassociated with some sordid infirmity or poverty was new to him;
for he had lived with people among whom old age meant, for the most
part, a grudged and degraded survival." Hyacinth has Yeats's awareness of
the dream that a great house embodies, that here the fountain of life
"overflows without ambitious pains,"

> And mounts more dizzy high the more it rains
> As though to choose whatever shape it wills
> And never stoop to a mechanical
> Or servile shape, at other's beck and call.

But no less than Yeats he has the knowledge that the rich man who builds
the house and the architect and artists who plan and decorate it are "bitter
and violent men" and that the great houses "but take our greatness with
our violence" and our "greatness with our bitterness."*

By the time Hyacinth's story draws to its end, his mind is in a perfect
equilibrium, not of irresolution but of awareness. His sense of the social
horror of the world is not diminished by his newer sense of the glory of
the world. On the contrary, just as his pledge of his life to the revolutionary cause had in effect freed him to understand human glory, so the sense
of the glory quickens his response to human misery—never, indeed, is he
so sensitive to the sordid life of the mass of mankind as after he has had
the revelation of art. And just as he is in an equilibrium of awareness, he
is also in an equilibrium of guilt. He has learned something of what may
lie behind abstract ideals, the envy, the impulse to revenge and to dominance. He is the less inclined to forgive what he sees because, as we must
remember, the triumph of the revolution presents itself to him as a certainty and the act of revolution as an ecstasy. There is for him as little
doubt of the revolution's success as there is of the fact that his mother had
murdered his father. And when he thinks of revolution it is as a tremendous tide, a colossal force; he is tempted to surrender to it as an escape
from his isolation—one would be lifted by it "higher on the sun-touched
billows than one could ever be by a lonely effort of one's own." But if the
revolutionary passion thus has its guilt, Hyacinth's passion for life at its

---

*"Ancestral Houses" in *Collected Poems*. The whole poem may be read as a most illuminating
companion-piece to *The Princess Casamassima*.

richest and noblest is no less guilty. It leads him to consent to the established coercive power of the world, and this can never be innocent. One cannot "accept" the suffering of others, no matter for what ideal, no matter if one's own suffering be also accepted, without incurring guilt. It is the guilt in which every civilization is implicated.

Hyacinth's death, then, is not his way of escaping from irresolution. It is truly a sacrifice, an act of heroism. He is a hero of civilization because he dares do more than civilization does: embodying two ideals at once, he takes upon himself, in full consciousness, the guilt of each. He acknowledges both his parents. By his death he instructs us in the nature of civilized life and by his consciousness he transcends it.

6

Suppose that truth be the expression, not of intellect, nor even, as we sometimes now think, of will, but of love. It is an outmoded idea, and yet if it has still any force at all it will carry us toward an understanding of the truth of *The Princess Casamassima*. To be sure, the legend of James does not associate him with love; indeed, it is a fact symptomatic of the condition of American letters that Sherwood Anderson, a writer who himself spoke much of love, was able to say of James that he was the novelist of "those who hate." Yet as we read *The Princess Casamassima* it is possible to ask whether any novel was ever written which, dealing with decisive moral action and ultimate issues, makes its perceptions and its judgments with so much loving kindness.

Since James wrote, we have had an increasing number of novels which ask us to take cognizance of those whom we call the underprivileged. These novels are of course addressed to those of us who have the money and the leisure to buy books and read them and the security to assail our minds with accounts of the miseries of our fellow men; on the whole, the poor do not read about the poor. And in so far as the middle class has been satisfied and gratified by the moral implications of most of these books, it is not likely to admire Henry James's treatment of the poor. For James represents the poor as if they had dignity and intelligence in the same degree as people of the reading class. More, he assumes this and feels no need to insist that it is so. This is a grace of spirit that we are so little likely to understand that we may resent it. Few of our novelists are able to write about the poor so as to make them something more than the pitied objects of our facile sociological minds. The literature of our liberal democracy pets and dandles its underprivileged characters, and, quite as if it had the right to do so, forgives them what faults they may have. But James is sure that in such people, who are numerous, there are the usual human gradations of understanding, interest, and goodness. Even if my conjecture about the family connection of the novel be wholly mistaken, it will at least suggest what is unmistakably true, that James could write about a working man quite as if he were as large, willful, and complex as the author of *The Principles of Psychology*. At the same time that everything in the story of *The Princess Casamassima* is based on social difference, everything is also based on the equality of the members of the human family. People at the furthest extremes of class are easily brought into relation because they are all contained in the novelist's affection. In that context it is natural for the Princess and Lady Aurora Langrish to make each other's acquaintance by the side of Rosy Muniment's bed and to contend for the notice of Paul. That James should create poor people so proud and intelligent as to make it impossible for anyone, even the reader who has paid for the privilege, to condescend to them, so proud and intelligent indeed that it is not wholly easy for them to be "good," is, one ventures to guess, an unexpressed, a never-to-be-expressed reason for finding him "impotent in matters sociological." We who are liberal and progressive know that the poor are our equals in every sense except that of being equal to us.

But James's special moral quality, his power of love, is not wholly comprised by his impulse to make an equal distribution of dignity among his characters. It goes beyond this to create his unique moral realism, his particular gift of human understanding. If in his later novels James, as many say he did, carried awareness of human complication to the point of virtuosity, he surely does not do so here, and yet his knowledge of complication is here very considerable. But this knowledge is not an analytical one, or not in the usual sense in which that word is taken, which implies a cool dissection. If we imagine a father of many children who truly loves them all, we may suppose that he will see very vividly their differences from one another, for he has no wish to impose upon them a similarity which would be himself; and he will be quite willing to see their faults, for his affection leaves him free to love them, not because they are faultless but because they are they; yet while he sees their faults he will be able, from long connection and because there is no reason to avoid the truth, to perceive the many reasons for their actions. The discriminations and modifications of such a man would be enormous, yet the moral realism they would constitute would not arise from an analytical intelligence as we usually conceive it but from love.

The nature of James's moral realism may most easily be exemplified by his dealings with the character of Rosy Muniment. Rosy is in many ways similar to Jennie Wren, the dolls' dressmaker of *Our Mutual Friend*; both are crippled, courageous, quaint, sharp-tongued, and dominating, and both are admired by the characters among whom they have their existence. Dickens unconsciously recognizes the cruelty that lies hidden in Jennie, but consciously he makes nothing more than a brusque joke of her habit of threatening people's eyes with her needle. He allows himself to be deceived and is willing to deceive us. But James manipulates our feelings about Rosy into a perfect ambivalence. He forces us to admire her courage, pride, and intellect and seems to forbid us to take account of her cruelty because she directs it against able-bodied or aristocratic people. Only at the end does he permit us the release of our ambivalence— the revelation that Hyacinth doesn't like Rosy and that we don't have to is an emotional relief and a moral enlightenment. But although we by the author's express permission are free to dislike Rosy, the author does not avail himself of the same privilege. In the family of the novel Rosy's status has not changed.

Moral realism is the informing spirit of *The Princess Casamassima* and it yields a kind of social and political knowledge which is hard to come by. It is at work in the creation of the character of Millicent Henning, whose strength, affectionateness, and warm sensuality move James to the series of remarkable prose arias in her praise which punctuate the book; yet while he admires her, he knows the particular corruptions which our civilization is working upon her, for he is aware not only of her desire to pull down what is above her but also of her desire to imitate and conform to it and to despise what she herself is. Millicent is proud of doing nothing with her hands, she despises Hyacinth because he is so poor in spirit as to consent to *make* things and get dirty in the process, and she values herself because she does nothing less genteel than exhibit what others have made; and in one of the most pregnant scenes of the book James involves her in the peculiarly corrupt and feeble sexuality which is associated in our culture with exhibiting and looking at luxurious objects.

But it is in the creation of Paul Muniment and the Princess that James's moral realism shows itself in fullest power. If we seek an explanation of why *The Princess Casamassima* was not understood in its own day, we find it in the fact that the significance of this remarkable pair could scarcely have emerged for the reader of 1886. But we of today can say that they and their relationship constitute one of the most masterly comments on modern life that has ever been made.

In Paul Muniment a genuine idealism coexists with a secret desire for personal power. It is one of the brilliances of the novel that his ambition is never made explicit. Rosy's remark about her brother, "What my brother really cares for—well, one of these days, when you know you'll tell me," is perhaps as close as his secret ever comes to statement. It is conveyed to us by his tone, as a decisive element of his charm, for Paul radiates what the sociologists, borrowing the name from theology, call charisma, the charm of power, the gift of leadership. His natural passion for power must never become explicit, for it is one of the beliefs of our culture that power invalidates moral purpose. The ambiguity of Paul Muniment has been called into being by the nature of modern politics in so far as they are moral and idealistic. For idealism has not changed the nature of leadership, but it has forced the leader to change his nature, requiring him to present himself as a harmless and self-abnegating man. It is easy enough to speak of this ambiguity as a form of hypocrisy, yet the opposition between morality and power from which it springs is perfectly well conceived. But even if well conceived, it is endlessly difficult to execute and it produces its own particular confusions, falsifications, and even lies. The moral realist sees it as the source of characteristically modern ironies, such as the liberal exhausting the scrupulosity which made him deprecate all power and becoming extravagantly tolerant of what he had once denounced, or the idealist who takes license from his ideals for the unrestrained exercise of power.

The Princess, as some will remember, is the Christina Light of James's earlier novel, *Roderick Hudson*, and she considers, as Madame Grandoni says of her, "that in the darkest hour of her life, she sold herself for a title and a fortune. She regards her doing so as such a terrible piece of frivolity that she can never for the rest of her days be serious enough to make up for it." Seriousness has become her ruling passion, and in the great sad comedy of the story it is her fatal sin, for seriousness is not exempt from the tendency of ruling passions to lead to error. And yet it has an aspect of heroism, this hunt of hers for reality, for a strong and final basis of life. "Then it's real, it's solid!" she exclaims when Hyacinth tells her that he has seen Hoffendahl and has penetrated to the revolutionary holy of holies. It is her quest for reality that leads her to the poor, to the very poorest poor she can find, and that brings a light of joy to her eye at any news of suffering or deprivation which must surely be, if anything is, an irrefrangible reality. As death and danger are—her interest in Hyacinth is made the more intense by his pledged death, and she herself eventually wants to undertake the mortal mission. A perfect drunkard of reality, she is ever drawn to look for stronger and stronger drams.

Inevitably, of course, the great irony of her fate is that the more passionately she seeks reality and the happier she becomes in her belief that she is close to it, the further removed she is. Inevitably she must turn away from Hyacinth because she reads his moral seriousness as frivolousness; and inevitably she is led to Paul who, as she thinks, affirms her in a morality which is as real and serious as anything can be, an absolute morality which gives her permission to devaluate and even destroy all that she has known of human good because it has been connected with her own frivolous, self-betraying past. She cannot but mistake the nature of reality, for she believes it is a thing, a position, a finality, a bedrock. She is, in short, the very embodiment of the modern will which masks itself in virtue, making itself appear harmless, the will that hates itself and finds its manifestations guilty and is able to exist only if it operates in the name of virtue, that despises the variety and modulations of the human story and longs for an absolute humanity, which is but another way of saying a nothingness. In her alliance with Paul she constitutes a striking symbol of that powerful part of modern culture that exists by means of its claim to political innocence and by its false seriousness—the political awareness that is not aware, the social consciousness which hates full consciousness, the moral earnestness which is moral luxury.

The fatal ambiguity of the Princess and Paul is a prime condition of Hyacinth Robinson's tragedy. If we comprehend the complex totality that James has thus conceived, we understand that the novel is an incomparable representation of the spiritual circumstances of our civilization. I venture to call it incomparable because, although other writers have provided abundant substantiation of James's insight, no one has, like him, told us the truth in a single luminous act of creation. If we ask by what magic James was able to do what he did, the answer is to be found in what I have identified as the source of James's moral realism. For the novelist can tell the truth about Paul and the Princess only if, while he represents them in their ambiguity and error, he also allows them to exist in their pride and beauty: the moral realism that shows the ambiguity and error cannot refrain from showing the pride and beauty. Its power to tell the truth arises from its power of love. James had the imagination of disaster and that is why he is immediately relevant to us; but together with the imagination of disaster he had what the imagination of disaster often destroys and in our time is daily destroying, the imagination of love.

Wordsworth and the Rabbis

1950

Our commemoration of the hundredth anniversary of Wordsworth's death must inevitably be charged with the consciousness that if Wordsworth were not kept in mind by the universities he would scarcely be remembered at all. In our culture it is not the common habit to read the books of a century ago, and very likely all that we can mean when we say that a writer of the past is "alive" in people's minds is that, to those who once read him as a college assignment or who have formed an image of him from what they have heard about him, he exists as an attractive idea, as an intellectual possibility. And if we think of the three poets whom Matthew Arnold celebrated in his "Memorial Verses," we know that Byron is still attractive and possible, and so is Goethe. But Wordsworth is not attractive and not an intellectual possibility. He was once the great, the speaking poet for all who read English. He spoke both to the ordinary reader and to the literary man. But now the literary man outside the university will scarcely think of referring to Wordsworth as one of the important events of modern literature; and to the ordinary reader he is likely to exist as the very type of the poet whom life has passed by, presumably for the good reason that he passed life by.

If we ask why Wordsworth is no longer the loved poet he once was, why, indeed, he is often thought to be rather absurd and even a little despicable, one answer that suggests itself is that for modern taste he is too Christian a poet. He is certainly not to be wholly characterized by the Christian element of his poetry. Nor can we say of him that he is a Christian poet in the same sense that Dante is, or Donne, or Hopkins. With them the specific Christian feeling and doctrine is of the essence of their matter and their conscious intention, as it is not with Wordsworth. Yet at the present time, the doctrinal tendency of the world at large being what it is, that which *is* Christian in Wordsworth may well seem to be more prominent than it ever was before, and more decisive. I have in mind his concern for the life of humbleness and quiet, his search for peace, his sense of the burdens of this life, those which are inherent in the flesh and spirit of man. Then there is his belief that the bonds of society ought to be inner and habitual, not merely external and formal, and that the strengthening of these bonds by the acts and attitudes of charity is a great and charming duty. Christian too seems his responsiveness to the idea that there is virtue in the discharge of duties which are of the great world and therefore dangerous to simple peace—his sense of affinity with Milton was as much with Milton's political as with his poetical career, and the Happy Warrior is the man who has, as it were, sacrificed the virtuous peace of the poet to the necessities of public life. There is his impulse to submit to the conditions of life under a guidance that is at once certain and mysterious; his sense of the possibility and actuality of enlightenment, it need scarcely be said, is one of the characteristic things about him. It was not he who said that the world was a vale of soul-making, but the poet who did make this striking paraphrase of the Christian sentiment could not have uttered it had not Wordsworth made it possible for him to do so.* And then, above all, there is his consciousness of the *neighbor*, his impulse to bring into the circle of significant life those of the neighbors who are simple and outside the circle of social pride, and also those who in the judgment of the world are queer and strange and useless: faith and hope were to him very great virtues, but he conceived that they rested upon the still greater virtue, charity.

Certainly what I have called Christian in Wordsworth scarcely approaches, let alone makes up, the sum of Christianity. But then no personal document or canon can do that, not even the work of a poet who is

---

*It is of some relevance to our argument that when Keats wrote the famous phrase he believed that he was controverting, not affirming, a tendency of Christian thought.

specifically Christian in the way of Dante, or of Donne, or of Hopkins. When we speak of a poet as being of a particular religion, we do not imply in him completeness or orthodoxy, or even explicitness of doctrine, but only that his secular utterance has the decisive mark of the religion upon it. And if a religion is manifold in its aspects and extensive in time, the marks that are to be found on the poets who are in a relation to it will be various in kind. It seems to me that the marks of Christianity on Wordsworth are clear and indelible. It is therefore worth trying the hypothesis that the world today does not like him because it does not like the Christian quality and virtues.

But the question at once arises whether this hypothesis is actually available to us. Professor Hoxie Neal Fairchild says that it is not. In the chapter on Wordsworth in the third volume of his *Religious Trends in English Poetry*, he tells us that Wordsworth was *not* a Christian poet and goes on to express his doubt that Wordsworth was ever properly to be called a Christian person even when he became a communicant of the Church and its defender. And Professor Fairchild goes so far as to tell us that as a poet Wordsworth is actually dangerous to the Christian faith. He is dangerous in the degree that he may be called religious at all, for his religion is said to be mere religiosity, the religion of nothing more than the religious emotion, beginning and ending in the mere sense of transcendence. Naked of dogma, bare of precise predication of God and the nature of man, this religiosity of Wordsworth's is to be understood as a pretentious and seductive rival of Christianity. It is the more dangerous because it gives license to man's pretensions—Professor Fairchild subscribes to the belief that romanticism must bear a large part of the responsibility for our present ills, especially for those which involve man's direct and conscious inhumanity to man.

We can surely admit the cogency of Professor Fairchild's argument within the terms of its intention. The nineteenth century was in many respects a very Christian century, but in the aspect of it which bulks largest in our minds it developed chiefly the ethical and social aspects of Christian belief, no doubt at the cost of the dogmatic aspect, which had already been weakened by the latitudinarian tendency of the eighteenth century. And it is probably true that when the dogmatic principle in religion is slighted, religion goes along for a while on generalized emotion and ethical intention—"morality touched by emotion"—and then loses the force of its impulse, even the essence of its being. In this sort of attentuation of religion, romanticism in general, and Wordsworth in particular, did indeed play a part by making the sense of transcendence and immanence so real and so attractive. During the most interesting and important period of his career, Wordsworth seems to have been scarcely aware of the doctrines of the Church in which he had been reared. He spoke of faith, hope, and charity without reference to the specifically Christian source and end of these virtues. His sense of the need for salvation did not take the least account of the Christian means of salvation. Of evil in the Christian sense of the word, of sins as an element of the nature of man, he also took no account.

And yet, all this being true, as we look at Wordsworth in the context of his own time and in the context of our time, what may properly be called the Christian element of his poetry can be made to speak to us, as it spoke to so many Christians in the nineteenth century, as it spoke to so many who were not Christians and made them in one degree or another accessible to Christianity.

"Any religious movement," says Christopher Dawson, an orthodox Christian scholar, "which adopts a purely critical and negative attitude to culture is . . . a force of destruction and disintegration which mobilizes against it the healthiest and most constructive elements in society—elements which can by no means be dismissed as worthless from the religious point of view." Romanticism in general was far from worthless to Christianity, far from worthless to that very Anglo-Catholicism which inclines to be so strict with it. And this is true of Wordsworth in particular. He certainly did not in his great period accept as adequate what the Church taught about the nature of man. But he was one of the few poets who really discovered something about the nature of man. What he discovered can perhaps be shown, if the argument be conducted by a comparison of formulas and doctrine, to be at variance with the teachings of Christianity. Yet I think it can also be shown that Wordsworth discovered much that a strong Christianity must take account of, and be easy with, and make use of. It can be shown too, I believe, that the Church has found advantage in what Wordsworth has told us of the nature of man.

Professor Fairchild, I need scarcely say, understands Christianity far better than I do, through his having studied it ever so much more than I have; and of course he understands it far better than I might ever hope to, because he has experienced it as a communicant. He has also, I am sure, tested his conclusions by the whole tendency of the Church to which he gives so strong and thoughtful an allegiance. My own reading of this tendency, at least as it appears in literature and in literary criticism, where it has been so influential, is that it is not inclined to accept Wordsworth as a Christian poet. And still, even against the force of Professor Fairchild's judgment, I cannot help feeling that there is an important element of Christianity with which Wordsworth has a significant affinity, even though this element is not at the present time of chief importance to Christian intellectuals.

But this is not an occasion for anything like contentiousness, and I ought not to seem to be forcing even a great poet into a faith whose members do not want him there. I am not, in any case, so much concerned to prove that Wordsworth is a Christian poet as to account for a certain quality in him which makes him unacceptable to the modern world. And so, without repudiating my first hypothesis, I shall abandon it for this fresh one: that the quality in Wordsworth that now makes him unacceptable is a Judaic quality.

My knowledge of the Jewish tradition is, I fear, all too slight to permit me to hope that I can develop this new hypothesis in any very enlightening way. Yet there is one Jewish work of traditional importance which I happen to know with some intimacy, and it lends a certain color of accuracy to my notion. This is the work called *Pirke Aboth*, that is, the sayings, the *sententiae*, of the Fathers. It was edited in the second century of the present era by the scholar and teacher who bore the magnificent name of Rabbi Jehudah the Prince, and who is traditionally referred to by the even more magnificent name of *Rabbi*—that is to say, *the* rabbi, the master teacher, the greatest of all. In its first intention *Pirke Aboth*, under the name *Aboth*, "Fathers," was one of the tractates of the Mishnah, which is the traditional Jewish doctrine represented chiefly by rabbinical decisions. But *Aboth* itself, the last of the tractates, does not deal with decisions; nor is it what a common English rendering of the longer title, "Ethics of the Fathers," would seem to imply, for it is not a system of ethics at all but simply a collection of maxims and *pensées*, some of them very fine and some of them very dull, which praise the life of study and give advice on how to live it.

In speaking of Wordsworth a recollection of boyhood cannot be amiss—my intimacy with *Pirke Aboth* comes from my having read it many times in boyhood. It certainly is not the kind of book a boy is easily drawn to read, and certainly I did not read it out of piety. On the contrary, indeed: for when I was supposed to be reading my prayers—very long, and in the Hebrew language, which I never mastered—I spent the required time and made it seem that I was doing my duty by reading the English translation of the *Pirke Aboth*, which, although it is not a devotional work, had long ago been thought of as an aid to devotion and included in the prayer book. It was more attractive to me than psalms, meditations, and supplications; it seemed more humane, and the Fathers had a curious substantiality. Just where they lived I did not know, nor just when, and certainly the rule of life they recommended had a very quaint difference from the life I knew, or, indeed, from any life that I wanted to know. Yet they were real, their way of life had the charm of coherence. And when I went back to them, using R. Travers Herford's scholarly edition and translation of their sayings,* I could entertain the notion that my early illicit intimacy with them had had its part in preparing the way for my responsiveness to Wordsworth, that between the Rabbis and Wordsworth an affinity existed.

But I must at once admit that a large difficulty stands in the way of the affinity I suggest. The *Aboth* is a collection of the sayings of masters of the written word. The ethical life it recommends has study as both its means and its end, the study of Torah, of the Law, which alone can give blessedness. So that from the start I am at the disadvantage of trying to make a conjunction between scholars living for the perpetual interpretation of a text and a poet for whom the natural world was at the heart of his doctrine and for whom books were barren leaves. The Rabbis expressed a suspiciousness of the natural world which was as extreme as Wordsworth's suspiciousness of study. That the warning was given at all seems to hint that it was possible for the Rabbis to experience the natural world as a charm and a temptation: still, the *Aboth* does warn us that whoever interrupts his study to observe the beauty of a fine tree or a fine meadow is guilty of sin. And yet I think it can be said without more extravagance than marks my whole comparison that it is precisely here, where they seem most to differ, that the Rabbis and Wordsworth are most at one. For between the Law as the Rabbis understood it and Nature as Wordsworth understood it, there is a pregnant similarity.

Pirke Aboth, edited with introduction, translation, and commentary, third edition (New York, 1945). I have also consulted the edition and translation of the Very Rev. Dr. Joseph H. Hertz, Chief Rabbi of the British Empire, and in my quotations I have drawn upon both versions, and sometimes, when it suited my point, I have combined two versions in a single quotation.

The Rabbis of the *Aboth* were Pharisees. I shall assume that the long scholarly efforts of Mr. Herford, as well as those of George Foot Moore, have by now made it generally known that the Pharisees were not in actual fact what tradition represents them to have been. They were anything but mere formalists, and of course they were not the hypocrites of popular conception. Here is Mr. Herford's statement of the defining principle of Pharisaism:

> The central conception of Pharisaism is Torah, the divine Teaching, the full and inexhaustible revelation which God had made. The knowledge of what was revealed was to be sought, and would be found, in the first instance in the written text of the Pentateuch; but the revelation, the real Torah, was the meaning of what was there written, the meaning as interpreted by all the recognized and accepted methods of the schools, and unfolded in ever greater fullness of detail by successive generations of devoted teachers. The written text of the Pentateuch might be compared to the mouth of a well; the Torah was the water which was drawn from it. He who wished to draw the water must needs go to the well, but there was no limit to the water which was there for him to draw. . . . The study of Torah . . . means therefore much more than the study of the Pentateuch, or even of the whole Scripture, regarded as mere literature, written documents. It means the study of the revelation made through those documents, the divine teaching therein imparted, the divine thought therein disclosed. Apart from the direct intercourse of prayer, the study of Torah was the way of closest approach to God; it might be called the Pharisaic form of the Beatific Vision. To study Torah was, to the devout Pharisee, to "think God's thoughts after him," as Kepler said.

The Rabbis, that is, found sermons in texts, tongues in the running commentary.

And Mr. Herford goes on to say that it might be observed of the *Aboth* that it makes very few direct references to God. "This is true," he says, "but it is beside the mark. Wherever Torah is mentioned, there God is implied. He is behind the Torah, the Revealer of what is Revealed."

What I am trying to suggest is that, different as the immediately present objects were in each case, Torah for the Rabbis, Nature for

Wordsworth, there existed for the Rabbis and for Wordsworth a great object, which is from God and might be said to represent Him as a sort of surrogate, a divine object to which one can be in an intimate passionate relationship, an active relationship—for Wordsworth's "wise passiveness" is of course an activity—which one can, as it were, handle, and in a sense create, drawing from it inexhaustible meaning by desire, intuition, and attention.

And when we turn to the particulars of the *Aboth* we see that the affinity continues. In Jewish tradition the great Hillel has a peculiarly Wordsworthian personality, being the type of gentleness and peace, and having about him a kind of *joy* which has always been found wonderfully attractive; and Hillel said—was, indeed, in the habit of saying: he "used to say"—"If I am not for myself, who, then, is for me? And if I am for myself, what then am I?" Mr. Herford implies that this is a difficult utterance. But it is not difficult for the reader of Wordsworth, who finds the Wordsworthian moral essence here, the interplay between individualism and the sense of community, between an awareness of the self that must be saved and developed, and an awareness that the self is yet fulfilled only in community.

Then there is this saying of Akiba's: "All is foreseen, and yet free will is given; and the world is judged by grace, and yet all is according to the work." With how handsome a boldness it handles the problem of fate and free will, or "grace" and "works," handles the problem by stating it as an antinomy, escaping the woeful claustral preoccupation with the alternatives, but not their grandeur. This refusal to be fixed either in fate or in free will, either in grace or in works, and the recognition of both, are characteristic of Wordsworth.

There are other parallels to be drawn. For example, one finds in the *Aboth* certain remarks which have a notable wit and daring because they go against the whole tendency of the work in telling us that the multiplication of words is an occasion for sin, and the chief thing is not study but action. One finds the injunction to the scholar to divide his time between study and a trade, presumably in the interest of humility. And the scholar is warned that the world must not be too much with him, that, getting and spending, he lays waste his powers. There is the concern, so typical of Wordsworth, with the "ages of man," with the right time in the individual's development for each of life's activities. But it is needless to multiply the details of the affinity, which in any case must not be insisted on too

far. All that I want to suggest is the community of ideal and sensibility between the *Aboth* and the canon of Wordsworth's work—the passionate
contemplation and experience of the great object which is proximate to
Deity; then the plain living that goes with the high thinking, the desire
for the humble life and the discharge of duty; and last, but not least important, a certain insouciant acquiescence in the anomalies of the moral
order of the universe, a respectful indifference to, or graceful surrender
before, the mysteries of the moral relation of God to man.

This last element, as it is expressed in the *pensée* of Akiba which I have
quoted, has its connection with something in the *Aboth* which for me is
definitive of its quality. Actually it is something not in the *Aboth* but left
out—we find in the tractate no implication of moral struggle. We find the
energy of assiduity but not the energy of resistance. We hear about sin,
but we do not hear of the sinful nature of man. Man in the *Aboth* guards
against sin but he does not struggle against it, and of evil we hear nothing
at all.

When we have observed this, it is natural to observe next that there is
no mention in the *Aboth* of courage or heroism. In our culture we connect the notion of courage or heroism with the religious life. We conceive
of the perpetual enemy within and the perpetual enemy without, which
must be "withstood," "overcome," "conquered"—the language of religion
and the language of fighting are in our culture assimilated to each other.
Not so in the *Aboth*. The enemy within seems not to be conceived of at
all. The enemy without is never mentioned, although the *Aboth* was compiled after the Dispersion, after the Temple and the nation had been destroyed—with what heroism in the face of suffering we know from
Josephus. Of the men whose words are cited in the *Aboth*, many met martyrdom for their religion, and the martyrology records their calm and fortitude in torture and death; of Akiba it records his heroic joy. And yet in
their maxims they never speak of courage. There is not a word to suggest
that the life of virtue and religious devotion requires the heroic quality.

As much as anything else in my boyhood experience of the *Aboth* it
was this that fascinated me. It also repelled me. It had this double effect
because it went so clearly against the militancy of spirit which in our culture is normally assumed. And even now, as I consider this indifference to
heroism of the *Aboth*, I have the old ambiguous response to it, so that I
think I can understand the feelings that readers have when they encounter

something similar in Wordsworth. It is what Matthew Arnold noted when in the "Memorial Verses" he compared Wordsworth with Byron, who was for Arnold the embodiment of militancy of spirit. Arnold said of Wordsworth that part of his peculiar value to us arose from his indifference to "man's fiery might," to the Byronic courage in fronting human destiny.

> The cloud of mortal destiny,
> Others will front it fearlessly—
> But who, like him, will put it by?

Arnold certainly did not mean that Wordsworth lacked courage or took no account of it. Wordsworth liked nothing better, indeed, than to recite examples of courage, but the Wordsworthian courage is different in kind from the Byronic. For one thing, it is never aware of itself, it is scarcely personal. It is the courage of mute, insensate things, and it is often associated with such things, "with rocks, and stones, and trees," or with stars. Michael on his hilltop, whose character is defined by the light of his cottage, which was called "The Evening Star," and by the stones of his sheepfold; or the Leech-gatherer, who is like some old, great rock; or Margaret, who, like a tree, endured as long as she might after she was blasted—of the Lesser Celandine it is said that its fortitude in meeting the rage of the storm is neither its courage nor its choice but "its necessity in being old," and the same thing is to be said of all Wordsworth's exemplars of courage: they endure because they are what they are, and we might almost say that they survive out of a kind of biological faith, which is not the less human because it is nearly an animal or vegetable faith; and, indeed, as I have suggested, it is sometimes nearly mineral. Even the Happy Warrior, the man in arms, derives his courage not from his militancy of spirit but from his calm submission to the law of things.

In Wordsworth's vision of life, then, the element of quietude approaches passivity, even insentience, and the dizzy raptures of youth have their issue in the elemental existence of which I have spoken. The scholars of the *Aboth* certainly had no such notion; they lived for intellectual sentience. But where the scholars and Wordsworth are at one is in the quietism, which is not in the least a negation of life, but, on the contrary, an affirmation of life so complete that it needed no saying. To the Rabbis, as

I read them, there life was, unquestionable because committed to a divine object. There life was—in our view rather stuffy and airless, or circumscribed and thin, but very intense and absolutely and utterly real, not needing to be affirmed by force or assertion, real because the object of its regard was unquestioned, and because the object was unquestionably more important than the individual person who regarded it and lived by it. To Wordsworth, as I read him, a similar thing was true in its own way. Much as he loved to affirm the dizzy raptures of sentience, of the ear and the eye and the mind, he also loved to move down the scale of being, to say that when the sentient spirit was sealed by slumber, when it was without motion and force, when it was like a rock or a stone or a tree, not hearing or seeing, and passive in the cosmic motion—that even then, perhaps especially then, existence was blessed.

Nothing could be further from the tendency of our Western culture, which is committed to an idea of consciousness and activity, of motion and force. With us the basis of spiritual prestige is some form of aggressive action directed outward upon the world, or inward upon ourselves. During the last century and a half this ideal has been especially strong in literature. If the religious personality of preceding times took to itself certain of the marks of military prestige, the literary personality now takes to itself certain of the marks of religious prestige, in particular the capacity for militant suffering.

A peculiarly relevant example of this lies to hand in T. S. Eliot's explanation of the decline of Wordsworth's genius from its greatness to what Mr. Eliot calls the "still sad music of infirmity." The small joke, so little characteristic of Mr. Eliot's humor, suggests something of the hostile uneasiness that Wordsworth can arouse in us. And Mr. Eliot's theory of the decline suggests the depth of our belief in the value of militancy, of militant suffering, for Mr. Eliot tells us that the trouble with Wordsworth was that he didn't have an eagle: it is that eagle which André Gide's Prometheus said was necessary for success in the spiritual or poetic life— "*Il faut avoir un aigle.*" As an explanation of Wordsworth's poetic career this is, we perceive, merely a change rung on the weary idea that Wordsworth destroyed his poetic genius by reversing his position on the French Revolution or by terminating his connection with Annette Vallon. Wordsworth had no need of an eagle for his greatness, and its presence or absence had nothing to do with the decline of his genius. His pain, when he suffered, was not of the kind that eagles inflict, and his power did not have its source in his pain. But we are disturbed by the absence of the validating, the poetically respectable bird, that *aigle obligatoire*. We like the fiercer animals. Nothing is better established in our literary life than the knowledge that the tigers of wrath are to be preferred to the horses of instruction, a striking remark which is indeed sometimes very true, although not always. We know that we ought to prefer the bulls in the ring to the horses, and when we choose between the two kinds of horses of Plato's chariot we all know that Plato was wrong, that it is the blacks, not the whites, which are to be preferred. We do not, to be sure, live in the fashion of the beasts we admire in our literary lives, but we cherish them as representing something that we all seek. They are the emblems of the *charisma*—to borrow from the sociologists a word they have borrowed from the theologians—which is the hot, direct relationship with Godhead, or with the sources of life, upon which depend our notions of what I have called spiritual prestige.

The predilection for the powerful, the fierce, the assertive, the personally militant, is very strong in our culture. We find it in the liberal-bourgeois admiration of the novels of Thomas Wolfe and Theodore Dreiser. On a lower intellectual level we find it in the long popularity of that curious underground work *The Fountainhead*. On a higher intellectual level we find it in certain aspects of the work of Yeats and Lawrence. We find it too, if not in our religion itself, then at least in one of our dominant conceptions of religion—to many intellectuals the violence of Dostoyevsky represents the natural form of the religious life, to many gentle spirits the ferocity of Léon Bloy seems quite appropriate to the way of faith; and although some years ago Mr. Eliot reprobated D. H. Lawrence, in the name of religion, for his addiction to this characteristic violence, yet for Mr. Eliot the equally violent Baudelaire is pre-eminently a Christian poet.*

I cannot give a better description of the quality of our literature with which I am concerned than by quoting the characterization of it which Richard Chase found occasion to make in the course of a review of a

---

*In his brief introduction to Father Tiverton's *D. H. Lawrence and Human Existence*, Mr. Eliot has indicated that he has changed his mind about Lawrence's relation to the religious life. I think he was right to do so. The revision of his opinion confirms, if anything, what I say of the place of violence in our conception of the religious life.

work on the nineteenth century by a notable English scholar, Professor Basil Willey. It is relevant to remark that Professor Willey deals with the nineteenth century from the point of view of the Anglican form of Christianity, and Mr. Chase is commenting on Professor Willey's hostility to a certain Victorian figure who, in any discussion of Wordsworth, must inevitably be in our minds—John Stuart Mill. His name seems very queer and shocking when it is spoken together with the names of the great figures of modern literature. Yet Mr. Chase is right when he says that "among the Victorians, it is Mill who tests the modern mind," and goes on to say that "in relation to him at least two of its weaknesses come quickly to light. The first is its morose desire for dogmatic certainty. The second is its hyperaesthesia: its feeling that no thought is permissible except an extreme thought: that every idea must be directly emblematic of concentration camps, alienation, madness, hell, history, and God; that every word must bristle and explode with the magic potency of our plight."

I must be careful not to seem to speak, as certainly Mr. Chase is not speaking, against the sense of urgency or immediacy, or against power or passion. Nor would I be taken to mean that the Wordsworthian quietism I have described is the whole desideratum of the emotional life. It obviously wasn't that for Wordsworth himself—he may be said to be the first poet who praised movement and speed for their own sakes, and dizziness and danger; he is the poet of rapture. No one can read Book v of *The Prelude* and remain unaware of Wordsworth's conception of literature as urgency and immediacy, as power and passion. Book v, which is about literature and the place of reading in our spiritual development, opens with an impressive eschatological vision, a vision of final events—Wordsworth shared in his own way our present sense of the possible end of man and of all the works of man's spirit, and it is important to observe that in the great dream of the Arab who hastens before the advancing flood to rescue Science and Poetry, represented by the Stone and the Shell he carries, the prophecy of the world destroyed is made to seem the expression of the very essence of literature. It is in this book that Wordsworth defends the violence and fearfulness of literature from the "progressive" ideas of his day; it is here that he speaks of the poet as "crazed/By love and feeling, and internal thought/Protracted among endless solitude," and of the "reason" that lies couched "in the blind and awful lair" of the poet's madness; and it is here that he defends the "maniac's" dedication at the cost of the domestic affections:

> Enow there are on earth to take in charge
> Their wives, their children, and their virgin loves,
> Or whatsoever else the heart holds dear;
> Enow to stir for these. . . .

As we speak of Wordsworth's quietism this opposite element of his poetry must be borne in mind. Then too, if we speak in anything like praise of his quietism, we must be conscious of the connection of his quietism with an aspect of his poetry that we rightly dread. When, in *The Excursion*, the Wanderer and the Poet and the Pastor sit upon the gravestones and tell sad stories of the deaths of other mild old men, for the benefit of the Solitary, who has had his fling at life and is understandably a little bitter, we know that something wrong is being done to us; we long for the winding of a horn or the drawing of a sword; we want someone to dash in on a horse—I think we want exactly a stallion, St. Mawr or another; for there can be no doubt about it: Wordsworth, at the extreme or perversion of himself, carries the element of quietude to the point of the denial of sexuality. And this is what makes the *Aboth* eventually seem to us quaint and oppressive, what, I suppose, makes a modern reader uneasy under any of the philosophies which urge us to the contemplative accord with a unitary reality and warn us that the accord will infallibly be disturbed and destroyed by the desires. Whether it be the Torah of the Rabbis, or the Cosmos of Marcus Aurelius, or the Nature of Spinoza or of Wordsworth, the accord with the unitary reality seems to depend upon the suppression not only of the sexual emotions but also of the qualities that are associated with sexuality: high-heartedness, wit, creative innovation, will.

But now, when we have touched upon the Wordsworthian quality that is very close to the Stoic *apatheia*, to not-feeling, let us remember what great particular thing Wordsworth is said to have accomplished. Matthew Arnold said that in a wintry clime, in an iron time, Wordsworth taught us to *feel*. This statement, extreme as it is, will be seen to be not inaccurate if we bring to mind the many instances of spiritual and psychological crisis in the nineteenth century in which affectlessness, the loss of the power to feel, played an important part. *Ennui, noia*—how often we meet with them in nineteenth-century biography; and the acedia which was once a disorder of the specifically religious life becomes now a commonplace of secular spirituality. Arnold, when he wrote the "Memorial Verses," could not, of course, have read Mill's autobiography, which so specifically and eloquently confirms Arnold's attribution to Wordsworth of a "healing power" through an ability to make us feel. And yet, although Arnold's statement is accurate so far as it goes, and is supported by Wordsworth's own sense of the overarching intention of his poetic enterprise, it does not go far enough. Wordsworth did, or tried to do, more than make us feel: he undertook to teach us how to *be*.

In *The Prelude*, in Book II, Wordsworth speaks of a particular emotion which he calls "the sentiment of Being." The "sentiment" has been described in this way: "There is, in sanest hours, a consciousness, a thought that arises, independent, lifted out from all else, calm, like the stars, shining eternal. This is the thought of identity—yours for you, whoever you are, as mine for me. Miracle of miracles, beyond statement, most spiritual and vaguest of earth's dreams, yet hardest basic fact, and only entrance to all facts." This, of course, is not Wordsworth, it is Walt Whitman, but I quote Whitman's statement in exposition of Wordsworth's "sentiment of Being" because it is in some respects rather more boldly explicit, although not necessarily better, than anything that Wordsworth himself wrote about the sentiment, and because Whitman goes on to speak of his "hardest basic fact" as a political fact, as the basis, and the criterion, of democracy.

Through all his poetic life Wordsworth was preoccupied by the idea, by the sentiment, by the problem, of being. All experience, all emotions lead to it. He was haunted by the mysterious fact that he existed. He could discover in himself different intensities and qualities of being—"Tintern Abbey" is the attempt to distinguish these intensities and qualities. Being is sometimes animal; sometimes it is an "appetite and a passion"; sometimes it is almost a suspension of the movement of the breath and blood. The *Lyrical Ballads* have many intentions, but one of the chief of them is the investigation of the problems of being. "We are Seven," which is always under the imputation of bathos, is established in its true nature when we read it as an ontological poem; its subject is the question, What does it mean when we say a person *is*? "The Idiot Boy," which I believe to be a great and not a foolish poem, is a kind of comic assertion of the actuality—and, indeed, the peculiar intensity—of being in a person who is outside the range of anything but our merely mechanical understanding. Johnny on the little horse, flourishing his branch of holly under the moon, is a creature of rapture, who, if he is not quite "human," is certainly elemental, magical, perhaps a little divine—"It was Johnny, Johnny everywhere." As much as anyone, and more than many—more than most—he *is*, and feels that he is.

From even the little I have said, it will be seen that as soon as the "sentiment of Being" is named, or represented, there arises a question of its degree of actuality or of its survival. "The glad animal movements" of the boy, the "appetite" and the "passion" of the young man's response to Nature easily confirm the sense of being. So do those experiences which are represented as a "sleep" or "slumber," when the bodily senses are in abeyance. But as the man grows older the stimuli to the experience of the sentiment of being grow fewer or grow less intense—it is this fact rather than any question of poetic creation (such as troubled Coleridge) that makes the matter of the Immortality Ode. Wordsworth, as it were, puts the awareness of being to the test in situations where its presence may perhaps most easily be questioned—in very old people. Other kinds of people also serve for the test, such as idiots, the insane, children, the dead, but I emphasize the very old because Wordsworth gave particular attention to them, and because we can all be aware from our own experience what a strain very old people put upon our powers of attributing to them personal being, "identity." Wordsworth's usual way is to represent the old man as being below the human condition, apparently scarcely able to communicate, and then suddenly, startlingly, in what we have learned to call an "epiphany," to show forth the intensity of his human existence. The old man in "Animal Tranquillity and Decay" is described as being so old and so nearly inanimate that the birds regard him as little as if he were a stone or a tree; for this, indeed, he is admired, and the poem says that his unfelt peace is so perfect that it is envied by the very young. He is questioned about his destination on the road—

> I asked him whither he was bound, and what
> The object of his journey; he replied,
> "Sir! I am going many miles to take
> A last leave of my son, a mariner,
> Who from a sea-fight has been brought to Falmouth,
> And there is dying in an hospital."

The revelation of the actuality of his being, of his humanness, quite dazzles us.*

The social and political implication of Wordsworth's preoccupation with ontology is obvious enough. It is not, however, quite what Wordsworth sometimes says it is. The direct political lesson that the poet draws from the Old Cumberland Beggar is interesting, but it is beside his real, his essential, point. "Deem not this man useless," he says in his apostrophe to the political theorists who have it in mind to put the Beggar into a workhouse, and he represents the usefulness of the Beggar as consisting in his serving as the object of a habitual charity and thus as a kind of communal institution, a communal bond. But this demonstrated utility of the Beggar is really secondary to the fact that he *is*—he is a person, he takes a pleasure, even though a minimal one, in his being, and therefore he may not in conscience be dealt with as a mere social unit. So with all the dramatis personae of the *Lyrical Ballads*—the intention of the poet is to require us to acknowledge their being and thus to bring them within the range of conscience, and of something more immediate than conscience, natural sympathy. It is an attractive thing about Wordsworth, and it should be a reassuring thing, that his acute sense of the being of others derives from, and serves to affirm and heighten, his acute sense of his own being.

I have spoken of Wordsworth's preoccupation with being as if it were unique, and as if it accounted for, or led to what accounts for, the contemporary alienation from his work and his personality. In some ways his preoccupation *is* unique, and certain aspects of it do lead to the present alienation from him. Yet from what I have said about him, it must be clear that between Wordsworth and the great figures of our literature there is a very close affinity indeed, if only in the one regard of the preoccupation with being. There is scarcely a great writer of our own day who has not addressed himself to the ontological crisis, who has not conceived of life as a struggle to be—not to live, but to be. They do so, to be sure, under a necessity rather different from Wordsworth's, and this necessity makes it seem appropriate that, with Byron, they assert "man's fiery might." (Blake suggests more aptly than Byron the quality of the mili-

---

*The concluding lines of the poem as originally printed in *Lyrical Ballads*, where the poem bears the title "Old Man Travelling," were deleted by Wordsworth in subsequent editions, which is a misfortune.

tancy of most modern writers, but I stay with the terms of the opposition as Arnold gives them to us.) They feel the necessity to affirm the personal qualities that are associated with a former time, presumably a freer and more personally privileged time—they wish, as a character in one of Yeats's plays says, "to bring back the old disturbed exalted life, the old splendor." Their image of freedom and personal privilege is often associated with violence, sometimes of a kind that does not always command the ready assent we are habituated to give to violence when it appears in moral or spiritual contexts. A tenant's sliced-off ear, which is an object of at least momentary pleasure to Yeats, a kick given by an employer to his employee, which wins the approval of Lawrence—these are all too accurately representative of the nature of the political fantasies that Yeats and Lawrence built upon the perception of the loss of freedom and privilege, the loss of the sense of being. Yet we know that this violence stands against an extreme fate of which we are all conscious. We really know in our time what the death of the word can be—for that knowledge we have only to read an account of contemporary Russian literature. We really know what the death of the spirit means—we have seen it overtake whole peoples. Nor do we need to go beyond our own daily lives to become aware, if we dare to, of how we have conspired, in our very virtues, to bring about the devaluation of whatever is bold and assertive and free, replacing it by the bland, the covert, the manipulative. If we wish to understand the violence, the impulse toward charismatic power, of so much of our literature, we have but to consider that we must endure not only the threat to being which comes from without but also the seduction to nonbeing which establishes itself within. We need, in Coleridge's words, something to "startle this dull pain, and make it move and live." Violence is a means of self-definition; the bad conscience, Nietzsche says, assures us of our existence.

Wordsworth, then, is not separated from us by his preoccupation with being, for it is our preoccupation. Yet he is separated from us. His conception of being seems different from ours.

In Book v of *The Prelude* Wordsworth gives us a satiric picture of the boy educated according to the "progressive" ideas of his day, and on the whole we follow him readily enough in the objections he makes to these ideas—this can be said even though it often happens that readers, misled by their preconceptions of Wordsworth, take his sarcasm seriously and suppose that he is actually praising "this model of a child." And we follow him when he speaks of the presumptuousness of pedagogical theorists, denouncing them as, in effect, engineers of the spirit: he flatters at least one element of our ambivalence toward the psychological expert. We are responsive to his notion of what a boy should be: "not . . . too good," "not unresentful where self-justified." Possibly we are not in perfect agreement with him on all points—perhaps we will feel that he has dealt rather too harshly with the alert political and social consciousness of the progressive child, or that he goes too far in thinking that a child's imagination should be fed on fanciful books; perhaps, too, the qualities of the boys he really admires would not be precisely the qualities we would specify—"Fierce, moody, patient, venturous, modest, shy." But on the whole his discussion of pedagogics appeals to the enlightened muddled concern with "adjustment" and "aggression" which occupies the P.T.A. segment of our minds, and if we have our reservation about details we can at least, as I say, follow Wordsworth through most of his argument. But I think we cease to follow him when, in the course of the argument, he rises to one of his great poetical moments. This is the passage "There was a Boy. . . ." It was perhaps rather finer when it stood alone as a poem in itself in *Lyrical Ballads*, but it is still very fine in its place in *The Prelude*, where it follows the description of the model child. The Boy is described as having had a trick of imitating the hooting of owls, and at night he would call across Windermere, trying to get the owls to answer; and often they did answer, but sometimes they did not, and then the silence would be strange and significant.

> . . . In that silence, while he hung
> Listening, a gentle shock of mild surprise
> Has carried far into his heart the voice
> Of mountain torrents; or the visible scene
> Would enter unawares into his mind,
> With all its solemn imagery, its rocks,
> Its woods, and that uncertain heaven, received
> Into the bosom of the steady lake.

We may be ready enough to acknowledge the "beauty" of the poem, but the chances are that we will be rather baffled by its intention. We perceive that the Boy is obviously intended to represent something very good and right, meant to be an example of very full being. But what baffles us, what makes us wonder what the poem has to do with education and the development of personality, is that the Boy exercises no will, or at least, when his playful will is frustrated, is at once content with the pleasures that follow upon the suspended will. And as likely as not we will be impelled to refer the poem to that "mysticism" which is supposed to be an element of Wordsworth's mind. Now Wordsworth's mind does have an element of mysticism—it is that "normal mysticism" which, according to a recent writer on the Rabbis, marked the Rabbinical mind.* Wordsworth's mysticism, if we wish to call it that, consists of two elements, his conception of the world as being semantic, and his capacity for intense pleasure. When we speak of him as a mystic in any other sense, we are pretty sure to be expressing our incomprehension of the intensity with which he experienced his own being, and our incomprehension of the relation which his sentiment of being bore to his will. Thus, we have no trouble understanding him when, in Book VI of *The Prelude*, in the remarkable episode of the crossing of the Alps, he speaks of the glory of the will.

> . . . Whither we be young or old,
> Our destiny, our being's heart and home,
> Is with infinitude, and only there;
> With hope it is, hope that can never die,
> Effort, and expectation, and desire,
> And something evermore about to be.

The note on which the will is affirmed is high, Miltonic—it echoes the accents of Satan's speech in the Council of Hell; and the passage resumes its movement with a line the martial tenor of which we happily respond to: "Under such banners militant, the soul . . ." But we are checked by what ensues:

*Max Kadushin, *The Rabbinical Mind* (New York, 1951). This impressive work of scholarship has received far less general notice than it deserves. I read it after I had written this essay—read it not only with admiration for its intellectual achievement but also with a peculiar personal pleasure, because its author, in his seminary days, had been one of the long-suffering men who tried to teach me Hebrew, with what success I have indicated; yet he did teach me—it was no small thing for a boy of twelve to be in relation with a serious scholar. Dr. Kadushin has been kind enough to tell me that what I have said about the Rabbis is not wrong. In revising my essay I have not tried to amend my primitive account by what is to be learned from Dr. Kadushin's presentation of the Rabbis in all their great complexity of thought. But the phrase "normal mysticism" seemed too apt not to quote.

> Under such banners militant, the soul
> Seeks for no trophies, struggles for no spoils
> That may attest her prowess, blest in thoughts
> That are their own perfection and reward,
> Strong in herself and in beatitude. . . .

The soul's energy is directed to the delight of the soul in itself.

Wordsworth is describing the action of what, at a later time, a man of very different mind, Hegel, was to call a new human faculty, the faculty of *Gemüt*. The word, I gather, is not entirely susceptible of translation—"heart," with the implication of responsiveness, and of high-heartedness and large-heartedness, is an approximation. Hegel defines his faculty of *Gemüt* as expressing itself as a desire, a will, which has "no particular aims, such as riches, honors, and the like; in fact, it does not concern itself with any worldly condition of wealth, prestige, etc., but with the entire condition of the soul—a general sense of enjoyment."

Much that I have said about the tendency of our culture would seem to deny the truth of Hegel's statement that *Gemüt* is one of the characteristics of our time, and much more evidence might be adduced to confirm the impression that nothing could be less characteristic of our time than the faculty of *Gemüt*, that we scarcely conceive of it, let alone exercise it. Yet at the same time I think it is true to say that it plays in our culture a covert but very important part.

Of our negative response to *Gemüt*, to the "sentiment of Being," Mr. Eliot provides an instance—again, for it is Mr. Eliot's high gift to be as pertinent when we think him wrong as when we think him right. In *The Cocktail Party* there is a description of the two virtuous ways of life, that of "the common routine" and that of the spiritual heroism of the saint and martyr. The two ways, Mr. Eliot tells us, are of equal value; the way of the saint is not better than that of the householder. Yet when it comes to describing the life of the common routine, Mr. Eliot says of those who elect it that they

> Learn to avoid excessive expectation,
> Become tolerant of themselves and others,
> Giving and taking in the usual actions
> What there is to give and take. They do not repine;
> And are contented with the morning that separates

And with the evening that brings together
For casual talk before the fire
Two people who know that they do not understand each other,
Breeding children whom they do not understand
And who will never understand them.

Well, few of us will want to say much for the life of the common routine, and no doubt, under the aspect of modern life with its terrible fatigues, and in the consciousness of its gross threats, the sort of thing that Mr. Eliot says here will be pretty nearly all that any of us will want to say. Yet if we think of the description of the common routine as being not merely the expression of one possible mood among many—and it is not merely that: it is what it says it is, the description of a "way"—we must find it very strange. There is in it no reference to the pain which is an essential and not an accidental part of the life of the common routine. There is no reference to the principles, the ethical discipline, by which the ordinary life is governed—all is habit. There is no reference to the possibility of either joy or glory—I use the Wordsworthian words by intention. The possibility of *Gemüt* does not appear. Mr. Eliot does not say that his couples are in Limbo, that they are in a condition of not-being, which would of course be a true thing to say of many householding couples: he is describing the virtuous way of life that is alternative to the way of the saint. This failure to conceive the actuality of the life of common routine is typical of modern literature since, say, Tolstoy. I do not say this in order to suggest that domestic life, the common routine, in itself makes an especially appropriate subject for literature—I don't think it does—but in order to suggest a limitation of our conception of the spiritual life. Mr. Eliot's representation of the two "ways" exemplifies how we are drawn to the violence of extremity. We imagine, with nothing in between, the dull not-being of life, the intense not-being of death; but we do not imagine being—we do not imagine that it can be a joy. We are in love, at least in our literature, with the fantasy of death. Death and suffering, when we read, are our only means of conceiving the actuality of life.

Perhaps this is not new and we but intensify what is indigenous in our culture. Perhaps this is in the nature of life as Western culture has long been fated to see it. Perhaps it is inescapable for us that the word "tragic" should be used as an ultimate recommendation of a sense of life. Yet we, when we use the word, do not really mean it in its old, complex, mysterious sense—we mean something like "violent" or "conclusive": we mean death. And just here lies a paradox and our point. For it is precisely what Wordsworth implies by his passionate insistence on being, even at a very low level of consciousness, pride, and assertiveness, as well as at the highest level of quasi-mystic intensity, that validates a conception of tragedy, and a conception of heroism. The saintly martyrdom which Mr. Eliot represents in his play is of course not intended to be taken as tragic: the idea of martyrdom precludes the idea of tragedy. But if we ask why the martyrdom seems as factitious as it does, must we not answer that this is because it is presented in a system of feeling which sets very little store by—which, indeed, denies the possibility of—the "beatitude" which Wordsworth thought was the birthright of every human soul? And this seems to be borne out by the emphasis which Mr. Eliot puts on the peculiar horror of the mode of the martyr's death, as if only by an extremity of pain could we be made to realize that a *being* was actually involved, that a life has been sacrificed—or, indeed, has been lived.

Wordsworth's incapacity for tragedy has often been remarked on, and accurately enough. Yet we cannot conclude that Wordsworth's relation to tragedy is wholly negative. The possibility of tragic art depends primarily upon the worth we ascribe not to dying but to living, and to living in "the common routine." The power of the Homeric tragedy, for example, derives from the pathos, which the poet is at pains to bring before us repeatedly, of young men dying, of not seeing ever again the trees of their native farmsteads, of their parents never again admiring and indulging them, of the cessation of their being in the common routine. The tragic hero, Achilles, becomes a tragic hero exactly because he has made a choice to give up the life of the common routine, which all his comrades desire, in favor of a briefer but more intense quality of being of transcendent glory. The pathos of his particular situation becomes the great thing it is because of the respondent pathos of Hector and Priam, which is the pathos of the family and the common routine, which we understand less and less and find ourselves more and more uncomfortable with. And I think it can be shown that every tragic literature owes its power to the high esteem in which it holds the common routine, and the sentiment of being which arises from it, the elemental *given* of biology. And that is what Wordsworth had in mind when, in the "Preface" of 1800, defending the idea that poetry should give "immediate pleasure," he said that this idea was "a homage paid to the native and naked dignity of man, to the grand elementary principle of pleasure, by which he knows, and feels, and lives, and moves."

Yet if we are aware of the tendency of our literature I have exemplified by the passage from Mr. Eliot's play, we must at the same time be aware of the equally strong counter-tendency. In speaking of our alienation from Wordsworth, it has not been my intention to make a separation between Wordsworth and the literature of our time. The separation cannot be made. Wordsworth and the great writers of our time stand, as I have said, on the common ground of the concern with being and its problems—Wordsworth, indeed, may be said to have discovered and first explored the ground upon which our literature has established itself. Our hyper-aesthesia, our preference for the apocalyptic subject and the charismatic style, do indeed constitute a taste which alienates many readers from Wordsworth, and no doubt the more if we believe, as some do, that it is a taste wholly appropriate to the actualities of our historical situation. Yet we can without too much difficulty become aware of how much of the Wordsworthian "mildness," which so readily irritates us, and how much of the Wordsworthian quietism (as I have called it), which dismays us, are in the grain of our literature, expressed through the very intensities which seem to deny them. Thus, to bring Wordsworth and James Joyce into conjunction might at first seem a joke or a paradox, or an excess of historicism, at best a mere device of criticism. We will at once be conscious of the calculated hauteur of Joyce's implied personality, the elaborations of his irony, the uncompromising challenge of his style and his manner, and by the association of contrast we will remember that horrendous moment in *The Prelude* when Wordsworth says, "My drift I fear/Is scarcely obvious." How can we fail to think only of the abysses of personality, theory, and culture that separate the two men? And yet when we have become acclimated to Joyce, when the charismatic legend becomes with familiarity not so fierce and the vatic paraphernalia of the style and method less intimidating, do we not find that we are involved in a conception of life that reiterates, in however different a tonality, the Wordsworthian vision? One of the striking things about *Ulysses* (to speak only of that work) is that the idea of evil plays so small a part in it. One hears a good deal about the essential Christian orthodoxy of Joyce, and perhaps this is an accurate opinion, but his orthodoxy, if he has it, takes no account of the evil which is so commonly affirmed by the literary expressions of orthodoxy; the conception of sin has but a tangential relevance to the book. The element of sexuality which plays so large a part in the story does not raise considerations of sin and evil; it is dealt with in the way of poetic naturalism. The character of Leopold Bloom, who figures in the life of Joyce's Poet much as the old men in Wordsworth figure in his life—met by chance and giving help of some transcendent yet essentially human kind—is conceived in Wordsworthian terms: in terms, that is, of his humbleness of spirit. If we speak of Wordsworth in reference to the Rabbis and their non-militancy, their indifference to the idea of evil, their acceptance of cosmic contradiction, are we not to say that Bloom is a Rabbinical character? It is exactly his non-militancy that makes him the object of general contempt and, on one occasion, of rage. It is just this that has captivated his author, as the contrast with the armed pride, the jealousy and desire for prestige, the bitter militancy of Stephen Dedalus. Leopold Bloom is deprived of every shred of dignity except the dignity of that innocence which for Joyce, as for Wordsworth, goes with the "sentiment of Being."

Again and again in our literature, at its most apocalyptic and intense, we find the impulse to create figures who are intended to suggest that life is justified in its elemental biological simplicity, and, in the manner of Wordsworth, these figures are conceived of as being of humble status and humble heart: Lawrence's simpler people or primitive people whose pride is only that of plants or animals; Dreiser's Jennie Gerhardt and Mrs. Griffiths, who stand as oases in the wide waste of their creator's dull representation of energy; Hemingway's waiters with their curious silent dignity; Faulkner's Negroes, of whom it is said, as so often it is said in effect of Wordsworth's people, *they endured*; and Faulkner's idiot boys, of whom it is to be said, *they are*—the list could be extended to suggest how great is the affinity of our literature with Wordsworth. And these figures express an intention which is to be discerned through all our literature—the intention to imagine, and to reach, a condition of the soul in which the will is freed from "particular aims," in which it is "strong in itself and in beatitude." At least as early as Balzac our literature has shown the will seeking its own negation—or, rather, seeking its own affirmation by its rejection of the aims which the world sets before it and by turning its energies upon itself in self-realization. Of this particular affirmation of the will Wordsworth is the proponent and the poet.

William Dean Howells
and the Roots of Modern Taste

1951

I

Every now and then in the past few years we have heard that we might soon expect a revival of interest in the work of William Dean Howells. And certainly, if this rumor were substantiated, there would be a notable propriety in the event. In the last two decades Henry James has become established as a great magnetic figure in our higher culture. In the same period Mark Twain has become as it were newly established—not indeed, like James, as a source and object of intellectual energy, but at least as a permanent focus of our admiring interest, as the representative of a mode of the American mind and temperament which we are happy to acknowledge. To say that Henry James and Mark Twain are opposite poles of our national character would be excessive, yet it is clear that they do suggest tendencies which are very far apart, so that there is always refreshment and enlightenment in thinking of them together. And when we do think of them together, diverse as they are, indifferent to each other as they mostly were, deeply suspicious of each other as they were whenever they became aware of each other, we naturally have in mind the man who stood between them as the affectionate friend of both, the happy admirer of their disparate powers, who saw so early the fullness of their virtues which we now take for granted. It would make a pleasant symmetry if we could know that William Dean Howells has become the object of renewed admiration, that he is being regarded, like his two great friends, as a large, significant figure in our literature.

But the rumor of the revival is surely false. A certain number of people, but a very small number, do nowadays feel that they might find pleasure in Howells, their expectation being based, no doubt, on an analogy with the pleasure that is being found in Trollope. And the analogy is fair enough. Howells produced in the free Trollopian way, and with the same happy yielding of the rigorous artistic conscience in favor of the careless flow of life; and now and then, even in our exigent age, we are willing to find respite from the strict demands of conscious art, especially if we can do so without a great loss of other sanctions and integrities. Howells, it is thought, can give us the pleasures of our generic image of the Victorian novel. He was a man of principle without being a man of heroic moral intensity, and we expect of him that he will involve us in the enjoyment of moral activity through the medium of a lively awareness of manners, that he will delight us by touching on high matters in the natural course of gossip.

This is a very attractive expectation and Howells does not really disappoint it. He is not Trollope's equal, but at his best he is in his own right a very engaging novelist. Whether or not he deserves a stronger adjective than this may for the moment be left open to question, but engaging he undoubtedly is. And yet I think that he cannot now engage us, that we cannot expect a revival of interest in him—his stock is probably quite as high in the market as it will go. The excellent omnibus volume of Howells which Professor Commager recently brought out was piously reviewed but it was not bought. And when, in a course of lectures on American literature, I imagined that it might be useful to my students to have a notion of the cultural and social situation which Howells described, and therefore spent a considerable time talking about his books, I received the first anonymous letter I have ever had from a student—it warned me that the lapse of taste shown by my excessive interest in a dull writer was causing a scandal in the cafeterias.

As a historical figure, Howells must of course always make a strong claim upon our attention. His boyhood and youth, to which he so often returned in memory in his pleasant autobiographical books, were spent in circumstances of which everyone must be aware who wishes to understand the course of American culture. Howells's induction into the intellectual life gives us one of the points from which we can measure what has happened to the humanistic idea in the modern world. If we want to know what was the estate of literature a hundred years ago, if we want to be made aware of how the nineteenth century, for all its development of science and technology, was still essentially a humanistic period, we have only to take Howells's account of the intellectual life of the Ohio towns in which he lived—the lively concern with the more dramatic aspects of European politics, the circulation of the great English reviews, the fond knowledge of the English and American literature of the century, the adoration of Shakespeare, the general, if naïve, respect for learning. It was certainly not elaborate, this culture of little towns that were almost of the frontier, and we must not exaggerate the extent to which its most highly developed parts were shared, yet it *was* pervasive and its assumptions were general enough to support Howells in his literary commitment. In a log cabin he read to the bottom of that famous barrel of books, he struggled to learn four or five languages, he determined on a life of literature, and his community respected his enterprise and encouraged him in it. And it is worth observing that, as he himself says, he devoted himself to a literary career not so much out of disinterested love for literature as out of the sense that literature was an institutional activity by which he might make something of himself in the worldly way.

Howells's historical interest for us continues through all his developing career. His famous pilgrimage to New England, his round of visits to the great literary figures of Massachusetts, is a *locus classicus* of our literary history. It culminated, as everyone remembers, in that famous little dinner which Lowell gave for him at the Parker House; it was the first dinner that Howells had ever seen that was served in courses, in what was then called the Russian style, and it reached its significant climax when Holmes turned to Lowell and said, "Well, James, this is the apostolic succession, this is the laying on of hands." Much has been made of this story, and indeed much must be made of it, for although Holmes probably intended no more than an irony-lightened kindliness to a very young man, his remark was previsionary, and the visit of Howells does mark a succession and an era, the beginning of an American literature where before, as Howells said, there had been only a New England literature. Then Howells's uprooting himself from Boston to settle in New York in 1888 marks, as Alfred Kazin observes, the shifting of the concentrations of literary capital from the one city to the other. And when, as old age came on and Howells was no longer a commanding figure with the New York publishers, when he suffered with characteristic mild fortitude the pain of having his work refused by a new generation of editors, the culture of the American nineteenth century had at last come to its very end.

Howells's historical importance is further confirmed by the position he attained in the institutional life of American letters. Not long after Howells died, H. L. Mencken, who had been at pains to make Howells's name a byword of evasive gentility, wrote to regret his death, because, as he said, with irony enough but also with some seriousness, there was now no American writer who could serve as the representative of American letters, no figure who, by reason of age, length of service, bulk of work, and public respect, could stand as a literary patriarch. And since Mencken wrote, no such figure has arisen. Howells was indeed patriarchal as he grew older, large and most fatherly, and if he exercised his paternity only in the mild, puzzled American way, still he was the head of the family and he took his responsibility seriously. He asserted the dignity of the worker in literature at the same time that he defined the writer's place as being economically and socially with the manual worker rather than with the business man. He was receptive to the new and the strange; his defense of Emily Dickinson, for example, does him great credit. His personal and cultural timidity about sexual matters made him speak harshly of writers more daring in such things than himself, yet he fought effectively for the acceptance of contemporary European literature, and he was tireless in helping even those of the young men who did not share his reticences. Edmund Wilson once defined the literary character of Stephen Crane by differentiating him from "the comfortable family men of whom Howells was chief," yet Crane was in Howells's debt, as were Boyesen, Hamlin Garland, Norris, and Herrick.

He was not a man of great moral intensity, but he was stubborn. His comportment in the Haymarket affair marks, I think, the beginning in our life of the problem of what came to be called the writer's "integrity," and his novel *A Hazard of New Fortunes* is probably the first treatment of the theme which became almost obsessive in our fiction in the 1930s, the intellectual's risking his class position by opposing the prejudices of his class. Some years ago, it seemed appropriate for almost any academic writer on American literature to condescend to Howells's social views as being, in comparison with the tradition of revolutionary Marxism, all too "mild," and quite foolish in their mildness, another manifestation of his "genteel" quality. The fact is that Howells's sense of the anomalies and injustices of an expanding capitalism was very clear and strong. What is more, it was very *personal*; it became a part, and a bitter part, of his temperament. In his criticism of American life, he was not like Henry Adams or Henry James, who thought of America in reference to their own grand ambitions. Howells's ambitiousness reached its peak in youth and then compromised itself, or democratized itself, so that in much of his work he is only the journeyman, a craftsman quite without the artist's expectably aristocratic notions, and in his life, although he was a child of light and a son of the covenant, he also kept up his connections with the philistines—he was, we remember, the original of James's Strether; and when such a man complains about America, we do not say that his case is special, we do not discount and resist what he says, we listen and are convinced. His literary criticism still has force and point because it is so doggedly partisan with a certain kind of literature and because it always had a social end in view.

It is of course in his novels that Howells is at his best as a social witness, and he can be very good indeed. The reader who wants to test for himself what were in actual fact Howells's powers of social insight, which have for long been slighted in most accounts of them, might best read *A Modern Instance*, and he would do well to read it alongside so perceptive a work of modern sociology as David Riesman's *The Lonely Crowd*, for the two books address themselves to the same situation, a change in the American character, a debilitation of the American psychic tone, the diminution of moral tension. Nothing could be more telling than Howells's description of the religious mood of the 1870s and 1880s, the movement from the last vestiges of faith to a genteel plausibility, the displacement of doctrine and moral strenuousness by a concern with "social adjustment" and the amelioration of boredom. And the chief figure of the novel, Bartley Hubbard, is worthy to stand with Dickens's Bradley Headstone, or James's Basil Ransom and Paul Muniment, or Flaubert's Sénécal, or Dostoyevsky's Smerdyakov and Shigalov, as one of a class of fictional characters who foretell a large social actuality of the future. Howells has caught in Hubbard the quintessence of the average sensual man as the most sanguine of us have come to fear our culture breeds him, a man somewhat gifted—and how right a touch that Hubbard should be a writer of sorts, how deep in our democratic culture is the need to claim some special undeveloped gift of intellect or art!—a man trading upon sincerity and half-truth; vain yet self-doubting; aggressive yet self-pitying; self-indulgent yet with starts of conscience; friendly and helpful yet not loyal; impelled to the tender relationships yet wishing above all to live to himself and by himself, essentially resenting all human ties. In the seventy years since *A Modern Instance* appeared, no American novelist has equaled Howells in the accuracy and cogency of his observation, nor in the seriousness with which he took the social and moral facts that forced themselves on his unhappy consciousness.

Yet if we praise Howells only as a man who is historically interesting, or if we praise him only as an observer who testifies truthfully about the American social fact of his time, we may be dealing as generously and as piously with his memory as the nature of his achievement permits, but we cannot be happy over having added to the number of American writers who must be praised thus circumspectly if they are to be praised at all. We have all too many American writers who live for us only because they can be so neatly "placed," whose life in literature consists in their being influences or precursors, or of being symbols of intellectual tendencies, which is to say that their life is not really in literature at all but in the history of culture.

Perhaps this is the fate to which we must abandon Howells. The comparison that is made between him and Trollope, while it suggests something of his quality, also proposes his limitations, which are considerable. As an American, and for reasons that Henry James made clear, he did not have Trollope's social advantages, he did not have at his disposal that thickness of the English scene and of the English character which were of such inestimable value to the English novelists as a standing invitation to energy, gusto, and happy excess. Nor did he have Trollope's assumption of a society essentially settled despite the changes that might be appearing; his consciousness of the past could not be of sufficient weight to balance the pull of the future, and so his present could never be as solid as Trollope's. "Life here," as he said, "is still for the future—it is a land of Emersons—and I like a little present moment in mine." He never got as much present moment as the novelist presumably needs, and his novels are likely to seem to most readers to be of the past because nothing in America is quite so dead as an American future of a few decades back, unless it be an American personage of the same time.

And yet it is still possible that Howells deserves something better than a place in the mere background of American literature. It is clear enough that he is not of a kind with Hawthorne, Melville, James, and Whitman; nor of a kind with Emerson and Thoreau; nor with Poe; nor with Mark Twain at his best. But neither is he of a kind with H. B. Fuller and Robert Herrick, whose names are usually mentioned with his as being in a line of descent from him. If Howells is experienced not as he exists in the textbooks, but as he really is on his own page, we have to see that there is something indomitable about him; at least while we are reading him he does not consent to being consigned to the half-life of the background of literature. For one thing, his wit and humor save him. Much must be granted to the man who created the wealthy, guilty, hypersensitive Clara Kingsbury, called her "a large blonde mass of suffering," and conceived that she might say to poor Marcia Hubbard, "Why, my child, you're a Roman matron!" and come away in agony that Marcia would think she meant her nose. And the man is not easily done with who at eighty-three, in the year of his death, wrote that strange "realistic" idyl *The Vacation of the Kelwyns*, with its paraphernalia of gypsies and dancing bears and its infinitely touching impulse to speak out against the negation and repression of emotion, its passionate wish to speak out for the benign relaxation of the will, for goodness and gentleness, for "life," for the reservation of moral judgment, for the charm of the mysterious, precarious little flame that lies at the heart of the commonplace. No one since Schiller has treated the genre of the idyl with the seriousness it deserves, yet even without a standard of criticism the contemporary reader will, I think, reach beyond the quaintness of the book to a sense of its profundity, or at least of its near approach to profundity. It will put him in mind of the early novels of E. M. Forster, and he will even be drawn to think of *The Tempest*, with which it shares the theme of the need for general pardon and the irony of the brave new world: Howells, setting his story in the year of the centennial of the Declaration of Independence, is explicit in his belief that the brave newness of the world is all behind his young lovers.

When we praise Howells's social observation, we must see that it is of a precision and subtlety which carry it beyond sociology to literature. It is literature and not sociology to understand with Howells's innocent clarity the relationship of the American social classes, to know that a lady from Cambridge and the farmer's wife with whom she boards will have a natural antagonism which will be expressed in the great cultural issue of whether the breakfast steak should be fried or broiled. Again, when we have said all that there is to say about Howells's theory of character, have taken full account of its intentional lack of glory, we must see that in its reasoned neutrality, in its insistence on the virtual equality in any person of the good and the bad, or of the interesting and the dull, there is a kind of love, perhaps not so much of persons as of persons in society, of the social idea. At the heart of Herrick there is deadness and even a kind of malice. At the heart of Fuller there is a sort of moral inertness. But at the heart of Howells there is a loving wonder at the fact that persons of the most mediocre sort somehow manage to make a society.

I don't mean by this to define the whole quality and virtue of Howells but only to offer enough in his defense to make his case at least doubtful, because I want to ask the question, How much is our present friendly indifference to him of his making and how much is it of ours? It is a question which cannot be fully answered at this time but only in some later generation that is as remote from our assumptions as from Howells's, yet it is worth attempting for what small self-knowledge the effort might bring.

2

Henry James's essay on Howells is well known, and in that essay there are three statements which by implication define the ground of our present indifference to Howells. They have the advantage for our inquiry of appearing in the friendliest possible context, and they are intended not as judgments, certainly not as adverse judgments, but only as descriptions.

This is the first statement: "He is animated by a love of the common, the immediate, the familiar, and the vulgar elements of life, and holds that in proportion as we move into the rare and strange we become vague and arbitrary; that truth of representation, in a word, can be achieved only so long as it is in our power to test and measure it."

Here is the second statement: "He hates a 'story,' and (this private feat is not impossible) has probably made up his mind very definitely as to what the pestilent thing consists of. Mr. Howells hates an artificial fable, a denouement that is pressed into service; he likes things to occur as in life, where the manner of a great many of them is not to occur at all."

And here is the third: "If American life is on the whole, as I make no doubt whatever, more innocent than that of any other country, nowhere is the fact more patent than in Mr. Howells's novels, which exhibit so constant a study of the actual and so small a perception of evil."

It will be immediately clear from these three statements how far from our modern taste Howells is likely to be. I have said they are objective statements, that they are descriptions and not judgments, yet we can hear in them some ambiguity of tone—some ambiguity of tone must inevitably be there, for James is defining not only his friend's work but, by inversion, his own. And almost in the degree that we admire James and defend his artistic practice, we are committed to resist Howells. But I think we must have the grace to see that in resisting Howells, in rejecting him, we are resisting and rejecting something more than a literary talent or temperament or method. There is in Howells, as I have tried to suggest, an odd kind of muted, stubborn passion which we have to take account of, and respect, and recognize for what it is, the sign of a commitment, of an involvement in very great matters—we are required to see that in making our judgment of him we are involved in considerations of way of life, of quality of being.

His passion and its meaning become apparent whenever he speaks of the commonplace, which was the almost obsessive object of his literary faith. "The commonplace? Commonplace? The commonplace is just that light, impalpable, aerial essence which [the novelists] have never got into their confounded books yet. The novelist who could interpret the common feelings of commonplace people would have the answer to 'the riddle of the painful earth' on his tongue." We might go so far as to grant that the passion of this utterance has a kind of intellectual illumination in it which commands our respect, but we in our time cannot truly respond to it. We are lovers of what James calls the rare and strange, and in our literature we are not responsive to the common, the immediate, the familiar, and the vulgar elements in life.

Or at least we have a most complicated relation to these elements. In our poetic language we do want something that has affinity with the common, the immediate, the familiar, and the vulgar. And we want a certain aspect or degree of these elements in all our literature—we want them in their extremity, especially the common and vulgar. We find an interest in being threatened by them; we like them represented in their extremity to serve as a sort of outer limit of the possibility of our daily lives, as a kind of mundane hell. They figure for us in this way in *Ulysses*, in *The Waste Land*, in Kafka's novels and stories, even in Yeats, and they account, I believe, for the interest of comfortable middle-class readers in James Farrell's *Studs Lonigan*. In short, we consent to the commonplace as it verges upon and becomes the rare and strange. The commonplace of extreme poverty or ultimate boredom may even come to imply the demonic and be valued for that—let life be sufficiently depressing and sufficiently boring in its commonplaceness and we shall have been licensed to give up quiet desperation and to become desperately fierce. We are attracted by the idea of human life in, as it were, putrefaction, in stewing corruption—we sense the force gathering in the fermentation. But of course Howells's kind of commonness suggests nothing of this. The objection that many readers made to his early work was that it was drab and depressing, the point of comparison being fiction of plot and melodramatic incident, what Howells called the "romantic." But after a time the objection was to his tame gentility, the comparison being then with Zola. Howells admired Zola enormously and fought for his recognition, but he eventually thought that Zola failed in realism and surrendered to "romanticism." He meant that the matter of Zola's realism would lead his readers away from the facts of their middle-class lives. For Howells the center of reality was the family life of the middle class.

The feeling for the family with which Howells's theory of the commonplace was bound up was very strong in him, and Mr. Wilson is accurate when he makes it definitive of Howells's quality. His family piety seems to have amounted almost to a superstitiousness, for as such we must interpret his having said to Mark Twain, "I would rather see and talk with you than with any other man in the world," and then feeling it necessary to add, "outside my own family." His sorrows were family sorrows; after his marriage the direction of his life was given chiefly by the family necessities. All this, we may well feel, is excessive, and very likely it accounts for the insufficiency of personality, of self, in Howells that makes the chief trouble in our relation with him. He is too much the *pius Aeneas* without having Aeneas's sad saving grace of being the sire of an enormous destiny. Yet this must not lead us to lessen the credit we give to Howells for being the only nineteenth-century American writer of large reputation who deals directly and immediately with the family.

I do not know whether or not anyone has remarked the peculiar power the idea of the family has in literature—perhaps it has never been worth anyone's while to remark what is so simple and obvious, so easily to be observed from the time of the Greek epics and of the Greek drama down through the course of European literature. Even today, when our sense of family has become much attenuated, the familial theme shows its power in our most notable literature, in Joyce, in Proust, in Faulkner, in Kafka. But our present sense of the family is of the family in dissolution, and although of course the point of any family story has always been a threatened or an actual dissolution, this was once thought to be calamity where with us it is the natural course of things. We are sure that the nineteenth-century family was an elaborate hoax and against nature. It is true that almost every second-rate novel will represent one of its good characters expressing the hope of a quiet home and charming and satisfying children; it is true that the family is at the center of the essential mythology of our social and economic life, the good and sufficient reason for accumulation and expenditure, and that the maintenance of the family in peace is the study of our psychological science, yet in our literature the family serves as but an ideality, a rather wistful symbol of peace, order, and continuity; it does not exist in anything like actuality.

This may explain our feeling of indifference to the realism of the commonplace. But our attitude toward the family must be understood in a very large context, as but one aspect of our attitude to the idea of "the conditioned," of the material circumstances in which spirit exists. From one point of view, no people has ever had so intense an idea of the relationship of spirit to its material circumstances as we in America now have. Our very preoccupation with *things*, as Mary McCarthy once observed, is really a way of dealing with the life of spirit in the world of matter—our possessions, although they have reference to status and comfort, have a larger reference to the future of our souls, to energy and the sense of cleanliness and fitness and health; our materialism cannot be represented as the Roman *luxus* has been represented—its style is not meant to imply ease and rest and self-indulgence but rather an ideal of alertness and readiness of spirit. And this sense of the conditioned is carried out in our elaborate theories of child-rearing, and the extravagant store we set by education; and in our theories of morality and its relation to social circumstance.

Yet it is to be seen that those conditions to which we do respond are the ones which we ourselves make, or over which we have control, which is to say conditions as they are virtually spirit, as they deny the idea of "the conditioned." Somewhere in our mental constitution is the demand for life as pure spirit.

The idea of unconditioned spirit is of course a very old one, but we are probably the first people to think of it as a realizable possibility and to make that possibility part of our secret assumption. It is this that explains the phenomenon of our growing disenchantment with the whole idea of the political life, the feeling that although we are willing, nay eager, to live in society, for we all piously know that man fulfills himself in society, yet we do not willingly consent to live in a particular society of the present, marked as it is bound to be by a particular economic system, by disorderly struggles for influence, by mere approximations and downright failures. Our aesthetic sense—I mean our deep comprehensive aesthetic sense, really our metaphysics—which is satisfied by the performance of a Bendix washing machine, is revolted by such a politically conditioned society. The wide disrepute into which capitalistic society has fallen all over the world is justified by the failures and injustices of capitalism; but if we want to understand the assumptions about politics of the world today, we have to consider the readiness of people to condemn the failures and injustices of that society as compared with their reluctance to condemn the failures and injustices of Communist society. The comparison will give us the measure of the modern preference for the unconditioned—to the modern more-or-less thinking man, Communist society is likely to seem a close approximation to the unconditioned, to spirit making its own terms.

The dislike of the conditioned is in part what makes so many of us dissatisfied with our class situation, and guilty about it, and unwilling to believe that it has any reality, or that what reality it may have is a possible basis of moral or spiritual prestige, the moral or spiritual prestige which is the most valuable thing in the world to those of us who think a little. By extension, we are very little satisfied with the idea of family life—for us it is part of the inadequate bourgeois reality. Not that we don't live good-naturedly enough with our families, but when we do, we know that we are "family men," by definition cut off from the true realities of the spirit. This, I venture to suppose, is why the family is excluded from American literature of any pretensions. Although not all families are thus excluded—for example, the family of Faulkner's *As I Lay Dying* is very happily welcomed. And on every account it should be, but probably one reason for our eager acceptance of it is that we find in that family's extremity of suffering a respite from the commonplace of the conditioned as we know it in our families, we actually find in it an intimation of liberty—when conditions become extreme enough there is sometimes a sense of deep relief, as if the conditioned had now been left quite behind, as if spirit were freed when the confining comforts and the oppressive assurances of civil life are destroyed.

But Howells was committed totally and without question to civil life, and when he wrote an essay called "Problems of Existence in Fiction," although he did include among the existential matters that the novelist might treat such grim, ultimate things as a lingering hopeless illness, it is but one item among such others as the family budget, nagging wives, daughters who want to marry fools, and the difficulties of deciding whom to invite to dinner.

In extenuation of Howells we remember that this is all the matter of Jane Austen, the high reverberations of whose touch upon the commonplace we have habituated ourselves to hear. But Howells does not permit us to defend him with the comparison; he is profligate in his dealings with the ordinary, and in *A Hazard of New Fortunes* he does not think twice about devoting the first six chapters to an account of the hero's search for an apartment. I have heard that someone has written to explicate the place of these chapters in the total scheme of the novel, and in perfect ignorance of this essay I hazard the guess that its intention is to rescue Howells from the appearance of an excess of literalness and ordinariness, and that, in the carrying out of this intention, Basil March's fruitless ringing of janitors' bells is shown to be a modern instance of the age-old theme of The Quest, or an analogue of the Twelve Tribes in the Wilderness, or of the flight into Egypt, or a symbol of the homelessness of the intellectual. But it is really just a house-hunt. Of course any house-hunt will inevitably produce lost and unhappy feelings, even a sense of cosmic alienation—so much in our dull daily lives really does make a significant part of man's tragic career on earth, which is what Howells meant by his passionate sentence about the charm and power of the commonplace. But when we yield to our contemporary impulse to enlarge all experience, to involve it as soon as possible in history, myth, and the oneness of spirit—an impulse with which, I ought to say, I have considerable sympathy—we are in danger of making experience merely typical, formal, and *representative*, and thus of losing one term of the dialectic that goes on between spirit and the conditioned, which is, I suppose, what we mean when we speak of man's tragic fate. We lose, that is to say, the actuality of the conditioned, the literality of matter, the peculiar authenticity and authority of the merely denotative.* To lose this is to lose not a material fact but a spiritual one, for it is a fact of spirit that it must exist in a world which requires it to engage in so dispiriting an occupation as hunting for a house. The knowledge of the antagonism between spirit and the conditioned—it is Donne's, it is Pascal's, it is Tolstoy's—may in literature be a cause of great delight because it is so rare and difficult; beside it the knowledge of pure spirit is comparatively easy.

3

To James's first statement about Howells, his second is clearly a corollary—"He hates a 'story' . . . [he] hates an artificial fable." We cannot nowadays be sure that all of our reading public loves a story in the way James did. Quite simple readers can be counted on to love a story, but there is a large, consciously intelligent middle part of our reading public that is inclined to suspect a story, in James's sense, as being a little dishonest. However, where theory of a certain complexity prevails, the implications of story, and even of "artificial fable," are nowadays easily understood. In these uplands of taste we comprehend that artificial devices, such as manipulated plot, are a way not of escaping from reality but of representing it, and we speak with vivacity of "imaginary gardens with real toads in them." Indeed, we have come to believe that the toad is the less real when the garden is also real. Our metaphysical habits lead us to feel the deficiency of what we call literal reality and to prefer what we call essential reality. To be sure, when we speak of literal reality, we are aware that there is really no such thing—that everything that is *per*ceived is in some sense *con*ceived, or created; it is controlled by intention and indicates intention; and so on. Nevertheless, bound as we are by society and convention, as well as by certain necessities of the mind, there still is a

---

*Students have a trick of speaking of money in Dostoyevsky's novels as "symbolic," as if no one ever needed, or spent, or gambled, or squandered the stuff—and as if to think of it as an actuality were subliterary.

thing that we persist in calling "literal reality," and we recognize in works of art a greater or less approximation to it. Having admitted the existence of literal reality, we give it a low status in our judgment of art. Naturalism, which is the form of art that makes its effects by the accumulation of the details of literal reality, is now in poor repute among us. We dismiss it as an analogue of an outmoded science and look to contemporary science to give authority to our preference for the abstract and conceptual; or we look to music to justify our impatience with the representational; and we derive a kind of political satisfaction from our taste, remembering that reactionary governments hate what we admire.

Our metaphysical and aesthetic prejudices even conspire to make us believe that our children have chiefly an "essential" sense of reality. We characterize the whole bent of their minds by their flights of fancy and by the extremity of distortion in their school paintings, preferring to forget that if they are in some degree and on some occasions essential realists, they are also passionately pedantic literalists—as they must be when their whole souls are so directed toward accommodation and control. The vogue of the "educational" toy with its merely essential representation is an adult vogue; the two-year-old wants the miniature Chevrolet with as many precise details as possible; it is not the gay chintz ball designed for the infant eye and grasp that delights him but rather the apple or the orange—its function, its use, its being valued by the family give him his pleasure; and as he grows older his pedantry of literalism will increase, and he will scorn the adult world for the metaphysical vagaries of its absurd conduct—until he himself is seduced by them.

Now we must admit that Howells's extravagance of literalism, his downright, declared hatred of a story, was on the whole not very intelligent. He said of Zola that "the imperfection of his realism began with the perfection of his form." That is, just where Zola appeals to us, just where he disregards his own syllabus of the experimental novel to introduce dramatic extravagance, he is disappointing to Howells. And Howells, in his character of programmatic literalist, spoke disrespectfully of Scott (one of the founders of realism), of Dickens, and of Balzac, saying that the truth was not in them; and he went so far as to express impatience with the romancing of George Eliot, despite the clear affinity his realism has with hers. It is difficult to know what he made of his adored Jane Austen. Clearly it never occurred to him, as he sought to learn from her, that some of her finest effects are due to her carefully contrived stories. We, of course, find it natural to say that the perfection of her realism begins with the perfection of her form.

It is perhaps an expression of our desire for unconditioned spirit that we have of late years been so preoccupied with artifice and form. We feel that the shape which the mind gives to what the mind observes is more ideally characteristic of the mind than is the act of observation. Possibly it is, and if the last decades of criticism have insisted rather too much that this is so,* it is possible that a view of our historical situation might lead us to justify the overemphasis, for in the historical perspective we perceive such a depressing plethora of matter and so little form. Form suggests a principle of control—I can quite understand that group of my students who have become excited over their discovery of the old animosity which Ezra Pound and William Carlos Williams bear to the iamb, and have come to feel that could they but break the iambic shackles, the whole of modern culture could find a true expression.

The value of form must never be denigrated. But by a perversity of our minds, just as the commitment to a particular matter of literature is likely to be conceived in terms of hostility to form, so the devotion to the power of form is likely to be conceived in terms of hostility to matter, to matter in its sheer literalness, in its stubborn denotativeness. The claims of form to pre-eminence over matter always have a certain advantage because of the feeling to which I have just referred, that the mind's power of shaping is more characteristic of mind than its power of observation. Certainly the power of shaping is more intimately connected with what Plato called the "spirited" part of man, with the will, while observation may be thought of as springing from the merely "vegetative" part. The eye, it cannot choose but see, we cannot bid the ear be still; things impress themselves upon us against or with our will. But the plastic stress of spirit is of the will in the sense that it strives against resistance, against the stubbornness of what Shelley called the dull, dense world—it compels "all new successions to the forms they wear."

But Shelley's description of the act of creation suggests that the plastic will cannot possibly exercise itself without the recalcitrance of stupid lit-

---

*Who can imagine any of our critics saying with Ruskin that "No good work whatever can be perfect, and the demand for perfection is always a sign of a misunderstanding of the ends of art"; and ". . . No great man ever stops working till he has reached his point of failure . . ."?

eral matter. When we consider what is going on in painting at this moment, we perceive what may happen in an art when it frees itself entirely from the objective. No doubt the defense of the legitimacy of nonobjective art which is made by referring to the right of music to be unindentured to an objective reality is as convincing as it ever was. Yet do we not have the unhappy sense that sterility is overtaking the painters, that by totally freeing themselves from the objective reality which they believed extraneous to their art, they have provided the plastic will with no resisting object, or none except itself as expressed by other painters, and are therefore beginning to express themselves in mere competitive ingenuity? It is no accident of the *Zeitgeist* that the classic painting of our time is Cubism. The Cubists, bold as they were, accepted the conditioned, and kept in touch with a world of literality. And this is the opinion of one of the greatest of the Cubists, Juan Gris. "Those who believe in abstract painting," he wrote in a letter of 1919, "are like weavers who think they can produce material with only one set of threads and forget that there has to be another set to hold these together. Where there is no attempt at plasticity how can you control representational liberties? And where there is no concern for reality how can you limit and unite plastic liberties?"

What is true of the Cubists is also true of the great classic writers of our time—the sense of *things* is stronger in them than in their expositors. They grew in naturalism, in literalism, and they in their way insist on it as much as Flaubert, or the Goncourts, or Zola. The impulse of succeeding writers to build on Joyce is pretty sure to be frustrated, for it is all too likely to be an attempt to build on Joyce's notions of form, which have force only in relation to Joyce's superb sense of literal fact, his solid simple awareness that in the work of art some things are merely denotative and do not connote more than appears, that they are *data* and must be permitted to exist as data.

4

The last of James's statements about Howells concerns his indifference to evil. For us today this constitutes a very severe indictment. We are all aware of evil; we began to be aware of it in certain quasi-religious senses a couple of decades or so ago; and as time passed we learned a great deal about the physical, political actuality of evil, saw it expressed in the political life in a kind of gratuitous devilishness which has always been in the world but which never before in western Europe had been organized and, as it were, rationalized. A proper sense of evil is surely an attribute of a great writer, and nowadays we have been drawn to make it almost a touchstone of greatness, drawn to do so in part by our revived religious feelings or nostalgia for religious feelings, but of course also in part by our desire that literature should be in accord with reality as we now know it.

Our responsiveness to the idea of evil is legitimate enough, yet we ought to be aware that the management of the sense of evil is not an easy thing. Be careful, Nietzsche said, when you fight dragons, lest you become a dragon yourself. There is always the danger, when we have insisted upon the fact of evil with a certain intensity, that we will go on to cherish the virtue of our insistence, and then the very fact we insist upon. I would make a distinction between the relation to evil of the creator of the literary work and that of the reader, believing that the active confrontation of the fact of evil is likelier to be healthy than is the passive confrontation—there is something suspect in making evil the object of, as it were, aesthetic contemplation. But not even the creator is nowadays immune from all danger. Consider that the awareness of evil is held by us to confer a certain kind of spiritual status and prestige upon the person who exercises it, a status and prestige which are often quite out of proportion to his general spiritual gifts. Our time has a very quick sensitivity to what the sociologists call charisma, which, in the socio-political context, is the quality of power and leadership that seems to derive from a direct connection with great supernal forces, with godhead. This power we respond to when we find it in our literature in the form of alliances with the dark gods of sexuality, or the huge inscrutability of nature, or the church, or history; presumably we want it for ourselves. This is what accounts in our theory of literature for our preference for the hidden and ambiguous, for our demand for "tension" and "tragedy." And evil has for us its own charisma. Hannah Arendt, in *The Origins of Totalitarianism*, speaking of the modern disintegration, remarks that with us today "to yield to the mere process of disintegration has become an irresistible temptation, not only because it has assumed the spurious grandeur of 'historical necessity' but also because everything outside it has begun to appear lifeless, bloodless, meaningless, and unreal." Disintegration itself fascinates us because it is a power. Evil has always fascinated men, not only because it is opposed to good but also because it is, in its own right, a power.

Lifeless, *bloodless*, *meaningless*, and *unreal*—without stopping to estimate just how much life, blood, meaning, and reality Howells actually has, we must observe that the modern reader who judges him to have little is not exactly in a position to be objective, that he is likely to deal with Howells under the aspect of a universal judgment by which it is concluded that very little in our life has life, blood, meaning, and reality.

The sentence in which Howells invites American novelists to concern themselves with the "more smiling aspects" of life as being the "more American" is well known and has done much harm to his reputation. In fairness to Howells, we ought to be aware that the sentence may not be quite so dreadful as is generally supposed. For one thing, it is rather ambiguous—when Howells says "we invite," it is not clear whether "we" is the editorial pronoun referring to himself or is meant to stand for the American people: the phrase, that is, may be read as simply descriptive of a disposition of American culture. And even if we take the sentence in its worst construction, we ought to recall that it appears in an essay on Dostoyevsky in which Howells urges the reading of Dostoyevsky; that when he speaks of the more smiling aspects of life as being the more American it is in the course of a comparison of America with the Russia of Dostoyevsky; that he is careful to remark that America is not exempt from the sorrows of the natural course of life, only from those which are peculiar to the poverty and oppression of Dostoyevsky's land; and that he says he is not sure that America is in every way the gainer by being so thoroughly in material luck, so rich in the smiling aspects. But let us leave all extenuation aside and take the sentence only as it has established itself in the legendary way, as the clear sign of Howells's blindness to evil, his ignorance of the very essence of reality. Taken so, it perhaps cannot be thought a very wise statement, but our interpretation of it, the vehemence with which we are likely to press its meaning, tells us, I think, more about ourselves than about Howells. It raises the question of why we believe, as we do believe, that evil is of the very essence of reality.

The management of the sense of evil, I have said, is not easy. The sense of evil is properly managed only when it is not allowed to be preponderant over the sense of self. The reason Shakespeare holds his place in our imagination is that in him the sense of evil and the sense of self are in so delicate and continuous a reciprocation. And the ground of Keats's greatness, I have come to feel, is that precarious reciprocation of self and evil, similar to Shakespeare's. He maintained this reciprocation in a more conscious and explicit way than Shakespeare found necessary. He called to his aid in the affirmation of self against the knowledge of evil his intense imagination of pleasure—of pleasure of all kinds, the simplest and most primitive, such as eating and drinking, as well as the highest. He boldly put pleasure, even contentment, at the center of his theory of poetry, and at one point in the development of his theory he spoke of poetry as being most itself when it tells "heart-easing things." It is just for this reason that some readers denigrate him; they quite miss the intensity of his sense of reality, for where they make a duality of the principle of pleasure and the principle of reality, Keats made a unity—for him pleasure was a reality; it was, as Wordsworth had taught him, the grand principle of life, of mind, and of self. And it was this commitment to pleasure that made it possible for him to write the greatest exposition of the meaning of tragedy in our literature.

When we are so eager to say how wrong Howells was to invite the novelist to deal with the smiling aspects of life, we have to ask ourselves whether our quick antagonism to this mild recognition of pleasure does not imply an impatience with the self, a degree of yielding to what Hannah Arendt calls the irresistible temptation of disintegration, of identification by submission to the grandeur of historical necessity which is so much more powerful than the self. It is possible that our easily expressed contempt for the smiling aspects and our covert impulse to yield to the historical process are a way of acquiring charisma. It is that peculiar charisma which has always been inherent in death. It was neither a genteel novelist nor a romantic poet who most recently defended the necessity of the smiling aspects and the heart-easing things—Dr. Bruno Bettelheim was first known in this country for his study, made at first hand, of the psychology of the inmates of the German concentration camps. Dr. Bettelheim recently found occasion to remark that "a fight for the very survival of civilized mankind is actually a fight to restore man to a sensitivity toward the joys of life. Only in this way can man be liberated and the survival of civilized mankind be assured. Maybe a time has come in which our main efforts need no longer be directed toward modifying the pleasure principle. [Dr. Bettelheim is speaking of the practice of psychoanalysis.] Maybe it is time we became concerned with restoring pleasure gratification to its dominant role in the reality principle; maybe this society needs less a modification of the pleasure principle by reality, and more assertion of the pleasure principle against an overpowering pleasure-denying reality." It cannot be said of Howells's smiling aspects that they represent a very intense kind of pleasure; yet for most men they will at least serve, in Keats's phrase, to bind us to the earth, to prevent our being seduced by the godhead of disintegration.

5

"Your really beautiful time will come," wrote Henry James to Howells on the occasion of his seventy-fifth birthday—what James characteristically meant was the time when the critical intelligence would begin to render Howells its tribute. The really beautiful time has come to James, but it has not yet come to Howells, and probably it will be a very long time coming. We are not easy with the quiet men, the civil personalities—the very word "civil," except as applied to disobedience or disorders, is uncomfortable in our ears. "Art inhabits temperate regions," said André Gide in 1940. Well, not always; but if the statement is perhaps a little inaccurate in the range of its generality, we can understand what led Gide to make it, for he goes on: "And doubtless the greatest harm this war is doing to culture is to create a profusion of extreme passions which, by a sort of inflation, brings about a devaluation of all moderate sentiments." And the devaluation of the moderate sentiments brings a concomitant devaluation of the extreme passions: "The dying anguish of Roland or the distress of a Lear stripped of power moves us by its exceptional quality but loses its special eloquence when reproduced simultaneously in several thousand copies." The extreme has become the commonplace of our day. This is not a situation which can be legislated or criticized out of existence, but while it endures we are not in a position to make a proper judgment of Howells, a man of moderate sentiments. It is a disqualification that we cannot regard with complacency, for if Gide is right, it implies that we are in a fair way of being disqualified from making any literary judgments at all.

The Poet as Hero:
Keats in His Letters

1951

In the history of literature the letters of John Keats are unique. All personal letters are interesting; the letters of great men naturally have an especial attraction; and among the letters of great men those of the great creative artists are likely to be the most intimate, the liveliest, and the fullest of wisdom. Yet even among the great artists Keats is perhaps the only one whose letters have an interest which is virtually equal to that of their writer's canon of created work. No other letters, for example, have ever been the occasion of such a warning as F. R. Leavis felt it necessary to give a few years ago. Dr. Leavis said that in thinking about Keats as a poet we must be sure to understand that the important documents are his poems, not his letters. No one will wish to dispute the point with Dr. Leavis. When we think about Keats as a poet, his letters are of course illuminating and suggestive, yet in relation to Keats as a poet they are not primary but secondary; they are no more than illuminating and suggestive. The fact is, however, that because of the letters it is impossible to think of Keats only as a poet—inevitably we think of him as something even more interesting than a poet, we think of him as a man, and as a certain kind of man, a hero.

To be sure, no hero, no man who fully engages our attention, is ever a man in the abstract but is always marked and distinguished by some particular role. We know him as he is a lover, a husband, a father, a son, and it is so much the better if we also know him through his profession, as, say, a king, or a soldier, or a poet. "Othello's *occupation*'s gone!"—the famous pathos of the cry reminds us that in a tragic story men are first vulnerable not in their abstract humanity but in the particular commitments of their lives. And so we cannot think of Keats as a man without thinking of him in his occupation of poet. At the same time, when once we have read his letters, we cannot help knowing that his being a poet was his chosen way of being a man.

The charm of Keats's letters is inexhaustible, and we can scarcely hope to define it wholly or to name all its elements. Yet we can be sure that some part of its effect comes from Keats's conscious desire to live life in the heroic mode. In a young man this is always most winning. Keats was situated in a small way of life, that of the respectable, liberal, intellectual middle part of the middle class; his field of action was limited to the small continuous duties of the family; his deportment was marked by quietness and modesty, at times by a sort of diffident neutrality. He nevertheless at every moment took life in the largest possible way and seems never to have been without the sense that to be, or to become, a man was an adventurous problem. The phrase in his letters that everyone knows, "life is a vale of soul-making," is his summing up of that sense, which, once we have become aware of its existence in him, we understand to have dominated his mind. He believed that life was given for him to find the right use of it, that it was a kind of continuous magical confrontation requiring to be met with the right answer. He believed that this answer was to be derived from intuition, courage, and the accumulation of experience. It was not, of course, to be a formula of any kind, not a piece of rationality, but rather a way of being and of acting. And yet it could in part be derived from taking thought, and it could be put, if not into a formula, then at least into many formulations. Keats was nothing if not a man of ideas.

His way of conceiving of life is characteristic of the spirited young man of high gifts—except that it is also characteristic of the very great older men whom the young men of spirit and gifts are most likely to take seriously. Its charm in Keats is the greater because its span is so short and so dramatically concise. Keats is twenty when the letters begin, and he is twenty-six when they end. But he was strikingly precocious—I am inclined to think even more precocious in his knowledge of the world than in poetry. He was one of that class of geniuses who early learn to trust themselves in an essential way, whatever moments of doubt they may have. He was remarkably lucky, or wise, in finding a circle of friends who believed in his powers before he had given much evidence of their existence beyond the communicated sense of his heroic vision, and these friends expected him to speak out. He therefore at a very early age passed beyond all self-conscious hesitation about looking deep into life and himself, about propounding the great questions and attempting the great answers, and about freely telling his thoughts. And so we have the first of the vital contradictions which make the fascination of Keats's mind—we have the wisdom of maturity arising from the preoccupations of youth. This wisdom is the proud, bitter, and joyful acceptance of tragic life which we associate pre-eminently with Shakespeare. It explains the force, as the sense of adventure explains the charm, of Keats's letters.

geniality

2

Bernard Shaw does not seem the likeliest person to help us toward an understanding of Keats as a man, and indeed the little essay on Keats which he once contributed to a memorial volume is for the most part perfunctory. Yet in the course of this essay Shaw speaks at some length of a quality of Keats which, at least for our time, may well be the one which we ought to recognize before any other. This quality is what Shaw calls Keats's "geniality."

The word is not in good repute nowadays. It is seldom used in common speech, and when it is used at all it is likely to be associated with men of middle age or of hale old age—to many readers it will imply precisely what is not young and fervent, and it will have overtones of a mediocre good will that verges upon a vulgar lack of personal discriminativeness. It will suggest anything but the dedication and impatient creative energy of a young poet. But the word was not always limited by these connotations. It was not thus limited in Keats's own time. It was then a word clearly applicable to a young man: Wordsworth speaks of "the genial sense of youth." And it was precisely applicable to the idea of creativeness: when Coleridge wants to express the idea that he has lost his creative powers, he says that his "genial spirits fail," and one sense of the word that he here intends is that which derives from "genius."*

The word is rich in other high meanings that will be worth noting in relation to Keats. But it will not do for us to ignore the single rather commonplace meaning which we now assign to it, the meaning of simple good-humoredness and sociability. Our notions about "the" poetic temperament being what they are, the sensitive reader is likely to shrink from Shaw's description of Keats as "not only a poet, but a merry soul, a jolly fellow, who could not only carry his splendid burthen of genius, but swing it around, toss it up and catch it again, and whistle a tune as he strode along." This is certainly not the way to describe Keats, yet it is righter than the impulse to consider this description of a poet somehow blasphemous. Nowadays our theory of poetic creation holds that the poet derives his power from some mutilation he has suffered. We take it for granted that he writes out of a darkness of the spirit or not at all. But this was not the belief of the great poets of Keats's own time, and it was not Keats's belief. Wordsworth and Coleridge thought that poetry depended upon a condition of positive health in the poet, a more than usual well-being. Keats himself seems to have had no analogous theory of the right circumstance for creation, but it is clear that for him the writing of poetry was first a regular work, his occupation, which he practiced with sober diligence, and then a great joy. For several obvious reasons, he was much concerned with health; the word occurs very frequently in his poems, and he hated ill health, whether physical or mental. Like any person, he had times of depression; and like any person of intellect, he might give expression to these moods in gloomy generalizations. Like any literary person, he had times when he seemed to feel nothing at all, in which he was without impulse and almost without personality. But he set no store by his dark hours. He was sure that negation was not of his essence, and that it must pass for him to be himself again. He writes to his brother George of a method he had devised for dealing with depression: "Whenever I

---

*For the Romantic poets the English word was no doubt reinforced by the German word, although *genial* in German had meanings that would not have recommended it to Wordsworth and Coleridge—when G. H. Lewes, in his *Life of Goethe*, describes the wild life of the young men of Weimar and their free sexuality, he says that their actions were understood and forgiven as being typical of the *genial* period and adds in a footnote: "It is difficult to find an English word to express the German *genial*, which means pertaining to genius. The genial period was the period when every extravagance was excused on the plea of genius." Even Goethe's bad spelling, as George Eliot notes in one of her letters from Germany, was spoken of as *genial*.

find myself growing vapourish, I rouse myself, wash and put on a clean shirt, brush my hair and clothes, tie my shoestrings neatly, and in fact adonize as I were going out—then all clean and comfortable I sit down to write. This I find the greatest relief."

"In fact adonize as I were going out"—how much this tells us about Keats. He never, he said, wrote a line with public intention, and yet when he wishes to summon up his most private faculties and bring them to high pitch, he does so by preparing himself as if for company. He had a passion for friendship and society. It is a statement that needs modification, but as at first we see him he has not the least impulse to hold himself aloof from the common pleasures of men—the community of pleasure, the generality of geniality are an important part of his daily life. And for quite a long time he believed that the development of his mind was scarcely less communal than were his pleasures. He felt that his friends, most of whom were older than he, had much to give him and were liberal in their giving. And very likely he was right. If we suppose that Keats's own large generosity perhaps estimated at too high a rate what they did give, we must also suppose that his generosity had the actual effect of calling forth a respondent generosity from them.

In his lively sense of social connection Keats was sharing a quality of his time: the life of art and intellect was then more genial than it is now. Men of the same artistic craft, or practitioners of different crafts who stood in the same relation to the public and to the established traditions, thought it becoming in them to admire and defend each other and to be often in each other's company for professional discussion, or merely for puns and jokes. Quarrels and jealousies of course developed, as we find them developing in Keats's circle, but the impulse was stronger than it is now toward the coterie, the *cénacle*, the little group that understood the purposes and legitimate ambitions of each of its members. The Romanticists revived the ideal of friendship, of comradeship in arms, which had been so commanding both in the Middle Ages and in the Renaissance. It was an ideal appropriate to a time that necessarily thought of new art as a political act, almost as a conspiracy.

To this strong tendency of sociability and friendship Keats happily contributed, and the quality of his letters is in part to be explained by it. Not all of Keats's friends were artists, but all lived in the ambience of the ideals of art and intellect, which, for young men, is likely to have the coloring of bohemianism. And the delicacy of feeling and the cogency of observation of Keats's letters would scarcely have appeared had not Keats been able carelessly to entrust his thoughts to his friends—and not his second thoughts but his first. We owe the wonderful, misspelled immediacy of the letters not only to confidence between friend and friend but also to the free manners of the group, which are of a piece with the generality of the masculine manners of the time. Men then, it would seem, made more occasions for exclusively masculine social diversion, and their habits were livelier than now. The set that Keats consorted with was by no means unmannerly. In the nature of the case, to be sure, there could be no emphasis on "family," and the claims of some of its members to be considered gentlemen might be disallowed by the old, almost technical definition of that rank. Nevertheless gentility was of its essence; and Keats himself, the grandson of a livery-stable keeper, the son of a former ostler and of a mother whose behavior and status became more than questionable, put a high value upon manners, and his own were, I think, exquisite. Yet Keats insisted on manners that were comfortable, and he happily tolerated those that were rowdy. Out of his admiration of Wordsworth the poet, he had every wish to excuse the failings of the man, but toward Wordsworth's stiffness in society no one could have been more severe than he. And with what enjoyment he writes of the raffish dinner of January 1818, with its extreme and elaborate sexual joking and its larking about chamber-pots. Keats would not have understood the ideal of delicacy of the later nineteenth century, which, so far as it manifested itself in the society of men, would have seemed to him strange and foolish.* The Regency manners did not in the least offend him, they suited him very well, and they account in some part for the directness and vigor of his correspondence. He and his friends attended bear-baitings and were fond of the raffish world of the prize ring. Keats, among whose books was a volume called *Fencing Familiarized*, was an excellent boxer, and he did not, we know, hesitate to engage a heavier opponent in earnest and with bare fists; he did very well on this occasion. For all his passion for what he called "abstractions," for all the ideality of his poetry, Keats loved the actuality of life; its coarseness and commonness delighted him. "Wonders are no wonders to me," he wrote in November 1819. "I am more at home

---

*It did not manifest itself quite so thoroughly as we have come to believe—the unpublished portions of Samuel Butler's notebooks give an enlightening account of the actual habits and conversation of the gentlemen of his period. But no doubt Butler's having been at such pains to record the facts suggests what the dominant behavior was.

amongst Men and Women. I would rather read Chaucer than Ariosto." His sense of actuality was quick and racy and in the line of the English poetic humorists from Chaucer and Skelton to Burns. "Dawlish Fair" and "Modern Love" are no doubt to be called exceptional among Keats's poems, but they are of the very stuff of his temperament as the letters show it.

In speaking of Keats's social geniality we shall not be accurate if we do not recognize that there was an element of his personality which acted to check it. His illness, of course, embittered him, separating him, as he grew more certain of his death, from those who still had the prospect of life, making him suspicious and jealous. But even before his illness he had already begun to withdraw from sociability. It was perhaps to be expected. Early in his career he had expressed to Bailey his confidence in his understanding of the springs of human action. It was an understanding which he was willing to say was exceptional. "As soon as I had known Haydon three days I had got enough of his character not to have been surprised at such a letter as he has hurt you with." "Before I felt interested in either Reynolds or Haydon—I was well read in their faults." But with the quick understanding of human failing goes a most profound tolerance: "—Men should bear with each other—there lives not the Man who may not be cut up, aye hashed to pieces on his weakest side." And the sure way of friendship, he says, "is first to know a man's faults, and then be passive—if after that he insensibly draws you toward him then you have no Power to break the link."

The tolerance was as affectionate as the understanding was undeceived, yet an understanding so undeceived could not allow Keats's social life to be a simple one. There came a time when he found that he was embarrassing himself and annoying his friends by replying not to their spoken remarks but to their unspoken intentions.

Modest as he was in all his relations, inclined as he was to a quiet generosity of admiration, Keats had nevertheless a lively and jealous pride. He early withdrew from Leigh Hunt because Hunt spoke patronizingly of his poetry. He was always cool to Shelley, suspecting condescension. He began to see that one reason for his being liked was his retiring quietness, a certain courteous withdrawal from social competitiveness which he practiced. "Think of my Pleasure in Solitude," he writes, "in comparison of my commerce with the world—there I am a child—there they do not know me, not even my most intimate acquaintance—I give into their feelings as though I were refraining from irritating a little child—Some think me middling, others silly, others foolish—everyone thinks he sees my weak side against my will, when in truth it is with my will—I am content to be thought all this because I have in my own breast so great a resource. This is one reason why they like me so; because they can all show to great advantage in a room, and eclipse from a certain tact one who is reckoned a good Poet—." And again: ". . . I suffer greatly by going into parties where from the rules of society and a natural pride I am obliged to smother my Spirit and look like an Idiot—because I feel that my impulses given way to would too much amaze them—I live under an everlasting restraint—never relieved except when I am composing—So I will write away."

Keats's separateness must indeed be mentioned but it must not be exaggerated. In part it was but what we all feel. Keats might say that he admired human nature and disliked men, but everybody says that, or says its converse, or both. We are all naturally not satisfied by the society around us. It never really lends itself to our purposes and expectations. Of Keats this was especially true. For him there was perhaps only one man, Shakespeare, who ever satisfied his notion of what men might be. But his separateness must also be understood as a normal aspect of his genius. It came to him in the natural course of his growing awareness of his power and identity, of the work there was for him to do and the destiny he must fulfill. The remarkable thing is not that he was separate, that he held the social world at some small distance by means of his knowledge of it, but rather that he was not more apart. His knowledge of men checked and controlled and dignified, but never limited, his geniality. Up to the end it expresses itself in his letters like an animal potency, strangely manifesting itself even when, in the bitterness of approaching death, he experiences spasms of hatred of the friends he loved.

3

When we think about Keats's social geniality, it is easy and natural for us to suppose that it is the development of his relation to his family. If Keats is genial, he is so in one of the elementary meanings of the word: he is of the *gens*, the family, and, by extension, the tribe, ultimately the nation. "I like, I love England," he said. Solitary as he might be in his mind, he was never a man for physical solitude. Company gave him pleasure. He lived but little alone. He could even compose in the same room with someone else. He liked, we may say, to reconstitute the family situation.

In the nineteenth century it came increasingly to be believed that alienation from the family was indispensable to the poet's growth, and nowadays our mythology of the poetic personality takes this for granted. But Keats would not have understood what we so easily assume. In him family feeling was enormously strong and perfectly direct. Or at least this is true of his feelings toward his brothers and sister. Of what he felt for his deceased parents we can speak only speculatively. But his affection for the brothers and sister is a definitive part of his character and legend. He devoted his life to the care of young Tom in the long last months of the boy's tuberculosis. His letters to George in America are those in which he most opened his heart and mind. To his sister Fanny he was unremitting in tenderness, and, so far as the Abbeys would permit, in solicitude; it was her image, together with that of the other Fanny, that haunted him on the Italian voyage. His familial feeling amounted to what he called a passion.

There is yet another aspect of Keats's geniality of which we must take account. This is his geniality toward himself. We cannot understand Keats's mind without a very full awareness of what powers of enjoyment he had and of how freely he licensed these powers. The pleasure of the senses was for him not merely desirable—it was the very ground of life. It was, moreover, the ground of thought. More than any other poet—more, really, than Shelley—Keats is Platonic, but his Platonism is not doctrinal or systematic: it was by the natural impulse of his temperament that his mind moved up the ladder of love which Plato expounds in *The Symposium*, beginning with the love of things and moving toward the love of ideas, with existences and moving toward essences, with appetites and moving toward immortal longings. But the movement is of a special kind, perhaps of a kind that the orthodox interpretation of Plato cannot approve. For it is not, so to speak, a biographical movement—Keats does not, as he develops, "advance" from a preoccupation with sense to a preoccupation with intellect. Rather it is his characteristic mode of thought all through his life to begin with sense and to move thence to what he calls "abstraction," but never to leave sense behind. Sense cannot be left behind, for of itself it generates the idea and remains continuous with it.

And the moral and speculative intensity with which Keats's poems and letters are charged has its unique grace and illumination because it goes along with, and grows out of, and conditions, but does not deny, the full autonomy of sense.

But it is not enough to speak of Keats's loyalty to sense, nor is it even enough to speak of his loyalty to the pleasures of the senses. *Sense* and *pleasures of the senses* may apply as well to Wordsworth as to Keats. We must make no mistake about it: when it comes to sense and pleasure, Keats is Wordsworth's disciple, and the great difference between the ways in which they understood the two words must not blind us to the similarities. Here, however, we are concerned with the significant difference. Our language distinguishes between the sensory, the sensuous, and the sensual. The first word is neutral as regards pleasure, the second connotes pleasure of varying degrees and kinds but is yet distinguished from the last, which suggests pleasure that is intense, appetitive, material, and which usually carries a strong pejorative overtone and almost always an implication of sexuality. For Wordsworth the pleasures of the senses are the clear sign of rightness of life, but virtually the only two sense-faculties of which he takes account are seeing and hearing, and, at that, the seeing and hearing of only a few kinds of things; and the matter of the senses' experience passes very quickly into what Wordsworth calls the "purer mind" and has been but minimally sensuous, let alone sensual. For Keats, however, there was no distinction of prestige among the senses, and to him the sensory, the sensuous, and the sensual were all one. Wordsworth would have happily concurred in the sentiment which Keats expresses when, writing to his friend Brown, he speaks of "the pleasures which it was your duty to procure," for Wordsworth had identified the "native and naked dignity of man" with the "grand elementary principle of pleasure, by which he knows, and feels, and lives, and moves." But Wordsworth would have withdrawn hastily when Keats urges the newly married Reynolds to "gorge the honey of life." Particularly because of the sexual context, but not because of that alone, he would have been dismayed by the appetitive image and the frankness of appetite amounting to greed.

But it is, of course, exactly the appetitive image and the frankness of his appetite that we cannot dispense with in our understanding of Keats. Eating and the delicacies of taste are basic and definitive in his experience and in his poetry. The story of his putting cayenne pepper on his tongue in order to feel the more intensely the pleasure of a draft of cold claret is apocryphal. Yet it is significant that Haydon, who told the story, was sufficiently aware of Keats's disposition to have invented it. It does not, after all, go beyond Keats's own account of his pleasure in the nectarine. "Talking of pleasure," he writes to Dilke, "this moment I was writing with one hand, and with the other holding to my mouth a Nectarine—good God how fine. It went down soft, slushy, oozy—all its delicious embonpoint melted down my throat like a beatified Strawberry."

We are ambivalent in our conception of the moral status of eating and drinking. On the one hand ingestion supplies the imagery of our largest and most intense experiences: we speak of the wine of life and the cup of life; we speak also of its dregs and lees, and sorrow is also something to be drunk from a cup; shame and defeat are wormwood and gall; divine providence is manna or milk and honey; we hunger and thirst for righteousness; we starve for love; lovers devour each other with their eyes; and scarcely a mother has not exclaimed that oh, she could eat her baby up; bread and salt are the symbols of peace and loyalty, bread and wine the stuff of the most solemn acts of religion. On the other hand, however, while we may represent all of significant life by the tropes of eating and drinking, we do so with great circumspection. Our use of the ingestive imagery is rapid and sparse, never developed; we feel it unbecoming to dwell upon what we permit ourselves to refer to.*

But with Keats the ingestive imagery is pervasive and extreme. He is possibly unique among poets in the extensiveness of his reference to eating and drinking and to its pleasurable or distasteful sensations. To some readers this is likely to be alienating, and indeed even a staunch admirer might well become restive under, for example, Keats's excessive reliance on the word "dainties" to suggest all pleasures, even the pleasures of literature. It is surely possible to understand what led Yeats to speak of Keats as a boy with his face pressed to the window of a sweet-shop. The mild and not unsympathetic derogation of Yeats's image suggests something of the reason for the negative part of our ambivalence toward eating and drinking. The ingestive appetite is the most primitive of our appetites, the

---

*The phrase "manna from heaven" is a common one, but no one ever says "quail from heaven," even though the quail were just as important as the manna in the diet which was divinely provided for the Children of Israel in the wilderness; manna, we might say, was but the divine dessert. Yet because manna was evanescent and is not to be identified with any known edible thing, it has come to serve as a metaphor for miraculous sustenance and spiritual comfort; the quail, being all too grossly actual, have been quite forgotten!

sole appetite of our infant state, and a preoccupation with it, an excessive emphasis upon it, is felt—and not without some reason—to imply the passivity and self-reference of the infantile condition. No doubt that is why Ciacco, the glutton of the *Inferno*, although not accounted the worst sinner in hell, is, as it were, the most dehumanized—not the most *inhuman* as we habitually use that word, but the most disgusting; he has not even grown into the adult activity which might lead to aggressive wickedness, but sits passive under the fall of stinking snow: his is the peculiar horribleness of a grown man who is still an infant. And religious satirists of modern life, such as Aldous Huxley, T. S. Eliot, or Graham Greene, when they wish to make a character represent the malign infantilism of our contemporary materialist culture, ascribe to him an undue and detailed interest in eating. In this connection it is worth noting that we consent to be delighted by the description of great feasts as in Homer, Rabelais, and Dickens; the communal aspect of the eating implies "maturity" and allays our fears of infantile narcissism. This is especially true if the food is plain and hearty and does not suggest cosseting, and if the appetites match it in this respect, for largeness of appetite has a moral sanction which fineness of appetite can never have.

But Keats did not share our culture's fear of the temptation to the passive self-reference of infancy. He did not repress the infantile wish; he confronted it, recognized it, and delighted in it. Food—and what for the infant usually goes with food, a cozy warmth—made for him the form, the elementary idea, of felicity. He did not fear the seduction of the wish for felicity, because, it would seem, he was assured that the tendency of his being was not that of regression but that of growth. The knowledge of felicity was his first experience—he made it the ground of all experience, the foundation of his quest for truth. Thus, for Keats, the luxury of food is connected with, and in a sense gives place to the luxury of sexuality. The best known example of this is the table spread with "dainties" beside Madeline's bed in *The Eve of St. Agnes*. And in that famous scene the whole paraphernalia of luxurious felicity, the invoked warmth of the south, the bland and delicate food, the privacy of the bed, and the voluptuousness of the sexual encounter, are made to glow into an island of bliss with the ultimate dramatic purpose of making fully apparent the cold surrounding darkness; it is the moment of life in the infinitude of not-being. As an image of man's life it has the force of the Venerable Bede's apologue of the sparrow that flew out of the night of winter storm through the warmth and light of the king's ale-hall and out again into darkness. Keats's capacity for pleasure implies his capacity for the apprehension of tragic reality.

It also serves his capacity for what he called "abstraction." I have said that he was the most Platonic of poets. Ideas, abstractions, were his life. He lived to perceive ultimate things, essences. This is what appetite, or love, was always coming to mean for him. Plato said that Love is the child of Abundance and Want, and for Keats it was just that. In one of the most remarkable passages of his letters he says that the heart "is the teat from which the mind or intelligence sucks identity." The first appetite prefigures the last; the first ingestive image is constant for this man who, in his last sonnet, speaks of "the palate of my mind," and who images the totality of life by the single grape which is burst against "the palate fine."

4

What I have called Keats's geniality toward himself, his bold acceptance of his primitive appetite and his having kept open a line of communication with it, had its decisive effect upon the nature of his creative intelligence. It had an effect no less decisive upon his moral character.

In speaking of Keats's appetitive inclination, we cannot ignore the element of heredity. There has been ascribed to his mother's father an extravagant concern with food—Mr. Jennings was said to have been so extreme in his love of eating that his wife and family spent four days in the week preparing for the Sunday dinner. His daughter, Keats's mother, was said to have resembled him in this gormandizing character, "but she was more remarkably the Slave of other Appetites attributable probably to this for their exciting Cause." The witness, to be sure, is Mr. Abbey, Keats's guardian, who was no doubt narrow in his views, and admirers of Keats naturally dislike him and allow him little credit or credence. Yet it was to the admirable John Taylor, Keats's publisher and loyal friend, that Abbey told his story; Taylor was an intelligent man and he must have known in some detail of the dealings of Abbey with the Keats children, yet Taylor speaks of Abbey as "kind hearted" and "good," and did not, as we are inclined to do, dismiss his testimony out of a pious partisanship but, on the contrary, thought him a man worthy of belief. And although

Abbey may well have been exaggerating, he was not necessarily making it up out of whole cloth when he said that the young Frances Jennings was so ardent in her passions that it was dangerous to be alone with her, and that at an early age she had told him that she must have and would have a husband. We make what discount we will for Mr. Abbey's susceptibility and for his narrowness of view, even for his spite, and still we cannot but suppose that Frances was of a lively and straightforward sexual temperament. Abbey said that she was a pretty little woman (but Cowden Clark says she was tall) with regular features, although her mouth was too wide. He remembered that she troubled a certain shopkeeper on rainy days because she held her skirts too high in crossing the street, showing "uncommonly handsome legs."*

Whether or not Frances Keats was, in the conventional sense, a good woman and a good mother is a hard judgment to make. The piety of biographers inclines to say that she was, or at least that she was not bad, and explains her second marriage three months after the death of her husband as a necessary practical step to maintain the livery stable, and dismisses as a mere canard Abbey's story that after leaving Rawlings, the unendurable second husband, she formed a liaison with a Jew named Abraham and became addicted to brandy. Yet it is a remarkable fact that in all of Keats's letters, many of which are to his brothers and sister, there is but a single reference to their mother, and this but a trifling one. (There is no mention at all of his father.) Keats was fifteen when his mother died (nine at the death of his father) so that he was certainly not without memory of her. We might suppose that in the normal course of things he would speak of her, that, in his tender letters to his sister Fanny, he would try to keep the mother's image alive in the little girl's mind. But we have not a word. There was much, it would seem, to be forgotten.

Yet it would also seem that there was much to be, in some fashion, remembered. Reynolds tells us that when John, at school, received the news of her death he was inconsolable. "When his mother died, which was suddenly—he gave way to such impassioned and prolonged grief—(hiding himself in a nook under the master's desk) as awakened the liveliest pity and sympathy in all who saw him." And George Keats, in a letter

---

*Abbey's account of Mrs. Keats is reported in a letter of John Taylor as given in *The Keats Circle*, edited by Hyder Edward Rollins (Cambridge, Massachusetts, 1948). The testimony of George Keats and of Reynolds, cited in the following pages, is from the same source.

to Dilke, makes what is, I believe, the only significant reference by one of the Keats children to their mother: he says she "resembled John very much in the face, was extremely fond of him and humored him in every whim, of which he had not a few." He adds: "She was a most excellent and affectionate parent and as I thought a woman of uncommon talents."

We may take George's estimate of his mother as the expression of filial decency, or as the truth, or as some part of the truth. Yet there would seem to be no reason to question, there is indeed reason to suppose, her affectionate and indulgent nature—what we may call a biological generosity. It is then not difficult to understand the genesis of Keats's preoccupation with a felicity of "dainties," kisses, and coziness.

But how are we to understand the heroic quality of Keats, the quality of moral energy? In part, it is clear, by reference to Keats's temperamental endowment. We read of the violent child of five who armed himself with a sword and brandished it on guard at the door and refused to let his mother leave the house; the story in this form is given by Haydon, who is not reliable, though usually apt, in the stories he tells; another version of the story is that Keats used the sword to keep anyone from entering his mother's room when she was ill. We read of the schoolboy who would fight anyone—he offered to fight one of the ushers who had boxed his brother Tom's ears—and of whom it was said that anyone might easily fancy he would become great, but rather in some military capacity than in literature. The traits that make up what Plato calls the "spirited" part of the soul were early and extreme in Keats. But Keats himself made, as we may, a clear genetic connection between felicity and manly energy. He who had stood guard at the door—whether to keep his mother safe from invaders or to keep her captive—wrote in *Endymion* of the happy pastoral people of Latmos as those fair creatures "whose young children's children bred / Thermopylae its heroes," and omitted all mention of any intervening period of Spartan training. When he laid down the program of his development as a poet, he stipulated that the first phase of his life in poetry be devoted to sensual felicity as a prelude to his confrontation of the noble pain of existence.

It is possible to say of Keats that the indulgence of his childhood goes far toward explaining the remarkable firmness of his character, what I have spoken of as his heroic quality. This is not the occasion to engage upon a discussion of the theory of child-rearing. Such discussions, as conducted by laymen, and even as conducted by experts, are all too likely to be unmodulated, contrasting an unqualified indulgence or "permissive-ness" with an equally unqualified disciplinary attitude. Indulgence is of many kinds and may be given in many contexts. Strength of character is also of different kinds, and it is necessary to ask what kind of strength our method of rearing seeks to inculcate. Thus there can be no doubt that a vigorous and strictly disciplinary training can indeed produce strength of a kind, even of an admirable kind. But, granting the complexity of the subject, I would yet venture to deal with it to the extent of proposing the idea that the person who was happily indulged as a child can in maturity—to use Keats's words—"bid these joys farewell" and "leave them for a nobler life," doing so of his own volition, with the moral advantages which attend upon free choice. His need of the childish joys has been satisfied, his will has not been fixed upon them.

"How strange it seems," says John Taylor after having retailed Mr. Abbey's account of Keats's parents, "that such a creature of the Elements as he should have sprung from such gross Realities—But how he refined upon the sensualities of his parents." How he refined indeed, but his relation to the "gross Realities" is not strange at all, or not strange in the way that Taylor meant. For the great and remarkable thing about Keats is that he did not refine by negation but by natural growth, by the tendency of life *to* refine. And when he had reached the top of the Platonic ladder of the appetites and had come as close as he could to what he called "fellow-ship with essence," he had no wish to kick over the ladder by which he had climbed. He felt free at any moment to climb down to the bottom-most rung, to put himself in touch with his first appetites. He was, as Taylor says, "a creature of the Elements," but he never forgot, as Taylor apparently did, that the elements include not only air, fire, and water, but also earth.

This license to put himself in touch with his first appetites, this un-questioning faith in pleasure, has played an important part in the developing estimate of Keats. It accounts for the need felt by certain of his partisans to insist that he was really a very manly young person. As the biographical and critical studies accumulate, the insistence is ever more strongly made, but even at its strongest it carries the implication that Keats was very manly *after all*, that we can see the manliness if we look close: the boy with his face pressed to the sweet-shop window is the image that persists, if only to be corrected.

But the fact is that Keats's mature masculinity is not something that is to be discovered by special perceptiveness. It is the essence of his being. One hesitates to say what one means by mature masculinity when the cultural anthropologists have been at such pains to disturb our old notions of it, and when in modern culture so much confusion exists about its nature and its value. Yet we may venture to say that in the traditional culture of Europe it has existed as an ideal that implies a direct relationship to the world of external reality, which, by activity, it seeks to understand, or to master, or to come to honorable terms with; and it implies fortitude, and responsibility for both one's duties and one's fate, and intention, and an insistence upon one's personal value and honor.

It is impossible to read Keats's letters without seeing that this was indeed his personal ideal. And the way he held it, the grace of his holding it, suggests to me that it grew easily and gently out of his happy relation with his infant appetites. To insist upon the growth of this ideal as a natural thing, and upon its not having negated what it grew out of, is not to deny all conflict. After all, Keats did institute a kind of antagonism between the idea of luxury and the idea of energetic morality. But in a complex and difficult culture the development of personality, even at its easiest and most natural, proceeds always by conflict—Freud speaks of the erroneous belief of laymen that all neuroses (i.e., psychic conflicts) "are entirely superfluous things which have no right whatever to exist." We may not unreasonably suppose of Keats that both the seductiveness and the disorderliness that attended his mother's biological generosity made conflict the more necessary and the more lively. But what is characteristic of Keats is that the conflict is never to the death, is never cruel. He seems never to have wished to injure or destroy any part of himself. The conflicting ideals seem to understand each other and to wish to come to terms with each other.

As good an instance as any of the firmness, the developed strength of Keats's character is his simple probity in money matters. Even to himself this simple virtue seemed of great significance. It was often necessary for him to draw upon his publishers, Taylor and Hessey, who treated him with a generosity which was no doubt made the easier for them by Keats's financial punctiliousness. To Taylor he writes of "the sense of squareness in me" and of his "desire to be correct in money matters." He generalizes upon this exactitude in a striking way: in August of 1819 he writes to Taylor explaining why, in taking an advance, he prefers to secure the money by a note endorsed by his friend Brown. "I must observe again," he says, "that it is not from want of reliance on your readiness to assist me that I offer a Bill; but as a relief to myself from too lax a Sensation of Life—which ought to be responsible, which requires chains for its own sake—duties to fulfill with the more earnestness the less strictly they are imposed."

I have referred to the remark made by an old schoolfellow that Keats was a boy whom anyone might easily have fancied would become great, but rather "in some military capacity than in literature." And there is indeed in Keats's character a sort of ideal military virtue whenever he confronts the difficulties of life. What he calls the "flint-worded" letter of August 16, 1819, to Fanny Brawne, is full of military references as he discusses their situation, his lack of money, his powers of work. "This Page as my eye skims over it I see is excessively unloverlike and ungallant—I cannot help it—I am no officer yawning in quarters." He is, that is to say, in action. He says he cannot, will not, be careless of his friends' money. "You see how I go on," he says, "like so many strokes of a Hammer. I cannot help it—I am impelled, driven to it. I am not happy enough for silken phrases, silver sentences. I can no more use soothing words to you than if I were at this moment engaged in a charge of Cavalry." He is hard at work—as he says, "in the fever." "I would feign, as my sails are set, sail on without interruption for a brace of Months longer." The sailing image is in his mind because he is about to tell Fanny of an incident of naval fortitude which had moved him to admiration: the ship in which he was sailing to Southampton had with its bowlines snapped the top of the mast of a Navy launch. "Had the mast been a little stouter they would have been upset. In so trifling an event I could not help admiring our Seamen—neither officer nor man in the whole Boat moved a Muscle—they scarcely notic'd it even with words—Forgive me this Flint-worded Letter, and believe that I cannot think of you without energy of some sort—though mal a propos."

This is Keats's characteristic tone when he confronts the necessity of action. We know with what dread he contemplates the Italian journey, but, as he writes to Shelley, he will undertake it "as a soldier marches up to a battery," and he uses the same image to Taylor. Poetry was his life, yet when he wishes to praise poetry he says, "I am convinced more and more day by day that fine writing is next to fine doing the top thing in the world. . . ." With him the deed comes before the word. The deed is, as it were, the guarantor of the word. Even the dull action of getting a living was charged for him with heroic meaning. Disappointed in the expectation of a financial competence and faced with the necessity of supporting himself, he came to understand that he could live only by his own exertions and self-denial. "I had got into the habit of looking towards you as a help in all difficulties," he writes to Brown. "This very habit would be the parent of idleness and difficulties. You will see it as a duty I owe myself to break the neck of it. I do nothing for my subsistence—make no exertion. At the end of another year you shall applaud me not for verses but for conduct." He was one, as he had said some years before, to "volunteer for uncomfortable hours." He had that in him "which would bear the buffets of the world."

The remarkable statement to Fanny Brawne, "I cannot think of you without some sort of energy," tells us much. Energy is of his essence. It is the basis of his conception of morality, although it may transcend morality. "Though a quarrel in the Streets is a thing to be hated, the energies displayed in it are fine; the commonest Man shows a grace in his quarrel—By a Superior being our reasonings may take the same tone—though erroneous they may be fine."

In his own life he recognizes two states of being which would seem equally opposed to energy. One is what he calls "agonie ennuiyeuse" or despair—"I must choose," he says, "between despair and Energy." The other is a happy passivity, what he calls indolence—"a sort of temper indolent and supremely careless"—or languor or laziness: "If I had teeth of pearl and the breath of lillies I should call it languor—but as I am [his own footnote here: "Especially as I have a black eye"] I must call it laziness." And he goes on: "In this state of effeminacy the fibres of the brain are relaxed in common with the rest of the body, and to such a happy degree that pleasure has no show of enticement and pain no unbearable frown."

"Agonie ennuiyeuse" is, of course, spleen, or melancholy, or acedia: it is the very opposite of energy. But there is no real antagonism between Keats's "indolence" and his energy. Keats's great statement of the principle of passivity is contained in the marvelous letter to Reynolds of February 19, 1818. This letter, unpremeditated as it is, has the effect of a work of contrived art as it accumulates its similitudes and intensifies its meaning until at last it becomes incandescent in the lovely blank-verse sonnet of the thrush, with its reiterated "O fret not after knowledge—I have none." It is the exposition of the principle of the *power* of passivity, of what Keats calls "diligent Indolence." The passivity in question is of course related to Wordsworth's "wise passiveness," but it is far more richly characterized. Significantly enough, it is characterized in a sexual way: "Who shall say between Man and Woman which is the most delighted?"—that is, in the sexual act.* And he has in mind the power of conception, incubation, gestation. It is not the least remarkable thing about Keats that, for all his "tendency to class women in my books with roses and sweetmeats,—they never see themselves dominant," he had an awareness, rare in our culture, of the female principle as a power, an energy. He does not shrink from experiencing its manifestation in himself, believing it to be half of his power of creation. Yet bold as he is in this, he must still assert the virtue of the specifically "masculine" energy: even the thrush assures him that "he's awake who thinks himself asleep," that by being conscious of his surrender to the passive, unconscious life he has affirmed the active principle.

5

The dialectic which Keats instituted between passivity and activity presents itself in another form, in the opposition between thought and sensation. The case against the notion that Keats was systematically anti-intellectual has been conclusively made by Professor Clarence Thorpe, but apparently for each new generation of readers the evidence of his hostility to intellect seems more dramatic and decisive than that of his almost extravagant respect for intellect. His having said, "Oh for a life of Sensation rather than Thoughts," his having with Lamb drunk confusion to Newton, his general concurrence in the antagonism to eighteenth-century rationalism which prevailed in his set, and perhaps especially what is usually understood to be the doctrine of *Lamia*, are taken to lend sanction to the belief that Keats was uniformly hostile to the exercise of the conscious mind. But Keats is far less simple than this

---

*It is perhaps worth recalling that an answer to this question is given in the classical dictionary which Keats used—Lemprière's. Tiresias, who had been transformed into a woman and then, after some years, restored to his original sex, was asked to settle a dispute between Juno and Jupiter and gave it as his opinion that women have ten times the pleasure of men. This so angered Juno that she deprived Tiresias of his eyesight; in compensation Jupiter bestowed upon him the gift of prophecy.

would make him out to be. The injunction of the thrush's song, "O fret not after knowledge," had great authority with him, yet he did fret after knowledge and thought it right to do so. When he speaks of applying himself energetically to poetry, he conceives of that application as being in part to reading and study. "I know nothing, I have read nothing and I mean to follow Solomon's direction of 'get Wisdom—get understanding'—I find cavalier days are gone by. I find that I can have no enjoyment in the World but a continual drinking of Knowledge— . . . There is one way for me—the road lies through application, study and thought."

The idea that Keats was anti-intellectual used to be easier to maintain when it was believed that, as one nineteenth-century critic put it, "Keats had no mind." To us the power of his mind is even more astonishing than the opinion that he had none, and we can scarcely be surprised that he should delight in its exercise. He did not think that difficult or abstract reading could corrupt his poetic impulse, and he was glad that he had kept his medical books; he found "every department of Knowledge . . . excellent and calculated towards a great whole." He conceived the emotional effect of knowledge to be analogous to that of poetry, which for him was successful when it led the reader to calmness. "An extensive knowledge is needful to thinking people—it takes away the heat and fever; and helps by widening speculation to ease the Border of the mystery." He said that "high Sensations" without knowledge induced anxiety—"horror"—but knowledge prevented fear. His judgment of his "Isabella" is that it has "too much inexperience of life and simplicity of knowledge in it."

He could, as we have seen, rate poetry inferior to action; he could also rate it inferior to philosophy. In the passage already referred to, in which he talks about how the charm of energy may be thought to redeem error, he says, "This is the very thing in which consists poetry; and if so it is not so fine a thing as philosophy—For the same reason that an eagle is not so fine a thing as a truth." He then goes on to say that he now understands from experience the force of Milton's line, "how charming is divine Philosophy." To Keats ideas were what Milton said they were, "musical as Apollo's lute," and he conceived that in heaven, where the potentiality of all things is realized, the nightingale will sing "not as a senseless tranced thing" but will utter philosophic truth.

If Keats did not accept the traditional antagonism between sensation and poetry on the one hand and intellect and knowledge on the other, it was because he understood intellect and knowledge in a certain way. He did not, that is, suppose that mind was an entity different in kind from and hostile to the sensations and emotions. Rather, mind came into being when the sensations and emotions were checked by external resistance or by conflict with each other, when, to use the language of Freud, the pleasure principle is confronted by the reality principle. Now, in Keats the reality principle was very strong. Was it ever by anyone more starkly asserted than in the phrase he used to Fanny Brawne: "I would mention that there are impossibilities in this world"? And it was strong in proportion to the strength of the pleasure principle. Philosophy and knowledge, the matter of the intellect, were for him associated in their old traditional way with the burden of life: to be "philosophical" means to acknowledge with the mind the pain of the world, and it means to derive courage from taking thought. "Until we are sick, we understand not;—in fine, as Byron says, 'Knowledge is Sorrow'; and I go on to say 'Sorrow is Wisdom.'"*

But the sentence does not end here. It goes on: "—and further for ought we know for certainty 'Wisdom is folly'!" This is perhaps a mere flourish to dismiss the subject. But it is also something more. It is an instance of Keats's urge toward the dialectical view of any large question, of his refusal to be fixed in a final judgment. As such it points toward that faculty of the mind to which Keats gave the name of "Negative Capability."

No one reading the letters of Keats can come on the phrase and its definition without feeling that among the many impressive utterances of the letters this one is especially momentous. It is, indeed, not too much to say that the power and quality of Keats's mind concentrate in this phrase, as does the energy of his heroism, for the conception of Negative Capability leads us to Keats's transactions with the problem of evil, and to know the high temper of his mind we must follow where it leads.

6

On 21 December 1817, Keats wrote to his brothers, telling them, among other things, of his having gone to the Christmas pantomime with his

---

*Byron actually said, "Sorrow is knowledge." (*Manfred* I. i. 10)

friends Brown and Dilke and that, while walking home with them, he had what he called "not a dispute but a disquisition" with Dilke. The disquisition touched on "various subjects" which are not specified, and Keats says that as it proceeded "several things dove-tailed in my mind and at once it struck me what quality went to make a man of Achievement, especially in literature. . . . I mean *Negative Capability*, that is, when a man is capable of being in uncertainties, mysteries, doubts, without any irritable reaching after fact and reason."

In an ideological age such as ours the faculty of Negative Capability is a rare one, and Keats's naming and defining it attracts a good deal of notice either for praise or blame. It is often misunderstood. Thus, it is sometimes taken to mean that poetry should have no traffic with ideas, and that the creative writer is exempt from the judgment of intellectual validity. This is not in the least Keats's intention. Keats thinks of Negative Capability as, precisely, an element of intellectual power. At a later time, taking up the subject again,* he says, "the only means of strengthening one's intellect is to make up one's mind about nothing—to let the mind be a thoroughfare for all thoughts. Not a select party. . . ."

But this statement, although it clears away any doubts of the specifically intellectual nature of Negative Capability, is in itself very questionable. On its face it is obviously not true—it is certainly not true that "to make up one's mind about nothing" is the only means of strengthening one's intellect. Exclusion is quite as much a part of the intellectual process as inclusion, and making up one's mind is not only the end of intellection but one of the means of intellection. Yet Keats's statement may well be true in reference to a certain kind of person and to a certain kind of problem—to a certain kind of person dealing with a certain kind of problem. It is essential to an understanding of what Keats meant that we have in mind the kind of person who was Keats's interlocutor in the "disquisition" during which the idea came to him, and also the kind of problem that was at the moment preoccupying Keats's thought.

Charles Wentworth Dilke was a man whom Keats knew to be not only very good but very intelligent. But Keats was of the settled opinion that Dilke was far too doctrinaire in his intellect. He calls him a "Godwin perfectibility man," and because it is not only the doctrine of human per-

---

*But he never uses the famous phrase again.

fectibility that is important in his judgment of Dilke—although it is *very* important—but also the over-systematic process of thought by which the doctrine is arrived at and maintained, he calls Dilke a "Godwin methodist." And he says of his friend that he "will never come at a truth so long as he lives; because he is always trying at it." This is a habit of mind which Dilke shares with Coleridge—in the passage in which Keats formulates the idea of Negative Capability, he cites Coleridge as an example of "irritable reaching after fact and reason." Coleridge, he says, was incapable of "remaining content with half-knowledge."

We are aware of a simple paradox, for traditionally truth must be striven for—*ad astra per aspera*. And half-knowledge is a sciolist's knowledge and "a dangerous thing." But we must consider the particular kind of problem to which the exercise of Negative Capability is appropriate. It will not be a scientific problem (although more than one great discoverer in science has said that at times it is well to suspend the irritable reaching after fact and reason, to let the mind be a thoroughfare for all thoughts or no thoughts, that then the data often speak unbidden). It will be a human problem—Shakespeare is Keats's example of a mind content with half-knowledge, "capable of being in uncertainties, mysteries, doubts." And in point of fact it is a particular and very large human problem, nothing less than the problem of evil.

This becomes apparent if we follow the line of thought that has been begun earlier in the letter. Before writing about the Christmas pantomime and Negative Capability, Keats tells his brothers that he has been to see Benjamin West's picture "Death on the Pale Horse." He says that "it is a wonderful picture, when West's age is considered" (West was nearly eighty), but that he does not really admire it. One objection to it that he makes is that "there is nothing to be intense upon; no woman one feels mad to kiss, no face smiling into reality." Another objection is the artist's way of handling what Keats calls "disagreeables." "The excellence of every art," he says, "is its intensity, capable of making all disagreeables evaporate, from their being in close relation with Beauty and Truth. Examine 'King Lear,' and you will find this exemplified throughout, but in this picture we have unpleasantness without any momentous depth of speculation excited in which to bury its repulsiveness." And this theme is picked up again when Keats brings to an end his definition of Negative Capability: when he has made the famous remark about half-knowledge and remaining in "uncertainties, mysteries, doubts," he says that the subject, if "pursued through volumes would perhaps take us not further than this, that with a great poet the sense of Beauty overcomes every other consideration, or rather obliterates all consideration."

With this sentence we are at the very center of Keats's theory of art. It is a theory of extreme complexity and I shall not attempt to deal with it here. But the element of the theory that chiefly makes for its complexity—and its power—must at least be mentioned. Keats's theory of art is, among other things, an effort to deal with the problem of evil.

A contemporary literate mind is likely to be made uncomfortable by certain of the things that Keats says about the representation of evil in art, by the open resistance he makes to "disagreeables." We find him, for example in "Sleep and Poetry," being very harsh with certain of his contemporaries, Byron in particular, over the subjects of their poetry. The themes, he says, are ugly clubs, the poets Polyphemes. And he quite shocks the modern literate mind by requiring of poetry that it should not "feed upon the burrs and thorns of life" and by judging those poets to be most worthy of respect "who simply tell the most heart-easing things." This is an opinion that will seem to us to have been dredged up from the depths of philistinism. We can scarcely understand how a true poet, let alone a great poet, could have uttered it.

Similarly, when Keats concludes his remarks about Negative Capability with the observation that "with a great poet the sense of Beauty overcomes every other consideration, or rather obliterates all consideration," meaning all considerations of what is disagreeable or painful, it may seem that he has evaded the issue, that, having raised the question of painful truth in art, he betrays it to beauty in a statement that really has no meaning. It is in this way that many readers understand the concluding aphorism, the "moral," of the "Ode to a Grecian Urn"—out of politeness to poetry they may consent to be teased, but they cannot suppose that they are enlightened by the statement "Beauty is truth, truth beauty," for, as they say, beauty is not all of truth, and not all truth is beautiful. Nor will they be the more disposed to find meaning in the notorious aphorism by the poet's extravagant assertion that in it is to be found "all/Ye know on earth, and all ye need to know."

But the statement "Beauty is truth, truth beauty," was not for Keats, and need not be for us, a "pseudo-statement," large, resonant, engaging, but without actual significance. Beauty was not for Keats, as it is for many, an inert thing, or a thing whose value lay in having no relevance to ordinary life: it was not a word by which he evaded, but a word by which he confronted, issues. What he is saying in his letter is that a great poet (e.g., Shakespeare) looks at human life, sees the terrible truth of its evil, but sees it so intensely that it becomes an element of the beauty which is created by his act of perception—in the phrase by which Keats describes his own experience as merely a reader of *King Lear*, he "burns through" the evil. To say, as many do, that "truth is beauty" is a false statement is to ignore our experience of the tragic art. Keats's statement is an accurate description of the response to evil or ugliness which tragedy makes: the matter of tragedy is ugly or painful truth seen as beauty. To see life in this way, Keats believes, is to see life truly: that is, as it must be seen if we are to endure to live it. Beauty is thus a middle term which connects and reconciles two kinds of truth—through the mediation of beauty, truth of fact becomes truth of affirmation, truth of life. For we must understand about Keats that he sought strenuously to discover the reason why we should live, and that he called those things good, or beautiful, or true, which induced us to live or which conduced to our health. (He had not walked the hospital wards for nothing.)

This way of seeing life, the poet's way, characterized by "intensity," is obviously anything but a "negative" capability—it is the most *positive* capability imaginable. But Keats understood it to be protected and made possible by Negative Capability: the poet avoids making those doctrinal utterances about the nature of life, about life's goodness or badness or perfectibility, which, if he rests in them, will prevent his going on to his full poetic vision.

At this point Keats's opinion of Dilke becomes important again. Keats believed that the Negative Capability which made possible the poetic vision of life depended upon a certain personal quality which he thought Dilke lacked. Of that poor Dilke who will never come at a truth so long as he lives because he is always trying at it, Keats says that he is "a man who cannot feel that he has a personal identity unless he has made up his mind about everything." Negative Capability, the faculty of not having to make up one's mind about everything, depends upon the sense of one's personal identity and is the sign of personal identity. Only the self that is certain of its existence, of its identity, can do without the armor of systematic certainties.* To remain content with half-knowledge is to remain content with contradictory knowledges; it is to believe that "sorrow is wisdom" and also that "wisdom is folly." It is not all of truth that Keats is concerned with but rather that truth which is to be discovered between the contradiction of love and death, between the sense of personal identity and the certainty of pain and extinction.

Along with other of the English romantic poets, Keats is often said to have lacked an adequate awareness of evil and to have failed to see it as a condition of life and a problem of thought. I have indicated my belief that the contrary of this is true, that the problem of evil lies at the very heart of Keats's thought. But for Keats the awareness of evil exists side by side with a very strong sense of personal identity and is for that reason the less immediately apparent. To some contemporary readers it will seem for the same reason the less intense. In the same way it may seem to a contemporary reader that, if we compare Shakespeare and Kafka, leaving aside the degree of genius each has, and considering both only as expositors of man's suffering and cosmic alienation, it is Kafka who makes the more intense and complete exposition. And indeed the judgment may be correct, exactly because for Kafka the sense of evil is not contradicted by the sense of personal identity. Shakespeare's world, quite as much as Kafka's, is that prison cell which Pascal says the world is, from which daily the inmates are led forth to die; Shakespeare no less than Kafka forces upon us the cruel irrationality of the conditions of human life, the tale told by an idiot, the puerile gods who torture us not for punishment but for sport; and no less than Kafka, Shakespeare is revolted by the fetor of the prison of this world, nothing is more characteristic of him than his imagery of disgust. But in Shakespeare's cell the company is so much better than in Kafka's; the captains and kings and lovers and clowns of Shakespeare are alive and complete before they die. In Kafka, long before the sentence is executed, even long before the malign legal process is ever instituted, something terrible has been done to the accused. We all know what that is—he has been stripped of all that is becoming to a man except his abstract humanity, which, like his skeleton, never is quite becoming to a man. He is without parents, home, wife, child, commitment, or ap-

*This is only apparently contradicted by certain notable remarks which Keats made about men of genius in poetry *lacking* personal identity. (See the letter to Bailey of 22 November 1817 and the letter to Woodhouse of 27 October 1818.) In these passages he is speaking of the poet as poet, not of the poet as man.

petite; he has no connection with power, beauty, love, wit, courage, loyalty, or fame, and the pride that may be taken in these. So that we may say that Kafka's knowledge of evil exists without the contradictory knowledge of the self in its health and validity, that Shakespeare's knowledge of evil exists with that contradiction in its fullest possible force.* It is therefore not hard to understand the virtually religious reverence in which Shakespeare began to be held in the nineteenth century, for when religion seemed no longer able to represent the actualities of life, it was likely to be Shakespeare who, to a thoughtful man, most fully confronted the truth of life's complex horror, while yet conveying the stubborn sense that life was partly blessed, not wholly cursed.

Now Keats's attachment to the principle of reality was, as I have said, a strong one. He perceived the fact of evil very clearly, and he put it at the very center of his mental life. He saw, as he said, "too far into the sea" and beheld there the "eternal fierce destruction" of the struggle for existence, and the shark and the hawk at prey taught him that the gentle and habitual robin was not less predatory, that life in its totality was cruel; he saw youth grow pale and specter-thin and die, saw life trod down by life, the hungry generations on the march. For all his partisanship with social amelioration, he had no hope whatever that life could be ordered in such a way that its condition might be anything but tragic. He was not a theological mind like Kafka—some other adjective of large import must be used to suggest the scope and dignity of the questions with which he was preoccupied—yet evil presented its problem to him in the theological or quasi-theological form in which alone it has any meaning. What is traditionally and technically called the problem of evil raises a question about the nature of God, who is said to be both benevolent and omnipotent, for man's experience of pain would seem to limit either God's benevolence or his power. And the evil which makes the problem truly a problem is neither that which is the natural outcome of man's wrong deeds, nor that which may be understood, by any human conception of justice, as divine punishment. In the Book of Job the problem of evil cannot be really stated until the ground has been cleared of the conventional apologetics which try to explain Job's suffering as punishment for his sins: the

---

*It would, of course, be less than accurate and fair not to remark of Kafka that he had a very intense knowledge of the self through its negation, that his great and terrible point is exactly the horror of the loss of the Shakespearean knowledge of the self.

divine voice itself says that the suffering is not a punishment. For Dostoyevsky the problem of evil must be stated in terms of the suffering of children—of human creatures, that is, of whom we cannot say that their pain is the consequence of their guilt. And Keats, who thought of women as exempt from the moral life of men, and therefore not to be held responsible or guilty, conceives the problem of evil with particular reference to them. "Why," he asks, "should women suffer?" And that *women* should "have cancers" is to him a conclusive instance of the unexplainable cruelty of the cosmos.

But at the same time that Keats had his clear knowledge of evil, he had his equally clear knowledge of the self. Most of us are conventional in our notions of reality and we suppose that what is grim and cruel is more real than what is pleasant. Like most conventionalities of thought, this one is a form of power-worship—evil and pain seem realer to us than the assertions of the self because we know that evil and pain always win in the end. But Keats did not share in our acquiescence. His attachment to reality was stronger and more complex than ours usually is, for to him the self was just as real as the evil that destroys it. The idea of reality and the idea of the self and its annihilation go together for him. "After all there is certainly something real in the World—. . . . Tom [his brother] has spit a leetle blood this afternoon, and that is rather a damper—but I know—the truth is there is something real in the World." He conceives of the energy of the self as at least one source of reality. "As Tradesmen say every thing is worth what it will fetch, so probably every mental pursuit takes its reality and worth from the ardour of the pursuer—being in itself a nothing." And again: "I am certain of nothing but of the holiness of the heart's affections and the truth of the Imagination—What the Imagination seizes as Beauty must be truth—whether it existed before or not—for I have the same Idea of all our Passions as of Love they are all, in their sublime, creative of essential Beauty. . . . The Imagination may be compared to Adam's dream [in *Paradise Lost*]—he awoke and found it truth."

He affirms, that is, the creativity of the self that opposes circumstance, the self that is imagination and desire, that, like Adam, assigns names and values to things, and that can realize what it envisions.

Keats never deceives himself into believing that the power of the imagination is sovereign, that it can make the power of circumstance of no account. His sense of the stubborn actuality of the material world is as stalwart as Wordsworth's. It is, indeed, of the very nature of his whole intellectual and moral activity that he should hold in balance the reality of self and the reality of circumstance. In another letter to Bailey he makes the two realities confront each other in a very telling way. He is speaking of the malignity of society toward generous enthusiasm and, as he goes on, his thought moves from the life of society to touch upon the cosmos, whose cruelty, as he thinks of it, impels him to reject the life in poetry and the reward of fame he so dearly wants. "Were it in my choice," he says, "I would reject a petrarchal coronation—on account of my dying day and because women have cancers." But then in the next sentence but one: "And yet I am not old enough or magnanimous enough to annihilate self. . . ." He has brought his two knowledges face to face, the knowledge of the world of circumstance, of death and cancer, and the knowledge of the world of self, of spirit and creation, and the delight in them. Each seems a whole knowledge considered alone; each is but a half-knowledge when taken with the other; both together constitute a truth.

It is in terms of the self confronting hostile or painful circumstance that Keats makes his magnificent effort at the solution of the problem of evil, his heroic attempt to show how it is that life may be called blessed when its circumstances are cursed. This occurs in the course of his dazzling letter to George and Georgiana Keats in Kentucky which he began on 14 February 1819, and sealed on 3 May. It is a massive journal-letter into which Keats copies, among lesser examples of his work, the sonnet "Why did I laugh to-night?," the two sonnets on fame, "La Belle Dame Sans Merci," the sonnet on sleep and the sonnet on rhyme, and the "Ode to Psyche." It is crammed full of gossip, personal, literary, and theatrical, and equally full of Keats's most serious and characteristic thought. The letter, indeed, is the quintessence of Keats's life-style, of his way of dealing with experience. It is one of the most remarkable documents of the culture of the century.

The climax of the letter occurs in the last full entry, that of 15 April, in which Keats makes his dead-set at the problem of evil. This entry is the first after that of 19 March, which in itself constitutes a very notable episode in Keats's intellectual life. The earlier entry is Keats's attempt to deal with the problem in aesthetic terms, as the later is his attempt to deal with it in moral terms. In the 19 March entry he writes that he is in a state of languorous relaxation in which "pleasure has no show of enticement and pain no unbearable frown," a condition which he calls "the only happiness." But at the moment of setting this down he receives a note from

Haslam telling of the imminently expected death of his friend's father, and he is led to speak of the ironic mutability of life. "While we are laughing the seed of some trouble is put into the wide arable land of event—while we are laughing it sprouts it grows and suddenly bears a poison fruit which we must pluck." Then follows a meditation on our inability really to respond to the troubles of our friends and on the virtue of "disinterestedness." This leads to the thought that disinterestedness, so great a virtue in society, is not to be found in "wild nature," where its presence, indeed, would destroy the natural economy of tooth and claw. But from the spectacle of self-interested cruelty of wild nature he snatches the idea of the brilliance of the energies that are in play in the struggle for existence. "This is what makes the Amusement of Life—to a speculative Mind. I go among the Fields and catch a glimpse of a Stoat or a field-mouse peeping out of the withered grass—the creature hath a purpose and its eyes are bright with it. I go among the buildings of a city and I see a Man hurrying along—to what? the creature hath a purpose and his eyes are bright with it." He thinks of the disinterestedness of Jesus and of how little it has established itself as against the self-interest of men, and again he snatches at the idea that perhaps life may be justified by its sheer energy: "May there not be superior beings amused by any graceful, though instinctive attitude my mind may fall into, as I am entertained with the alertness of a Stoat or the anxiety of a Deer? Though a quarrel in the Streets is a thing to be hated, the energies displayed in it are fine; the commonest Man shows a grace in his quarrel—By a superior being our reasonings may take the same tone—though erroneous they may be fine—This is the very thing in which consists poetry—"

It is very brilliant, very fine, but it does not satisfy him; "amusement," "entertainment" are not enough. Even poetry is not enough. Energy is the very thing "in which consists poetry"—"and if so it is not so fine a thing as philosophy—For the same reason that an eagle is not so fine a thing as a truth."

"Give me credit—" he cries across the broad Atlantic. "Do you not think I strive—to know myself? Give me this credit—" We cannot well refuse it.

The simple affirmation of the self in its vital energy means much to him, but it does not mean enough, and in the time intervening between the entry of 19 March and that of 15 April his mind has been moving toward the reconciliation of energy and truth, of passion and principle. He has been reading, he says, Robertson's *America* and Voltaire's *Siècle de Louis XIV* and his mind is full of the miseries of man in either a simple or a highly civilized state. He canvasses the possibilities of amelioration of the human fate and concludes that our life even at its conceivable best can be nothing but tragic, the very elements and laws of nature being hostile to man. Then, having stated as extremely as this the case of human misery, he breaks out with sudden contempt for those who call the world a vale of tears. "What a little circumscribed straightened notion!" he says. "Call the world if you please 'The vale of Soul-making!' . . . I say *'Soul making'*—Soul as distinguished from an Intelligence—There may be intelligences or sparks of the divinity in millions—but they are not Souls till they acquire identities, till each one is personally itself."

There follows a remarkable flight into a sort of transcendental psychology in the effort to suggest how intelligences become souls, and then: "Do you not see how necessary a World of Pains and troubles is to school an Intelligence and make it a Soul? A Place where the heart must feel and suffer in a thousand different ways." And the heart is "the teat from which the Mind or intelligence sucks its identity."

He writes with an animus against Christian doctrine, but what he is giving, he says, is a sketch of *salvation*. And for the purpose of his argument he assumes immortality, he assumes a deity who makes beings in an infinite variety of identities, each identity being a "spark" of God's "essence"; he assumes that the soul may return to God enhanced by its acquisition of identity. This assumed, "I began by seeing how man was formed by circumstances—and what are circumstances?—but touchstones of his heart—? and what are touchstones? but proovings of his heart? and what are proovings of his heart but fortifiers or alterers of his nature? and what is his altered nature but his Soul?—and what was his Soul before it came into the world and had these provings and alterations and perfectionings?—An intelligence—without Identity—and how is this Identity to be made through the medium of the heart? And how is the heart to become this Medium but in a world of Circumstances?"

The faculty of Negative Capability has yielded doctrine—for the idea of soul-making, of souls creating themselves in their confrontation of circumstance, is available to Keats's conception only because he has remained with half-knowledge, with the double knowledge of the self and of the world's evil.

7

So far as the idea of soul-making is doctrine—so far, that is, as it is something more than a moving rationale of heroism—it will probably not withstand the kind of scrutiny that today we are likely to give it. We have lost the *mystique* of the self. We cannot conceive of the self as having the same nature and the same value that Keats ascribed to it; we cannot respond to the justification of life by the heroic definition of self; and, having lost our knowledge of one term of Keats's equation, we are certain to find the reasons why his conclusion is wrong.

But when we deal adversely with Keats's notion of soul-making, we must at the same time deal with two greater poets than Keats. So far as Keats's resolution of the problem of evil is doctrinal, it leads us back to Milton. Here is Milton's characteristic doctrine of the conjoint nature of good and evil—"Good and evil we know in the field of this world grow up together almost inseparably. . . . Perhaps this is that doom which Adam fell into of knowing good and evil, that is to say, of knowing good by evil." Here is the Miltonic satisfaction at the expulsion from Eden, for from that great event all events follow, the life of "circumstances" has been instituted, history has been initiated, the human drama has begun, and now man may define his soul in the open and strenuous world of freedom as he never could in Eden—it is this, we feel, and not the great arguments of his theodicy that for Milton justify God's ways to man. And no one since Milton has put better and more feelingly the Miltonic doctrine of maturing freedom and responsibility in the field of this world than the young man who harked back incessantly to his Eden, to the primal bliss of satisfying the appetites without effort and without tears, who conceived the heroic vision of life because he first understood felicity.

Keats's doctrine of soul-making leads us not only to Milton, whose very theology was shaped by his love of the tragic poets, Shakespeare among them, but also to Shakespeare himself. What Keats calls "the bitter sweet of this Shakespearean fruit" is nothing else than the hard process of "provings and alterations and perfectionings" by which an "intelligence" acquires "identity" and becomes a "soul." The characterization of the "Shakespearean fruit" appears in the sonnet "On Sitting Down to Read 'King Lear' Once Again," and *King Lear* is precisely the history of the definition of a soul by circumstance. The sonnet begins with a farewell to "golden-tongued Romance with serene lute"—Romance is precisely not "circumstances." And what Keats says he is leaving Romance for is "the fierce dispute,/Betwixt Hell torment and impassion'd clay"*—between, that is, the knowledge of evil and the knowledge of self. We can understand why Keats's admiration of Shakespeare was so much more than a literary admiration, why Shakespeare had for him something of the magnitude of a religious idea, figuring in his letters as a sort of patron saint or guardian angel, almost as a Good Shepherd. Shakespeare suggested the only salvation that Keats found it possible to conceive, the tragic salvation, the soul accepting the fate that defines it.

Whether his heroic resolution of the problem of evil means much or little to us, we cannot doubt that to Keats himself it was a felt reality. It was not a doctrine formulated to guide his life if it might—rather it is a statement, as accurate as such a statement can be, of the nature of his being. It is impossible not to be moved to extreme pity by Keats's last days, by the young man doomed to death at the very moment that his genius has come into the full power that it had promised, at the moment too when he was at last able to feel the long-awaited passion of love. Sometimes he is buoyed up by the euphoria which is characteristic of his disease, but more often he is bitter, jealous, and resentful; the cup is being taken from him, and he is in despair. And yet, however great our pity may be, we cannot miss, unless we willfully and perversely wish to miss, the hard core of self which remains in the man. "I know the color in that blood—it is arterial blood—I cannot be deceived in that color; that drop is my death warrant. I must die." These are the words that he is reported to have uttered on the occasion of his first hemorrhage, and they suggest the heroic quality of his last days. He permitted nothing to be falsified. There are impossibilities in this world, and he knew them. His tortured fancy sometimes overpowered him—he imagined that Fanny Brawne might be unchaste, that Brown was not faithful, that the Hunts spied on him: his self was nearly maddened by the certainty of its extinction. Yet the dominant note is of fortitude, of courage, and of heroic concern for those he loved. As he lay on his deathbed, he asked Severn, "Did you ever see anyone die?" Severn never had. "Well then I pity you, poor Severn. What trouble and danger you have got into for me. Now you must be firm for it will not last long. I shall soon be laid in the quiet grave. Thank

---

*The line appears so in the version of the sonnet in the Letters. Keats later revised "Hell torment" to "damnation."

God for the quiet grave. . . ." And at the end: "Severn, lift me up, for I am dying. I shall die easy. Don't be frightened! Thank God it has come."

The tone, we feel, is not ours. To identify it we go back in time, and say, perhaps, that it is of the Renaissance, of Shakespeare. We do not have what produces this tone, the implicit and explicit commitment to the self even in the moment of its extinction. Events, it would seem, have destroyed this commitment—and there are those who will rise to say that it was exactly the romantic commitment to the self that has produced the dire events of our day, that the responsibility for our present troubles, and for the denial of the self which our troubles entail, is to be laid to the great romantic creators. And even those who know better than this will yet find it all too easy to explain why Keats's heroic vision of the tragic life and the tragic salvation will not serve us now. They will tell us that we must, in our time, confront circumstances which are so terrible that the soul, far from being defined and developed by them, can only be destroyed by them. This may be so, and if it is so it makes the reason that Keats is not less but more relevant to our situation. As we see him in his letters he has for us a massive importance—he has, as we say, a historical importance. He stands as the last image of health at the very moment when the sickness of Europe began to be apparent—he with his intense naturalism that took so passionate an account of the mystery of man's nature, reckoning as boldly with pleasure as with pain, giving so generous a credence to growth, development, and possibility; he with his pride that so modestly, so warmly and delightedly, responded to the idea of community. The spiritual and moral health of which he seems the image we cannot now attain by wishing for it. But we cannot attain it without wishing for it, and clearly imagining it. "The imagination may be compared to Adam's dream—he awoke and found it truth."

George Orwell and the
Politics of Truth

1952

George Orwell's *Homage to Catalonia* is one of the important documents of our time. It is a very modest book—it seems to say the least that can be said on a subject of great magnitude. But in saying the least it says the most. Its manifest subject is a period of the Spanish Civil War, in which, for some months, until he was almost mortally wounded, its author fought as a soldier in the trenches. Everyone knows that the Spanish war was a decisive event of our epoch, everyone said so when it was being fought, and everyone was right. But the Spanish war lies a decade and a half behind us, and nowadays our sense of history is being destroyed by the nature of our history—our memory is short and it grows shorter under the rapidity of the assault of events. What once occupied all our minds and filled the musty meeting halls with the awareness of heroism and destiny has now become chiefly a matter for the historical scholar. George Orwell's book would make only a limited claim upon our attention if it were nothing more than a record of personal experiences in the Spanish war. But it is much more than this. It is a testimony to the nature of modern political life. It is also a demonstration on the part of its author of one of the right ways of confronting that life. Its importance is therefore of the present moment and for years to come.

A politics which is presumed to be available to everyone is a relatively new thing in the world. We do not yet know very much about it. Nor have most of us been especially eager to learn. In a politics presumed to be available to everyone, ideas and ideals play a great part. And those of us who set store by ideas and ideals have never been quite able to learn that, just because they do have power nowadays, there is a direct connection between their power and another kind of power, the old, unabashed, cynical power of force. We are always being surprised by this. The extent to which Communism made use of unregenerate force was perfectly clear years ago, but many of us found it impossible to acknowledge this fact because Communism spoke boldly to our love of ideas and ideals. We tried as hard as we could to believe that politics might be an idyl, only to discover that what we took to be a political pastoral was really a grim military campaign or a murderous betrayal of political allies, or that what we insisted on calling agrarianism was in actuality a new imperialism. And in the personal life what was undertaken by many good people as a moral commitment of the most disinterested kind turned out to be an engagement to an ultimate immorality. The evidence of this is to be found in a whole literary genre with which we have become familiar in the last decade, the personal confession of involvement and then of disillusionment with Communism.

Orwell's book, in one of its most significant aspects, is about disillusionment with Communism, but it is not a confession. I say this because it is one of the important positive things to say about *Homage to Catalonia*, but my saying it does not imply that I share the *a priori* antagonistic feelings of many people toward those books which, on the basis of experience, expose and denounce the Communist party. About such books people of liberal inclination often make uneasy and rather vindictive jokes. The jokes seem to me unfair and in bad taste. There is nothing shameful in the nature of these books. There is a good chance that the commitment to Communism was made in the first place for generous reasons, and it is certain that the revulsion was brought about by more than sufficient causes. And clearly there is nothing wrong in wishing to record the painful experience and to draw conclusions from it. Nevertheless, human nature being what it is—and in the uneasy readers of such books as well as in the unhappy writers of them—it is a fact that public confession does often appear in an unfortunate light, that its moral tone is less simple and true than we might wish it to be. But the moral tone of Orwell's book is uniquely simple and true. Orwell's ascertaining of certain political facts was not the occasion for a change of heart, or for a crisis of the soul. What he learned from his experiences in Spain of course pained him very much, and it led him to change his course of conduct. But it did not destroy him; it did not, as people say, cut the ground from under him. It did not shatter his faith in what he had previously believed, or weaken his political impulse, or even change its direction. It produced not a moment of guilt or self-recrimination.

Perhaps this should not seem so very remarkable. Yet who can doubt that it constitutes in our time a genuine moral triumph? It suggests that Orwell was an unusual kind of man, that he had a temper of mind and heart which is now rare, although we still respond to it when we see it.

It happened by a curious chance that on the day I agreed to write this essay as the introduction to the new edition of *Homage to Catalonia*, and indeed at the very moment that I was reaching for the telephone to tell the publisher that I would write it, a young man, a graduate student of mine, came in to see me, the purpose of his visit being to ask what I thought about his doing an essay on George Orwell. My answer, naturally, was ready, and when I had given it and we had been amused and pleased by the coincidence, he settled down for a chat about our common subject. But I asked him not to talk about Orwell. I didn't want to dissipate in talk what ideas I had, and also I didn't want my ideas crossed with his, which were sure to be very good. So for a while we merely exchanged bibliographical information, asking each other which of Orwell's books we had read and which we owned. But then, as if he could not resist making at least one remark about Orwell himself, he said suddenly in a very simple and matter-of-fact way, "He was a virtuous man." And we sat there, agreeing at length about this statement, finding pleasure in talking about it.

It was an odd statement for a young man to make nowadays, and I suppose that what we found so interesting about it was just this oddity— its point was in its being an old-fashioned thing to say. It was archaic in its bold commitment of sentiment, and it used an archaic word with an archaic simplicity. Our pleasure was not merely literary, not just a response to the remark's being so appropriate to Orwell, in whom there was indeed a quality of an earlier and simpler day. We were glad to be able to say it about anybody. One doesn't have the opportunity very often. Not that there are not many men who are good, but there are few men who, in addition to being good, have the simplicity and sturdiness and activity which allow us to say of them that they are virtuous men, for somehow to say that a man "is good," or even to speak of a man who "is virtuous," is not the same thing as saying, "He is a virtuous man." By some quirk of the spirit of the language, the form of that sentence brings out the primitive meaning of the word "virtuous," which is not merely moral goodness, but also fortitude and strength in goodness.

Orwell, by reason of the quality that permits us to say of him that he was a virtuous man, is a figure in our lives. He was not a genius, and this is one of the remarkable things about him. His not being a genius is an element of the quality that makes him what I am calling a figure.

It has been some time since we in America have had literary figures— that is, men who live their visions as well as write them, who *are* what they write, whom we think of as standing for something as men because of what they have written in their books. They preside, as it were, over certain ideas and attitudes. Mark Twain was in this sense a figure for us, and so was William James. So, too, were Thoreau, and Whitman, and Henry Adams, and Henry James, although posthumously and rather uncertainly. But when in our more recent literature the writer is anything but anonymous, he is likely to be ambiguous and unsatisfactory as a figure, like Sherwood Anderson, or Mencken, or Wolfe, or Dreiser. There is something about the American character that does not take to the idea of the figure as the English character does. In this regard, the English are closer to the French than to us. Whatever the legend to the contrary, the English character is more strongly marked than ours, less reserved, less ironic, more open in its expression of willfulness and eccentricity and cantankerousness. Its manners are cruder and bolder. It is a demonstrative character—it shows itself, even shows off. Santayana, when he visited England, quite gave up the common notion that Dickens's characters are caricatures. One can still meet an English snob so thunderingly shameless in his worship of the aristocracy, so explicit and demonstrative in his adoration, that a careful, modest, ironic American snob would be quite bewildered by him. And in modern English literature there have been many writers whose lives were demonstrations of the principles which shaped their writing. They lead us to be aware of the moral personalities that stand behind the work. The two Lawrences, different as they were, were alike in this: that they assumed the roles of their belief and acted them out on the stage of the world. In different ways this was true of Yeats, and of Shaw, and even of Wells. It is true of T. S. Eliot, for all that he has spoken against the claims of personality in literature. Even E. M. Forster, who makes so much of privacy, acts out in public the role of the private man, becoming for us the very spirit of the private life. He is not merely a writer, he is a figure.

Orwell takes his place with these men as a figure. In one degree or another they are geniuses, and he is not; if we ask what it is he stands for, what he is the figure of, the answer is: the virtue of not being a genius, of confronting the world with nothing more than one's simple, direct, undeceived intelligence, and a respect for the powers one does have and the work one undertakes to do. We admire geniuses, we love them, but they discourage us. They are great concentrations of intellect and emotion, we feel that they have soaked up all the available power, monopolizing it and leaving none for us. We feel that if we cannot be as they, we can be nothing. Beside them we are so plain, so hopelessly threadbare. How they glitter, and with what an imperious way they seem to deal with circumstances, even when they are wrong! Lacking their patents of nobility, we might as well quit. This is what democracy has done to us, alas—told us that genius is available to anyone, that the grace of ultimate prestige may be had by anyone, that we may all be princes and potentates, or saints and visionaries and holy martyrs, of the heart and mind. And then when it turns out that we are no such thing, it permits us to think that we aren't much of anything at all. In contrast with this cozening trick of democracy, how pleasant seems the old, reactionary Anglican phrase that used to drive people of democratic leanings quite wild with rage—"my station and its duties."

Orwell would very likely have loathed that phrase, but in a way he exemplifies its meaning. And it is a great relief, a fine sight, to see him doing this. His novels are good, quite good, some better than others, some of them surprising us by being so very much better than their modesty leads us to suppose they can be, all of them worth reading; but they are clearly not the work of a great or even of a "born" novelist. In my opinion, his satire on Stalinism, *Animal Farm*, was overrated—I think people were carried away by someone's reviving systematic satire for serious political purposes. His critical essays are almost always very fine, but sometimes they do not fully meet the demands of their subject—as, for example, the essay on Dickens. And even when they are at their best, they seem to have become what they are chiefly by reason of the very plainness of Orwell's mind, his simple ability to look at things in a downright, undeceived way. He seems to be serving not some dashing daimon but the plain, solid Gods of the Copybook Maxims. He is not a genius—what a relief! What an encouragement. For he communicates to us the sense that what he has done any one of us could do.

Or could do if we but made up our mind to do it, if we but surrendered a little of the cant that comforts us, if for a few weeks we paid no attention to the little group with which we habitually exchange opinions, if we took our chance on being wrong or inadequate, if we looked at things simply and directly, having in mind only our intention of finding out what they really are, not the prestige of our great intellectual act of looking at them. He liberates us. He tells us that we can understand our political and social life merely by looking around us; he frees us from the need for the inside dope. He implies that our job is not to be intellectual, certainly not to be intellectual in this fashion or that, but merely to be intelligent according to our lights—he restores the old sense of the democracy of the mind, releasing us from the belief that the mind can work only in a technical, professional way and that it must work competitively. He has the effect of making us believe that we may become full members of the society of thinking men. That is why he is a figure for us.

In speaking thus of Orwell, I do not mean to imply that his birth was presided over only by the Gods of the Copybook Maxims and not at all by the good fairies, or that he had no daimon. The good fairies gave him very fine free gifts indeed. And he had a strong daimon, but it was of an old-fashioned kind and it constrained him to the paradox—for such it is in our time—of taking seriously the Gods of the Copybook Maxims and putting his gifts at their service. Orwell responded to truths of more than one kind, to the bitter, erudite truths of the modern time as well as to the older and simpler truths. He would have quite understood what Karl Jaspers means when he recommends the "decision to renounce the absolute claims of the European humanistic spirit, to think of it as a stage of development rather than the living content of faith." But he was not interested in this development. What concerned him was survival, which he connected with the old simple ideas that are often not ideas at all but beliefs, preferences, and prejudices. In the modern world these had for him the charm and audacity of newly discovered truths. Involved as so many of us are, at least in our literary lives, in a bitter metaphysics of human nature, it shocks and dismays us when Orwell speaks in praise of such things as responsibility, and orderliness in the personal life, and fair play, and

physical courage—even of snobbery and hypocrisy because they sometimes help to shore up the crumbling ramparts of the moral life.

It is hard to find personalities in the contemporary world who are
analogous to Orwell. We have to look for men who have considerable intellectual power but who are not happy in the institutionalized life of intellectuality; who have a feeling for an older and simpler time, and a
guiding awareness of the ordinary life of the people, yet without any
touch of the sentimental malice of populism; and a strong feeling for the
commonplace; and a direct, unabashed sense of the nation, even a conscious love of it. This brings Péguy to mind, and also Chesterton, and I
think that Orwell does have an affinity with these men—he was probably
unaware of it—which tells us something about him. But Péguy has been
dead for quite forty years, and Chesterton (it is a pity) is at the moment
rather dim for us, even for those of us who are Catholics. And of course
Orwell's affinity with these men is limited by their Catholicism, for although Orwell admired some of the effects and attitudes of religion, he
seems to have had no religious tendency in his nature, or none that went
beyond what used to be called natural piety.

In some ways he seems more the contemporary of William Cobbett
and William Hazlitt than of any man of our own century. Orwell's radicalism, like Cobbett's, refers to the past and to the soil. This is not uncommon nowadays in the social theory of literary men, but in Orwell's
attitude there is none of the implied aspiration to aristocracy which so often marks literary agrarian ideas; his feeling for the land and the past simply serve to give his radicalism a conservative—a conserving—cast, which
is in itself attractive, and to protect his politics from the ravages of ideology. Like Cobbett, he does not dream of a new kind of man, he is content
with the old kind, and what moves him is the desire that this old kind of
man should have freedom, bacon, and proper work. He has the passion
for the literal actuality of life as it is really lived which makes Cobbett's
Rural Rides a classic, although a forgotten one; his own *The Road to
Wigan Pier* and *Down and Out in Paris and London* are in its direct line.
And it is not the least interesting detail in the similarity of the two men
that both had a love affair with the English language. Cobbett, the self-
educated agricultural laborer and sergeant major, was said by one of his
enemies to handle the language better than anyone of his time, and he
wrote a first-rate handbook of grammar and rhetoric; Orwell was obsessed by the deterioration of the English language in the hands of the

journalists and pundits, and nothing in *Nineteen Eighty-Four* is more memorable than his creation of Newspeak.

Orwell's affinity with Hazlitt is, I suspect, of a more intimate temperamental kind, although I cannot go beyond the suspicion, for I know much less about Orwell as a person than about Hazlitt. But there is an unquestionable similarity in their intellectual temper which leads them to handle their political and literary opinions in much the same way. Hazlitt remained a Jacobin all his life, but his unshakable opinions never kept him from giving credit when it was deserved by a writer of the opposite persuasion, not merely out of chivalrous generosity but out of respect for the truth. He was the kind of passionate democrat who could question whether democracy could possibly produce great poetry, and his essays in praise of Scott and Coleridge, with whom he was in intense political disagreement, prepare us for Orwell on Yeats and Kipling.

The old-fashionedness of Orwell's temperament can be partly explained by the nature of his relation to his class. This was by no means simple. He came from that part of the middle class whose sense of its status is disproportionate to its income, his father having been a subordinate officer in the Civil Service of India, where Orwell was born. (The family name was Blair, and Orwell was christened Eric Hugh; he changed his name, for rather complicated reasons, when he began to write.) As a scholarship boy he attended the expensive preparatory school of which Cyril Connolly has given an account in *Enemies of Promise*. Orwell appears there as a school "rebel" and "intellectual." He was later to write of the absolute misery of the poor boy at a snobbish school. He went to Eton on a scholarship, and from Eton to Burma, where he served in the police. He has spoken with singular honesty of the ambiguousness of his attitude in the imperialist situation. He disliked authority and the manner of its use, and he sympathized with the Burmese; yet at the same time he saw the need for authority and he used it, and he was often exasperated by the natives. When he returned to England on leave after five years of service, he could not bring himself to go back to Burma. It was at this time that, half voluntarily, he sank to the lower depths of poverty. This adventure in extreme privation was partly forced upon him, but partly it was undertaken to expiate the social guilt which he felt he had incurred in Burma. The experience seems to have done what was required of it. A year as a casual worker and vagrant had the effect of discharging Orwell's guilt, leaving him with an attitude toward the working class that was entirely affectionate and perfectly without sentimentality.

His experience of being declassed, and the effect which it had upon him, go far toward defining the intellectual quality of Orwell and the particular work he was to do. In the 1930s the middle-class intellectuals made it a moral fashion to avow their guilt toward the lower classes and to repudiate their own class tradition. So far as this was nothing more than a moral fashion, it was a moral anomaly. And although no one can read history without being made aware of what were the grounds of this attitude, yet the personal claim to a historical guilt yields but an ambiguous principle of personal behavior, a still more ambiguous basis of thought. Orwell broke with much of what the English upper middle class was and admired. But his clear, uncanting mind saw that, although the morality of history might come to harsh conclusions about the middle class and although the practicality of history might say that its day was over, there yet remained the considerable residue of its genuine virtues. The love of personal privacy, of order, of manners, the ideal of fairness and responsibility—these are very simple virtues indeed and they scarcely constitute perfection of either the personal or the social life. Yet they still might serve to judge the present and to control the future.

Orwell could even admire the virtues of the lower middle class, which an intelligentsia always finds it easiest to despise. His remarkable novel *Keep the Aspidistra Flying* is a *summa* of all the criticisms of a commercial civilization that have ever been made, and it is a detailed demonstration of the bitter and virtually hopeless plight of the lower-middle-class man. Yet it insists that to live even in this plight is not without its stubborn joy. Péguy spoke of "fathers of families, those heroes of modern life"—Orwell's novel celebrates this biological-social heroism by leading its mediocre, middle-aging poet from the depths of splenetic negation to the acknowledgment of the happiness of fatherhood, thence to an awareness of the pleasures of marriage, and of an existence which, while it does not gratify his ideal conception of himself, is nevertheless his own. There is a dim, elegiac echo of Defoe and of the early days of the middle-class ascendancy as Orwell's sad young man learns to cherish the small personal gear of life, his own bed and chairs and saucepans—his own aspidistra, the ugly, stubborn, organic emblem of survival.

We may say that it was on his affirmation of the middle-class virtues that Orwell based his criticism of the liberal intelligentsia. The characteristic error of the middle-class intellectual of modern times is his tendency to abstractness and absoluteness, his reluctance to connect idea with fact, especially with personal fact. I cannot recall that Orwell ever related his criticism of the intelligentsia to the implications of *Keep the Aspidistra Flying*, but he might have done so, for the prototypical act of the modern intellectual is his abstracting himself from the life of the family. It is an act that has something about it of ritual thaumaturgy—at the beginning of our intellectual careers we are like nothing so much as those young members of Indian tribes who have had a vision or a dream which gives them power on condition that they withdraw from the ordinary life of the tribe. By intellectuality we are freed from the thralldom to the familial commonplace, from the materiality and concreteness by which it exists, the hardness of the cash and the hardness of getting it, the inelegance and intractability of family things. It gives us power over intangibles and imponderables, such as Beauty and Justice, and it permits us to escape the cosmic ridicule which in our youth we suppose is inevitably directed at those who take seriously the small concerns of the material quotidian world, which we know to be inadequate and doomed by the very fact that it is so absurdly *conditioned*— by things, habits, local and temporary customs, and the foolish errors and solemn absurdities of the men of the past.

The gist of Orwell's criticism of the liberal intelligentsia was that they refused to understand the conditioned nature of life. He never quite puts it in this way but this is what he means. He himself knew what war and revolution were really like, what government and administration were really like. From first-hand experience he knew what Communism was. He could truly imagine what Nazism was. At a time when most intellectuals still thought of politics as a nightmare abstraction, pointing to the fearfulness of the nightmare as evidence of their sense of reality, Orwell was using the imagination of a man whose hands and eyes and whole body were part of his thinking apparatus. Shaw had insisted upon remaining sublimely unaware of the Russian actuality; Wells had pooh-poohed the threat of Hitler and had written off as anachronisms the very forces that were at the moment shaping the world—racial pride, leader-worship, religious belief, patriotism, love of war. These men had trained the political intelligence of the intelligentsia, who now, in their love of abstractions, in their wish to repudiate the anachronisms of their own emotions, could not conceive of directing upon Russia anything like the same stringency of criticism they used upon their own nation. Orwell observed of them that their zeal for internationalism had led them to constitute Russia their new fatherland. And he had the simple courage to point out that the pacifists preached their doctrine under condition of the protection of the British navy, and that, against Germany and Russia, Gandhi's passive resistance would have been of no avail.

He never abated his anger against the established order. But a paradox of history had made the old British order one of the still beneficent things in the world, and it licensed the possibility of a social hope that was being frustrated and betrayed almost everywhere else. And so Orwell clung with a kind of wry, grim pride to the old ways of the last class that had ruled the old order. He must sometimes have wondered how it came about that he should be praising sportsmanship and gentlemanliness and dutifulness and physical courage. He seems to have thought, and very likely he was right, that they might come in handy as revolutionary virtues—he remarks of Rubashov, the central character of Arthur Koestler's novel *Darkness at Noon*, that he was firmer in loyalty to the revolution than certain of his comrades because he had, and they had not, a bourgeois past. Certainly the virtues he praised were those of survival, and they had fallen into disrepute in a disordered world.

Sometimes in his quarrel with the intelligentsia Orwell seems to sound like a leader-writer for *The Times* in a routine wartime attack on the highbrows.

> The general weakening of imperialism, and to some extent of the whole British morale, that took place during the nineteen thirties, was partly the work of the left-wing intelligentsia, itself a kind of growth that sprouted from the stagnation of the Empire.

> The mentality of the English left-wing intelligentsia can be studied in half a dozen weekly and monthly papers. The immediately striking thing about all these papers is their generally negative querulous attitude, their complete lack at all times of any constructive suggestion. There is little in them except the irresponsible carping of people who have never been and never expect to be in a position of power.

During the past twenty years the negative faineant outlook which has been fashionable among the English left-wingers, the sniggering of the intellectuals at patriotism and physical courage, the persistent effort to chip away at English morale and spread a hedonistic, what-do-I-get-out-of-it attitude to life, has done nothing but harm.

But he was not a leader-writer for *The Times*. He had fought in Spain and nearly died there, and on Spanish affairs his position had been the truly revolutionary one. The passages I have quoted are from his pamphlet, *The Lion and the Unicorn*, a persuasive statement of the case for socialism in Britain.

Toward the end of his life Orwell discovered another reason for his admiration of the old middle-class virtues and his criticism of the intelligentsia. Walter Bagehot used to speak of the political advantages of *stupidity*, meaning by the word a concern for one's own private material interests as a political motive which was preferable to an intellectual, theoretical interest. Orwell, it may be said, came to respect the old bourgeois virtues because they were stupid—that is, because they resisted the power of abstract ideas. And he came to love things, material possessions, for the same reason. He did not in the least become what is called "anti-intellectual"—this was simply not within the range of possibility for him—but he began to fear that the commitment to abstract ideas could be far more maleficent than the commitment to the gross materiality of property had ever been. The very stupidity of things has something human about it, something meliorative, something even liberating. Together with the stupidity of the old unthinking virtues it stands against the ultimate and absolute power which the unconditioned idea can develop. The essential point of *Nineteen Eighty-Four* is just this, the danger of the ultimate and absolute power which mind can develop when it frees itself from conditions, from the bondage of things and history.

But this, as I say, is a late aspect of Orwell's criticism of intellectuality. Through the greater part of his literary career his criticism was simpler and less extreme. It was as simple as this: that the contemporary intellectual class did not think and did not really love the truth.

In 1937 Orwell went to Spain to observe the civil war and to write about it. He stayed to take part in it, joining the militia as a private. At that time each of the parties still had its own militia units, although these were in process of being absorbed into the People's Army. Because his letters of introduction were from people of a certain political group in England, the Independent Labour Party, which had connections with the POUM,* Orwell joined a unit of that party in Barcelona. He was not at the time sympathetic to the views of his comrades and their leaders. During the days of interparty strife, the POUM was represented, in Spain and abroad, as being a Trotskyist party. In point of fact it was not, although it did join with the small Trotskyist party to oppose certain of the policies of the dominant Communist party. Orwell's own preference, at the time of his enlistment, was for the Communist party line, and because of this he looked forward to an eventual transfer to a Communist unit.

It was natural, I think, for Orwell to have been a partisan of the Communist program for the war. It recommended itself to most people on inspection by its apparent simple common sense. It proposed to fight the war without any reference to any particular political idea beyond a defense of democracy from a fascist enemy. When the war was won, the political and social problems would be solved, but until the war should be won, any debate over these problems was to be avoided as leading only to the weakening of the united front against Franco.

Eventually Orwell came to understand that this was not the practical policy he had at first thought it to be. His reasons need not be reiterated here—he gives them with characteristic cogency and modesty in the course of this book, and under the gloomy but probably correct awareness that, the economic and social condition of Spain being what it was, even the best policies must issue in some form of dictatorship. In sum, he believed that the war was revolutionary or nothing, and that the people of Spain would not fight and die for a democracy which was admittedly to be a bourgeois democracy.

But Orwell's disaffection from the Communist party was not the result of a difference of opinion over whether the revolution should be instituted during the war or after it. It was the result of his discovery that the Communist party's real intention was to prevent the revolution from ever being instituted at all—"The thing for which the Communists were working was not to postpone the Spanish revolution till a more suitable time, but to make sure it never happened." The movement of events, led by the Communists who had the prestige and the supplies of Russia, was

*Partido Obrero de Unificación Marxista—Party of Marxist Unification.

always to the right, and all protest was quieted by the threat that the war would be lost if the ranks were broken, which in effect meant that Russian supplies would be withheld if the Communist lead was not followed. Meanwhile the war was being lost because the government more and more distrusted the non-Communist militia units, particularly those of the Anarchists. "I have described," Orwell writes, "how we were armed, or not armed, on the Aragon front. There is very little doubt that arms were deliberately withheld lest too many of them should get into the hands of the Anarchists, who would afterwards use them for a revolutionary purpose; consequently, the big Aragon offensive which would have made Franco draw back from Bilbao and possibly from Madrid, never happened."

At the end of April, after three months on the Aragon front, Orwell was sent to Barcelona on furlough. He observed the change in morale that had taken place since the days of his enlistment—Barcelona was no longer the revolutionary city it had been. The heroic days were over. The militia, which had done such splendid service at the beginning of the war, was now being denigrated in favor of the People's Army, and its members were being snubbed as seeming rather queer in their revolutionary ardor, not to say dangerous. The tone of the black market and of privilege had replaced the old idealistic puritanism of even three months earlier. Orwell observed this but drew no conclusions from it. He wanted to go to the front at Madrid, and in order to do so he would have to be transferred to the International Column, which was under the control of the Communists. He had no objection to serving in a Communist command and, indeed, had resolved to make the transfer. But he was tired and in poor health and he waited to conclude the matter until another week of his leave should be up. While he delayed, the fighting broke out in Barcelona.

In New York and in London the intelligentsia had no slightest doubt of what had happened—could not, indeed, have conceived that anything might have happened other than what they had been led to believe had actually happened. The Anarchists, together with the "Trotskyist" POUM—so it was said—had been secreting great stores of arms with a view to an uprising that would force upon the government their premature desire for collectivization. And on 3 May their plans were realized when they came out into the streets and captured the Telephone Exchange, plus breaking the united front in an extreme manner and endangering the progress of the war. But Orwell in Barcelona saw nothing like this. He was under the orders of the POUM, but he was not committed to its lines, and certainly not to the Anarchist line, and he was sufficiently sympathetic to the Communists to wish to join one of their units. What he saw he saw as objectively as a man might ever see anything. And what he records is now, I believe, accepted as the essential truth by everyone whose judgment is worth regarding. There were no great stores of arms cached by the Anarchists and the POUM—there was an actual shortage of arms in their ranks. But the Communist-controlled government had been building up the strength of the Civil Guard, a gendarmerie which was called "non-political" and from which workers were excluded. That there had indeed been mounting tension between the government and the dissident forces is beyond question, but the actual fighting was touched off by acts of provocation committed by the government itself—shows of military strength, the call to all private persons to give up arms, attacks on Anarchist centers, and, as a climax, the attempt to take over the Telephone Exchange, which since the beginning of the war had been run by the Anarchists.

It would have been very difficult to learn anything of this in New York or London. The periodicals that guided the thought of left-liberal intellectuals knew nothing of it, and had no wish to learn. As for the aftermath of the unhappy uprising, they appeared to have no knowledge of that at all. When Barcelona was again quiet—some six thousand Assault Guards were imported to quell the disturbance—Orwell returned to his old front. There he was severely wounded, shot through the neck; the bullet just missed the windpipe. After his grim hospitalization, of which he writes so lightly, he was invalided to Barcelona. He returned to find the city in process of being purged. The POUM and the Anarchists had been suppressed; the power of the workers had been broken and the police hunt was on. The jails were already full and daily becoming fuller—the most devoted fighters for Spanish freedom, men who had given up everything for the cause, were being imprisoned under the most dreadful conditions, often held incommunicado, often never to be heard of again. Orwell himself was suspect and in danger because he had belonged to a POUM regiment, and he stayed in hiding until, with the help of the British consul, he was able to escape to France. But if one searches the liberal periodicals, which have made the cause of civil liberties their own, one can find no mention of this terror. Those members of the intellectual class who prided themselves upon their political commitment were committed not to the fact but to the abstraction.*

And to the abstraction they remained committed for a long time to come. Many are still committed to it, or nostalgically wish they could be. If only life were not so tangible, so concrete, so made up of facts that are at variance with each other; if only the things that people say are good things were really good; if only the things that are pretty good were entirely good and we were not put to the everlasting necessity of qualifying and discriminating; if only politics were not a matter of power—*then* we should be happy to put our minds to politics, *then* we should consent to think!

But Orwell had never believed that the political life could be an intellectual idyl. He immediately put his mind to the politics he had experienced. He told the truth, and told it in an exemplary way, quietly, simply, with due warning to the reader that it was only one man's truth. He used no political jargon, and he made no recriminations. He made no effort to show that his heart was in the right place, or the left place. He was not interested in where his heart might be thought to be, since he knew where it was. He was interested only in telling the truth. Not very much attention was paid to his truth—*Homage to Catalonia* sold poorly in England, it had to be remaindered, it was not published in America, and the people to whom it should have said most responded to it not at all.

Its particular truth refers to events now far in the past, as in these days we reckon our past. It does not matter the less for that—this particular truth implies a general truth which, as now we cannot fail to understand, must matter for a long time to come. And what matters most of all is our sense of the man who tells the truth.

---

*In looking through the files of *The Nation* and *The New Republic* for the period of the Barcelona fighting, I have come upon only one serious contradiction of the interpretation of events that constituted the editorial position of both periodicals. This was a long letter contributed by Bertram Wolfe to the correspondence columns of *The Nation*. When this essay first appeared, some of my friends took me to task for seeming to imply that there were no liberal or radical intellectuals who did not accept the interpretations of *The Nation* and *The New Republic*. There were indeed such liberal or radical intellectuals. But they were relatively few in number and they were treated with great suspiciousness and even hostility by the liberal and radical intellectuals as a class. It is as a class that Orwell speaks of the intellectuals of the Left in the 1930s, and I follow him in this.

The Situation of
the American Intellectual
at the Present Time

1952

The editors of *Partisan Review* have long been thought to give a rather special credence and sympathy to the idea of "alienation," particularly to the alienation of the modern artist, most of all to the alienation of the American artist. When, therefore, they instituted a symposium on the attitude of American intellectuals toward America at the present time, it was inevitable that a certain significance should be thought to attach to their having proposed the subject at this point in history. To some it seemed to suggest that the editors perceived—and perhaps condoned and even welcomed—a lessening of the degree of alienation which they had observed, and which they had both deplored and cherished. The symposium was called "Our Country and Our Culture," and one of the twenty-four participants found in the use of the possessive pronoun the clear evidence of the end of the fighting spirit in *Partisan Review* and in the whole of the intellectual class—*our* country? *our* culture?—and this attitude was shared in greater or less degree by two other contributors. But the other twenty-one, among whom were the editors themselves, treated the subject on its merits, and most of them were willing to say or imply that they could indeed discover in themselves a diminution of the sense of alienation which at some earlier time they would have taken for granted. No one expressed himself as being enraptured by the cultural situation, but most of those who wrote did seem to be saying that they were truly involved in it, and with some sufficient hope, with some aggressive joy at engaging in the conflict of interests which every reasonably healthy culture is.

The nature of the questions (as well as the nature of the contributors) perhaps made it inevitable that "culture" should be conceived of in a certain way, what might be called an institutional way. In point of fact, of course, when you speak of your degree of alienation, greater or less, you are not responding merely to the chances of making a living as an artist or an intellectual, or to the quality of the books the publishing houses are bringing out, or to the number of art galleries, symphonic orchestras, and literary reviews, or to the state of the universities. These things are no doubt of prime importance, but, as much as to them, when you speak of your relation with your country and your culture, you are responding to a tone and a style in your compatriots, to their tempo of movement, the inflection of their voices, the look on their faces. You trust or you do not trust. You penetrate beneath the manner and the manners to the intention which the manner and manners stand for, you become aware of your compatriots' estimate of the future, of their relation to life and death. Sometimes, as you meditate upon yourself in your individuality, insisting upon that individuality for the moment or for an extended time, your fellow beings simply do not seem very real to you. They do not seem to exist sufficiently. You have lost the power to understand their intentions. Or, if you understand, you are repelled or frightened. At such moments, the people of a foreign nation may become very attractive. Our literary and cultural history is full of the records of romances with other cultures, or, sometimes, with other classes. Haunted as we all are by unquiet dreams of peace and wholeness, we are eager and quick to find them embodied in another people. Other peoples may have for us the same beautiful integrity that, from childhood on, we are taught to find in some period of our national or ethnic pasts. Truth, we feel, must *somewhere* be embodied in man. Ever since the nineteenth century, we have been fixing on one kind of person or another, on one group of people or another, to satisfy our yearning—the peasant and the child have served our purpose; so has woman; so has the worker; for the English, there has been a special value in Italians and Arabs; most nations of Europe have set high store upon the Chinese; Americans have made use of the English, the French rural classes, and Negroes. And so on, everyone searching for innocence, for simplicity and integrity of life.

But there also comes a moment when the faces, the gait, the tone, the manner and manners of one's own people become just what one needs, and the whole look and style of one's culture seems appropriate, seems perhaps not good but intensely *possible*. What your compatriots are silently saying about the future, about life and death, may seem suddenly very accessible to you, and not wrong. You are at a gathering of people, or you are in a classroom, and, being the kind of unpleasant person you are, you know that you might take one individual after another and make yourself fully aware of his foolishness or awkwardness and that you might say, "And this is my country! And this is my culture!" But instead of doing that, you let yourself become aware of something that is really in the room, some common intention of the spirit, which, although it may be checked and impeded, is not foolish or awkward but rather graceful, and not wrong. This can be a very real experience, and just because it can be so real—because, that is, the category of culture is so deeply implanted in the modern mind—it can be easily falsified and must therefore be subjected to critical analysis of the strictest kind. Every country has its false language of at-homeness. The American false language of at-homeness, of contented national consciousness, can be dreadfully boring. Not vicious, just boring. I am not speaking of political chauvinism, but of a kind of cultural idealism that can be served by so decent a man as Stephen Vincent Benét, or by so good a poet as Hart Crane, or by so gifted a person as Thomas Wolfe, not to mention lesser writers than these, not to mention the writers of advertisements. But beyond that false language there really is the possibility of a real feeling, which is likely to express itself in indirect and ironic ways, and critically, and wryly.

Something of this sort of feeling is, I think, at work among American intellectuals at this time. I take occasion to refer to it because, although it was not mentioned by any of the contributors to the *Partisan* symposium, I venture to think that it was actually one of the conditions of their thought. Needless to say, this more intangible aspect of "culture" is not unrelated to the institutional aspects about which the contributors did write.

What follows is what I wrote for the symposium, somewhat expanded in detail. The questions which were put by the *Partisan Review* editors, intended rather to suggest the direction of what was written than to be replied to directly, are these:

1. To what extent have American intellectuals actually changed their attitude toward America and its institutions?

2. Must the American intellectual and writer adapt himself to mass culture? If he must, what forms can his adaptation take? Or, do you believe that a democratic society necessarily leads to a leveling of culture, to a mass culture which will overrun intellectual and aesthetic values traditional to Western civilization?

3. Where in American life can artists and intellectuals find the basis of strength, renewal, and recognition, now that they can no longer depend fully on Europe as a cultural example and a source of vitality?

4. If a reaffirmation and rediscovery of America is under way, can the tradition of critical nonconformism (going back to Thoreau and Melville and embracing some of the major expressions of American intellectual history) be maintained as strongly as ever?

It is certainly true that in recent years—say the last ten—American intellectuals have considerably, even radically, revised their attitude toward America. It is no longer the case, as it once used to be, that an avowed aloofness from national feeling is the young intellectual's first ceremonial step into the life of thought.

The ritual of seeming to repudiate one's nation, of denying, in one degree or another, the intellectual and emotional and moral value of the national idea, was not, of course, peculiar to the initiation of the American intellectual. It is part of a tendency of Western culture which developed along with the belief that the national state was in the control and at the service of the *bourgeoisie*. Certainly it was no less common in England than in America, as we know if only through the writings of that remarkable man George Orwell. Himself an intellectual, and an intellectual of the left, and a man who had little use for conventional notions as such, Orwell nevertheless had a reasoned but strong attachment to the idea of England, and he characterized in a very stringent way those intellectuals who treated this idea with habitual contempt. (As much as anything else, I am sure, it was the mere habituality of the attitude that aroused Orwell's anger.) The gist of his criticism was that the English intellectuals of the Left threw out the actuality of social life with the idea of the nation; that they expressed by their anti-nationalism their ignorance of the conditioned nature of all social and political life and their indifference to responsibility; and that, in preferring ideology to nationality, they blinded themselves to the truth that the nation, in the present historical crisis, might represent a principle of freedom as against the tyrannical actuality of any existing ideology.

A prime reason for the change in the American intellectual's attitude toward his nation is of course America's new relation with the other nations of the world. Even the most disaffected American intellectual must nowadays respond, if only in the way of personal interestedness, to the growing isolation of his country amid the hostility which is directed against it. He has become aware of the virtual uniqueness of American security and well-being, and, at the same time, of the danger in which they stand. Perhaps for the first time in his life, he has associated his native land with the not inconsiderable advantages of a whole skin, a full stomach, and the right to wag his tongue as he pleases. (And despite both American and European belief to the contrary, it is true, and true in a very simple way, that he does have the right to wag his tongue as he pleases.)

He also responds to the fact that there is now no longer any foreign cultural ideal to which he can possibly fly from that American stupidity and vulgarity, the institutionalized awareness of which was once likely to have been the mainspring of his mental life. The ideal of the Workers' Fatherland systematically destroyed itself some time back—even the dullest intellectual now knows better than to choose Kronos for a foster father. Nor can he any longer entertain the ideal of the bright cosmopolis of artists and thinkers, usually localized in Paris.

But the change in the American intellectual's attitude toward his country is not merely the result of his having been driven back to within its borders. The American situation has changed in a way that is not merely relative. There is an unmistakable improvement in the American cultural situation of today over that of, say, thirty years ago. This statement is, of course, much too simple and I make it with the awareness that no cultural situation is ever really good, culture being not a free creation but a continuous bargaining with life, an exchange in which one may yield less or more, but never nothing. Yet as against the state of affairs of three decades ago, we are notably better off.

The improvement is manifold. I shall choose only one aspect of it and remark the change in the relation of wealth to intellect. In many civilizations there comes a point at which wealth shows a tendency to submit itself, in some degree, to the rule of mind and imagination, to apologize for its existence by a show of taste and sensitivity. In America the signs of this submission have for some time been visible. For assignable reasons which cannot be here enumerated, wealth inclines to be uneasy about itself. I do not think that in a commercial civilization the acquisition of money can be anything but a prime goal, but I do think that acquisition as a way of life has become conscious of the effective competition of other ways of life.

And one of the chief competitors is intellect. We cannot, to be sure, put money and mind in entire opposition to each other. At a certain risk—for I know how intellectuals value their perfect purity—I shall advance the idea that the intellect of a society may be thought of as a function of the money of a society, not merely of the wealth in general, but specifically of the money. Like money, intellect is conceptual, critical, and fluent. Where money concentrates, intellect concentrates; and money finds that it needs intellect, just as intellect finds that it needs money. But this symbiosis may at times be attenuated or suspended, or the two parties may not be aware of it, and the appearance, or even the reality, of opposition may develop between them. In such an opposition as formerly obtained in this country, money was the stronger of the parties, and this superiority and the moral anomaly it represents are recorded in every developed literature of the nineteenth and twentieth centuries.

But at the present time the needs of our society have brought close to the top of the social hierarchy a large class of people of considerable force and complexity of mind. This is to be observed in most of the agencies of our society, in, for example, government, finance, industry, journalism. The Luce periodicals have for many years been an established butt of the progressive intellectuals, who hate them for their politics and their pretentiousness. The progressive intellectuals are not entirely wrong in their judgment, yet the fact is that the Luce organizations have always been explicit in their desire for the best possible intellectual talent and have been able, by and large, to satisfy their wish. The use to which this talent is put is not frequently defensible, but I am not arguing the point of intellectual virtue—I am making a neutral sociological observation of the place of intellect in our society. Intellect has associated itself with power, perhaps as never before in history, and is now conceded to be in itself a kind of power. The American populist feeling against mind, against the expert, the theorist, and the brain truster, is no doubt still strong. But it has not prevented the entry into our political and social life of an ever-growing class which we must call intellectual, although it is not necessarily a class of "intellectuals."

The strength of this class, its pervasion through our national life, is indicated by the phenomenon of Governor Stevenson. His defeat in the national election is not to the point, and in any case, it is to be accounted for by very complex causes. What is to the point is that, having avowed himself to be an intellectual (in an almost unduly ostentatious way, with a touch of the intellectual's masochism we know all too well), he yet won the Democratic nomination, aroused enormous enthusiasm, and received a strikingly large popular vote despite the obvious apathy and inefficiency of the Democratic machine. To be sure, Governor Stevenson's tone led his successful opponent to express himself in a manner calculated to appeal to the relatively ignorant and anti-intellectual (a manner, it is to be noted, very different from the admirable one in which he could address an academic audience), and this undoubtedly played its part in General Eisenhower's victory. But I do not for a moment undertake to say that there is not a very large element of our population which responds hostilely to intelligence. Any national population, as Walter Bagehot remarked, is a kind of geological formation of culture in which the most primitive coexists with the most highly developed.

The new intellectual class to which I refer is to be accounted for not only by the growing complexity of the administration of our society but also by the necessity of providing a new means of social mobility. Our many bureaus and authorities, our new employments for people of some trained intellectual capacity, were created not only as a response to the social needs which they serve, but also as a response to the social desires of their personnel. They have the function of making jobs and careers for a large class of people whose minds are their only capital. The social principle here at work may or may not be conscious, but it is omnipresent and very strong; and it would seem to be of the very essence of a modern democracy. It may be observed not only in government but in the policy of the powerful labor unions, which are drawing to themselves and carefully training young college graduates to carry out their increasingly complex undertakings. It is to be observed in the increased prestige of the universities. The university teacher now occupies a place in our social hierarchy which is considerably higher than he could have claimed three decades ago. The academic career is now far more attractive to members of all classes than it used to be. One cannot but be struck by the number of well-to-do students who, presumably with their parents' consent, now elect the academic life, just as one cannot but be struck by the even more significant number of students making the same election who, even ten years ago, would have thought themselves debarred from the academic life by class or ethnic considerations, or who would not have consented to think that the rewards of the academic life, now available to them by reason of the increased social mobility, would have been sufficient compensation for their own efforts or their parents' sacrifices.

My own observation of the new tendency does not give me unalloyed delight. As I look, for example, at the present academic situation, I become aware that the movement toward the university is charged with the special impurity that is to be discovered in the professions which are not in their nature gainful. The motives for the study of the humanities often seem to me to be those of laziness, or indecisiveness, or fear, the fear of the contamination of the brisk world, or the simple desire for the degree of prestige that has newly been attached to the profession. And in general I do not believe that a high incidence of conscious professional intellect in a society necessarily makes for a good culture. It is even possible to imagine that a personnel of considerable intellectual power would have little interest in what is called the intellectual life, and even less interest in art. But this is at present not quite the case. The members of the newly expanded intellectual class that I have been describing, partly by reason of the old cultural sanctions, which may operate only as a kind of snobbery but which still do operate, and partly because they know that the mental life of practical reality does have a relation to the mental life of theory and free imagination, are at least potentially supporters and consumers of high culture. They do not necessarily demand the best, but they demand what is called the best; they demand something. The dreadful haste and overcrowding of their lives prevents them from getting as much as they might want and need. So does the stupidity of the entrepreneurs of culture, such as publishers, who, in this country, have not had a new idea since they invented the cocktail party.* So does the nature of the commit-

---

*In 1956 I must modify this harsh statement about publishers by taking note of the remarkable new phenomenon of the paper-bound book.

ment of most of the people who produce the cultural commodity, that is, the actual "intellectuals." Yet it seems to me that art and thought are more generally and happily received and recognized—if still not wholly loved—than they have ever been in America.

A country like ours, as big as ours, compounded of so many elements of a heterogeneous sort, makes it difficult for us to think that ideas such as might be entertained by anything resembling an elite can have any direct influence in the country at large. And it is undoubtedly true that there is a considerable inertia that must be taken into account as we calculate the place of mind in our national life. But we should be wrong to conclude that the inertia is wholly definitive of our cultural situation. This is a characteristic mistake of the American intellectual, particularly the literary intellectual, with whom I am naturally most concerned. His sense of an inert American mass resistant to ideas, entirely unenlightened, and hating enlightenment, is part of the pathos of liberalism in the 1920s and 1930s, which is sedulously maintained despite the fact that the liberal ideas of the 1920s and 1930s are, I will not say dominant—this might, at the present juncture of affairs, be misleading—but strong and established, truly powerful. That the resistance to these ideas often takes an ugly, mindless form I should not think of denying, but this must not blind us to the power of ideas among us, to the existence of a very considerable class which is moved by ideas.

The literary intellectual is likely to be unaware of this, because he is ignorant of the channels through which opinion flows. He does not, for example, know anything about the existence and the training and the influence of, say, high-school teachers, or ministers, or lawyers, or social workers, the people of the professions whose stock in trade is ideas of some kind. Nor does he have any real awareness of the ideas which pass current among these people, or the form in which they are found acceptable. He is likely to think of ideas, of "real" ideas as being limited to the most highly developed, the most "advanced," the most esoteric ideas that he himself is capable of absorbing and of finding aesthetic pleasure in. And when he tests society for the presence of the ideas to which he gives his attention, he finds what he expects to find—no, they are not present, or they are not present in the form in which he knows them. But ideas of some kind, and by no means of a bad or retrograde kind, are indeed present.

I was able to make my own test of this when I recently had occasion to meet with two groups, one of high-school teachers, the other of men concerned in a professional way with the revision of our penal code. In both cases, I ought to say, the participants were the best of their professions—the teachers having been selected for fellowships in leading universities, the penal group consisting of professors of law, judges, psychiatrists, and penologists—yet they did not, I ought also to say, by any means comport themselves as isolated and desperate minorities but rather as people who, by their choice among ideas and their avowed intention of making them prevail, could effect change and make improvements in the conduct of their professions. And my sense of the seriousness of these people, of their commitment to ideas, of their willingness to examine ideas, my sense of their appropriate intellectual humility, by which I mean their willingness to test ideas by experience and by the criterion of human welfare, was to me what it should not have been, a revelation. Should not have been: for to the literary intellectual any profession other than that of literature condemns itself by the mere fact of its being a profession.

From what I have said about the increased power of mind in the nation, something of my answer to the question about mass culture may be inferred. Although mass culture is no doubt a very considerable threat to high culture, there is a countervailing condition in the class I have been describing. As for mass culture itself, one never knows, of course, what may happen in any kind of cultural situation. It is possible that mass culture, if it is not fixed and made static, might become a better thing than it now is, that it might attract genius and discover that it has an inherent law of development. But at the moment I am chiefly interested in the continuation of the traditional culture in the traditional forms. I am therefore concerned with the existence and effect of the large intellectual elite I have described. This group will not be—is not—content with mass culture as we now have it, because for its very existence it requires new ideas, or at the least the simulacra of new ideas.

The social complexion of the new large intellectual class which I have been hypostasizing must be taken fully into account as we estimate the cultural situation it makes. The intellectual and quasi-intellectual classes of contemporary America characteristically push up from the bottom. They are always new. Very little is taken for granted by them. Very little can be taken for granted in instructing them or in trying to influence them. They have, as it were, only a very small cultural reserve. In some ways this is deplorable, making it difficult to think of the refinement of ideas, making it almost impossible to hope for grace and vivacity in the intellectual life. But in some ways it is an advantage, for it assures for the intellectual life a certain simplicity and actuality, an ever-renewed energy of discovery.

From my sense of this there follows my answer to the question: where in American life can the artists and intellectuals find the basis of strength, renewal, and recognition, now that they can't depend on Europe as a cultural example?

In attempting an answer, I shall not speak of the artist, only of the intellectual. For purposes of the artist's salvation, it is best not to speak of the artist at all. It is best to think of him as crazy, foolish, inspired—as an unconditionable kind of man—and to make no provision for him until he appears in person and demands it. Our attitude to the artist is deteriorating as our sense of his need increases. It seems to me that the more we think about doing something for the artist, the less we think of him as Master, and the more we think of him as Postulant or Apprentice. Indeed, it may be coming to be true that for us the Master is not the artist himself, but the great philanthropic Foundation, which brings artists into being, whose creative act the artist is. All the signs point toward our desire to institutionalize the artist, to integrate him into the community. By means of university courses which teach the "technique" of writing, or which arrange for the communication of the spirit from a fully initiated artist to the neophyte, by means of doctoral degrees in creativity, by means of summer schools and conferences, our democratic impulses fulfill themselves and we undertake to prove that art is a profession like another, in which a young man of reasonably good intelligence has a right to succeed. And this undertaking, which is carried out by administrators and by teachers of relatively simple mind, is in reality the response to the theory of more elaborate and refined minds—of intellectuals—who conceive of the artist as the Commissioner of Moral Sanitation, and who demand that he be given his proper statutory salary without delay. I do not hold with the theory that art grows best in hardship. But I become uneasy—especially if I consider the nature of the best of modern art, its demand that it be wrestled with before it consents to bless us—whenever I hear of plans for its early domestication. These plans seem to me an aspect of the modern fear of being cut off from the social group even for a moment, of the modern indignation at the idea of entering the life of the spirit without proper provision having been made for full security.

But intellectuals are in a different case. It is possible that plans can be made for their welfare without diminishing their function. They can be trained. They can, I believe, be taught to think, or at least to think better. It is not improper to discuss what kind of work they should be doing, and their manner of doing it, and the conditions of their doing it, and the influences to which they might submit.

In a way it is wrong, or merely academic, to talk of the *influence* of European thought on American thought, since the latter is continuous with the former. But in so far as the American intellectual conceived of the continuity as being an influence, it no doubt was exactly that, and, in being that, it was, in its time, useful. If that influence has now come to an end, we must truly regret the reasons for its termination, we must be sad over what it may suggest of a diminution of free intercourse, of which we can never have enough. And yet it seems to me that if the European influence, as a large, definitive, conscious experience of the American intellectual, has indeed come to an end, this is, at the moment, all to the good.

For the fact is that the American intellectual never so fully expressed his provincialism as in the way he submitted to the influence of Europe. He was provincial in that he thought of culture as an abstraction and as an absolute. So long as Marxism exercised its direct influence on him, he thought of politics as an absolute. So long as French literature exercised its direct influence upon him, he thought of art as an absolute. To put it another way, he understood himself to be involved primarily with the discipline he had elected. To be sure, the times being what they were, he did not make the mistake of supposing that the elected discipline was not connected with reality. But the reality that he conceived was abstractly conceived, or it was conditioned by circumstances which were more specifically local than the American intellectual could quite perceive.

The "society" which the American intellectual learned about from Europe was in large part a construct of Marxism, or a construct of the long war of the French intellectuals with the French *bourgeoisie*. Ideas, of course, are transferrable: there was no reason why the American intellectual might not have transferred to America what he had learned from Europe, why he should not have directed the impatience, the contempt, the demand, the resistance, which are necessary elements of the life of the critical intellect—and, as I think, of a large part of the creative life as well—upon the immediate, the local, the concrete phenomena of American life. I do not say that he did not display impatience, contempt, demand, and resistance, but only that he did not direct them where they should have gone, that he was general and abstract where he should have been specific and concrete. His sense of himself as an intellectual, his conception of the function of criticism, led him always away from the variousness and complexity of phenomena to an abstract totality of perception which issued in despair or disgust, to which he attached a very high degree of spiritual prestige.

The literary mind, more precisely the historical-literary mind, seems to me the best kind of critical mind that we have, better than the theological, better than the philosophical, better than the scientific and the social-scientific. But the literary intellectuals of today, possibly because they are still fascinated by certain foreign traditions, do not look at our culture with anything like the precise critical attention it must have. If we are to maintain the organic pluralism we have come to value more highly than ever before, it is not enough to think of it in its abstract totality—we must be aware of it in its multifarious, tendentious, competitive details.

For example, it is a truism that universal education is one of the essential characteristics of modern democracy and that the quality and content of the education provided is a clear indication of the quality and tendency of the democracy that provides it. What, then, is the condition of American education? The question has been allowed to fall into the hands of reactionaries of the most vicious kind, and of progressives and liberals whose ideas must evoke sympathy and whose goals are probably right in general, but who live in a cave of self-commiseration into which no ray of true criticism ever penetrates. Who among the intellectuals really knows what is being taught in the great teachers' colleges, which have not only great doctrinal influence but also a very considerable practical control of the schools? Those of us who have any awareness of these colleges at all are likely to hold them in contempt because of what we suppose to be their anti-intellectualism, their emphasis on "method" as against "content," or because of their foolish language of "areas" and "frames of reference" and "implementation," or because of their statistical preoccupations, or because of their absurd claims for their profession which lead them to say such things as that education is coextensive with life. Our impression is probably a just one, yet we can by no means be sure. It may be that they are making foolish formulations of something that they perceive with sufficient accuracy. They are in touch with the matrix of our culture; perhaps their theories do not wholly misrepresent what they see there. In one way or another, we who are intellectuals go back in our tradition of schooling to Colet or Dr. Boyer, by which I do not mean to imply that we have been trained in the classical languages, but that at some point or other in our careers, often in the face of our actual schooling, we have submitted ourselves to learning, to what is called a "discipline." But the teachers' colleges may have become aware that the very idea of submission to a discipline is deeply repugnant to the modern American personality, so that any drill or memorizing (which is necessary for certain kinds of learning) is impossible, and all teaching must depend upon "interest" and must have as its goal not knowledge but "attitudes." Or it is possible that the teachers' colleges have discovered that so many agencies in our culture have failed to provide children with the material of an adequate ethos that it really does devolve upon the schools to make the provision.

If my suppositions are true, they involve the idea of a crisis in culture being dealt with by intellectual agencies of considerable magnitude and power—why should not the intellectuals be concerned with it? Yet it scarcely enters our consciousness, except when one of the Luce periodicals makes one of its heedless and malicious attacks on John Dewey, who, in the demonology of the Luce editors, is the particular imp responsible for virtually every fault of American schooling. And yet, although I would not mitigate the characterization of these attacks as heedless and malicious, they do at least suggest a recognition of the importance of ideas in a democracy.

We know nothing of the directives that are issued by the superintendents of the great school systems. Most of us are not aware that these directives are based on the most elaborate theories of society and the individual. Who among us has any adequate idea about the quality of the teaching staffs of the schools? What is the literary curriculum of our high schools? What is taught in "Social Studies"? What actually happens in a "progressive" school—I mean apart from what everybody jokes about? What happens in colleges? These are questions which the intellectuals have been content to leave to the education editor of *The New York Times*. With the result that Dr. Benjamin Fine, a man with, properly enough, his own ax to grind and his own tears to shed, is far more influential in our culture than any intellectual who reads this, or writes it, is ever likely to be.

Psychology is a science to which literary intellectuals feel a natural affinity. But who knows just what is happening in psychology? Dr.

Fromm, and the late Dr. Horney, and the late Dr. Sullivan, and their disciples have great influence upon many members of the elite. What actually do they say? What is the worth of what they say? Their theories, like the theories of the teachers' colleges, are a response, and, I suspect, a subtle response, to the American cultural personality. I suspect that they are responding to the American feeling that things cannot possibly be as bad as that, i.e., as bad as Freud says they are, or as deeply rooted in biology, that if we could only get together and talk over our attitudes and social arrangements, and revise our culture a little, things would be ever so much better and there would be less neurosis and no wars. But what intellectual takes the time to take these theories seriously?* All literary intellectuals know enough about Dr. Wilhelm Reich to gossip about his theories of sexuality. But nowhere have I read a considered critical examination of what he says. Nor are there any signs of late years that the ethics of sexuality is to be considered a serious subject. What is happening to the development of Freud's ideas by those who are called orthodox Freudians? I speak under correction but I suspect that very little indeed is happening and I regret this very much. One result of what I have come to believe to be the otiosity of the Freudian psychoanalyst is that the intellectual public has withdrawn its sympathy—and its understanding—from the Freudian ideas. For a good many years now I have assigned *Civilization and Its Discontents* to one or another group of students, and I can report how the response to the book has deteriorated from the puzzled respect of some years ago to the present blithe, facetious dismissal. Again and again the public is told, and is very content to hear, that we have got well beyond Freud's possibly useful but certainly primitive and limiting ideas. In point of fact, we have not yet made a beginning in the realization of these ideas—Freud's doctrine has been with us for nearly fifty years and it contains the elements of a most complex moral system, yet I know of no attempt to deal seriously with its implications, or even a true awareness of their existence. Meanwhile the Bollingen Foundation, at considerable expense, is asking us to admire Jung's discovery—made, as it happens, a century ago by a general of the American Army†—that the al-

*In 1956, this question can no longer be asked with the expectation of receiving only the implied answer. Several intellectuals have recently written studies of various schools of psychoanalytical thought.

†See *Ethan Allen Hitchcock: Soldier, Humanitarian, Scholar, Discoverer of the "True Subject" of the Hermetic Art*, by I. Bernard Cohen (Worcester, Massachusetts, 1952).

chemists were men of the profoundest wisdom, concerned with the trans-mutation not of metals but of psychic and moral qualities. Jung contin-ues, I believe, to have influence among some sections of the intellectual population; yet, although we do have the admirable, acidulous book of the English Freudian Dr. Glover, I know of no American who has ven-tured to deal critically with him except for the tireless Mr. Parelhof, who has made it his life work to demonstrate that Jung's relations with Nazism and his stand on anti-Semitism do him no credit.

Departments of psychology in the universities are detaching them-selves from the faculties of philosophy in order to enter the faculties of pure science, on the ground that their science is wholly experimental. What is the value of the very considerable vested interests of this academic psychology? We are as little equipped to give an answer as the laboratory rats themselves. Colleges nowadays give courses in Marriage and Sex, and who knows what is the received doctrine in these courses, let alone in what tone of voice it is delivered?

I could go on with my question at very great length, for I have chosen my two examples pretty much at random from an inexhaustible number. But there is no need for me to go on. My simple point is surely plain. As I make it, I see that it answers the last question which the editors put, about how a reaffirmation and rediscovery of America can go hand in hand with the tradition of critical nonconformism. The editors, to iden-tify the great American tradition of critical nonconformism, speak of it as "going back to Thoreau and Melville." I am glad that they have done so, for it saves me the trouble of defending myself from those to whom it will seem that I recommend an elaborate prostitution of the literary mind to trivialities, to whom it will seem that I have suppressed and betrayed art by my emphasis on the local particularities of culture, and if not art, which I expressly exempted from consideration, then those larger and finer and more transcendent matters to which the most gifted intellectu-als are naturally drawn. I think I should be rather more sensitive to the possibility of this rebuke were I aware that in the larger and finer and more transcendent matters the most gifted intellectuals were as knowl-edgeable and eager as I would wish them to be in grosser and more im-mediate things. But although everybody knows that there is "a great interest in religion" among American literary intellectuals, I see very little evidence of acquaintance with the documents of religion, except those provided by Graham Greene, and very little confrontation of the actuality of religion; nor do American literary intellectuals give any signs of re-sponsiveness to either music or the plastic arts.

Whatever the particular facts of our cultural situation may turn out to be, the recollection of Thoreau and Melville will sustain me in my certi-tude that the kind of critical interest I am asking the literary intellectual to take in the life around him is a proper interest of the literary mind, and that it is the right ground on which to approach transcendent things. More: it is the right ground for the literary art to grow in—the right ground for satire, for humor, for irony, for tragedy, for the personal vi-sion affirming itself against the institutional with the peculiar passionate-ness of art. Art, strange and sad as it may be to have to say it again, really is the criticism of life.

Mansfield Park

1954

Sooner or later, when we speak of Jane Austen, we speak of her irony, and it is better to speak of it sooner rather than later because nothing can so far mislead us about her work as a wrong understanding of this one aspect of it. Most people either value irony too much or fear it too much. This is true of their response to irony in its first simple meaning, that of a device of rhetoric by which we say one thing and intend its opposite, or intend more, or less, than we say. It is equally true of their response to irony in its derived meaning, the loose generalized sense in which we speak of irony as a quality of someone's mind, Montaigne's for example.* Both the excessive valuation and the excessive fear of irony lead us to misconceive the part it can play in the intellectual and moral life. To Jane Austen, irony does not mean, as it means to many, a moral detachment or the tone of superiority that goes with moral detachment. Upon irony so conceived she has made her own judgment in the figure of Mr. Bennet of *Pride and Prejudice*, whose irony of moral detachment is shown to be the cause of his becoming a moral nonentity.

Jane Austen's irony is only secondarily a matter of tone. Primarily it is

*See "Irony" in Fowler's *Modern English Usage*.

a method of comprehension. It perceives the world through an awareness of its contradictions, paradoxes, and anomalies. It is by no means detached. It is partisan with generosity of spirit—it is on the side of "life," of "affirmation." But it is preoccupied not only with the charm of the expansive virtues but also with the cost at which they are to be gained and exercised. This cost is regarded as being at once ridiculously high and perfectly fair. What we may call Jane Austen's first or basic irony is the recognition of the fact that spirit is not free, that it is conditioned, that it is limited by circumstance. This, as everyone knows from childhood on, is indeed an anomaly. Her next and consequent irony has reference to the fact that only by reason of this anomaly does spirit have virtue and meaning.

In irony, even in the large derived sense of the word, there is a kind of malice. The ironist has the intention of practicing upon the misplaced confidence of the literal mind, of disappointing comfortable expectation. Jane Austen's malice of irony is directed not only upon certain of the characters of her novels but also upon the reader himself. We are quick, too quick, to understand that *Northanger Abbey* invites us into a snug conspiracy to disabuse the little heroine of the errors of her corrupted fancy—Catherine Morland, having become addicted to novels of terror, has accepted their inadmissible premise, she believes that life is violent and unpredictable. And that is exactly what life is shown to be by the events of the story: it is we who must be disabused of our belief that life is sane and orderly. The shock of our surprise at the disappointment of our settled views is of course the more startling because we believe that we have settled our views in conformity with the author's own. Just when we have concluded in *Sense and Sensibility* that we ought to prefer Elinor Dashwood's sense to Marianne Dashwood's sensibility, Elinor herself yearns toward the anarchic passionateness of sensibility. In *Emma* the heroine is made to stand at bay to our adverse judgment through virtually the whole novel, but we are never permitted to close in for the kill—some unnamed quality in the girl, some trait of vivacity or will, erects itself into a moral principle, or at least a vital principle, and frustrates our moral blood-lust.

This interference with our moral and intellectual comfort constitutes, as I say, a malice on the part of the author. And when we respond to Jane Austen with pleasure, we are likely to do so in part because we recognize in her work an analogue with the malice of the experienced universe, with the irony of circumstance, which is always disclosing more than we bargained for.

But there is one novel of Jane Austen's, *Mansfield Park*, in which the characteristic irony seems not to be at work. Indeed, one might say of this novel that it undertakes to discredit irony and to affirm literalness, that it demonstrates that there are no two ways about anything. And *Mansfield Park* is for this reason held by many to be the novel that is least representative of Jane Austen's peculiar attractiveness. For those who admire her it is likely to make an occasion for embarrassment. By the same token, it is the novel which the depreciators of Jane Austen may cite most tellingly in justification of their antagonism.

About this antagonism a word must be said. Few writers have been the object of an admiration so fervent as that which is given to Jane Austen. At the same time, she has been the object of great dislike. Lord David Cecil has said that the people who do not like Jane Austen are the kind of people "who do not like sunshine and unselfishness," and Dr. Chapman, the distinguished editor of Jane Austen's novels and letters, although dissenting from Lord David's opinion, has speculated that perhaps "a certain lack of charity" plays a part in the dislike. But Mark Twain, to take but one example, manifestly did not lack charity or dislike sunshine and unselfishness, and Mark Twain said of Jane Austen that she inspired in him an "animal repugnance." The personal intensity of both parties to the dispute will serve to suggest how momentous, how elemental, is the issue that Jane Austen presents.

The *animality* of Mark Twain's repugnance is probably to be taken as the male's revulsion from a society in which women seem to be at the center of interest and power, as a man's panic fear at a fictional world in which the masculine principle, although represented as admirable and necessary, is prescribed and controlled by a female mind. Professor Garrod, whose essay "Jane Austen, A Depreciation" is a *summa* of all the reasons for disliking Jane Austen, expresses a repugnance which is very nearly as feral as Mark Twain's; he implies that a direct sexual insult is being offered to men by a woman author who "describes everything in the youth of women which does not matter" in such a way as to appeal to "that age in men when they have begun to ask themselves whether anything matters." The sexual protest is not only masculine—Charlotte Brontë despised Jane Austen for representing men and women as nothing but ladies and gentlemen.

The sexual objection to Jane Austen is a very common one, even when it is not made explicit. It is not valid, yet it ought to be taken seriously into account. But then there is Emerson with his characteristic sexual indifference, his striking lack of animality, and Emerson's objection to Jane Austen is quick and entire, is instinctual. He says that she is "sterile" and goes on to call her "vulgar." Emerson held this opinion out of his passion of concern for the liberty of the self and the autonomy of spirit, and his holding it must make us see that the sexual reason for disliking Jane Austen must be subsumed under another reason which is larger, and, actually, even more elemental: the fear of imposed constraint. Dr. Chapman says something of this sort when he speaks of "political prejudice" and "impatient idealism" as perhaps having something to do with the dislike of Jane Austen. But these phrases, apart from the fact that they prejudge the case, do not suggest the biological force of the resistance which certain temperaments offer to the idea of society as a limiting condition of the individual spirit.

Such temperaments are not likely to take Jane Austen's irony as a melioration of her particular idea of society. On the contrary, they are likely to suppose that irony is but the engaging manner by which she masks society's crude coercive power. And they can point to *Mansfield Park* to show what the social coercion is in all its literal truth, before irony has beglamoured us about it and induced us to be comfortable with it—here it is in all its negation, in all the force of its repressiveness. Perhaps no other work of genius has ever spoken, or seemed to speak, so insistently for cautiousness and constraint, even for dullness. No other great novel has so anxiously asserted the need to find security, to establish, in fixity and enclosure, a refuge from the dangers of openness and chance.

There is scarcely one of our modern pieties that it does not offend. Despite our natural tendency to permit costume and manners to separate her world from ours, most readers have no great difficulty in realizing that all the other novels of Jane Austen are, in essential ways, of our modern time. This is the opinion of the many students with whom I have read the novels; not only do the young men controvert by their enthusiasm the judgment of Professor Garrod that Jane Austen appeals only to men of middle age, but they easily and naturally assume her to have a great deal to say to them about the modern personality. But *Mansfield Park* is the exception, and it is bitterly resented. It scandalizes the modern assumptions about social relations, about virtue, about religion, sex, and art. Most troubling of all is its preference for rest over motion. To deal with the world by condemning it, by withdrawing from it and shutting it out, by making oneself and one's mode and principles of life the very center of existence and to live the round of one's days in the stasis and peace thus contrived—this, in an earlier age, was one of the recognized strategies of life, but to us it seems not merely impracticable but almost wicked.

Yet *Mansfield Park* is a great novel, its greatness being commensurate with its power to offend.

Mansfield Park was published in 1814, only one year after the publication of *Pride and Prejudice*, and no small part of its interest derives from the fact that it seems to controvert everything that its predecessor tells us about life. One of the striking things about *Pride and Prejudice* is that it achieves a quality of transcendence through comedy. The comic mode typically insists upon the fact of human limitation, even of human littleness, but *Pride and Prejudice* makes comedy reverse itself and yield the implication of a divine enlargement. The novel celebrates the traits of spiritedness, vivacity, celerity, and lightness, and associates them with happiness and virtue. Its social doctrine is a generous one, asserting the right of at least the *good* individual to define himself according to his own essence. It is animated by an impulse to forgiveness. One understands very easily why many readers are moved to explain their pleasure in the book by reference to Mozart, especially *The Marriage of Figaro*.

Almost the opposite can be said of *Mansfield Park*. Its impulse is not to forgive but to condemn. Its praise is not for social freedom but for social stasis. It takes full notice of spiritedness, vivacity, celerity, and lightness, but only to reject them as having nothing to do with virtue and happiness, as being, indeed, deterrents to the good life.

Nobody, I believe, has ever found it possible to like the heroine of *Mansfield Park*. Fanny Price is overtly virtuous and consciously virtuous. Our modern literary feeling is very strong against people who, when they mean to be virtuous, believe they know how to reach their goal and do reach it. We think that virtue is not interesting, even that it is not really virtue unless it manifests itself as a product of "grace" operating through a strong inclination to sin. Our favorite saint is likely to be Augustine; he is sweetened for us by his early transgressions. We cannot understand how any age could have been interested in Patient Griselda. We admire Milton only if we believe with Blake that he was of the Devil's party, of which we are fellow travelers; the paradox of the *felix culpa* and the "fortunate fall" appeals to us for other than theological reasons and serves to validate all sins and all falls, which we take to be the signs of life.

It does not reconcile us to the virtue of Fanny Price that it is rewarded by more than itself. The shade of Pamela hovers over her career. We take failure to be the mark of true virtue and we do not like it that, by reason of her virtue, the terrified little stranger in Mansfield Park grows up to be virtually its mistress.

Even more alienating is the state of the heroine's health. Fanny is in a debilitated condition through the greater part of the novel. At a certain point the author retrieves this situation and sees to it that Fanny becomes taller, prettier, and more energetic. But the first impression remains of a heroine who cannot cut a basket of roses without fatigue and headache.

Fanny's debility becomes the more striking when we consider that no quality of the heroine of *Pride and Prejudice* is more appealing than her physical energy. We think of Elizabeth Bennet as in physical movement; her love of dancing confirms our belief that she moves gracefully. It is characteristic of her to smile; she likes to tease; she loves to talk. She is remarkably responsive to all attractive men. And to outward seeming, Mary Crawford of *Mansfield Park* is another version of Elizabeth Bennet, and Mary Crawford is the antithesis of Fanny Price. The boldness with which the antithesis is contrived is typical of the uncompromising honesty of *Mansfield Park*. Mary Crawford is conceived—is calculated—to win the charmed admiration of almost any reader. She is all pungency and wit. Her mind is as lively and competent as her body; she can bring not only a horse but a conversation to the gallop. She is downright, open, intelligent, impatient. Irony is her natural mode, and we are drawn to think of her voice as being as nearly the author's own as Elizabeth Bennet's is. Yet in the end we are asked to believe that she is not to be admired, that her lively mind compounds, by very reason of its liveliness, with the world, the flesh, and the devil.

This strange, this almost perverse, rejection of Mary Crawford's vitality in favor of Fanny's debility lies at the very heart of the novel's intention. "The divine," said T. E. Hulme in *Speculations*, "is not life at its intensest. It contains in a way an almost anti-vital element." Perhaps it cannot quite be said that "the divine" is the object of Fanny's soul, yet she is a Christian heroine. Hulme expresses with an air of discovery what was once taken for granted in Christian feeling. Fanny is one of the poor in spirit. It is not a condition of the soul to which we are nowadays sympathetic. We are likely to suppose that it masks hostility—many modern readers respond to Fanny by suspecting her. This is perhaps not unjustified, but as we try to understand what Jane Austen meant by the creation of such a heroine, we must have in mind the tradition which affirmed the peculiar sanctity of the sick, the weak, and the dying. The tradition perhaps came to an end for literature with the death of Milly Theale, the heroine of Henry James's *The Wings of the Dove*, but Dickens exemplifies its continuing appeal in the nineteenth century, and it was especially strong in the eighteenth century. Clarissa's sickness and death confirm her Christian virtue, and in Fielding's *Amelia*, the novel which may be said to bear the same relation to *Tom Jones* that *Mansfield Park* bears to *Pride and Prejudice*, the sign of the heroine's Christian authority is her loss of health and beauty.

Fanny is a Christian heroine: it is therefore not inappropriate that the issue between her and Mary Crawford should be concentrated in the debate over whether or not Edmund Bertram shall become a clergyman. We are not, however, from our reading of the novel, inclined to say more than that the debate is "not inappropriate"—it startles us to discover that ordination was what Jane Austen said her novel was to be "about." In the letter in which she tells of having received the first copies of *Pride and Prejudice*, and while she is still in high spirits over her achievement, she says, "Now I will try and write something else, and it shall be a complete change of subject—ordination." A novelist, of course, presents a new subject to himself, or to his friends, in all sorts of ways that are inadequate to his real intention as it eventually will disclose itself—the most unsympathetic reader of *Mansfield Park* would scarcely describe it as being about ordination. Yet the question of ordination is of essential importance to the novel.

It is not really a religious question, but, rather, a cultural question, having to do with the meaning and effect of a *profession*. Two senses of that word are in point here, the open avowal of principles and beliefs as well as a man's commitment to a particular kind of life work. It is the latter sense that engages us first. The argument between Fanny and Mary is over what will happen to Edmund as a person, as a *man*, if he chooses to become a clergyman. To Mary, every clergyman is the Mr. Collins of *Pride and Prejudice*; she thinks of ordination as a surrender of manhood. But Fanny sees the Church as a career that claims a man's best manly energies; her expressed view of the churchman's function is that which was to develop through the century, exemplified in, say, Thomas Arnold, who found the Church to be an adequate field for what he called his talents for command.

The matter of a man's profession was of peculiar importance to Jane Austen. It weighs heavily against Mr. Bennet that, his estate being entailed, he has made no effort to secure his family against his death, and by reason of his otiosity he is impotent to protect his family's good name from the consequences of Lydia's sexual escapade. He is represented as being not only less a man but also less a gentleman than his brother-in-law Gardiner, who is in trade in London. Jane Austen's feelings about men in relation to their profession reach their highest intensity in *Persuasion*, in the great comic scene in which Sir Walter Elliot is flattered by Mrs. Clay's telling him that every profession puts its mark upon a man's face, and that a true gentleman will avoid this vulgar injury to his complexion. And in the same novel much is made of the professional pride of the Navy and the good effect it has upon the personal character.

In nineteenth-century England the ideal of professional commitment inherits a large part of the moral prestige of the ideal of the gentleman. Such figures as the engineer Daniel Doyce of *Little Dorrit* or Dr. Lydgate of *Middlemarch* represent the developing belief that a man's moral life is bound up with his loyalty to the discipline of his calling. The concern with the profession was an aspect of the ethical concept which was prepotent in the spiritual life of England in the nineteenth century, the concept of duty. The Church, in its dominant form and characteristic virtue, was here quite at one with the tendency of secular feeling; its preoccupation may be said to have been less with the achievement of salvation than with the performance of duty.

The word grates upon our moral ear. We do what we should do, but we shrink from giving it the name of duty. "Cooperation," "social-mindedness," the "sense of the group," "class solidarity"—these locutions do not mean what duty means. They have been invented precisely for the purpose of describing right conduct in such a way as *not* to imply what duty implies—a self whose impulses and desires are very strong, and a willingness to subordinate these impulses and desires to the claim of some external nonpersonal good. The new locutions are meant to suggest that right action is typically to be performed without any pain to the self.

The men of the nineteenth century did not imagine this possibility. They thought that morality was terribly hard to achieve, at the cost of renunciation and sacrifice. We of our time often wonder what could have made the difficulty. We wonder, for example, why a man like Matthew Arnold felt it necessary to remind himself almost every day of duty, why he believed that the impulses must be "bridled" and "chained down," why he insisted on the "strain and labour and suffering" of the moral life. We are as much puzzled as touched by the tone in which F. W. H. Myers tells of walking with George Eliot in the Fellows' Garden at Trinity "on an evening of rainy May," and she, speaking of God, Immortality, and Duty, said how inconceivable was the first, how unbelievable the second, "yet how peremptory and absolute the third." "Never, perhaps, have sterner accents affirmed the sovereignty of impersonal and unrecompensing Law. I listened, and night fell; her grave majestic countenance turned towards me like a sybil's in the gloom; it was as though she withdrew from my grasp, one by one, the two scrolls of promise, and left me the third scroll only, awful with inevitable fate."*

The diminution of faith in the promise of religion accounts for much but not for all the concern with duty in nineteenth-century England. It was not a crisis of religion that made Wordsworth the laureate of duty. What Wordsworth asks in his great poem "Resolution and Independence" is how the self, in its highest manifestation, in the Poet, can preserve itself from its own nature, from the very sensibility and volatility that define it, from its own potentiality of what Wordsworth calls with superb explicitness "despondency and madness." Something has attenuated the faith in the self of four years before, of "Tintern Abbey," the certitude that "Nature never did betray/The heart that loved her": a new

---

*But if we are puzzled by the tone of this, we cannot say that it is a tone inappropriate to its subject. The idea of duty was central in the English culture of the nineteenth century, and in general when Englishmen of the period speak about duty *in propria persona* they speak movingly. This makes it all the stranger that when they express the idea through a literary form they scarcely ever do so in an elevated manner. They seem to have thought of duty as an ideal to be associated in literature chiefly with domestic life or with dullness. As a consequence, everyone was delighted with the jig in *Ruddigore*: "For duty, duty must be done,/ The rule applies to everyone./ Unpleasant though that duty be,/ To shirk the task were fiddledeedee." It was left to foreigners to deal with the idea as if it were of *tragic* import. Melville in *Billy Budd* and Vigny in his military stories exploited the moral possibilities of the British naval tradition of Nelson and Collingwood, which even Wordsworth had been able to represent only abstractly and moralistically in his "character" of the Happy Warrior; and Conrad is the first English novelist to make the idea of duty large and interesting. It is hard to believe that the moral idea which Emily Dickinson celebrates in her brilliant poem on Thermopylae and associates with high intelligence is the same idea that Tennyson celebrates in "The Charge of the Light Brigade" and associates with stupidity.

Paraclete is needed and he comes in the shape of the Old Leech-gatherer, a man rocklike in endurance, rocklike in insensibility, annealed by a simple, rigorous religion, preserved in life and in virtue by the "anti-vital element" and transfigured by that element.

That the self may destroy the self by the very energies that define its being, that the self may be preserved by the negation of its own energies—this, whether or not we agree, makes a paradox, makes an irony, that catches our imagination. Much of the nineteenth-century preoccupation with duty was not a love of law for its own sake, but rather a concern with the hygiene of the self. If we are aware of this, we are prepared to take seriously an incident in *Mansfield Park* that on its face is perfectly absurd.

The great fuss that is made over the amateur theatricals can seem to us a mere travesty on virtue. And the more so because it is never made clear why it is so very wrong for young people in a dull country house to put on a play. The mystery deepens, as does our sense that *Mansfield Park* represents an unusual state of the author's mind, when we know that amateur theatricals were a favorite amusement in Jane Austen's home. The play is Kotzebue's *Lovers' Vows* and it deals with illicit love and a bastard, but Jane Austen, as her letters and novels clearly show, was not a prude. Some of the scenes of the play permit Maria Bertram and Henry Crawford to make love in public, but this is not said to be decisively objectionable. What is decisive is a traditional, almost primitive, feeling about dramatic impersonation. We know of this, of course, from Plato, and it is one of the points on which almost everyone feels superior to Plato, but it may have more basis in actuality than we commonly allow. It is the fear that the impersonation of a bad or inferior character will have a harmful effect upon the impersonator, that, indeed, the impersonation of any other self will diminish the integrity of the real self.

A right understanding of the seemingly absurd episode of the play must dispel any doubt of the largeness of the cultural significance of *Mansfield Park*. The American philosopher George Mead has observed that the "assumption of roles" was one of the most important elements of Romanticism. Mead conceived of impersonation as a new mode of thought appropriate to that new sense of the self which was Romanticism's characteristic achievement. It was, he said further, the self's method of defining itself. Involved as we all are in this mode of thought and in this method of self-definition, we are not likely to respond sympathetically to Jane Austen when she puts it under attack as being dangerous to the integrity of the self as a moral agent. Yet the testimony of John Keats stands in her support—in one of his most notable letters Keats says of the poet that, as poet, he cannot be a moral agent; he has no "character," no "self," no "identity"; he is concerned not with moral judgment but with "gusto," subordinating his own being to that of the objects of his creative regard. Wordsworth implies something of a related sort when he contrasts the poet's volatility of mood with the bulking permanence of identity of the Old Leech-gatherer. And of course not only the poet but the reader may be said to be involved in the problems of identity and of (in the literal sense) integrity. Literature offers the experience of the diversification of the self, and Jane Austen puts the question of literature at the moral center of her novel.

The massive ado that is organized about the amateur theatricals and the dangers of impersonation thus has a direct bearing upon the matter of Edmund Bertram's profession. The election of a profession is of course in a way the assumption of a role, but it is a permanent impersonation which makes virtually impossible the choice of another. It is a commitment which fixes the nature of the self.

The ado about the play extends its significance still further. It points, as it were, to a great and curious triumph of Jane Austen's art. The triumph consists in this—that although on a first reading of *Mansfield Park* Mary Crawford's speeches are all delightful, they diminish in charm as we read the novel a second time. We begin to hear something disagreeable in their intonation: it is the peculiarly modern bad quality which Jane Austen was the first to represent—insincerity. This is a trait very different from the *hypocrisy* of the earlier novelists. Mary Crawford's intention is not to deceive the world but to comfort herself; she impersonates the woman she thinks she ought to be. And as we become inured to the charm of her performance we see through the moral impersonation and are troubled that it should have been thought necessary. In Mary Crawford we have the first brilliant example of a distinctively modern type, the person who cultivates the *style* of sensitivity, virtue, and intelligence.

Henry Crawford has more sincerity than his sister, and the adverse judgment which the novel makes on him is therefore arrived at with greater difficulty. He is conscious of his charm, of the winningness of his personal style, which has in it—as he knows—a large element of *natural* goodness and generosity. He is no less conscious of his lack of weight and solidity; his intense courtship of Fanny is, we may say, his effort to add the gravity of principle to his merely natural goodness. He becomes, however, the prey to his own charm, and in his cold flirtation with Maria Bertram he is trapped by his impersonation of passion—his role requires that he carry Maria off from a dull marriage to a life of boring concupiscence. It is his sister's refusal to attach any moral importance to this event that is the final proof of her deficiency in seriousness. Our modern impulse to resist the condemnation of sexuality and of sexual liberty cannot properly come into play here, as at first we think it should. For it is not sexuality that is being condemned, but precisely that form of asexuality that incurred D. H. Lawrence's greatest scorn—that is, sexuality as a game, or as a drama, sexuality as an expression of mere will or mere personality, as a sign of power, or prestige, or autonomy: as, in short, an impersonation and an insincerity.

A passage in one of her letters of 1814, written while *Mansfield Park* was in composition, enforces upon us how personally Jane Austen was involved in the question of principle as against personality, of character as against style. A young man has been paying court to her niece Fanny Knight, and the girl is troubled by, exactly, the effect of his principledness on his style. Her aunt's comment is especially interesting because it contains an avowal of sympathy with Evangelicism, an opinion which is the reverse of that which she had expressed in a letter of 1809 and had represented in *Pride and Prejudice*, yet the religious opinion is but incidental to the affirmation that is being made of the moral advantage of the profession of principle, whatever may be its effect on the personal style.

Mr. J. P.—— has advantages which do not often meet in one person. His only fault indeed seems Modesty. If he were less modest, he would be more agreeable, speak louder & look Impudenter;— and is it not a fine Character of which Modesty is the only defect?—I have no doubt that he will get more lively & more like yourselves as he is more with you;—he will catch your ways if he belongs to you. And as to there being any objection from his *Goodness*, from the danger of his becoming even Evangelical, I cannot admit *that*. I am by no means convinced that we ought not all to be Evangelicals, & am at least persuaded that they who are so from

Reason and Feeling, must be happiest & safest. Do not be frightened from the connection by your Brothers having most wit. Wisdom is better than Wit, & in the long run will certainly have the laugh on her side; & don't be frightened by the idea of his acting more strictly up to the precepts of the New Testament than others.

The great charm, the charming greatness, of *Pride and Prejudice* is that it permits us to conceive of morality as style. The relation of Elizabeth Bennet to Darcy is real, is intense, but it expresses itself as a conflict and reconciliation of styles: a formal rhetoric, traditional and rigorous, must find a way to accommodate a female vivacity, which in turn must recognize the principled demands of the strict male syntax. The high moral import of the novel lies in the fact that the union of styles is accomplished without injury to either lover.

Jane Austen knew that *Pride and Prejudice* was a unique success and she triumphed in it. Yet as she listens to her mother reading aloud from the printed book, she becomes conscious of her dissatisfaction with one element of the work. It is the element that is likely to delight us most, the purity and absoluteness of its particular style.

The work [she writes in a letter to her sister Cassandra] is rather too light, and bright, and sparkling; it wants to be stretched out here and there with a long chapter of sense, if it could be had; if not, of solemn specious nonsense, about something unconnected with the story; an essay on writing, a critique on Walter Scott, or the history of Buonaparté, or anything that would form a contrast, and bring the reader with increased delight to the playfulness and epigrammatism of the general style.

Her overt concern, of course, is for the increase of the effect of the "general style" itself, which she believes would have been heightened by contrast. But she has in mind something beyond this technical improvement—her sense that the novel is a genre that must not try for the shining outward perfection of style; that it must maintain a degree of roughness of texture, a certain hard literalness; that, for the sake of its moral life, it must violate its own beauty by incorporating some of the irreducible prosy actuality of the world. It is as if she were saying of *Pride and Prejudice* what Henry James says of one of the characters of his story "Crapy

Cornelia": "Her grace of ease was perfect, but it was all grace of ease, not a single shred of it grace of uncertainty or of difficulty."*

Mansfield Park, we may conceive, was the effort to encompass the grace of uncertainty and difficulty. The idea of morality as achieved style, as grace of ease, is not likely ever to be relinquished, not merely because some writers will always assert it anew, but also because morality itself will always insist on it—at a certain point in its development, morality seeks to express its independence of the grinding necessity by which it is engendered, and to claim for itself the autonomy and gratuitousness of art. Yet the idea is one that may easily deteriorate or be perverted. Style, which expresses the innermost truth of any creation or action, can also hide the truth; it is in this sense of the word that we speak of "mere style." *Mansfield Park* proposes to us the possibility of this deception. If we perceive this, we cannot say that the novel is without irony—we must say, indeed, that its irony is more profound than that of any of Jane Austen's other novels. It is an irony directed against irony itself.

In the investigation of the question of character as against personality, of principle as against style and grace of ease as against grace of difficulty, it is an important consideration that the Crawfords are of London. Their manner is the London manner, their style is the *chic* of the metropolis. The city bears the brunt of our modern uneasiness about our life. We think of it as being the scene and the cause of the loss of the simple integrity of the spirit—in our dreams of our right true selves we live in the country. This common mode of criticism of our culture is likely to express not merely our dissatisfaction with our particular cultural situation but

---

*This may be the place to remark that although the direct line of descent from Jane Austen to Henry James has often been noted, and although there can be no doubt of the lineage, James had a strange misconception of the nature of the art of his ancestress. "Jane Austen, with her light felicity," he says in *The Lesson of Balzac*, "leaves us hardly more curious of her process, or of the experience that fed it, than the brown thrush who tells his story from the garden bough." He says of her reputation that it is higher than her intrinsic interest and attributes it to "the body of publishers, editors, illustrators, producers of the present twaddle of magazines, who have found their 'dear,' our dear, everybody's dear, Jane so infinitely to their material purpose." An acid response to the "dear Jane" myth is always commendable, but it seems to have led James into a strange obtuseness: "The key to Jane Austen's fortune with posterity has been in part the extraordinary grace of her facility, in part of her unconsciousness . . ." This failure of perception (and syntax) is followed by a long, ambiguous, and unfortunate metaphor of Jane Austen musing over her "work-basket, her tapestry flowers, in the spare, cool drawing room of other days." Jane Austen was, it need scarcely be said at this date, as little unconscious as James himself either in her intentions or (as the remarks about the style of *Pride and Prejudice* show) in her "process."

our dislike of culture itself, or of any culture that is not a folk culture, that is marked by the conflict of interests and the proliferation and conflict of ideas. Yet the revulsion from the metropolis cannot be regarded merely with skepticism; it plays too large and serious a part in our literature to be thought of as nothing but a sentimentality.

To the style of London Sir Thomas Bertram is the principled antagonist. The real reason for not giving the play, as everyone knows, is that Sir Thomas would not permit it were he at home; everyone knows that a sin is being committed against the absent father. And Sir Thomas, when he returns before his expected time, confirms their consciousness of sin. It is he who identifies the objection to the theatricals as being specifically that of impersonation. His own self is an integer and he instinctively resists the diversification of the self that is implied by the assumption of roles. It is he, in his entire identification with his status and tradition, who makes of Mansfield Park the citadel it is—it exists to front life and to repel life's mutabilities, like the Peele Castle of Wordsworth's "Elegiac Verses," of which it is said that it is "cased in the unfeeling armor of old time." In this phrase Wordsworth figures in a very precise way the Stoic doctrine of *apatheia*, the principled refusal to experience more emotion than is forced upon one, the rejection of sensibility as a danger to the integrity of the self.

Mansfield stands not only against London but also against what is implied by Portsmouth on Fanny's visit to her family there. Fanny's mother, Lady Bertram's sister, had made an unprosperous marriage, and the Bertrams' minimal effort to assist her with the burdens of a large family had been the occasion of Fanny's coming to live at Mansfield nine years before. Her return to take her place in a home not of actual poverty but of respectable sordidness makes one of the most engaging episodes of the novel, despite our impulse to feel that it ought to seem the most objectionable. We think we ought not be sympathetic with Fanny as, to her slow dismay, she understands that she cannot be happy with her own, her natural, family. She is made miserable by the lack of cleanliness and quiet, of civility and order. We jib at this, we remind ourselves that for the seemliness that does indeed sustain the soul, men too often sell their souls, that warmth and simplicity of feeling may go with indifference to disorder. But if we have the most elementary honesty, we feel with Fanny the genuine pain not merely of the half-clean and the scarcely tidy, of confusion and intrusion, but also of the vulgarity that thrives in these surroundings. It is beyond human ingenuity to define what we mean by vulgarity, but in Jane Austen's novels vulgarity has these elements: smallness of mind, insufficiency of awareness, assertive self-esteem, the wish to devalue, especially to devalue the human worth of other people. That Fanny's family should have forgotten her during her long absence was perhaps inevitable; it is a vulgarity that they have no curiosity about her and no desire to revive the connection, and this indifference is represented as being of a piece with the general indecorum of their lives. We do not blame Fanny when she remembers that in her foster father's house there are many rooms, that hers, although it was small and for years it had been cold, had always been clean and private, that now, although she had once been snubbed and slighted at Mansfield, she is the daughter of Sir Thomas's stern heart.

Of all the fathers of Jane Austen's novels, Sir Thomas is the only one to whom admiration is given. Fanny's real father, Lieutenant Price of the Marines, is shallow and vulgar. The fathers of the heroines of *Pride and Prejudice*, *Emma*, and *Persuasion*, all lack principle and fortitude; they are corrupted by their belief in their delicate vulnerability—they lack *apatheia*. Yet Sir Thomas is a father, and a father is as little safe from Jane Austen's judgment as he is from Shelley's. Jane Austen's masculine ideal is exemplified by husbands, by Darcy, Knightley, and Wentworth, in whom principle and duty consort with a ready and tender understanding. Sir Thomas's faults are dealt with explicitly—if he learns to cherish Fanny as the daughter of his heart, he betrays the daughters of his blood. Maria's sin and her sister Julia's bad disposition are blamed directly upon his lack of intelligence and sensibility. His principled submission to convention had issued in mere worldliness—he had not seen to it that "principle, active principle" should have its place in the rearing of his daughters, had not given them that "sense of duty which alone can suffice" to govern inclination and temper. He knew of no other way to counteract the low worldly flattery of their Aunt Norris than by the show of that sternness which had alienated them from him. He has allowed Mrs. Norris, the corrupter of his daughters and the persecutor of Fanny, to establish herself in the governance of his home; "she seemed part of himself."

So that Mansfield is governed by an authority all too fallible. Yet Fanny thinks of all that comes "within the view and patronage of Mansfield Park" as "dear to her heart and thoroughly perfect in her eyes." The judgment is not ironical. For the author as well as for the heroine, Mansfield Park is the good place—it is The Great Good Place. It is the house "where all's accustomed, ceremonious," of Yeats's "Prayer for His Daughter"—

How but in custom and ceremony
Are innocence and beauty born?

Yet Fanny's loving praise of Mansfield, which makes the novel's last word, does glance at ironies and encompasses ironies. Of these ironies the chief is that Lady Bertram is part of the perfection. All of Mansfield's life makes reference and obeisance to Sir Thomas's wife, who is gentle and without spite, but mindless and moveless, concerned with nothing but the indulgence of her mild, inexorable wants. Middle-aged, stupid, maternal persons are favorite butts for Jane Austen, but although Lady Bertram is teased, she is loved. Sir Thomas's authority must be qualified and tutored by the principled intelligence, the religious intelligence—Fanny's, in effect—but Lady Bertram is permitted to live unregenerate her life of cushioned ease.

I am never quite able to resist the notion that in her attitude to Lady Bertram Jane Austen is teasing herself, that she is turning her irony upon her own fantasy of ideal existence as it presented itself to her at this time. It is scarcely possible to observe how *Mansfield Park* differs from her work that had gone before and from her work that was to come after without supposing that the difference points to a crisis in the author's spiritual life. In that crisis fatigue plays a great part—we are drawn to believe that for the moment she wants to withdraw from the exigent energies of her actual self, that she claims in fancy the right to be rich and fat and smooth and dull like Lady Bertram, to sit on a cushion, to be a creature of habit and an object of ritual deference, not to be conscious, especially not to be conscious of herself. Lady Bertram is, we may imagine, her mocking representation of her wish to escape from the requirements of personality.

It was Jane Austen who first represented the specifically modern personality and the culture in which it had its being. Never before had the moral life been shown as she shows it to be, never before had it been conceived to be so complex and difficult and exhausting. Hegel speaks of the "secularization of spirituality" as a prime characteristic of the modern epoch, and Jane Austen is the first to tell us what this involves. She is the first novelist to represent society, the general culture, as playing a part in the moral life, generating the concepts of "sincerity" and "vulgarity" which no earlier time would have understood the meaning of, and which for us are so subtle that they defy definition, and so powerful that none can escape their sovereignty. She is the first to be aware of the Terror which rules our moral situation, the ubiquitous anonymous judgment to which we respond, the necessity we feel to demonstrate the purity of our secular spirituality, whose dark and dubious places are more numerous and obscure than those of religious spirituality, to put our lives and styles to the question, making sure that not only in deeds but in *décor* they exhibit the signs of our belonging to the number of the secular-spiritual elect.

She herself is an agent of the Terror—we learn from her what our lives should be and by what subtle and fierce criteria they will be judged, and how to pass upon the lives of our friends and fellows. Once we have comprehended her mode of judgment, the moral and spiritual lessons of contemporary literature are easy—the metaphysics of "sincerity" and "vulgarity" once mastered, the modern teachers, Lawrence and Joyce, Yeats and Eliot, Proust and Gide, have but little to add save in the way of contemporary and abstruse examples.

To what extremes the Terror can go she herself has made all too clear in the notorious passage in *Persuasion* in which she comments on Mrs. Musgrove's "large, fat sighings" over her dead scapegrace son. "Personal size and mental sorrow have certainly no necessary proportions," she says. "A large bulky figure has as good a right to be in deep affliction as the most graceful set of limbs in the world. But fair or not fair, there are unbecoming conjunctions, which reason will patronize in vain—which taste cannot tolerate, which ridicule will seize." We feel this to be unconscionable, and Henry James and E. M. Forster will find occasion to warn us that it is one of the signs of the death of the heart to regard a human being as an object of greater or less *vertu*; in fairness to Jane Austen we must remember that the passage occurs in the very novel which deals mercilessly with Sir Walter Elliot for making just this illegitimate application of taste to life. But although this aesthetic-spiritual snobbery is for Jane Austen a unique lapse, it is an extension, an extravagance of her characteristic mode of judgment, and it leads us to see what is implied by the "secularization of spirituality," which requires of us that we judge not merely the moral act itself but also, and even more searchingly, the quality of the agent. This is what Hegel has in mind when he is at such pains to make his distinction between character and personality and to show how the development of the idea of personality is one of the elements of the secularization of spirituality. Dewey followed Hegel in this when, in his *Ethics*, he said that moral choice is not really dictated by the principle or the maxim that is applicable to the situation but rather by the "kind of selfhood" one wishes to "assume." And Nietzsche's conception of the Third Morality, which takes cognizance of the *real*—that is, the unconscious—intention of the agent, is the terrible instrument of criticism of this new development of the moral life. We are likely to feel that this placing of the personality, of the quality of being, at the center of the moral life is a chief glory of spirit in its modern manifestation, and when we take pleasure in Jane Austen we are responding to her primacy and brilliance in the exercise of this new mode of judgment. Yet we at times become aware of the terrible strain it imposes upon us, of the exhausting effort which the concept of personality requires us to make and of the pain of exacerbated sensitivity to others, leading to the *disgust* which is endemic in our culture.

Jane Austen's primacy in representing this mutation in the life of the spirit constitutes a large part of her claim to greatness. But in her representation of the modern situation *Mansfield Park* has a special place. It imagines the self safe from the Terror of secularized spirituality. In the person of Lady Bertram it affirms, with all due irony, the bliss of being able to remain unconscious of the demands of personality (it is a bliss which is a kind of virtue, for one way of being solid, simple, and sincere is to be a vegetable). It shuts out the world and the judgment of the world. The sanctions upon which it relies are not those of culture, of quality of being, of personality, but precisely those which the new conception of the moral life minimizes, the sanctions of principle, and it discovers in principle the path to the wholeness of the self which is peace. When we have exhausted our anger at the offense which *Mansfield Park* offers to our conscious pieties, we find it possible to perceive how intimately it speaks to our secret inexpressible hopes.

Isaac Babel

1955

A good many years ago, in 1929, I chanced to read a book which disturbed me in a way I can still remember. The book was called *Red Cavalry*; it was a collection of stories about Soviet regiments of horse operating in Poland. I had never heard of the author, Isaac Babel—or I. Babel, as he signed himself—and nobody had anything to tell me about him, and part of my disturbance was the natural shock we feel when, suddenly and without warning, we confront a new talent of great energy and boldness. But the book was disturbing for other reasons as well.

In those days one still spoke of the "Russian experiment" and one might still believe that the light of dawn glowed on the test-tubes and crucibles of human destiny. And it was still possible to have very strange expectations of the new culture that would arise from the Revolution. I do not remember what my own particular expectations were, except that they involved a desire for an art that would have as little ambiguity as a proposition in logic. Why I wanted this I don't wholly understand. It was as if I had hoped that the literature of the Revolution would realize some simple, inadequate notion of the "classical" which I had picked up at college; and perhaps I was drawn to this notion of the classical because I was afraid of the literature of modern Europe, because I was scared of its terrible intensities, ironies, and ambiguities. If this is what I really felt, I can't say that I am now wholly ashamed of my cowardice. If we stop to think of the museum knowingness about art which we are likely to acquire with maturity, of our consumer's pride in buying only the very best spiritual commodities, the ones which are sure to give satisfaction, there may possibly be a grace in those moments when we lack the courage to confront, or the strength to endure, some particular work of art or kind of art. At any rate, here was Babel's book and I found it disturbing. It was obviously the most remarkable work of fiction that had yet come out of revolutionary Russia, the only work, indeed, that I knew of as having upon it the mark of exceptional talent, even of genius. Yet for me it was all too heavily charged with the intensity, irony, and ambiguousness from which I wished to escape.

There was anomaly at the very heart of the book, for the Red Cavalry of the title were Cossack regiments, and why were Cossacks fighting for the Revolution, they who were the instrument and symbol of Tsarist repression? The author, who represented himself in the stories, was a Jew; and a Jew in a Cossack regiment was more than an anomaly, it was a joke, for between Cossack and Jew there existed not merely hatred but a polar opposition. Yet here was a Jew riding as a Cossack and trying to come to terms with the Cossack ethos. The stories were about violence of the most extreme kind, yet they were composed with a striking elegance and precision of objectivity, and also with a kind of lyric *joy*, so that one could not at once know just how the author was responding to the brutality he recorded, whether he thought it good or bad, justified or not justified. Nor was this the only thing to be in doubt about. It was not really clear how the author felt about, say, Jews; or about religion; or about the goodness of man. He had—or perhaps, for the sake of some artistic effect, he pretended to have—a secret. This alienated and disturbed me. It was impossible not to be overcome by admiration for *Red Cavalry*, but it was not at all the sort of book that I had wanted the culture of the Revolution to give me.

And, as it soon turned out, it was not at all the sort of book that the Revolution wanted to give anyone. No event in the history of Soviet culture is more significant than the career, or, rather, the end of the career, of Isaac Babel. He had been a protégé of Gorky, and he had begun his career under the aegis of Trotsky's superb contempt for the pieties of the conventional "proletarian" aesthetics. In the last years of the 1920s and in the early 1930s he was regarded as one of the most notable talents of Soviet literature. This judgment was, however, by no means an official one. From the beginning of his career, Babel had been under the attack of the literary bureaucracy. But in 1932 the Party abolished RAPP—the Russian Association of Proletarian Writers—and it seemed that a new period of freedom had been inaugurated. In point of fact, the reactionary elements of Soviet culture were established in full ascendancy, and the purge trials of 1937 were to demonstrate how absolute their power was. But in the five intervening years the Party chose to exercise its authority in a lenient manner. It was in this atmosphere of seeming liberality that the first Writers' Congress was held in 1934. Babel was one of the speakers at the Congress. He spoke with considerable jauntiness, yet he spoke as a penitent—the stories he had written since *Red Cavalry* had been published in a volume at the end of 1932 and since that time he had written nothing, he had disappointed expectation.

His speech was a strange performance.* It undertook to be humorous; the published report is punctuated by indications of laughter. It made the avowals of loyalty that were by then routine, yet we cannot take it for granted that Babel was insincere when he spoke of his devotion to the Revolution, to the government, and to the state, or when he said that in a bourgeois country it would inevitably have been his fate to go without recognition and livelihood. And perhaps he was sincere even when he praised Stalin's literary style, speaking of the sentences "forged" as if of steel, of the necessity of learning to work in language as Stalin did. Yet beneath the orthodoxy of this speech there lies some hidden intention. One feels this in the sad vestiges of the humanistic mode that wryly manifest themselves. It is as if the humor, which is often of a whimsical kind, as if the irony and the studied self-depreciation were forlorn affirmations of freedom and selfhood; it is as if Babel were addressing his fellow writers in a dead language, or in some slang of their student days, which a few of them might perhaps remember.

---

*I am indebted to Professor Rufus Mathewson for the oral translation of Babel's speech which he made for me. Professor Mathewson was kindness itself in helping me to information about Babel; he is, of course, not accountable for any inaccuracy or awkwardness that may appear in my use of the facts.

Everything, he said at one point in his speech, is given to us by the Party and the government; we are deprived of only one right, the right to write badly. "Comrades," he said, "let us not fool ourselves: this is a very important right, and to take it away from us is no small thing." And he said, "Let us give up this right, and may God help us. And if there is no God, let us help ourselves. . . ."

The right to write badly—how precious it seems when once there has been the need to conceive of it! Upon the right to write badly depends the right to write at all. There must have been many in the audience who understood how serious and how terrible Babel's joke was. And there must have been some who had felt a chill at their hearts at another joke that Babel had made earlier in his address, when he spoke of himself as practicing a new literary genre. This was the genre of silence—he was, he said, "the master of the genre of silence."

Thus he incriminated himself for his inability to work. He made reference to the doctrine that the writer must have respect for the reader, and he said that it was a correct doctrine. He himself, he said, had a very highly developed respect for the reader; so much so, indeed, that it might be said of him that he suffered from a hypertrophy of the faculty of respect—"I have so much respect for the reader that I am dumb." But then he takes a step beyond irony; he ventures to interpret, and by his interpretation to challenge, the social doctrine of "respect for the reader." The reader, he says, asks for bread, and he should indeed be given what he asks for, but not in the way he expects it. He must be surprised by what he gets; he ought not be given what he can easily recognize as "a certified true copy" of life—the essence of art is unexpectedness.

The silence for which Babel apologized was not broken. In 1937 he was arrested. He died in a concentration camp in 1939 or 1940. It is not known for certain whether he was shot or died of typhus. Both accounts of the manner of his death have been given by people who were inmates of the camp at the time. Nor is it known for what specific reason he was arrested. Raymond Rosenthal, in an admirable essay on Babel published in *Commentary* in 1947, says, on good authority, that Babel did not undergo a purge but was arrested for having made a politically indiscreet remark. It has been said that he was arrested when Yagoda was purged, because he was having a love-affair with Yagoda's sister. It has also been said that he was accused of Trotskyism, which does indeed seem possible, especially if we think of Trotsky as not only a political but a cultural figure.*

But it may be that no reason for the last stage of the extinction of Isaac Babel need be looked for beyond that which is provided by his stories, by their method and style. If ever we want to remind ourselves of the nature and power of art, we have only to think of how accurate reactionary governments are in their awareness of that nature and that power. It is not merely the content of art that they fear, not merely explicit doctrine, but whatever of energy and autonomy is implied by the aesthetic qualities a work may have. Intensity, irony, and ambiguousness, for example, constitute a clear threat to the impassivity of the state. They constitute a *secret*.

Babel was not a political man except as every man of intelligence was political at the time of the Revolution. Except, too, as every man of talent or genius is political who makes his heart a battleground for conflicting tendencies of culture. In Babel's heart there was a kind of fighting—he was captivated by the vision of two ways of being, the way of violence and the way of peace, and he was torn between them. The conflict between the two ways of being was an essential element of his mode of thought. And when Soviet culture was brought under full discipline, the fighting in Babel's heart could not be permitted to endure. It was a subversion of discipline. It implied that there was more than one way of being. It hinted that one might live in doubt, that one might live by means of a question.

It is with some surprise that we become aware of the centrality of the cultural, the moral, the *personal* issue in Babel's work, for what strikes us first is the intensity of his specifically aesthetic preoccupation. In his schooldays Babel was passionate in his study of French literature; for several years he wrote his youthful stories in French, his chief masters being Flaubert and Maupassant. When, in an autobiographical sketch, he means to tell us that he began his mature work in 1923, he puts it that in that year

---

*In the introduction to her edition in English of Babel's letters to his family, *The Lonely Years*, 1964, Miss Nathalia Babel, his daughter by his first marriage, says that it is not true that Babel had an affair with Yagoda's sister. Although Babel's life and work have in recent years been quite intensively studied by Western scholars of Soviet literature, I believe that the actual reasons for the arrest have not yet been disclosed.

he began to express his thoughts "clearly, and not at great length." This delight in brevity became his peculiar mark. When Eisenstein spoke of what it was that literature might teach the cinema, he said that "Isaac Babel will speak of the extreme laconicism of literature's expressive means—Babel, who, perhaps, knows in practice better than anyone else that great secret, 'that there is no iron that can enter the human heart with such stupefying effect, as a period placed at just the right moment.' "* A reminiscence of Babel by Konstantin Paustovsky tells of his intense admiration of Kipling's "iron prose" and of his sense of affinity with the style of Julius Caesar.† Babel's love of the laconic implies certain other elements of his aesthetic, his commitment (it is sometimes excessive) to *le mot juste*, to the search for the word or phrase that will do its work with a ruthless speed, and his remarkable powers of significant distortion, the rapid foreshortening, the striking displacement of interest and shift of emphasis—in general his pulling all awry the arrangement of things as they appear in the "certified true copy."

Babel's preoccupation with form, with the aesthetic surface, is, we soon see, entirely at the service of his moral concern. James Joyce has taught us the word "epiphany," a showing forth—Joyce had the "theory" that suddenly, almost miraculously, by a phrase or a gesture, a life might thrust itself through the veil of things and for an instant show itself forth, startling us by its existence. In itself the conception of the epiphany makes a large statement about the nature of human life; it suggests that the human fact does not dominate the scene of our existence—for something to "show forth" it must first be hidden, and the human fact is submerged in and subordinated to a world of circumstance, the world of *things*; it is known only in glimpses, emerging from the danger or the sordidness in which it is implicated. Those writers who by their practice subscribe to the theory of the epiphany are drawn to a particular aesthetic. In the stories of Maupassant, as in those of Stephen Crane, and Hemingway, and the Joyce of *Dubliners*, as in those of Babel himself, we perceive the writer's intention to create a form which shall in itself be shapely and autonomous and at the same time unusually responsible to the truth of external reality, the truth of things and events. To this end he concerns

---

*Eisenstein quotes from Babel's story "Guy de Maupassant." The reference to Babel occurs in the essay of 1932, "A Course in Treatment," in the volume *Film Form: Essays in Film Theory*, edited and translated by Jay Leyda (1949).

†This was kindly communicated to me in translation by Mrs. Rachel Erlich.

himself with the given moment, and, seeming almost hostile to the continuity of time, he presents the past only as it can be figured in the present. In his commitment to event he affects to be indifferent to "meanings" and "values"; he seems to be saying that although he can tell us with unusual accuracy what is going on, he does not presume to interpret it, scarcely to understand it, certainly not to judge it. He arranges that the story shall tell itself, as it were; or he tells it by means of a narrator who somehow makes it clear that he has no personal concern with the outcome of events—what I have called Babel's lyric joy in the midst of violence is in effect one of his devices for achieving the tone of detachment. We are not, of course, for very long deceived by the elaborate apparatus contrived to suggest the almost affectless detachment of the writer. We soon enough see what he is up to. His intense concern with the hard aesthetic surface of the story, his preoccupation with things and events, are, we begin to perceive, cognate with the universe, representative of its nature, of the unyielding circumstance in which the human fact exists; they make the condition for the epiphany, the showing forth; and the apparent denial of immediate pathos is a condition of the ultimate pathos the writer conceives.

All this, as I say, is soon enough apparent in Babel's stories. And yet, even when we have become aware of his pathos, we are, I think, surprised by the kind of moral issue that lies beneath the brilliant surface of the stories, beneath the lyric and ironic elegance—we are surprised by its elemental simplicity. We are surprised, too, by its passionate subjectivity, the intensity of the author's personal involvement, his defenseless commitment of himself to the issue.

The stories of *Red Cavalry* have as their principle of coherence what I have called the anomaly, or the joke, of a Jew who is a member of a Cossack regiment—Babel was a supply officer under General Budenny in the campaign of 1920. Traditionally the Cossack was the feared and hated enemy of the Jew. But he was more than that. The principle of his existence stood in total antithesis to the principle of the Jew's existence. The Jew conceived his own ideal character to consist in his being intellectual, pacific, humane. The Cossack was physical, violent, without mind or manners. When a Jew of eastern Europe wanted to say what we mean by "a bull in a china shop," he said "a Cossack in a *succah*"—in, that is, one of the fragile decorated booths or tabernacles in which the meals of the harvest festival of Succoth are eaten: he intended an image of animal violence, of aimless destructiveness. And if the Jew was political, if he thought beyond his own ethnic and religious group, he knew that the Cossack was the enemy not only of the Jew—although him especially— but of all men who thought of freedom; he was the natural and appropriate instrument of ruthless oppression.

There was, of course, another possible view of the Cossack, one that had its appeal for many Russian intellectuals, although it was not likely to win the assent of the Jew. Tolstoy had represented the Cossack as having a primitive energy, passion, and virtue. He was the man as yet untrammeled by civilization, direct, immediate, fierce. He was the man of enviable simplicity, the man of the body—and of the horse, the man who moved with speed and grace. We have devised an image of our lost freedom which we mock in the very phrase by which we name it: the noble savage. No doubt the mockery is justified, yet our fantasy of the noble savage represents a reality of our existence; it stands for our sense of something unhappily surrendered, the truth of the body, the truth of full sexuality, the truth of open aggressiveness. Babel's view of the Cossack was more consonant with that of Tolstoy than with the traditional view of his own people. For him the Cossack was indeed the noble savage, all too savage, not often noble, yet having in his savagery some quality that might raise strange questions in a Jewish mind.

I have seen three pictures of Babel, and it is a puzzle to know how he was supposed to look. The most convincing of the pictures is a photograph, to which the two official portrait-sketches bear but little resemblance. The sketch which serves as the frontispiece to Babel's volume of stories of 1932 makes the author look like a Chinese merchant—his face is round, impassive, and priggish; his nose is low and flat; he stares through rimless glasses with immovable gaze. The sketch in the *Soviet Literary Encyclopedia* lengthens his face and gives him horn-rimmed spectacles and an air of amused and knowing assurance: a well-educated and successful Hollywood writer who has made the intelligent decision not to apologize for his profession except by his smile. But in the photograph the face is very long and thin, charged with emotion and internality; bitter, intense, very sensitive, touched with humor, full of consciousness and contradiction. It is "typically" an intellectual's face, a scholar's face, and it has great charm. I should not want to speak of it as a Jewish face, but it is a kind of face which many Jews used to aspire to have, or hoped their sons would have. It was, surely, this face, or one much like it, that Babel took with him when he went among the Cossacks.*

We can only marvel over the vagary of the military mind by which Isaac Babel came to be assigned as a supply officer to a Cossack regiment. He was a Jew of the ghetto. As a boy—so he tells us in his autobiographical stories—he had been of stunted growth, physically inept, subject to nervous disorders. He was an intellectual, a writer—a man, as he puts it in striking phrase, with spectacles on his nose and autumn in his heart. The orders that sent him to General Budenny's command were drawn either by a conscious and ironical Destiny with a literary bent—or at his own personal request. For the reasons that made it bizarre that he should have been attached to a Cossack regiment are the reasons why he was there. He was there to be submitted to a test, he was there to be initiated. He was there because of the dreams of his boyhood. Babel's talent, like that of many modern writers, is rooted in the memory of boyhood, and Babel's boyhood was more than usually dominated by the idea of the test and the initiation. We might put it that Babel rode with a Cossack regiment because, when he was nine years old, he had seen his father kneeling before a Cossack captain who wore lemon-colored chamois gloves and looked ahead with the gaze of one who rides through a mountain pass.†

Isaac Babel was born in Odessa, in 1894. The years following the accession of Nicholas II were dark years indeed for the Jews of Russia. It was the time of the bitterest official anti-Semitism, of the Pale, of the Beilis trial, of the Black Hundreds and the planned pogroms. And yet in Odessa the Jewish community may be said to have flourished. Odessa was the great port of the Black Sea, an eastern Marseilles or Naples, and in such cities the transient, heterogeneous population dilutes the force of

*Apparently it was hard to know what Babel looked like even if one met him face to face. Here is Paustovsky trying to cope with the difficulty: "I had never met a person who looked less like a writer than Babel. Stocky, almost no neck . . . a wrinkled forehead, an oily twinkle in the small eyes; he did not arouse any interest. He could be taken for a salesman, a broker. But of course this was true only as long as he didn't open his mouth . . . Many people could not look into Babel's burning eyes. He was by nature an 'unmasker,' he liked to put people into impossible positions and he had the reputation of being a difficult and dangerous person. . . . Then Babel took off his glasses, and his face became at once helpless and good. . . ."

†Miss Babel denies that Babel was being literally autobiographical in the stories in which he speaks in the first person of the experiences of a boy-protagonist; she casts particular doubt upon the narratives having to do with a pogrom.

law and tradition, for good as well as for bad. The Jews of Odessa were in some degree free to take part in the general life of the city. They were, to be sure, debarred from the schools, with but few exceptions. And they were sufficiently isolate when the passions of a pogrom swept the city. Yet all classes of the Jewish community seem to have been marked by a singular robustness and vitality, by a sense of the world, and of themselves in the world. The upper classes lived in affluence, sometimes in luxury, and it was possible for them to make their way into a Gentile society in which prejudice had been attenuated by cosmopolitanism. The intellectual life was of a particular energy, producing writers, scholars, and journalists of very notable gifts; it is in Odessa that modern Hebrew poetry takes its rise with Bialyk and Tchernichovsky. As for the lower classes, Babel himself represents them as living freely and heartily. In their ghetto, the Moldavanka, they were far more conditioned by their economic circumstances than by their religious ties; they were not at all like the poor Jews of the *shtetln*, the little towns of Poland, whom Babel was later to see. These Odessa ghetto Jews are of a Brueghel-like bulk and brawn; they have large, coarse, elaborate nicknames; they are draymen and dairy-farmers; they are gangsters—the Jewish gangs of the Moldavanka were famous; they made upon the young Babel an ineradicable impression and to them he devoted a remarkable group of comic stories.

It was not Odessa, then, it was not even Odessa's ghetto, that forced upon Babel the image of the Jew as a man not in the actual world, a man of no body, a man of intellect, or wits, passive before his secular fate. Not even his image of the Jewish intellectual was substantiated by the Odessa actuality—Bialyk and Tchernichovsky were anything but men with spectacles on their noses and autumn in their hearts, and no one who ever encountered in America the striking figure of Dr. Chaim Tchernowitz, the great scholar of the Talmud and formerly the Chief Rabbi of Odessa, a man of Jovian port and large, free mind, would be inclined to conclude that there was but a single season of the heart available to a Jew of Odessa.

But Babel had seen his father on his knees before a Cossack captain on a horse, who said, "At your service," and touched his fur cap with his yellow-gloved hand and politely paid no heed to the mob looting the Babel store. Such an experience, or even a far milder analogue of it, is determinative in the life of a boy. Freud speaks of the effect upon him when, at twelve, his father told of having accepted in a pacific way the insult of having his new fur cap knocked into the mud by a Gentile who shouted at him, "Jew, get off the pavement." It is clear that Babel's relation with his father defined his relation to his Jewishness. Benya Krik, the greatest of the gangsters, he who was called King, was a Jew of Odessa, but he did not wear glasses and he did not have autumn in his heart—it is in writing about Benya that Babel uses the phrase that sets so far apart the intellectual and the man of action. The exploration of Benya's pre-eminence among gangsters does indeed take account of his personal endowment— Benya was a "lion," a "tiger," a "cat"; he "could spend the night with a Russian woman and satisfy her." But what really made his fate was his having had Mendel Krik, the drayman, for his father. "What does such a father think about? He thinks about drinking a good glass of vodka, of smashing somebody in the face, of his horses—and nothing more. You want to live and he makes you die twenty times a day. What would you have done in Benya Krik's place? You would have done nothing. But *he* did something. . . ." But Babel's father did not think about vodka, and smashing somebody in the face, and horses; he thought about large and serious things, among them respectability and fame. He was a shop-keeper, not well to do, a serious man, a failure. The sons of such men have much to prove, much to test themselves for, and, if they are Jewish, their Jewishness is ineluctably involved in the test.

Babel spoke with bitterness of the terrible discipline of his Jewish education. He thought of the Talmud Torah as a prison shutting him off from all desirable life, from reality itself. One of the stories he tells—perhaps the incident was invented to stand for his feelings about his Jewish schooling—is about his father's having fallen prey to the Messianic delusion which beset the Jewish families of Odessa, the belief that any one of them might produce a prodigy of the violin, a little genius who could be sent to be processed by Professor Auer in Petersburg, who would play before crowned heads in a velvet suit, and support his family in honor and comfort. Such miracles occurred in Odessa, whence came Elman, Zimbalist, and Heifetz. Babel's father hoped for wealth, but he would have forgone wealth if he could have been sure, at a minimum, of fame. Being small, the young Babel at fourteen might pass for eight and a prodigy. In point of fact, Babel had not even talent, and certainly no vocation. He was repelled by the idea of becoming a musical "dwarf," one of the "big-headed freckled children with necks as thin as flower stalks and an epileptic flush on their cheeks." This was a Jewish fate and he fled from it, escaping to the port and the beaches of Odessa. Here he tried to learn to swim and could not: "the hydrophobia of my ancestors—Spanish rabbis and Frankfurt moneychangers—dragged me to the bottom." But a kindly proofreader, an elderly man who loved nature and children, took pity on him. "How d'you mean, the water won't hold you? Why shouldn't it hold you?"—his specific gravity was no different from anybody else's and the good Yefim Nikitich Smolich taught him to swim. "I came to love that man," Babel says in one of the very few of his sentences over which no slightest irony plays, "with the love that only a boy suffering from hysteria and headaches can feel for a real man."

The story is called "Awakening" and it commemorates the boy's first effort of creation. It is to Nikitich that he shows the tragedy he has composed and it is the old man who observes that the boy has talent but no knowledge of nature and who undertakes to teach him how to tell one tree or one plant from another. This ignorance of the natural world— Babel refers to it again in his autobiographical sketch—was a Jewish handicap to be overcome. It was not an extravagance of Jewish self-consciousness that led him to make the generalization—Maurice Samuel remarks in *The World of Sholom Aleichem* that in the Yiddish vocabulary of the Jews of eastern Europe there are but two flower names (rose, violet) and no names for wild birds.

When it was possible to do so, Babel left his family and Odessa to live the precarious life, especially precarious for a Jew, of a Russian artist and intellectual. He went to Kiev and then, in 1915, he ventured to St. Petersburg without a residence certificate. He was twenty-one. He lived in a cellar on Pushkin Street, and wrote stories which were everywhere refused until Gorky took him up and in 1916 published two stories in his magazine. To Gorky, Babel said, he was indebted for everything. But Gorky became of the opinion that Babel's first work was successful only by accident; he advised the young man to abandon the career of literature and to "go among the people." Babel served in the Tsar's army on the Rumanian front; after the Revolution he was for a time a member of the Cheka; he went on grain-collecting expeditions in 1918; he fought with the northern army against Yudenich. In 1920 he was with Budenny in Poland, twenty-six years old, having seen much, having endured much, yet demanding initiation, submitting himself to the test.

The test, it is important to note, is not that of courage. Babel's affinity with Stephen Crane and Hemingway is close in many respects, of which not the least important is his feeling for his boyhood and for the drama of the boy's initiation into manhood. But the question that Babel puts to himself is not the one that means so much to the two American writers; he does not ask whether he will be able to meet danger with honor. This he seems to know he can do. Rather, the test is of his power of direct and immediate, and violent, action—not whether he can endure being killed but whether he can endure killing. In the story "After the Battle" a Cossack comrade is enraged against him not because, in the recent engagement, he had hung back, but because he had ridden with an unloaded revolver. The story ends with the narrator imploring fate to "grant me the simplest of proficiencies—the ability to kill my fellow men."

The necessity for submitting to the test is very deeply rooted in Babel's psychic life. This becomes readily apparent when we read the whole of Babel's canon and perceive the manifest connection between certain of the incidents of *Red Cavalry* and those of the stories of the Odessa boyhood. In the story "My First Goose" the newcomer to the brigade is snubbed by the brilliant Cossack commander because he is a man with spectacles on his nose, an intellectual. "Not a life for the brainy type here," says the quartermaster who carries his trunk to his billet. "But you go and mess up a lady, and a good lady too, and you'll have the boys patting you on the back. . . ." The five new comrades in the billet make it quite clear that he is an outsider and unwanted; they begin at once to bully and haze him. Yet by one action he overcomes their hostility to him and his spectacles. He asks the old landlady for food and she puts him off, whereupon he kills the woman's goose in a particularly brutal manner, and, picking it up on the point of a sword, thrusts it at the woman and orders her to cook it. Now the crisis is passed; the price of community has been paid. The group of five re-forms itself to become a group of six. All is decent and composed in the conduct of the men. There is a general political discussion, then sleep. "We slept, all six of us, beneath a wooden roof that let in the stars, warming one another, our legs intermingled. I dreamed: and in my dreams I saw women. But my heart, stained with bloodshed, grated and brimmed over." We inevitably read this story in the light of Babel's two connected stories of the 1905 pogrom, "The Story of My Dovecot" and "First Love," recalling the scene in which the crippled cigarette vender, whom all the children loved, crushes the boy's newly bought and long-desired pigeon and flings it in his face. Later the pigeon's blood and entrails are washed from the boy's cheek by the young Russian woman who is sheltering the Babel family and whom the boy adores. It is after her caress that the boy sees his father on his knees before the Cossack captain; the story ends with his capitulation to nervous illness. And now again a bird has been brutally killed, now again the killing is linked with sexuality, but now it is not his bird but another's, now he is not passive but active.

Yet no amount of understanding of the psychological genesis of the act of killing the goose makes it easy for us to judge it as anything more than a very ugly brutality. It is not easy for us—and it is not easy for Babel. Not easy, but we must make the effort to comprehend that for Babel it is not violence in itself that is at issue in his relation to the Cossacks, but something else, some quality with which violence does indeed go along, but which is not in itself merely violent. This quality, whatever it is to be called, is of the greatest importance in Babel's conception of himself as an intellectual and an artist, in his conception of himself as a Jew.

It is, after all, not merely violence and brutality that make the Cossacks what they are. This is not the first violence and brutality that Babel has known—when it comes to violence and brutality a Western reader can scarcely have, unless he sets himself to acquire it, an adequate idea of their place in the life of eastern Europe. The impulse to violence, as we have learned, seems indigenous in all mankind. Among certain groups the impulse is far more freely licensed than among others. Americans are aware and ashamed of the actuality or potentiality of violence in their own culture, but it is as nothing to that of the East of Europe; the people for whom the mass impalings and the knout are part of their memory of the exercise of authority over them have their own ways of expressing their rage. As compared with what the knife, or the homemade pike, or the boot, can do, the revolver is an instrument of delicate amenity and tender mercy—this, indeed, is the point of one of Babel's stories. Godfrey Blunden's description of the method of execution used by the Ukrainian peasant bands is scarcely to be read.

The point I would make is that the Cossacks were not exceptional for their violence. It was not their violence in itself that evoked Tolstoy's admiration. Nor was it what fascinated Babel. Rather he was drawn by what the violence goes along with, the boldness, the passionateness, the simplicity and directness—and the grace. Thus the story "My First Goose" opens with a description of the masculine charm of the brigade commander Savitsky. His male grace is celebrated in a shower of tropes—the "beauty of his giant's body" is fully particularized: we hear of the decorated chest "cleaving the hut as a standard cleaves the sky," of "the iron and flower of that youthfulness," of the long legs, which were "like girls sheathed to the neck in shining riding boots." Only the openness of the admiration and envy—which constitutes, also, a qualifying irony—keeps the description from seeming sexually perverse. It is remarkably *not* perverse; it is as "healthy" as a boy's love of his hero of the moment. And Savitsky's grace is a real thing. Babel has no wish to destroy it by any of the means which are so ready to the intellectual confronted by this kind of power and charm; he does not diminish the glory he perceives by confronting it with the pathos of human creatures less glorious physically, having more, or a higher, moral appeal because they are weaker and because they suffer.

The grace that Babel saw and envied in the Cossacks is much the same thing that D. H. Lawrence was drawn to in his imagination of archaic cultures and personalities and of the ruthlessness, even the cruelty, that attended their grace. It is what Yeats had in mind in his love of "the old disturbed exalted life, the old splendor." It is what even the gentle Forster represents in the brilliant scene in *Where Angels Fear to Tread* in which Gino, the embodiment of male grace, tortures Stephen by twisting his broken arm.

Babel carries as far as he can his sympathy with the fantasy that an ultimate psychic freedom is to be won through cruelty conceived of as a spiritual exercise. One of the famous and fascinating leaders of horse is "the headstrong Pavlichenko" who tells of his peasant origin, of the insults received from his aristocratic landlord, of how, when the Revolution came, he had wiped out the insult. "Then I stamped on my master Nikitinsky; trampled on him for an hour or maybe more. And in that time I got to know life through and through. With shooting . . . you only get rid of a chap. Shooting's letting him off, and too damn easy for yourself. With shooting you'll never get at the soul, to where it is in a fellow and how it shows itself. But I don't spare myself, and I've more than once trampled an enemy for over an hour. You see, I want to get to know what life really is. . . ." This is all too *raffiné*—we are inclined, I think, to forget Pavlichenko and to be a little revolted by Babel.*

*The celebration of the Cossack ethos gave no satisfaction to General Budenny, who, when some of Babel's *Red Cavalry* stories appeared in a magazine before their publication in a volume, attacked Babel furiously, and with a large display of literary pretentiousness, for the cultural corruption and political ignorance which, he claimed, the stories displayed.

In our effort to understand Babel's complex involvement with the Cossack ethos we must be aware of the powerful and obsessive significance that violence has for the intellectual. Violence is, of course, the contradiction of the intellectual's characteristic enterprise of rationality. Yet at the same time it is the very image of that enterprise. This may seem a strange thing to say. Since Plato we have set violence and reason over against each other in reciprocal negation. Yet it is Plato who can tell us why there is affinity between them. In the most famous of the Platonic myths, the men of the Cave are seated facing the interior wall of the Cave, and they are chained by their necks so that it is impossible for them to turn their heads. They can face in but one direction, they can see nothing but the shadows that are cast on the wall by the fire behind them. A man comes to them who has somehow freed himself and gone into the world outside the Cave. He brings them news of the light of the sun; he tells them that there are things to be seen which are real, that what they see on the wall are but shadows. Plato says that the men chained in the Cave will not believe this news. They insist that it is not possible, that the shadows are the only reality. But suppose they do believe the news! Then how violent they will become against their chains as they struggle to free themselves so that they may look at what they believe is there to be seen. They will think of violence as part of their bitter effort to know what is real. To grasp, to seize—to *apprehend*, as we say—reality from out of the deep dark cave of the mind—this is indeed a very violent action.

The artist in our time is perhaps more overtly concerned with the apprehension of reality than the philosopher is, and the image of violence seems often an appropriate way of representing his mode of perception. "The language of poetry naturally falls in with the language of power," says Hazlitt in his lecture on *Coriolanus,* and goes on to speak in several brilliant passages of "the logic of the imagination and the passions" which makes them partisan with representations of proud strength. Hazlitt carries his generalization beyond the warrant of literary fact yet all that he says is pertinent to Babel, who almost always speaks of art in the language of force. The unexpectedness which he takes to be the essence of art is that of a surprise attack. He speaks of the maneuvers of prose, of "the army of words, . . . the army in which all kinds of weapons may be brought into play." In one of his most remarkable stories, "Di Grasso," he describes the performance of a banal play given by an Italian troupe in Odessa; all is dreariness until in the third act the hero sees his betrothed in converse with the villainous seducer, and, leaping miraculously, with the power of levitation of a Nijinsky or a panther, soars across the stage and drops upon the villain to destroy him. That leap of the actor Di Grasso makes the fortune of the Italian company with the exigent Odessa audience; that leap, we are given to understand, is art. And as the story continues, Babel is explicit—if also ironic—in what he demonstrates of the moral effect that may be produced by this violence of virtuosity and power.

The spectacles on his nose were for Babel of the first importance in his conception of himself. He was a man to whom the perception of the world outside the Cave came late and had to be apprehended, by strength and speed, against the parental or cultural interdiction, the Jewish interdiction. The violence of the Revolution, its sudden leap, was cognate with this feral passion for perception—to an artist the Revolution might well have seemed the rending not only of the social but of the perceptual chains, those that held men's gaze upon the shadows on the wall; it may have suggested the rush of men from the darkness of the Cave into the light of reality. Something of this is conveyed in a finely wrought story, "Line and Color," in which Kerensky is represented as defending his myopia, refusing to wear glasses, because, as he argues very charmingly, there is so much that myopia protects him from seeing; imagination and benign illusion are thus given a larger license. But at a great meeting in the first days of the Revolution he cannot perceive the disposition of the crowd, and the story ends with Trotsky coming to the rostrum and saying in his implacable voice, "Comrades!"

But when we have followed Babel into the depths of his experience of violence, when we have imagined something of what it meant in his psychic life and in the developing conception of his art, we must be no less aware of his experience of the principle that stands opposed to the Cossack principle.

We can scarcely fail to see that when in the stories of *Red Cavalry* Babel submits the ethos of the intellectual to the criticism of the Cossack ethos, he intends a criticism of his own ethos not merely as an intellectual but as a Jew. It is always as an intellectual, never as a Jew, that he is denounced by his Cossack comrades, but we know that he has either suppressed, for political reasons, the denunciations of him as a Jew that were actually made, or, if none were actually made, that he has in his heart supposed that they were made. These criticisms of the Jewish ethos, as he embodies it, Babel believes to have no small weight. When he implores fate to grant him the simplest of proficiencies, the ability to kill his fellow man, we are likely to take this as nothing but an irony, and as an ironic assertion of the superiority of his moral instincts. But it is only in part an irony. There comes a moment when he should kill a fellow man. In "The Death of Dolgushov," a comrade lies propped against a tree; he cannot be moved, inevitably he must die, for his entrails are hanging out; he must be left behind and he asks for a bullet in his head so that the Poles will not "play their dirty tricks" on him. It is the narrator whom he asks for the *coup de grâce*, but the narrator flees and sends a friend, who, when he has done what had to be done, turns on the "sensitive" man in a fury of rage and disgust. "You bastards in spectacles have about as much pity for us as a cat has for a mouse." Or again, the narrator has incurred the enmity of a comrade through no actual fault—no moral fault—of his own, merely through having been assigned a mount that the other man passionately loved, and riding it so badly that it developed saddle galls. Now the horse has been returned, but the man does not forgive him, and the narrator asks a superior officer to compound the quarrel. He is rebuffed. "You're trying to live without enemies," he is told. "That's all you think about, not having enemies." It comes at us with momentous force. This time we are not misled into supposing that Babel intends irony and a covert praise of his pacific soul; we know that in this epiphany of his refusal to accept enmity he means to speak adversely of himself in his Jewish character.

But his Jewish character is not the same as the Jewish character of the Jews of Poland. To these Jews he comes with all the presuppositions of an acculturated Jew of Odessa, which were perhaps not much different from the suppositions of an acculturated Jew of Germany. He is repelled by the conditions of their life; he sees them as physically uncouth and warped; many of them seem to him to move "monkey-fashion." Sometimes he affects a wondering alienation from them, as when he speaks of "the occult crockery that the Jews use only once a year at Eastertime." His complexity and irony being what they are, the Jews of Poland are made to justify the rejection of the Jews among whom he was reared and the wealthy assimilated Jews of Petersburg. "The image of the stout and jovial Jews of the South, bubbling like cheap wine, takes shape in my memory, in sharp contrast to the bitter scorn inherent in these long bony backs, these tragic yellow beards." Yet the Jews of Poland are more than a stick with which

Babel beats his own Jewish past. They come to exist for him as a spiritual fact of consummate value.

Almost in the degree that Babel is concerned with violence in the stories of *Red Cavalry*, he is concerned with spirituality. It is not only Jewish spirituality that draws him. A considerable number of the stories have to do with churches, and although they do indeed often express the anticlerical feeling expectable in the revolutionary circumstances, the play of Babel's irony permits him to respond in a positive way to the aura of religion. "The breath of an invisible order of things," he says in one story, "glimmers beneath the crumbling ruin of the priest's house, and its soothing seduction unmanned me." He is captivated by the ecclesiastical painter Pan Apolek, he who created ecclesiastical scandals by using the publicans and sinners of the little towns as the models for his saints and Virgins. Yet it is chiefly the Jews who speak to him of the life beyond violence, and even Pan Apolek's "heretical and intoxicating brush" had achieved its masterpiece in his Christ of the Berestechko church, "the most extraordinary image of God I had ever seen in my life," a curly-headed Jew, a bearded figure in a Polish greatcoat of orange, barefoot, with torn and bleeding mouth, running from an angry mob with a hand raised to ward off a blow.

Hazlitt, in the passage to which I have referred, speaking of the "logic of the imagination and the passions," says that we are naturally drawn to the representation of what is strong and proud and feral. Actually that is not so: we are, rather, drawn to the representation of what is real. It was a new species of reality that Babel found in the Jews of the Polish provinces. "In these passionate, anguish-chiseled features there is no fat, no warm pulsing of blood. The Jews of Volhynia and Galicia move jerkily, in an uncontrolled and uncouth way; but their capacity for suffering is full of a somber greatness, and their unvoiced contempt for the Polish gentry unbounded."

Here is the counterimage to the captivating Savitsky, the denial of the pride in the glory of the flesh to which, early or late, every artist comes, to which he cannot come in full sincerity unless he can also make full affirmation of the glory. Here too is the image of art that is counter to that of Di Grasso's leap, counter to the language armed to stab—it is through the Jews of the Polish provinces that Babel tells us of the artist's suffering, patience, uncouthness, and scorn.

If Babel's experience with the Cossacks may be understood as having reference to the boy's relation to his father, his experience of the Jews of Poland has, we cannot but feel, a maternal reference. To the one, Babel responds as a boy; to the other, as a child. In the story "Gedali" he speaks with open sentimentality of his melancholy on the eve of Sabbaths—"On those evenings my child's heart was rocked like a little ship upon enchanted waves. O the rotted Talmuds of my childhood! O the dense melancholy of memories!" And when he has found a Jew, it is one who speaks to him in this fashion: ". . . All is mortal. Only the mother is destined to immortality. And when the mother is no longer living, she leaves a memory which none yet has dared to sully. The memory of the mother nourishes in us a compassion that is like the ocean, and the measureless ocean feeds the rivers that dissect the universe."

He has sought the Jew Gedali in his gutted curiosity shop ("Where was your kindly shade that evening, Dickens?") to ask for "a Jewish glass of tea, and a little of that pensioned-off God in a glass of tea." He does not, that evening, get what he asks for; what he does get is a discourse on revolution, on the impossibility of a revolution made in blood, on the International that is never to be realized, the International of the good.

It was no doubt the easier for Babel to respond to the spiritual life of the Jews of Poland because it was a life coming to its end and having about it the terrible pathos of its death. He makes no pretense that it could ever claim him for its own. But it established itself in his heart as an image, beside the image of the other life that also could not claim him, the Cossack life. The opposition of these two images made his art—but it was not a dialectic that his Russia could permit.

The Morality of Inertia

1955

A theological seminary in New York planned a series of lectures on "The Literary Presentations of Great Moral Issues," and invited me to give one of the talks. Since I have a weakness for the general subject, I was disposed to accept the invitation. But I hesitated over the particular instance, for I was asked to discuss the moral issues in *Ethan Frome*. I had not read Edith Wharton's little novel in a good many years, and I remembered it with no pleasure or admiration. I recalled it as not at all the sort of book that deserved to stand in a list which included *The Brothers Karamazov* and *Billy Budd, Foretopman*. If it presented a moral issue at all, I could not bring to mind what that issue was. And so I postponed my acceptance of the invitation and made it conditional upon my being able to come to terms with the subject assigned to me.

Ethan Frome, when I read it again, turned out to be pretty much as I had recalled it, not a great book or even a fine book, but a factitious book, perhaps even a cruel book. I was puzzled to understand how it ever came to be put on the list, why anyone should want to have it discussed as an example of moral perception. Then I remembered its reputation, which, in America, is very considerable. It is sometimes spoken of as an American classic. It is often assigned to high-school and college students as a text for study.

But the high and solemn repute in which it stands is, I am sure, in large part a mere accident of American culture. *Ethan Frome* appeared in 1911, at a time when, to a degree that we can now only wonder at, American literature was committed to optimism, cheerfulness, and gentility. What William Dean Howells called the "smiling aspects of life" had an importance in the literature of America some fifty years ago which is unmatched in the literature of any other time and place. It was inevitable that those who were critical of the prevailing culture and who wished to foster in America higher and more serious literature should put a heavy stress upon the grimmer aspects of life, that they should equate the smiling aspects with falsehood, the grimmer aspects with truth. For these devoted people, sickened as they were by cheerfulness and hope, the word "stark" seemed to carry the highest possible praise a critical review or a blurb could bestow, with "relentless" and "inevitable" as its proper variants. *Ethan Frome* was admired because it was "stark"—its action, we note, takes place in the New England village of Starkville—and because the fate it describes is *relentless* and *inevitable*.

No one would wish to question any high valuation that may be given to the literary representation of unhappy events—except, perhaps, as the high valuation may be a mere cliché of an intellectual class, except as it is supposed to seem the hallmark of the superior sensibility and intelligence of that class. When it is only this, we have the right, and the duty, to look sniffishly at starkness, and relentlessness, and inevitability, to cock a skeptical eye at grimness. And I am quite unable to overcome my belief that *Ethan Frome* enjoys its high reputation because it still satisfies our modern snobbishness about tragedy and pain.

We can never speak of Edith Wharton without some degree of respect. She brought to her novels a strong if limited intelligence, notable powers of observation, and a genuine desire to tell the truth, a desire which in some part she satisfied. But she was a woman in whom we cannot fail to see a limitation of heart, and this limitation makes itself manifest as a literary and moral deficiency of her work, and of *Ethan Frome* especially. It appears in the deadness of her prose, and more flagrantly in the suffering of her characters. Whenever the characters of a story suffer, they do so at the behest of their author—the author is responsible for their suffering and must justify his cruelty by the seriousness of his moral intention. The author of *Ethan Frome*, it seemed to me as I read the book again to test my memory of it, could not lay claim to any such justifica-

"Dead book" product of will

No moral issue

tion. Her intention in writing the story was not adequate to the dreadful fate she contrived for her characters. She indulges herself by what she contrives—she is, as the phrase goes, "merely literary." This is not to say that the merely literary intention does not make its very considerable effects. There is in *Ethan Frome* an image of life-in-death, of hell-on-earth, which is not easily forgotten: the crippled Ethan, and Zeena, his dreadful wife, and Matty, the once charming girl he had loved, now bedridden and querulous with pain, all living out their death in the kitchen of the desolate Frome farm—a perpetuity of suffering memorializes a moment of passion. It is terrible to contemplate, it is unforgettable, but the mind can do nothing with it, can only endure it.

My new reading of the book, then, did not lead me to suppose that it justified its reputation, but only confirmed my recollection that *Ethan Frome* was a dead book, the product of mere will, of the cold hard literary will. What is more, it seemed to me quite unavailable for any moral discourse. In the context of morality, there is nothing to say about *Ethan Frome*. It presents no moral issue at all.

For consider the story it tells. A young man of good and gentle character is the only son of a New England farm couple. He has some intellectual gifts and some desire to know the world, and for a year he is happy attending a technical school. But his father is incapacitated by a farm accident, and Ethan dutifully returns to manage the failing farm and sawmill. His father dies; his mother loses her mental faculties, and during her last illness she is nursed by a female relative whom young Ethan marries, for no other reason than that he is bemused by loneliness. The new wife, Zeena, immediately becomes a shrew, a harridan, and a valetudinarian— she lives only to be ill. Because Zeena now must spare herself, the Fromes take into their home a gentle and charming young girl, a destitute cousin of the wife. Ethan and Matty fall in love, innocently but deeply. The wife, perceiving this, plans to send the girl away, her place to be taken by a servant whose wages the husband cannot possibly afford. In despair at the thought of separation Matty and Ethan attempt suicide. They mean to die by sledding down a steep hill and crashing into a great elm at the bottom. Their plan fails: both survive the crash, Ethan to be sorely crippled, Matty to be bedridden in perpetual pain. Now the wife Zeena surrenders her claim to a mysterious pathology and becomes the devoted nurse and jailer of the lovers. The terrible tableau to which I have referred is ready for inspection.

& bossy

unduly anxious about one's neglect

It seemed to me that it was quite impossible to talk about this story. This is not to say that the story is without interest as a story, but what interest it may have does not yield discourse, or at least not moral discourse.

But as I began to explain to the lecture committee why I could not accept the invitation to lecture about the book, it suddenly came over me how very strange a phenomenon the book made—how remarkable it was that a story should place before us the dreadful image of three ruined and tortured lives, showing how their ruin came about, and yet propose no moral issue of any kind. And if "issue" seems to imply something more precisely formulated than we have a right to demand of a story, then it seemed to me no less remarkable that the book had scarcely any moral reverberation, that strange and often beautiful sound we seem to hear generated in the air by a tale of suffering, a sound which is not always music, which does not always have a "meaning," but which yet entrances us, like the random notes of an Aeolian harp, or merely the sound of the wind in the chimney. The moral sound that *Ethan Frome* makes is a dull thud. And this seemed to me so remarkable, indeed, that in the very act of saying why I could not possibly discuss *Ethan Frome*, I found the reason why it must be discussed.

It is, as I have suggested, a very great fault in *Ethan Frome* that it presents no moral issue, sets off no moral reverberation. A certain propriety controls the literary representation of human suffering. This propriety dictates that the representation of pain may not be, as it were, gratuitous; it must not be an end in itself. The naked act of representing, or contemplating, human suffering is a self-indulgence, and it may be a cruelty. Between a tragedy and a spectacle in the Roman circus there is at least this much similarity, that the pleasure both afford derives from observing the pain of others. A tragedy is always on the verge of cruelty. What saves it from the actuality of cruelty is that it has an intention beyond itself. This intention may be so simple a one as that of getting us to do something practical about the cause of the suffering or to help actual sufferers, or at least to feel that we should; or it may lead us to look beyond apparent causes to those which the author wishes us to think of as more real, such as Fate, or the will of the gods, or the will of God; or it may challenge our fortitude or intelligence or piety.

A sense of the necessity of some such intention animates all considerations of the strange paradox of tragedy. Aristotle is concerned to solve the

Aristotle on tragedy
paradox of tragedy

riddle of how the contemplation of human suffering can possibly be plea-surable, of why its pleasure is permissible. He wanted to know what liter-ary conditions were needed to keep a tragedy from being a display of horror. Here it is well to remember that the Greeks were not so con-cerned as we have been led to believe to keep all dreadful things off the stage—in the presentation of Aristotle's favorite tragedy, the audience saw Jocasta hanging from a beam, it saw the representation of Oedipus's bloody eyesockets. And so Aristotle discovered, or pretended to discover, that tragedy did certain things to protect itself from being merely cruel. It chose, Aristotle said, a certain kind of hero; he was of a certain social and moral stature; he had a certain degree of possibility of free choice; he must justify his fate, or seem to justify it, by his moral condition, being neither wholly good nor wholly bad, having a particular fault that collab-orates with destiny to bring about his ruin. The purpose of all these spec-ifications for the tragic hero is to assure us that we observe something more than mere passivity when we witness the hero's suffering, that the suffering has, as we say, some meaning, some show of rationality.

Aristotle's theory of tragedy has had its way with the world to an ex-tent which is perhaps out of proportion to its comprehensiveness and ac-curacy. Its success is largely due to its having dealt so openly with the paradox of tragedy. It serves to explain away any guilty feelings that we may have at deriving pleasure from suffering.

But at the same time that the world has accepted Aristotle's theory of tragedy, it has also been a little uneasy about some of its implications. The element of the theory that causes uneasiness in modern times is the mat-ter of the stature of the hero. To a society based in egalitarian sentiments, the requirement that the hero be a man of rank seems to deny the pre-sumed dignity of tragedy to men of lesser status. And to a culture which questions the freedom of the will, Aristotle's hero seems to be a little be-side the point. Aristotle's prescription for the tragic hero is clearly con-nected with his definition, in his *Ethics*, of the nature of an ethical action. He tells us that a truly ethical action must be a free choice between two al-ternatives. This definition is then wonderfully complicated by a further requirement—that the moral man must be so trained in making the right choice that he makes it as a matter of habit, makes it, as it were, instinc-tively. Yet it *is* a choice, and reason plays a part in its making. But we, of course, don't give to reason the same place in the moral life that Aristotle gave it. And in general, over the last hundred and fifty years, dramatists

and novelists have tried their hand at the representation of human suffering without the particular safeguards against cruelty which Aristotle perceived, or contrived. A very large part of the literature of western Europe
may be understood in terms of an attempt to invert or criticize the heroic
prescription of the hero, by burlesque and comedy, or by the insistence
on the commonplace, the lowering of the hero's social status and the
diminution of his power of reasoned choice. The work of Fielding may
serve as an example of how the mind of Europe has been haunted by the
great image of classical tragedy, and how it has tried to lay that famous
ghost. When Fielding calls his hero Tom Jones, he means that his young
man is not Orestes or Achilles; when he calls him a foundling, he is suggesting that Tom Jones is not, all appearances to the contrary notwithstanding, Oedipus.

Edith Wharton was following where others led. Her impulse in conceiving the story of Ethan Frome was not, however, that of moral experi-
mentation. It was, as I have said, a purely literary impulse, in the bad
sense of the word "literary." Her aim is not that of Wordsworth in any of
his stories of the suffering poor, to require of us that we open our minds
to a realization of the kinds of people whom suffering touches. Nor is it
that of Flaubert in *Madame Bovary*, to wring from solid circumstances all
the pity and terror of an ancient tragic fable. Nor is it that of Dickens or
Zola, to shake us with the perception of social injustice, to instruct us in
the true nature of social life and to dispose us to indignant opinion and
action. These are not essentially literary intentions; they are moral intentions. But all that Edith Wharton has in mind is to achieve that grim
tableau of which I have spoken, of pain and imprisonment, of life-in-
death. About the events that lead up to this tableau, there is nothing she
finds to say, nothing whatever. The best we can conclude of the meaning
of her story is that it might perhaps be a subject of discourse in the context of rural sociology—it might be understood to exemplify the thesis
that love and joy do not flourish on poverty-stricken New England farms.
If we try to bring it into the context of morality, its meaning goes no further than certain cultural considerations—that is, to people who like their
literature to show the "smiling aspects of life," it may be thought to say,
"This is the aspect that life really has, as grim as this"; while to people
who repudiate a literature that represents only the smiling aspects of life it
says, "How intelligent and how brave you are to be able to understand
that life is as grim as this." It is really not very much to say.

And yet there is in *Ethan Frome* an idea of considerable importance. It is there by reason of the author's deficiencies, not by reason of her powers—because it suits Edith Wharton's rather dull intention to be content with telling a story about people who do not make moral decisions, whose fate cannot have moral reverberations. The idea is this: that moral inertia, the *not* making of moral decisions, constitutes a large part of the moral life of humanity.

This isn't an idea that literature likes to deal with. Literature is charmed by energy and dislikes inertia. It characteristically represents morality as positive action. The same is true of the moral philosophy of the West—has been true ever since Aristotle defined a truly moral act by its energy of reason, of choice. A later development of this tendency said that an act was really moral only if it went against the inclination of the person performing the act: the idea was parodied as saying that one could not possibly act morally to one's friends, only to one's enemies.

Yet the dull daily world sees something below this delightful preoccupation of literature and moral philosophy. It is aware of the morality of inertia, and of its function as a social base, as a social cement. It knows that duties are done for no other reason than that they are said to be duties; for no other reason, sometimes, than that the doer has not really been able to conceive of any other course, has, perhaps, been afraid to think of any other course. Hobbes said of the Capitol geese that saved Rome by their cackling that they were the salvation of the city, not because they were they but there. How often the moral act is performed not because we are we but because we are there! This is the morality of habit, or the morality of biology. This is Ethan Frome's morality, simple, unquestioning, passive, even masochistic. His duties as a son are discharged because he is a son; his duties as a husband are discharged because he is a husband. He does nothing by moral election. At one point in his story he is brought to moral crisis—he must choose between his habituated duty to his wife and his duty and inclination to the girl he loves. It is quite impossible for him to deal with the dilemma in the high way that literature and moral philosophy prescribe, by reason and choice. Choice is incompatible with his idea of his existence; he can only elect to die.

Literature, of course, is not wholly indifferent to what I have called the morality of habit and biology, the morality of inertia. But literature, when it deals with this morality, is tempted to qualify its dullness by endowing it with a certain high grace. There is never any real moral choice

Neither courage nor choice =
But necessity LIONEL TRILLING *morality of*
inertia

for the Félicité of Flaubert's story "A Simple Heart." She is all pious habit of virtue, and of blind, unthinking, unquestioning love. There are, of course, actually such people as Félicité, simple, good, loving—quite stupid in their love, not choosing where to bestow it. We meet such people frequently in literature, in the pages of Balzac, Dickens, Dostoyevsky, Joyce, Faulkner, Hemingway. They are of a quite different order of being from those who try the world with their passion and their reason; they are by way of being saints, of the less complicated kind. They do not really exemplify what I mean by the morality of inertia. Literature is uncomfortable in the representation of the morality of inertia or of biology, and overcomes its discomfort by representing it with the added grace of that extravagance which we denominate saintliness.

But the morality of inertia is to be found in very precise exemplification in one of Wordsworth's poems. Wordsworth is pre-eminent among the writers who experimented in the representation of new kinds and bases of moral action—he has a genius for imputing moral existence to people who, according to the classical morality, should have no moral life at all. And he has the courage to make this imputation without at the same time imputing the special grace and interest of saintliness. The poem I have in mind is ostensibly about a flower, but the transition from the symbol to the human fact is clearly, if awkwardly, made. The flower is a small celandine, and the poet observes that it has not, in the natural way of flowers, folded itself against rough weather:

> But lately, one rough day, this Flower I passed
> And recognized it, though in altered form,
> Now standing as an offering to the blast,
> And buffeted at will by rain and storm.

> I stopped, and said with inly-muttered voice,
> It doth not love the shower nor seek the cold;
> This neither is its courage nor its choice,
> But its necessity in being old.

Neither courage nor choice, but necessity: it cannot do otherwise. Yet it acts as if by courage and choice. This is the morality imposed by brute circumstance, by biology, by habit, by the unspoken social demand which we have not the strength to refuse, or, often, to imagine refusing. People are scarcely ever praised for living according to this morality—we do not suppose it to be a morality at all until we see it being broken.

This is morality as it is conceived by the great mass of people in the world. And with this conception of morality goes the almost entire negation of any connection between morality and destiny. A superstitious belief in retribution may play its part in the thought of simple people, but essentially they think of catastrophes as fortuitous, without explanation, without reason. They live in the moral universe of the Book of Job. In complex lives, morality does in some part determine destiny; in most lives it does not. Between the moral life of Ethan and Matty and their terrible fate we cannot make any reasonable connection. Only a moral judgment cruel to the point of insanity could speak of it as anything but accidental.

I have spoken of the morality of inertia not in order to praise it but only to recognize it, to suggest that when we keep our minds fixed on what the great invigorating books tell us about the moral life, we obscure the large bulking dull mass of moral fact. Morality is not only the high, torturing dilemmas of Ivan Karamazov and Captain Vere. It is also the deeds performed without thought, without choice, perhaps even without love, as Zeena Frome ministers to Ethan and Matty. The morality of inertia, of the dull, unthinking round of duties, may, and often does, yield the immorality of inertia; the example that will most readily occur to us is that of the good simple people, so true to their family responsibilities who gave no thought to the concentration camps in whose shadow they lived. No: the morality of inertia is not to be praised, but it must be recognized. And Edith Wharton's little novel must be recognized for bringing to our attention what we, and literature, so easily forget.

"That Smile of Parmenides
Made Me Think"

1956

One doesn't have to read very far in Santayana's letters to become aware that it might be very hard to like this man—that, indeed, it might be remarkably easy to dislike him. And there is no point in struggling against the adverse feeling. The right thing to do is to recognize it, admit it into consciousness, and establish it beside that other awareness, which should come as early and which should be the stronger of the two—that Santayana was one of the most remarkable men of our time and that his letters are of classic importance.

To say that they are among the best of modern letters is not to say much, if anything. I can think of no modern collections of letters—D. H. Lawrence's and Shaw's excepted—that aren't deeply depressing in their emptiness and lack of energy, in their frightening inability to suggest living spirit. To find an adequate point of comparison for Santayana's letters one has to go back to the nineteenth century. Santayana isn't, of course, equal to Keats as a letter writer, but that one can even think to say that he isn't is a considerable compliment. I am led to make the comparison not because the letters of Santayana and of Keats are similar in kind but because they are similar in effect. No recent book has taken possession of my mind as this one has, commanding not assent (or not often) but concurrence—I mean a literal "running along with," the desire to follow where the writer leads. One of the effects of Keats's letters is to suggest that the writer holds in his mind at every moment a clear image of the actual quotidian world and also an image of the universe and of a mode of existence beyond actuality yet intimately related to actuality and, in a sense, controlling it. I don't pretend to understand Santayana's doctrine of essences, not having read the works in which he expounds it; nor, indeed, do I wholly understand Keats's doctrine of essences, although I do perceive that it was central to his thought. I suspect that the two doctrines have much in common and I recommend the exploration of this possibility to a competent philosopher. But quite apart from any connection that may be found between Santayana's thought and Keats's—it was certainly not an influence: Santayana read Keats in the old nineteenth-century way, and was skeptical of the idea that Keats *thought* at all—what one finds in the two men as letter writers is the force and seduction of their manner of thought, their impulse to think about human life in relation to a comprehensive vision of the nature of the universe.

It is this that accounts for the exhilaration that Santayana's letters induce, a sense of the mind suddenly freed, happily disenchanted, active in a new way. Santayana has several times reminded us how close he was to the men of the English late nineteenth century, how great a part Ruskin and Arnold and Pater played in the formation of his thought. What one becomes aware of from the letters is how close he was to the English Romantics. For the kind of mental sensation he imparts is what the Romantic poets thought of as peculiarly appropriate to the mind, and they often represented it by images of the mind "soaring" or on a mountain peak: it was thus that they proposed the escape from the "bondage" of "earth," the ability to move at will in a sustaining yet unresisting medium, the possibility of looking at life in detachment, from a "height." This is a nearly forgotten possibility of the mind; it is not approved by the hidden, prepotent Censor of modern modes of thought. To look within is permitted; to look around is encouraged; but best not to look down—not realistic, not engaged, not democratic. One experiences the unsanctioned altitude with as much guilt as pleasure.

For this pleasure, or the reminder of pleasure, we are of course grateful to Santayana and drawn to him. Yet at the same time there is the easy possibility of disliking him, or at least of regarding him with ready suspicion. It shouldn't matter. It should, indeed, constitute an added charm. Let us just call it "tension" or "ambiguity" or "irony" or whatever name serves to remind us that there is a special intellectual satisfaction in admiring where we do not love, in qualifying our assent, in keeping our distance.

My own antagonism to Santayana goes back to my college days. Irwin Edman, as all his students knew, was a great admirer of Santayana and was said actually to be on terms of friendship with the great man. Edman had an amazing gift as a teacher. He could summarize the thought of a philosopher in a way both to do justice to his subject and to make it comprehensible to the meanest intelligence. Or, if the meanest intelligence didn't actually comprehend, it certainly had the sentiment of comprehension. This I can testify to, because, when it came to philosophy, I was the meanest intelligence going. I found it virtually impossible to know what issues were involved; I could scarcely begin to understand the questions, let alone the answers. But when Edman spoke with that wonderful systematic lucidity of his, all things seemed clear. With, for me, the exception of Santayana. Edman could never make plain to me what Santayana was up to.

If Santayana could now be consulted about why this was so, he would very likely explain that it was because Edman didn't really understand him. He seems to have come to think that no Jew and no Columbia man was likely to understand him. And of course Edman's allegiance to Santayana gradually abated, and in the essay which he contributed to Professor Schilpp's *The Philosophy of George Santayana* he maintains that the later developments of the thought of the man who had been his master verged on the irrelevant and, perhaps, the immoral. And in the reply to his critics which Santayana makes in the same volume, Santayana permits himself to speak of Edman's objections as showing a "personal animus."

Yet I have no doubt that Edman's account of Santayana was perfectly just and accurate. What stood in the way of my understanding it was a cherished prejudice. The college group to which I belonged, many of whom were more or less close to Edman, resisted that part of his thought which led him to understand and praise detachment. We were very down on Walter Pater, very hostile to what we called "aestheticism," and we saw Edman's enthusiasm for Santayana as of a piece with his admiration for Pater and as a proof of his mere "aestheticism." I have come to think that Pater is a very remarkable writer, much misrepresented by the critics and literary historians. But at the time we took him to be everything that was disembodied and precious. Santayana seemed to some of us to be in the line of Pater, brought there if only by his prose, which even now I think is only occasionally really good because all too much of it is "beautiful," as the philosophers never weary of telling us. The famous "perfection of rottenness," which William James said that Santayana's thought represented, was wholly apparent to us, and we did not use the phrase with any touch of the admiration that James really did intend.

In short, what Edman (if I read him aright) eventually came to feel about Santayana after a close study of the later work, I felt out of a prejudice based on hearsay. Against this prejudice not even Edman's lucidity and the sympathy he then had with Santayana's mind could make any headway. When an undergraduate entertains a critical prejudice against a literary or philosophical figure, the last person in the world who can change his mind is his teacher.

My case, of course, was not unique. The feeling against Santayana in America is endemic and almost inevitable. It is indeed very difficult for an American, *qua* American—to use the crow-like expression of professional philosophers—to like him or trust him. Of course among the majority of the academic historians of American culture his name is mud. They hustle him off into the limbo they reserve for "aristocratic critics of American democracy." They find it wonderfully convenient to think of him as the "perfection of rottenness"—he is the Gilbert Osmond of their *Portrait of a Lady*, the Lady being America in the perfection of her democracy and innocence: he is a spoiled American, all too elegant, all too cultivated, all too knowing, all too involved with aesthetic values. Actually they are much mistaken. For one thing, Santayana was very severe in his attitude toward the aesthetic experience—as severe as William James and for rather better reasons. This is one of the remarkable and salutary things about him. He was not in the least taken in by the modern pieties about art; and as he grew older art meant less and less to him, and he thought that it should. As for his rejection of America, it is a good deal more complex, not to say cogent, than historians of American culture usually care to remember. America, it is true, seemed to have affected him adversely in an almost physical way, making him anxious and irritable. But it was to a particular aspect of American life that he directed his antagonism, the aspect of what we, with him, may call its gentility, the aspect of its high culture. And what the academic historian of American culture would do without Santayana's phrase "the genteel tradition" is impossible to imagine. Santayana was ill at ease everywhere in America, but what offended his soul was New England, especially Boston, especially Cambridge. For the America of raw energy, the America of material concerns, the America that he could see as young and barbaric and in the line of history he had a tolerance and affection that were real and not merely condescending. Some years ago the late Bernard De Voto raised a storm of protest and contempt among American intellectuals because he wrote in praise of a certain research on the treatment of third-degree burns and insisted that this was a cultural achievement of the first order, that it was an intellectual achievement; he said that it was a fault in American intellectuals that they were not aware of it and did not take pride in it as a characteristic achievement of the American mind. Santayana would have been in agreement with De Voto. In a letter of 1921 to Logan Pearsall Smith, he writes of high American culture as being ineffectual and sophomoric.

> But notice: *all* learning and "mind" in America is not of this ineffectual Sophomoric sort. There is your Doctor at Baltimore who is a great expert, and *really knows how to do things*: and you will find that, in the service of material life, all the arts and sciences are prosperous in America. But it must be in the service of material life; because it is material life (of course with the hygiene, morality, and international good order that can minister to material life) that America has and wants to have and may perhaps bring to perfection. Think of that! If material life could be made perfect, as (in a very small way) it was perhaps for a moment among the Greeks, would not that of itself be a most admirable achievement, like the creation of a new and superior mammal, who would instinctively suck only the bottle? . . . And possibly on that basis of perfected material life, a new art and philosophy would grow unawares, not similar to what we call by those names, but having the same relation to the life beneath which art and philosophy amongst us ought to have had, but never have had actually. You see I am content to let the past bury its dead. It does not seem to me that we can impose on America the task of imitating Europe. The more different it can come to be, the better; and we must let it take its own course, going a long way round, perhaps, before it can shake

off the last trammels of alien tradition, and learn to express itself simply, not apologetically, after its own heart.

Here, surely, is the perfect dream, the shaping Whitmanesque principle, of the academic historian of American culture. Santayana, it is true, formulates it with a touch of irony and indeed on another occasion he avowed his belief that everything good in "the ultimate sense" would come to America from Europe only, and from Latin Europe; and of course he was glad that he would not live to see the new American culture come into being. Yet he had too strong a sense of history, too clear an understanding of cultures, not to be as serious as he was ironic.

No, it is not really Santayana's open rejection of America that troubles us about him. His feelings about America go very deep, go to his first principles. That is why they cannot be related to the shabby canting anti-Americanism of the intellectual middle class of England or of the Continent. A good many things may no doubt be said in dispraise of Santayana, but it cannot be said of him that he had a vulgar mind, that he could possibly think as *The New Statesman* thinks. There was no malice in Santayana's feeling about America, nor does he ever give evidence that he had ever been *offended* by America—he had none of the provincial burgher's hurt vengeful pride which led Dostoyevsky to write *A Winter Diary* to get in his licks at France, or Graham Greene to write *The Quiet American*.

What does alienate Americans from Santayana is the principles upon which his rejection of America is founded. That is, what troubles us is not his negations of America, but the affirmation upon which he based his sense of himself as a European. These disturb us, they put questions to us which we cannot endure.

It isn't possible to speak of Santayana as a representative European. To do so would be to give modern Europe more credit than it deserves. But he was, we might say, the Platonic "idea" of a European. To the development of this idea America was necessary. It was not enough for him to have been Santayana of Avila in Castile; there had also to be the Sturgis connection, and Boston, and Harvard. Santayana repelled the belief that as a boy in Boston he had lived an isolated and unhappy life because he was of foreign birth. He was, he writes, the lieutenant-colonel of the Boston Latin School regiment, he acted in the Hasty Pudding plays at

Harvard, he was devoted—"(as a spectator)"—to football. Yet he did stand apart; and he was able to look at the culture into which he had been transplanted with a degree of consciousness that was available to no other lieutenant-colonel and to no other leading lady of a Hasty Pudding play. He knew it to be not his culture, and he lived to develop its opposite principle, the idea of a European culture. This was, to be sure, not mono-lithically European; England, France, Spain, Italy, Greece were all sepa-rate to him, sharp, clear entities which had different values for him at different stages of his life. But, in contrast to America, they came together as a single idea, they made the idea of Europe.

If we ask what it was that Santayana thought of as separating him from America, as making him characteristically and ideally European (and a philosopher), the answer is that it was his materialism. He seems to have found it very difficult to convince people that he really was a materi-alist. No doubt in his more technical works there are grounds for the re-sistance to his claim that his materialism was basic to all his thought; of these I have no knowledge. But one reason for the resistance is that we don't expect materialists to compose in highly wrought prose, exquisite and sometimes all too exquisite; we don't expect subtlety and vivacity, supposing, no doubt that materialists must partake of the dull density of "matter"; we don't expect them to give a very high value to poetry and all fictions, especially the fictions of religions. In 1951 Santayana finds it nec-essary to write, "Naturalism . . . is something to which I am so thor-oughly wedded that I like to call it materialism, so as to prevent all confusion with *romantic* naturalism, like Goethe's, for instance, or that of Bergson. Mine is the hard, non-humanistic naturalism of the Ionian philosophers, of Democritus, Lucretius, and Spinoza." And he goes on: "Those professors at Columbia who tell you that in my *Idea of Christ in the Gospels* I incline to theism have not read that book sympathetically. They forget that my naturalism is fundamental and includes man, his mind, and all his works, products of the generative order of nature."

From Santayana's materialism comes his detachment. Maybe, of course, if we want to look at it psychologically, it is the other way around—the materialism rationalizes the detachment which was tempera-mental. But certainly the two things go together in Santayana, just as they did in Spinoza, who was perhaps Santayana's greatest hero of thought. The world is matter, and follows the laws of matter. The world is even, he is willing to say, a machine, and follows the laws of its devising. The world is not spirit, following the laws of spirit, made to accommodate spirit, available to full comprehension by spirit. It permits spirit to exist, but this is by chance and chancily: no intention is avowed. And the world, we might go on to say, is Boston to the boy from Avila; the world is the Sturgis family to the young Santayana—not hostile, yet not his own, not continuous with him. It is, as he says, his host, and he must have reflected that the word implies not only a guest but a parasite!

When Bouvard and Pecuchet gave themselves to the study of Spinoza, Flaubert's favorite philosopher, they felt as if they were in "a balloon at night, in glacial coldness, carried on an endless journey towards a bottomless abyss and with nothing near but the unseizable, the motionless, the eternal." We do not feel *quite* this as we read Santayana's letters. They are far too full of intended grace, of conscious charm, too full of the things of this world. But the abyss is there, and his dreadful knowledge of it is what Americans fear in Santayana, just as it is the American avoidance of the knowledge of the abyss that made Santayana fear America and flee it. The knowledge of the abyss, the awareness of the discontinuity between man and the world, this is the forming perception of Santayana's thought as it comes to us in the letters. It is already in force at the age of twenty-three—it makes itself manifest in the perfectly amazing self-awareness and self-possession of the letters he writes from his first trip abroad just after his graduation from Harvard. The philosophical detachment is wholly explicit; and we see at once that it is matched by a personal detachment no less rigorous. For Santayana friendship was always of high special importance. He could be a loyal and devoted friend, as witness his constancy to the unfortunate and erratic Frank Russell, Bertrand Russell's elder brother, his predecessor in the earldom; he could be finely sympathetic, as witness his letter to Iris Origo on the death of her only son. But friendship had for him a status in his life like that of art. Art, however lovely, however useful, was not reality; at best it was an element of reality; and sometimes, he said, it interfered with the apprehension of reality. So too he never deceived himself about friendship; its limits were clear to him very early and he never permitted himself to be deceived into thinking that a friend was himself. Nothing could be more striking than Santayana's equal devotion and remoteness in his youthful letters to his friends. He put all his intelligence and all his sympathy at their service, but never himself. It is, in its own way, very fine; but no American reader, I think, can help being made uncomfortable by this stern and graceful self-possession, this rigorous objectivity, this strict limitation, in so very young a man.

And our American discomfort is the more intense, I believe, because we cannot but perceive that Santayana's brilliant youthful reserve is his response to his youthful consciousness of what I have called the abyss. His friend Henry Ward Abbott writes to him out of one of those states of cosmological despair which were common enough among young men even as late as 1887, asking Santayana to consider the problem of life from "the point of view of the grave"; Santayana replies in this fashion:

What you call the point of view of the grave is what I should call the point of view of the easy chair. [That is, the point of view of detached philosophic contemplation.] From that the universal joke is indeed very funny. But a man in his grave is not only apathetic, but also invulnerable. That is what you forget. Your dead man is not merely amused, he is also brave, and if his having nothing to gain makes him impartial his having nothing to lose makes him free. "Is it worth while after all?" you ask. What a simple-hearted question. Of course it isn't worth while. Do you suppose when God made up his mind to create this world after his own image, he thought it was worth while? I wouldn't make such an imputation on his intelligence. Do you suppose he existed there in his uncaused loneliness because it was worth while? Did Nothing ask God before God existed, whether he thought it would be worth while to try life for a while? or did Nothing have to decide the question? Do you suppose the slow, painful, nasty, bloody process, by which things in this world grow, is worth having for the sake of the perfection of a moment? Did you come into the world because you thought it worth while? No more do you stay in it because you do. The idea of demanding that things should be worth doing is a human impertinence.

But then, when Abbott continues the question in a later letter, Santayana says, "The world may have little in it that is good: granted. But that little is really and inalienably good. Its value cannot be destroyed because of the surrounding evil." It is a startling thing for a youth to say, as startling as his exposition of the point of view of the grave, and these two utterances may surely be thought of as definitive of Santayana's later thought. Whatever his materialism leads Santayana to, it does not lead him to a radical relativism pointing to an ultimate nihilism. It does not lead him to a devaluation of life, to the devaluation of anything that might be valued. On the contrary—it is the basis of his intense valuation. Here indeed, we might almost say, is one *intention* of his materialism, that it should lead to a high valuation of what may be valued at all. If we are in a balloon over an abyss, let us at least value the balloon. If night is all around, then what light we have is precious. If there is no life to be seen in the great emptiness, our companions are to be cherished; so are we ourselves. And this, I think, is the essence of the European view of life as it differs from the American. Willa Cather is not in my opinion a very intelligent or subtle mind, but she did show in her novels an understanding of the European attachment to *things* and how it differed from the American attachment. The elaborate fuss that she made about cuisine, about wine, and salads, and bread, and copper pots, was an expression of her sense of the unfeeling universe; cookery was a ritual in which the material world, some tiny part of it, could be made to serve human ends, could be made human; and in so far as she represents cookery as a ritual, it is the paradigm of religious belief, and goes along with her growing sympathy for Catholicism, of which the chief attraction seemed to be not any doctrinal appeal it had but rather its being *so very European*. That is, what hope the Catholic religion offered her took its sanction from the European confrontation of the abyss—the despair that arises from the knowledge of the material nature of the world validates all rituals and all fictions that make life endurable in the alien universe.

If I apprehend Santayana aright, what Miss Cather felt in a very simple way, he felt in a very elaborate way. That is why he was so acutely uncomfortable in America. Santayana knew that America was not materialistic, not in the philosophic sense and not really in the moral sense. What he says about America's concern with the practical life and with "material well-being" does not contradict this. If anything, it substantiates it.

For if the Americans were truly materialistic, they would recognize the necessity of dualism, they would have contrived a life of the spirit apart from and in opposition to the life of material concern. But for the American consciousness the world is the natural field of the spirit, laid out to be just that, as a baseball diamond or a tennis court is laid out for a particular kind of activity; and what the American wins is not enjoyed as a possession but, rather, cherished as a trophy. The European sees the world as hard and resistant to spirit; whatever can be won is to be valued, protected, used, and enjoyed. But the high valuation of the material life makes, as it were, the necessity for its negation in an intense respect for the life of spirit.

What exasperated Santayana was the American refusal to confront the hard world that materialism proposes, the American preference for seeing the world as continuous with spirit. His animus against Emerson's transcendentalism was extreme, and what he felt about Emerson he felt about all of American philosophic thought, as we see from the brilliant *Character and Opinion in the United States*. The inclusion of the word "character" in that title is significant. One of the things that must especially involve our interest in Santayana's letters is what we perceive to be a chief preoccupation of the writer—the concern for character, for self-definition, for self-preservation. This concern is intimately related to Santayana's materialism. Santayana defined himself in the universe by detachment from it. And what is true of him in the largest possible connection is also true of him in smaller connections. Thus, he had no sooner received his first Harvard appointment than he began to think of the moment when he could retire from Harvard, which he did at the first possible opportunity. It was not merely that he was a foreigner, or that he saw himself as of a different breed from the American academic, or that he could not support what, in an early letter, he calls the "damnable worldliness and snobbishness prevalent at Harvard." It was rather that he needed to define himself by withdrawal.

And how very precise his self-definition is. We see it in the cool self-possession of his dealings with William James. In his early relation with Santayana, James as a teacher is in a very different role from that in which we find him in that all too famous anecdote of Gertrude Stein at Radcliffe, when, to Gertrude Stein's having written nothing in her examination book except the statement that the afternoon was too fine for examinations, James replied with agreement and an A for the course. I have never admired James for this—it seems to me that he gave an unfortunate impetus to all the contemporary student cant about how teachers ought to behave, that, for example, they should be *human*. I like much better James's coming down on Santayana for not having done the conventional thing with his traveling fellowship; I like it in part because it gave Santayana the opportunity to stand up to his superior and to affirm himself and to hold himself ready to take the consequences. And this he does in a way that no American youth could have equaled, with a sincere regard for James, with a perfect if not wholly ingenuous courtesy, with the full sanction of his view of the world, an entire readiness to wipe out his academic career before it should have begun. It isn't exactly endearing; it makes the beginning of our sense that we shall not like Santayana at all. But it is very impressive, it is even very fortifying.

That sense of himself which Santayana shows in his letters to James was what he saw lacking in American life. His novel, *The Last Puritan*, is, as he says, about a man who, with all the personal and material gifts, "peters out," and the tragedy of this he felt to be so terrible that he "actually cried over the writing of it." He speaks of the petering out of most of the young American poets who do not escape to hibernate in Europe. And petering out was, it seems, the fate of most of his Harvard friends—it was not that they were worn out by American life, nor that they were hampered by economic circumstances, or perverted by bad ideals; it was that they did not know how to define themselves, they did not know how to grasp and possess; we might say that they did not know how to break their hearts on the idea of the hardness of the world, to admit the defeat which is requisite for any victory, to begin their effective life in the world by taking the point of view of the grave. Perhaps the whole difference between Santayana and America is summed up in an exchange between him and William Lyons Phelps. No two men could have been more worlds apart than Phelps and Santayana, but Santayana liked Phelps—he was American academic life, and American kindliness, he was all the massive excitement of the Yale-Harvard game, which Santayana relished, making it a point always to stay with the Phelpses whenever the game was in New Haven. When *The Last Puritan* appeared, Phelps was distressed by the book and Santayana had to deal with his objection that he did not "love life" and also with the objection that there were no "good people" in the book. To which Santayana replied, "I don't think you like *good* people, really, only sweet people—like Annabel [Mrs. Phelps] and you!" The sentence seems to me momentous in its definition of American life. In that life sweetness is an endemic trait, and very lovely and valuable it is. But we find it very hard to imagine that definition of character which is necessary for the strain of what Santayana calls goodness.

As for Santayana himself, his effort of self-definition had, in some ways, an amazing success. He was manifestly not a sweet man, although there are some engagingly kind letters to people whose defenses he knew to be weak, students, young philosophers, old friends who suddenly called themselves to mind after half a century. That he was a good man has been questioned and the question seems to me a very reasonable one—there is certainly something deeply disquieting about his temperament. But there can be no doubt of the firmness of his self-definition; there can be no doubt that he did not peter out. The surrender of hope that he made at an early age, the admission of defeat that many interpret as an essential cynicism or even as a kind of malevolence, may not be life-giving to most of his readers; but it was a regimen that preserved him in life in a way that must astound us. He lived to be nearly ninety, and up to the end there is no intellectual event that he does not respond to with full alertness and full power and full involvement. His comments on Edna St. Vincent Millay make a definitive estimate of her; a few years later he is no less precise about Faulkner. He absorbed Freud far better than most intellectuals, and his essay on *Beyond the Pleasure Principle* deals in a remarkable way with Freud's materialistic assumptions that would make Santayana sympathetic to him. He is much interested in the poetry of Robert Lowell, and also in the stories of Somerset Maugham, the point of his interest in the latter being his "wonder at anybody wishing to write such stories." In general he is responsive to the modern element in literature—he is fascinated by Joyce and captivated by Proust; but he says he has no enthusiasm for D. H. Lawrence, Dostoyevsky, and Nietzsche: he has had from Aristotle all they can give him. The vivacity and cogency of his mind never abate.

In the letter to Abbott which I quoted earlier he had written that "the point of view of the grave is not to be attained by you or me everytime we happen to want anything in particular. It is not gained except by renunciation. Pleasure must first cease to attract and pain to repel, and this, you will confess, is no easy matter. But meantime, I beg of you, let us remember that the joke of things is one at our expense. It is very funny, but it is exceedingly unpleasant." The ironic smile at the universal joke never left the face of his writing, but neither, I think, did the sense of how unpleasant the joke was. The smile drove philosophers to distraction and led some of them to say that he wasn't a philosopher at all—maybe a poet. "If you took [my lucubrations] more lightly perhaps you would find them less aggravating," he wrote to Professor Lamprecht. He himself thought a smile might say much—in a letter to Father Munson he speaks of the importance in his philosophic life of a passage of Plato's *Parmenides* "about 'ideas' of filth, rubbish, etc., which the moralistic young Socrates recoils from as not beautiful, making old Parmenides smile. That smile of Parmenides made me think." How much for a smile to do! Yet Santayana's does no less.

The Last Lover

1958

I

Vladimir Nabokov's novel *Lolita* was first published in Paris in 1955. Its reputation was not slow to reach the country in which it had been written and in which, presumably, it could not be published. Reviews of the book appeared in some of the more advanced literary journals, and in 1956 *The Anchor Review* published a sizable portion of the novel, together with a thoughtful comment on the whole work by F. W. Dupee. Copies of the book in the Olympia Press edition were brought back to the United States by returning travelers and were passed from hand to hand in a manner somewhat reminiscent of the early circulation of *Ulysses* in the 1920s and *Lady Chatterley's Lover* in the 1930s.

I use the qualifying "somewhat" because the borrowing and lending of *Lolita* did not proceed in the aura of righteous indignation which had attended the private circulation of the two earlier books. The bland acceptance of what would once have been called censorship and denounced as such—actually there never was an American legal ruling on *Lolita*, only a caginess on the part of the American publishers—was perhaps the result of a general cultural change from the 1920s and 1930s, an aspect of the diminished capacity for indignation that has often been noted of the 1950s.

Or it may imply the recognition that Mr. Nabokov's book, in tune with the temper of the times, is very much less weighty and solemn than Joyce's or Lawrence's, that it does not proclaim itself to be, and is not, a work of genius. Or, again, it may suggest that readers have discovered that *Lolita* really is, as the conditions of its first publication would lead us to suppose, a shocking and scandalous book.

Certainly its scandalous reputation was affirmed by the action of the French government in suppressing it. When I was in Paris not long after its publication I tried to buy a copy, and as I stood at that foremost counter in Galignani's on which are piled the standard dirty books for English and American tourists, I was told by the clerk that the sale of *Lolita* had been made illegal just the day before. This was at a time when the French were going in for suppressing books on a rather large scale. I heard it said that they were doing so in response to representations made by the English government, which was concerned to stop the flow of indecent or questionable literature across the Channel. Perhaps this was true, although it is really not necessary to account in any special and elaborate way for the displays of literary squeamishness that the French make every now and then. But this time their heart was not in it, and shortly after my visit *Lolita* became again available.

So much for the pre-history of *Lolita*. Now the book has been brought out by an American publishing firm of entire respectability and everyone may buy it and read it and judge it for himself.

The legitimizing of *Lolita* must not mislead us about its nature. It must not tempt us into taking the correct enlightened attitude—"Well, now, what was all the fuss about? Here is the book brought into the full light of day, and of course we can very plainly see that there is nothing shocking about it." The fact is that *Lolita* is indeed a shocking book. It means to be shocking and it succeeds in its intention.

But it is not shocking in the way that books which circulate in secret are usually said to be shocking. I shall presently try to say in what ways— there are several—the book does, or should, shock us. Now I shall simply report that *Lolita* is not pornographic as that word would be used in any legal complaint that might conceivably be made against it.

I specify the legal use of the word in order to distinguish that from my own use of it. As I use the word, its meaning is neutrally descriptive, not pejorative.* I take it to mean the explicit representation in literature (or the graphic arts—or music, for that matter) of the actual sexual conduct of human beings. (I suppose I should include anthropomorphic gods, demons, etc.) It seems to me that this representation is a perfectly acceptable artistic enterprise. I expect that, if it is carried out with some skill, it will raise lustful thoughts in the reader, and I believe that this in itself provides no ground for objection.

I should like to be entirely clear on this point. I am not taking the position of liberal and progressive lawyers and judges. I am not saying that literature should be permitted its moments of pornography because such moments are essential to the moral truth which a particular work of literature is aiming at; or because they are essential to its objective truth; or because, when taken in context, they cannot really arouse the normal mature reader to thoughts of lust. I am saying that I see no reason in morality (or in aesthetic theory) why literature should not have as one of its intentions the arousing of thoughts of lust. It is one of the effects, perhaps one of the functions, of literature to arouse desire, and I can discover no ground for saying that sexual pleasure should not be among the objects of desire which literature presents to us, along with heroism, virtue, peace, death, food, wisdom, God, etc.

This, as I say, is not the position taken by the liberal lawyers and judges. And having read a good many of the American legal opinions in matters of literary censorship, I have come to think that the liberal line of argument, although it comes out on the right side in some ways, is shallow and evasive. I have been told by lawyers that there is no other way for them to go about things, that they must defend indicted books by taking a hypocritical view of their sexual passages, owlishly arguing that these passages when "read in context" have no special significance or effect, that they are "essential" to the "total artistic effect of the work." No doubt the forensic necessity is what the lawyers say it is, but their submission to it does not advance the cause of honesty.

My position in this matter does not lead me to argue that censorship is always indefensible. My use of the word "pornographic" follows, of course, that of D. H. Lawrence in his famous essay "Pornography and

*I am aware that a pejorative meaning is, as it were, built into the word, that it derives from *porne*, the Greek word for prostitute. But we have no other word to express the idea; and the attempt to invent a prettier one is bound to compromise the position I wish to maintain.

Obscenity," and I go along with Lawrence in distinguishing the pornographic from the obscene. It seems to me that if we are going to be frank in our demand that sexuality be accepted as an element of human life which should be available to literature like any other, we must be no less frank in recognizing its unique nature as a literary subject. For most people it is the very most interesting subject, the subject that is most sought for, even though with shame and embarrassment. It is, if we look at it truthfully, a uniquely influential subject—no part of the individual life is so susceptible to literature as the sexual expectations and emotions. As Lawrence said in effect, there are discriminations to be made among kinds of lust, of which some tend to humanize, others to dehumanize us. This gives society an unusually high stake in sexuality as a literary subject, and although I have no great confidence in the ability of society, through the agency of the courts of law, to make the discrimination accurately, it seems to me natural that the effort at discrimination should be made, and appropriate that it should be made through the courts.

The purpose of my digression on censorship is simply to make plain the grounds for my saying that in the sense in which the courts use the word, it is not possible to call *Lolita* a pornographic book. It is, to be sure, the story of an erotic episode, and the story is told in such a way that erotic emotions and sensations are always before the reader. By my own definition of pornography, there is one scene to which the word can be applied—other readers may perhaps find more—but it is unlikely that any court, working under the standards of acceptation that have been established over the last few years, would apply the word in the legal sense even to that scene. And, indeed, *Lolita* takes very little of the wide latitude in the representation of sexual behavior that is nowadays permitted to fiction, in point either of language or of explicitness of description.

That is what I mean when I say that if *Lolita* is, as I have called it, a shocking book, it is not for the reason that books are commonly thought to be shocking.

2

Lolita is the story of the love of a man in his forties for a girl of twelve. The narrative is in the first person, the memoir or confession of the lover, written by him while awaiting trial for murder. Upon his sudden death before the trial begins, his manuscript is edited by John Ray, Jr., Ph.D., presumably a professor of psychology.

Humbert Humbert is the fictitious name under which the narrator presents himself. It is, as the "editor" remarks in his solemn preface, a bizarre name, and Humbert himself says that of the possible pseudonyms that had occurred to him, this one "expresses the nastiness best." It is in some way indicative of his nature that he takes a kind of pleasure in its being misheard and misremembered; he adopts the distortions and represents himself variously as Humbug, Humbird, Humburger, Hamburg, Homberg. He is, as the editor says, "a mixture of ferocity and jocularity that betrays supreme misery perhaps, but is not conducive to attractiveness." He is indeed anything but attractive. The jocularity can sometimes rise to wit, sometimes to wildness, but it can also sink to facetiousness and reach the brink of silliness. Humbert is a man without friends, and he desires none. His characteristic mode of thought is contemptuous and satirical, but we do not know what makes his standard of judgment, for it is never clear what, besides female beauty of a certain kind, has ever won his admiration. His ferocity takes the form of open brutality to women. He is the less attractive by reason of the style in which he chiefly writes about himself—whoever has tried to keep a journal and has been abashed at reading it by the apologetic, self-referring, self-exculpating whine of the prose, and by the very irony which is used to modify this deplorable tone, will recognize the manner of most of *Lolita*. Humbert himself recognizes it and asks forgiveness for it—he is nothing if not self-conscious and he is as self-contemptuous as he is self-defensive.

By no means attractive, then. Yet he does not fail to effect an intimacy with us. His unrelenting self-reference, his impious greediness, seduce us into kinship with him. He is in every way a nonhero, an anti-hero; but his lack of all admirable qualities leaves perfectly clear—was no doubt devised to leave perfectly clear—the force of the obsessive passion of which he is capable.

Humbert is the son of a generally European (Swiss, French, Austrian, Danubian) father, who owned a luxury hotel on the Riviera, and of an English mother. His European birth and rearing are of considerable importance, for if the narrative is primarily the history of his love-affair with an American girl-child, it is incidentally the history of his love-affair with America. It is a relationship sufficiently ambivalent, charged with as much scorn and dislike as tenderness and affection, but perhaps for that reason the more interesting, and yielding a first-rate account of the life of the American road, of hotels and motels, of dead towns and flashy resorts, of skating-rinks and tourist caves, of Coke machines and juke boxes, of all that pertains to mobility and transience, to youth and uninvolvement.

By the time he has reached maturity H.H. (as he sometimes calls himself) has come to the realization of the most important fact about his nature. Grown women repel him, not in the degree that he cannot have sexual relations with them, but in the degree that they can give him no pleasure. His sexual desire can be aroused and truly gratified only by girls between the ages of nine and fourteen.

The social sanctions against the indulgence of this taste being of the most extreme sort, H.H. lives a deprived life. On several occasions he has had to take refuge in mental hospitals. He makes no great claims for his sanity, all he insists on is the madness of psychiatrists, and it is a chief dogma of his view of his erotic idiosyncrasy that no explanation of it can possibly be made. He tells us that his "very photogenic mother died in a freak accident (picnic, lighting)" when he was three, and nothing seems to him more absurd than the idea that his passional life might have been influenced by this event. It is probable that the author does not intend an irony here, that he quite agrees with Humbert in thinking the idea comical.

But Humbert does trace the strict condition imposed upon his love to a childhood episode, to his first passionate attachment, experienced as a boy one summer on the Riviera. The object of his passion, who reciprocated it, was a little girl named Annabel, who soon after died of typhus. Her name and her fate are significant, intended to recall the Annabel Lee of Poe's poem. The marriage of Poe to the fourteen-year-old Virginia Clemm is touched upon several times in the course of the story, and can, I think, be made to throw light on what the novel is up to.

The image of the lost Annabel fixes itself upon H.H.'s mind. To girls of her kind, having her beauty, charm, and sexual responsiveness, he gives the name "nymphets." "Between the age limits of nine and fourteen there occur maidens who, to certain bewitched travellers, twice or many times older than they, reveal their true nature which is not human, but nymphic (that is, demoniac); and those chosen creatures I propose to designate as 'nymphets.'" [The accent should probably come on the first syllable, otherwise we get, as someone pointed out to me when I put it on the second, the heavy sound and eventually the ugly appearance of "nymphette," which must inevitably suggest the very opposite of a nymphet, a drum-majorette.] The further description of the nymphet emphasizes the demoniac quality—"the fey grace, the elusive, shifty, soul-shattering, insidious charm"—upon which the Greeks based their idea of the disease of nympholepsy and later peoples their conceptions of Undines, Belles Dames Sans Merci, and White Goddesses.

In middle age, in a New England town, Humbert discovers Dolores Haze, called Lolita, a middle-class schoolgirl of twelve, and conceives for her an irresistible desire. In order to be near Lolita and to make opportunity to possess her, Humbert marries her mother. It cannot be said that he exactly murders his new wife—it is only that, having read his diary in which he had set forth his reasons for marrying her and the details of his dislike of her, she runs distractedly out of the house and is providentially hit by a passing car. The way is now quite clear for the stepfather. Believing that Lolita's innocence must not be offended, he has for some time made elaborate plans to drug the child, but in the end it is Lolita who ravishes Humbert; a month at a summer camp had served to induct her into the mysteries of sex, which to her are no mysteries at all, and she considers that H.H. is rather lacking in address.

The relation that is now established between Humbert and Lolita is of a double kind. His sexual obsession, so far from abating, grows by what it feeds on. Lolita accepts his sensuality with cool acquiescence, and even responds to it physically, but she is not moved by desire, and she is frequently bored and has to be bribed into compliance. Sensuality, however, does not comprise the whole of Humbert's feeling. He is *in loco parentis*—I have forgotten whether or not he makes a joke on this—and his emotions are in some part paternal. Lolita passes for his daughter, and his brooding concern for her, his jealousy of her interest in other males, his nervous desire to please or to placate her, constitute a mode of behavior not very different from that of any American father to his adolescent daughter. Nor is Lolita's response to Humbert very different from that which American girls of her age make to their fathers. She maintains toward him the common alternation of remote indifference and easy acceptance, and finds his restriction of her freedom a burden which is not much lightened by his indulgence.

Inevitably, of course, she undertakes to "get away," and inevitably she makes another man the instrument of an escape from a tyranny which for her is less that of a lover than of a father. All Humbert's jealous fantasies come true; Lolita takes up with a perverse middle-aged playwright—who is as much concerned to torture Humbert as to win Lolita—and after a period of very skillful deception, runs off with her lover. Her desertion of Humbert brings his life to an end and he exists only to dream of regaining her love and of destroying her seducer. After the passage of some years, he does at last find Lolita; she is married, not to the perverse lover but to a deaf and worthy young technician, by whom she is pregnant. At seventeen, her status as a nymphet has quite gone, yet for Humbert her charm is unabated, still absolute. It is so even though he observes "how womanish and somehow never seen that way before was the shadowy division between her pale breasts." He begs her to return to him. She refuses—it is to her a surprising idea that he loves her or had ever loved her: she is as unrecognizing of his feeling for her as if she were indeed his daughter—and Humbert goes off to murder the playwright. We learn from the editor's preface that Lolita dies in childbed. Humbert dies of heart disease.

3

This, then, is the story of *Lolita* and it is indeed shocking. In a tone which is calculatedly not serious, it makes a prolonged assault on one of our unquestioned and unquestionable sexual prohibitions, the sexual inviolability of girls of a certain age (and compounds the impiousness with what amounts to incest).

It is all very well for us to remember that Juliet was fourteen when she was betrothed to Paris and gave herself, with our full approval, to Romeo. It is all very well for us to find a wry idyllic charm in the story of the aged David and the little maid Abishag. And gravely to receive Dante's account of being struck to the heart by an eight-year-old Beatrice. And to say that distant cultures—H.H. gives a list of them to put his idiosyncrasy in some moral perspective—and hot climates make a difference in ideas of the right age for female sexuality to begin. All very well for us to have long ago got over our first horror at what Freud told us about the sexuality of children, and to receive blandly what he has told us about the "family romance" and its part in the dynamics of the psyche. All very well for the family and society to take approving note of the little girl's developing sexual charms, to find a sweet comedy in her growing awareness of them and her learning to use them, and for her mother to be open and frank and delighted and ironic over the teacups about the clear signs of the explosive force of her sexual impulse. We have all become so nicely clear-eyed, so sensibly Coming-of-Age-in-Samoa. But let an adult male seriously think about the girl as a sexual object and all our sensibility is revolted.

The response is not reasoned but visceral. Within the range of possible heterosexual conduct, this is one of the few prohibitions which still seem to us to be confirmed by nature itself. Virginity once seemed so confirmed, as did the marital fidelity of women, but they do so no longer. No novelist would expect us to respond with any moral intensity to his representing an unmarried girl having a sexual experience, whether in love or curiosity; the infidelity of a wife may perhaps be a little more interesting, but not much. The most serious response the novelist would expect from us is that we should "understand," which he would count on us to do automatically.

But our response to the situation that Mr. Nabokov presents to us is that of shock. And we find ourselves the more shocked when we realize that, in the course of reading the novel, we have come virtually to condone the violation it presents. Charles Dickens, by no means a naïve man, was once required to meet a young woman who had lived for some years with a man out of wedlock; he was dreadfully agitated at the prospect, and when he met the girl he was appalled to discover that he was not confronting a piece of depravity but a principled, attractive young person, virtually a lady. It was a terrible blow to the certitude of his moral feelings. That we may experience the same loss of certitude about the sexual behavior that *Lolita* describes is perhaps suggested by the tone of my summary of the story—I was plainly not able to muster up the note of moral outrage. And it is likely that any reader of *Lolita* will discover that he comes to see the situation as less and less abstract and moral and horrible, and more and more as human and "understandable." Less and less, indeed, do we see a *situation*; what we become aware of is people. Humbert is perfectly willing to say that he is a monster; no doubt he is, but we find ourselves less and less eager to say so. Perhaps his depravity is the easier to accept when we learn that he deals with a Lolita who is not innocent, and who seems to have very few emotions to be violated; and I suppose we naturally incline to be lenient toward a rapist—legally and by intention H.H. is that—who eventually feels a deathless devotion to his victim!

But we have only to let the immediate influence of the book diminish a little with time, we have only to free ourselves from the rationalizing effect of H.H.'s obsessive passion, we have only to move back into the real world where twelve-year-olds are being bored by Social Studies and plagued by orthodonture, to feel again the outrage at the violation of the sexual prohibition. And to feel this the more because we have been seduced into conniving in the violation, because we have permitted our fantasies to accept what we know to be revolting.

What, we must ask, is Mr. Nabokov's purpose in making this occasion for outrage?

I have indicated that his purpose cannot be explained by any interest in the "psychological" aspects of the story; he has none whatever. His novel is as far as possible from being a "study of " the emotions it presents. The malice which H.H. bears to psychiatry is quite Mr. Nabokov's own; for author as for character, psychiatric concepts are merely occasions for naughty irreverence. Psychiatry and the world may join in giving scientific or ugly names to Humbert's sexual idiosyncrasy; the novel treats of it as a condition of love like another.

And we can be sure that Mr. Nabokov has not committed himself to moral subversion. He is not concerned to bring about a sexual revolution which will make paedophilia a rational and respectable form of heterosexuality. Humbert's "ferocity and jocularity," what we might call his moral facetiousness reaching the point of anarchic silliness, make the pervasive tone of the narrative, and that tone does have its curious influence upon us, as does the absoluteness of Humbert's passional obsession. Yet any anarchic power to which we may respond in the novel is quite negated when, near the end of the history, H.H. reflects, in a tone never used before, on the havoc he has made of Lolita's life.

It is of course possible that Mr. Nabokov wanted to shock us merely for shocking's sake, that he had in mind the intention of what might be called general satire, the purpose of which is to make us uneasy with ourselves, less sure of our moral simplicity than we have been: this he brings about by contriving the effect I have described, of leading us to become quite at ease with a sexual situation that should outrage us and then facing us with our facilely given acquiescence.

And then of course Mr. Nabokov may be intending a more particular satire, upon the peculiar sexual hypocrisy of American life. I have in mind the perpetual publicity we give to sexuality, the unending invitation made by our popular art and advertising to sexual awareness, competence, and competition. To what end is a girl-child taught from her earliest years to consider the brightness and fragrance of her hair, and the shape of her body, and her look of readiness for adventure? Why, what other end than that she shall some day be a really capable airline hostess? Or that she shall have the shining self-respect which, as we know, underlies all true virtue and efficiency? Or that her husband and her children shall not be ashamed of her but, on the contrary, proud to claim her as their own? So say the headmistresses, the principals, the deans of women, the parents. But in every other culture that Mr. Nabokov is aware of, which is a good many, the arts of the boudoir were understood to point to the bed, and if they were taught early, they were understood to point to the bed early.

But I think that the real reason why Mr. Nabokov chose his outrageous subject matter is that he wanted to write a story about love.

4

Lolita is about love. Perhaps I shall be better understood if I put the statement in this form: *Lolita* is not about sex, but about love. Almost every page sets forth some explicit erotic emotion or some overt erotic action and still it is not about sex. It is about love.

This makes it unique in my experience of contemporary novels. If our fiction gives accurate testimony, love has disappeared from the Western world, just as Denis de Rougemont said it should. The contemporary novel can tell us about sex, and about sexual communion, and about mutuality, and about the strong fine relationships that grow up between men and women; and it can tell us about marriage. But about love, which was once one of its chief preoccupations, it can tell us nothing at all.

My having mentioned Denis de Rougemont and his curious, belated, supererogatory onslaught on love will indicate that I have in mind what I seem to remember he calls passion-love, a kind of love with which European literature has dealt since time immemorial but with especial intensity since the Arthurian romances and the code of courtly love. Passion-love was a mode of feeling not available to everyone—the authorities on the subject restricted it to the aristocracy—but it was always of the greatest interest to almost everyone who was at all interested in the feelings, and it had a continuing influence on other kinds of love and on the literary conventions through which love was represented.

The essential condition of this kind of love was that it had nothing to do with marriage and could not possibly exist in marriage. Alanus Capellanus in his manual on courtly love set it down as perfectly obvious doctrine that a husband and wife cannot be lovers. The reason was that theirs was a practical and contractual relationship, having reference to estates and progeny. It was not a relation of the heart, and the inclination and the situation of the lady made it impossible for her to give herself in free-will because it was expected that she give herself in obedience. That the possibility of love could exist only apart from and more or less in opposition to marriage has been, by and large, the traditional supposition of the European upper classes, which have placed most of their expectations of erotic pleasure outside of marriage.

It was surely one of the most interesting and important of cultural revisions when the middle classes, which had been quite specifically excluded from the pleasure and dignity of love (one cannot be both busy and a lover), began to appropriate the prestige of this mode of feeling and to change it in the process of adopting it. For they assimilated it to marriage itself, and required of married love that it have the high brilliance and significance of passion-love. Something of that expectation still persists—it is still the love-poetry and the love-music and the love-dramas of passion-love in its later forms that shape our notions of what the erotic experience can be in intensity, in variety, in grace.

But inevitably the sexual revolution of our time brought the relationship between marriage and passion-love to a virtual end. Perhaps all that the two now have in common is the belief that the lovers must freely choose each other and that their choice has the highest sanctions and must not be interfered with. Apart from this, every aspect of the new relationship is a denial of the old ideal of love. If one can rely on the evidence of fiction to discover the modern idea of the right relation between a man and a woman, it would probably begin with a sexual meeting, more or less tentative or experimental, and go on to sexual communion, after which marriage would take place. There would follow a period in which husband and wife would each make an effort to get rid of their *merely symbolic* feelings for the other *partner* in the marriage and to learn to see each other *without illusion* and as they are *in reality*. To do this is the sign of *maturity*. It enables husband and wife to *build a life together*. In the *mutuality* and *warmth* of their *togetherness* their children are included. Toward each other, as toward their children, they show *tolerance* and *understanding*, which they find it easier to do if they have a *good sexual relationship*.

The condition toward which such a marriage aspires is *health*—a marriage is praised by being called a *healthy* marriage. This will suggest how far the modern ideal of love is from passion-love. The literal meaning of the word "passion" will indicate the distance. Nowadays we use the word chiefly to mean an intense feeling, forgetting the old distinction between a passion and an emotion, the former being an emotion before which we are helpless, which we have to *suffer*, in whose grip we are *passive*. The passion-lover was a sick man, a *patient*. It was the convention for him to say that he was sick and to make a show of his physical and mental derangement. And indeed by any modern standard of emotional health what he was expected to display in the way of obsessional conduct and masochism would make his condition deserve some sort of pretty grave name. His passion filled his whole mind to the exclusion of everything else; he submitted himself to his *mistress* as her *servant*, even her *slave*, he gloried in her *power* over him and expected that she would make him suffer, that she would be *cruel*.

Obviously I am dealing with a convention of literature, not describing the actual relationship between men and women. But it was a convention of a peculiar explicitness and force and it exerted an influence upon the management of the emotions down through the nineteenth century. At that time, it may be observed, the creative genius took over some of the characteristics of the lover: his obsessiveness, his masochism, his noble subservience to an ideal, and his antagonism to the social conventions, his propensity for making a scandal.

For scandal was of the essence of passion-love, which not only inverted the marital relationship of men and women but subverted marriage itself. It could also subvert a man's social responsibility, his honor. In either case, a scandal resulted, the extent of which measured the force of the love. Typically it led to disaster for the lovers, to death. For one aspect of the pathology of love was that it made of no account certain established judgments, denying the reality and the good of much in the world that is indeed real and good. In this respect lovers were conceived of much as we conceived of the artist—that is, as captivated by a reality and a good that are not of the ordinary world.

Now it may well be that all this is absurd, and really and truly a kind of pathology, and that we are much the better for being quite done with it, and that our contemporary love-ideal of a firm, tolerant, humorous, wry, happy marriage is a great advance from it. The world seems to be agreed that this is so—the evidence is to be found in a wide range of testimony from the most elementary fiction and the simplest handbook of marriage up to psychoanalysis and the works of D. H. Lawrence, for whom "love" was anathema. But the old ideal, as I have said, still has its charm for us—we still understand it in some degree; it still speaks to us of an intensity and grace of erotic emotion and behavior that we do not want to admit is entirely beyond our reach.

If a novelist wanted, for whatever strange reason, to write a novel about the old kind of love, how would he go about it? How would he find or contrive the elements that make love possible?

For example, if love requires scandal, what could the novelist count on to constitute a scandal? Surely not—as I have already suggested—adultery. The very word is archaic; we recognize the possibility of its use only in law or in the past. Marital infidelity is not thought of as necessarily destructive of marriage, and, indeed, the word "unfaithful," which once had so terrible a charge of meaning, begins to sound quaint, seeming to be inappropriate to our modern code. A few years ago William Barrett asked, *à propos* the effect of *Othello* on a modern audience, whether anyone nowadays could really comprehend and be interested in the spectacle of Othello's jealousy. I think that both comprehension and interest are possible. There are more than enough of the old feelings still left—nothing is ever thrown out of the attic of the mind—to permit us to understand perfectly well what Othello feels. Here we must be aware of the difference between life and literature. It is of course not true that people do not feel sexual jealousy; it is still one of the most intense of emotions. But they find it ever harder to believe that they are justified in feeling it, that they do right to give this emotion any authority. A contemporary writer would not be able to interest us in a situation like Othello's because, even if he had proof in his own experience of the actuality of jealousy, he could not give intellectual credence, or expect his readers to give it, to an emotion which in Shakespeare was visceral, unquestionable, of absolute authority.

But the breaking of the taboo about the sexual unavailability of very young girls has for us something of the force that a wife's infidelity had for Shakespeare. H.H.'s relation with Lolita defies society as scandalously as did Tristan's relation with Iseult, or Vronsky's with Anna. It puts the lovers, as lovers in literature must be put, beyond the pale of society.

Then the novelist, if he is to maintain the right conditions for a story of passion-love, must see to it that his lovers do not approach the condition of marriage. That is, their behavior to each other must not be touched by practicality, their virtues must not be of a kind that acknowledges the claims of the world. As soon as mutuality comes in, and common interests, and cooperation, and tolerance, and a concern for each other's welfare or prestige in the world, the ethos of the family, of marriage, has asserted itself and they lose their status of lovers. Their behavior to each other must be precisely not what we call "mature"—they must see each other and the world with the imperious absolutism of children. So that a man in the grip of an obsessional lust and a girl of twelve make the ideal couple for a story about love written in our time. At least at the beginning of his love for Lolita there are no practical moral considerations, no practical personal considerations, that qualify H.H.'s behavior. As for Lolita, there is no possibility of her bringing the relation close to the condition of marriage because she cannot even imagine the female role in marriage. She remains perpetually the cruel mistress; even after her lover has won physical possession of her, she withholds the favor of her feeling, for she has none to give, by reason of her age, possibly by reason of her temperament.

Then the novelist must pay due attention to making the lover's obsession believable and not ridiculous. Nowadays we find it difficult to give credence to the idea that a man might feel that his reason and his very life depended on the response to him of a particular woman. Recently I read *Liber Amoris* with some graduate students and found that they had no understanding whatever of Hazlitt's obsessive commitment to Sarah Walker. They could see no reason why a man could not break the chains of a passion so unrewarding, so humiliating. I later regretted having been cross at their stupidity when I found myself doubting the verisimilitude of

Proust's account of the relation of Swann to Odette. But our doubts are allayed if the obsession can be accounted for by the known fact of a sexual peculiarity, an avowed aberration. Pathology naturalizes the strange particularity of the lover's preference.

I may seem to have been talking about *Lolita* as if in writing it Mr. Nabokov had undertaken a job of emotional archaeology. This may not be quite fair to Mr. Nabokov's whole intention, but it does suggest how regressive a book *Lolita* is, how, although it strikes all the most approved modern postures and attitudes, it is concerned to restore a foredone mode of feeling. And in nothing is *Lolita* so archaic as in its way of imaging the beloved. We with our modern latitude in these matters are likely to be amused by the minor details of his mistress's person that caught the lover's fancy in the novels of the nineteenth century—the expressiveness of the eyes, a certain kind of glance, a foot, an ankle, a wrist, an ear, a ringlet; with our modern reader's knowledge of the size and shape of the heroine's breasts, thighs, belly, and buttocks, these seem trifling and beside the point. Yet the interest in the not immediately erotic details of the female person was not forced on the lover or the novelist by narrow conventions; rather, it was an aspect of the fetishism which seems to attend passion-love, a sort of synecdoche of desire, in which the part stands for the whole, and even the glove or the scarf of the beloved has an erotic value. This is the mode of H.H.'s adoration of Lolita, and against the background of his sexual greed, which he calls "ape-like," it comes over us as another reason for being shocked, that in recent fiction no lover has thought of his beloved with so much tenderness, that no woman has been so charmingly evoked, in such grace and delicacy, as Lolita; the description of her tennis game, in which even her racket has an erotic charm, is one of the few examples of rapture in modern writing.

It seems to me that it is impossible to miss the *parti pris* in Mr. Nabokov's archaeological undertaking, the impulse to mock and discredit all forms of progressive rationalism not only because they are stupid in themselves but because they have brought the madness of love to an end. But Mr. Nabokov is not partisan to the point of being dishonest about the true nature of love. It is H.H., that mixture of ferocity and jocularity, who reminds us that "Love seeketh only self to please. . . . And builds a Hell in Heaven's despite." The passages in which Humbert gives voice to this judgment are not as well done as one might wish; they stand in an awkward relation to the tone and device of the book. Yet perhaps for that very reason they are the more startling and impressive (if we do not read them in a mood which makes them seem to verge upon the maudlin).

And in the end H.H. succumbs, and happily, to the dialectic of the history of love. I have represented passion-love as being the antithesis of marriage and as coming to an end when the conditions characteristic of marriage impose themselves, by whatever means, upon the lovers. Yet it is always to marriage that passion-love aspires, unique marriage, ideal marriage, marriage available to no other pair, but marriage nonetheless, with all the cramping vows and habitualness of marriage. And it is just this that H.H. eventually desires. Mr. Nabokov is, among his other accomplishments, an eminent entomologist and I shall leave it to some really rigorous close-reader of fiction to tell us what an entomological novelist wants us to do with the fact that "nymph" is the name for the young of an insect without complete metamorphosis. Probably nothing. But he is also a scholar of languages and he knows that "nymph" is the Greek word for "bride." He does not impart this information to us, yet he is at pains, as I have remarked, to put us in mind of the rapturous, tortured marriage of Poe and Virginia, and one of his last meditations on Lolita is of the constancy she evokes from him despite the ravages of time having destroyed the old incitements to lust:

> . . . There she was with her ruined looks and her adult, rope-veined narrow hands and her goose-flesh white arms, and her shallow ears, and her unkempt armpits, there she was (my Lolita), hopelessly worn at seventeen, with that baby, dreaming already in her of becoming a big shot and retiring around 2020 A.D.—and I looked and looked at her, and knew as clearly as I know I am to die, that I loved her more than anything I had ever seen or imagined on earth, or hoped for anywhere else. She was only the faint violet whiff and dead leaf echo of the nymphet I had rolled myself upon with such cries in the past; an echo on the brink of a russet ravine, with a far wood under a white sky, and brown leaves choking the brook and one last cricket in the crisp weeds . . . but thank God it was not that echo alone that I worshipped. What I used to pamper among the tangled vines of my heart, *mon grand péché radieux*, had dwindled in its essence: sterile and selfish vice, all that I cancelled and cursed. You may jeer at me, and threaten to clear

the court, but until I am gagged and half-throttled, I will shout my poor truth. I insist the world know how much I loved my Lolita, *this* Lolita, pale and polluted, and big with another's child, but still grey-eyed, still sooty-lashed, still auburn and almond. . . .

I am not sure just how I respond to the moral implication of this passage—I am not sure that with it, as with other passages in which H.H. speaks of the depth and wild solemnity of his love and remorse, Mr. Nabokov has not laid an emotional trap for the reader, that perhaps H.H.'s last intensities ought not to be received with considerably more irony than at first they call for. I don't say this with the least certitude. It may be that Mr. Nabokov really wants us to believe with entire seriousness that we are witnessing the culmination of H.H.'s moral evolution. Perhaps he even wants us to believe that his ascent from "ape-like" lust to a love which challenges the devils below and the angels up over the sea to ever dissever his soul from the soul of the lovely Annabel Lee constitutes the life-cycle of the erotic instinct. I can, I think, manage to take seriously a tragic Humbert, but I find myself easier with Humbert the anti-hero, with Humbert as cousin-german to Rameau's nephew.

I don't want to put my uneasiness with the tragic Humbert as an objection. Indeed, for me one of the attractions of *Lolita* is its ambiguity of tone—which is pretty well exemplified in the passage I have quoted—and its ambiguity of intention, its ability to arouse uneasiness, to throw the reader off balance, to require him to change his stance and shift his position and move on. *Lolita* gives us no chance to settle and sink roots. Perhaps it is the curious moral mobility it urges on us that accounts for its remarkable ability to represent certain aspects of American life.

A Speech on Robert Frost:
A Cultural Episode

1959

On 26 March 1959, Henry Holt and Company, the publishers of Robert Frost, gave Mr. Frost a dinner at the Waldorf-Astoria in celebration of his eighty-fifth birthday. I was the speaker at the dinner. I am publishing what I said about Mr. Frost not because I think it to be especially interesting in itself but because it made the occasion for a disturbance of some magnitude and I should like to answer the question that has often been put to me: What did I say that could so nearly have approached a scandal?

Some of the substance of my speech was made public by J. Donald Adams in his column in *The New York Times Book Review* of 12 April. Mr. Adams wrote from a copy of my manuscript which, with my permission, had been made available to him by Holt, and he reported with sufficient accuracy those parts of the speech to which he took exception. It should be said of Mr. Adams's reply to me that it took exception only to the critical judgment I had expressed. Mr. Adams did not question my taste or tact except in one small and perhaps facetious instance—he thought it "unfortunate . . . in view of Frost's shock of white hair," that I should have "identified the poet with the Bald Eagle." (But every American worthy of the name knows that the Bald Eagle is not bald at all and that in maturity it is distinguished by its shock of white hair.) Nevertheless the reply of Mr. Adams created the impression with some people that, so far from my having paid tribute to a venerable man at a celebration of his life and achievement, I had actually offered him an affront. I gather that the chief cause of the presumed offense was my having spoken of Mr. Frost as "a terrifying poet."

Certainly what I had said as reported by Mr. Adams offered an affront to some part of American opinion. It was a very deep affront if I can judge by the letters, published in the *Book Review* of 26 April, which applauded Mr. Adams for his reply to me. There were nine such letters and all of them sounded a note of bitterness, or of personal grievance, or of triumph over my having been so thoroughly taken down by Mr. Adams. I must confess to being surprised by the low personal and intellectual tone of these letters. My estimate of the present state of American culture had not prepared me for it. "Trilling doesn't have the good sense to know when he is out of his field or his depth or whatever it is." "Frost might have had the Nobel Prize if so many New York critics hadn't gone whoring after European gods." "This Trilling fella had it coming to him for some time." "I hope Robert Frost was having a nice plate of buckwheat cakes and Vermont maple syrup as he read Mr. Adams's remarks. He couldn't have done better unless he had taken the so-called professor out to the woodshed." "I am a Freudian psychoanalyst, but I couldn't agree with Mr. Adams more. Imagine calling Frost a 'terrifying poet.' Professor Trilling never got lost in the Freudian wood. He is just enmeshed in a Trilling world." (In his column Mr. Adams had urged me "to come out of the Freudian wood . . . and face the facts of life." It will be seen that I make no mention of Freud in my speech, but I do speak of D. H. Lawrence, and Mr. Adams said that Lawrence was a genius but hadn't understood "the American experience" because, like me, he was "lost in the Freudian wood." Lawrence, of course, hated Freud and took every occasion to denounce him.)

The personal and intellectual quality of the letters is especially interesting because of the professions of the people who wrote them: in addition to the "Freudian psychoanalyst," the writers included the editor of *The Atlantic Monthly*, the publisher of *The Saturday Review*, two fairly well-known poets, a member of the Federal Trade Commission, a well-known and quite literate writer of fiction and biography, a very distinguished literary scholar. Only one of the writers, Mr. Weeks of *The Atlantic Monthly*, knew at first hand what I had said, having been present at the dinner. He expressed himself as finding my remarks "ill-judged and condescending for an occasion which was intended to be appreciative," and went on to say that "it would have been more appropriate had the introduction been entrusted to W. H. Auden, particularly in view of England's early acceptance of Frost's work, in which case we should have been spared the long Freudian self-analysis which few could have come to hear." All the other writers knew what I had said only from Mr. Adams's reply to it. That the literary scholar was among their number made a circumstance to which I couldn't fail to respond with some unhappiness, for I had first been Professor Emery Neff's student when I was an undergraduate at Columbia College and I had worked in his field and under his direction as a graduate student; I have always thought of Mr. Neff as the teacher from whom I had learned the methods and attitudes of the scholar; that he should so far have abrogated the rule and spirit of scholarship as to write in support of Mr. Adams's rebuke (as he chose to call it) without having seen the text of what I had said disturbed me deeply in a way I shall not now attempt to describe.

I have no doubt that the episode will yield cultural conclusions to whoever wants to draw them.

Because I am publishing the speech as a document, I give it exactly as I spoke it, not even mitigating the donnish humor of the opening paragraphs.

Mr. Rigg, Ladies and Gentlemen
(and I shall address Mr. Frost presently):

I am sure that anyone standing in my place to-night, charged with the happy office of greeting Mr. Frost on his birthday, on his massive, his Sophoclean birthday, would be bound to feel, as I do indeed feel, a considerable measure of diffidence.

For our occasion, although it isn't solemn, is surely momentous. We all of us know that we celebrate something that lies beyond even Mr. Frost's achievement as a poet. No person here tonight, no matter how high his regard for Mr. Frost as a poet may be, is under any illusion that Mr. Frost, at this point in his career, exists in the consciousness of Americans as only a poet. Just what he does exist as may perhaps be best understood by the archaeologists of a few millenniums hence. They will observe, those ardent students of our culture, how, at the time of the vernal equinox, feasts were held to celebrate the birth of this personage, and how, at a later time in the spring, at that ceremony which the ancient North Americans, with their infallible instinct for beauty, called by the lovely name of *Commencement*, it was customary to do him honor by a rite in which it was pretended that he was a scholar, a man of immense learning—a doctor—and no American university was thought to be worthy of the name until it had duly performed this rite, which was quaintly called *conferring a degree*. The time of year at which these ritual observances took place makes it plain to the archaeologists that they are almost certainly not dealing with an historical individual but rather with a solar myth, a fertility figure. They go on to expound the subtle process of myth which is to be observed in the fact that this vernal spirit was called *Frost*, a name which seems to contradict his nature and function. In their effort to explain this anomaly, they take note of evidence which suggests that the early North Americans believed that there were once two brothers, Robert Frost and Jack Frost, of whom one, Jack, remained unregenerate and hostile to mankind, while the other brother became its friend. But of course the archaeologists understand that this is a mere folk-explanation which explains nothing. They say, cogently enough, that mythical figures often embody contradictory principles, that just as Apollo was both destroyer and preserver, so Robert Frost was at one and the same time both ice and sun, and they point to a dark saying attributed to him: "Like a piece of ice on a hot stove, the poem must ride on its own melting."

Thus the ultimate myth. It tells us much about the nature of Robert Frost and I am glad to be able to communicate it to you.

But there is also the myth that is nearer at hand. We do not need to wait upon the archaeologists of the future to understand that Robert Frost exists not only in a human way but also in a mythical way. We know him, and have known him so for many years, as nothing less than a national fact. We have come to think of him as virtually a symbol of America, as something not unlike an articulate, an actually poetic, Bald Eagle. When we undertake to honor him, we do indeed honor him as a poet, but also as a tutelary genius of the nation and as a justification of our national soul.

This mythical existence of Robert Frost determines the nature of our occasion and makes it momentous. It substantiates my statement that anyone who speaks publicly about Mr. Frost tonight must do so under the constraints of an extreme diffidence.

Yet I must be more weighed down by diffidence than many others who might speak here. I must almost entertain a doubt of the appropriateness of my speaking here at all. For I cannot help knowing that the manifest America of Robert Frost's poems is not the America that has its place in my own mind. The manifest America of Mr. Frost's poems is rural, and, if I may say so, it is rural in a highly moralized way, in an aggressively moralized way. It thus represents an ideal that is common to many Americans, perhaps especially to Americans of the literary kind, who thus express their distaste for the life of the city and for all that the city implies of excessive complexity, of uncertainty, of anxiety, and of the demand that is made upon intellect to deal with whatever are the causes of complexity, uncertainty, anxiety.

I do not share this ideal. It is true that the image of the old America has a great power over me—that old America with which the America of Mr. Frost's poems seems to be continuous. And I think I know from experience—there are few Americans who do not—how intense can be the pleasure in the hills and the snow, in the meadows and woods and swamps that make the landscape of Mr. Frost's manifest America; and know, too, how great a part this pleasure can play in a man's moral being. But these natural things that give me pleasure constitute my notion of the earthly paradise, they are not the ruling elements of my imagination of actual life. Those elements are urban—I speak here tonight incongruously as a man of the city. I teach in an urban university. The magazine I most enjoy writing for is *Partisan Review*, to which, as I know, there is often imputed an excess of city intellectuality, even to the point of its being thought scarcely American at all.

Of course I have imagination enough to hate the city. And of course I have sensibility enough to be bored and exasperated by the intellectual life that is peculiar to the city, as that is lived not only by others but by myself. But to the essential work that is done by the critical intellect (I use the term in its widest sense), that work which, wherever it is carried on, must sooner or later relate itself to the metropolis or must seek, wherever it is carried on, to create around itself the intensity and variety that traditionally characterize the intellectual life of the metropolis—to that work I give a partisan devotion. I know all that can be charged against the restless, combative, abstract urban intellect: I know perhaps more than is known by its avowed antagonists. I also know that when it flags, something goes out of the nation's spirit, and that if it were to cease, the state of the nation would be much the worse.

It is a fact which I had best confess as simply as possible that for a long time I was alienated from Mr. Frost's great canon of work by what I saw in it that either itself seemed to denigrate the work of the critical intellect or that gave to its admirers the ground for making the denigration. It was but recently that my resistance, at the behest of better understanding, yielded to admiration—it is probable that there is no one here tonight who has not admired Mr. Frost's poetry for a longer time than I have.

This will begin to explain why I am so especially diffident standing in this place. I have yet more to confess. I have to say that my Frost—*my Frost*: what airs we give ourselves when once we believe that we have come into possession of a poet!—I have to say that my Frost is not the Frost I seem to perceive existing in the minds of so many of his admirers. He is not the Frost who confounds the characteristically modern practice of poetry by his notable democratic simplicity of utterance: on the contrary. He is not the Frost who controverts the bitter modern astonishment at the nature of human life: the opposite is so. He is not the Frost who reassures us by his affirmation of old virtues, simplicities, pieties, and ways of feeling: anything but. I will not go so far as to say that my Frost is not essentially an American poet at all: I believe that he is quite as American as everyone thinks he is, but not in the way that everyone thinks he is.

In the matter of the Americanism of American literature one of my chief guides is that very remarkable critic D. H. Lawrence. Here are the opening sentences of Lawrence's great outrageous book about classic American literature: "We like to think of the old fashioned American classics as children's books. Just childishness on our part. The old American art speech contains an alien quality which belongs to the American continent and to nowhere else." And this unique alien quality, Lawrence goes on to say, the world has missed. "It is hard to hear a new voice," he says, "as hard as to listen to an unknown language. . . . Why? Out of fear. The world fears a new experience more than it fears anything. It can pigeonhole any idea. But it can't pigeonhole a real new experience. It can only dodge. The world is a great dodger, and the Americans the greatest. Because they dodge their own very selves." I should like to pick up a few more of Lawrence's sentences, feeling the freer to do so because they have an affinity to Mr. Frost's prose manner and substance: "An artist is usually a damned liar, but his art, if it be art, will tell you the truth of his day. And that is all that matters. Away with eternal truth. Truth lives from day to day. . . . The old American artists were hopeless liars. . . . Never trust the artist. Trust the tale. The proper function of the critic is to save the tale from the artist who created it. . . . Now listen to me, don't listen to him. He'll tell you the lie you expect, which is partly your fault for expecting it."

Now in point of fact Robert Frost is *not* a liar. I would not hesitate to say that he was if I thought he was. But no, he is not. In certain of his poems—I shall mention one or two in a moment—he makes it perfectly plain what he is doing; and if we are not aware of what he is doing in other of his poems, where he is not quite so plain, that is not his fault but our own. It is not from him that the tale needs to be saved.

I conceive that Robert Frost is doing in his poems what Lawrence says the great writers of the classic American tradition did. That enterprise of theirs was of an ultimate radicalism. It consisted, Lawrence says, of two things: a disintegration and sloughing off of the old consciousness, by which Lawrence means the old European consciousness, and the forming of a new consciousness underneath.

So radical a work, I need scarcely say, is not carried out by reassurance, nor by the affirmation of old virtues and pieties. It is carried out by the representation of the terrible actualities of life in a new way. I think of Robert Frost as a terrifying poet. Call him, if it makes things any easier, a tragic poet, but it might be useful every now and then to come out from under the shelter of that literary word. The universe that he conceives is a terrifying universe. Read the poem called "Design" and see if you sleep the better for it. Read "Neither Out Far nor In Deep," which often seems to me the most perfect poem of our time, and see if you are warmed by anything in it except the energy with which emptiness is perceived.

But the *people*, it will be objected, the *people* who inhabit this possibly terrifying universe! About them there is nothing that can terrify; surely the people in Mr. Frost's poems can only reassure us by their integrity and solidity. Perhaps so. But I cannot make the disjunction. It may well be that ultimately they reassure us in some sense, but first they terrify us, or should. We must not be misled about them by the curious tenderness with which they are represented, a tenderness which extends to a recognition of the tenderness which they themselves can often give. But when ever have people been so isolated, so lightning-blasted, so tried down and cabined by life, so reduced, each in his own way, to some last irreducible core of being. Talk of the disintegration and sloughing off of the old consciousness! The people of Robert Frost's poems have done that with a vengeance. Lawrence says that what the Americans refused to accept was "the post-Renaissance humanism of Europe," "the old European spontaneity," "the flowing easy humor of Europe," and that seems to me a good way to describe the people who inhabit Robert Frost's America. In the interests of what great other thing these people have made this rejection we cannot know for certain. But we can guess that it was in the interest of truth, of some truth of the self. This is what they all affirm by their humor (which is so *not* "the easy flowing humor of Europe"), by their irony, by their separateness and isolateness. They affirm *this* of themselves: that they are what they are, that this is their truth, and that if the truth be bare, as truth often is, it is far better than a lie. For me the process by which they arrive at that truth is always terrifying. The manifest America of Mr. Frost's poems may be pastoral; the actual America is tragic.

And what new consciousness is forming underneath? That I do not know, possibly because I have not been long enough habituated to the voice that makes the relatively new experience I am having. I am still preoccupied with the terrifying process of the disintegration and sloughing off of the old consciousness.

Mr. Frost:

I hope that you will not think it graceless of me that on your birthday I have undertaken to say that a great many of your admirers have not understood clearly what you have been doing in your life in poetry. I know that you will not say which of us is in the right of the matter. You will behave like the Secret whose conduct you have described:

> We dance around in a ring and suppose.
> But the Secret sits in the middle and knows.

And I hope that you will not think it graceless of me that on your birthday I have made you out to be a poet who terrifies. When I began to speak I called your birthday Sophoclean and that word has, I think, controlled everything I have said about you. Like you, Sophocles lived to a great age, writing well; and like you, Sophocles was the poet his people loved most. Surely they loved him in some part because he praised their common country. But I think that they loved him chiefly because he made plain to them the terrible things of human life: they felt, perhaps, that only a poet who could make plain the terrible things could possibly give them comfort.

On the Teaching of
Modern Literature

1961

I propose to consider here a particular theme of modern literature which
appears so frequently and with so much authority that it may be said to
constitute one of the shaping and controlling ideas of our epoch. I can
identify it by calling it the disenchantment of our culture with culture itself—it seems to me that the characteristic element of modern literature,
or at least of the most highly developed modern literature, is the bitter
line of hostility to civilization which runs through it. It happens that my
present awareness of this theme is involved in a personal experience, and
I am impelled to speak of it not abstractly but with the husks of the experience clinging untidily to it. I shall go so far in doing this as to describe
the actual circumstances in which the experience took place. These circumstances are pedagogic—they consist of some problems in teaching
modern literature to undergraduates and my attempt to solve these problems. I know that pedagogy is a depressing subject to all persons of sensibility, and yet I shall not apologize for touching upon it because the
emphasis upon the teaching of literature and especially of modern literature is in itself one of the most salient and significant manifestations of
the culture of our time. Indeed, if, having in mind Matthew Arnold's lecture "On the Modern Element in Literature," we are on the hunt for *the*

modern element in modern literature, we might want to find it in the susceptibility of modern literature to being made into an academic subject.

For some years I have taught the course in modern literature in Columbia College. I did not undertake it without misgiving and I have never taught it with an undivided mind. My doubts do not refer to the value of the literature itself, only to the educational propriety of its being studied in college. These doubts persist even though I wholly understand that the relation of our collegiate education to modernity is no longer an open question. The unargued assumption of most curriculums is that the real subject of all study is the modern world; that the justification of all study is its immediate and presumably practical relevance to modernity; that the true purpose of all study is to lead the young person to be at home in, and in control of, the modern world. There is really no way of quarreling with the assumption or with what follows upon it, the instituting of courses of which the substance is chiefly contemporary or at least makes ultimate reference to what is contemporary.

It might be asked why anyone should *want* to quarrel with the assumption. To that question I can return only a defensive, eccentric, self-depreciatory answer. It is this: that to some of us who teach and who think of our students as the creators of the intellectual life of the future, there comes a kind of despair. It does not come because our students fail to respond to ideas, rather because they respond to ideas with a happy vagueness, a delighted glibness, a joyous sense of power in the use of received or receivable generalizations, a grateful wonder at how easy it is to formulate and judge, at how little resistance language offers to their intentions. When that despair strikes us, we are tempted to give up the usual and accredited ways of evaluating education, and instead of prizing responsiveness and aptitude, to set store by some sign of personal character in our students, some token of individual will. We think of this as taking the form of resistance and imperviousness, of personal density or gravity, of some power of supposing that ideas are real, a power which will lead a young man to say what Goethe thought was the modern thing to say, "But is this really true—is it true for *me*?" And to say this not in the facile way, not following the progressive educational prescription to "think for yourself," which means to think in the progressive pieties rather than in the conservative pieties (if any of the latter do still exist), but to say it from his sense of himself as a person rather than as a bundle of attitudes and responses which are all alert to please the teacher and the progressive community.

We can't do anything about the quality of personal being of our students, but we are led to think about the cultural analogue of a personal character that is grave, dense, and resistant—we are led to think about the past. Perhaps the protagonist of Thomas Mann's story "Disorder and Early Sorrow" comes to mind, that sad Professor Cornelius with his intense and ambivalent sense of history. For Professor Cornelius, who is a historian, the past is dead, is death itself, but for that very reason it is the source of order, value, piety, and even love. If we think about education in the dark light of the despair I have described, we wonder if perhaps there is not to be found in the past that quiet place at which a young man might stand for a few years, at least a little beyond the competing attitudes and generalizations of the present, at least a little beyond the contemporary problems which he is told he can master only by means of attitudes and generalizations, that quiet place in which he can be silent, in which he can *know* something—in what year the Parthenon was begun, the order of battle at Trafalgar, how Linear B was deciphered: almost anything at all that has nothing to do with the talkative and attitudinizing present, anything at all but variations on the accepted formulations about *anxiety*, and *urban society*, and *alienation*, and *Gemeinschaft* and *Gesellschaft*, all the matter of the academic disciplines which are founded upon the modern self-consciousness and the modern self-pity. The modern self-pity is certainly not without its justification; but, if the circumstances that engender it are ever to be overcome, we must sometimes wonder whether this work can be done by minds which are taught in youth to accept these sad conditions of ours as the only right objects of contemplation. And quite apart from any practical consequences, one thinks of the simple aesthetic personal pleasure of having to do with young minds, and maturing minds, which are free of cant, which are, to quote an old poet, "fierce, moody, patient, venturous, modest, shy."

This line of argument I have called eccentric and maybe it ought to be called obscurantist and reactionary. Whatever it is called, it is not likely to impress a Committee on the Curriculum. It was, I think, more or less the line of argument of my department in Columbia College, when, up to a few years ago, it would decide, whenever the question came up, not to carry its courses beyond the late nineteenth century. But our rationale could not stand against the representations which a group of students made to our Dean and which he communicated to us. The students wanted a course in modern literature—very likely, in the way of

students, they said that it was a scandal that no such course was being offered in the College. There was no argument that could stand against this
expressed desire: we could only capitulate, and then, with pretty good
grace, muster the arguments that justified our doing so. Was not the
twentieth century more than half over? Was it not nearly fifty years since
Eliot wrote "Portrait of a Lady"? George Meredith had not died until
1909, and even the oldest among us had read one of his novels in a college
course—many American universities had been quick to bring into their
purview the literature of the later nineteenth century, and even the early
twentieth century; there was a strong supporting tradition for our capitulation. Had not Yeats been Matthew Arnold's contemporary for twenty-
three years?

Our resistance to the idea of the course had never been based on an
adverse judgment of the literature itself. We are a department not only of
English but of comparative literature, and if the whole of modern literature is surveyed, it could be said—and we were willing to say it—that no
literature of the past surpassed the literature of our time in power and
magnificence. Then too, it is a difficult literature, and it is difficult not
merely as defenders of modern poetry say that all literature is difficult. We
nowadays believe that Keats is a very difficult poet, but his earlier readers
did not. We now see the depths and subtleties of Dickens, but his contemporary readers found him as simply available as a plate of oysters on
the half shell. Modern literature, however, shows its difficulties at first
blush; they are literal as well as doctrinal difficulties—if our students were
to know their modern literary heritage, surely they needed all the help
that a teacher can give?

These made cogent reasons for our decision to establish, at long last,
the course in modern literature. They also made a ground for our display
of a certain mean-spirited, last-ditch vindictiveness. I recall that we said
something like, Very well, if they want the modern, let them have it—let
them have it, as Henry James says, full in the face. We shall give the
course, but we shall give it on the highest level, and if they think, as students do, that the modern will naturally meet them in a genial way, let
them have their gay and easy time with Yeats and Eliot, with Joyce and
Proust and Kafka, with Lawrence, Mann, and Gide.

Eventually the course fell to me to give. I approached it with an uneasiness which has not diminished with the passage of time—it has, I
think, even increased. It arises, this uneasiness, from my personal relation

with the works that form the substance of the course. Almost all of them have been involved with me for a long time—I invert the natural order not out of lack of modesty but taking the cue of W. H. Auden's remark that a real book reads us. I have been read by Eliot's poems and by *Ulysses* and by *Remembrance of Things Past* and by *The Castle* for a good many years now, since early youth. Some of these books at first rejected me; I bored them. But as I grew older and they knew me better, they came to have more sympathy with me and to understand my hidden meanings. Their nature is such that our relationship has been very intimate. No literature has ever been so shockingly personal as that of our time—it asks every question that is forbidden in polite society. It asks us if we are content with our marriages, with our family lives, with our professional lives, with our friends. It is all very well for me to describe my course in the College catalogue as "paying particular attention to the role of the writer as a critic of his culture"—this is sheer evasion: the questions asked by our literature are not about our culture but about ourselves. It asks us if we are content with ourselves, if we are saved or damned—more than with anything else, our literature is concerned with salvation. No literature has ever been so intensely spiritual as ours. I do not venture to call it actually religious, but certainly it has the special intensity of concern with the spiritual life which Hegel noted when he spoke of the great modern phenomenon of the secularization of spirituality.

I do not know how other teachers deal with this extravagant personal force of modern literature, but for me it makes difficulty. Nowadays the teaching of literature inclines to a considerable technicality, but when the teacher has said all that can be said about formal matters, about verse-patterns, metrics, prose conventions, irony, tension, etc., he must confront the necessity of bearing personal testimony. He must use whatever authority he may possess to say whether or not a work is true; and if not, why not; and if so, why so. He can do this only at considerable cost to his privacy. How does one say that Lawrence is right in his great rage against the modern emotions, against the modern sense of life and ways of being, unless one speaks from the intimacies of one's own feelings, and one's own sense of life, and one's own wished-for way of being? How, except with the implication of personal judgment, does one say to students that Gide is perfectly accurate in his representation of the awful boredom and slow corruption of respectable life? Then probably one rushes in to say that this doesn't of itself justify homosexuality and the desertion of one's dying wife, certainly not. But then again, having paid one's *devoirs* to morality, how does one rescue from morality Gide's essential point about the supreme rights of the individual person, and without making it merely historical, academic?

My first response to the necessity of dealing with matters of this kind was resentment of the personal discomfort it caused me. These are subjects we usually deal with either quite unconsciously or in the privacy of our own conscious minds, and if we now and then disclose our thoughts about them, it is to friends of equal age and especial closeness. Or if we touch upon them publicly, we do so in the relative abstractness and anonymity of print. To stand up in one's own person and to speak of them in one's own voice to an audience which each year grows younger as one grows older—that is not easy, and probably it is not decent.

And then, leaving aside the personal considerations, or taking them merely as an indication of something wrong with the situation, can we not say that, when modern literature is brought into the classroom, the subject being taught is betrayed by the pedagogy of the subject? We have to ask ourselves whether in our day too much does not come within the purview of the academy. More and more, as the universities liberalize themselves and turn their beneficent imperialistic gaze upon what is called Life Itself, the feeling grows among our educated classes that little can be experienced unless it is validated by some established intellectual discipline, with the result that experience loses much of its personal immediacy for us and becomes part of an accredited societal activity. This is not entirely true and I don't want to play the boring academic game of pretending that it *is* entirely true, that the university mind wilts and withers whatever it touches. I must believe, and I do believe, that the university study of art is capable of confronting the power of a work of art fully and courageously. I even believe that it can discover and disclose power where it has not been felt before. But the university study of art achieves this end chiefly with works of art of an older period. Time has the effect of seeming to quiet the work of art, domesticating it and making it into a classic, which is often another way of saying that it is an object of merely habitual regard. University study of the right sort can reverse this process and restore to the old work its freshness and force—can, indeed, disclose unguessed-at power. But with the works of art of our own present age, university study tends to accelerate the process by which the radical and subversive work becomes the classic work, and university study does this in the degree that it is vivacious and responsive and what is called nonacademic. In one of his poems Yeats mocks the literary scholars, the "bald heads forgetful of their sins," the "old, learned, respectable bald heads," who edit the poems of the fierce and passionate young men.

> Lord, what would they say
> Did their Catullus walk this way?

Yeats, of course, is thinking of his own future fate, and no doubt there is all the radical and comical discrepancy that he sees between the poet's passions and the scholars' close-eyed concentration on the text. Yet for my part, when I think of Catullus, I am moved to praise the tact of all those old heads, from Heinsius and Bentley to Munro and Postgate, who worked on Codex G and Codex O and drew conclusions from them about the lost Codex V—for doing only this and for not trying to realize and demonstrate the true intensity and the true quality and the true cultural meaning of Catullus's passion and managing to bring it somehow into eventual accord with their respectability and baldness. Nowadays we who deal with books in universities live in fear that the World, which we imagine to be a vital, palpitating, passionate, reality-loving World, will think of us as old, respectable, and bald, and we see to it that in our dealings with Yeats (to take him as the example) his wild cry of rage and sexuality is heard by our students and quite thoroughly understood by them as—what is it that we eventually call it?—*a significant expression of our culture*. The exasperation of Lawrence and the subversiveness of Gide, by the time we have dealt with them boldly and straightforwardly, are notable instances of the *alienation of modern man as exemplified by the artist*. "Compare Yeats, Gide, Lawrence, and Eliot in the use which they make of the theme of sexuality to criticize the deficiencies of modern culture. Support your statement by specific references to the work of each author. [Time: one hour.]" And the distressing thing about our examination questions is that they are not ridiculous, they make perfectly good sense—such good sense that the young person who answers them can never again know the force and terror of what has been communicated to him by the works he is being examined on.

Very likely it was with the thought of saving myself from the necessity of speaking personally and my students from having to betray the full harsh meaning of a great literature that I first taught my course in as *liter-*

ary a way as possible. A couple of decades ago the discovery was made that a literary work is a structure of words: this doesn't seem a surprising thing to have learned except for its polemical tendency, which is to urge us to minimize the amount of attention we give to the poet's social and personal will, to what he wants to happen outside the poem as a result of the poem; it urges us to fix our minds on what is going on inside the poem. For me this polemical tendency has been of the greatest usefulness, for it has corrected my inclination to pay attention chiefly to what the poet *wants*. For two or three years I directed my efforts toward dealing with the matter of the course chiefly as structures of words, in a formal way, with due attention paid to the literal difficulty which marked so many of the works. But it went against the grain. It went against my personal grain. It went against the grain of the classroom situation, for formal analysis is best carried on by question-and-answer, which needs small groups, and the registration for the course in modern literature in any college is sure to be large. And it went against the grain of the authors themselves—structures of words they may indeed have created, but these structures were not pyramids or triumphal arches, they were manifestly contrived to be not static and commemorative but mobile and aggressive, and one does not describe a quinquereme or a howitzer or a tank without estimating how much *damage* it can do.

Eventually I had to decide that there was only one way to give the course, which was to give it without strategies and without conscious caution. It was not honorable, either to the students or to the authors, to conceal or disguise my relation to the literature, my commitment to it, my fear of it, my ambivalence toward it. The literature had to be dealt with in the terms it announced for itself. As for the students, I have never given assent to the modern saw about "teaching students, not subjects"— I have always thought it right to teach subjects, believing that if one gives his first loyalty to the subject, the student is best instructed. So I resolved to give the course with no considerations in mind except my own interests. And since my own interests lead me to see literary situations as cultural situations, and cultural situations as great elaborate fights about moral issues, and moral issues as having something to do with gratuitously chosen images of personal being, and images of personal being as having something to do with literary style, I felt free to begin with what for me was a first concern, the animus of the author, the objects of his will, the things he wants or wants to have happen.

My cultural and nonliterary method led me to decide that I would begin the course with a statement of certain themes or issues that might especially engage our attention. I even went so far in nonliterariness as to think that my purposes would best be served if I could contrive a "background" for the works we would read—I wanted to propose a history for the themes or issues that I hoped to discover. I did not intend that this history should be either very extensive or very precise. I wanted merely to encourage a *sense* of a history, some general intuition of a past, in students who, as it seems to me, have not been provided with any such thing by their education and who are on the whole glad to be without it. And because there is as yet no adequate general work of history of the culture of the last two hundred years, I asked myself what books of the age just preceding ours had most influenced our literature, or, since I was far less concerned with showing influence than with discerning a tendency, what older books might seem to fall into a line the direction of which pointed to our own literature and thus might serve as a prolegomenon to the course.

It was virtually inevitable that the first work that should have sprung to mind was Sir James Frazer's *The Golden Bough*, not, of course, the whole of it, but certain chapters, those that deal with Osiris, Attis, and Adonis. Anyone who thinks about modern literature in a systematic way takes for granted the great part played in it by myth, and especially by those examples of myth which tell about gods dying and being reborn— the imagination of death and rebirth, reiterated in the ancient world in innumerable variations that are yet always the same, captivated the literary mind at the very moment when, as all accounts of the modern age agree, the most massive and compelling of all the stories of resurrection had lost much of its hold upon the world.

Perhaps no book has had so decisive an effect upon modern literature as Frazer's. It was beautifully to my purpose that it had first been published ten years before the twentieth century began. Yet forty-three years later, in 1933, Frazer delivered a lecture, very eloquent, in which he bade the world be of good hope in the face of the threat to the human mind that was being offered by the Nazi power. He was still alive in 1941. Yet he had been born in 1854, three years before Matthew Arnold gave the lecture "On the Modern Element in Literature." Here, surely, was history, here was the past I wanted, beautifully connected with our present. Frazer was wholly a man of the nineteenth century, and the more so because the eighteenth century was so congenial to him—the lecture of 1933 in which he predicted the Nazi defeat had as its subject Condorcet's *Progress of the Human Mind*; when he took time from his anthropological studies to deal with literature, he prepared editions of Addison's essays and Cowper's letters. He had the old lost belief in the virtue and power of rationality. He loved and counted on order, decorum, and good sense. This great historian of the primitive imagination was in the dominant intellectual tradition of the West which, since the days of the pre-Socratics, has condemned the ways of thought that we call primitive.

It can be said of Frazer that in his conscious intention he was a perfect representative of what Arnold meant when he spoke of a modern age. And perhaps nothing could make clearer how the conditions of life and literature have changed in a hundred years than to note the difference between the way in which Arnold defines the modern element in literature and the way in which we must define it.

Arnold used the word "modern" in a wholly honorific sense. So much so that he seems to dismiss all temporal idea from the word and makes it signify certain timeless intellectual and civic virtues—his lecture, indeed, was about the modern element in the ancient literatures. A society, he said, is a modern society when it maintains a condition of repose, confidence, free activity of the mind, and the tolerance of divergent views. A society is modern when it affords sufficient material well-being for the conveniences of life and the development of taste. And, finally, a society is modern when its members are intellectually mature, by which Arnold means that they are willing to judge by reason, to observe facts in a critical spirit, and to search for the law of things. By this definition Periclean Athens is for Arnold a modern age, Elizabethan England is not; Thucydides is a modern historian, Sir Walter Raleigh is not.

I shall not go into further details of Arnold's definition or description of the modern.* I have said enough, I think, to suggest what Arnold was

---

*I leave out of my summary account the two supreme virtues that Arnold ascribes to the most successful examples of a "modern" literature. One is the power of effecting an "intellectual deliverance," by which Arnold means leading men to comprehend the "vast multitude of facts" which make up "a copious and complex present, and behind it a copious and complex past." The other is "adequacy," the ability to represent the complex high human development of a modern age "in its completest and most harmonious" aspect, doing so with "the charm of that noble serenity which always accompanies true insight."

up to, what he wanted to see realized as the desideratum of his own society, what ideal he wanted the works of intellect and imagination of his own time to advance. And at what a distance his ideal of the modern puts him from our present sense of modernity, from our modern literature! To anyone conditioned by our modern literature, Arnold's ideal of order, convenience, decorum, and rationality might well seem to reduce itself to the small advantages and excessive limitations of the middle-class life of a few prosperous nations of the nineteenth century. Arnold's historic sense presented to his mind the long, bitter, bloody past of Europe, and he seized passionately upon the hope of true civilization at last achieved. But the historic sense of our literature has in mind a long excess of civilization to which may be ascribed the bitterness and bloodiness both of the past and of the present and of which the peaceful aspects are to be thought of as mainly contemptible—its order achieved at the cost of extravagant personal repression, either that of coercion or that of acquiescence; its repose otiose; its tolerance either flaccid or capricious; its material comfort corrupt and corrupting; its taste a manifestation either of timidity or of pride; its rationality attained only at the price of energy and passion.

For the understanding of this radical change of opinion nothing is more illuminating than to be aware of the doubleness of mind of the author of *The Golden Bough*. I have said that Frazer in his conscious mind and in his first intention exemplifies all that Arnold means by the modern. He often speaks quite harshly of the irrationality and the orgiastic excesses of the primitive religions he describes, and even Christianity comes under his criticism both because it stands in the way of rational thought and because it can draw men away from intelligent participation in the life of society. But Frazer had more than one intention, and he had an unconscious as well as a conscious mind. If he deplores the primitive imagination, he also does not fail to show it as wonderful and beautiful. It is the rare reader of *The Golden Bough* who finds the ancient beliefs and rituals wholly alien to him. It is to be expected that Frazer's adduction of the many pagan analogues to the Christian mythos will be thought by Christian readers to have an adverse effect on faith, it was undoubtedly Frazer's purpose that it should, yet many readers will feel that Frazer makes all faith and ritual indigenous to humanity, virtually biological; they feel, as DeQuincey put it, that not to be at least a *little* superstitious is to lack generosity of mind. Scientific though his purpose was, Frazer had the effect of validating those old modes of experiencing the world which modern men, beginning with the Romantics, have sought to revive in order to escape from positivism and common sense.

The direction of the imagination upon great and mysterious objects of worship is not the only means men use to liberate themselves from the bondage of quotidian fact, and although Frazer can scarcely be held accountable for the ever-growing modern attraction to the extreme mental states—to rapture, ecstasy, and transcendence, which are achieved by drugs, trance, music and dance, orgy, and the derangement of personality—yet he did provide a bridge to the understanding and acceptance of these states; he proposed to us the idea that the desire for them and the use of them for heuristic purposes is a common and acceptable manifestation of human nature.

This one element of Frazer's masterpiece could scarcely fail to suggest the next of my prolegomenal works. It is worth remarking that its author was in his own way as great a classical scholar as Frazer himself—Nietzsche was Professor of Classical Philology at the University of Basel when, at the age of twenty-seven, he published his essay *The Birth of Tragedy*. After the appearance of this stunningly brilliant account of Greek civilization, of which Socrates is not the hero but the villain, what can possibly be left to us of that rational and ordered Greece, that modern, that eighteenth-century, Athens that Arnold so entirely relied on as the standard for judging all civilizations? Professor Kaufmann is right when he warns us against supposing that Nietzsche exalts Dionysus over Apollo and tells us that Nietzsche "emphasizes the Dionysiac only because he feels that the Apollonian genius of the Greeks cannot be fully understood apart from it." But no one reading Nietzsche's essay for the first time is likely to heed this warning. What will reach him before due caution intervenes, before he becomes aware of the portentous dialectic between Dionysus and Apollo, is the excitement of suddenly being liberated from Aristotle, the joy of finding himself acceding to the author's statement that "art rather than ethics constitutes the essential metaphysical activity of man," that tragedy has its source in the Dionysiac rapture, "whose closest analogy is furnished by physical intoxication," and that this rapture, in which "the individual forgets himself completely," was in itself no metaphysical state but an orgiastic display of lust and cruelty, "of sexual promiscuity overriding every form of tribal law." This sadic and masochistic frenzy, Nietzsche is at pains to insist, needs the taming hand of Apollo before it can become tragedy, but it is the primal stuff of great art, and to the modern experience of tragedy this explanation seems far more pertinent than Aristotle's, with its eagerness to forget its origin in its achievement of a state of noble imperturbability.

Of supreme importance in itself, Nietzsche's essay had for me the added pedagogic advantage of allowing me to establish a historical line back to William Blake. Nothing is more characteristic of modern literature than its discovery and canonization of the primal, nonethical energies, and the historical point could be made the better by remarking the correspondence of thought of two men of different nations and separated from each other by a good many decades, for Nietzsche's Dionysian orgy and Blake's Hell are much the same thing.

Whether or not Joseph Conrad read either Blake or Nietzsche I do not know, but his *Heart of Darkness* follows in their line. This very great work has never lacked for the admiration it deserves, and it has been given a kind of canonical place in the legend of modern literature by Eliot's having it so clearly in mind when he wrote *The Waste Land* and his having taken from it the epigraph to "The Hollow Men." But no one, to my knowledge, has ever confronted in an explicit way its strange and terrible message of ambivalence toward the life of civilization. Consider that its protagonist, Kurtz, is a progressive and a liberal and that he is the highly respected representative of a society which would have us believe it is benign, although in fact it is vicious. Consider too that he is a practitioner of several arts, a painter, a writer, a musician, and into the bargain a political orator. He is at once the most idealistic and the most practically successful of all the agents of the Belgian exploitation of the Congo. Everybody knows the truth about him which Marlow discovers—that Kurtz's success is the result of a terrible ascendancy he has gained over the natives of his distant station, an ascendancy which is derived from his presumed magical or divine powers, that he has exercised his rule with an extreme of cruelty, that he has given himself to unnamable acts of lust. This is the world of the darker pages of *The Golden Bough*. It is one of the great points of Conrad's story that Marlow speaks of the primitive life of the jungle not as being noble or charming or even free but as being base and sordid—and for *that* reason compelling: he himself feels quite overtly its dreadful attraction. It is to this devilish baseness that Kurtz has yielded himself, and yet Marlow, although he does indeed treat him with hostile irony, does not find it possible to suppose that Kurtz is anything but a hero of the spirit. For me it is still ambiguous whether Kurtz's famous deathbed cry, "The horror! The horror!" refers to the approach of death or to his experience of savage life. Whichever it is, to Marlow the fact that Kurtz could utter this cry at the point of death, while Marlow himself, when death threatens him, can know it only as a weary grayness, marks the difference between the ordinary man and a hero of the spirit. Is this not the essence of the modern belief about the nature of the artist, the man who goes down into that hell which is the historical beginning of the human soul, a beginning not outgrown but established in humanity as we know it now, preferring the reality of this hell to the bland lies of the civilization that has overlaid it?

This idea is proposed again in the somewhat less powerful but still very moving work with which I followed *Heart of Darkness*, Thomas Mann's *Death in Venice*. I wanted this story not so much for its account of an extravagantly Apollonian personality surrendering to forces that, in his Apollonian character, he thought shameful—although this was certainly to my purpose—but rather for Aschenbach's fevered dreams of the erotic past, and in particular that dream of the goat-orgy which Mann, being the kind of writer he is, having the kind of relation to Nietzsche he had, might well have written to serve as an illustration of what *The Birth of Tragedy* means by religious frenzy, the more so, of course, because Mann chooses that particular orgiastic ritual, the killing and eating of the goat, from which tragedy is traditionally said to have been derived.

A notable element of this story in which the birth of tragedy plays an important part is that the degradation and downfall of the protagonist is not represented as tragic in the usual sense of the word—that is, it is not represented as a great deplorable event. It is a commonplace of modern literary thought that the tragic mode is not available even to the gravest and noblest of our writers. I am not sure that this is the deprivation that some people think it to be and a mark of our spiritual inferiority. But if we ask why it has come about, one reason may be that we have learned to think our way back through tragedy to the primal stuff out of which tragedy arose. If we consider the primitive forbidden ways of conduct which traditionally in tragedy led to punishment by death, we think of them as being the path to reality and truth, to an ultimate self-realization. We have always wondered if tragedy itself may not have been saying just this in a deeply hidden way, drawing us to think of the hero's sin and death as somehow conferring justification, even salvation of a sort—no doubt this is what Nietzsche had in mind when he said that "tragedy denies ethics." What tragedy once seemed to hint, our literature now is willing to say quite explicitly. If Mann's Aschenbach dies at the height of his intellectual and artistic powers, overcome by a passion that his ethical reason condemns, we do not take this to be a defeat, rather a kind of terrible rebirth: at his latter end the artist knows a reality that he had until now refused to admit to consciousness.

Thoughts like these suggested that another of Nietzsche's works, *The Genealogy of Morals*, might be in point. It proposes a view of society which is consonant with the belief that art and not ethics constitutes the essential metaphysical activity of man and with the validation and ratification of the primitive energies. Nietzsche's theory of the social order dismisses all ethical impulse from its origins—the basis of society is to be found in the rationalization of cruelty: as simple as that. Nietzsche has no ultimate Utopian intention in saying this, no hope of revising the essence of the social order, although he does believe that its pain can be mitigated. He represents cruelty as a social necessity, for only by its exercise could men ever have been induced to develop a continuity of will: nothing else than cruel pain could have created in mankind that memory of intention which makes society possible. The method of cynicism which Nietzsche pursued—let us be clear that it is a method and not an attitude—goes so far as to describe punishment in terms of the pleasure derived from the exercise of cruelty: "Compensation," he says, "consists in a legal warrant entitling one man to exercise his cruelty on another." There follows that most remarkable passage in which Nietzsche describes the process whereby the individual turns the cruelty of punishment against himself and creates the bad conscience, the consciousness of guilt which manifests itself as a pervasive anxiety. Nietzsche's complexity of mind is beyond all comparison, for in this book which is dedicated to the liberation of the conscience, Nietzsche makes his defense of the bad conscience as a decisive force in the interests of culture. It is much the same line of argument that he takes when, having attacked the Jewish morality and the priestly existence in the name of the health of the spirit, he reminds us that only by his sickness does man become interesting.

From *The Genealogy of Morals* to Freud's *Civilization and Its Discontents* is but a step, and some might think that, for pedagogic purposes, the step is so small as to make the second book supererogatory. But although Freud's view of society and culture has indeed a very close affinity to Nietzsche's, Freud does add certain considerations which are essential to our sense of the modern disposition.

For one thing, he puts to us the question of whether or not we want to *accept* civilization. It is not the first time that the paradox of civilization has been present to the mind of civilized people, the sense that civilization makes men behave worse and suffer more than does some less developed state of human existence. But hitherto all such ideas were formulated in a moralizing way—civilization was represented as being "corrupt," a divagation from a state of innocence. Freud had no illusions about a primitive innocence, he conceived no practicable alternative to civilization. In consequence, there was a unique force to the question he asked: whether we wished to accept civilization, with all its contradictions, with all its pains—pains, for "discontents" does not accurately describe what Freud has in mind. He had his own answer to the question—his tragic, or stoic, sense of life dictated it: we do well to accept it, although we also do well to cast a cold eye on the fate that makes it our better part to accept it. Like Nietzsche, Freud thought that life was justified by our heroic response to its challenge.

But the question Freud posed has not been set aside or closed up by the answer that he himself gave to it. His answer, like Nietzsche's, is essentially in the line of traditional humanism—we can see this in the sternness with which he charges women not to interfere with men in the discharge of their cultural duty, not to claim men for love and the family to the detriment of their free activity in the world. But just here lies the matter of Freud's question that the world more and more believes Freud himself did not answer. The pain that civilization inflicts is that of the instinctual renunciation that civilization demands, and it would seem that fewer and fewer people wish to say with Freud that the loss of instinctual gratification, emotional freedom, or love is compensated for either by the security of civilized life or by the stern pleasures of the masculine moral character.

With Freud's essay I brought to a close my list of prolegomenal books for the first term of the course. I shall not do much more than mention the books with which I introduced the second term, but I should like to do at least that. I began with *Rameau's Nephew*, thinking that the peculiar moral authority which Diderot assigns to the envious, untalented, unregenerate protagonist was peculiarly relevant to the line taken by the ethical explorations of modern literature. Nothing is more characteristic of the literature of our time than the replacement of the hero by what has come to be called the anti-hero, in whose indifference to or hatred of ethical nobility there is presumed to lie a special authenticity. Diderot is quite overt about this—he himself in his public character is the deuteragonist, the "honest consciousness," as Hegel calls him, and he takes delight in the discomfiture of the decent, dull person he is by the Nephew's nihilistic mind.

It seemed to me too that there was particular usefulness in the circumstance that this anti-hero should avow so openly his *envy*, which Tocqueville has called the ruling emotion of democracy, and that, although he envied anyone at all who had access to the creature-comforts and the social status which he lacked, what chiefly animated him was envy of men of genius. Ours is the first cultural epoch in which many men aspire to high achievement in the arts and, in their frustration, form a dispossessed class which cuts across the conventional class lines, making a proletariat of the spirit.

Although *Rameau's Nephew* was not published until fairly late in the century, it was known in manuscript by Goethe and Hegel; it suited the temper and won the admiration of Marx and Freud for reasons that are obvious. And there is ground for supposing that it was known to Dostoyevsky, whose *Notes from Underground* is a restatement of the essential idea of Diderot's dialogue in terms both more extreme and less genial. The Nephew is still on the defensive—he is naughtily telling secrets about the nature of man and society. But Dostoyevsky's underground man shouts aloud his envy and hatred and carries the ark of his self-hatred and alienation into a remorseless battle with what he calls "the good and the beautiful," mounting an attack upon every belief not merely of bourgeois society but of the whole humanist tradition. The inclusion of *Notes from Underground* among my prolegomenal books constituted something of a pedagogic risk, for if I wished to emphasize the subversive tendency of modern literature, here was a work which made all subsequent subversion seem like affirmation, so radical and so brilliant was its negation of our traditional pieties and its affirmation of our new pieties.

I hesitated in compunction before following *Notes from Underground* with Tolstoy's *Death of Ivan Ilyitch*, which so ruthlessly and with such dreadful force destroys the citadel of the commonplace life in which we all believe we can take refuge from ourselves and our fate. But I did assign it and then two of Pirandello's plays which, in the atmosphere of the sordidness of the commonplace life, undermine all the certitudes of the commonplace, common-sense mind.

From time to time I have raised with myself the question of whether my choice of these prolegomenal works was not extravagant, quite excessively tendentious. I have never been able to believe that it is. And if these works do indeed serve to indicate in an accurate way the nature of modern literature, a teacher might find it worth asking how his students respond to the strong dose.

One response I have already described—the readiness of the students to engage in the process that we might call the socialization of the antisocial, or the acculturation of the anticultural, or the legitimization of the subversive. When the term-essays come in, it is plain to me that almost none of the students have been taken aback by what they have read: they have wholly contained the attack. The chief exceptions are the few who simply do not comprehend, although they may be awed by, the categories of our discourse. In their papers, like poor hunted creatures in a Kafka story, they take refuge first in misunderstood large phrases, then in bad grammar, then in general incoherence. After my pedagogical exasperation has run its course, I find that I am sometimes moved to give them a queer respect, as if they had stood up and said what in fact they don't have the wit to stand up and say: "Why do you harry us? Leave us alone. We are not Modern Man. We are the Old People. Ours is the Old Faith. We serve the little Old Gods, the gods of the copybook maxims, the small, dark, somewhat powerful deities of lawyers, doctors, engineers, accountants. With them is neither sensibility nor *angst*. With them is no disgust—it is they, indeed, who make ready the way for 'the good and the beautiful' about which low-minded doubts have been raised in this course, that 'good and beautiful' which we do not possess and don't want to possess but which we know justifies our lives. Leave us alone and let us worship our gods in the way they approve, in peace and unawareness." Crass, but—to use that interesting modern word which we have learned from the curators of museums—authentic. The rest, the minds that give me the A papers and the B papers and even the C+ papers, move through the terrors and mysteries of modern literature like so many Parsifals, asking no questions at the behest of wonder and fear. Or like so many seminarists who have been sytematically instructed in the constitution of Hell and the ways to damnation. Or like so many *readers*, entertained by moral horror stories. I asked them to look into the Abyss, and, both dutifully and gladly, they have looked into the Abyss, and the Abyss has greeted them with the grave courtesy of all objects of serious study, saying: "Interesting, am I not? And *exciting*, if you consider how deep I am and what dread beasts lie at my bottom. Have it well in mind that a knowledge of me contributes materially to your being whole, or well-rounded, men."

In my distress over the outrage I have conspired to perpetrate upon a great literature, I wonder if perhaps I have not been reading these papers too literally. After all, a term-essay is not a diary of the soul, it is not an occasion for telling the truth. What my students might reveal of their true feelings to a younger teacher they will not reveal to me; they will give me what they conceive to be the proper response to the official version of terror I have given them. I bring to mind their faces, which are not necessarily the faces of the authors of these unperturbed papers, nor are they, not yet, the faces of fathers of families, or of theatergoers, or of buyers of modern paintings: not yet. I must think it possible that in ways and to a degree which they keep secret they have responded directly and personally to what they have read.

And if they have? And if they have, am I the more content?

What form would I want their response to take? It is a teacher's question that I am asking, not a critic's. We have decided in recent years to think of the critic and the teacher of literature as one and the same, and no doubt it is both possible and useful to do so. But there are some points at which the functions of the two do not coincide, or can be made to coincide only with great difficulty. Of criticism we have been told, by Arnold, that "it must be apt to study and praise elements that for fulness of spiritual perfection are wanted, even though they belong to a power which in the practical sphere may be maleficent." But teaching, or at least undergraduate teaching, is not given the same licensed mandate—cannot be given it because the teacher's audience, which stands before his very eyes, as the critic's audience does not, asks questions about "the practical sphere," as the critic's audience does not. For instance, on the very day that I write this, when I had said to my class all I could think of to say about *The Magic Mountain* and invited questions and comments, one student asked, "How would you generalize the idea of the educative value of illness, so that it would be applicable not only to a particular individual, Hans Castorp, but to young people at large?" It makes us smile, but it was asked in all seriousness, and it is serious in its substance, and it had to be answered seriously, in part by the reflection that this idea, like so many ideas encountered in the books of the course, had to be thought of as having reference only to the private life; that it touched the public life only in some indirect or tangential way; that it really ought to be encountered in solitude, even in secrecy, since to talk about it in public and in our academic setting was to seem to propose for it a public practicality and thus to distort its meaning. To this another student replied; he said that, despite the public ritual of the classroom, each student inevitably experienced the books in privacy and found their meaning in reference to his own life. True enough, but the teacher sees the several privacies coming together to make a group, and they propose—no doubt the more because they come together every Monday, Wednesday, and Friday at a particular hour—the idea of a community, that is to say, "the practical sphere."

This being so, the teacher cannot escape the awareness of certain circumstances which the critic, who writes for an ideal, uncircumstanced reader, has no need to take into account. The teacher considers, for example, the social situation of his students—they are not of patrician origin, they do not come from homes in which stubbornness, pride, and conscious habit prevail, nor are they born into a culture marked by these traits, a culture in which other interesting and valuable things compete with and resist ideas; they come, mostly, from "good homes" in which authority and valuation are weak or at least not very salient and bold, so that ideas have for them, at their present stage of development, a peculiar power and preciousness. And in this connection the teacher will have in mind the special prestige that our culture, in its upper reaches, gives to art, and to the ideas that art proposes—the agreement, ever growing in assertiveness, that art yields more truth than any other intellectual activity. In this culture what a shock it is to encounter Santayana's acerb skepticism about art, or Keats's remark, which the critics and scholars never take notice of, presumably because they suppose it to be an aberration, that poetry is "not so fine a thing as philosophy—For the same reason that an eagle is not so fine a thing as a truth." For many students no ideas that they will encounter in any college discipline will equal in force and sanction the ideas conveyed to them by modern literature.

The author of *The Magic Mountain* once said that all his work could be understood as an effort to free himself from the middle class, and this, of course, will serve to describe the chief intention of all modern literature. And the means of freedom which Mann prescribes (the characteristic irony notwithstanding) is the means of freedom which in effect all of modern literature prescribes. It is, in the words of Clavdia Chauchat, *"se perdre et même . . . se laisser dépérir,"* and thus to name the means is to make plain that the end is not merely freedom from the middle class but freedom from society itself. I venture to say that the idea of losing oneself up to the point of self-destruction, of surrendering oneself to experience without regard to self-interest or conventional morality, of escaping wholly from the societal bonds, is an "element" somewhere in the mind of every modern person who dares to think of what Arnold in his unaffected Victorian way called "the fulness of spiritual perfection." But the teacher who undertakes to present modern literature to his students may not allow that idea to remain in the *somewhere* of his mind; he must take it from the place where it exists habitual and unrealized and put it in the conscious forefront of his thought. And if he is committed to an admiration of modern literature, he must also be committed to this chief idea of modern literature. I press the logic of the situation not in order to question the legitimacy of the commitment, or even the propriety of expressing the commitment in the college classroom (although it does seem odd!), but to confront those of us who do teach modern literature with the striking actuality of our enterprise.

The Leavis-Snow Controversy

1962

I

It is now nearly eighty years since Matthew Arnold came to America on his famous lecture tour. Of his repertory of three lectures, none was calculated to give unqualified pleasure to his audience. The lecture on Emerson praised the then most eminent of American writers only after it had denied that he was a literary figure of the first order. The lecture called "Numbers" raised disturbing questions about the relation of democracy to excellence and distinction. "Literature and Science" was the least likely to give offense, yet even this most memorable of the three *Discourses in America* was not without its touch of uncomfortableness. In 1883 America was by no means committed—and, indeed, never was to be committed—to the belief that the right education for the modern age must be predominantly scientific and technical, and Arnold, when he cited the proponents of this idea, which of course he opposed, mentioned only those who were English. Yet his audience surely knew that Arnold was warning them against what would seem to be the natural tendency of an industrial democracy to devalue the old "aristocratic" education in favor of studies that are merely practical.

Arnold wrote "Emerson" and "Numbers" especially for his American tour, but he had first composed "Literature and Science" as the Rede Lecture at Cambridge in 1882. Its original occasion cannot fail to have a peculiar interest at this moment, for C. P. Snow's *The Two Cultures and the Scientific Revolution*, around which so curious a storm rages in England, was the Rede Lecture of 1959.

Sir Charles did not mention his great predecessor in the lectureship, although his own discourse was exactly on Arnold's subject and took a line exactly the opposite of Arnold's. And F. R. Leavis, whose admiration of Arnold is well known and whose position in respect to the relative importance of literature and of science in education is much the same as Arnold's, did not mention Arnold either, when, in his Richmond Lecture at Downing College, he launched an attack of unexampled ferocity upon the doctrine and the author of *The Two Cultures*.

In its essential terms, the issue in debate has not changed since Arnold spoke. Arnold's chief antagonist was T. H. Huxley—it was he who, in his lecture "Culture and Education," had said that literature should, and inevitably would, step down from its pre-eminent place in education, that science and not "culture" must supply the knowledge which is necessary for an age committed to rational truth and material practicality. What is more, Huxley said, science will supply the very basis of the assumptions of modern ethics. In effect Snow says nothing different.

The word "culture" had been Arnold's personal insigne ever since the publication of *Culture and Anarchy* in 1867, and Huxley made particular reference to the views on the value of humanistic study which Arnold had expressed in that book.* Arnold's reply in "Literature and Science" could not have been simpler, just as it could not have been more temperate, although it surely did not surpass in temperateness Huxley's statement of his disagreement with Arnold's ideas; the two men held each other in high admiration and were warm friends. Arnold said that he had not the least disposition to propose that science be slighted in education. Quite apart from its practical value, scientific knowledge is naturally a delight to the mind, no doubt engaging certain mental temperaments more than others but holding out the promise of intellectual pleasure to all. Yet of itself science does not, as Arnold put it, "serve" the instinct for conduct and the instinct for beauty, or at least it does not serve these instincts as they

*Arnold, I need scarcely say, did not use the word in the modern sense in which it is used by anthropologists, sociologists, and historians of thought and art; this is, more or less, the sense in which it is used by Snow. For Arnold, "culture" was "the best that has been thought and said in the world" and also an individual person's relation to this body of thought and expression. My own use of the word in this essay is not Arnold's.

exist in most men. This service, which includes the relating of scientific knowledge to the whole life of man, is rendered by culture, which is not to be thought of as confined to literature—to *belles lettres*—but as comprising all the humane intellectual disciplines. When Dr. Leavis asserts the primacy of the humanities in education, he refers more exclusively to literature than Arnold did, but in general effect his position is the same.

It may seem strange, and a little tiresome, that the debate of eighty years ago should be instituted again today. Yet it is perhaps understandable in view of the "scientific revolution" about which Sir Charles tells us. This revolution would seem to be one of the instances in which a change of quantity becomes a change in kind—science can now do so much more and do it so much more quickly than it could a generation ago, let alone in the last century, that it has been transmuted from what the world has hitherto known. One of the consequences of this change—to Sir Charles it is the most salient of all possible consequences—is the new social hope that is now held out to us, of life made better in material respects, not merely in certain highly developed countries but all over the world and among peoples that at the moment are, by Western standards, scarcely developed at all.

The new power of science perhaps justifies a contemporary revival of the Victorian question. But if we consent to involve ourselves in the new dialectic of the old controversy, we must be aware that we are not addressing ourselves to a question of educational theory, or to an abstract contention as to what kind of knowledge has the truest affinity with the human soul. We approach these matters only to pass through them. What we address ourselves to is politics, and politics of a quite ultimate kind, and to the disposition of the modern mind.

2

The Two Cultures has had a very considerable currency in England and America ever since its publication in 1959, and in England it was for a time the subject of lively discussion. Indeed, the general agreement in England that it was a statement of great importance, to the point of its being used as an assigned text in secondary schools, was what aroused Dr. Leavis to make his assault on the lecture this long after the first interest in it had subsided. The early discussions of *The Two Cultures* were of a substantive kind, but the concerns which now agitate the English in response to Dr. Leavis's attack have scarcely anything to do with literature and science, or with education, or with social hope. These matters have now been made a mere subordinate element in what amounts to a scandal over a breach of manners. The published comments on Dr. Leavis's attack on *The Two Cultures* were, with few exceptions, directed to such considerations as the exact degree of monstrousness which Dr. Leavis achieved in speaking of Sir Charles as he did; whether or not he spoke out of envy of Sir Charles's reputation; whether or not he has, or deserves to have, any real standing as a critic; or writes acceptable English; or represents, as he claims he does, "the essential Cambridge."

Dr. Leavis's Richmond Lecture, "The Significance of C. P. Snow," was delivered in the Hall of Downing College, Cambridge, on 28 February 1962, and published in *The Spectator* of 9 March.* In the next week's issue of *The Spectator*, seventeen letters appeared, all defending Snow and most of them expressing anger at, or contempt for, Leavis. The following week brought fifteen more communications, of which eight expressed partisanship with Leavis; several of these deplored the tone of the previous week's correspondence. Many of the correspondents who defended Snow were of distinguished reputation; of the defenders of Leavis, the only one known to me was Mr. Geoffrey Wagner, who wrote from America to communicate his belief that the attack on Snow was much needed, for, despite a parody in *New Left Review* in which Snow appears as C. P. Sleet, despite, too, his own adverse criticism of Snow in *The Critic*, "the hosannas obediently continued on this side of the Atlantic, both from the Barzun-Trilling syndrome and the Book-of-the-Month Club, the worst of both worlds, as it were." Three of the writers of the Snow party touched upon the question of literature and science, the scientist J. D. Bernal, the historian of science Stephen Toulmin, and the literary critic G. S. Fraser. In a miasma of personality-mongering, their letters afforded a degree of relief, but they said little that was of consequence. Of the Leavis party two dons of the University of Birmingham in a joint letter touched rapidly but with some cogency on the relation between literature and science, deplor-

---

*In an editorial note, Dr. Leavis is quoted as saying, "The lecture was private and representatives of the press who inquired were informed that there was no admission and that no reporting was to be permitted. The appearance in newspapers of garbled reports has made it desirable that the lecture should appear in full."

ing any attempt to prefer one above the other, concluding that if one must be preferred, it should be, for reasons not stated, literature.

From the *Spectator* letters, so many of them expressing small and rather untidy passions, there are no doubt conclusions to be drawn, of a sufficiently depressing sort, about the condition of intellectual life at the moment. But no awareness that we may have of the generally bad state of intellectual affairs ought to blind us to the particular fault of Dr. Leavis in his treatment of Sir Charles Snow. Intelligent and serious himself, Dr. Leavis has in this instance been the cause of stupidity and triviality in other men.

There can be no two opinions about the tone in which Dr. Leavis deals with Sir Charles. It is a bad tone, an impermissible tone. It is bad in a personal sense because it is cruel—it manifestly intends to wound. It is bad intellectually because by its use Dr. Leavis has diverted attention, his own included, from the matter he sought to illuminate. The doctrine of *The Two Cultures* is a momentous one, and Dr. Leavis obscures its large significance by bringing into consideration such matters as Sir Charles's abilities as a novelist, his club membership, his opinion of his own talents, his worldly success, and his relation to worldly power. Anger, scorn, and an excessive consciousness of persons have always been elements of Dr. Leavis's thought—of the very process of his thought, not merely of his manner of expressing it. They were never exactly reassuring elements, but they could be set aside and made to seem of relatively small account in comparison with the remarkable cogency in criticism which Dr. Leavis so often achieved. But as they now appear in his valedictory address—for, in effect, that is what the Richmond Lecture was, since Dr. Leavis retired that year from his university post—they cannot be easily set aside, they stand in the way of what Dr. Leavis means to say.

And, indeed, our understanding of what he means to say is to be derived less from the passionate utterance of the lecture itself than from our knowledge of the whole direction of his career in criticism. That direction was from the first determined by Dr. Leavis's belief that the human faculty above all others to which literature addresses itself is the moral consciousness, which is also the source of all successful creation, the very root of poetic genius. The extent of his commitment to this idea results in what I believe to be a fault in his critical thought—he does not give anything like adequate recognition to those aspects of art which are gratuitous, which arise from high spirits and the impulse to play. One would suppose that the moral consciousness should, for its own purposes, take account of those aspects of art and life that do not fall within its dominion. But if the intensity of Dr. Leavis's commitment to the moral consciousness contrives to produce this deficiency of understanding, it is no less responsible for the accuracy and force which we recognize as the positive characteristics of his work. For Dr. Leavis's, literature is what Matthew Arnold said it is, *the criticism of life*—he can understand it in no other way. Both in all its simplicity and in all its hidden complexity, he has made Arnold's saying his own, and from it he has drawn his strength.

If, then, Dr. Leavis now speaks with a very special intensity in response to *The Two Cultures*, we must do him the justice of seeing that the Rede Lecture denies, and in an extreme way, all that he has ever believed about literature—it is, in fact, nothing less than an indictment of literature on social and moral grounds. It represents literature as constituting a danger to the national well-being, and most especially when it is overtly a criticism of life.

Not only because Charles Snow is himself a practitioner of literature but also because he is the man he is, the statement that his lecture has this purport will be shocking and perhaps it will be thought scarcely credible. And I have no doubt that, in another mood and on some other occasion, Sir Charles would be happy to assert the beneficent powers of literature. But there can be no other interpretation of his lecture than that it takes toward literature a position of extreme antagonism.

The Two Cultures begins as an objective statement of the lack of communication between scientists and literary men. This is a circumstance which must have been often observed and often deplored. Perhaps nothing in our culture is so characteristic as the separateness of the various artistic and intellectual professions. As between, say, poets and painters, or musicians and architects, there is very little discourse, and perhaps the same thing could be remarked of scientists of different interests, biologists and physicists, say. But the isolation of literary men from scientists may well seem to be the most extreme of these separations, if only because it is the most significant, for a reason which Sir Charles entirely understands: the especially close though never fully defined relation of these two professions with our social and political life.

The even-handedness with which Sir Charles at first describes the split between the two "cultures" does not continue for long. He begins by telling us that scientists and literary men are equally to blame for the separation—they are kept apart by "a gulf of mutual incomprehension," by distorted images of each other which give rise to dislike and hostility. But as Sir Charles's lecture proceeds, it becomes plain that, although the scientists do have certain crudities and limitations, they are in general in the right of things and the literary men in the wrong of them. The matter which causes the scales to shift thus suddenly is the human condition. This, Sir Charles tells us, is of its nature tragic: man dies, and he dies alone. But the awareness of the ineluctably tragic nature of human life makes a moral trap, "for it tempts one to sit back, complacent in one's unique tragedy," paying no heed to the circumstances of everyday life, which, for the larger number of human beings, are painful. It is the literary men, we are told, who are the most likely, the scientists who are the least likely, to fall into this moral trap; the scientists "are inclined to be impatient to see if something can be done: and inclined to think that it can be done, until it's proved otherwise." It is their spirit, "tough and good and determined to fight it out at the side of their brother men," which has "made scientists regard the other [i.e., the literary] culture's social attitudes as contemptible."

"This is too facile," Sir Charles says in mild rebuke of the scientists, by which he of course means that essentially they are right. There follows a brief consideration of a question raised not by Sir Charles in his own person but by "a scientist of distinction" whom he quotes. "Yeats, Pound, Wyndham Lewis, nine out of ten of those who have dominated literary sensibility in our time, weren't they not only politically silly, but politically wicked? Didn't the influence of all they represent bring Auschwitz that much nearer?" And Sir Charles in answer grants that Yeats was a magnanimous man and a great poet, but he will not, he says, defend the indefensible—"the facts . . . are broadly true." Sir Charles in general agrees, that is, that the literary sensibility of our time brought Auschwitz nearer. He goes on to say that things have changed considerably in the literary life in recent years, even if slowly, for "literature changes more slowly than science."

From the mention of Auschwitz onward, the way is open to the full assertion by Sir Charles of the virtues of the scientist. Although they are admitted to be sometimes gauche or stupidly self-assertive, although Sir Charles concedes of some of them that "the whole literature of the traditional culture doesn't seem relevant to [their] interests" and that, as a result, their "imaginative understanding" is diminished, he yet finds scientists to be men of a natural decency; they are free from racial feelings, they are lovers of equality, they are cooperative. And chief among their virtues, as Sir Charles describes them, is the fact that they "have the future in their bones."

Indeed, it turns out that it is the future, and not mere ignorance of each other's professional concerns, that makes the separation between the culture of science and the culture of literature. Scientists have the future in their bones. Literary men do not. Quite the contrary—"If the scientists have the future in their bones, then the traditional culture responds by wishing that the future did not exist." The future that the scientists have in their bones is understood to be nothing but a good future; it is very much like the history of the Marxists, which is always the triumph of the right, never possibly the record of defeat. In fact, to entertain the idea that the future might be bad is represented as being tantamount to moral ill-will—in a note appended to the sentence I have just quoted, Sir Charles speaks of George Orwell's *1984* as "the strongest possible wish that the future shall not exist."

It is difficult to credit the implications of this astonishing remark and to ascribe them to Sir Charles. As everyone recalls, Orwell's novel is an imagination of the condition of the world if the authoritarian tendencies which are to be observed in the present develop themselves—logically, as it were—in the future, the point being that it is quite within the range of possibility that this ultimate development should take place. In Orwell's representation of an absolute tyranny, science has a part, and a polemical partisan of science might understand this as the evidence of a literary man's malice toward science. But it is much more likely that, when Orwell imagined science as one of the instruments of repression, he meant to say that science, like everything else that is potentially good, like literature itself, can be perverted and debased to the ends of tyranny. Orwell was a man who, on the basis of actual and painful experience, tried to tell the truth about politics, even his own politics. I believe that he never gave up his commitment to socialism, but he refused to be illusioned in any way he could prevent; it lay within the reach of his mind to conceive that even an idealistic politics, perhaps especially an idealistic politics, can pervert itself. We must be puzzled to know what can be meant when such a man is said to entertain the strongest possible wish that the future shall not exist.

Having characterized the culture of literature, or, as he sometimes calls it, "the traditional culture," by its hostility to the future, Sir Charles goes on to say that "it is the traditional culture, to an extent remarkably little diminished by the emergence of the scientific one, which manages the Western world." This being so, it follows that the traditional culture must be strictly dealt with if the future is to be brought into being: what is called "the existing pattern" must be not merely changed but "broken." Only if this is done shall we be able to educate ourselves as we should. As for the need to educate ourselves: "To say, we have to educate ourselves or perish is perhaps a little more melodramatic than the facts warrant. To say, we have to educate ourselves or watch a steep decline in our lifetime is about right." And Sir Charles indicates our possible fate by the in-stance—he calls it a "historical myth"—of the Venetian Republic in its last half-century:

> Its citizens had become rich, as we did, by accident. They had ac-quired immense political skill, just as we have. A good many of them were tough-minded, realistic, patriotic men. They knew, just as clearly as we know, that the current of history had begun to flow against them. Many of them gave their minds to working out ways to keep going. It would have meant breaking the pattern into which they had been crystallized. They were fond of the pattern, just as we are fond of ours. They never found the will to break it.

I quoted without comment Sir Charles's statement of the idea on which, we may say, the whole argument of *The Two Cultures* is based: "It is the traditional culture, to an extent remarkably little diminished by the emergence of the scientific one, which manages the Western world." It is a bewildering statement. In what way can we possibly understand it? That the Western world is managed by some agency which is traditional is of course comprehensible. And we can take in the idea that this agency may be described, for particular purposes of explanation, in terms of a certain set of mind, a general tendency of thought and feeling which, being per-vasive, is hard to formulate, and that this is to be called a "culture." But for Sir Charles the words "traditional" and "literary" are interchangeable, and that this culture, as we agree to call it, is *literary*, that it bears the same relation to actual literary men and their books that what is called the "sci-entific culture" bears to scientists and their work in laboratories, is truly a staggering thought. The actions of parliaments and congresses and cabinets in directing the massive affairs of state, the negotiations of embassies, the movement of armies and fleets, the establishment of huge scientific projects for the contrivance of armaments and of factories for the production of them, the promises made to citizens, and the choices made by voters at the polls—these, we are asked to believe, are in the charge of the culture of literature. Can we possibly take this to be so?

It can of course be said that literature has some part in the management of the Western world, a part which is limited but perhaps not wholly unimportant. If, for example, we compare the present condition of industrial England with the condition of industrial England in the early nineteenth century, we can say that the present condition is not, in human respects, anything like what men of good will might wish it to be, but that is very much better than it was in the early years of the Industrial Revolution. And if we then ask what agencies brought about the improvement, we can say that one of them was literature. Certain literary men raised the "Condition of England Question" in a passionate and effective way and their names are still memorable to us—Coleridge, Carlyle, Mill (I take him to be a man of letters; he was certainly a good literary critic), Dickens, Ruskin, Arnold, William Morris. They made their effect only upon individuals, but the individuals they touched were numerous, and by what they said they made it ever harder for people to be indifferent to the misery around them or to the degradation of the national life in which they came to think themselves implicated. These literary men helped materially, some would say decisively, to bring about a change in the state of affairs. This is not exactly management, but it is a directing influence such as literature in the modern time often undertakes to have and sometimes does have.

Yet in Sir Charles's opinion this directing influence of the literary men of the nineteenth century deserves no praise. On the contrary, his description of their work is but another count in the indictment of the culture of literature. Speaking of the response which literary men made to the Industrial Revolution, he says:

> Almost everywhere . . . intellectual persons did not comprehend what was happening. Certainly the writers didn't. Plenty of them shuddered away, as though the right course for a man of feeling was to contract out; some, like Ruskin and William Morris and Thoreau and Emerson and Lawrence, tried various kinds of fan-

cies, which were not much in effect more than screams of horror. It is hard to think of a writer of high class who really stretched his imaginative sympathy, who could see at once the hideous back-streets, the smoking chimneys, the internal price—and also the prospects of life that were opening out for the poor. . . .

Nothing could be further from the truth. No great English writer of the nineteenth century, once he had become aware of the Industrial Revolution, ever contracted out. This is not the place to rehearse the miseries that were acquiesced in by those who comforted the world and their own consciences with the thought of "the prospects of life that were opening out for the poor." It is enough to say that there were miseries in plenty of a brutal and horrifying kind, by no means adequately suggested by phrases like "the hideous back-streets, the smoking chimneys, the internal price." (Auschwitz, since it has been mentioned, may be thought of as the development of the conditions of the factories and mines of the earlier Industrial Revolution.) If the writers "shuddered away," it was not in maidenly disgust with machines and soot; if they uttered "screams of horror," it was out of moral outrage at what man had made of man—and of women and little children. Their emotions were no different from those expressed by Karl Marx in his chapter on the working day, nor from those expressed in Blue Books by the factory inspectors, those remarkable men of the middle class whom Marx, in a moving passage of *Capital*, praises and wonders at for their transcendence of their class feelings.

I have mentioned Matthew Arnold among those writers who made the old conditions of the Industrial Revolution ever less possible. Like many of his colleagues in this undertaking, he did entertain "fancies"—they all found modern life ugly and fatiguing and in some way false, and they set store by certain qualities which are no doubt traditional to the point of being archaic. But Arnold's peculiar distinction as a literary critic is founded on the strong sensitivity of his response to the modern situation. He uniquely understood what Hegel had told the world, that the French Revolution marked an absolute change in the condition of man. For the first time in history, Hegel said, Reason—or Idea, or Theory, or Creative Imagination—had become decisive in human destiny. Arnold's argument in "Literature and Science" was the affirmation of the French Revolution; he was speaking on behalf of the illumination and refinement of that Reason by which man might shape the conditions of his own existence. This is the whole purport of his famous statement, "Literature is the criticism of life."

That saying used to have a rough time of it, perhaps because people found the word "criticism" narrow and dour and wished to believe that life was worthier of being celebrated than criticized. But less and less, I think, will anyone find the ground on which to quarrel with it. Whatever else we also take literature to be, it must always, for us now, be the criticism of life.

But it would seem to be precisely the critical function of literature that troubles Sir Charles. And perhaps that is why, despite all that he says about the need to educate ourselves, he does not make a single substantive proposal about education.

If we undertake to say what the purpose of modern education is, our answer will surely be suggested by Arnold's phrase, together with the one by which he defined the particular function of criticism: "to see the object as in itself it really is." Whenever we undertake to pass judgment on an educational enterprise, the import of these two phrases serves as our criterion: we ask that education supply the means for a criticism of life and teach the student to try to see the object as in itself it really is. Yet when Sir Charles speaks of the need to break the "existing pattern" and to go on to the right education which will help us to establish the necessary new pattern, he does not touch upon any such standard of judgment. Although he would seem to be the likeliest person in the world to speak intelligently about the instruction in science of students who do not intend to be scientists, actually he says nothing more on the subject than that ignorance of the Second Law of Thermodynamics is equivalent to ignorance of Shakespeare, or that the Yang-Lee experiment at Columbia should have been a topic of general conversation at college High Tables.

Nor does he propose anything for the education of the scientist, except, of course, science. He does say that scientists need to be "trained not only in scientific but in human terms," but he does not say how. Scientists—but eventually one begins to wonder if they are really scientists and not advanced technologists and engineers—are to play a decisive part in the affairs of mankind, but nowhere does Sir Charles suggest that, if this is so, they will face difficulties and perplexities and that their education should include the study of books—they need not be "literary," they need not be "traditional": they might be contemporary works of history, sociology, anthropology, psychology, philosophy—which would raise the difficult questions and propose the tragic complexity of the human condition, which would suggest that it is not always easy to see the object as in itself it really is.

Well, it isn't beyond belief that a professional corps of high intellectual quality, especially if it is charged with great responsibility, should learn to ask its own questions and go on to make its own ethos, perhaps a very good one. But Sir Charles would seem to be asking for more than the right of scientists to go their own way. What he seems to require for scientists is the right to go their own way *with no questions asked*. The culture of literature, having done its worst, must now be supplanted; it is not even to play the part of a loyal opposition. How else are we to understand Sir Charles's belief in the endemic irresponsibility of the literary mind, his curious representation of the literary culture as having the management of the Western world, that is to say, as being answerable for all the anomalies, stupidities, and crimes of the Western world, for having made the "existing pattern" which must now be broken if the West is to survive or at least not suffer steep decline? It is manifest that the literary culture has lost the right to ask questions.

No one could possibly suppose of Charles Snow that he is a man who wants to curtail the rights of free criticism. The line which he takes in *The Two Cultures* is so far from the actuality of his temperament in this respect that we can only suppose that he doesn't mean it, not in all the extravagance of its literalness. Or we suppose that he means it at the behest of some large preoccupation of whose goodness he is so entirely convinced that he will seek to affirm it even in ways that would take him aback if the preoccupation were not in control of his thought. And this, I think, is the case. I believe that the position of *The Two Cultures* is to be explained by Sir Charles's well-known preoccupation with a good and necessary aim, with the assuring of peace, which is to say, with the compounding of the differences between the West and the Soviet Union. It is an aim which, in itself, can of course only do Sir Charles credit, yet it would seem to have implicit in it a strange, desperate method of implementing itself.

For the real message of *The Two Cultures* is that an understanding between the West and the Soviet Union could be achieved by the culture of scientists, which reaches over factitious national and ideological differences. The field of agreement would be the scientists' common perception of the need for coming together to put the possibilities of the scientific revolution at the disposal of the disadvantaged of all nations. The bond between scientists, Sir Charles has told us, is virtually biological: they all have the future in their bones. Science brings men together in despite of all barriers—speaking of the way in which the very wide differences in the social origins of English scientists were overcome to make the scientific culture of England (and seeming to imply that this is a unique grace of scientists, that English men of letters never had differences of social class to overcome), Sir Charles says, "Without thinking about it, they respond alike. That is what a culture means." And in the same way, "without thinking about it," the scientists of the West and the scientists of the Soviet Union may be expected to "respond alike." And, since "that is what a culture means," they will have joined together in an entity which will do what governments have not done, the work of relieving the misery of the world. But in the degree to which science naturally unites men, literature separates them, and the scientists of the world cannot form this beneficent entity until we of the West break the existing pattern of our traditional culture, the literary culture, which is self-regarding in its complacent acceptance of tragedy, which is not only indifferent to human suffering but willing to inflict it, which asks rude and impertinent questions about the present and even about the future.

It is a point of view which must, I suppose, in desperate days, have a show of reason. In desperate days, it always seems wise to throw something or someone overboard, preferably Jonah or Arion, the prophet or the poet. Mr. G. S. Fraser, for example, seems to understand what Sir Charles wants, and he is rather willing to go along with him, rather open to the idea that the achievement of peace may require some adverse judgment on literature. "It does not matter," he says, "whether we save the real Cambridge within the actual Cambridge . . .; what we want to save is our actual human world with all the spots on it. This will not be done by teaching English at universities; men like Snow, at home both in Russia and America, and in a simple blunt way trying to teach these two blunt simple giants to understand each other, may in the end prove greater benefactors than Dr. Leavis."

No, the world will not be saved by teaching English at universities, nor, indeed, by any other literary activity. It is very hard to say what will save the world. But we can be perfectly certain that denying the actualities of the world will not work its salvation. Among these actualities politics is one. And it can be said of *The Two Cultures* that it communicates the strongest possible wish that we should forget about politics. It mentions national politics once, speaking of it as the clog upon the activity of scientists, as the impeding circumstance in which they must work. But the point is not developed and the lecture has the effect of suggesting that the issue is not between the abilities and good intentions of scientists and the inertia or bad will of governments; the issue is represented as being between the good culture of science and the bad culture of literature.

In this denial of the actuality of politics, Sir Charles is at one with the temper of intellectuals today—we all want politics not to exist, we all want that statement of Hegel's to be absolutely and immediately true, we dream of reason taking over the whole management of the world, and soon. No doubt a beneficent eventuality, but our impatience for it is dangerous if it leads us to deny the actuality of politics in the present. While we discuss, at Sir Charles's instance, the relative merits of scientific philosopher-kings as against literary philosopher-kings, politics goes on living its own autonomous life, of which one aspect is its massive resistance to reason. What is gained by describing the resistance to reason as other than it is, by thinking in the specious terms of two opposing "cultures"?

But of course the fact is that politics is not finally autonomous. It may be so massively resistant to reason that we are led to think of its resistance as absolute—in bad times we conceive politics to be nothing but power. Yet it cannot be said—at least not so long as politics relies in any degree upon ideology—that politics is never susceptible to such reason as is expressed in opinion, only that it is less susceptible in some nations and at some times than in other nations and at other times. And nowhere and at no time is politics exempt from moral judgment, whether or not that judgment is effectual. But if we make believe, as *The Two Cultures* does, that politics does not exist at all, then it cannot be the object of moral judgment. And if we deny all authority to literature, as *The Two Cultures* does, going so far as to say that this great traditional agency of moral awareness is itself immoral, then the very activity of moral judgment is impugned, except for that single instance of it which asserts the rightness of bringing the benefits of science to the disadvantaged of the world. In short, Sir Charles, seeking to advance the cause of understanding between the West and the Soviet Union, would seem to be saying that this under-standing will come if we conceive both that politics cannot be judged (be-cause it does not really exist) and that it should not be judged (because the traditional agency of judgment is irresponsible).

3

I take *The Two Cultures* to be a book which is mistaken in a very large way indeed. And I find the failure of Dr. Leavis's criticism of it to consist in his addressing himself not to the full extent of its error but to extrane-ous matters. From reading the Richmond Lecture one gains the impres-sion that the substance of the Rede Lecture is extremely offensive to Dr. Leavis, that all his sensibilities are outraged by it: we conclude that Sir Charles wants something which is very different from what Dr. Leavis wants, and that Dr. Leavis thinks that what Sir Charles wants is crude and vulgar. But we can scarcely suppose from Dr. Leavis's response that what Sir Charles says has a very wide reference—for all we can tell, he might have been proposing a change in the University curriculum which Dr. Leavis is repelling with the violence and disgust that are no doubt often felt though not expressed at meetings of curriculum committees. For Dr. Leavis, who has always attached great importance to educational matters, the proposed change is certainly important beyond the University. He understands it both as likely to have a bad effect on the national culture and as being the expression of something already bad in the national cul-ture. But this, we suppose, he would feel about any change in the cur-riculum.

In short, Dr. Leavis, in dealing with the Rede Lecture, has not seen the object as in itself it really is, just as Sir Charles, in dealing with the cul-ture of literature in its relation to politics, has not seen the object as in it-self it really is.

An example of the inadequacy of Dr. Leavis's criticism of *The Two Cul-tures* is his response to what Sir Charles says, in concert with that "scien-tist of distinction," about the political posture of the great writers of the modern period. That statement, if we stop short of its mention of Auschwitz—which makes a most important modification—certainly does have a color of truth. It is one of the cultural curiosities of the first three decades of the twentieth century that, while the educated people, the readers of books, tended to become ever more liberal and radical in their thought, there is no literary figure of the very first rank (although many of the next rank) who, in his work, makes use of or gives credence to liberal or radical ideas. I remarked on this circumstance in an essay of 1946. "Our educated class," I said,

> has a ready if mild suspiciousness of the profit motive, a belief in progress, science, social legislation, planning, and international co-operation, perhaps especially where Russia is in question. These beliefs do great credit to those who hold them. Yet it is a comment, if not on our beliefs then on our way of holding them, that not a single first-rate writer has emerged to deal with these ideas, and the emotions that are consonant with them, in a great literary way. . . . If we name those writers who, by the general consent of the most serious criticism, by consent, too, of the very class of educated people of which we speak, are thought of as the monumental figures of our time, we see that to these writers the liberal ideology has been at best a matter of indifference. Proust, Joyce, Lawrence, Yeats, Mann [as novelist], Kafka, Rilke, Gide [also as novelist]—all of them have their own love of justice and the good life, but in not one of them does it take the form of a love of the ideas and emotions which liberal democracy, as known by our educated class, has declared respectable.

To which it can be added that some great writers have in their work given utterance or credence to conservative and even reactionary ideas, and that some in their personal lives have maintained a settled indifference to all political issues, or a disdain of them. No reader is likely to derive political light from either the works or the table talk of a modern literary genius, and some readers (of weak mind) might even be led into bad political ways.

If these writers are to be brought to the bar of judgment, anyone who speaks as their advocate is not, as Sir Charles says, defending the indefensible. The advocacy can be conducted in honest and simple ways. It is not one of these ways to say that literature is by its nature or by definition innocent. Literature is powerful enough for us to suppose that it has the capability of doing harm. But the ideational influence of literature is by no means always as direct as, for polemical purposes, people sometimes say it is. As against the dismay of Sir Charles and the distinguished scientist at the reactionary tendencies of modern literary geniuses, there is the fact that the English poets who learned their trade from Yeats and Eliot, or even from Pound, have notably had no sympathy with the social ideas and attitudes of their poetical masters.

Every university teacher of literature will have observed the circumstance that young people who are of radical social and political opinion are virtually never troubled by the opposed views or the settled indifference of the great modern writers. This is not because the young exempt the writer from dealing with the serious problems of living, or because they see him through a mere aesthetic haze. It is because they know—and quite without instruction—that, in D. H. Lawrence's words, they are to trust the tale and not the teller of the tale. They perceive that the tale is always on the side of their own generous impulses. They know that, if the future is in the bones of anyone, it is in the bones of the literary genius, and exactly because the present is in his bones, exactly because the past is in his bones. They know that if a work of literature has any true artistic existence, it has value as a criticism of life; in whatever complex way it has chosen to speak, it is making a declaration about the qualities that life should have, about the qualities life does not have but should have. They feel, I think, that it is simply not possible for a work of literature that comes within the borders of greatness *not* to ask for more energy and fineness of life, and, by its own communication of awareness, bring these qualities into being. And if, in their experience of such a work, they happen upon an expression of contempt for some idea which they have connected with political virtue, they are not slow to understand that it is not the idea in its ideal form that is being despised, but the idea as it passes current in specious form, among certain and particular persons. I have yet to meet the student committed to an altruistic politics who is alienated from Stephen Dedalus by that young man's disgust with political idealism, just as I have yet to meet the student from the most disadvantaged background who feels debarred from what Yeats can give him by the poet's slurs upon shopkeepers or by anything else in his inexhaustible fund of snobbery.

If ever a man was qualified to state the case for literature, and far more persuasively than I have done, it is Dr. Leavis. His career as a critic and a teacher has been devoted exactly to the exposition of the idea that literature presents to us "the possibilities of life," the qualities of energy and fineness that life might have. And it is, of course, the intention of the Richmond Lecture to say just this in answer to Sir Charles's indictment. Yet something checks Dr. Leavis. When it is a question of the defense, not of literature in general, but of modern literature, he puts into countervailing evidence nothing more than a passage in which Lawrence says something, in a wry and grudging way, on behalf of social equality. This does not meet the charge; against it Sir Charles might cite a dozen instances in which Lawrence utters what Sir Charles—and perhaps even Dr. Leavis himself—would consider "the most imbecile expressions of antisocial feeling."

There is only one feasible approach to the antisocial utterances of many modern writers, and that is to consider whether their expressions of antisocial feeling are nothing but imbecile. It is the fact, like it or not, that a characteristic cultural enterprise of our time has been the questioning of society itself, not its particular forms and aspects but its very essence. To this extreme point has the criticism of life extended itself. On the ways of dealing with this phenomenon, that of horror and dismay, such as Sir Charles's, is perhaps the least useful. Far better, It seems to me, is the effort to understand what this passionate hostility to society implies, to ask whether it is a symptom, sufficiently gross, of the decline of the West, or whether it is not perhaps an act of critical energy on the part of the West, an act of critical energy on the part of society itself—the effort of society to identify in itself that which is but speciously good, the effort to understand afresh the nature of the life it is designed to foster. I would not anticipate the answer, but these questions make, I am sure, the right way to come at the phenomenon.

It is not the way that Dr. Leavis comes at the phenomenon, despite his saying that the university study of literature must take its stand on "the intellectual-cultural frontier." Actually, when it is a question of the frontier, he prefers—it is an honorable preference—to remain behind it or to take a position at certain check-points. For example, of the two D. H. Lawrences, the one who descended from the social-minded nineteenth century and who did in some sort, affirm the social idea, and the other, at least equally important, for whom the condition of salvation was the total negation of society, Dr. Leavis can be comfortable only with the former. His commitment to the intellectual-cultural frontier is sincere but chiefly theoretical; he has, as is well known, sympathy with very few modern writers, and he therefore cannot in good grace come to their defense against Sir Charles's characterization of them.

Mr. Walter Allen, writing in *The New York Times Book Review* shortly after the publication of the Richmond Lecture and the *Spectator* letters attacking and defending it, accurately remarked on "the common areas of agreement" between Dr. Leavis and Sir Charles. "One would expect . . . that Snow would be sympathetic to Leavis's emphasis on the all-importance of the moral center of literature," Mr. Allen said. "Both have attacked experiment in literature. Neither of them, to put it into crude shorthand, are Flaubert-and-Joyce men." The similarities go further. In point of social background the two men are not much apart, at least to the untutored American eye. Both spring from the provincial middle class in one or another of its strata, and whatever differences there may have been in the material advantages that were available or lacking to one or the other, neither was reared in the assumption of easy privilege. From these origins they derived, we may imagine, their strong sense of quotidian actuality and a respect for those who discharge the duties it imposes, and a high regard for the domestic affections, a quick dislike of the frivolous and merely elegant. Neither, as I have suggested, has any least responsiveness to the tendencies of modern thought or literature which are existential or subversive. A lively young person of advanced tastes would surely say that if ever two men were committed to England, Home, and Duty, they are Leavis and Snow—he would say that in this they are as alike as two squares.

There is one other regard, an especially significant one, in which they are similar. This is their feeling about social class. One of the chief interests of Sir Charles's novels is their explicitness about class as a determinative of the personal life, and in this respect *The Two Cultures* is quite as overt as the novels—its scientists make a new class by virtue of their alienation from the old class attitudes, and Sir Charles's identification of literary men with the traditional culture which supposedly manages the Western world implies that they are in effect the representatives of an aristocratic ruling class, decadent but still powerful. The work of Dr. Leavis is no less suffused by the idea of social class, even though its preoccupation with the subject is far less explicit. To my recollection, Dr. Leavis does not make use of any of the words which denote the distinctions of English society—he does not refer to an aristocracy, a gentry, an upper middle or lower middle or working class. For him a class defines itself by its idea of itself—that is, by its tastes and style. Class is for him a cultural entity. And when he conceives of class power, as he often does, it is not economic or political power but, rather, cultural power that he thinks of. It is true that cultural power presents itself to his mind as being in some way suggestive of class power, but the actualities of power or influence are for him always secondary to the culture from which they arose or to which they give rise.

And indeed, no less than Sir Charles, Dr. Leavis is committed to the creation of a new class. This, we might even say, is the whole motive of his work. The social situation he would seem to assume is one in which there is a fair amount of mobility which is yet controlled and limited by the tendency of the mobile people to allow themselves to be absorbed into one of the traditional classes. As against the attraction exerted by a quasi-aristocratic, metropolitan upper middle class, Dr. Leavis has taken it to be his function to organize the mobile people, those of them who are gifted and conscious, into a new social class formed on the basis of its serious understanding of and response to literature, chiefly English literature. In this undertaking he has by no means been wholly unsuccessful. One has the impression that many of the students he has trained think of themselves, as they take up their posts in secondary schools and universities, as constituting at least a social cadre.

The only other time I wrote about Dr. Leavis I remarked that the Cromwellian Revolution had never really come to an end in England and that Dr. Leavis was one of the chief colonels of the Roundhead party. His ideal readers are people who "are seriously interested in literature," and it is on their behalf that he wages war against a cultural-social class which, when it concerns itself with literature, avows its preference for the qualities of grace, lightness, and irony, and deprecates an overt sincerity and seriousness. "To a polished nation," said Gibbon, "poetry is an amusement of the fancy, not a passion of the soul," and all through his career it is against everything that Gibbon means by a polished nation and might mean by a polished class that Dr. Leavis has set his face. Bloomsbury has been his characteristic antagonist. But now, in Charles Snow, he confronts an opponent who is as Roundhead as himself, and as earnest and *intentional*.

To this confrontation Dr. Leavis is not adequate. It is not an adequate response to the massive intention of *The Two Cultures* for Dr. Leavis to meet Sir Charles's cultural preferences with his own preferences; or to seek to discredit Sir Charles's ideas chiefly by making them out to be vulgar ideas or outmoded ("Wellsian") ideas; or to offer, as against Sir Charles's vision of a future made happier by science, the charms of primitive peoples "with their marvellous arts and skills and vital intelligence." I do not mean to say that Dr. Leavis does not know where Sir Charles goes wrong in the details of his argument—he is as clear as we expect him to be in rebuking that large unhappy blunder about the Victorian writers. Nor, certainly, do I mean that Dr. Leavis does not know what the great fundamental mistake of Sir Charles's position is—he does, and he can be eloquent in asserting against a simplistic confidence in a scientific "future" the need of mankind, in the face of a rapid advance of science and technology, "to be in full intelligent possession of its full humanity (and 'possession' here means, not confident ownership of that which belongs to *us*—our property, but a basic living deference towards that to which, opening as it does into the unknown and itself immeasurable, we know we belong)." But such moments of largeness do not save the Richmond Lecture from its general parochialism. For example, of the almost limitless political implications of Sir Charles's position it gives no evidence of awareness. And if we undertake to find a reason for the inadequacy of Dr. Leavis's response, we will find, I think, that it is the same as the reason which accounts for Sir Charles having been in the first place so wholly mistaken in what he says—both men set too much store by the idea of *culture* as a category of thought.

The concept of culture is an idea of great attractiveness and undoubted usefulness. We may say that it begins in the assumption that all human expressions or artifacts are indicative of some considerable tendencies in the life of social groups or sub-groups, and that what is indicative is also causative—all cultural facts have their consequences. To think in cultural terms is to consider human expressions not only in their overt existence and avowed intention, but in, as it were, their secret life, taking cognizance of the desires and impulses which lie behind the open formulation. In the judgments which we make when we think in the category of culture we rely to a very large extent upon the style in which an expression is made, believing that style will indicate, or betray, what is not intended to be expressed. The aesthetic mode is integral to the idea of culture, and our judgments of social groups are likely to be made chiefly on an aesthetic basis—we like or do not like what we call their life-styles, and even when we judge moralities, the criterion by which we choose between two moralities of, say, equal strictness or equal laxness is likely to be an aesthetic one.

The concept of culture affords to those who use it a sense of the liberation of their thought, for they deal less with abstractions and mere objects, more with the momentous actualities of human feelings as these shape and condition the human community, as they make and as they indicate the quality of man's existence. Not the least of the attractions of the cultural mode of thought are the passions which attend it—because it assumes that all things are causative or indicative of the whole of the cultural life, it proposes to us those intensities of moralized feeling which seem appropriate to our sense that all that is good in life is at stake in every cultural action. An instance of mediocrity or failure in art or thought is not only what it is but also a sin, deserving to be treated as such. These passions are no doubt vivifying: they have the semblance of heroism.

And if we undertake to say what were the circumstances that made the cultural mode of thought as available and as authoritative as it now is, we must refer to Marx, and to Freud, and to the general movement of existentialism, to all that the tendencies of modernity imply of the sense of contingency in life, from which we learn that the one thing that can be disputed, and that is worth disputing, is preference or taste. The Rede Lecture and the Richmond Lecture exemplify the use to which the idea of culture can be put in shaking the old certainties of class, in contriving new social groups on the basis of taste.

All this does indeed give the cultural mode of thought a very considerable authority. Yet sometimes we may wonder if it is wholly an accident that so strong an impulse to base our sense of life, and conduct of the intellectual life, chiefly upon the confrontations of taste should have developed in an age dominated by advertising, the wonderful and terrible art which teaches us that we define ourselves and realize our true being by choosing the right style. In our more depressed moments we might be led to ask whether there is a real difference between being the Person Who defines himself by his commitment to one or another idea of morality, politics, literature, or city-planning, and being the Person Who defines himself by wearing trousers without pleats.

We can, I suppose, no more escape from the cultural mode of thought than we can escape from culture itself. Yet perhaps we must learn to cast a somewhat colder eye upon it for the sake of whatever regard we have for the intellectual life, for the possibility of rational discourse. Sir Charles envisages a new and very powerful social class on the basis of a life-style which he imputes to a certain profession in contrast with the life-style he imputes to another profession, and he goes on from there to deny both the reality of politics and the possibility of its being judged by moral standards. Dr. Leavis answers him with a passion of personal scorn which obscures the greater part of the issue and offers in contradiction truth indeed but truth so hampered and hidden by the defenses of Dr. Leavis's own choice in life-styles that it looks not much different from a prejudice. And the *Spectator* correspondents exercise their taste in life-styles and take appropriate sides. It is at such a moment that our dispirited minds yearn to find comfort and courage in the idea of mind, that faculty whose ancient potency our commitment to the idea of culture denies. To us today, mind must inevitably seem but a poor gray thing, for it always sought to detach itself from the passions (but not from the emotions, Spinoza said, and explained the difference) and from the conditions of time and place. Yet it is salutary for us to contemplate it, whatever its grayness, because of the bright belief that was once attached to it, that it was the faculty which belonged not to professions, or to social classes, or to cultural groups, but to man, and that it was possible for men, and becoming to them, to learn its proper use, for it was the means by which they could communicate with each other.

It was on this belief that science based its early existence, and it gave to the men who held it a character which is worth remarking. Sir Charles mentions Faraday among those scientists who overrode the limitations of social class to form the "scientific culture" of England. This is true only so far as it can be made consonant with the fact that Faraday could not have imagined the idea of a "scientific culture" and would have been wholly repelled by it. It is told of Faraday that he refused to be called a *physicist*; he very much disliked the new name, as being too special and particular, and insisted on the old one, *philosopher*, in all its spacious generality: we may suppose that this was his way of saying that he had not overridden the limiting conditions of class only to submit to the limitations of profession. The idea of mind which had taught the bookbinder's apprentice to embark on his heroic enterprise of self-instruction also taught the great scientist to place himself beyond the specialness of interest which groups prescribe for their members. Every personal episode in Tyndall's classic account of his master, *Faraday as a Researcher*, makes it plain that Faraday undertook to be, in the beautiful lost sense of the word, a *disinterested* man. From his belief in mind, he derived the certitude that he had his true being not as a member of this or that profession or class, but as—in the words of a poet of his time—"a man speaking to men."

No one now needs to be reminded of what may befall the idea of mind in the way of excess and distortion. The literature of the nineteenth century never wearied of telling us just this, of decrying the fatigue and desiccation of spirit which result from an allegiance to mind that excludes impulse and will, and desire and preference. It was, surely, a liberation to be made aware of this, and then to go on to take serious account of those particularities of impulse and will, of desire and preference, which differentiate individuals and groups—to employ what I have called the cultural mode of thought. We take it for granted that this, like any other mode of thought, has its peculiar dangers, but there is cause for surprise and regret that it should be Sir Charles Snow and Dr. Leavis who have jointly demonstrated how far the cultural mode of thought can go in excess and distortion.

The Fate of Pleasure

1963

Of all critical essays in the English language, there is none that has established itself so firmly in our minds as Wordsworth's Preface to *Lyrical Ballads*. Indeed, certain of the statements that the Preface makes about the nature of poetry have come to exist for us as something like proverbs of criticism. This is deplorable, for the famous utterances, in the form in which we hold them in memory, can only darken counsel. A large part of the literate world believes that Wordsworth defines poetry as the spontaneous overflow of powerful feelings. With such a definition we shall not get very far in our efforts to think about poetry, and in point of fact Wordsworth makes no such definition. Much less does he say, as many find it convenient to recall, that poetry is emotion recollected in tranquillity. Yet the tenacity with which we hold in mind our distortions of what Wordsworth actually does say suggests the peculiar power of the essay as a whole, its unique existence as a work of criticism. Its cogency in argument is notable, even if intermittent, but the Preface is not regarded by its readers only as an argument. By reason of its eloquence, and because of the impetuous spirit with which it engages the great questions of the nature and function of poetry, it presents itself to us not chiefly as a discourse, but rather as a dramatic action, and we are prepared to respond to its utterances less for their truth than for their happy boldness.

This being so, it should be a matter for surprise that one especially bold utterance of the Preface has not engaged us at all and is scarcely ever cited. I refer to the sentence in which Wordsworth speaks of what he calls "the grand elementary principle of pleasure," and says of it that it constitutes "the naked and native dignity of man," that it is the principle by which man "knows, and feels, and lives, and moves."

This is a statement which has great intrinsic interest, because, if we recognize that it is bold at all, we must also perceive that it is bold to the point of being shocking, for it echoes and controverts St. Paul's sentence which tells us that "we live, and move, and have our being" in God (Acts 17:28). And in addition to its intrinsic interest, it has great historical interest, not only because it sums up a characteristic tendency of eighteenth-century thought but also because it bears significantly upon a characteristic tendency of our contemporary culture. Its relation to that culture is chiefly a negative one—our present sense of life does not accommodate the idea of pleasure as something which constitutes the "naked and native dignity of man."

The word "pleasure" occurs frequently in the Preface. Like earlier writers on the subject, when Wordsworth undertakes to explain why we do, or should, value poetry, he bases his explanation upon the pleasure which poetry gives. Generally he uses the word in much the same sense that was intended by his predecessors. The pleasure which used commonly to be associated with poetry was morally unexceptionable and not very intense—it was generally understood that poetry might indeed sometimes excite the mind but only as a step toward composing it. But the word has, we know, two separate moral ambiences and two very different degrees of intensity. The pleasures of domestic life are virtuous; the pleasures of Imagination or Melancholy propose the idea of a cultivated delicacy of mind in those who experience them; the name of an English pipe-tobacco, "Parson's Pleasure," although derived from the place on the river at Oxford where men have traditionally bathed naked, is obviously meant to suggest that the word readily consorts with ideas of mildness. None of these point to what Byron had in mind when he wrote, "O pleasure! you're indeed a pleasant thing,/ Although one must be damn'd for you no doubt." The *Oxford English Dictionary* takes due note of what it calls an "unfavorable" sense of the word: "Sensuous enjoyment as a chief object of life, or end, in itself," and informs us that in this pejorative sense it is "sometimes personified as a female deity." The Oxford lexicographers do not stop there but go on to recognize what they call a "strictly physical" sense, which is even lower in the moral scale: "the indulgence of the appetites, sensual gratification." The "unfavorable" significations of the word are dramatized by the English career of the most usual Latin word for pleasure, *voluptas*. Although some Latin-English dictionaries, especially those of the nineteenth century, say that *voluptas* means "pleasure, enjoyment, or delight of body or mind in a good or a bad sense," the word as it was used in antiquity seems to have been on the whole morally neutral and not necessarily intense. But the English words derived from *voluptas* are charged with moral judgment and are rather excited. We understand that it is not really to the minds of men that a voluptuous woman holds out the promise of pleasure, enjoyment, or delight. We do not expect a voluptuary to seek his pleasures in domesticity, or in the Imagination of Melancholy, or in smoking a pipe.

It is obvious that any badness or unfavorableness of meaning that the word "pleasure" may have relates to the primitiveness of the enjoyment that is being referred to. Scarcely any moralist will object to pleasure as what we may call a secondary state of feeling, as a charm or grace added to the solid business of life. What does arouse strong adverse judgment is pleasure in its radical aspect, as it is the object of an essential and definitive energy of man's nature. It was because Bentham's moral theory represented pleasure in this way that Carlyle called it the Pig-philosophy. He meant, of course, that it impugned man's nature to associate it so immediately with pleasure. Yet this is just how Wordsworth asks us to conceive man's nature in the sentence I have spoken of—it is precisely pleasure in its primitive or radical aspect that he has in mind. He speaks of "the grand *elementary* principle of pleasure," which is to say, pleasure not as a mere charm or amenity but as the object of an instinct, of what Freud, whose complex exposition of the part that pleasure plays in life is of course much in point here, was later to call a "drive." How little concerned was Wordsworth, at least in this one sentence, with pleasure in its mere secondary aspect is suggested by his speaking of it as constituting the *dignity* of man, not having in mind such dignity as is conferred by society but that which is *native* and *naked*.

When Carlyle denounced Bentham's assertion that pleasure is, and must be, a first consideration of the human being, it was exactly man's dignity that he was undertaking to defend. The traditional morality to which Carlyle subscribed was certainly under no illusion about the crude force of man's impulse to self-gratification, but it did not associate man's dignity with this force—on the contrary, dignity, so far as it was personal and moral, was thought to derive from the resistance which man offers to the impulse to pleasure.

For Wordsworth, however, pleasure was the defining attribute of life itself and of nature itself—pleasure is the "impulse from the vernal wood" which teaches us more of man and his moral being "than all the sages can." And the fallen condition of humanity—"what man has made of man"—is comprised by the circumstance that man alone of natural beings does not experience the pleasure which, Wordsworth believes, moves the living world. It is of course a commonplace of Wordsworth criticism that, although the poet sets the highest store by the idea of pleasure, the actual pleasures he represents are of a quite limited kind. Certainly he ruled out pleasures that are "strictly physical," those which derive from "the indulgence of the appetites" and "sensual gratification," more particularly erotic gratification. His living world of springtime is far removed from that of Lucretius: nothing in it is driven by the irresistible power of *alma Venus*. This is not to say that there is no erotic aspect to Wordsworth's mind; but the eroticism is very highly sublimated—Wordsworth's pleasure always tended toward *joy*, a purer and more nearly transcendent state. And yet our awareness of this significant limitation does not permit us to underrate the boldness of his statement in the Preface about the primacy of pleasure and the dignity which derives from the principle of pleasure, or to ignore its intimate connection with certain radical aspects of the moral theory of the French Revolution.*

For an understanding of the era of the Revolution, there is, I think, much to be gained from one of the works of the German economic historian Werner Sombart, whose chief preoccupation was the origins of capitalism. In his extensive monograph *Luxury and Capitalism*, Sombart develops the thesis that the first great accumulations of capital were achieved by the luxury trades in consequence of that ever-increasing demand for the pleasures of the world, for comfort, sumptuousness, and el-

---

*And we ought not let go unheeded the explicit connection that Wordsworth makes between poetry and sexuality. Explaining the pleasure of metrical language, he says that it is "the pleasure which the mind derives from the perception of similitude in dissimilitude." And he goes on: "This principle is the great spring of the activity of our minds and their chief feeder. From this principle the direction of the sexual appetite, and all the passions connected with it, take their origin."

egance, which is observed in Western Europe between the end of the Middle Ages and the end of the eighteenth century. As a comprehensive explanation of the rise of capitalism, this theory, I gather, has been largely discredited. Yet the social and cultural data which Sombart accumulates are in themselves very interesting, and they are much to our point.

Sombart advances the view that the European preoccupation with luxury took its rise in the princely courts and in the influence of women which court life made possible; he represents luxury as being essentially an expression of eroticism, as the effort to refine and complicate the sexual life, to enhance, as it were, the quality of erotic pleasure. The courtly luxury that Sombart studies is scarcely a unique instance of the association of pleasure with power, of pleasure being thought of as one of the signs of power and therefore to be made not merely manifest but conspicuous in the objects that constitute the *décor* of the lives of powerful men—surely Egypt, Knossos, and Byzantium surpassed Renaissance Europe in elaborateness of luxury. But what would seem to be remarkable about the particular phenomenon that Sombart describes is the extent of its proliferation at a certain period—the sheer amount of luxury that got produced, its increasing availability to classes less than royal or noble, the overtness of the desire for it, and the fierceness of this desire. Sombart's data on these points are too numerous to be adduced here, but any tourist, having in mind what he has even casually seen of the secondary arts of Europe from the centuries in question, the ornaments, furniture, and garniture of certain stations of life, will know that Sombart does not exaggerate about the amount of luxury produced. And any reader of Balzac will recognize the intensity of the passions which at a somewhat later time attended the acquisition of elaborate and costly objects which were desired as the means or signs of pleasure.

What chiefly engages our interest is the influence that luxury may be discovered to have upon social and moral ideas. Such an influence is to be observed in the growing tendency of power to express itself mediately, by signs or indices, rather than directly, by the exercise of force. The richness and elaboration of the objects in a princely establishment were the indices of a power which was actual enough, but they indicated an actual power which had no need to avow itself in action. What a prince conceived of as his dignity might, more than ever before, be expressed by affluence, by the means of pleasure made overt and conspicuous.

And as the objects of luxury became more widely available, so did the dignity which luxury was meant to imply. The connection between dignity and a luxurious style of life was at first not self-evident—in France in 1670 the very phrase *bourgeois gentilhomme* was thought to be comical. In the contemporary English translation of the title of Molière's comedy, *The Cit Turned Gentleman*, it was funny, too, but the English laugh was neither so loud nor so long as the French, with what good consequences for the English nation Tocqueville has made plain. Yet in France as in England, the downward spread of the idea of dignity, until it eventually became an idea that might be applied to man in general, was advanced by the increasing possibility of possessing the means or signs of pleasure. That idea, it need scarcely be said, established itself at the very heart of the radical thought of the eighteenth century. And Diderot himself, the most uncompromising of materialists as he was the most subtle and delicate, could not have wanted a more categorical statement of his own moral and intellectual theory than Wordsworth's assertion that the grand elementary principle of pleasure constitutes the native and naked dignity of man, and that it is by this principle that man knows, and lives, and breathes, and moves.

Nothing so much connects Keats with Wordsworth as the extent of his conscious commitment to the principle of pleasure. But of course nothing so much separates Keats from his great master as his characteristic way of exemplifying the principle. In the degree that for Wordsworth pleasure is abstract and austere, for Keats it is explicit and voluptuous. No poet ever gave so much credence to the idea of pleasure in the sense of "indulgence of the appetites, sensual gratification," as Keats did, and the phenomenon that Sombart describes, the complex of pleasure-sensuality-luxury, makes the very fabric of his thought.

Keats's preoccupation with the creature-pleasures, as it manifests itself in his early work, is commonly regarded, even by some of his warmest admirers, with an amused disdain. At best, it seems to derive from the kind of elegant minuscule imagination that used to design the charming erotic scenes for the lids of enameled snuff boxes. At worst, in the explicitness of its concern with luxury, it exposes itself to the charge of downright vulgarity that some readers have made. The word "luxury" had a charm for Keats, and in his use of it he seems on the point of reviving its older meaning, which is specifically erotic and nothing but erotic; for Chaucer and Shakespeare "luxury" meant lust and its indulgence. Women present themselves to Keats's imagination as luxuries: "All that soft luxury/ that nestled in his arms." A poem is described as "a posy/ Of luxuries, bright, milky, soft and rosy." Poetry itself is defined by reference to objects of luxury, and even in its highest nobility, its function is said to be that of comforting and soothing.

Nor is the vulgarity—if we consent to call it that—confined to the early works; we find it in an extreme form in a poem of Keats's maturity. The lover in *Lamia* is generally taken to be an innocent youth, yet the most corrupt young man of Balzac's scenes of Parisian life would scarcely have spoken to his mistress or his fiancée as Lycius speaks to Lamia when he insists that she display her beauty in public for the enhancement of his prestige. Tocqueville said that envy was the characteristic emotion of plutocratic democracy, and it is envy of a particularly ugly kind that Lycius wishes to excite. "Let my foes choke," he says, "and my friends shout afar,/ While through the thronged streets your bridal car/ Wheels round its dazzling spokes." I am not sure that we should be at pains to insist that this is wholly a dramatic utterance and not a personal one, that we ought entirely to dissociate Keats from Lycius. I am inclined to think that we should suppose Keats to have been involved in all aspects of the principle of pleasure, even the ones that are vulgar and ugly. Otherwise we miss the full complication of that dialectic of pleasure which is the characteristic intellectual activity of Keats's poetry.

The movement of this dialectic is indicated in two lines from an early poem in which Keats speaks of "the pillowy silkiness that rests/ Full in the speculation of the stars"—it is the movement from the sensual to the transcendent, from pleasure to knowledge, and knowledge of an ultimate kind. Keats's intellect was brought into fullest play when the intensity of his affirmation of pleasure was met by the intensity of his skepticism about pleasure. The principle of pleasure is for Keats, as it is for Wordsworth, the principle of reality—by it, as Wordsworth said, we *know*. But for Keats it is also the principle of illusion. In *The Eve of St. Agnes*, to take the most obvious example, the moment of pleasure at the center of the poem, erotic pleasure expressed in the fullest possible imagination of the luxurious, is the very essence of reality: it is all we know on earth and all we need to know. And it is the more real as reality and it is the more comprehensive as knowledge exactly because in the poem it exists surrounded by what on earth denies it, by darkness, cold, and death, which make it transitory, which make the felt and proclaimed reality mere illusion.

But we must be aware that in Keats's dialectic of pleasure it is not only external circumstances that condition pleasure and bring it into question as the principle of reality, but also the very nature of pleasure itself. If for Keats erotic enjoyment is the peak and crown of all pleasures, it is also his prime instance of the way in which the desire for pleasure denies itself and produces the very opposite of itself.

> Love in a hut, with water and a crust,
> Is—Love, forgive us—cinders, ashes, dust;
> Love in a palace is perhaps at last
> More grievous torment than a hermit's fast.

This opening statement of the second part of *Lamia* is not, as it is often said to be, merely a rather disagreeable jaunty cynicism but one of Keats's boldest expressions of his sense that there is something perverse and self-negating in the erotic life, that it is quite in the course of nature that we should feel "Pleasure . . . turning to Poison as the bee-mouth sips." He insists on the seriousness of the statement in a way that should not be hard to interpret—referring to the lines I have just quoted, he says

> That is a doubtful tale from faery land,
> Hard for the non-elect to understand.

That faery land we know very well—in the Nightingale Ode, Keats's epithet for the region is *forlorn*; it is the country of La Belle Dame sans Merci, the scene of erotic pleasure which leads to devastation, of an erotic fulfillment which implies castration.

Keats, then, may be thought of as the poet who made the boldest affirmation of the principle of pleasure and also as the poet who brought the principle of pleasure into the greatest and *sincerest* doubt. He therefore has for us a peculiar cultural interest, for it would seem to be true that at some point in modern history the principle of pleasure came to be regarded with just such ambivalence.

This divided state of feeling may be expressed in terms of a breach between politics and art. Modern societies seek to fulfill themselves in affluence, which of course implies the possibility of pleasure. Our political morality is more than acquiescent to this intention. Its simple and on the whole efficient criterion is the extent to which affluence is distributed among individuals and nations. But another morality, which we may describe as being associated with art, regards with a stern and even minatory gaze all that is implied by affluence, and it takes a dim or at best a very complicated view of the principle of pleasure. If we speak not only of the two different modes of morality, the political and the artistic, but also of the people who are responsive to them, we can say that it is quite within the bounds of possibility, if not of consistency, for the same person to respond, and intensely, to both of the two moral modes: it is by no means uncommon for an educated person to base his judgment of politics on a simple affirmation of the principle of pleasure, and to base his judgment of art, and also his judgment of personal existence, on a complex antagonism to that principle. This dichotomy makes one of the most significant circumstances of our cultural situation.

A way of testing what I have said about the modern artistic attitude to pleasure is afforded by the conception of poetry which Keats formulates in "Sleep and Poetry." This poem does not express everything that Keats thought about the nature and function of poetry, but what it does express is undeniably central to his thought, and for the modern sensibility it is inadmissible and even repulsive. It tells us that poetry is gentle, soothing, cheerful, healthful, serene, smooth, regal; that the poet, in the natural course of his development, will first devote his art to the representation of the pleasures of appetite, of things that can be bitten and tasted, such as apples, strawberries, and the white shoulders of nymphs, and that he will give his attention to the details of erotic enticement amid grateful sights and odors, and to sexual fulfillment and sleep. The poem then goes on to say that, as the poet grows older, he will write a different kind of poetry, which is called nobler; this later kind of poetry is less derived from and directed to the sensuality of youth and is more fitted to the gravity of mature years, but it still ministers to pleasure and must therefore be strict in its avoidance of ugly themes; it must not deal with those distressing matters which are referred to as "the burrs and thorns of life"; the great end of poetry, we are told, is "to soothe the cares, and lift the thoughts of man."

Such doctrine from a great poet puzzles and embarrasses us. It is, we say, the essence of philistinism.

The conception of the nature and function of poetry which Keats propounds is, of course, by no means unique with him—it can be understood as a statement of the common assumptions about art which prevailed through the Renaissance up to some point in the nineteenth century, when they began to lose their force.* Especially in the eighteenth century, art is closely associated with luxury—with the pleasure or at least the comfort of the consumer, or with the quite direct flattery of his ego. The very idea of Beauty seems to imply considerations of this sort, which is perhaps why the eighteenth century was so much drawn to the idea of the Sublime, for that word would seem to indicate a kind of success in art which could not be called Beauty because it lacked the smoothness and serenity (to take two attributes from Keats's catalogue) and the immediacy of gratification which the idea of Beauty seems to propose. But the Sublime itself of course served the purposes of egoism—thus, that instance of the Sublime which was called the Grand Style, as it is described by its great English exponent in painting, Sir Joshua Reynolds, is said to be concerned with "some instance of heroic action or heroic suffering" and its proper effect, Reynolds explains, is to produce the emotion which Bouchardon reported he felt when he read Homer: "His whole frame appeared to himself to be enlarged, and all nature which surrounded him diminished to atoms."†

In connection with the art of the eighteenth century I used the disagreeable modern word "consumer," meaning thus to suggest the affinity that art was thought to have with luxury, its status as a commodity which is implied by the solicitude it felt for the pleasure and the comfort of the person who was to own and experience it. Certainly Wordsworth was

*One of the last significant exponents of the old assumptions was the young Yeats. He was "in all things pre-Raphaelite"—a partisan, that is, not of the early and austere pre-Raphaelite mode, but of the later sumptuous style, tinged with a sort of mystical eroticism—and he stubbornly resisted the realism of Carolus Duran and Bastien-Lepage, which was being brought back to England by the painters who had gone to study in Paris. His commitment to the "beautiful," as against truthful ugliness, was an issue of great moment between him and his father.

†All writers on the Sublime say in effect what Bouchardon says—that, although the sublime subject induces an overpowering emotion, even fear or terror, it does so in a way that permits us to rise superior to it and thus gives us occasion to have a good opinion of our power of intellect and of ourselves generally. The Sublime has this direct relation to comfort and luxury, that it induces us "to regard as small those things of which we are wont to be solicitous" (Kant, *Critique of Aesthetic Judgment*). A more ambitious treatment of my subject would require a much fuller exposition of the theory of the Sublime. Of this theory, which so much occupied the writers on art of the eighteenth century, it can be said that it has much more bearing upon our own literature than modern critics have recognized. The classic study in English is Samuel H. Monk's *The Sublime*, first published in 1935.

pre-eminent in the movement to change this state of affairs,* yet Wordsworth locates the value of metrical language as lying in its ability to protect the reader from the discomfort of certain situations that poetry may wish to represent and he compares the effect of such situations in novels with their effect in Shakespeare, his point being that in novels they are "distressful" but in Shakespeare they are not.† It was, we know, an explanation which did not satisfy Keats, who was left to puzzle out why it is that in King Lear "all disagreeables evaporate." He discovers that this effect is achieved by "intensity," and we of our day are just at the point of being comfortable with him when he disappoints our best hopes by hedging: he is constrained to say that the "disagreeables" evaporate not only by the operation of intensity but also by "their being in close connection with Beauty & Truth." But we do at last find ourselves at one with him when, in his sonnet "On Sitting Down to Read 'King Lear' Once Again," he dismisses all thought of pleasure and prepares himself for the pain he is in duty bound to undergo:

> . . . Once again, the fierce dispute
> Betwixt damnation and impassion'd clay
> Must I burn through; once more humbly assay
> The bitter-sweet of this Shakespearian fruit.

He is by no means certain that the disagreeables really will evaporate and that he will emerge whole and sound from the experience, and he prays to Shakespeare and "the clouds of Albion" that they will guard him against

---

*" . . . Men . . . who talk of Poetry as a matter of amusement and idle pleasure; who will converse with us as gravely about a *taste* for Poetry, as they express it, as if it were a thing as indifferent as a taste for rope-dancing, or Frontiniac, or Sherry."

†The strength of Wordsworth's impulse to suppress the "distressful" is suggested by the famous passage in *The Prelude* in which the poet explains how his childhood reading served to inure him to the terrors of actuality. He recounts the incident, which occurred when he was nine years old, of his seeing a drowned man brought up from the bottom of Esthwaite Lake. He was, he says, not overcome by fear of the "ghastly face," because his "inner eye" had seen such sights before in fairy tales and romances. And then he feels it necessary to go further, to go beyond the bounds of our ready credence, for he tells us that from his reading came "a spirit" which hallowed the awful sight

> With decoration and ideal grace
> A dignity, a smoothness, like the works
> Of Grecian Art, and purest poetry.

wandering "in a barren dream," and that, when he is "consumed in the fire," they will contrive his Phoenix-resurrection.

This we of our time can quite understand. We are repelled by the idea of an art that is consumer-directed and comfortable, let alone luxurious. Our typical experience of a work which will eventually have authority with us is to begin our relation to it at a conscious disadvantage, and to wrestle with it until it consents to bless us. We express our high esteem for such a work by supposing that it judges us. And when it no longer does seem to judge us, or when it no longer baffles and resists us, when we begin to feel that we *possess* it, we discover that its power is diminished. In our praise of it we are not likely to use the word "beauty": we consented long ago—more than four decades ago—to the demonstration made by I. A. Richards in collaboration with Ogden and Wood that the concept of Beauty either could not be assigned any real meaning, or that it was frivolously derived from some assumed connection between works of art and our sexual preferences, quite conventional sexual preferences at that. "Beauty: it curves: curves are beauty," says Leopold Bloom, and we smile at so outmoded an aesthetic—how like him! With a similar amusement we read the language in which the young Yeats praised beauty in *The Secret Rose* (1896)—he speaks of those who are so fortunate as to be "heavy with the sleep/Men have named beauty."*

In short, our contemporary aesthetic culture does not set great store by the principle of pleasure in its simple and primitive meaning and it may even be said to maintain an antagonism to the principle of pleasure. Such a statement of course has its aspect of absurdity, but in logic only. There is no psychic fact more available to our modern comprehension than that there are human impulses which, in one degree or another, and

---

*Mr. Bloom's observation (which goes on to "shapely goddesses Venus, Juno: curves the world admires" and "lovely forms of women sculped Junonian") follows upon his lyrical recollection of his first sexual encounter with Molly; Yeats's phrase occurs in the course of a poem to Maud Gonne. I think it is true to say of Joyce (at least up through *Ulysses*) and of Yeats that they were among the last devotees of the European cult of Woman, of a Female Principle which, in one way or another, *ziegt uns hinan*, and that Molly and Maud are perhaps the last women in literature to be represented as having a transcendent and on the whole beneficent significance (although Lara in *Dr. Zhivago* should be mentioned—it is she who gives that novel much of its archaic quality). The radical change in our sexual mythos must surely be considered in any speculation about the status of pleasure in our culture. It is to the point, for example, that in Kafka's account of the spiritual life, which is touched on below, women play a part that is at best ambiguous.

sometimes in the very highest degree, repudiate pleasure and seek gratification in—to use Freud's word—unpleasure.

The repudiation of pleasure in favor of the gratification which may be found in unpleasure is a leading theme of Dostoyevsky's great *nouvelle*, *Notes from Underground*. Of this extraordinary work Thomas Mann has said that "its painful and scornful conclusions," its "radical frankness . . . ruthlessly transcending all novelistic and literary bounds," have "long become parts of our moral culture." Mann's statement is accurate but minimal—the painful and scornful conclusions of Dostoyevsky's story have established themselves not only as parts of our moral culture but as its essence, at least so far as that culture makes itself explicit in literature.

Notes from Underground is an account, given in the first person, of the temperament and speculations of a miserable clerk, disadvantaged in every possible way, who responds to his unfortunate plight by every device of bitterness and resentment, by hostility toward those of mankind who are more unfortunate than he is, and also by the fiercest contempt for his more fortunate fellow beings, and for the elements of good fortune. He hates all men of purposeful life, and reasonable men, and action, and happiness, and what he refers to as "the sublime and the beautiful," and pleasure. His mind is subtle, complex, and contradictory almost beyond credibility—we never know where to have him and in our exhaustion we are likely to explain his perversity in some simple way, such as that he hates because he is envious, that he despises what he cannot have: all quite natural. But we are not permitted to lay this flattering unction to our souls—for one thing, he himself beats us to that explanation. And although it is quite true, it is only a small part of the truth. It is also true that he does not have because he does not wish to have; he has arranged his own misery—arranged it in the interests of his dignity, which is to say, of his freedom. For to want what is commonly thought to be appropriate to men, to want whatever it is, high or low, that is believed to yield pleasure, to be active about securing it, to use common sense and prudence to the end of gaining it, this is to admit and consent to the *conditioned* nature of man. What a distance we have come in the six decades since Wordsworth wrote his Preface! To know and feel and live and move at the behest of the principle of pleasure—this, for the Underground Man, so far from constituting his native and naked dignity, constitutes his humiliation in bondage. It makes him, he believes, a mechanic thing, the puppet of whoever or whatever can offer him the means of pleasure. If pleasure is indeed the principle of his being, he is as *known* as the sum of 2 and 2; he is a mere object of reason, of that rationality of the revolution which is established upon the primacy of the principle of pleasure.

At one point in his narrative, the protagonist of *Notes from Underground* speaks of himself as an "anti-hero." He is the eponymous ancestor of a now-numerous tribe. He stands as the antagonistic opposite to all the qualities which are represented by that statue of Sophocles which Professor Margarete Bieber tells us we are to have in mind when we try to understand the Greek conception of the hero, the grave beauty of the countenance and physique expressing the strength and order of the soul; the Underground Man traces his line of descent back to Thersites. It is in his character of anti-hero that he addresses the "gentlemen," as he calls them, the men of action and reason, the lovers of "the sublime and the beautiful," and brags to them, "I have more life in me than you have."

More life: perhaps it was this boast of the Underground Man that Nietzsche recalled when he said, "Dostoyevsky's Underman and my Overman are the same person clawing his way out of the pit [of modern thought and feeling] into the sunlight." One understands what Nietzsche meant, but he is mistaken in the identification, for his own imagination is bounded on one side by that word "sunlight," by the Mediterranean world which he loved: by the tradition of humanism with its recognition of the value of pleasure. He is ineluctably constrained by considerations of society and culture, however much he may despise his own society and culture, but the Underground Man is not. To be sure, the terms of the latter's experience are, in the first instance, social; he is preoccupied by questions of status and dignity, and he could not, we may suppose, have come into existence if the fates of the heroes of Balzac and Stendhal had not previously demonstrated that no object of desire or of the social will is anything but an illusion and a source of corruption, society being what it is. But it is the essence of the Underground Man's position that his antagonism to society arises not in response to the deficiencies of social life, but, rather, in response to the insult society offers his freedom by aspiring to be beneficent, to embody "the sublime and the beautiful" as elements of its being. The anger Dostoyevsky expresses in *Notes from Underground* was activated not by the bad social condition of Russia in 1864 but by the avowed hope of some people that a good social condition could be brought into being. A Utopian novel of the day, Chernyshevsky's *What Is to Be Done?*, seemed to him an especially repugnant expression of this hope.* His disgust was aroused by this novel's assumption that man would be better for a rationally organized society, by which was meant, of course, a society organized in the service of pleasure. Dostoyevsky's reprobation of this idea, begun in *Notes from Underground*, reached its climax in Ivan Karamazov's poem of the Grand Inquisitor, in which again, but this time without the brilliant perversities of the earlier work, the disgust with the specious good of pleasure serves as the ground for the affirmation of spiritual freedom.

I have taken the phrase "specious good" from a passage in Wallace Fowlie's little book on Rimbaud, in which Mr. Fowlie discusses what he calls "the modern seizure and comprehension of spirituality." Without evasion, Mr. Fowlie identifies a chief characteristic of our culture which critics must inevitably be conscious of and yet don't like to name. If we are to be aware of the spiritual intention of modern literature, we have to get rid of certain nineteenth-century connotations of the word "spiritual," all that they may imply to us of an overrefined and even effeminate quality, and have chiefly in mind what Mr. Fowlie refers to when he speaks of a certain type of saint and a certain type of poet and says of them that "both the saint and the poet exist through some propagation of destructive violence." And Mr. Fowlie continues: "In order to discover what is the center of themselves, the saint has to destroy the world of evil, and the poet has to destroy the world of specious good."

The destruction of what is considered to be specious good is surely one of the chief literary enterprises of our age. Whenever in modern literature we find violence, whether of represented act or of expression, and an insistence upon the sordid and the disgusting, and an insult offered to the prevailing morality or habit of life, we may assume that we are in the

*"A Utopian novel of the day" does not, of course, give anything like an adequate notion of the book's importance in the political culture of Russia. Dostoyevsky chose his antagonist with the precision that was characteristic of him, for Chernyshevsky, who thought of himself as the heir of the French Enlightenment, by his one novel exercised a decisive influence upon the Russian revolutionaries of the next two generations, most notably upon Lenin, who borrowed its title for one of his best-known pamphlets and whose moral style was much influenced by the character Rakhmetov. This paragon of revolutionists, although very fond of the luxury in which he was reared, embraces an extreme asceticism because, as he says, "We demand that men may have a complete enjoyment of their lives, and we must show by our example that we demand it, not to satisfy our personal passions, but for mankind in general; that what we say we say from principle and not from passion, from conviction and not from personal desire." Only one pleasure is proof against Rakhmetov's iron will—he cannot overcome his love of expensive cigars.

presence of the intention to destroy specious good, that we are being confronted by that spirituality, or the aspiration toward it, which subsists upon violence against the specious good.

The most immediate specious good that a modern writer will seek to destroy is, of course, the habits, manners, and "values" of the bourgeois world, and not merely because these associate themselves with much that is bad, such as vulgarity, or the exploitation of the disadvantaged, but for other reasons as well, because they clog and hamper the movement of the individual spirit toward freedom, because they prevent the attainment of "more life." The particular systems and modes of thought of the bourgeois world are a natural first target for the modern spirituality. But it is not hard to believe that the impulse to destroy specious good would be as readily directed against the most benign socialist society, which, by modern definition, serves the principle of pleasure.

In the characteristically modern conception of the spiritual life, the influence of Dostoyevsky is definitive. By comparison with it, the influence of Nietzsche is marginal. The moral and personal qualities suggested by a particular class, the aristocracy, had great simple force with Nietzsche and proposed to his imagination a particular style of life. Despite the scorn he expressed for liberal democracy and socialist theory as he knew them, he was able to speak with sympathy of future democracies and possible socialisms, led to do so by that element of his thought which served to aerate his mind and keep it frank and generous—his awareness of the part played in human existence by the will to power, which, however it figures in the thought of his epigones and vulgarizers, was conceived by Nietzsche himself as comprising the whole range of the possibilities of human energy, creativity, libido. The claims of any social group to this human characteristic had weight with him. And he gave ready credence to the pleasure that attends one or another kind of power; if he was quick to judge people by the pleasures they chose—and woe to those who preferred beer to wine and *Parsifal* to *Carmen*!—the principle of pleasure presented itself to him as constituting an element of the dignity of man. It is because of this humanism of his, this naturalistic acceptance of power and pleasure, that Nietzsche is held at a distance by the modern spiritual sensibility. And the converse of what explains Nietzsche's relative marginality explains Dostoyevsky's position at the very heart of the modern spiritual life.

If we speak of spirituality, we must note that it is not only humanism that is negated by the Underground Man but Christianity as well, or at least Christianity as western Europe understands it. For not only humanism but the Christianity of the West bases reason upon pleasure, upon pleasure postponed and purified but analogous in kind to worldly pleasure. Dostoyevsky's clerk has had his way with us: it would seem to be true that, in the degree that the promises of the spiritual life are made in terms of pleasure—of comfort, rest, and beauty—they have no power over the modern imagination. If Kafka, perhaps more than any other writer of our time, lends the color of reality to the events of the spiritual life, his power to do so lies in his characterizing these events by unpleasure, by sordidness and disorder, even when, as in *The Castle*, the spiritual struggle seems to yield a measure of success. He understood that a divinity who, like Saint Augustine's, could be spoken of as gratifying all the senses, must nowadays be deficient in reality and that a heaven which is presented to us as well ordered, commodious, beautiful—as *luxurious*—cannot be an object of hope. Yeats tells us that "Berkeley in his youth described the summum bonum and the reality of Heaven as physical pleasure, and thought this conception made both more intelligible to simple men." To simple men perhaps, but who now is a simple man? How far from our imagination is the idea of "peace" as the crown of spiritual struggle! The idea of "bliss" is even further removed. The two words propose to us a state of virtually infantile passivity which is the negation of the "more life" that we crave, the "more life" of spiritual militancy. We dread Eden, and of all Christian concepts there is none we understand so well as the *felix culpa* and the "fortunate fall"; not, certainly, because we anticipate the salvation to which these Christian paradoxes point, but because by means of the sin and the fall we managed to escape the seductions of peace and bliss.

My first intention in trying to make explicit a change in the assumptions of literature which everybody is more or less aware of has been historical and objective. But it must be obvious that my account of the change has not been wholly objective in the sense of being wholly neutral. It asks a question which is inevitably adversary in some degree, if only by reason of the irony which is implicit in the historical approach to a fact of moral culture. It suggests that the modern spirituality, with its devaluation of the principle of pleasure, because it came into being at a particular time, may be regarded as a contingent and not a necessary mode of thought. This opens the way to regarding it as a mode of thought which is "received" or "established" and which is therefore, like any other received or established mode of thought, available to critical scrutiny.

And that possibility is by no means comfortable. We set great store by the unillusioned militancy of spirit which deals violently with the specious good. Upon it we base whatever self-esteem we can lay claim to—it gives us, as one of D. H. Lawrence's characters says of it (or something very much like it), our "last distinction"; he feels that to question it is a "sort of vulgarity."* To what end, with what intention, is it to be questioned? Can an adversary scrutiny of it point away from it to anything else than an idiot literature, to "positive heroes" who know how to get the good out of life and who have "affirmative" emotions about their success in doing so? The energy, the consciousness, and the wit of modern literature derive from its violence against the specious good. We instinctively resent questions which suggest that there is fault to be found with the one saving force in our moral situation—that extruded "high" segment of our general culture which, with its exigent, violently subversive spirituality, has the power of arming us against, and setting us apart from, all in the general culture that we hate and fear.

Then what justification can there be for describing with any degree of adversary purpose the diminished status of the principle of pleasure which characterizes this segment of our culture?

Possibly one small justification can be brought to light by reference to a famous passage in the *Confessions* of Saint Augustine, the one in which Augustine speaks of an episode of his adolescence and asks why he entered that orchard and stole those pears. Of all the acts of his unregenerate days which he calls sinful and examines in his grim, brilliant way, there is none that he nags so persistently, none that seems to lie so far beyond the reach of his ready comprehension of sin. He did not steal the pears because he was hungry. He did not steal them because they were delicious—they were pears of rather poor quality, he had better at home. He did not steal them to win the admiration of the friends who were with him, although this comes close, for, as he says, he would not have stolen them if he had been alone. In all sin, he says, there is a patent motivating

*Gerald Crich, in Chapter XXIX of *Women in Love*.

desire, some good to be gained, some pleasure for the sake of which the act was committed. But this sin of the stolen pears is, as it were, pure—he can discover no human reason for it. He speaks again of the presence of the companions, but although their being with him was a necessary condition of the act, it cannot be said to have motivated it. To the mature Augustine, the petty theft of his youth is horrifying not only because it seems to have been a sin committed solely for the sake of sinning, but because, in having no conceivable pleasure in view, it was a sort of negative transcendence—in effect, a negation—of his humanity. This is not strange to us—what I have called the extruded high segment of our general culture has for some time been engaged in an experiment in the negative transcendence of the human, a condition which is to be achieved by freeing the self from its thralldom to pleasure. Augustine's puzzling sin is the paradigm of the modern spiritual enterprise, and in his reprobation of it is to be found the reason why Dostoyevsky condemned and hated the Christianity of the West, which he denounced as, in effect, a vulgar humanism.

To be aware of this undertaking of negative transcendence is, surely, to admire the energy of its desperateness. And we can comprehend how, for the consumer of literature, for that highly developed person who must perforce live the bourgeois life in an affluent society, an aesthetic ethos based on the devaluation of pleasure can serve, and seem to save, one of the two souls which inhabit his breast. Nearly overcome as we are by the specious good, insulted as we are by being forced to acquire it, we claim the right of the Underground Man to address the "gentlemen" with our assertion, "I have more life in me than you have," which consorts better with the refinement of our sensibility than other brags that men have made, such as "I am stronger than you," or "I am holier than thou." Our high culture invites us to transfer our energies from the bourgeois competition to the spiritual competition. We find our "distinction"—last or penultimate—in our triumph over the miserable "gentlemen," whether they are others or ourselves, whether our cry be, "I have more life in me than you have" or "I have more life in me than I have."

Now and then it must occur to us that the life of competition for spiritual status is not without its own peculiar sordidness and absurdity. But this is a matter for the novelist—for that novelist we do not yet have but must surely have one day, who will take into serious and comic account the actualities of the spiritual career of our time.

More immediately available to our awareness and more substantive and simple in itself is the effect which the devaluation of pleasure has upon the relation between our high literature and our life in politics, taking that word in its largest possible sense. There was a time when literature assumed that the best ideals of politics were naturally in accord with its own essence, when poetry celebrated the qualities of social life which had their paradigmatic existence in poetry itself. Keats's *Poems* of 1817 takes for its epigraph two lines from Spenser which are intended to point up the political overtone of the volume: "What more felicity can fall to creature/Than to enjoy delight with liberty." Even when Wordsworth is deep in Toryism and Stoic Christianity, it is natural for him to assert the Utopian possibility.

> Paradise and groves
> Elysian, Fortunate Fields—like those of old
> Sought in the Atlantic Main—why should they be
> A history only of departed things,
> Or a mere fiction of what never was?

He goes on to say categorically that these imaginations may become, at the behest of rationality and good will, "a simple produce of the common day." But the old connection between literature and politics has been dissolved. For the typical modern literary personality, political life is likely to exist only as it makes an occasion for the disgust and rage which are essential to the state of modern spirituality, as one particular instance of the irrational, violent, and obscene fantasy which life in general is, as licensing the counter-fantasy of the poet.

In a recent essay,* William Phillips described in an accurate and telling way the division that has developed between modern literature and a rational and positive politics, and went on to explain why, for literature's sake, the separation must be maintained. "It now looks," Mr. Phillips said, "as though a radical literature and a radical politics must be kept apart. For radical politics of the modern variety has really served as an antidote to literature. The moral hygiene, the puritanism, the benevolence—all the virtues that sprout on the left—work like a cure for the perverse and morbid idealism of the modern writer. If writing is to be thought of as radi-

*"What Happened in the 30's," *Commentary*, September 1962.

cal, it must be in a deeper sense, in the sense not simply of cutting across the grain of contemporary life but also of reaching for the connections between the real and the forbidden and the fantastic. The classic example is Dostoyevsky."

The situation that Mr. Phillips describes will scarcely be a matter of indifference to those of us who, while responding to the force of the perverse and morbid idealism of modern literature, are habituated to think of literature and politics as naturally having affinity with each other. We cannot but feel a discomfort of mind at the idea of their hostile separation, and we are led to ask whether the breach is as complete as Mr. Phillips says it is. His description, it seems to me, so far as it bears upon the situation of the moment, upon the situation as it presents itself to the practitioner of literature, needs no modification. But if we consider the matter in a more extended perspective, in the long view of the cultural historian, it must occur to us to speculate—even at the risk of being "hygienic"—whether the perverse and morbid idealism of modern literature is not to be thought of as being precisely political, whether it does not express a demand which in its own way is rational and positive and which may have to be taken into eventual account by a rational and positive politics.

If we do ask this question, we will be ready to remind ourselves that the devaluation of the pleasure principle, or, as perhaps we ought to put it, the imagination of going *beyond the pleasure principle*, is, after all, not merely an event of a particular moment in culture. It is, as Freud made plain in his famous essay, a fact of the psychic life itself. The impulse to go beyond the pleasure principle is certainly to be observed not only in modern literature but in all literature, and of course not only in literature but in the emotional economy of at least some persons in all epochs. But what we can indeed call an event in culture is that at a particular moment in history, in our moment, this fact of the psychic life became a salient and dominant theme in literature, and also that it has been made explicit as a fact in the psychic life and forced upon our consciousness by Freud's momentous foray into metapsychology. And this cultural event may indeed be understood in political terms, as likely to have eventual political consequences, just as we understood in political terms and as having had political consequences the eighteenth-century assertion that the dignity of man was to be found in the principle of pleasure.

We deal with a change in quantity. It has always been true of some men that to pleasure they have preferred unpleasure. They imposed upon themselves difficult and painful tasks, they committed themselves to strange, "unnatural" modes of life, they sought out distressing emotions, in order to know psychic energies which are not to be summoned up in felicity. These psychic energies, even when they are experienced in self-destruction, are a means of self-definition and self-affirmation. As such, they have a social reference—the election of unpleasure, however isolate and private the act may be, must refer to society if only because the choice denies the valuation which society in general puts upon pleasure; and of course it often receives social approbation in the highest degree, even if at a remove of time: it is the choice of the hero, the saint and martyr, and, in some cultures, the artist. The quantitative change which we have to take account of is this: what was once a mode of experience of a few has now become an ideal of experience of many. For reasons which, at least here, must defy speculation, the ideal of pleasure has exhausted itself, almost as if it had been actually realized and had issued in satiety and ennui. In its place, or, at least, beside it, there is developing—conceivably at the behest of literature!—an ideal of the experience of those psychic energies which are linked with unpleasure and which are directed toward self-definition and self-affirmation. Such an ideal makes a demand upon society for its satisfaction: it is a political fact. It surely asks for gratification of a sort which is not within the purview of ordinary democratic progressivism.

What I have called the spirituality of modern literature can scarcely be immune to irony, and the less so as we see it advancing in the easy comprehension of increasing numbers of people, to the point of its becoming, through the medium of the stage and the cinema, the stuff of popular entertainment—how can irony be withheld from an accredited subversiveness, an established moral radicalism, a respectable violence? But although the anomalies of the culture of the educated middle class do indeed justify an adversary response, and perhaps a weightier one than that of irony, a response that is nothing but adversary will not be adequate.

We often hear it said nowadays, usually by psychoanalysts and by writers oriented toward psychoanalysis, that the very existence of civilization is threatened unless society can give credence to the principle of pleasure and learn how to implement it. We understand what is meant, that repressiveness and oppression will be lessened if the principle of pleasure is established in our social arrangements, and we readily assent. Yet secretly we know that the formula does not satisfy the condition it addresses itself to—it leaves out of account those psychic energies which press beyond the pleasure principle and even deny it.

It is possible to say that—whether for good or for bad—we confront a mutation in culture by which an old established proportion between the pleasure-seeking instincts and the ego instincts is being altered in favor of the latter.* If we follow Freud through the awesome paradoxes of *Beyond the Pleasure Principle*, we may understand why the indications of this change should present themselves as perverse and morbid, for the other name that Freud uses for the ego instincts is the death instincts. Freud's having made the ego instincts synonymous with the death instincts accounts, more than anything else in his dark and difficult essay, for the cloud of misunderstanding in which it exists. But before we conclude that *Beyond the Pleasure Principle* issues, as many believe, in an ultimate pessimism or "negation," and before we conclude that the tendencies in our literature which we have remarked on are nothing but perverse and morbid, let us recall that although Freud did indeed say that "the aim of all life is death," the course of his argument leads him to the statement that "the organism wishes to die only in its own fashion," only through the complex fullness of its appropriate life.

---

*See the remarks on tragedy in "On the Teaching of Modern Literature" (p. 381) and also Lionel Abel's brilliant chapter on tragedy in *Metatheatre*. For a full and detailed account of the modern devaluation of that good fortune the destruction of which once pained us in tragedy, see Thomas Munro, "The Failure Story: A Study of Contemporary Pessimism," *The Journal of Aesthetics and Art Criticism*, Vol. XVII, No. 2, December 1958.

James Joyce in His Letters

1967

In 1935, near the end of a long affectionate letter to his son George in America, James Joyce wrote: "Here I conclude. My eyes are tired. For over half a century they have gazed into nullity, where they have found a lovely nothing."

It is not a characteristic utterance. Joyce was little given to making large statements about the nature of existence. As Dr. Johnson said of Dryden, he knew how to complain, but his articulate grievances were not usually of a metaphysical kind. They referred to particular circumstances of practical life, chiefly the lets and hindrances to his work; at least in his later years, such resentment as he expressed was less in response to what he suffered as a person than to the impediments that were put in his way as an artist.

And actually we cannot be certain that Joyce did indeed mean to complain when he wrote to George of his long gaze into *"nulla"*—his letters to his children were always in Italian—or that he was yielding to a metaphysical self-pity when he said he had found in it *"un bellissimo niente."* The adjective may well have been intended not ironically but literally and Joyce can be understood to say that human existence is nullity right enough, yet if it is looked into with a vision such as his, the nothing that can be perceived really *is* lovely, though the maintenance of the vision is fatiguing work.

To read the passage in this way is in accord with our readiness nowadays to see Joyce as pre-eminently a "positive" writer, to be aware of the resistance he offered to nullity through his great acts of creation. From the famous climactic epiphany of *A Portrait of the Artist as a Young Man*, in which life "calls" in all imaginable erotic beauty and is answered in ecstasy, he went on to celebrate human existence even in the pain, defeat, and humiliation that make up so large a part of its substance. He consciously intended Molly Bloom's ultimate "Yes" as a doctrinal statement, a judgment in life's favor made after all the adverse evidence was in. He contrived a rich poetry out of the humble and sordid, the sad repeated round of the commonplace, laying a significant emphasis on the little, nameless, unremembered acts of kindness and of love—it is much to the point that Joyce as a young man could speak of Wordsworth in superlative praise, for much of the power of his own work derives from the Wordsworthian purpose of discovering a transcendence by which life, in confrontation with nullity, is affirmed.

But this does not tell the whole story of the relation in which Joyce stood to nullity. He was not only resistant to it but also partisan with it. He loved it and sought to make it prevail. The transcendent affirmation of hypostatized life went along with a profound indifference, even a hostility, to a great many of the particularities in which the energies of life embody themselves. He could speak in thrilling archaic phrase of "the fair courts of life" yet the elaborations of developed society were for the most part of no account to him, and to much of the redundancy of culture as it proliferates in objects and practices that are meant to be pleasing he was chiefly apathetic. His alienation from so many of the modes and conditions of human existence is sometimes chilling.

Among life's processes, that of entropy makes an especial appeal to Joyce. The "paralysis" which is represented in *Dubliners* as the pathology of a nation at a particular moment of its history was also known to him as a general condition of life itself, and if he found it frightening, he also found it tempting. *Dubliners* does indeed have the import of social criticism that its author often said it was meant to have. This "chapter in the moral history" of his nation levels an accusation to which the conscience of his race, when at last it will have been forged in the smithy of his soul, must be sensitive. But if the devolution of energy to the point of "paralysis" is, in a moral and social view, a condition to be deplored and reversed, it is also for Joyce a sacred and powerful state of existence. The attraction it had for him is nearly overt in the first story of *Dubliners*, "The Sisters," and in the last, "The Dead." "The special odor of corruption which, I hope, floats over my stories" is the true scent by which life is to be tracked to its last authenticity. It is not without reason that Samuel Beckett is often said to have represented Joyce in the Hamm of *Endgame*, the terrible blind storyteller who presides over the quietus of Nature, himself on the verge of extinction but grimly cherishing and ordering what little life remains, setting against the ever-encroaching void, which he himself has helped bring about, an indomitable egoism that is itself an emptiness.

The power of Joyce's work derives, we must see, not only from the impulse to resist nullity but also, and equally, from the impulse to make nullity prevail. Something of the destructive force was remarked by T. S. Eliot when, taking tea with Virginia Woolf and trying to convince his hostess that *Ulysses* was not to be dismissed as the work of one or another kind of "underbred" person, he characterized the author's achievement and the magnitude of his power by saying that his book "destroyed the whole of the nineteenth century." Eliot meant that Joyce by his radical innovations of style had made obsolete the styles of the earlier time, and also that, as a result of or in concomitance with the obsolescence that Joyce had effected, the concerns and sentiments to which the old styles were appropriate had lost their interest and authority. In 1922 the nineteenth century was not in high repute and one might suppose that the report of its having been killed would make an occasion for hope: with the old concerns and sentiments out of the way, those of the new day might be expected to flourish. But Eliot expressed no such expectation. Although he took it to be part of the great achievement of *Ulysses* that it had shown up "the futility of all the English styles," he went on to say that Joyce had destroyed his own future, for now there was nothing left for him to write about. Nor for anyone else: Eliot later said that with *Ulysses* Joyce had brought to an end the genre of the novel.

If there is truth in Eliot's observation, a phrase of Walter Pater's helps us understand what concerns and sentiments of the nineteenth century Joyce may be said to have killed. In a famous paragraph of the Conclusion to *The Renaissance*, Pater spoke of "success in life." It doesn't matter that he was saying that success in life was the ability to burn with a hard gemlike flame, to make all experience into an object of aesthetic contemplation. The point is that, at the high moment of his exposition of a doctrine directed against crass practicality, Pater could use a phrase that to us now can seem only vulgar, a form of words which scarcely even stockbrokers, headmasters, and philistine parents would venture to use. In the nineteenth century a mind as exquisite and detached as Pater's could take it for granted that upon the life of an individual person a judgment of success or failure might be passed. And the nineteenth-century novel was in nothing so much a product of its time as in its assiduity in passing this judgment.

It was of course moral or spiritual success that the novel was concerned with, and this "true" success often—though not always—implied failure as the world knows it. But a characteristic assumption of the novel was that the true success brought as much gratification as conventional opinion attributed to worldly success, that it was just as real and nearly as tangible. The conception of moral or spiritual achievement was, we may say, sustained and controlled by the society from whose conventions the triumph was wrested. The houses, servants, carriages, plate, china, linen, cash, credit, position, honor, power that were the goods of the conventional world served to validate the goods of the moral or spiritual life. At the heart of the novel is the idea that the world, the worldly world, Henry James's "great round world itself," might have to be given up in the interests of integrity or even simple decency. What made this idea momentous was the assumption that the surrender is of something entirely real, and in some way, in the forcible way of common sense, much to be desired. Upon the valuation of what is given up depends much of the valuation of what is gotten in exchange. Poor Julien Sorel! Poor Pip! Poor Phineas Finn! It was a dull-spirited reader indeed who did not feel what a pity it was that the young man could not make a go of Things As They Are and at the same time possess his soul in honor and peace. But since the soul was one of the possible possessions, it was of course to be preferred to all others, the more because the price paid for it was thought real and high. In the degree that the novel gave credence to the world while withholding its assent, it established the reality of the moral or spiritual success that is defined by the rejection of the world's values.

Credence given, assent withheld: for a time this position of the novel *vis-à-vis* the world was of extraordinary interest. At a certain point in the novel's relatively short history, in the first quarter of this century, there burst upon our consciousness a realization of how great had been its accomplishment, how important its function. It was on all sides seen to be what Henry James in effect said it was, what D. H. Lawrence explicitly called it, "the book of life."

Yet no sooner had the novel come to this glory than it was said, not by Eliot alone, to have died. In all likelihood the report is true. The question of the viability of the novel today is probably to be answered in the spirit of the man who, when asked if he believed in baptism, replied that of course he did, he had seen it performed many times. Novels are still ceaselessly written, published, reviewed, and on occasion hailed, but the old sense of their spiritual efficacy is ever harder to come by. One thing is certain: to whatever purposes the novel now addresses itself, it has outgrown the activity which, in the nineteenth century and in the early days of the twentieth, was characteristic of the genre, virtually definitive of it, the setting of the values of the moral and spiritual life over against the values of the world. This is a confrontation that no longer engages our interest. Which is by no means to say that getting and spending are not of great moment, or that moral and spiritual sensibility have declined. As to the latter, indeed, it flourishes in a way that is perhaps unprecedented—it may well be that never before have so many people undertaken to live enlightened lives, to see through the illusions that society imposes, doing this quite easily, without strain or struggle, having been led to the perception of righteousness by what literature has told them of the social life. Whatever we may *do* as persons in the world, however we behave as getters and spenders, in our other capacity, as readers, as persons of moral sensibility, we *know* that the values of the world do not deserve our interest. We know it: we do not discover it, as readers once did, with the pleasing excitement that the novel generated as it led toward understanding. It is a thing taken for granted. That the world is a cheat, its social arrangements a sham, its rewards a sell, was patent to us from our moral infancy, whose first spoken words were, "Take away that bauble."

So entirely, and, as it were, so naturally do we withhold our assent from the world that we give it scarcely any credence. As getters and spenders we take it to be actual and there; as readers our imagination repels it, or at most accepts it as an absurdity. What in the first instance is a moral judgment on the world intensifies and establishes itself as a habit of thought to the point where it transcends its moral origin and becomes a metaphysical judgment.

More and more the contemporary reader requires of literature that it have a metaphysical rather than a moral aspect. Having come to take nullity for granted, he wants to be enlightened and entertained by statements about the nature of nothing, what its size is, how it is furnished, what services the management provides, what sort of conversation and amusements can go on in it. The novel in some of its experimental and theoretical developments can gratify the new taste, but this is more easily accomplished by the theater, which on frequent occasions in its long tradition has shown its natural affinity for ultimate and metaphysical considerations. By means of the irony which it generates merely through turning a conscious eye on its traditional devices of illusion, the theater easily escapes from its servitude to morality into free and radical play with the nature of existence as morality assumes it to be. That life is a dream, that all the world's a stage, that right you are if you think you are—such propositions can be forcibly demonstrated by the theater, which, defined by its function of inducing us to accept appearance as reality, delights in discovering in itself the power of showing that reality is but appearance, in effect nothing.

At least at one point in his life Joyce rated drama above all literary forms and made what he called the "dramatic emotion" the type of the "aesthetic emotion" in general. With the metaphysical potentialities of drama he was not concerned in an immediate way, but his famous account of the "dramatic emotion" has an obvious bearing upon the theater's ability to control, even to extirpate, the credence given to the worldly reality. Dedalus explains to Lynch that this emotion is "static," that it is brought into being by the "arrest" of the mind. "The feelings excited by improper art are kinetic, desire and loathing. Desire urges us to possess, to go to something; loathing urges us to abandon, to go from something. The arts which excite them, pornographical or didactic, are therefore improper arts. The aesthetic emotion (I use the general term) is therefore static. The mind is arrested and raised above desire and loathing."

Nothing, of course, could be further from the aesthetic of the novel in its classic phase. The novel was exactly, in Joyce's sense of the words, both pornographical and didactic, having the intention to generate desire and loathing, to urge the possession of the good, the abandonment of the bad. Assuming the prepotency of the will, the novel sought to educate and direct it by discriminating among the objects to which it might address itself. But Joyce characteristically represents the will in entropy, in its movement through ambiguity and paralysis to extinction. In *Ulysses*, for example, the objects of desire or intention of virtually all the characters are either of no great moment as the world judges, or they exist in unrealizable fantasy, or in the past.

There is one exception. The will of one person is represented as being, although momentarily in abeyance, on the point of becoming prepotent, and its object is represented as both capable of attainment and worth attaining: Stephen Dedalus means to become a great writer and we know, of course, that he does. The will of the artist is accepted in all its legendary power and authority, fully licensed. And the worldly traits of the particular artist Stephen Dedalus are entirely acknowledged—his bitter intention of fame, his pride, his vanity, his claim to unique personal superiority, touched with class feeling, his need to be ascendant in every situation. Yet the world to which these traits refer, that world to which Yeats—the admirer of Balzac!—gave so lively a recognition, in which the artist wins his prizes, has no existence in *Ulysses*. On the evidence that the book provides, there is nothing that can signalize the artist's achievement of success in life. There is no person, let alone a social agency, component and empowered to judge his work and tell him that he has triumphed with it, that he has imposed his will upon the world and is now to be feared and loved. The honor he deserves cannot be accorded him, since the traditional signs of honor are wanting—there is no fine house to inhabit, no comfort or elegance that can gratify his heroic spirit after strenuous days, no acclaim or deference appropriate to his genius. His prepotent will lifts him above the primitive life, the everlasting round of birth, copulation, and death, making him peerless: his only possible peers are a certain few of the pre-eminent dead, among whom God is one, on the whole the most congenial of the small company. It is chiefly in emulation of the work of this particular colleague that Joyce undertakes his own creation, intending that his book shall be read as men formerly "read" the "book of the universe." In his eyes a thousand years are as but a day, or the other way around, and the fall of the sparrow does not go unnoticed. The round of birth, copulation, and death receives his sanction under the aspect of eternity and in the awful silence of the infinite spaces, and his inscrutable but on the whole affectionate irony is directed upon all that men contrive in their cities for their survival, with a somewhat wryer glance toward what they contrive for their delight. Who that responds to the subtle power of his work can ever again, as a reader, give serious thought to the appointments of the house, the ribbon in the buttonhole, the cash in the bank and the stocks in the portfolio, the seemliness of the ordered life, the claims of disinterested action (except as they refer to certain small dealings between one person and another, especially between father and child), the fate of the nation, the hope of the future? And however else we read *Finnegans Wake*, we cannot fail to understand that it is a *contra-Philosophie der Geschichte*, that its transcendent genial silliness is a spoof on those figments of the solemn nineteenth-century imagination—History, and World Historical Figures, and that wonderful Will of theirs which, Hegel tells us, keeps the world in its right course toward the developing epiphany of *Geist*.

But if Joyce did indeed kill the nineteenth century, he was the better able to do so because the concerns and sentiments he destroyed made so considerable a part of the fabric of his being. To read his letters as we now have them is to be confirmed in our sense of his denial of the world, but it is also to become aware that what is denied was once affirmed with an extraordinary intensity. It is to understand how entirely Joyce was a man of the century in which he was born, how thoroughgoing was his commitment to its concerns and sentiments, how deeply rooted he was in its ethos and its mythos, its beliefs and its fantasies, its greedy desires, its dream of entering into the fair courts of life.

In 1957 Stuart Gilbert brought out a volume called *Letters of James Joyce* which gave us most, though not all, of the letters that were available at the time. Taken as a whole, the collection proved disappointing. It included relatively few letters of the early years, always likely to be the most interesting period of a writer's correspondence; by far the greater number date from the years of maturity, beginning at a time when, although not yet famous, Joyce was already a figure, and of these a great many are devoted to business in the unremitting and often trifling detail in which Joyce carried it on. Nothing that bears upon Joyce's life can fail to command attention, but there is not much in Mr. Gilbert's collection that goes beyond the well-known public aspects of the career to make the appeal of intimacy.

It is true that some reviewers remarked on a quality of warmth and gaiety that they found in the letters and on how much more "human" this showed Joyce to be than had hitherto been supposed. By his middle years Joyce had developed a talent, if not for friendship, then at least for friendliness; whatever else his friends may have been to him, they were his aides, adjutants, and ambassadors, and in the letters in which he did business with them and through them there sounds a note of geniality, often of a whimsical kind, which, as the reviewers noted, is at variance with what is often reported of his forbidding reserve. But it is possible to feel that the genial air is rather *voulu*, even contrived,* and at least one reviewer put the matter of the "humanness" in a qualified way—Philip Toynbee said no more than that the letters "reveal a far less inhuman man than the myth had led us to believe." They may be thought to reveal a man who, out of his sense of what is seemly, or perhaps for reasons of policy, wished to conceal the full extent of his "inhumanness," of his detachment from the affections. On the evidence of the first published letters only one event of his middle age seems ever actually to have reached Joyce, his daughter's extreme mental illness. Even here the *apatheia* is to some degree in force, in part through the self-deception as to the true state of affairs that Joyce practiced, although we are in no doubt about the bitterness of his grief.† For the rest, the personal life seems to have been burned out, calcined. The difficulties of the once-obsessing marriage appear to have been settled one way or another and no new erotic interests are to be discerned. The dialectic of temperament has come to an end—there are scarcely any indications of an interplay between the self and the life around it, the existence of which is recognized only as the world rejects or accepts Joyce's art.

Immediately after the appearance of Mr. Gilbert's collection there came to light a great trove of Joyce's letters, preserved through many vicissitudes. They were available to Richard Ellmann in the research for his definitive life of Joyce, and Professor Ellmann has edited them with the erudition and intelligence that make his biography the superlative work it is. The two collections have been conjoined to make a new *Letters of James Joyce* in three volumes, of which Mr. Gilbert's is now Volume I, Professor

---

*The letters to Frank Budgen are exceptional in suggesting Joyce's actual enjoyment of a relationship with another person.

†Joyce's long refusal to recognize the seriousness of Lucia's condition was abetted by the doctors, who, whether out of ignorance or compunction, seem never to have offered a firm diagnosis.

Ellmann's Volumes II and III. The arrangement is anomalous and of course awkward, since the collections cover the same span of time although in different degrees of completeness. But the practical nuisance should not be exaggerated. The Joyce scholars are inured to worse difficulties than those to which the arrangement subjects them. And the general reader will inevitably conclude that Volumes II and III make the corpus of the *Letters* to which Volume I serves as a supplement. His conclusion will be based not merely on the greater scope of the later volumes but on the extent of their interest, which is beyond comparison with that of their predecessor.

The letters of the mature years that are given in Professor Ellmann's collection do not change in any decisive way the impression made by those of Volume I, although they do modify it in some respects. It turns out not to be true, for example, that there are no moments of crisis in the marriage after the removal to Paris. In 1922 Nora Joyce went off to Ireland with the children, threatening that she would not return. Joyce writes in desperate appeal to "my darling, my love, my queen," telling her that the check for her fur is on the way, that he will live anywhere with her so long as he can be "alone with her dear self without family and without friends. Either this must occur or we must part for ever, though it will break my heart." He goes on to report in detail his "fainting fit in Miss Beach's shop," and concludes: "O my dearest, if you would only turn to me even now and read that terrible book which has now broken the heart in my breast* and take me to yourself alone to do with me what you will!"

The substance of the marital correspondence at forty is not different from that of the twenties: the same belief in the importance of gifts, especially of fur; the extravagant demand for devotion made through the avowal of infantile weakness; the plea to be dealt with ruthlessly in his total and pathic dependence. But as compared with the earlier letters of similar import that we now have, the energy of this one seems but dutiful, almost perfunctory. It appears early in Volume III and is the last expression not only of erotic feeling but of strong personal emotion of any kind.

From here on, the new letters of the later years are at one with those of the 1957 collection in suggesting that, however powerful Joyce's cre-

---

*Even two years later Nora had not yet consented to read *Ulysses*.

ative will continued to be, his affective will had been outlived. *"Only dis-connect!"* had long been an avowed principle of his life, but not until now had it been put fully in force. It is true that the paternal tenderness and solicitude do not abate, that the form of courteous geniality is main-tained, that an enterprise of helpfulness is not precluded, such as involved Joyce with the career of the tenor Sullivan, and we must suppose that some other magnetism in addition to that of his genius drew many peo-ple to his service. But nothing in the ordinary way of "humanness" con-tradicts our sense that the letters of the years of fame were written by a being who had departed this life as it is generally known and had become such a ghost as Henry James and Yeats imagined, a sentient soul that has passed from temporal existence into nullity yet still has a burden of en-ergy to discharge, a destiny still to be worked out.

We are tempted to deal with the uncanny condition by bringing it into the comfortable circle of morality. Joyce's disconnection from the world, we may want to say, is the ground of his indomitable courage, be-fore which we stand in awed admiration. The man who had ventured and won so much with *Ulysses* now pushes on with *Finnegans Wake* under the encroaching shadow of blindness and to the disapproval of his patron and virtually all his supporters: how else save by a disconnection amounting to "inhumanness" can he pursue the enterprise? Or our moralizing takes the adversary tack and notes the occasions when the disconnection issues in an ugly coarseness of behavior in regard to others. Joyce, who con-cerned himself with every detail of the promotion of his own books and enlisted everyone he could in the enterprise, when asked to support one of the posthumous novels of Italo Svevo, whose work he admired, not only refuses the request but sneers at the very idea of literary publicity. When his daughter-in-law, Giorgio's first wife, suffers an extreme mental collapse, he writes of the disaster in anger and describes the deranged conduct with contemptuous bitterness.

Eventually, however, we come to feel that no moral judgment can re-ally be to the point of Joyce's state of being in his latter years. And psy-chology seems as limited in its pertinence as morality. It is inevitable that psychological speculation will be attracted to the often strange and ex-treme emotional phenomena that the new letters record, especially to what the early ones tell us of the extravagant energy of affective will that was to devolve into the disconnection from the world, the existence in nullity. Neither Joyce's representation of himself as Dedalus, nor Professor Ellmann's detailed account of his youthful temperament, nor yet the two taken together quite prepare us for the intimacy and violence of Joyce's early relation to the world, the urgency with which he sought to requisition the world's goods. And certainly the devolution (if that is the word) from this early egotism of the world to the later egotism of nullity is a biographical event that asks for explanation. But however brilliant and even true may be the insights into the disposition of the internal forces that brought it about, they will fail to do justice to its significance, which is finally not personal but cultural. The process recorded by the letters proposes itself as a paradigm of the nineteenth-century will *in extremis*. It leads us to reflect less on what transpired in the life of James Joyce than on what could formerly happen and cannot happen again— never in our time will a young man focus this much power of love and hate into so sustained a rage of effectual intention as Joyce was capable of, so ferocious an ambition, so nearly absolute a commitment of himself to himself.

Joyce was of course not exceptional in being a continuator of the titanism of the nineteenth-century artistic personality. The literary culture of the first quarter of the twentieth century is differentiated from that of our own time by nothing so much as the grandiosity, both in purpose and in achievement, of its pre-eminent figures. In this respect their sense of life is alien from ours and is not uncommonly felt to alienate them from us. In one point of temperament, in the unremitting energy of their inner-direction, they have a closer affinity with their nineteenth-century predecessors than with their successors. But as compared with Joyce, none of the great modern chieftains of art put himself so directly and, as one might say, so *naïvely*, in the line of the powerful personalities of the age before his own. None so cherished the purpose of imposing himself upon the world, of being a king and riding in triumph through Persepolis.

If Joyce did indeed derive the impetus to his achievement from his acceptance of the ethos and mythos of the nineteenth century, a first salient example is his response to an idea that we take to be characteristic of the ideology of the period, the idea of the nation. One of the best-known things about Joyce is his ambivalence toward Ireland, of which the hatred was as relentless as the love was unfailing. With this passionate relation-

ship his lust for pre-eminence and fame is bound up, and the more so because his erotic life is intricately involved with it. He is twenty-seven and
on his first visit to Dublin after his exile and he is writing to Nora, telling
her of the part she plays in his inspiration. "My darling," he says, "tonight
I was in the Gresham Hotel and was introduced to about twenty people
and to all of them the same story was told: that I was going to be the
great writer of the future in my country. All the noise and flattery around
me hardly moved me. I thought I heard my country calling to me or
her eyes were turned toward me expectantly." He goes on to tell Nora
that she is more important to him than the world and that everything
comes from her. But in his thought of fame he cannot separate her from
the nation, the "race": "O take me into your soul of souls and then I will
indeed become the poet of my race." And among the things he has loved
in her—"the image of the beauty of the world, the mystery and beauty of
life itself . . . the images of spiritual purity and pity which I believed in as
a boy"—there are "the beauty and doom of the race of whom I am a
child." He calls her "my love, my life, my star, my little strange-eyed Ireland!"

And yet, of course, "I loathe Ireland and the Irish. They themselves
stare at me in the street though I was born among them. Perhaps they
read my hatred in my eyes." The hatred was of the essence of his ambition
quite as much as the love. Three years later he is again in Dublin and he
writes: "The Abbey Theatre will be open and they will give plays of Yeats
and Synge. You have a right to be there because you are my bride and I
am one of the writers of this generation who are perhaps creating at last a
conscience in the soul of this wretched race."

Some considerable part of Joyce's ambition consisted of what the
nineteenth century called aspiration and conceived to be a mode of feeling peculiarly appropriate to generous minds, artists perhaps especially
but also soldiers, statesmen, engineers, industrialists. Aspiration was the
desire for fame through notable and arduous achievement. The end in
view which defined it was the realization of one's own powers. That in order to reach this end one might be involved in competition with others,
seeking to surpass and overcome them, was a frequent but accidental circumstance of aspiration which was not thought to qualify its noble disinterestedness. That this is a reasonable way of looking at the matter is
suggested by the astonishing letter the nineteen-year-old Joyce addressed

to Ibsen. He makes a full and grandiose communication of his admiration and then goes on to say to the sick old man, "Your work on earth draws to a close and you are near the silence. It is growing dark for you." But there is a comfort that he can offer, the assurance that One—an unnamed but unmistakable One—comes after to carry on the great work. It is in all conscience a crueller letter than the young writer chose to know, yet the competition with the Father, the Old King, is sanctioned not only by tradition but by the very nature of life, and Joyce invests it with an absurd but genuine nobility by which the Master Builder, after a wince or two, might well have been grimly pleased.

But Joyce's competitiveness, which was extreme, was not always, not characteristically, in the grand style; as it showed itself in his relations with his age-mates it was often vindictive and coarse. Through all the early years in Trieste and Rome, Joyce lived in bitter jealous hatred of his former friends and companions in Dublin. He cannot mention them and their little successes without an expression of disgust: "Their writings and their lives nauseate [me] to the point of vomiting." The new letters make clear to how great an extent Joyce in his youth conceived of his art as a weapon to be used in personal antagonism, especially in vengeance. "Give me for Christ' sake a pen and an ink-bottle and some peace of mind and then, by the crucified Jaysus, if I don't sharpen that little pen and dip it into fermented ink and write tiny little sentences about the people who betrayed me send me to hell." The chief object of his bitterness, of course, was Gogarty, from whom, after the quarrel, he would accept no tender of reconciliation. It was his belief that the man who had so terribly offended him sought to make peace out of fear of how he would be delineated— the belief finds expression in the first chapter of *Ulysses*: "He fears the lancet of my art as I fear that of his. Cold steelpen."—and as early as 1905 it was assumed by Joyce's Dublin friends that a great revenge was in train; the form it would take was already known. "[Elwood] says," writes Stanislaus Joyce, "he would not like to be Gogarty when you come to the Tower episode. Thanks be to God he never kicked your arse or anything." Gogarty himself had every expectation that revenge would be duly taken, and Joyce coolly confirmed him in this; he reports that in refusing Gogarty's attempt to renew the friendship, he had said: "I bear you no ill will. I believe you have some points of good nature. You and I of 6 years ago are both dead. But I must write as I have felt!" To which Gogarty replied, "I don't care a damn what you say of me so long as it is litera-ture."*

The unremitting bitterness with which Joyce remembered and com-memorated his relation with Gogarty serves to remind us of the great au-thority that the ideal of male friendship formerly had. In this, as in so many other respects, the nineteenth century maintained its connection with the courtly cultures of earlier epochs. Out of the dream of the true friend arose the possibility of the false friend, and it is an element of the *Heldenleben*, as the nineteenth century understood the genre, that the hero is beset by treacherous comrades envious of his powers and eager to subvert them. Had these dwarfish natures been lacking in the actuality of his life, Joyce would have been quick to supply the want. His genius throve upon his paranoia, which was capable of anything—it is quite in his style to say in an early letter to Lady Gregory that the college authori-ties were determined that he should not study medicine, "wishing I dare say to prevent me from securing any position of ease from which I might speak out my heart." A belief in a hostile environment, in persecution and personal betrayal, was necessary to his mission. But in point of fact the false friends and the malice of their envy were real enough; they were fos-tered by Dublin life before they were cherished by Joyce as a condition of his art and the testimony of his being a dedicated spirit, singled out. Long before Joyce had anything like a career his promise of genius was taken for granted by those who knew him, and Stanislaus's diary records the envy with which he was regarded by his contemporaries. In his early days of exile, when his thoughts turned homeward, it was to inquire what these lesser impotent beings said of his courage, his freedom, his uncon-ventional marriage, and, as time passed, his approach to success. Their mischievous impulses in relation to him came fully to light in the strange episode of his friend Cosgrove telling him, falsely and seemingly out of the gratuitous impulse to play Iago to this Othello, that before the elope-

*In the event this proved not to be true—Gogarty cared many a damn when *Ulysses* appeared. As well he might, if only because Joyce led all the world to believe forever that he and not Gogarty-Mulligan was the rightful tenant of the tower and that the famous key was his: any statement of the fact of the matter, that the opposite was the case, will always be received with surprise and in-credulity and soon forgotten. Such is the power of the literary imagination in the service of self-justification. Partisans of simple justice—alas, there are virtually none of Gogarty—may find some encouragement in the display of the actual lease in the tower; that a signboard calls the tower James Joyce's should not dismay them: the rights of the ultimate possession are now ab-solute.

ment Nora had been unfaithful to him, a communication that for a time had all its intended effect of making chaos come again.

The social life of late nineteenth-century Dublin as Joyce's class situation permitted him to know it was obviously in most respects quite elementary, but it was certainly not wanting in concern with social status, in judging who was "better" and stood higher than whom, and to such questions the young Joyce gave the most solemn attention. It was surely an important circumstance of the last interview with Gogarty that it took place in Gogarty's elaborate house and that the former friend, now set up in medical practice, well-to-do and well married, should have invited Joyce to come with him in his motorcar to have lunch in his country home. The social advantages that Gogarty had previously enjoyed, perhaps especially his having gone to Oxford, were of the greatest moment to Joyce, who was at constant pains to enforce the idea that, when it came to social establishment, Stephen Dedalus, if the truth were seen, was the superior of anyone.* Joyce was in nothing so much a man of the nineteenth century as in the sensitivity of his class feelings. No less than Dickens he was concerned to be a *gentleman* and he was as little shy as Dickens about using the word, the Victorian force of which maintained itself for at least two of the Joyces in the face of the family's rapid downward mobility. In the midst of an expression of disgust with his situation at Rome James remarks to Stanislaus, "I feel somehow that I am what Pappie said I wasn't [,] a gentleman."† He was at the time working in a bank as a correspondence clerk; he lived with his wife and infant son in a single small room; often his wages did not meet his weekly expenses and the letters of the period are chiefly to Stanislaus in Trieste, their whole burden being that money must be sent at once. The conversation of his fellow clerks, as

---

*In the tower scene Mulligan tells Stephen, "You know, Dedalus, you have the real Oxford manner." And he speculates that this is why Haines, the Englishman who is staying with them, can't make Stephen out. Haines is rich and himself an Oxford man and Mulligan twice remarks that he thinks Stephen isn't a gentleman.

†The occasion of the judgment was John Joyce's reading *Gas From a Burner*. Stanislaus seems not to have shared the social feelings of his father and elder brother. Perhaps it was his puritanical rationalism that led him to adopt a rather plebeian stance. The youngest surviving Joyce brother, Charles, apparently laid no continuing claim to being a gentleman; when last we hear of him he is a postal clerk in London. The idea of social status was part of the fabric of the Joyce family life—it is well known how preoccupied John Joyce was with the superiority of his own family to his wife's, which of course had some bearing on James's choice of a wife whose pretensions to breeding were notably less than his own.

he describes it, is simian; he has no ordinarily decent social intercourse with anyone, yet he finds it in his heart to describe his circumstances not as unfit for a human being but as unfit for a gentleman.

His feeling for the social forms could be strict, often in a genteel, lower-middle-class way. Although in 1910 black-edged writing paper was still used by proper people in a period of mourning, the faintly barbaric custom was not universally observed, but Joyce, at the death of his uncle John Murray, thought it necessary to his sense of how things should be done.* When he was virtually starving during his first sojourn in Paris, he regretted that he could not attend the Irish Ball because he had no dress suit. He is still working as a Berlitz teacher in Trieste and the family in Dublin is on the verge of destitution, but he directs his father to arrange to sit for his portrait. The family crest was his treasured possession.

At the present time feelings about class in their old form are in at least literary abeyance and it is hard to remember the force they once had and the extent to which they defined the character and aspirations of the artist.† In an age when the middle classes seemed to be imposing their stamp upon the world, a young writer was led to set store by what he imagined to be the aristocratic qualities of grace, freedom, and indifference to public opinion, and the aristocratic mode of life seemed the model for what all men's lives should be. It was the rare writer who did not think himself to be "well born" in some sense of the phrase, and if he had any reason to think that he was actually of distinguished blood, he was pretty sure to find the circumstance of value. George Moore said no more than the simple truth when he remarked that "Yeats's belief in his lineal descent from the great Duke of Ormonde was part of his poetic equipment." Writing in admiration of Tolstoy, Joyce associates his genius with his class position and his ability to remember "the Christian name of his great-great-grandfather." And the young man who felt himself excluded from the patrician literary circle of Dublin and expressed his re-

---

*Joyce took account in *Ulysses* of his response to the claims of funeral pomp. "He can't wear them," Mulligan says when his offer of a pair of gray trousers has been refused by Dedalus because he is in mourning for his mother. "Etiquette is etiquette. He kills his mother but he can't wear gray trousers."

†A few years ago I had occasion to remark in an essay that my students, no matter what their social origins, were not prevented by Yeats's snobbery from responding to his poetry. One reviewer took me sternly to task for obscuring the transcendent achievement of the great poet by speaking of him as a snob. What made especially interesting the view of life and letters implied by the rebuke was that the reviewer was Leon Edel, the biographer of Henry James.

sentment in rude mockery of its members shared Yeats's dream of the culture—the word is Joyce's own—of the great houses and the ancient families. Writing to Nora, who had been a chambermaid in a Dublin hotel
when he had first met her and whose lack of grammar he was not above
mocking to his brother, he explains to her the inspiration of *Chamber
Music*: "You were not in a sense the girl for whom I had dreamed and
written the verses you now find so enchanting. She was perhaps (as I saw
her in my imagination) a girl fashioned into a curious grave beauty by the
culture of generations before her, the woman for whom I wrote poems
like 'Gentle Lady' or 'Thou leanest to the shell of night.' " He goes on,
surely in entire sincerity: "But then I saw that the beauty of your soul out-
shone that of my verses. There was something in you higher than anything I had put into them. And so for this reason the book of verses is for
you. It holds the desire of my youth, and you, darling, were the fulfillment of that desire." Yet the discrepancy between the robust, barely literate chambermaid who had to be told not to copy her love-letters out of a
letter-book and the girl fashioned into a curious grave beauty by her lineage was often a pain to Joyce, and much as he needed Nora's earthy
strength, he flinched at the rudeness—so he called it—that went with it.
It was certain that he was a gentleman, but whatever else Nora was, she
was, alas, no lady.

That Joyce's preoccupation with his social status should go along with
an avowed interest in subverting the society in which he held his valued
rank does not make a contradiction. It was quite common in the nineteenth century for gifted men to find sanction for their subversive intentions toward society in such aristocracy or gentility as they could claim.*
But that Joyce should ever have been political at all will for most of his
readers make an occasion for surprise. For a few years of his young manhood, between the ages of twenty-two and twenty-five, Joyce called himself a socialist. Again and again in his letters to Stanislaus he insists on the
importance to the artist of a radical political position: "I believe that Ibsen and Hauptmann separate from the herd of writers because of their
political aptitude—eh?" "It is a mistake for you to imagine that my political opinions are those of a universal lover: but they are those of a social-
istic artist." He scolds Stanislaus for not sharing his "detestation of the
stupid, dishonest, tyrannical and cowardly burgher class." He explains the

*This was especially true of the anarchists in Russia, France, and Italy.

opposition of the Church to "the quite unheretical theory of socialism" as being an expression of the belief that a socialist government would expropriate ecclesiastical "landed estates . . . and invested moneys." His cogent objection to the Irish nationalist movement is that it takes no account of economic realities and is not aware that "if the Irish question exists, it exists for the Irish proletariat chiefly." And it is a further black mark against Gogarty that his political views exclude economic considerations. "Gogarty would jump into the Liffey to save a man's life but he seems to have little hesitation in condemning generations to servitude."*

Joyce never committed himself to political action or association, and although he had a knowledgeable interest in the Italian radical parties, he seems never to have put himself to the study of socialist theory; the only reference to Karl Marx occurs in the course of an excited and rather confused account of the apocalyptic Jewish imagination derived from Ferrero's *Young Europe*. By 1907 his socialism had evaporated, leaving as its only trace the sweet disposition of Leopold Bloom's mind to imagine the possibility of rational and benevolent social behavior and the brotherhood of man. This, however, is a residue of some importance in the history of literature: it makes *Ulysses* unique among modern classics for its sympathy with progressive social ideas.

In one of his early poems Yeats speaks of the places where men meet "to talk of love and politics." To us at our remove in time the conjunction of the two topics of conversation seems quaint, for of course by love Yeats did not mean the rather touching interfusion of *eros* and *agape* that young people have lately come to use as a ground of social and political dissidence: he meant a love much more personal and egotistic, that ultimate relation between a man and a woman the conception of which had descended from courtly love, the "gay science" of the late Middle Ages, to become one of the powerful myths of the nineteenth century. Its old force has greatly diminished, perhaps to the point of extinction. No matter how gravely and idealistically we may use our contemporary names for the relation between a man and a woman, "sex" and "marriage," and even the phrase that is a vestige of the old name, "in love with," do not suggest, as "love" did for an age in whose sensibility *Tristan and Isolde* occupied a central position, the idea of life realized and transfigured by the erotic

---

*Joyce's disgust with Gogarty on political grounds was made the more intense by Gogarty's anti-Semitism.

connection, fulfilled by its beauty, sustained by the energy and fidelity that constituted its ethos.* In the nineteenth century, politics was a new activity of free spirits and it naturally found affinity with a conception of love that made large promises of perceptivity, liberty, and happiness. Love was understood to be art's true source and best subject, and those who lived for love and art did harm to no one, lived the right life of humanity: so Tosca in a passion that reaches B-flat informs the tyrant Scarpia. The operatic example is much in point, for opera was the genre in which love and political virtue joined hands to make a lyric affirmation of life. The contemptuous indifference in which opera is held by our intellectual culture is not qualified by recognition of its political tendency. For Joyce, as everyone knows, opera was a passion. With a most engaging simplicity he gave the genre the response it asked for; he found it, as people used to say, ravishing. He would have been astonished and dismayed by the contemporary snootiness to Puccini; he held *Madama Butterfly* to be a work of transcendent beauty and power, most especially the aria *"Un bel dì"* which at one period seems to have woven itself into the very fabric of his emotional life; when Butterfly sang the "romance of her hope" of what would come to her over the sea, his soul (as he wrote bitterly to Nora, who was not similarly moved) "sway[ed] with languor and longing": in the face of the harshness of circumstance, life is affirmed in erotic ecstasy, as when, in *A Portrait of the Artist*, Stephen has sight of the girl on the strand, gazing out to sea. For Joyce, as still for many men of the time in which he was young, human existence was justified by the rapture—lost archaic word!—of love.

Perhaps nothing in Joyce's life is more poignant and more indicative of the extent to which his imagination was shaped by the mythos of his time than the episode, on the threshold of his middle age, in which the famous vision of the lovely girl standing with high-kilted skirts at the water's edge, the most grandiose of the epiphanies, seemed to have presented itself as an attainable actuality. Martha Fleischmann was a young woman, seemingly Jewish, though not so in fact, beautiful, provocative, but apparently not disposed to go beyond elaborate flirtation, whom Joyce came to know in Zurich in the autumn of 1918. As Martha recalled their meeting nearly a quarter of a century later, the scene stands all ready

---

*For an account of what *Tristan and Isolde* meant to the epoch, see Elliot Zuckermann's admirable *The First Hundred Years of Wagner's Tristan* (New York, 1964).

for the librettist. She was coming home "one evening at dusk" when a passerby stopped and looked at her "with an expression of such wonder on his face that she hesitated for just a moment before entering the house." The stranger spoke, explaining his astonishment by saying that she reminded him of a girl he had once seen "standing on the beach of his home country."* Martha's erotic temperament was ambiguous to a degree. She had a devoted "guardian," as she called him, and he expressed jealousy of her relation with Joyce, but there is some question as to whether her connection with this man was sexual in any ordinary sense of the word. On one occasion Joyce addressed her as "Nausikaa," signing himself "Odysseus,"† and it would seem that the Gerty MacDowell of the "Nausikaa" episode of *Ulysses* commemorates her genteel narcissism and sentimentality. Joyce's own erotic disposition at this time was scarcely of a more direct kind. His lust, like Mr. Bloom's, was chiefly of the eye and the mind. What seems to have been the climactic assignation of these two fantasts of love took place in Frank Budgen's studio on 2 February, which was Joyce's birthday and the feast of Candlemas, and Joyce borrowed from a Jewish friend a *Menorah* so that he might gaze on Martha's beauty by candlelight, perhaps the sole intention of the meeting.‡ With the passage of years the exquisite virgin, *La Princesse lointaine*, came to be represented in the great "Nausikaa" episode as nothing more than the sad, silly figment of ladies' magazines, and the dream of love-and-beauty as an occasion of masturbation. But at the time his feelings for Martha seemed to Joyce to challenge comparison with Dante's for Beatrice and Shake-

*The quoted passages are from Professor Straumann's account of his interview with Martha when, in Zurich in 1941, she called to inquire about selling the four letters and the postcard that Joyce had written to her. Professor Straumann did not make the purchase on that occasion, but he did so at a later time, in 1943, when, Martha being ill, her affairs were in the charge of her sister—at least he bought the letters; the postcard had vanished. Professor Straumann's account of the relationship of Martha and Joyce appears as a preface to the letters as given in Volume II, pp. 426–36; it is less full and circumstantial than Professor Ellmann's earlier account in his biography.

†The salutation and the subscription were, Professor Straumann says, the whole message of the lost postcard.

‡Candlemas commemorates the purification of the Virgin Mary and the presentation of Christ in the Temple. "The blessing of candles is now the distinctive rite of this day. . . . Beeswax candles, which are blessed, distributed, and lit whilst the Nunc Dimittis is sung, are carried in a procession commemorating the entrance of Christ, the 'True Light' (cf. Jn. 1.9) into the Temple."—*The Oxford Dictionary of the Christian Church.* In his second letter to Martha, remarking on his impression that she was a Jewess, Joyce says, "If I am wrong, you must not be offended. Jesus Christ put on his human body: in the womb of a Jewish woman."

speare's for the Dark Lady; at least he meant them to. "And through the night of the bitterness of my soul," he wrote in the last of his letters to Martha, "the kisses of your lips fell on my heart, soft as rosepetals gentle as dew," and concludes, "O rosa mistica [*sic*], ora pro me."

One of the four letters is mutilated—we are told that Martha "tore off the lower right-hand edge of the second sheet . . . because it contained what she considered an indelicate expression." The judgment on the offending word or phrase cannot be set aside out of hand as one of Martha's neurotic gentilities. The chances are that Joyce did actually write an indelicacy, even an obscenity, for his concern that the erotic object and situation be of an extreme refinement and beauty went together with a no less exigent desire for all that is commonly thought to sully, besmirch, and degrade the erotic activity, and he derived a special pleasure from expressing this desire in writing.

The dialectic between the essential innocence and the essential shamefulness of the sexual act has in our time lost much of its old force, at least overtly. If nowadays we obey the command of Blake's Los to "Consider Sexual Organization," it does not seem naturally to follow, as the demiurge thought it would, that we "hide . . . in the dust" for shame. Crazy Jane's observation that love has pitched his mansion in the place of excrement is received as an interesting reminder of the actual state of affairs rather than as the expression of a distressing (or exciting) thought in the forefront of consciousness. The words of Yeats's poem echo those of another divine utterance in *Jerusalem*: "For I will make their places of love and joy excrementitious," but the circumstance as Yeats refers to it is not conceived to be a curse: we understand Yeats to be remarking on an anomaly that makes human existence more complex and difficult than his long celebration of the *Rosa Mystica* would suggest, or more "ironic," or more "tragic," but for that reason more substantive and the more interesting. His sense of the shameful arrangements of the erotic life stands midway between the neutralizing view of them that our contemporary educated consciousness seems determined to take and the eager response to them made by Joyce, for whom shame was a chief condition of sexual fulfillment.

In the course of the two visits he made to Ireland in 1909, Joyce in his letters to Nora ran through the whole gamut of his erotic emotions and in full voice. Within a week of his first arrival in Dublin, Cosgrove imparted the news of Nora's double dealing in the betrothal time, and although the false friend spoke only of kisses, Joyce of course imagined more and questioned whether Nora had actually come to him a virgin—"I remember that there was very little blood that night. . . ."—and whether Giorgio is in truth his son. He is shattered by the dreadful revelation—"I shall cry for days"—but a fortnight has not passed before he can report blandly that everything has been cleared up by Byrne's having said that Cosgrove's tale is "all a 'blasted lie' "; and after having called himself a "worthless fellow," he vows to be "Worthy of your love, dearest," and goes on to speak of a shipment of cocoa he has sent, that same cocoa that he later urges Nora to drink a good deal of so that she will increase the size of "certain parts" of her body, pleasing him by becoming more truly womanly. His marital resentments are bitter and explicit: Nora, whose great fault is her rudeness, had called him an imbecile, had disagreed with his expressed opinion that priests are disgusting, had been indifferent to *"Un bel di"*; his apologies, when his recriminations have proved offensive, are abject. He is much given to expressions of tender and poetic regard and is engagingly proud of the courtly ingenuity of a gift of jewelry he has designed and had executed, a necklace of gold links, five cubes of old ivory and an ivory plaque bearing in ancient lettering words from one of his poems, which is to symbolize the lovers' years together and their sadness and suffering when they are divided; his Christmas present is *Chamber Music* copied out of his own hand on parchment, bound with his family crest, on the cover the lovers' interlaced initials. But his lively imagination of the elegances of love goes along with fantasies and solicitation that, as he says, make him the object of his own disgust and, he insists on supposing, of Nora's.

Professor Ellmann has not found it possible to carry out his intention of publishing in its entirety the group of obscene love-letters from Dublin preserved in the Cornell Library. What he is able to publish does indeed, as he says, suggest the tenor of these extraordinary documents (the adjective is Joyce's) but not the force and the strange dignity that they seemed to me to have when I read them at Cornell some years ago. It may be, of course, that my memory plays me false, but I recall the letters read in the completeness of the holograph as making the effect of having been written under a more driving compulsion, a more exigent possession, than appears in the curtailed printed version. Perhaps it was the holograph itself that contributed to the impressiveness, enforcing the situation in something like the awesomeness that Joyce himself felt it to have: the man who may well be the greatest literary genius of his age submits to the necessity of taking in hand his sacred cold steel pen and with it to sully sheet after virgin sheet of paper with the filthy words that express all that he feels in the way of delight at the dirtiness of his exalted nature. The words themselves have for him a terrifying potency. One of his letters has induced Nora in her reply to use what he can refer to in no other way than as "a certain word." The sight of it, he says, excites him terribly— "There is something obscene and lecherous in the very look of the letters. The sound of it too is like the act itself, brief, brutal, irresistible and devilish."

His longed-for perversities and depravities—we had best call them that without permissive apologies, since he thought of them so and we ought not deny the ground of his pleasure—were not of an especially esoteric kind. He expresses the wish to be flogged and not merely in show but fiercely, to the end of his feeling real pain; he blames himself for writing "filth" and instructs Nora, if she is insulted by it, to bring him to his senses "with the lash, as you have done before." Nora is an "angel" and a "saint" who guides him to his great destiny, and he longs to "nestle" in her womb, and he seeks to "degrade" and "deprave" her, he wants her to be insolent and cruel and obscene. Perhaps the controlling and to him most puzzling and most significant component of his polymorphous perversity is his delight in the excrementitiousness of the places of love and joy, what he called his "wild beast-like craving . . . for every secret and shameful part" of his wife's body, "for every odor and act of it." "Are you offended because I said I loved to look at the brown stain that comes behind on your girlish white drawers? I suppose you think me a filthy wretch."

No one, I think, will be so armored in objectivity as not to be taken aback by the letters. But their shocking interest fades as we become habituated to them, or to the idea of them. In the way of all drastic personal facts, especially in our time, they cease to be dismaying or amazing soon after they are brought into the light of common day and permitted to assume their institutional status—one might say their prestige—as biographical data. What does not fade, however, is the interest of the literary use to which Joyce put the erotic tendencies that the letters disclose and indulge.

To a reader of *Ulysses* nothing in the substance of the letters comes as a surprise. All the fantasies are familiar to us through our having made acquaintance with them in the mind of Leopold Bloom. But what exists in the mind of Mr. Bloom is of a quite different import from the apparently identical thing as it exists in the mind of James Joyce or might exist in the mind of his surrogate Stephen Dedalus. The reader of the letters will not fail to conclude that it required a considerable courage for Joyce to write them. His doing so went against the grain of a decisive and cherished part of his nature, his austere, almost priestly propriety. "As you know, dearest," he writes in one of the letters, "I never use obscene phrases in speaking. You have never heard me, have you, utter an unfit word before others. When men tell in my presence here filthy or lecherous stories I hardly smile." Yet he put on paper and sent through the mail what was not to be countenanced and, although he urged Nora to be watchful in guarding the secrecy of the letters, since he did not destroy them when he might have done so, he must be thought to have wished that they be preserved. One thing, however, he would not—could not—do: attribute the fantasies of the letters to the mind of Stephen Dedalus.

By assigning them to Mr. Bloom, he of course quite changes their character. As elements of Mr. Bloom's psyche, they become comic, which is to say morally neutral. Our laughter, which is gentle, cognizant, forgiving, affectionate, has the effect of firmly distancing them and at the same time of bringing them within the circle of innocence and acceptability. We understand that nothing very terrible is here, nothing awesome, or devilish, or wild-beast-like—only what we call, with a relishing domesticating chuckle, *human*. And the chuckle comes the more easily because we recognize in Mr. Bloom, as we are intended to, the essential innocence of the child; his polymorphous perversity is appropriate to his infantile state. This innocence, it would appear, is part of Joyce's conception of Jews in general, who, he seems to have felt, through some natural grace were exempt from the complexities of the moral life as it was sustained by Christians. Writing to Stanislaus of his son having been born early, with nothing prepared, he says, "However, our landlady is a Jewess and gave us everything we wanted." The implication is that a Christian might or might not have provided the necessary things; Christian kindness would result from the making of a choice between doing the good deed and not doing it, and would therefore, by the Aristotelian definition, be moral; but a Jewish good deed was a matter of instinct, natural rather than moral. It is in natural goodness rather than in morality that Mr. Bloom has his being, and in the ambience of his mind the perverse fantasies have nothing of the fearsome significance they had for Joyce when he entertained them.

It is possible to say that the translation of the fantasies as they existed in the mind of James Joyce, and might have existed in the mind of Stephen Dedalus, into what they become in the mind of Leopold Bloom is a derogation of Joyce's courage as an artist. A Stephen Dedalus whose rigorous moral being is assailed and torn by sinful desires is readily received as a heroic figure so long as the desires can be supposed sinful in a received way. But a polymorphous-perverse hero would make a difficulty, would be thought a contradiction in terms. For Joyce the Aristotelian categories of tragedy and comedy, the one showing men as "better," i.e., more dignified, than they really are, the other showing men as "worse," i.e., more ignoble, than they really are, had an authority that, at the time of *Ulysses*, was not to be controverted.

It is also possible to say that Joyce's refusal to assign the perverse fantasies to Stephen is a derogation of personal courage. A polymorphous-perverse Leopold Bloom stands as testimony to his author's astonishing powers of imagination, of sympathetic insight into the secret places of nature at the furthest remove from his own. But a polymorphous-perverse Stephen Dedalus must advertise the polymorphous perversity of the author whose fictive surrogate he is inevitably understood to be. To this personal disclosure Joyce could not consent.

His fictional disposition of the polymorphous perversity must make a salient question in any attempt to understand the mind of James Joyce. What I have called—with, I should make plain, no pejorative force—a derogation of courage is an answer that has a kind of provisional cogency. But a comment on the obscene letters made by Professor Ellmann in his Introduction seems to me to initiate an explanation that goes deeper. Professor Ellmann says of the letters that they have an "ulterior purpose," that Joyce, in writing them, had an intention beyond immediate sexual gratification. One thing he intended was "to anatomize and reconstitute and crystallize the emotion of love." And, Professor Ellmann says, "he goes further still; like Richard Rowan in *Exiles*, he wishes to possess his wife's soul, and have her possess his, in nakedness. To know someone else in love and hate, beyond vanity and remorse, *beyond human possibility almost* [my italics], is his extravagant desire."

If this is so, as I think it is, it brings the obscene letters into accord with what I have proposed as the controlling tendency of Joyce's genius—to move through the fullest realization of the human, the all-too-human, to that which transcends and denies the human. It was a progress he was committed to make, yet he made it with some degree of reluctance. Had the obscene fantasies been assigned to Stephen Dedalus, they would have implied the import that Professor Ellmann supposes they had for Joyce himself. But Joyce, we may believe, did not want, not yet, so Hyperborean a hero as he then would have had. The ethos and mythos of the nineteenth century could still command from him some degree of assent. The merely human still engaged him, he was not wholly ready to go beyond it. The fair courts of life still beckoned invitation and seemed to await his entrance. He was to conclude that their walls and gates enclosed nothing. His genius is defined by his having concluded this rather than taking it for granted, as many of the generation that came after him have found it possible to do.

Mind in the Modern World

1972

I

In 1946, in the last year of his life, H. G. Wells published a little book which is surely one of the saddest and possibly one of the most portentous documents of our century. Much of its sadness lies in how far it is from being a good book. Wells was old and ill and sunk in despair over the Second World War; he still wrote with his characteristic assertiveness, but he no longer commanded the lucidity which had marked his prose for fifty years, and this last utterance is neither orderly in its argument nor perspicuous in its expression. Yet it does communicate its informing idea, which is as heartbreaking as the incoherence in which it is set forth. Actually, the whole import of the essay is contained in its title, *Mind at the End of Its Tether*. With that weary and desperate phrase Wells repudiated his once passionately held belief that the human race might find salvation, which is to say happiness, in the right exercise of its mental powers.

The creed had been simple and unequivocal. If mind were cleared of its inherited illusions and prejudices, if it put itself to two tasks, that of perceiving the physical universe as it really is and that of comprehending its own nature, then what had long been accepted as the inevitable rule of harsh necessity might be overthrown and mankind would achieve the felicity which was both its immemorial dream and its clear evolutionary destiny. This expectation, once the root and ground of his thought, was now said by Wells to be false. He had come to see that the power of mind which mankind required not only for the winning of felicity but even for survival was not to be counted on. Mind was at the end of its tether.

It need scarcely be said that Wells's little book made no place for itself in the intellectual life of the quarter-century after it appeared. Nor would it have done so if its mode of discourse had more nearly approached a persuasive coherence. The war, which had led Wells to abandon all hope for mind and the human race, did not have a similar effect generally. In the face of the dreadful suffering the war had entailed, in the face, too, of the close approximation to success that had been made by the brutish antirational doctrine of Nazism, as well as of the unimaginable destructive power of the new weapons that mind had brought into being, the prevailing mood was one of chastened optimism, which involved the expectation that mind would play a beneficent part in human existence.

Yet now, in this year of 1972, as I say the title of Wells's book, *Mind at the End of Its Tether*, there will, I think, be some among us, and perhaps many, who will hear it with the sense that it has a chill appositeness to our present time. Of those who entertain an apprehension about the future of mind, there may be those who do so on Wells's absolute ground, that the tasks which are now imposed upon mind are beyond its inherent capabilities. Some will locate the cause of their anxiety in the paradoxes about the nature of mind which seem to be proposed by mind itself through the realization of its powers. Others are made uneasy by what they discern of a complex tendency of our contemporary culture to impugn and devalue the very concept of mind. Whichever way the foreboding points, I venture to believe that there will be no difficulty in understanding how it might happen that, as I first contemplated speaking under the bright aegis of the name and spirit of Thomas Jefferson, there should have arisen out of the depths of memory the dark portent of Wells's phrase.

Between Thomas Jefferson and H. G. Wells there was no affinity of personal temperament or of class tradition, and certainly none of political view. And although both men put the pursuit of happiness at the center of their speculations about man's existence, the meanings each of them attached to that enterprise were widely disparate. But they were at one in the firm confidence they placed in mind, Jefferson until his dying day,

Wells up to his last years. Historically speaking they stood in the same line.

In some respects this is a very long line indeed. It goes back to the philosophers of ancient Greece both in what might be called its aesthetic appreciation of mind, its admiration of the mental faculties almost for their own sake, apart from what practical ends they might achieve, and also in its assumption that mind can play a decisive part in the moral life of the individual person. In other respects its extent is relatively short, going back only to the Renaissance in its belief that what mind might encompass of knowledge of the physical universe has a direct bearing upon the quality of human existence, and also in its certitude that mind can, and should, be decisive in political life. In the eighteenth century, this belief established itself so firmly and extensively as to become the chief characteristic of the intellectual culture of the age.

When we consider the enthusiasm with which Jefferson assented to this master belief of his time and the assiduity with which he implemented it in the conduct of his own life, it is possible to make too much of his own mental endowment and by doing so to obscure one of the most important significances he has for us. Thus, if we apply to him the word "genius," we ought to use it, as he did, in the quiet, unassertive sense that prevailed in the eighteenth century, to mean distinguished ability, rather than in the sense it later came to have, that of a unique power, an originating power, which puts the person who possesses it into a class apart. A unique originating power of mind Jefferson did not in fact have. He was, for example, a devoted student of philosophy, and it is possible for scholars to write learned books on the philosophy of Thomas Jefferson, yet none of them asserts that Jefferson was, in the modern sense of the word, a genius of speculative thought. He did not give new answers to old questions or propose questions never asked before. He possessed himself of the ideas of the philosophical originators of his own time and of the past; he chose among these ideas and made use of them.

I make this point, it will be plain, not to depreciate Jefferson's native gifts of intellect but to describe their nature as he himself understood it. We may say that it was on the basis of this understanding that he conceived the place of mind in the future of the United States. He held the view, which was characteristic of the eighteenth century, that men were essentially equal in their mental faculties. This is not to say that all men have the same speed, or agility, or strength of mind, only that all men have reason and that the intellectual resources of a nation are invested not in a few but held in common.

Jefferson's estimate of the intellectual capability of the whole people is part of the fabric of American history. A great scholar of our past has traced in detail the long unhappy course of anti-intellectualism in American life, but Richard Hofstadter also made it plain to us, through his studies of higher education in the United States, how strong in our culture is the opposite tendency, to conceive of intellect as a cherished element of democracy. Of this tendency Jefferson is the presiding spirit. A sense of what he expected of the American people in the way of intellect may be readily gained from one detail of the plan of popular education which he set forth in 1783 in his *Notes on the State of Virginia*. He is speaking of the instruction that is to be given in the earliest of the three stages of schooling he proposed, not the primary skills of reading, writing, and figuring, which he takes for granted, but the substantive matter by which the minds of children are to be formed. This is to be, he says, "chiefly historical"—the memories of the pupils are "to be stored with the most useful facts of Greek, Roman, European, and American history." Consider what he understands to follow in the way of intellectual process: "History by apprising them of the past will enable them to judge the future; it will avail them of the experiences of other times and nations; it will qualify them as judges of the actions and designs of men."

I shall not pursue in further detail Jefferson's views on education as they illustrate his confidence in the mind of the people but shall allow this one project to speak for the whole. It can tell us much about the fortunes of mind in the course of two centuries. Jefferson hoped that most of the children who were to receive the instruction he envisaged would become farmers or be engaged in occupations connected with agriculture, and it seemed to him natural and right that men in this walk of life should have had their memories stored with "the useful facts of the past" against the day when, as citizens responsible for their own happiness, they would bring them to bear upon the events of their own time and place. The facts of the past were useful because they gave rise to ideas, and in ideas Jefferson perceived a power which would countervail the power of property and thus make for social equality in the Republic.

Scarcely anybody nowadays will judge Jefferson's plan to be beyond debate. Our contemporary pedagogic theory will be distressed by the idea of storing what it would call the mere memories of children with what it would call mere facts and, at that, facts about the conduct of the alien race of adults in far distant times and places, having nothing to do with the desires and instincts of children. And searching questions are sure to be raised about the present state of the subject which Jefferson makes pre-eminent in elementary education. It will be asked, for instance, whether his view of history was not, as compared with ours, a naïve one. He did, of course, understand that history might be biased, that party-interest might obscure or distort the facts. But he did not doubt that the facts were to be known and that the narrative of them, which they themselves would dictate to any honest mind, would be the truth and, as such, uni-tary and canonical. This belief the historiography of our day teaches us to regard with skepticism.

It can be said of Jefferson that his sense of the past was definitive of his intellectual life. From earliest youth into his old age the intense imag-ination of the past gave impetus to his mind—as, of course, it gave impe-tus to all the shaping minds of the eighteenth and nineteenth centuries. Voltaire, Diderot, Rousseau, Goethe, Hegel, Darwin, Marx, Freud—all were rooted in their sense of the past, from which derived the force with which they addressed themselves to the present. None of them could have imagined that event of our day which one eminent historian, Profes-sor J. H. Plumb, has called the "death of the past," that mutation of cul-ture, represented by Professor Plumb as following inevitably from the full development of industrial society, which makes the idea of the past supererogatory and, for many, nothing but limiting and obstructive.* This profound alteration of our culture is explicit in the ever-diminishing place that history is given in the curriculums of our schools and colleges. The efflorescence of mind in the two centuries before our own seems so closely bound up with the vivid imagination of the past that we are led to conclude that the urgent recollection of what man has already done and undergone in pursuit of his destiny is a necessary condition of compre-hending and intending mind. And if now we may be aware of a dimin-ished confidence in mind, of a disposition to withdraw our credence from it, we might conjecture that this is, if not a consequence, then at least a

The Death of the Past (Boston, 1969).

concomitance of our diminished awareness of the past, of our disaffection from history.

2

What mind is, and what it should be, and what part it ought to play in human existence became an issue of public policy at least as early as the eighteenth century. If we regard the history of Europe between the Puritan revolution of the seventeenth century in England and the yet more drastic revolution in France at the end of the eighteenth century, we cannot fail to be aware of a new element in the life of mankind—the ever-growing power of ideas. Professor Michael Walzer has said of the Puritan clergymen of England in the seventeenth century that they were "the first instance of 'advanced' intellectuals in a traditional society," that is to say, the first of a class of men who bring ideas, publicly expressed, to bear upon the nature of the polity, making it a question for debate how society should be constructed.* With the French Revolution this new element in human life reached a further development. Hegel said of the French Revolution that it was the first time in history that mankind recognized the principle that "thought ought to govern spiritual reality."

An early consequence of this new expectation of mind was that it gave rise to a certain coarseness of intellectual procedure—to what we call, with some adverse force, rationalism. To be rational, to be reasonable, is a good thing, but when we say of a thinker that he is committed to rationalism, we mean to convey a pejorative judgment. It expresses our sense that he conceives of the universe and man in a simplistic way, and often it suggests that his thought proceeds on the assumption that there is a close analogy to be drawn between man and a machine. This analogy, if for some it guaranteed optimism about the possibility of the control and direction of life, was for others the cause of an intense anxiety, as seeming to limit the freedom and dignity of man. To the principle of the machine the antagonists of rationalism opposed the principle of the organism, the view that man and his institutions are not designed and contrived but

---

*The Revolution of the Saints (Cambridge, Mass., 1965).

have their autonomous existence through the inherent laws of their growth and development.

The powerful cultural tendency to which we give the name Romanticism is defined by its effort to correct the theory of the mind which had become dominant in the eighteenth century. Opposing itself to what Pascal had called the "spirit of geometry," that is to say, the programmatic isolation of the cognitive process from feeling, imagination, and will, Romanticism insisted that these faculties were integral to any right conception of mind. Wordsworth's great autobiographical poem *The Prelude* gives the classic account of the damage done to the mind of the individual, to its powers of cognition no less than to its vital force, by the scientistic conception of mind that prevailed among intellectuals at the time of the French Revolution. The explanatory subtitle of the poem is "The Growth of the Poet's Mind"—for Wordsworth, the poet's mind was the normative mind of man. It grew, he said, not through the strengthening of its powers of analysis and abstraction but through the development of feeling, imagination, and will.

Wordsworth's attitude toward science has a peculiar pertinence to any canvass of the situation of mind in our own culture. One of the best remembered things about Wordsworth is the antagonism to science he expressed, but it is scarcely less characteristic of his thought that he did not consent to see the poetic mind and the scientific mind as being in final opposition to each other. On the contrary, he asserted that there was a natural affinity between them. "Poetry," he said, ". . . is the impassioned expression which is on the countenance of all science," and he predicted that the day would come when the discoveries of scientists would be "as proper objects of the Poet's art as any which can be employed." There was, however, one condition which he said must prevail before this happy state of affairs could come about—that the substance of science should become familiar to those who are not scientists. No one will suppose that this familiarity has been achieved. Physical science in our day lies beyond the intellectual grasp of most men. The newspapers inform us in a loose, general way of its great dramatic events. We have our opinions of its practical consequences, but its operative conceptions are alien to the mass of educated persons. They generate no cosmic speculations, they do not engage emotion or challenge imagination. Our poets are indifferent to them.

The old humanistic faith conceived science, together with mathematics, to be almost as readily accessible to understanding and interest as literature and history. Jefferson took this for granted. The belief that the fully developed man—the "whole man," as the phrase goes, or went—must have, and would want to have, *some* knowledge of science and mathematics was until recently taken for granted in the American theory of higher education and was implemented in the requirements of the curriculum. These requirements, it is well known, are undergoing severe attrition and in many colleges have been abolished. No successful method of instruction has been found, and the need for finding one no longer seems pressing, which can give a comprehension of science in its present state of development to those students who are not professionally committed to its mastery and especially endowed to achieve it.

This exclusion of most of us from the mode of thought which is habitually said to be the characteristic achievement of the modern age is bound to be experienced as a wound given to our intellectual self-esteem. About this humiliation we all agree to be silent, but can we doubt that it has its consequences, that it introduces into the life of mind a significant element of dubiety and alienation which must be taken into account in any estimate that is made of the present fortunes of mind?

But surely, it might be said, when it comes to the actual living of life this exclusion from science is not of decisive consequence. When Adam in *Paradise Lost* says that he wants to understand the mysteries of the cosmos, the archangel Raphael tells him not to puzzle his head over these abstruse matters and assures him that the "prime Wisdom" is to know "that which before us lies in daily life." The good sense of the angelic advice is confirmed when we consider that our scientific friends and colleagues do not seem any further advanced in the prime Wisdom than any of the rest of us. They see no more clearly than we do what lies before us in daily life.

But this reassurance loses some of its efficacy when we observe that, as compared with the relation in which we stand to physical science, most of us do not come any closer to the contemporary intellectual disciplines which address themselves to the affairs of daily life. Economics may serve as an example. In 1848, John Stuart Mill published his *Principles of Political Economy*. The book was at once a great popular success; over the next fifty years thirty-two editions of it appeared in England alone. The most widely read author of the day, whom Mill referred to as "that creature Dickens," wrote a novel, *Hard Times*, which undertook to demonstrate how deplorable were the human implications of Mill's views. John Ruskin, until then known only as a critic of art, attacked the assumptions of the work in a great series of essays which Thackeray published in his *Cornhill Magazine* until the outraged subscribers threatened to cancel. That is to say, Mill's treatise on economics entered into the general culture of its time; it was an object of the general intellect of the nation. We know that in our day no work of economic theory comparable to Mill's in completeness and authority could be similarly received, that any contemporary economist must think and write in terms which by their abstractness and technicality put his subject at a hopeless distance from the layman. In one or another degree this is true of the practitioners of the other social sciences.

In the humanistic disciplines the situation is similar. I have already spoken of the deteriorating status of history. Philosophy would appear to have become a technical subject for specialists and no longer consents to accommodate the interest and effort of any reasonably strong general intelligence. With my own discipline of literary study the case is somewhat more complicated. Over recent decades much of the study of literature has proceeded on the assumption—how it would have astonished Jefferson!—that literary works are not so readily accessible to the understanding as at first they might look to be, and there have developed elaborate and sophisticated methods for their comprehension which cannot but have tended to make literature seem an esoteric subject available only to expert knowledge. As long as twenty years ago some literary critics of high repute complained that the hyperactivity of criticism and scholarship had come to stand as a barrier between the ordinary reader and the literary work. This objection did not question the usefulness of literary study itself. On the contrary, it affirmed the faith in the inherent instructive power of literature which had long characterized American higher education. At the present time, however, that faith is being brought into ultimate question. Within the literature-teaching profession itself there is now a significant body of opinion which holds that literature, so far from having an educative power, can only obscure truth and impede virtue.

This view has been put forward by a person no less eminent in the profession than a recent president of the Modern Language Association, Professor Louis Kampf, who in his presidential address of 1971 assured his colleagues that the teaching of literature in American colleges is now virtually at its end, having lost all rational justification. Professor Kampf made reference to what he correctly takes to have been Matthew Arnold's shaping influence upon the literature-teaching profession in America. But he did not locate that influence in the part of Arnold's theory of literature where it truly resides, in the continuing force of the famous characterization of literature as "a criticism of life" and in Arnold's definition of criticism as the effort "to see the object as in itself it really is," the objects upon which it directs itself being not literature alone but also ideas in general and most especially ideas about society. Professor Kampf characterizes literature in a way that is at an opposite pole from Arnold's—literature, he says, is nothing but "a diversion and a spectacle," it exists wholly in what he calls the "realm of aesthetics" and thus stands at an ultimate remove from "practical activity." That is to say, it has no possible bearing upon the matters which must be the chief or only objects of concern, the anomalies and injustices of American life. Why, if the dereliction of literature from seriousness is this absolute, the totalitarian countries are so fearful of it Professor Kampf does not tell us. He is prepared, however, to name the exact moment when, after generations during which teachers were animated by their faith in the educative powers of literature, they came at last to understand that theirs was a commitment to a corrupting frivolity— the year was 1968, the occasion was the campus uprisings which, in Professor Kampf's view, at long last forced social and political reality upon the consciousness of students and teachers alike. Since 1968, Professor Kampf says, "the young go into the profession with dread; the old can scarcely wait for retirement; and those of the middle years yearn for sabbaticals." He speaks as the elected chief officer of the professional association of teachers of literature: in his estimate of the morale of his constituency there must be some quantum of truth. We can therefore say that in our time the mind of a significant part of a once proud profession has come to the end of its tether.

3

I have touched upon certain developments in the organized intellectual life of our day which may be thought to make an individual person's participation in it difficult or fruitless. But if it is indeed the case that an uneasiness has come into our relation to mind, we ought to consider whether this might not be something other than a response to particular alienating circumstances, whether it is not rather the expression of an attitude toward mind which is more nearly autonomous, an adverse judgment passed upon mind in its very essence.

It is a commonplace of our day to speak of crises of authority, and the glibness with which we use the phrase does not derogate from the salient actuality of what it denotes. One such crisis of authority, we might suppose, is taking place in relation to mind. Certainly a chief characteristic of mind is the claims which it makes, or which are made for it, to a very high authority indeed. Of these claims one goes so far as to identify mind with divinity itself, and it was once usual to express the idea of intellectual authority in terms which were explicitly analogous with social authority and the status pertaining to it. The classic example is Plato's account of mind, which asserts the superiority of thought to all other activities and represents it as free and noble while condemning physical occupations, however necessary and skilled, as mechanical and servile; in Plato's ideal polity all authority is vested in men of mind, the Philosopher-Kings. Aristotle can imagine the right development of individual mind as taking place only in men of high rank. The association of mind with social authority continues into modern times, when, however, the emphasis is placed upon the aggressive activity by which authority is achieved and asserted— in the nineteenth century the received way of praising mind was to connect it with the aristocratic-military ideal: we hear of "the march of mind," of "man's unconquerable mind," of "the imperial intellect," of "heroes of thought."

But at the end of the nineteenth century a voice was raised to say that mind in its traditional authoritative and aggressive character was so far from being in the service of mankind as actually to constitute a principle of social evil. The voice was that of William Morris in *News from Nowhere*, the enchanting romance in which he envisioned a society of perfect felicity. Two ideals were to be realized in Morris's utopia: one was equality; the other was rest, the cessation of all anxious effort. To this end Morris excluded science, philosophy, and high art from his community. His happy people occupy themselves with what he had elsewhere called the "lesser arts," those modest enterprises of the hand which produce useful and decorative objects of daily life. Morris wanted neither the aggressivity of comprehension and control which highly developed mind directs upon the world nor the competitiveness and self-aggrandizement which obtain among those individual persons who commit themselves to the life of thought and creation and which he associates with the worst traits of capitalist enterprise. He wanted no geniuses to distress their less notable fellows by their pre-eminent ability to tell the truth or be interesting, and to shine brighter than the general run of mankind, requiring our submission to the authority of their brilliance, disturbing us with novel ideas and difficult tastes, perhaps tempting some few to emulate them by giving up rest in order to live laborious days and incur the pains of mental fight. As Morris's young friend William Butler Yeats was to put it, mind says, "Thou fool," and Morris wanted no such divisive antiegalitarian manners in his society. He would not even allow teachers into it, justifying their exclusion by his certitude that anybody could learn all by himself all that he wanted and needed to know.

News from Nowhere has always been regarded with a sort of affectionate condescension—most readers have been charmed by its vision of unvexed life but have felt that its attitude toward mind made it impossible for them to take it seriously. We in our time will be less disposed to condescend to the book which eight decades ago stated the case against mind that is now being openly litigated in our culture. This adversary proceeding represents mind as having two maleficent effects. One is that the authority accorded to mind leads to the negation of social equality. The other is that mind works a personal deformation in those who commit themselves to its service.

That mind could be thought to make a principle of inequality would once have bewildered any man of good will and advanced views. Jefferson thought that it was virtually of the essence of mind that it pointed toward equality, and his system of education had the specific goal of countervailing the power of property by the power of ideas, which he assumed to be accessible to all men equally. Yet we must see that whatever inherent antagonism there may be between ideas and property, they are not in all respects dissimilar. Between ideas and one form of property, money, there is actually a close analogy to be drawn. At a certain point in history money began to play a part in society which can be thought of as ideational—in England in the late Renaissance, in a society in which the aristocratic land-owning class was prepotent, money had a disintegrating effect upon the nation's class structure and hence upon its moral and intellectual assumptions. As Shakespeare said in the famous speech in *Timon of Athens*, which Karl Marx found so apt to his own purpose, money has the power to bring into question every certitude and every piety. It was the ever-growing power of money that proposed and propagated equality as a social ideal. And then, to carry the analogy further, it can be said of ideas that they are, like money, a mobile and mobilizing form of property. They are, to be sure, accessible to all and held in common, but as they come to have power in the world, it is plain that a peculiar power or, at the least, status accrues to the individuals who first conceive them, or organize them, or make them public. Men of ideas, perhaps even more rapidly than men of money, move toward equality with men of birth. Voltaire, Rousseau, and Diderot appear on the eighteenth-century scene as sovereign princes of intellect.

This, of course, was not what Jefferson meant when he spoke of ideas as making for equality, nor was it what the French Revolution meant when it emblazoned the word on its banners. But with the exception of equality before the law, it was all that established society was ready for. Napoleon's maxim, "Careers open to talents," seemed in its time a quite sufficient, even a bold, definition of social equality. In 1856, Alexis de Tocqueville, the great historian of the modern ideal of equality and of its developing force in the world, judged England to be notably advanced over France in egalitarianism because in England it was not required that a man be of gentle lineage in order for him to be received into good society and full participation in the political and cultural life of the nation. In England there had long been growing up a strong mercantile, middle-class culture which celebrated the kind of man it called "self-made," who rose from humble or simple origins to wealth, status, and influence through his talents and efforts alone, beholden to no one. The careers of men of mind might follow the same course; the necessitous childhoods of such imposing figures as Michael Faraday, Thomas Carlyle, and Charles Dickens were part of their legend of glory. And as the professions proliferated and their practitioners grew in number, more and more careers were opened not only to transcendent talent but even to ordinary competence.

No one said that this was equality, only that it was equality of opportunity. In England it had created the class of gentlemen which Tocqueville admired because it seemed so effectual a means of preventing the revolutions which plagued France, but there was no disposition of English society to go further. Carlyle and Ruskin in their impassioned demands for social justice were quite explicit in excluding equality from its conception.

In 1876, when Arnold gave his famous lecture on equality before the Royal Institute, he observed that everyone in England repelled the idea of equality, and he went so far as to say that the English had "a religion of inequality," which accounted for what he judged to be the poor tone and style of the national life. Expectably enough, Arnold saw the cause of equality as being best served by the improvement and spread of the education available to the lower-middle and working classes, and in England in relatively recent times this has become an avowed national purpose, although its realization proceeds slowly by American standards. In America for more than a century higher education, to speak only of that, has spread among the population at an ever-accelerating rate, and nothing has so much confirmed the nation's happy certitude of its commitment to equality.

We know, of course, that this sanguine view of the equalizing potential of higher education no longer prevails in its old force. Indeed, in some quarters, it has given place to a view which holds that higher education is one of the citadels of social privilege. This change in opinion has led to a radically revised conception of the nature and function of our colleges and universities.

Up to a few years ago, when our colleges and universities were still generally thought to be a successful means of upward social mobility, this one of their imputed functions was allowed to remain at least partially tacit and they could still be viewed in the light of the ideal intellectual and cultural purpose which they traditionally avowed. Everyone was perfectly aware of their being a way to social advancement, but much of the complex interest they had for the American people, much of the esteem and even affection in which they were held, derived from the purposes of general enlightenment and humanization which they claimed, from their conceiving themselves to be in the service of disinterested mind. Now, however, with the rapidly developing opinion that our colleges and universities do not further equality to the extent that was once supposed, their equalizing function is being made fully explicit and the tendency grows ever stronger to say that they must be wholly defined by the function in which they are now said to fail. It is coming to be taken for granted that they are primarily agencies of social accreditation. They may still claim, though they do so ever less often and less firmly, that they are in the service of those ideals which are announced by the Latin mottoes on their corporate seals, ideals of "light" and "truth," but it is increasingly believed that their real duty is to enable as many people as possible to pass from a lower to a higher position in society. By an inevitable inference, the intellectual disciplines in which they give instruction are to be regarded not as of intrinsic value, but, at best, as elements of a rite of social passage and, at worst, as devices of social exclusion.

I think I do not exaggerate a view of our academic institutions which in recent years has become widely established. It scarcely need be said that such a view can lead to no practicable program of change, that serious thought about the nature and function of education in our society cannot proceed from its cynicism and intellectual nihilism. Yet we cannot fail to take gravely the extremity of its negation, understanding it to be the index of how bitterly felt is the *de facto* situation of inequality which does indeed exist in our system of higher education. If higher education is, among other things, an institutionalized means of upward social movement, it must be recognized that many members of our society are debarred from its process by reason of an ever more galling circumstance of their disadvantaged position, a limited acculturation and an early schooling of extreme inadequacy.

The redress of this state of affairs is imperative. To all appearances, our society's commitment to the correction of the inequality is genuine, even if, like all large commitments of any democratic society, it is not perfectly single-minded. And I think there can be no doubt that our colleges and universities themselves are especially active in moving toward it. Yet if we consider some of the assumptions on which the effort of redress has so far been made by our society through its government, we must see that they constitute telling evidence of that uneasy or ambivalent or actually disaffected relation to mind which has come to mark our culture. And no less significant in this respect is the silence of our colleges and universities about what is implied for their continuing life by the particular means our society has chosen to remedy the injustice.

I have in view the posture toward colleges and universities which of recent years has been taken by the Department of Health, Education, and Welfare. This, of course, does not bear directly upon the inaccessibility of higher education to the members of disadvantaged ethnic groups but upon the social situation that follows from it, the low representation of these ethnic groups in the academic profession. To this the Department of

Health, Education, and Welfare has responded with its directive that institutions of higher education which receive government funds shall move at once toward bringing about a statistically adequate representation on their faculties of ethnic minority groups.* The directive does not pretend that this purpose is to be accomplished without change in the standards of excellence of the academic profession. Since it is of the essence of the situation which is being redressed that certain ethnic groups, by reason of circumstances beyond their control, have not yet produced any large number of persons trained for the academic profession, the prescribed representations—the word "quota" is strenuously resisted by HEW—are to be achieved by the appointment of persons who are not competitively qualified but only equal in professional attainments to the least qualified person who in a given past period has been appointed to the academic unit in question.

To the general and ideal goal of this directive every person of good will is bound to give happy assent. And it is perhaps possible to find in its particular stipulations an arguable merit. It might be argued, for example, that if certain ethnic minorities are to enter the full stream of the nation's cultural life, a good way of bringing this about is simply to put them there. It might also be contended that for members of ethnic minorities who are students in colleges and universities, the process of their education will go better if members of their own groups, even if they have been appointed without particular regard to their academic qualifications, have some decisive part in it, offering by their mere presence a needed reassurance and hope. As against such cogency as these positions may be thought to have, it must nevertheless be urged that there will be serious adverse consequences for the academic profession if it is required to surrender an essential element of its traditional best sense of itself, its belief that no considerations extraneous to those of professional excellence

*The affirmative action program, as it is called, applies not only to certain ethnic groups but also to women. In the text of my lecture as it was delivered, the latter stipulation was included in my paraphrase of the program's directive. I omit it here because what I go on to say about the effect of the program on academic standards does not bear immediately upon it. At the present time the number of trained academic women is perhaps large enough to support the frequently expressed belief that no lowering of academic standards can result from the requirement that women be proportionately represented on faculties. Doubtless it will eventually be possible to say the same thing of the disadvantaged groups, the sooner the better. When that time comes, the anomaly of prescribed social or sexual representation in the life of the mind will perhaps seem necessary to no one.

should bear upon the selection of its personnel.* These consequences, we must know, will be felt not within the academic community alone but within the cultural life of our society as a whole, not least, we may be sure, by that part of it to which the disadvantaged ethnic groups will themselves look for sustenance.

This issue I do not now mean to debate; my point is only that the academic profession does not debate it. The profession must have noted that, by way of justifying the drastic sanctions which are being invoked against it, its traditional standards of training and achievement have been explicitly and as it were officially impugned, actually charged with having no other purpose than that of discriminatory exclusion. Surely it says much about the status of mind in our society that the profession which is consecrated to its protection and furtherance should stand silent under the assault, as if suddenly deprived of all right to use the powers of mind in its own defense.

The diminished morale which marks the academic profession in its official existence is, we may suppose, of a piece with the growing intellectual recessiveness of college and university faculties, their reluctance to formulate any coherent theory for higher education, to discover what its best purposes are, and to try to realize them through the requirements of the curriculum. And no observation of the decline in academic confidence can leave out of account the effect of a tendency which of recent years has established itself within the academic community, among teachers as well as students, the ideological trend which rejects and seeks to discredit the very concept of mind. This adversary position is now highly developed and its influence is of considerable extent. However specious we may judge the position to be, we must see that it is not merely captious—those who hold it are persuaded that the concept of mind which is traditional to Western civilization is an informing principle of modern culture in those of its aspects which are most dehumanizing and life-denying.

One ground for this opinion I have already touched on: the analogy

---

*I would not wish to be understood as saying that the academic profession has invariably acted on this belief or that, even when it has, its selection of its personnel has been unimpeachable. I mean to say only that, whatever the profession's inadequacies may be, the requirement that it act as if professional excellence is not of first importance is certain to have a drastically deteriorating effect upon its ethos, which, taking one thing with another, has hitherto been a reasonably good one.

that may be drawn between the authority claimed by mind, or for it, and an exigent and even repressive social authority. Implicit in the concept of mind is the idea of order, even of hierarchy, the subordination of some elements of thought to others. And in the carrying out of the enterprises of mind a hierarchy of persons prevails—those who are recruited to such undertakings must rise from the ranks, usually by slow stages, although some are inequitably privileged to rise faster and higher than others. In the institutionalized training of mind, some persons are given, or arrogate, the right to prescribe to others a certain degree of proficiency, to specify the means by which they are to attain it, and to test the extent to which they have done so. Such personal gratification as mind affords is likely to be of the postponed kind. Sometimes, it is true, the mind makes exhilarating leaps, but not often, and if its ethos has at times been associated with the aristocratic-military ethos, which, though deplorably aggressive, is at least spirited, a more common association is with another ethos of later growth and less vivid character, the work ethos of early capitalism, whose defining virtues are patience, the taking of pains, and the denial of spontaneous impulse.

The resentful view of mind cannot be wholly new, else the word "docile," which originally meant only teachable, would not have long ago come to mean submissive. In our time, however, the social compensations for the sacrifice of personal autonomy which mind is presumed to exact have been drastically devalued, and, as a consequence, resentment of the authority of mind has grown to the point of becoming a virtually political emotion.

Another ground, a more comprehensive one, on which mind is now impeached is its commitment to the ideal of objectivity. What has been called the myth of objective consciousness* is held to be pre-eminently responsible for the dehumanizing tendency of our culture. It is said that objectivity has come to control and pervert our mental life through the agency of technology, which has established as a model of mental process in general the quite special psychology implicit in the method of science. The consequences imputed to the domination of the psychology of sci-

---

*The phrase is used by Theodore Roszak in *The Making of a Counter-Culture* (Garden City, N.Y., 1969), which is perhaps the best-known and also the best-tempered defense of the ideologized antagonism to mind.

ence over our way of perceiving the world are readily identified, for, except that they are more extreme, they are those which the Romanticists saw as following from the ascendancy of scientific thought. One of these consequences is said to be the devaluation of the objects of our perception—even if these objects are human beings or human situations, the objective consciousness is accused of not permitting them to exist in their full integral being but only so far as they can be known in abstract and quantifiable terms. Another consequence is that because the psychology of science postulates that all the human faculties shall be subordinate to the one faculty of abstract cognition, we who as perceivers are under the sway of that psychology suffer a deformation of our personal existence, an acute diminution of our humanity. Our instinctual life is curtailed; joy becomes ever less available to us; our natural impulse of sympathy with our fellow men and with the universe we inhabit is thwarted.

No one, I think, can fail to take seriously this description of the mental life of our society. The anxiety it expresses has been with mankind for more than two centuries, at some times less overt than at other times but always there. In 1856, when the technological dispensation was as yet nothing like so encompassing as it has since become, Emerson saw it as having a malevolent power over mental life—"A terrible machine," he said, "has possessed itself of the ground, the air, and the men and women, and hardly even thought is free." The consciousness that some alien power has taken possession of human existence is now of the very substance of our life in culture. In one or another degree we all share it, we all are aware of some diminution which technology works upon our humanity.

But when we have given this much assent to the common characterization of the mental life of our time, we must see that what distresses us has nothing whatever to do with the intellectual ideal of objectivity as that has traditionally been understood and striven for. Objectivity is by no means an invention of science. It is by no means a limitation upon the range of perception. It does not imply the devaluation of the object that is perceived, its characteristic purpose is not reductive.

Actually the opposite is so. The aim of what we properly call objectivity is the fullest possible recognition of the integral and entire existence of the object. It has always seemed to me that the simplest and best definition of objectivity is contained in that phrase of Matthew Arnold's which

I quoted earlier—objectivity is the effort "to see the object as in itself it really is." The object, whether it be a phenomenon of nature, or a work of art, or an idea or system of ideas, or a social problem, or, indeed, a person, is not to be seen as it, or he or she, appears to our habitual thought, to our predilections and prejudices, to our casual or hasty inspection, but as it really is *in itself*, in its own terms, in these alone. Objectivity, we might say, is the respect we give to the object as object, as it exists apart from us. Eventually we will probably, and properly, see the object in more terms than its own—what in itself it is seen really to be will make it an object of admiration, or an object of affection or compassion, or an object of detestation. This way of seeing the object, as something we move toward or away from, even as something we wish to destroy, is not precluded by the ideal of objectivity, which requires only that, before the personal response is given, the effort to see the object as in itself it really is be well and truly made.

It is an effort which can never wholly succeed. That it must at least partially fail, that the object as in itself it really is can never finally be known, is guaranteed by the nature of individual persons, by the nature of society, even, the philosophers tell us, by the nature of mind itself. In the face of the certainty that the effort of objectivity will fall short of what it aims at, those who undertake to make the effort do so out of something like a sense of intellectual honor and out of the faith that in the practical life, which includes the moral life, some good must follow from even the relative success of the endeavor.

We know that these reasons for making the effort of objectivity have never been universally compelling. And we can scarcely fail to be aware that at the present time their moderateness confirms the belief that mind is discredited because it cannot be in an immediate relation to experience, but must always stand merely proximate to it, that through mind we can never know the world in a way which is, to use a favorite modern word, authentic—that is to say, real, true, wholly to be relied on. These are, of course, the qualities of experience which mind itself cherishes. But as authenticity is conceived by those who take an adversary position toward mind, it stipulates that only those things are real, true, and to be relied on which are experienced without the intervention of rational thought. And it is on the basis of this judgment that the contemporary ideology of irrationalism proceeds, celebrating the attainment of an immediacy of experience and perception which is beyond the power of rational mind. The means to this end are not new; they are known from of old. They include intuition, inspiration, revelation; the annihilation of selfhood perhaps through contemplation but also through ecstasy and the various forms of intoxication; violence; madness.

The impulse to transcend rational mind would seem to be very deeply rooted in man's nature. Before modern anthropology taught us not to despise or condescend to it, the highest literary and philosophical tradition of Western civilization took sympathetic cognizance of it, together with the various means by which it is thought to be realized. Madness, for example, figures memorably in the work of Plato, Shakespeare, Cervantes, Nietzsche, and Yeats, all of whom represent it as a condition productive of truths which are not accessible to our habitual and socially countenanced mode of perception and constitute an adverse judgment upon it. No one is ever in doubt that their representation of madness is of the profoundest and most cogent import, yet no one ever supposes them to be urging it upon us that madness, because of the heuristic and moral powers they ascribe to it, is a state of existence which is to be desired and sought for and, as it were, socially established. To say that madness is for them merely a figure of speech would not, I think, state the case accurately. But while their representation of the powers of madness is doubtless something more than a metaphorical construct, it does not ask for credence as a practicable actuality. In our day it has become possible to claim just such credence for the idea that madness is a beneficent condition, to be understood as the paradigm of authentic existence and cognition. This view is advanced not only by speculative laymen but also by a notable section of post-Freudian psychiatric opinion with wide influence in the intellectual community. The position is argued on grounds which are quite overtly political. The line is taken that insanity is directly related to the malign structures and forces of society, not as a mere passive effect but, rather, as an active and significant response to society's destructive will. Insanity is represented as a true perception appropriately acted out—society itself is insane, and when this is understood, the apparent aberration of the individual appears as rationality, as liberation from the delusions of the social madness. From individual madness, its heartbreaking pain, isolation, and distraction blithely ignored, is to be derived the principle by which society may recover its lost reason and humanity. The project may be taken as the measure of how desperate is the impulse to impugn and transcend the limitations of rational mind.

4

In what I have said this evening I have tried to canvass the situation in which mind stands in our nation at the present time. My emphasis has been on the vicissitudes of the situation, on those circumstances of several kinds which might be thought to limit a free, general participation in the activities of mind or to baffle its intentions and fatigue its energies.

As we look back over history, it is difficult to say what part mind has played in the life of nations. A nation's life gets carried on by many agencies, of which conscious and self-conscious mind has seldom over the long past seemed the most salient. Mere habit and inertia are powerful elements of a national life, as are old pieties, as are commitments to particular social interests or classes. And intelligence has always been of moment, what we call practical intelligence, which, in the degree to which it is effectual, is probably more than simply practical. But at a point in relatively recent history, about four centuries ago, there would seem to have developed some obscure unarticulated idea that mind, in the sense in which I have been speaking of it, ought to have a place in the national enterprise. I refer to a phenomenon of English life in the sixteenth century which Professor J. H. Hexter describes in an interesting essay:* the sudden movement of the aristocracy and gentry into the schools and the two universities. These had hitherto been the preserve of boys and young men of the lower classes who were preparing for careers in the Church. But now, to an extent which in some quarters was thought to be scandalous, their places were pre-empted by young gentlemen. The new tendency was the more surprising because it went against the settled tradition of aristocratic education, which had concerned itself wholly with manners and graces and had quite explicitly excluded all intellectual training as unsuitable to a man of gentle birth. Professor Hexter discovers no documented reason for the sudden change; he speculates, however, that it was brought

---

* "The Education of the Aristocracy in the Renaissance," in *Reappraisals in History* (Evanston, Ill., 1961).

about by the growing intention of the upper classes to take a more immediate and active part in the government of the nation. What their sons
would learn at Winchester and Eton, at Oxford and Cambridge, the disciplines of theology and classical philology in which they would be
schooled, could of course have not the slightest bearing upon what they
might actually do in governing the nation, but this seems to have caused
no dissatisfaction; no one said that the curriculum was not relevant. Apparently the upper classes had somehow got hold of the idea that mind,
not in one or another of its specific formal disciplines but in what any one
disciple might imply of the essence of mind, was of consequence in state-
craft and in the carrying on of the national life. What they would seem
suddenly to have identified and wanted to capture for themselves was
what nowadays we might call the *mystique* of mind—its energy, its intentionality, its impulse toward inclusiveness and completeness, its search for
coherence with due regard for the integrity of the elements which it
brings into relation with each other, its power of looking before and after.
In some inchoate way these ambitious upper-class parents of the sixteenth
century sought the characteristic traits of mind which they might incor-
porate into the activities of government; and in so doing, in pursuing
their inarticulate intuition that mind made the model of the practical activity of society, they proposed the ideal nature of the modern nation-
state.

With the passage of time that dim perception has achieved a fuller
consciousness—we now judge societies and their governments by the
same criteria we use in estimating the rightness of the conduct of mind.
We judge them by their energy, their intentionality, their impulse toward
inclusiveness, by their striving toward coherence with due regard for the
integrity of the disparate elements they comprise, by their power of looking before and after. Plato, when he undertook to say what the right conduct of mind should be, found the paradigm in the just society. We
reverse that procedure, finding the paradigm of a just society in the right
conduct of mind.

In describing some of the special vicissitudes which at the present
time attend the right conduct of mind, it has not been my intention to
suggest that these, though disquieting, are overwhelming. I have not
meant to say that mind, in Wells's phrase, is at the end of its tether. In my
account of its present situation I have represented mind through its ideal
purposes and through the procedures and attitudes by which it moves to-

ward the realization of these ends, through its criteria of order, inclusiveness, and coherence. To speak of mind only in this way is not to describe the life of mind in its full actuality as a human phenomenon. Seen in its totality, seen historically, the life of mind consists as much in its failed efforts as in its successes, in its false starts, its mere approximations, its very errors. It is carried on, we may say, even in the vicissitudes it makes for itself, including its mistrust or denial of its own ideal nature. All these are manifestations of the energies of mind, and William James, a philosopher in whose peculiar largeness of spirit we may perceive an affinity with Jefferson's, was at pains to remind us that they, in all their ill-conditioned disorder, are actually a function of mind's ideal achievement. Mind does not move toward its ideal purposes over a royal straight road but finds its way through the thicket of its own confusions and contradictions.

This thought must always be with us as we make our judgment of the intellectual temper of a culture. Yet we know that when we cast up the fortunes of mind at any given moment in history, what makes the object of our concern is mind as it defines itself by its ideal purposes, by its power to achieve order, inclusiveness, and coherence. It is when we take mind in this sense that I believe there is reason for disquietude about its future, discerning as I do within the intellectual life of the nation, and not of our nation alone, a notable retraction of spirit, a falling off in mind's vital confidence in itself. The history of mind has of course never been a bland continuity. There have always been periods when mind shines forth with a special luminosity and periods when it withdraws into the shadows. In the past, when a retraction of mind took place, it might well seem to affect only such specific and discrete intellectual life as a society had developed: what was thought of as an ornament of the general life was no longer there and yet the general life went its habitual way. In our time this cannot be the case. When mind, far from being ornamental, part of the super-structure of society, is the very model of the nation-state, as now it is for us, any falling off of its confidence in itself must be felt as a diminution of national possibility, as a lessening of the social hope. It is out of this belief that I have ventured to urge upon you the awareness that mind at the present time draws back from its own freedom and power, from its own delight in itself. That my having done so is not a counsel of despair is assured by one characteristic of mind, its wish to be conscious of itself, with what this implies of its ability to examine a course it has taken and to correct it.

Art, Will, and Necessity

1973

I

It is one of the defining characteristics of our contemporary civilization that in the degree we cherish art and make it the object of our piety we see it as perpetually problematical. From the eighteenth century onward, enlightened opinion has held that art plays an important part in the life of the individual and of society, some would say a decisive part. But although art is regarded as momentous in its function, which is sometimes said to be no less than that of providing the significance of life, nothing is more typical of our cultural activity than our periodic discovery that art is not so serviceable as it was supposed to be or that it has lost some measure of the power it once had. Art, we might say, exists for us through our crises of belief in its potency. We experience it not through pleasure, as men did in former times, but through anxiety—through our uneasiness over its status and over its chances of survival, and through our sense that we do it injury by holding false ideas about its nature and about the ways in which it works for our good.

Sometimes we are saddened that our devotion to art finds no mode of expression more carefree than this. But it does not. Our gray, moralistic relation to art appears to be an element of the modern fate. And this fate I submit to when in my talk here this evening I undertake to speculate about our cultural situation at the present time by remarking on the part that is played in art, and in our experience of art, by the faculty—as once it was called—of the will.

The concept of the will no longer figures significantly in the systematic psychology of our day. Those of us who are old enough to have been brought up in the shadow of the nineteenth century can recall how important the will was once thought to be in the conduct of the personal life, how confidently our parents and teachers pointed to the practical as well as the moral advantages of having a will of developed strength and discipline. Nothing could be more alien to the contemporary style of rearing and teaching the young. In the nineteenth century the will was a central and controlling topic in psychological and ethical theory—as how could it not be, given an economic system in which the unshakeable resolve of the industrial entrepreneur was of the essence, and given the temperaments of its great cultural figures? Goethe, Byron, Balzac, Dickens—to name just these few practitioners of the single art of literature is to suggest how salient was the will in the personal life of individual artists and the extent to which it preoccupied the moral imagination of the age. A chief subject of the literature of the nineteenth century was the physiology and hygiene of the will, what its normality consisted in, what were its pathologies of excess or deficiency, what were its right and wrong goals.

For us, as I say, the will has lost virtually all this former standing. This does not mean, however, that it can no longer be thought about, if only anonymously. And in fact I am going to talk this evening about two recent critical documents which seem to me to be of high significance in what they imply of the present state of our artistic culture and in both these documents the will, though not spoken of by name, is plainly a chief matter of concern.

One of these documents, the first I shall touch on, is a recent book by Harold Rosenberg, who for some two decades has been the most widely read critic of the visual arts in this country. The book is called *The De-Definition of Art* and it presents in unhappy detail its author's sense of a crisis which now obtains in the visual arts, perhaps threatening their very existence.

The other document is an essay published two years ago in *New Literary History* by Robert Scholes, an American scholar and critic of literature, who advances the view that the contemporary novel in its best manifestations is transforming the aesthetic of fiction in such a way as to promise a beneficent change, an actual mutation, in the moral and political life of mankind.

This summary description of the two documents makes them out to be dissimilar almost to the point of contradicting each other, yet I think it will eventually appear that they are in essential accord with each other in what they tell us of the attitude toward the will which at the present time informs our high culture.

2

An understanding of the dramatic significance of Mr. Rosenberg's book should perhaps begin with a reference to the provenance of the essays of which it consists. With one exception, all the essays first appeared in *The New Yorker*, the magazine for which Mr. Rosenberg writes regularly about art. From the beginning of its nearly half-century of existence, *The New Yorker* has directed itself to that section of the affluent middle class of America which, while not committed to the most urgent aspects of the cultural life, yet wishes not to be philistine. In its early days the magazine was commonly described by an adjective which has since fallen into disrepute: it was said to be "sophisticated." Actually *The New Yorker* soon transcended this description and achieved a kind of bright, modest, decent awareness. This was signalized by the good-tempered wryness of its witty cartoons and by its famous prose style, which was obsessively concerned to be correct, lucid, and level, resistant to the intensities as well as the vagaries of current American writing. In its critical departments it was committed to an ideal of cool intelligence which confronted the vanguard of any of the arts with a grave amenity, a curiosity which was at once diffident and imperturbable.

But then in the 1960s the advanced culture began to press harder upon the middle-class consciousness than it had formerly done and *The New Yorker* bestirred itself to respond to this new exigency. The expression of its always liberal political views became more highly charged, and for its critical columns and major articles it increasingly recruited serious writers of note, many of whom had come to reputation as exponents of left-wing views in both politics and art.

Of these Mr. Rosenberg was one. It was exactly his intransigent dedication to the most extreme tendencies of modern painting that *The New Yorker* was honoring when it called Mr. Rosenberg to its staff.

As art critic of *The New Yorker* Mr. Rosenberg continued to put his strong and agile mind at the service of—to use the phrase with which his name came to be associated—"the tradition of the new." As Mr. Rosenberg saw it, this tradition had never been anything but exigent. In modern art, each succeeding instance of the new entails its own peculiar difficulty, which is not to be overcome merely by habituation. Taste and what it implies of learning to be comfortable with a new mode of art have very little to do with the understanding of modern art, which is not, Mr. Rosenberg tells us, to be regarded as exclusively a visual experience; it is also, and perhaps more decisively, a conceptual experience. The individual work of art can be rightly known only if we grasp the theory that brought it into being. Which is to say, as Mr. Rosenberg does say, that our response to the *words* that express these concepts is no less essential to our experience of the tradition of the new than is sensory perception. "The basic substance of art" (I quote Mr. Rosenberg) "has become the protracted discourse in words and materials, echoed back and forth from artist to artist, work to work, art movement to art movement, on all aspects of contemporary civilization and of the place of creation in it. . . ." He continues: "Begin by explaining a single painting (and the more empty of content it is the better) and if you continue describing it, you will find yourself touching on more subjects to investigate—philosophical, social, political, historical, scientific, psychological—than are needed for an academic degree."

The effort is indeed an arduous one and perhaps it needs to be justified by what Mr. Rosenberg goes on to tell us of art's beneficence, its unique redemptive power. The arts, he says (I quote him again), "have never been more indispensable than they are today. With its accumulated insights, its disciplines, its inner conflicts, painting (or poetry, or music) provides a means for the active self-development of individuals—perhaps the only means. Given the patterns in which mass-behavior, including mass-education, is presently organized, art is the one vocation that keeps a space open for the individual to realize himself in knowing himself."

In the virtually Victorian eloquence of Mr. Rosenberg's profession of faith in art's high function you will perhaps have discerned a note of conscious pathos. If so, you will have heard aright. Mr. Rosenberg's statement comes at the end of the first essay of his book and it is in this essay, which is in effect the manifesto of his developing position, that he expresses his belief that art at the present time is being deprived of its redemptive power and that it may even be threatened with extinction. This, I need scarcely say, is a grimly significant statement to come from the prophet of the tradition of the new.

The danger in which Mr. Rosenberg believes art to stand derives from none of the circumstances which are commonly known to be hostile to art. There is no question of a repressive government forbidding what is new or strange or likely to subvert conformity. Nor does Mr. Rosenberg suggest that the survival of art is being endangered by the indifference of a materialistic society. Even mass-behavior and mass-education aren't the source of the threat. No—the present plight of art derives, according to Mr. Rosenberg, from art itself. And herein lies the drama of his book: the threat to art of which Mr. Rosenberg warns us is a development of its own nature. It is the logical outcome of its own chosen relation to society.

How that logic has unfolded I shall try to say as briefly as possible. The account begins with the coming into vogue, in the early nineteenth century, of the word "philistine" to suggest the character of society and why art stands in opposition to it. Confronting bourgeois society in the materialism of its aims and the insensibility of its power are those persons who, by creating art or by giving it their loyalty, become the new Chosen People. These Children of Light set at naught the objects worshipped in the crass life of bourgeois capitalism. But bourgeois society, it turns out, is not so Goliath-like as at first it appears to be. It does not wish to be philistine if it can help it—it is not inaccessible to shame. Beginning in the nineteenth century, at first tentatively, then more boldly, eventually by official action, society set out to claim art for its own. And in fact it was precisely those paintings which were most overt in their antagonism to society and which had once been refused by the Salon which came to have the highest value for bourgeois collectors, for museums and ministries of culture.

Certainly, as Mr. Rosenberg makes plain, no work of art in our day is so extreme in the outrage it offers to society as to prevent its being given social canonization. Almost in the degree that art expresses its contempt of all that is established and official, it is sought and paid for—which is to say: taken into camp and deprived of its antagonistic force. The readiness of capitalist society to accept the art that avows its antagonism to capitalist society is therefore anything but the evidence of art's power; it is exactly the means by which art is made impotent. The expectation that art will supply the principle by which society can be redeemed is little more than a self-congratulatory fantasy. No redemption has occurred; all that has happened is that the highest achievement of the free subversive spirit has been co-opted to lend the color of spirituality to the capitalist enterprise.

To this situation the profession of painting—of the visual arts in general, but I follow Mr. Rosenberg in speaking most particularly of painting—has had but a single response: to step up the rate of its inventiveness, style succeeding style and theory superseding theory in an ever more urgent attempt to outstrip society's relentlessly accelerating accommodation to it. But the heightened rate of inventiveness has proved to be of no avail. Such has become society's appetite for new art that it will gag at nothing, and indeed in the last few years it has reached the point where not only the output of individual painters but the very idea of painting has been appropriated by society. To this the response of painting has been as nearly ultimate as possible: it is as if art would sooner negate itself than be gulped down in this fashion. Mr. Rosenberg puts the matter with a terrifying succinctness; "Painting today," he says "is a profession one of whose aspects is the pretense of overthrowing it." That is to say, painting is in the process of "de-defining" itself, of denying the attributes of its former identity. And as Mr. Rosenberg proceeds with his exposition, he puts less emphasis on the element of pretense in art's overthrow of itself—in Mr. Rosenberg's judgment the de-definition of art will in all probability issue in the actual extinction of art.

In the course of outlining this belief, Mr. Rosenberg speaks of our present situation as one in which art is no longer thought to consist of specifically *created* objects. In a striking phrase he refers to "the heroic concept of masterpieces"—it is no longer the intention of the vanguard artist, Mr. Rosenberg tells us, that his effort should be controlled by "the heroic concept of masterpieces." The word "masterpiece" has traditionally suggested the exercise of the creative will in its highest and purest form. It implies that the creative will freely elects to meet resistance, not only that which is inherent in whatever genre is being explored but also that which the will, in its happy consciousness of its powers, seeks out or invents. It is from the kind of difficulty which the creative will acknowledges, or chooses, or invents, and from its manner of mastering this difficulty that the value of a masterpiece derives. Through the overcoming of resistance the masterpiece is produced and then itself becomes an object which offers resistance to the will of the viewer. For Mr. Rosenberg this process is a paradigm of what he characterizes as virtually the essential undertaking of human existence, the overcoming of passivity, the realization of self through self-knowledge, the forming of an autonomous personal character.

I need scarcely say that Mr. Rosenberg doesn't believe that it is inevitably in the nature of vanguard art that it should reject the idea of masterpieces. Nothing could be further from his thought. The great "tradition of the new" with which Mr. Rosenberg's name is associated, the movement of American vanguard art in the 1950s of which the preeminent figures were Gorky, Pollock, Rothko, Newman, Gottlieb, and de Kooning, was assuredly extreme, perhaps even outrageous in its practice, but it never lost its commitment to the heroic concept of masterpieces. Whatever hostility it directed to the bourgeois social principle, it was in this far social, and in this far traditionally humanistic, that it invited the individual viewer to enter into a complex transaction with its works. Implicit in its programs was the expectation that the product of its creative will would speak to persons who similarly valued the will and who, too, were intent upon overcoming their passivity to the social environment.

By Mr. Rosenberg's account, it is precisely this transaction that the vanguard art of recent years seeks to disrupt. We have not the time to follow Mr. Rosenberg in his adverse characterization of the particular schools of contemporary art he refers to—Pop art; minimal art; *arte povera*; earthworks; World Game; the staging of autonomous events which go under the name of happenings; art in which the project is described rather than executed. What all these artistic modes have in common is the wish to deny the validity of the traditional aesthetic experience. Which is to say that their ultimate goal is to deny the will as we traditionally know it.

This animus against the will, we must understand, does not always present itself explicitly and directly. Sometimes it takes the form of a paradox of a most extravagant kind, for nothing is more typical of contemporary vanguard art than the enormous claims it makes for the power of the will of the artist. Mr. Rosenberg tells us that (I quote him) "an excited view, recently become prevalent in advanced artistic and academic circles, holds that all kinds of problems are waiting to be solved by the magical touch of the artist. . . . So intense is this enthusiasm for what the artist might accomplish that mere painting and sculpture are presented as undeserving of the intention of the serious artist. . . ." And he goes on: "In contrast to the meagerness of art, the artist is blown up to gigantic proportions. . . . The artist has become, as it were, too big for art . . .": the only undertaking that is now thought to be appropriate to his status and function is, as Mr. Rosenberg puts it, "a super-art presumably able to encompass all experience." One does not need to be deeply instructed in the contradictions of the unconscious to understand that the surest negation of the potent will is the fantasy of the omnipotent will.

The situation which Mr. Rosenberg describes can have, he is certain, but one outcome. He tells us that "except as a figure of popular nostalgia," a mere fiction, the "post-art" or "beyond-art" artist is fated for dissolution. And of the art which transcends art he says that such existence as it may continue to have will (I quote) "blend into the communications and entertainment media."

To most of us, even those who are ambiguous in their relation to vanguard art, the prediction is a dire one. We cannot be surprised, however, that there are those who are anything but distressed by it, among them, for example, Douglas Davis, who is the art critic of *Newsweek*, a magazine whose readers are numbered in the millions. In reviewing *The De-Definition of Art* in *The New York Times Book Review* Mr. Davis acknowledges the intimacy that has developed between vanguard art and the public media and he finds it nothing but beneficent. He puts the case with a passionate intensity which obscures his precise meaning but not his general purport. "The media," he says, "the pulse of rapid information, is a fact of life. We cannot expect artists to labor at inclusive tasks for generations. They find and meet problems more quickly now because the rhythm of the aesthetic dialogue demands it. The media have plunged us not into Post Art but into Total Art." By Total Art Mr. Davis means an art which is momently present to the public consciousness and which we do not confront and contemplate but of which we are an element.

A similar response to the idea that art is moving away from aesthetic discreteness to a generalized state which approximates extinction is taken account of by Mr. Rosenberg himself in the essay he devotes to a French book called in translation *Art and Confrontation*, a symposium occasioned by the student uprising in Paris in the spring of 1968, in which, as you will recall, artistic culture was a salient topic. The contributors to the symposium were all of them Marxists, which perhaps makes it curious that they found it impossible to imagine that the creative will could any longer express itself to some good human purpose—several of them took the view that art, in any conception of it whatever, is so hopelessly compromised by its social acceptance that it had best be liquidated. In this they echoed and supported the animus against humanistic culture which the insurgent students expressed in their posters and graffiti, in which they rejected the whole tradition of personal development which is represented in Mr. Rosenberg's characterization of art as "the one vocation that keeps a space open for the individual to realize himself by knowing himself." According to the insurgent French students, art thus conceived, so far from being the agent of freedom, constitutes a tyranny: the will of the individual is being coerced by the will of art. What they oppose to art's traditional function of advancing self-realization is a concept of art as simultaneously a total environment and a total participation. As one contributor put it: "Art doesn't exist. Art is you."

3

I turn now from Mr. Rosenberg's book about the visual arts to Professor Scholes's essay about the destiny of the novel, with which I shall deal far more briefly. To make this move is to pass from the darkling plain of crisis to what is presented to us as the bright upland of order and confident hope. While the visual artists have been desperately de-defining their profession, the new novelists—so Mr. Scholes tells us—have quietly jettisoned the old idea of the novel and, without any polemical fuss, have got on with the development of an entirely different order of creation, as firmly defined as its predecessor and apparently no less committed to the heroic concept of masterpieces. This new genre seeks no help from systematic theory. But it stands, if not under the banner, under the aegis of the mode of thought known as structuralism, whose implications for the moral and political life of our time are, as Mr. Scholes sees it, of the very greatest positive value.

To all appearances, that is, no two situations could be more unlike than those to which our two authors turn their thought. Yet quite as much as the situation in the visual arts which distresses Mr. Rosenberg, the situation in the novel about which Mr. Scholes is so sanguine proposes the idea which concerns me this evening: the devaluation of will in our present-day high culture.

I am afraid that I must begin what I say about Mr. Scholes's essay by explaining that I am implicated in its argument. The essay is called "The Illiberal Imagination" and this may suggest to some of you that Mr. Scholes states his position by reference to a book of mine. *The Liberal Imagination* was published in 1950; it is a collection of critical essays which I wrote over the preceding decade. Mr. Scholes finds the book convenient to his purpose of explicating the new novel because he feels that it sums up the assumptions and values which once informed fiction but which fiction now repudiates.

Mr. Scholes's transaction with my book calls for no defensiveness on my part not only because Mr. Scholes characterizes my views with unfailing generosity but also because the issue between us plainly transcends personal opinion. That issue, which I believe must occupy the consciousness of our culture for a long time to come, is whether life is the better or the worse for putting a high valuation on the will. It is my position that it is the better. Mr. Scholes takes the opposite view.

The essays of *The Liberal Imagination* were not concerned exclusively with literature and those that did deal with literature were not only about the novel, but Mr. Scholes is justified in concentrating upon what I said about that genre. What I said was not remarkable for its originality. I spoke of the novel as an especially useful agent of the moral imagination, as the literary form which most directly reveals to us the complexity, the difficulty, and the interest of life in society, and which best instructs us in our human variety and contradiction. All this had been said many times before and if any particular interest attached to my saying it in the decade of the 1940s, it was because I said it with a polemical purpose and with reference to a particular political-cultural situation.

At our distance in time the significance of this situation is perhaps not easily recalled. I speak of the commitment that a large segment of the intelligentsia of the West gave to the degraded version of Marxism known as Stalinism. No one, of course, called himself a Stalinist; it was the pejorative designation used by those members of the class of advanced intellectuals who were its opponents. At its center was the belief that the Soviet Union had resolved all social and political contradictions and was well on the way toward realizing the highest possibilities of human life. The facts which refuted this certitude were not hard to come by but the wish to ignore them was resolute, which is to say that the position of the Stalinist intellectuals of the West was not, in any true conception of politics, a political position at all but, rather, the expression of a settled disgust with politics, or at least with what politics entails of contingency, vigilance, and effort. In an imposed monolithic government they saw the promise of rest from the particular acts of will which are needed to meet the many, often clashing requirements of democratic society. The Stalinists of the West were not commonly revolutionaries, they were what used to be called fellow-travelers but they cherished the idea of revolution as the final, all-embracing act of will which would forever end the exertions of our individual wills. Failing the immediate actuality of revolution, their animus against individual will expressed itself in moral and cultural attitudes which devalued all the gratuitous manifestations of feeling, of thought, and of art, of all such energies of the human spirit as are marked by spontaneity, complexity, and variety.

All my essays of the 1940s were written from my sense of this dull, repressive tendency of opinion which was coming to dominate the old ethos of liberal enlightenment. The opposition I offered to it was of the simplest kind, consisting of not much more than my saying to people who prided themselves on being liberals that liberalism was 1) a political position and 2) a political position that affirmed the value of individual existence in all its variousness, complexity, and difficulty, and that, since this was so, literature had a bearing upon political conduct because literature, especially the novel, is the human activity that takes the fullest and most precise account of variousness, complexity, difficulty—and possibility.

Well, I wrote at the mid-point of our century, and in the years that have intervened the novel has undergone a mutation which manifestly makes my old characterization of it obsolete. To Mr. Scholes the change is a welcome one. Its best and most significant aspects result, he says, from the novel's having come under the influence of structuralism, which he speaks of as "the most vigorous current of thought in modern life." Structuralism, according to Mr. Scholes's description, is a mode of thought defined by the emphasis it puts upon "the universal and systematic at the expense of the individual and idiosyncratic." Its effect upon the novel is most clearly revealed in the way in which the characters who figure in fictional narrative are conceived. The novel in its traditional form confirmed the liberal ethos by its loving and enthusiastic account of individual characters, by the attention it paid to the particularities of individual personality—to what, with a certain condescension, Mr. Scholes calls individual *quirkiness*—even though this principle of individuation went along with another and opposite principle, that of typification—the representation, that is, of certain categories of humanity. The novelists of today, however—and Mr. Scholes refers to Iris Murdoch, Barth, Pynchon, Fowles, Coover—are no longer interested in individual fates, but only in one or another mode of typification, and as an aspect of this programmatic preference they represent human existence not as a series of contingencies but as a *structure*, a discernible pattern of reiterated destinies in which personal intention is but one of several formal elements.

And it is in this concentration upon the pattern of events and circumstances and in the subordination of personal intention that Mr. Scholes discovers the momentous moral implications of the new novel. He does not put it so, but we cannot fail to see that what gratifies him in the new fiction is its desire to purge itself of its old concern, its undeviating nineteenth-century concern, with the will of its characters, who want so much from life—money, rank, achievement, fame, each other—and with the will of the reader who wants these things, too, and seeks to learn what are his chances of getting them and at what cost; and not least with the will of the novelist himself, so all too imperious, Mr. Scholes tells us, in encompassing and directing his world, controlling his characters, assigning them their fates, instructing his readers in the way life goes and in how they ought to feel about it and what they ought to do about it.

And how much it all was thought to matter! Pain was momentous, so also were relief and joy, because it was believed that each person happened only once and would never recur—which is to say, each life, like the culture in which it was lived out, was a history. It began, it developed, it came to an end. And in this history what was decisive was its end—for it was the end that suggested the extent to which things mattered and the reason why the will had better exert itself to the fullest extent of its power.

But if things are not singular, as once was believed and as the traditional novel urged us to believe, if a life is not to be seen as a history, then the end, if we are to conceive it at all, is not decisive. Things do not matter to the degree that we once supposed and the will need not exert itself as was once expected. In other words, if I read Mr. Scholes aright, what constitutes the tremendous moral significance he attributes to the new novel is the diminished demand it makes upon the will. Indeed, so great is his estimate of the redemptive power of the structuralist vision that it permits him to speak of the new novel as portending a "politics of love," thus licensing the hope—did we not make its acquaintance some decades ago, in the program of Stalinist liberalism?—that the conflict of wills may be brought to an end and order made to prevail in the conduct of human affairs.

4

There is a point in *The De-Definition of Art*—it is in the essay on the French symposium to which I have referred—where Mr. Rosenberg uses a phrase with which I should like to lead to my conclusion. He has been speaking of the importance which is now commonly attached to eliminating the distance between audience and art-object or art-event; he refers particularly to the success in this regard of American rock festivals. The store that is nowadays put upon merging the audience with the art-object or art-event he explains as arising from the wish to (I quote him) "dispense with ego-values." In the context it is unmistakable that he is using the word "ego" in its precise Freudian meaning.

According to Freud, in the very earliest stages of infancy, the self is not experienced, let alone conceived, as separate from its environment. In the first months of life the universe is, as it were, contained within the infant's sensory system. Only by gradual stages in the process of maturation does the infant come to perceive that the world is external to it and independent of it, and learns to surrender the omnipotence of its subjectivity. Recognizing the imperative nature of the objectified universe, the infant acquires the ability to deal with the external world in individual acts of will. Thus it survives, and to the agency of its survival, to that element of the psychic economy which has guided the infant in making this necessary differentiation between itself as subject and the world as object, Freud gave the name of ego.

The development of the ego is a process of infinite complexity, of which one aspect is its periodic reluctance to go forward in its growth. Sometimes it is tempted to regress to a less active and effectual stage, even to turn back to the comfortable condition of subjective omnipotence, to the megalomania of infantile narcissism. Yet, typically, of course, the positive tendency of the ego is strong, so strong, in fact, that the ego goes well beyond its primary function of seeing to the survival of the individual and comes to define itself in activities—art, sport, speculation, invention, play of all kinds—which are not dictated by necessity but are, as we say, gratuitous, undertaken only for the sake of the ego's delight in itself.

We assess these gratuitous undertakings of the ego more complicatedly than we are readily aware of. In general, we value them highly: they make the substance of our imagination of freedom and happiness. Yet at the same time we regard them with a certain disquiet because, while the ego does indeed find delight in going beyond necessity, it also looks to necessity for the assurance of its integrity and authority, which necessity had evoked and continues to affirm. We happily assent to Schiller's idea that "man is most fully human when he plays," yet we have but to read about an imagined society, such as William Morris depicts in *News from Nowhere*, where there is almost no necessity and where virtually every activity is a form of play, to know from the anxiety that is aroused in us by this state of affairs how much we count on necessity to assure us that the ego is actual and authoritative. Nietzsche, speaking of the condition of mind which would follow from the realization that God is dead, said that for some time to come men would experience the uncomfortable state which he called *weightlessness*. The word may be used to describe the similarly unhappy state which is associated with the sense that necessity has lost its imperative force.

It is possible, I think, to write the psycho-cultural history of the nineteenth century in terms of its anxious concern over the threat to the ego when necessity is diminished in power. The issue was tersely stated by William James as the nineteenth century drew to its close. "If this life be not a real fight," James wrote, "in which something is eternally gained for the universe by success, it is no better than a game of private theatricals from which we may withdraw at will." James was not able to say with certitude that life *was* a real fight, though what he could say seems to have served his purpose: "But it *feels* like a fight." His culture made it possible for him to affirm necessity in at least this far: that *something* demanded of him the exercise of his will and that therefore his ego had the traditional evidence that it was actual.

The careful balance between will and necessity which the nineteenth century undertook to maintain was no mere psychological construct. It reflected realities of the culture, in particular the technological situation of the time. Although it was a day in which the practical requirements of life were met with confidence and ingenuity, there could be no promise that the attainment of goals was inevitable. Too, although society had become measurably more open and the rate of mobility, at least within the middle class, had increased, the making of a career was still far from something that even a member of the middle class could take for granted. There were far fewer professions than we know today, and those there were were not rationalized. Society was penetrable only by the few, and even by these only with great effort. A life had to be shaped, devised, battled for. Necessity, in short, made the actual condition of human experience.

But of course it still does, however we may try to persuade ourselves to the contrary—except that we no longer believe that it *should*. A perfecting technology, a growing confidence in rational system, a new drama of social mobility—all these elements of modernity have had their effect on us. And, in consequence, necessity figures in the modern imagination as only contingently necessary, in fact as an anomaly which continues in existence not because it cannot be mastered but only because we have not yet put ourselves with sufficient energy to getting rid of it. What would be the human outcome were necessity indeed obliterated and there were no fight in which the ego took shape and then went on to gratuitous activity—this is a question we have no wish to ask ourselves.

Perhaps, however, the two documents I have talked about this evening force the question upon our unwilling attention. Both tell us, if we read them with due awareness, of the really quite dramatic degree to which the contemporary ego is baffled by the diminishing credence we give to the idea of necessity. At the beginning of this lecture I said that the older members of this audience would have the remembrance of a time when our parents and teachers held the training of the will to be a chief concern of their pedagogy. What I had in mind in using the word "will" in this context was that element of character which we mobilize to meet the demands of necessity—it is the "will" of that now discredited phrase "willpower." But there was, of course, another form of will to which the old pedagogy was addressed, negatively: that is, will as willfulness, or will associated, most familiarly in very young children, with the narcissistic fantasy of omnipotence and thus constituting a counter-force to the will we associate with the developed ego. The prepotency of will which is asserted by the present-day artists of whom Mr. Rosenberg writes plainly belongs in the narcissistic category; it is the will of the undeveloped ego, unresponsive to necessity. From Mr. Rosenberg's book we learn of the possibility that in the present state of vanguard art the effectual will, the will of ego, has in fact so far neutralized itself that art has been brought to meaninglessness and that it is even moving toward extinction. And from Mr. Scholes's essay we similarly learn of the reduced condition of the will of developed ego: Mr. Scholes invites us to a world where, indeed, the will is to be so thoroughly abrogated that life will virtually cease to have meaning except in its formal aspects. In both documents we confront the evidence of a regressive impulse which may be of some considerable significance in the human destiny.

Why We Read Jane Austen

1975

My subject is of a speculative kind and as it develops it will lead us away from Jane Austen and toward the consideration of certain aspects and functions of literature and art generally. It did not have its origin in reflections upon our author's canon of work in itself but was proposed by a phenomenon of our contemporary high culture, the large and ever-growing admiration which Jane Austen's work is being given. This phenomenon may be thought the more significant because, contrary to what would have been the case at an earlier time, young people have a salient part in it, and what I shall begin by talking about is the intensity of feeling which students at my university directed to Jane Austen when I gave a course in her novels two years ago.

An account of the incident I refer to must touch upon some dull scholastic details. As I envisaged my course, it was not to be given in lectures but as a "class." That is to say, each of its two meetings a week would start with my remarking on some significant aspect of the novel that was being considered and to this the members of the class would address themselves, developing or disagreeing with what I and then their fellow-students had said. This method of instruction is likely to be held in greater regard than it deserves. In any class there will be students who cannot be induced to say anything at all, and there will be those who cannot be kept from trying to say everything, and of course even a measured articulateness does not ensure the cogency of what is said. But if through luck or cunning one can get the method working at all well, it has a quite special pedagogic value.

For this way of teaching, the optimum number of students would seem to be twenty and a practicable maximum probably cannot be higher than thirty. To my amazement and distress the number of students who attended the first meeting of the course was something like 150. Although there was no clear principle by which I could choose among such a number, I was determined to stay with the method of instruction I had originally proposed to myself. I addressed my little multitude and said that the course as I had planned it could not accommodate nearly as many students as were now gathered, and that beginning at once and going on for as long as was necessary, I would interview students in my office and post a list of those who might register. There were the conventional student sounds of dismay but no polemical challenge was offered to my decision and by the time I reached my office a long line had formed outside it.

All through that afternoon, through the whole of the next day and the day after that I conducted interviews, and with each one the absurdity of the procedure became more apparent. As I have said, there was no reasonable criterion by which I might judge the applicants. I had to see that the comments I jotted down about each student were subjective and in some sense discriminatory; they expressed my estimate of the applicant's intellectual aptitude, range of knowledge, and—inevitably—personal interestingness. Yet despite my growing discomfort, I continued as I had begun, feeling that I had made my decision for good reason.

The reason deserves some notice. It had to do with my ambiguous feelings about the position Jane Austen had come to occupy in our literary culture and about the nature of the esteem and the degree of attention she was being given by scholars and critics. If I looked back over the period of my life during which I was at all aware of Jane Austen, I had of course to recognize that a decisive change had taken place in the way she was being thought about. One could not adequately describe this change by saying that she stood now in higher esteem than formerly. A glance through Chapman's critical bibliography makes plain to what heights the esteem had long ago ascended, how grand were the terms in which admiration had been expressed, including comparison with Shakespeare. Indeed, when it came to the question of how much praise she deserved, a personage no less authoritative than Henry James could say that she was given too much of it, or at least that it was of the wrong sort and given by people of the wrong sort. And as if at the instance of Henry James's little burst of temper over this state of affairs, the regard in which Jane Austen was held began to change its nature in a radical way—she ceased to be a darling and a pet, she ceased to be what James deplored her being, "dear Jane." She became ever less the property of people who, through being nice people, were excluded from the redemptive strenuosities of the intellectual life. One was the less disposed to share the views of this order of her admirers because it had been shown that Jane Austen herself actually hated such people. And now having been delivered from their deplorable adulation, she was safe and presumably happy in the charge of scholars and critics of the most enlightened and energetic kind.

Instructed and lively intellects do not make pets and darlings and dears out of the writers they admire but they do make them into what can be called "figures"—that is to say, creative spirits whose work requires an especially conscientious study because in it are to be discerned significances, even mysteries, even powers, which carry it beyond what in a loose and general sense we call literature, beyond even what we think of as very good literature, and bring it to as close an approximation of a sacred wisdom as can be achieved in our culture. Flaubert is of course a figure *par excellence*; Stendhal somewhat less of one; Balzac, though certainly much admired, remains a writer. Dickens became a figure quite some time back; there has been a large increase in the admiration we now give Trollope, but it is unlikely that he will ever become a figure. Kafka was a figure from the first; Gide was a figure twenty-five years ago but seems now to have lost much of his figurative ground.

The making of Jane Austen into a figure has of recent years been accelerated, probably in part by the contemporary demand for female figures, though certainly not for that reason alone. I find it difficult to say why I am not on comfortable terms with the figurative process generally and as it touches Jane Austen in particular, but a chief reason for my not wanting to give the course as lectures was that lectures would almost certainly have to take account of the enormous elaboration of articulate sensibility which has developed around Jane Austen and would put me under the obligation of trying to add to it. Perhaps because I somewhere held the primitive belief that there really was such a thing as life itself, which I did not want interfered with by literature or by the ingenuities of academic criticism, I did not wish either to encompass or to augment the abundant, the superabundant, the ever more urgent intellectual activity that was being directed toward a body of work whose value I would be the first to assert.

How, then, did I want my students to think of Jane Austen? Was she perhaps to be thought of as nothing more than a good read? I do not accept that my purpose can be thus described, though now that we have before us that British locution, which Americans have lately taken to using, the question might be asked why the phrase should have come to express so much force of irony and condescension, why a good read should necessarily imply a descent into mere creature-comfort, into downright coziness. As my case stood, I would have granted that we must get beyond the unexamined pleasure with which we read in childhood and be prepared to say why and how it is that pleasure comes to us from stories; we keep it in mind here that some of my students were in graduate school and going on to the teaching of literature as their profession. But it seemed to me that the enterprise of consciousness could best be forwarded, could best be kept direct and downright, by the colloquial give-and-take of class discussion rather than by lectures.

As the interviews got under way, however, I found myself becoming doubtful that the directness and downrightness I hoped for could actually be achieved, for such qualities of literary discourse did not consort well with the prevailing emotional tone of the interviews. Many of these did of course proceed in, if I may put it so, a normal enough way. An undergraduate had read *Pride and Prejudice*, had liked it and wanted more of the same; a graduate student concentrating in the Romantic period might naturally wish to give close attention to the six novels. But most of the students had no special scholarly reason for reading Jane Austen and yet displayed a degree of anxiety about their admission to the course which seemed to say that their motive was something other than that of ordinary literary interest. There was something they wanted, not from me, as was soon apparent, but from Jane Austen, something that was making for an intensity in their application for the course such as I had no preparation for in all my teaching career. So far as I could make out, they did not think it absurd that they should be required to formulate reasons why they should be allowed to take the course—why should not the sincerity of their vocation be tested? Several of them, after their interviews, wrote me pleading notes. Several sought out colleagues of mine with whom they were in good repute and asked them to intercede with me. Two messages came from friends who taught in other colleges in the city telling me that certain graduate students who had worked with them as undergraduates deserved my most thoughtful consideration.

When at last I posted my roster, with all due misgiving and such compunction as led me to revise upward to forty my notion of what is a feasible number for classroom discussion, there were appeals made to me to reconsider my decisions. There were even expressions of bitterness.

The course as it was given must have gone well enough, for I recall that I enjoyed giving it. The bizarre show of almost hysterical moral urgency which marked its beginning disappeared as soon as we got down to business. Although there might have been some pedagogic value in my doing so, I did not revert to that uncanny episode to try to explain it. But the occurrence deserves some effort of explanation.

One line of understanding which inevitably proposes itself is that the students were so especially eager to take the course because they had formed the impression that Jane Austen's novels presented a mode of life which brought into question the life they themselves lived and because it offered itself to their fantasy as an alternative to their own mode of life. If this was indeed the case, nothing could have been more characteristic of our high culture—we have built into the structure of our thought about society the concept of *Gemeinschaft* in its standing criticism of *Gesellschaft* and we can readily suppose that the young men and women who so much wanted to study Jane Austen believed that by doing so they could in some way transcend our sad contemporary existence, that, from the world of our present weariness and desiccation, they might reach back to a world which, as it appears to the mind's eye, is so much more abundantly provided with trees than with people, a world in whose green shade life for a moment might be a green thought.

The use of social-political terms to explain the literary predilection I was dealing with is lent a degree of substantiation by the circumstance that five years before there had been given to another English literary figure a devotion which, though of a different kind, was as intense as that which was now being given to Jane Austen and which clearly received its impetus from feelings about social existence. American undergraduates seem to be ever more alienated from the general body of English literature, but they had for some time made an exception of William Blake, pledging him their unquestioning allegiance, and in 1968, when the large majority of the students at my university were either committed to or acquiescent in its disruption, they found him uniquely relevant to their spiritual aspirations. It might seem that, no less than Blake, Jane Austen offered a position from which to scrutinize modern life with adverse intention. The style phases of our culture are notoriously short; it was not to be thought anomalous that at one moment disgust with modern life should be expressed through devotion to a figure proposing impulse, excess, and the annihilation of authority, and then a scant five years later through devotion to the presiding genius of measure, decorum, and irony.

It is not hard to say what are the attributes of the world of Jane Austen's novels which might make it congenial to the modern person who feels himself ill-accommodated by his own time. I have referred in passing to an aspect of the visual character of that world, its abundance of trees as compared with the number of people who come into our or each other's ken; and in general it is a thing taken for granted by readers that the novels represent a world which is distinctly, even though implicitly, gratifying to the eye and to the whole sensory and cognitive system. We are seldom required by Jane Austen to envision a displeasing scene, such as Fanny Price's parental home, and almost all places, even those that are not particularly described, seem to have some degree of pleasantness imputed to them. Notable among the elements of visuality which lead to the effect of amenity is that of *scale*, the relation in size between human beings and the components of their environment. No one needs to be reminded that the dialectic over what sort of scale is to be preferred is ancient and ceaseless—sometimes the hygiene of the soul is thought to be best served by spaces and objects whose magnitude overawes and quiets the will, or, alternatively, challenges it to heroic assertion; sometimes the judgment goes that the most salubrious situation is one in which moderate though generous size conveys the idea of happy accommodation. At the present time the sensibility of educated persons is likely to set particular store by this latter sort of scale as it is represented in Jane Austen's novels.

But it is plain that the charming visual quality of Jane Austen's "world," even when we grant it all the moral significance it can in fact have, will not of itself account for the present appeal that the novels make. If it could do so, we might expect that William Morris's *News from Nowhere* would rival the Austen novels in interest, for no one ever gave so much moral weight as Morris did to the *look* of human existence, especially to the question of scale, making it one of the traits of his redeemed Londoners of the future that they should hold in contempt the dimensions of St. Paul's and the coarseness of the mind of Christopher Wren in having fixed upon them. But of course to the modern taste Morris's utopian romance is little more than a pleasing curiosity. It is a tribute to Morris's honesty that we can so easily perceive why this is so, for Morris is explicit in saying that the one discontent that at least a few of the inhabitants of Nowhere might be expected to feel is that being a person is not interesting in the way that novelists had shown it to be in the old unregenerate time.

It might be said that Morris, for his own reasons, adumbrates the programmatic negation of character which increasingly marks the novel of our day, the contemporary novelist finding it ever more beside the point to deal with destinies as if they were actually personal, or at least to do so in any other way than that of pastiche and parody. Surely one obvious reason why the students turned so eagerly to Jane Austen is that they felt the need to see persons represented as novels once typically represented them; that, without formulating their need, they were in effect making a stand against the novel in its contemporary mode. We should never take it for granted that young people inevitably respond affirmatively to what is innovative and antitraditional in the high artistic culture of their time; there is the distinct possibility that the students with whom I was dealing saw the contemporary novel as being of a piece with those elements of the modern dispensation which they judged to be maleficent, such as industrialism, urbanization, the multiversity. This maleficence would have to do with the reduction of their selfhood, and presumably it could be neutralized by acquaintance with the characters of Jane Austen's novels, an association that was indeed licensed by the aesthetic of the works. That is, these fictive persons would be experienced as if they had actual existence, as if their "values" were available to assessment, as if their destinies bore upon one's own, and as if their styles of behavior and feeling must inevitably have a consequence in one's own behavior and feeling.

If this was really what the students felt in reading Jane Austen, they were of course fulfilling the aim of traditional humanistic education. In reading about the conduct of other people as presented by a writer highly endowed with moral imagination and in consenting to see this conduct as relevant to their own, they had undertaken an activity which humanism holds to be precious, in that it redeems the individual from moral torpor; its communal effect is often said to be decisive in human existence.

Humanism does not in the least question the good effect of reading about the conduct of other people of one's own time, but it does put a special value upon ranging backward in time to find in a past culture the paradigms by which our own moral lives are put to test. In its predilection for the moral instructiveness of past cultures, humanism is resolute in the belief that there is very little in this transaction that is problematic; it is confident that the paradigms will be properly derived and that the judgments made on the basis they offer will be valid. Humanism takes for granted that any culture of the past out of which has come a work of art that commands our interest must be the product, and also, of course, the shaping condition, of minds which are essentially the same as our own.

Perhaps this is so, but after the Jane Austen course had gone on for a time, the enormous qualifying power of that word "essentially" became manifest to me. Essentially like our own that past culture and those minds, or selves, which created it and were created by it doubtless were, but between them and us there stretched a great range of existential differences.

The word "code" has a traditional place in discourse about society, but in our day it has acquired a new force which isn't quite continuous with what used to be intended by such phrases as "the social code" or "the code of honor." The question I tried to raise with my class was the extent to which any of us who delighted in Jane Austen's novels and found them so charged with moral significance could comprehend the elaborately encoded values of the society they depicted and read accurately the signals being sent out.

A certain amount of difficulty was produced by the question of what kind of society was being represented by the novels. There was a general readiness among the students to say that the society was "aristocratic," but one young man remarked that it was an aristocracy without any nobles— he actually used that by now oddly vulgar word. This observation had the effect of somewhat relaxing the inhibition which American students are likely to feel about taking note of social gradations and we managed to achieve a reasonably complicated view of the system of status and deference on which the novels are based. I had the sense, however, that the students were never quite easy with it and didn't finally believe in its actuality.

Then, following my observation that Jane Austen does not find the relation between servants and their masters or mistresses as interesting as many English novelists do and therefore gives but little help to the modern reader in understanding the part servants played in the life of her time, I had to particularize for the students such matters as what it was that servants were needed for and how many were required for one or another kind of domestic establishment. It turned out that most of the students, though of the middle class, had no real conception of what a servant was or did and could not imagine what the existence of a servant class might imply for a culture—to take a simple example, what effect, for good or ill, their relationships with servants might have upon the children of the house.

We gave some attention to the nature of familial and personal relationships. In the fall of 1973, when my course was being given, the debate in *The Times Literary Supplement* over how brothers and sisters might naturally have felt toward each other early in the nineteenth century had not yet begun, but we remarked the relations between sister and sister in Jane Austen's novels and agreed that this relation was represented as having the possibility of greater closeness than is now likely. And at a moment when notions of youthful solidarity and community were strong, we came to the conclusion that the ideal of friendship had become considerably less vivid than it once was.

We remarked on the circumstance that no one in the novels sought personal definition through achievement. For instance, to none of her heroines and to none of her male characters does Jane Austen attribute her own impulse to literary composition. In 1973 the "work ethic" was still under a cloud, yet I could not fail to see that for all their readiness to be wry about "performance" and "roles," the students expected the interest of life to be maintained by some enterprise requiring effort. But although they could perceive that the idea of vocation lent dignity to Mr. Gardner or Charles Bertram or Captain Wentworth, it did not occur to them to find alien to their conception a society in which most persons naturally thought that life consisted not of doing but only of being.

And then there was the question of the way and the degree in which a person might be morally conscious. The students were not in the least inclined to cynicism but they were gently amused when Eleanor Dashwood, in response to Marianne's question, says that what had sustained her in a bad time was the consciousness that she was doing her duty. They thought it downright quaint of Anne Elliot to say to Captain Wentworth that she had been right in submitting to Lady Russell because a "strong sense of duty is no bad part of a woman's portion," and we did what we could to take account of the cultural implications of that highly charged word "portion."

Inevitably we went into manners in its several meanings, including, of course, the one that Hobbes assigns to it when he says that manners are small morals. I sought to elicit an explanation of the legendary propriety of the novels in relation to what might be concluded about the sexual mores of the age and about those curious moments in the author's published letters which E. M. Forster speaks of as the "deplorable lapses of taste over carnality."

All this might well suggest that the direction of the discussion was toward subverting the basic assumption of humanistic literary pedagogy: so far from wishing to bring about the realization of how similar to ourselves are the persons of a past society, it was actually the dissimilarity between them and us that I pressed upon. At the time, I was conscious of no reason why I inclined to cast doubt upon the procedure by which humanism puts literature at the service of our moral lives, but my more or less random undertaking has since been given a measure of rationalization by certain formulations which have been put forward by a distinguished anthropologist.

I refer to the lecture, delivered in the spring of 1974, in which Professor Clifford Geertz examines the epistemology of cultures, asking what knowledge we can have of cultures unlike our own and what are the means by which we gain this knowledge.* The chief intention of the lecture is to say that, contrary to common belief, the faculty of empathy plays but a minimal part in the knowledge an anthropologist gains of unfamiliar cultures and to describe the means by which reliable understanding actually is achieved. Drawing upon his own experience, Mr. Geertz puts the matter thus:

*"From the Native's Point of View: On the Nature of Anthropological Understanding," *Bulletin of the American Academy of Arts and Sciences*, Vol. XXVIII, No. 1.

In all three of the societies I have studied intensively, Javanese, Balinese, and Moroccan, I have been concerned, among other things, with attempting to determine how the people who live there define themselves as persons, what enters into the idea they have (but . . . only half realize they have) of what a self, Javanese, Balinese, or Moroccan style, is.

He goes on:

In each case I have tried to arrive at this most intimate of notions not by imagining myself as someone else—a rice peasant or a tribal sheikh, and then seeing what I thought—but by searching out and analyzing the symbolic forms—words, images, institutions, behaviors—in terms of which, in each place, people actually represent themselves to themselves and to one another.

Mr. Geertz then specifies the method by which these symbolic forms are to be induced to yield up their meaning: he tells us that one follows "what Dilthey called the hermeneutic circle," in which a conceived whole is referred to its particularities and then the particularities are referred to the conceived whole, and so on in ceaseless alternation.

Mr. Geertz cites two examples of the hermeneutic circle, or, as it sometimes appears, the hermeneutic spiral. One of these is the process by which we comprehend a baseball game. "In order to follow a baseball game, one must understand what a bat, a hit, an inning, a left fielder, a squeeze play, a hanging curve, or a tightened infield are, and what the game in which these 'things' are elements is all about." The second example of the hermeneutic circle or spiral is one that I shall have occasion to return to. It is the attempt of "an *explication de texte* critic like Leo Spitzer" to interpret Keats's "Ode on a Grecian Urn." The attempt, Mr. Geertz says, will involve the critic in "repetitiously asking himself the alternating questions, 'What is the whole poem about?' and 'What exactly has Keats seen (or chosen to show us) depicted on the urn he is describing?'; at the end of an advancing spiral of general observations and specific remarks he emerges with a reading of the poem as an assertion of the aesthetic mode of perception over the historical."

With reference to the two examples of the hermeneutic process which Mr. Geertz considers appropriate to ethnology, he says, "In the same way, when a meanings-and-symbols ethnographer like myself attempts to find out what some pack of natives* conceives a person to be, he moves back and forth between asking himself, 'What is the general form of this life?' and 'What exactly are the vehicles in which that form is embodied?', emerging at the end of a similar sort of spiral with the notion that they see the self as a composite, or a persona, or a point in a pattern."

No student of literature can read Mr. Geertz's lecture without having it borne in upon him that anthropologists conceive unfamiliar cultures to be much more difficult to comprehend than do humanist scholars or the ordinary readers they instruct. Mr. Geertz spends years trying to discover the concepts on which the members of one or another unfamiliar culture base their sense of being persons or selves, and eventually, by following the hermeneutic circle or spiral, he is able to tell us what these concepts are. By and large, the humanist way of dealing with alien cultures feels itself to be under no such necessity. I recently read for the first time the well-known Icelandic story called "Audun and the Bear," which tells about a rather poorly-off man from the Westfirths who takes ship for Greenland and there buys a bear, said to be "an absolute treasure," which he wants to present as a gift to King Svein of Denmark; King Harald of Norway, Svein's enemy, would like to have this treasure of a bear for himself but behaves very well about it, and there follows a series of incidents in which Audun and the two kings adumbrate a transcendent ethos of magnanimity and munificence. I had no difficulty in "understanding" this story. I did exactly what Mr. Geertz says he does not do when he wants to arrive at the understanding of what a self is in an alien culture: I made use of empathy, I imagined myself someone else, a not very well-off man from the Westfirths, and this seemed to suit my purpose admirably, leading me to know all that I felt I needed to know about bears and their excellence, and kings, and gift-giving.

But actually, of course, if Mr. Geertz is right, I don't know anything at all about Audun and his bear and his two kings, or at best I know something that merely approximates the cultural fact—and it was in this pleasant but wholly imprecise way of empathy that my students knew the culture represented in Jane Austen's novels. Humanism brushes aside

---

*The phrase is used by Mr. Geertz with ironic force: it expresses his uneasiness over the condescension which is implicit in the situation of someone "studying" a group of strangers in whose land he sojourns.

the imprecision, and doubtless would brush aside gross error if it were proved; humanism takes the line that we are to be confident of our intuitive understanding of behavior in Iceland a thousand years ago; we understand it because it is part of "Western" culture and as such pretty directly continuous with our own culture of the present time. Just so we know all about Abraham or Achilles because of what we call the "Judaeo-Hellenic tradition," which constitutes a considerable part of the tradition we conceive ourselves to be in. Of course neither the Jews nor the Greeks thought like humanists—they believed that nothing could be, or should be, more incomprehensible than alien cultures, the ways that *goyim* or *barbaroi* chose to go about being persons or selves.

In thinking about the cultures of the past which are presumably continuous with our own, humanists of our time do of course acknowledge one striking and quite invincible alienation—they know that we of the present time may not do certain things that were done in the cultures of the past even though they are things upon which we bestow the very highest praise. For example, although we are of course enlightened and exalted and generally made better by the art of, say, Giotto or Michelangelo, we know that we must not make use of the idioms of their art or of the art of their epochs in our own creative enterprises. When we bring into conjunction with each other the certitude that great spiritual good is to be derived from the art of the past and the no less firmly held belief that an artistic style cannot be validly used in any age other than that in which it was invented, we confront what is surely one of the significant mysteries of man's life in culture.

It is at this point, when I may have succeeded in bringing at least a little complication to humanism's rather simple view of the relation in which our moral lives stand to other cultures, that I should like to recur to the second of the two examples offered by Mr. Geertz as he explains the hermeneutic circle. This is the one in which he speaks of Keats's "Ode on a Grecian Urn" as it is interpreted by a critic of Leo Spitzer's persuasion. Whether or not Mr. Geertz consciously framed the example to this end, we must see, I think, that Keats's poem bears decisively upon the question of how we respond to observed cultures.

I myself should not say of "Ode on a Grecian Urn," as Mr. Geertz does say, following Mr. Spitzer, that it asserts "the aesthetic mode of perception over the historical." Actually, indeed, I think that the poem may be said to assimilate the two modes to each other in that it conceives the essence of the aesthetic object as having *pastness* as one of its attributes. The aesthetic essence of what is depicted on the urn is that it will never proceed into the future; the culture of the little hillside town is no longer in process. This is true also of the dramatic action represented on the urn—although the lover pursues his beloved, it is of decisive consequence in the poem that neither he nor she is in motion; the distance between them will never change. They exist in an eternal present which momently becomes the past. In the comparison which the poem institutes between them and actual persons, they are represented as lacking in certain of the attributes of life, as being in some degree or in some sense *dead*, and it is in their being so that we find their significance.

This significance consists in the paradox that their motion is to be seen as fixity; its evanescence has, through representation, become permanence. In "Disorder and Early Sorrow" Thomas Mann speaks of the impulse of the historian—which of course is what the urn is explicitly said to be—to bring the processes of life to a stop so as to be able to conceive and, as it were, *possess*, a coherent and comprehensible event. "The past is immortalized; that is to say, it is dead," says the protagonist of the story, Professor Cornelius, ". . . and death is the root of godliness and of all abiding significance." And Mann suggests that this death, which brings everlastingness and abiding significance, may be a decisive element in personal love. The father in Mann's great story, who actually is a historian, wants his beloved little daughter to be always as she now is, as he now knows her and loves her; he fears the changes that the processes of life will bring. That is why, in a moment of distressing perception, he is able to say that in his love for his little daughter "there is something not perfectly right and good." He wishes to believe that he and she can exist in the fixity of conception, of art, like Keats's lovers, that forever will he love and she be a child and his darling; his desire is, in effect, that she forgo her development, or, to put the matter in Yeats's terms, her life in nature. It is not alone the art and thought of Yeats's Byzantium that has in it the element of fixity, of movelessness, or what I am calling death—all thought and art, all conceptual possession of the processes of life, even that form which we call love, has inherent in its celebration and sanctification of life some element of this negation of life. We seek to lay hold of the fluidity of time and to make perdurable the cherished moments of existence. Committed to will as we of the West are, we yet on certain occasions seek to qualify and even to negate its authority and to assert the life-affirming power of idea, or, to use the word that has been proposed by the latest translator of Schopenhauer's great work, to say that life is best affirmed by *representation*, by will realized and negated. Nowadays it is not often observed as a paradox of the human spirit in the West that, for all its devotion to will in action, it finds pleasure and the image of perfection in what is realized and brought to its end—in the perception that art, even when it is at pains to create the appearance of intense and vigorous action, has the effect of transmuting that which is alive into that which has the movelessness and permanence of things past, assimilating it in some part to death.

And surely what can be said of love and thought and art can also be said of culture, more, doubtless, of some cultures than of others, but in a measure of all cultures. Of the three cultures Mr. Geertz touches on his lecture, at least two of them, the Javanese and the Balinese, may readily be thought of as bringing life under the dominion of some form of conceptual or aesthetic "death." Javanese culture may indeed verge upon the bizarre in the overtness of its intention to control, up to the point of actually negating, what we think of as the characteristic processes of life.

Among the Javanese, Mr. Geertz tells us, the problem of the person or self is pursued with "the sort of intensity which would be very rare with us." The person is conceived by means of two dualities; the terms of one of them may be given as "inside"/"outside," of the other as "refined"/"vulgar." The goal of the Javanese person-system is to order inward feelings and outward actions in such a way that the result may be described as "refined" (or "polished," "exquisite," "ethereal," "subtle," "civilized": the native word is *alus*) rather than as "vulgar" (or "impolite," "insensitive," "rough," "uncivilized," "coarse": the native word is *kaser*). Mr. Geertz tells us how this effort is to be achieved:

> Through meditation the civilized man thins out his emotional life to a kind of constant hum; through etiquette, he both shields that life from external disruptions and regularizes his outer behavior in such a way that it appears to others as a predictable, undisturbing, elegant, and rather vacant set of choreographed motions and settled forms of speech.

It might, Mr. Geertz says, lie beyond our powers to take seriously the possibility of such a conception of selfhood, being kept from doing so "by our own notions of the intrinsic honesty of deep feeling and the moral importance of personal sincerity." Perhaps, he says, it can have credibility for us only when we have seen, as he has,

> a young man whose wife—a woman he has raised from childhood and who had been the center of his life—has suddenly and inexplicably died, greeting everyone with a set smile and formal apologies for his wife's absence and trying by mystical techniques to flatten out, as he himself put it, the hills and valleys of his emotion into an even level plain. ("That is what you have to do," he said to me, "be smooth inside and out.")

The Javanese sense of personhood is indeed at a far remove from our own, yet surely it is considerably more accessible to us than Mr. Geertz says it is. Doubtless if any of us were to see a friend respond to the death of his wife as the Javanese young man did, we would conclude that he was in a state of severe mental pathology. But when we regard the Javanese behavior apart from the context of our own lives, we do not, I think, experience an insuperable difficulty in giving credence to the concepts on which it is based, and, what is more, for many of us it will be not merely comprehensible but actually may have quite considerable charm.

If I try to account for the possibility of our forming this judgment, I almost certainly must begin by observing that the Javanese culture has as one of its definitive functions to induce its members to become as much as possible like works of art: the human individual is to have the shapedness, the coherence, the changelessness of an object, if not actually of high art, then at least of *vertu*. This, it needs scarcely be said, is at the furthest possible remove from the dominant avowed intentions of Western culture in regard to personhood, yet we ought to consider that not all the intentions of Western culture in regard to personhood are avowed, and that some of them, even though they are not actually dominant, are quite strong. However committed to expressive action and significant utterance the Western paradigm of personhood may be, the Western person, as I have suggested, is not wholly without the capability of finding value in what is fixed, moveless, and silent.

For example, it will not, I believe, carry us beyond the bounds of rationality if we consider whether there is not a similarity to be discerned between the charm which we can discover in the Javanese ideal of personhood as embodied in the young widower and the gratification which we experience as we watch a tragic drama approach its end. We know that soon now, for Hamlet or Macbeth or Lear, the process of destiny must come to a stop: a point is reached at which each hero ceases to be a manifestation of will and comes to exist for us as idea or representation, as an object completed and, as it were, perfected. We may speculate that somewhere involved in the tragic gratification is the security which we derive from seeing what is intrinsically and ineluctably painful when it is an element of the experience of will being transmuted into an object of representation, carried by appropriate death beyond the reach of contingency. Tragic drama generates and confirms a supposition which we cherish: that life may be transmuted into art and thus put into our possession and control.

The culture of Bali may not engage us for even so long as that of Java has done, though certainly it commands no less interest by its overt purpose of bringing life within the presumably reassuring categories of art. Mr. Geertz tells us "that there is in Bali a persistent and systematic attempt to stylize all aspects of personal expression to the point where anything idiosyncratic, anything characteristic of the individual mainly because he is who he is physically, psychologically, or biographically, is muted in favor of his assigned place in the continued, and so it is thought, never changing pageant that is Balinese life. It is dramatis personae, not actors, that in the proper sense really exist. Physically men come and go—mere incidents in a happenstance history of no importance even to themselves. But the masks they wear, the stage they occupy, the parts they play"—Mr. Geertz later particularizes such parts as "king," "grandmother," "third-born," "Brahman," all of them unimpassioned, or, as we say, undramatic parts—"and, most important, the spectacle they mount remain and comprise not the façade but the substance of things, not least the self. . . . There is no make-believe; of course players perish, but the play doesn't and it is the latter, the performed rather than the performer, that really matters."

It has become part of the jargon of our Western selfhood and society to speak of the "roles" which we "play," but this location manifestly has only a metaphorical intention as compared with the literal force that the idea of a dramaturgic existence has for the Balinese. Sometimes, Mr. Geertz tells us, it happens that a Balinese person becomes aware that there is a core of personality (as we would call it) which can break through and dissolve "the standardized public identity" and that for this to happen would be thought a disaster, though the normal expectation is that it will not happen but that all will go well, which is to say that the integrity of the dramaturgic mode will be maintained.

That people—that an organized culture—should deal with life in this way cannot fail, at some point in our encounter with the possibility, to be received incredulously. Life, we do indeed believe, is real, life is earnest, and for it to achieve a praiseworthy aesthetic condition through a negation of its lifelikeness is not its goal. Yet at the same time we cannot deny that in some fashion, for some reason, our hearts go out to this dramatis-personification of personhood, just as our hearts go out to the Javanese transformation of persons into objects of art or of *vertu*.

We of the West perhaps cannot ever do quite what the Balinese and the Javanese do in the way of turning life into art. We believe, indeed, that we ought not to do it. Yet there are moments of fantasy, of fantasy that may barely be conscious of what it is, in which we are drawn to deal with our personhood somewhat in this manner, when we find in the negation of the literal and immediate actuality of Western personhood such gratification as comes with the promise of integration or perfection of being. The communal life of the little town on Keats's Grecian urn is part of what is apostrophized in the poem as an "attitude" ("O Attic shape! Fair attitude!"), which is the technical term for an archaic device of dramaturgic presentation, that in which all the actors simultaneously "freeze," holding themselves motionless in whatever posture the moment of attitude has caught them. It is thus that the participants in the festival have their existence, and, yet more memorably, the two lovers, she fixed in the attitude of flight, he in that of pursuit. All these persons are imbued with life, yet they do not live as we live, we of the West. They are, in the matter of speaking I have taken license to use, touched with death, in that they are stopped in all vital process, made motionless and changeless, yet by very reason of the deprived condition of their existence, are thought to celebrate and perpetuate life.

This we understand, and at moments, as I have said, it makes a strong appeal to us. But then again, when we consciously regard such cultures as those of Java and Bali, we can be aware that, along with the complex gratification which we take in their approximation to art, there exists a certain condescension. Surely, we find ourselves asking, this cannot be the way cultures, or individuals, ought to confront their destinies, their lives as given? Surely it is not by being urged toward becoming a kind of simulacrum of art that life can be given its right meed of dignity? We of the West are never finally comfortable with the thought of life's susceptibility to being made into an aesthetic experience, not even when the idea is dealt with as one of the received speculations of our intellectual culture—sooner or later, for example, we find ourselves becoming uneasy with Schiller's having advanced, on the basis of Kant's aesthetic theory, the idea that life will be the better for transforming itself into art, and we are uneasy again with Huizinga's having advanced the proposition, on the basis of Schiller's views, that life actually does transform itself into art: we feel that both authors deny the earnestness and literalness—the necessity—of which, as we of the West ultimately feel, the essence of life consists.

It is, I think, open to us to believe that our alternations of view on this matter of life seeking to approximate art are not a mere display of cultural indecisiveness but, rather, that they constitute a dialectic, with all the dignity that inheres in that word. . . .

APPENDIXES

Under Forty

1944

It is never possible for a Jew of my generation to "escape" his Jewish origin. In order to be sure of this I have only to remember how, when I was a child beginning to read for pleasure, certain words would leap magnetically to my eye from the page before I had reached them in the text. One such word was "snake"; others were words of such sexual explicitness as a child is likely to meet in his reading; and there was the word "Jew." These were words, that is, which struck straight to the unconscious, where fear, shame, attraction and repulsion are indistinguishable. Yet there was no dramatic or even specific reason why the word "Jew" should produce (as it still produces) so deep, so visceral, a reverberation. I was never a victim of prejudice or persecution. My family was fairly well established; although my parents were orthodox in the form of their religion they had a strong impulse to partake of the general life and to want it for me. My childhood was spent in a comfortable New York suburb where a Jewish group formed around the synagogue an active community large enough to be both interesting and protective; at the same time we Jewish children were perfectly at home in the pleasant public school. Those were days in which Jews lived with an ampler hope than now; yet even then the word "Jew" could have for a Jewish child an emotional charge as strong as I have described.

A childhood feeling so intense obviously does not disappear. It is clear to me that my existence as a Jew is one of the shaping conditions of my temperament, and therefore I suppose it must have its effect on my intellect. Yet I cannot discover anything in my professional intellectual life which I can specifically trace back to my Jewish birth and rearing. I do not think of myself as a "Jewish writer." I do not have it in mind to serve by my writing any Jewish purpose. I should resent it if a critic of my work were to discover in it either faults or virtues which he called Jewish.

In what I might call my life as a citizen my being Jewish exists as a point of honor. The phrase is grandiloquent although I do not mean it to be. I can have no pride in seeing a long tradition, often great and heroic, reduced to this small status in me, for I give only a limited respect to points of honor: they are usually mortuary and monumental, they have being without desire. For me the point of honor consists in feeling that I would not, even if I could, deny or escape being Jewish. Surely it is at once clear how minimal such a position is—how much it hangs upon only a resistance (and even only a passive one) to the stupidity and brutality which make the Jewish situation as bad as it is.

The position I have described as mine is perhaps the position of most American writers of Jewish birth. It creates no surprise and no resentment until it is formulated. And when it is formulated it has, I suppose, a certain gracelessness—if only because millions of Jews are suffering simply because they have the heritage that I so minimize in my own intellectual life. I do not want to "answer" this confrontation—to do so, except at great length and with many modulations, could only make the position appear more graceless than it must seem to some. I would say, however, that we are on all sides required to imagine the unimaginable sufferings of masses of men and that while the most common failure of the imagination will certainly be insensibility, there is also the failure of merely symbolic action, of mere guilty gesture.

But the position I have described brings with it no feeling of guilt toward the American Jewish community. I hope I have enough knowledge and sympathy to understand what has led this community to its impasse of sterility, but understanding does not mitigate the perception of the unhappy fact. If what I have called my "point of honor" is minimal and even negative, if, that is, it does not *want* enough and is nothing more than a resistance to an external force, it seems to me that the position of the

American Jewish community is to be described in much the same way. There is, I know, much show and talk of affirmation, but only to the end that the negative, or neuter, elements may be made more acceptable. As I see it, the great fact for American Jews is their exclusion from certain parts of the general life and every activity of Jewish life seems to be a response to this fact.

Jewish religion is, I am sure, very liberal and intelligent and modern. Its function is to provide, chiefly for people of no strong religious impulse, a social and rational defense against the world's hostility. A laudable purpose surely, but not a sufficient basis for a religion; and one has only to have the experience of modern Judaism trying to deal with a death ritual to have the sense of its deep inner uncertainty, its lack of grasp of life which must eventually make even its rational social purpose quite abortive. Modern Jewish religion at its best may indeed be intelligent and soaked in university knowledge, but out of it there has not come a single voice with the note of authority—of philosophical, or poetic, or even of rhetorical, let alone of religious, authority.

Of Jewish cultural movements I know something at first hand, for I once served as a minor editor of a notable journal of Jewish culture. The effort this journal represented was, it even now seems to me, a generous one; but its results were sterile at best. I was deep in—and even contributed to—the literature of Jewish self-realization of which Ludwig Lewisohn was the best-known exponent. This was a literature which attacked the sin of "escaping" the Jewish heritage; its effect, it seems to me, was to make easier the sin of "adjustment" on a wholly neurotic basis. It fostered a willingness to accept exclusion and even to intensify it, a willingness to be provincial and parochial. It is in part accountable for the fact that the Jewish social group on its middle and wealthy levels—that is, where there is enough leisure to allow a conscious consideration of social and spiritual problems—is now one of the most self-indulgent and self-admiring groups it is possible to imagine.

To describe this situation is almost to account for it. And to account for it is, in one sense, to forgive it. But in one sense only: for history does not forgive the results of the unfortunate conditions it brings, and, contrary to the popular belief, suffering does not confer virtue. As the Jewish community now exists, it can give no sustenance to the American artist or intellectual who is born a Jew. And so far as I am aware, it has not done so in the past. I know of writers who have used their Jewish experience as the subject of excellent work; I know of no writer in English who has added a micromillimeter to his stature by "realizing his Jewishness," although I know of some who have curtailed their promise by trying to heighten their Jewish consciousness.

Preface to The Liberal Imagination

1950

The essays of this volume were written over the last ten years, the greater number within the last three or four years. I have substantially revised almost all of them, but I have not changed the original intent of any.

Although the essays are diverse in subject, they have, I believe, a certain unity. One way, perhaps the quickest way, of suggesting what this unity is might be to say that it derives from an abiding interest in the ideas of what we loosely call liberalism, especially the relation of these ideas to literature.

In the United States at this time liberalism is not only the dominant but even the sole intellectual tradition. For it is the plain fact that nowadays there are no conservative or reactionary ideas in general circulation. This does not mean, of course, that there is no impulse to conservatism or to reaction. Such impulses are certainly very strong, perhaps even stronger than most of us know. But the conservative impulse and the reactionary impulse do not, with some isolated and some ecclesiastical exceptions, express themselves in ideas but only in action or in irritable mental gestures which seek to resemble ideas.

This intellectual condition of conservatism and reaction will perhaps seem to some liberals a fortunate thing. When we say that a movement is "bankrupt of ideas" we are likely to suppose that it is at the end of its powers. But this is not so, and it is dangerous for us to suppose that it is so, as the experience of Europe in the last quarter-century suggests, for in the modern situation it is just when a movement despairs of having ideas that it turns to force, which it masks in ideology. What is more, it is not conducive to the real strength of liberalism that it should occupy the intellectual field alone. In the course of one of the essays of this book I refer to a remark of John Stuart Mill's in his famous article on Coleridge— Mill, at odds with Coleridge all down the intellectual and political line, nevertheless urged all liberals to become acquainted with this powerful conservative mind. He said that the prayer of every true partisan of liberalism should be,

> "Lord, enlighten thou our enemies . . ."; sharpen their wits, give acuteness to their perceptions and consecutiveness and clearness to their reasoning powers. We are in danger from their folly, not from their wisdom: their weakness is what fills us with apprehension, not their strength.

What Mill meant, of course, was that the intellectual pressure which an opponent like Coleridge could exert would force liberals to examine their position for its weaknesses and complacencies.

We cannot very well set about to contrive opponents who will do us the service of forcing us to become more intelligent, who will require us to keep our ideas from becoming stale, habitual, and inert. This we will have to do for ourselves. It has for some time seemed to me that a criticism which has at heart the interests of liberalism might find its most useful work not in confirming liberalism in its sense of general rightness but rather in putting under some degree of pressure the liberal ideas and assumptions of the present time. If liberalism is, as I believe it to be, a large tendency rather than a concise body of doctrine, then as that large tendency makes itself explicit, certain of its particular expressions are bound to be relatively weaker than others, and some even useless and mistaken. If this is so, then for liberalism to be aware of the weak or wrong expressions of itself would seem to be an advantage to the tendency as a whole.

Goethe says somewhere that there is no such thing as a liberal idea, that there are only liberal sentiments. This is true. Yet it is also true that certain sentiments consort only with certain ideas and not with others. What is more, sentiments become ideas by a natural and imperceptible process. "Our continued influxes of feeling," said Wordsworth, "are modified and directed by our thoughts, which are indeed the representatives of all our past feelings." And Charles Péguy said, "*Tout commence en mystique et finit en politique*"—everything begins in sentiment and assumption and finds its issue in political action and institutions. The converse is also true: just as sentiments become ideas, ideas eventually establish themselves as sentiments.

If this is so, if between sentiments and ideas there is a natural connection so close as to amount to a kind of identity, then the connection between literature and politics will be seen as a very immediate one. And this will seem especially true if we do not intend the narrow but the wide sense of the word politics. It is the wide sense of the word that is nowadays forced upon us, for clearly it is no longer possible to think of politics except as the politics of culture, the organization of human life toward some end or other, toward the modification of sentiments, which is to say the quality of human life. The word liberal is a word primarily of political import, but its political meaning defines itself by the quality of life it envisages, by the sentiments it desires to affirm. This will begin to explain why a writer of literary criticism involves himself with political considerations. These are not political essays, they are essays in literary criticism. But they assume the inevitable intimate, if not always obvious, connection between literature and politics.

The making of the connection requires, as I have implied, no great ingenuity, nor any extravagant manipulation of the word "literature" or, beyond taking it in the large sense specified, of the word "politics." It is a connection which is quickly understood and as quickly made and acted upon by certain governments. And although it is often resisted by many very good literary critics, it has for some time been accepted with enthusiasm by the most interesting of our creative writers; the literature of the modern period, of the last century and a half, has been characteristically political. Of the writers of the last hundred and fifty years who command our continuing attention, the very large majority have in one way or another turned their passions, their adverse, critical, and very intense passions, upon the condition of the polity. The preoccupation with the research into the self that has marked this literature, and the revival of the concepts of religion that has marked a notable part of it, do not controvert but rather support the statement about its essential commitment to politics.

When Mill urged liberals to read Coleridge, he had in mind not merely Coleridge's general power of intellect as it stood in critical opposition to the liberalism of the day; he had also in mind certain particular attitudes and views that sprang, as he believed, from Coleridge's nature and power as a poet. Mill had learned through direct and rather terrible experience what the tendency of liberalism was in regard to the sentiments and the imagination. From the famous "crisis" of his youth he had learned, although I believe he never put it in just this way, that liberalism stood in a paradoxical relation to the emotions. The paradox is that liberalism is concerned with the emotions above all else, as proof of which the word "happiness" stands at the very center of its thought, but in its effort to establish the emotions, or certain among them, in some sort of freedom, liberalism somehow tends to deny them in their full possibility. Dickens's *Hard Times* serves to remind us that the liberal principles upon which Mill was brought up, although extreme, were not isolated and unique, and the principles of Mill's rearing very nearly destroyed him, as in fact they did destroy the Louisa Gradgrind of Dickens's novel. And nothing is more touching than the passionate gratitude which Mill gave to poetry for having restored him to the possibility of an emotional life after he had lived in a despairing apathy which brought him to the verge of suicide. That is why, although his political and metaphysical disagreement with Coleridge was extreme, he so highly valued Coleridge's politics and metaphysics—he valued them because they were a poet's, and he hoped that they might modify liberalism's tendency to envisage the world in what he called a "prosaic" way and recall liberals to a sense of variousness and possibility. Nor did he think that there was only a private emotional advantage to be gained from the sense of variousness and possibility—he believed it to be an intellectual and political necessity.

Contemporary liberalism does not depreciate emotion in the abstract, and in the abstract it sets great store by variousness and possibility. Yet, as is true of any other human entity, the conscious and the unconscious life of liberalism are not always in accord. So far as liberalism is active and positive, so far, that is, as it moves toward organization, it tends to select the emotions and qualities that are most susceptible of organization. As it carries out its active and positive ends it unconsciously limits its view of the world to what it can deal with, and it unconsciously tends to develop theories and principles, particularly in relation to the nature of the human mind, that justify its limitation. Its characteristic paradox appears again, and in another form, for in the very interests of its great primal act of imagination by which it establishes its essence and existence—in the interests, that is, of its vision of a general enlargement and freedom and rational direction of human life—it drifts toward a denial of the emotions and the imagination. And in the very interest of affirming its confidence in the power of the mind, it inclines to constrict and make mechanical its conception of the nature of mind. Mill, to refer to him a last time, understood from his own experience that the imagination was properly the joint possession of the emotions and the intellect, that it was fed by the emotions, and that without it the intellect withers and dies, that without it the mind cannot work and cannot properly conceive itself. I do not know whether or not Mill had particularly in mind a sentence from the passage from Thomas Burnet's *Archaeologiae Philosophicae* which Coleridge quotes as the epigraph to *The Ancient Mariner*, the sentence in which Burnet says that a judicious belief in the existence of demons has the effect of keeping the mind from becoming "narrow, and lapsed entirely into mean thoughts," but he surely understood what Coleridge, who believed in demons as little as Mill did, intended by his citation of the passage. Coleridge wanted to enforce by that quaint sentence from Burnet what is the general import of *The Ancient Mariner* apart from any more particular doctrine that exegesis may discover—that the world is a complex and unexpected and terrible place which is not always to be understood by the mind as we use it in our everyday tasks.

It is one of the tendencies of liberalism to simplify, and this tendency is natural in view of the effort which liberalism makes to organize the elements of life in a rational way. And when we approach liberalism in a critical spirit, we shall fail in critical completeness if we do not take into account the value and necessity of its organizational impulse. But at the same time we must understand that organization means delegation, and agencies, and bureaus, and technicians, and that the ideas that can survive delegation, that can be passed on to agencies and bureaus and technicians, incline to be ideas of a certain kind and of a certain simplicity: they give up something of their largeness and modulation and complexity in order to survive. The lively sense of contingency and possibility, and of those exceptions to the rule which may be the beginning of the end of the rule—this sense does not suit well with the impulse to organization. So that when we come to look at liberalism in a critical spirit, we have to expect that there will be a discrepancy between what I have called the primal imagination of liberalism and its present particular manifestations.

The job of criticism would seem to be, then, to recall liberalism to its first essential imagination of variousness and possibility, which implies the awareness of complexity and difficulty. To the carrying out of the job of criticizing the liberal imagination, literature has a unique relevance, not merely because so much of modern literature has explicitly directed itself upon politics, but more importantly because literature is the human activity that takes the fullest and most precise account of variousness, possibility, complexity, and difficulty.

Preface to Beyond Culture

1965

From time to time the essays I have published are reproached for making use of the pronoun "we" in a way that is said to be imprecise and indiscriminate. Sometimes the objection is made with considerable irritation—the writer angrily declines to be included in the "we" that is being proposed, and denounces my presumptuousness in putting him where he does not belong. But one writer, reviewing a book of mine in *The Times Literary Supplement,* dealt with my "we" in a quiet and considerate way and inevitably his words came home to me. He said that when I spoke of what "we" think or feel it was often confusing because sometimes it meant "just the people of our time as a whole; more often still Americans in general; most often of all a very narrow class, consisting of New York intellectuals as judged by [my] own brighter students in Columbia."

This may well be an all too accurate description of my practice, although I would wish to claim for my awareness of the narrow class of New York intellectuals a rather fuller experience than is here imputed to me. For the rest, if I try to discern the range of my pronoun, I would say that it very likely does move among the entities of diverse size that the writer names. As a minor rhetorical device, employed in the effort to describe the temper of our age, it is not remarkable for its ingenuity, and I can see that it might be confusing: no doubt its implied assumption that there is a natural continuity among those groups so different in size involves me in loose and contradictory formulations.

Yet the assumption of cultural continuities is not easily put down. In the face of the chanciness of the generalizations it leads to, it insists on its interest and on its right to be tested. Between the intellectual temperament of an educated Englishman and an educated American the differences are very notable despite the common language and the easy flow of books and persons between the two countries. And if between England and America the differences are great, then how much greater are those between nations that do not have so many things in common. Yet the sense of the dissimilarities even between England and America must go along with the perception of what is similar or congruent in the cultures of the two nations, less in what they may be thought to derive from their respective pasts than in what they are in process of choosing from among the possibilities of the present. The differences are of rate or phase. The same may be said of certain of the differences among other nations. One cannot be aware of the large sub-culture (as we have learned to call it) of youth, of those characteristics that are shared by the young of many lands, without giving credence to the supposition that a world-wide continuity of culture tends to come into being and that it is possible to make predications about it.

If such predications can be made at all, even those that seem to be based on that "very narrow class" to which my fluctuating "we" has sometimes referred may have at least a tentative validity. The class of New York intellectuals is not remarkable for what it originates, and perhaps it says something about its nature that an eminent member of this class, an intelligent and eager-minded younger critic, could recently have found it possible to publish a volume of critical essays in which the sad word "sophisticated" was repeatedly used as a term of praise. Yet as a group it is busy and vivacious about ideas and, even more, about attitudes. Its assiduity constitutes an authority. The structure of our society is such that a class of this kind is bound by organic filaments to groups less culturally fluent which are susceptible to its influence. The great communications industries do not exactly rely for their content and methods upon the class of New York intellectuals, yet journalism and television show its effects. At least one of the ways in which the theater and the cinema prosper is by suiting the taste which this "narrow class" has evolved. And between this small class and an analogous class in, say, Nigeria, there is pretty sure to be a natural understanding.

If one speaks of the tendency toward homogeneity in modern culture, one is necessarily implicated in the semantic difficulties of the word "culture." These are notorious. Everyone is conscious of at least two meanings of the word. One of them refers to that complex of activities which includes the practice of the arts and of certain intellectual disciplines, the former being more salient than the latter. It is this meaning that we have in mind when we talk about popular culture as distinguished from "high" culture, or about a Ministry of Culture, or about the cultural attaché of an embassy.

The other meaning is much more inclusive. It comprises a people's technology, its manners and customs, its religious beliefs and organization, its systems of valuation, whether expressed or implicit. (If the people in question constitutes a highly developed modern nation, its social organization and its economy are usually excluded from the concept of culture and considered separately, although the reciprocal influence of social-economic and cultural factors are of course taken into account.) When the word is used in the second and larger sense, the extent of its reference includes a people's art and thought, but only as one element among others. The two meanings of the word, so different in their scope, permit us to say—it is a dubious privilege—that a certain culture sets a higher store by culture than does some other culture.

The title of this book is meant to propose both significations of the word. In its reference to the larger meaning, the phrase "beyond culture" can be said to make nonsense, for if all the implications of the word's definition are insisted on, it is not possible to conceive of a person standing beyond his culture. His culture has brought him into being in every respect except the physical, has given him his categories and habits of thought, his range of feeling, his idiom and tones of speech. No aberration can effect a real separation: even the forms that madness takes, let alone the way in which madness is evaluated, are controlled by the culture in which it occurs. No personal superiority can place one beyond these influences: the unique gifts of genius are understood to have been conditioned by the cultural conditions in which they developed; only in that time and place could they have appeared. Even when a person rejects his culture (as the phrase goes) and rebels against it, he does so in a culturally determined way: we identify the substance and style of his rebellion as having been provided by the culture against which it is directed.

Yet of course this total power that the strict definition of culture, in the large sense of the word, seems to claim for itself can have only a mere formal reality. The belief that it is possible to stand beyond the culture in some decisive way is commonly and easily held. In the modern world it is perhaps a necessary belief. When we turn from the large meaning of the word to the smaller, we readily see the extent to which the art and thought of the modern period assume that it is possible for at least some persons to extricate themselves from the culture into which they were born. Any historian of the literature of the modern age will take virtually for granted the adversary intention, the actually subversive intention, that characterizes modern writing—he will perceive its clear purpose of de-taching the reader from the habits of thought and feeling that the larger culture imposes, of giving him a ground and a vantage point from which to judge and condemn, and perhaps revise, the culture that produced him.

What I am calling the modern period had its beginning in the latter part of the eighteenth century and its apogee in the first quarter of the twentieth century. We continue the direction it took. The former energy of origination is very much diminished, but we still do continue the di-rection: the conscious commitment to it is definitive of the artistic and in-tellectual culture of our time. It is a belief still pre-eminently honored that a primary function of art and thought is to liberate the individual from the tyranny of his culture in the environmental sense and to permit him to stand beyond it in an autonomy of perception and judgment.

But if the program of our present artistic and intellectual culture has not changed from that of forty or fifty years ago, the circumstances in which it has its existence have changed materially. In the doctrinal way its relation to the inclusive culture is pretty much what it once was; in the ac-tual and operative way the relation is very different. The difference can be expressed quite simply, in numerical terms—there are a great many more people who adopt the adversary program than there formerly were. Be-tween the end of the first quarter of this century and the present time there has grown up a populous group whose members take for granted the idea of the adversary culture. This group is to be described not only by its increasing size but by its increasing coherence. It is possible to think of it as a class. As such, it of course has its internal conflicts and contradictions, but also its common interests and presuppositions and a considerable efficiency of organization, even of an institutional kind.

The present position of the university in American life tells us much about this new state of affairs. Dr. Clark Kerr recently set forth his vision of the super-university he expects to come into being. His prophecy stipulates that this intellectual imperium, to which he gives the Baconian name of Ideopolis, shall provide a commodious place for what Dr. Kerr calls "pure creative effort," that is to say, the arts. There will perhaps be some people who regard this prospect with dismay. They will be moved by certain apprehensions which once commonly attended thoughts of bigness, of institutions, and of the academic, all of which were believed to be fatal to art. Their fears are surely anachronistic. No one who knows how things now really stand is afraid of the university. Dr. Kerr's prophecy is but a reasonable projection into the future of a condition already established and regarded with satisfaction by those who might be thought to be most jealous for the freedom of art and thought.

Three or four decades ago the university figured as the citadel of conservatism, even of reaction. It was known that behind what used to be called its walls and in its ivory towers reality was alternately ignored and traduced. The young man who committed himself to an academic career was understood to have announced his premature surrender. Now it is scarcely possible for him to be so intransigent that the university cannot be thought the proper field for his undertakings. Between the university and reality there now exists the happiest, most intimate relation. Nothing in life is so mundane and practical or so rarefied and strange that the university will not take it into sympathetic consideration.

In two of the essays of this volume I have referred to Mr. Harold Rosenberg's account of one of the conditions in which our taste in painting nowadays exists, that is, under the constantly exerted influence of a very active and authoritative criticism which is able to bring about rapid and radical changes in our aesthetic views. Objects that at one moment are not to be thought of as deserving inclusion in the category of art are at another moment firmly established in the category; criticism can also reverse this process, and our most cherished works of art (Mr. Rosenberg gives as examples the paintings of Michelangelo, Vermeer, Goya, and Cézanne) can, if an "extreme ideology" so decides, be made "not art" and may even come to seem "creatures of darkness." In the process itself there is nothing very new; for about two hundred years taste has increasingly come under the control of criticism, which has made art out of what is not art and the other way around. What *is* new is the nature of the critical agent, which perhaps explains the expeditious power it is said to have—Mr. Rosenberg tells us that the making and unmaking of art is in the hands of university art departments and the agencies which derive from them, museums and professional publications.

I cite the changed character of the university as but an example, although a particularly striking one, of the new circumstances in which the adversary culture of art and thought now exists. The change has come about, we may say, through the efforts of the adversary culture itself. It has not dominated the whole of its old antagonist, the middle class, but it has detached a considerable force from the main body of the enemy and has captured its allegiance.

The situation calls for at least a little irony. Given the legend of the free creative spirit at war with the bourgeoisie, it isn't possible to be wholly grave as we note, say, the passion that contemporary wealth feels for contemporary painting. But not more than a little irony is appropriate. For how else are civilizations ever formed save by reconciliations that were once unimaginable, save by syntheses that can be read as paradoxes? It is often true that the success of a social or cultural enterprise compromises the virtues that claimed our loyalty in its heroic, hopeless beginning, but there is a kind of vulgarity in the easy assumption that this is so always and necessarily.

Yet around the adversary culture there has formed what I have called a class. If I am right in identifying it in this way, then we can say of it, as we say of any other class, that it has developed characteristic habitual responses to the stimuli of its environment. It is not without power, and we can say of it, as we can say of any other class with a degree of power, that it seeks to aggrandize and perpetuate itself. And, as with any other class, the relation it has to the autonomy of its members makes a relevant question, and the more, of course, by reason of the part that is played in the history of its ideology by the ideal of autonomy. There is reason to believe that the relation is ambiguous.

Most of the essays in this volume were written out of an awareness of this ambiguity. Some of them propose the thought that we cannot count upon the adversary culture to sustain us in such efforts toward autonomy of perception and judgment as we might be impelled to make, that an adversary culture of art and thought, when it becomes well established, shares something of the character of the larger culture to which it was—to which it still is—adversary, and that it generates its own assumptions and preconceptions, and contrives its own sanctions to protect them. The early adversary movement of European art and thought, it has been said, based itself on the question, "Is it true? Is it true for me?" The characteristic question of our adversary culture is, "Is it true? Is it true for us?" This a good question, too, it has its particular social virtues, but it does not yield the same results as the first question, and it may even make it harder for anyone to ask the first question. The difference between the force of the two questions is suggested by the latter part of my essay on Freud. The second question is asked by the group of psychiatrists to whom I refer; it serves an unquestionably useful purpose. The first question was asked by Freud himself.

Several of the essays touch on the especial difficulty of making oneself aware of the assumptions and preconceptions of the adversary culture by reason of the dominant part that is played in it by art. My sense of this difficulty leads me to approach a view which will seem disastrous to many readers and which, indeed, rather surprises me. This is the view that art does not always tell the truth or the best kind of truth and does not always point out the right way, that it can even generate falsehood and habituate us to it, and that, on frequent occasions, it might well be subject, in the interests of autonomy, to the scrutiny of the rational intellect. The history of this faculty scarcely assures us that it is exempt from the influences of the cultures in which it has sought its development, but at the present juncture its informing purpose of standing beyond any culture, even an adversary one, may be of use.

"The world doesn't fear a new idea. It can pigeonhole any idea. But it can't pigeonhole a new experience." This statement of D. H. Lawrence's is often quoted. It is a saying that has a canonical authority in our adversary culture, and it does indeed tell us much of what that culture, in its great days, intended in the way of liberation, in the way of autonomy. By an experience Lawrence meant, of course, an experience of art, and, we may suppose, of such art as derives from an experience of life. Lawrence's saying suggests that the experience speaks, as no idea ever can, to the full actuality of the person who exposes himself to it, requiring him to respond in an active way; by that response he is confirmed in his sense of personal being and its powers, and in the possibility of autonomy. If Lawrence's statement is true, surely its truth pertains to a situation in which the artist is alone and in which his audience is small and made up of isolate individuals. It has much less truth now that we are organized for the reception and accommodation of new experiences. Thus, in the process of making and unmaking art that Mr. Rosenberg describes, it is plain that experiences of painting, even of a very intense kind, submit quite docilely to being pigeonholed. Every group that organizes itself around an experience constitutes an effective pigeonhole, with the result that the demarcation between experience and idea that Lawrence took for granted as clear and certain is now hard to discern. In our adversary culture such experience as is represented in and proposed by art moves toward becoming an idea, even an ideology, as witness the present ideational and ideological status of sex, violence, madness, and art itself. If in this situation the rational intellect comes into play, it may be found that it works in the interests of experience.

Bibliographical Notes

"The America of John Dos Passos." A review of *U.S.A.* by John Dos Passos, in *Partisan Review*, April 1938; republished posthumously in *Speaking of Literature and Society*, New York: Harcourt Brace Jovanovitch, 1980.

"Hemingway and His Critics." A review of *The Fifth Column* and *The First Forty-Nine Stories* by Ernest Hemingway, in *Partisan Review*, Winter 1939; republished posthumously in *Speaking of Literature and Society*, 1980.

"T. S. Eliot's Politics." An essay originally entitled "Elements That Are Wanted," in *Partisan Review*, September–October 1940; Trilling considered and rejected it for inclusion in *The Liberal Imagination* and it was published posthumously in *Speaking of Literature and Society*, 1980.

"The Immortality Ode." A lecture at the English Institute, September 1941. Published in *The English Institute Annual, 1941*, Columbia University Press, 1942; republished in *The Liberal Imagination*, New York: The Viking Press, 1950.

"Kipling." First published in *The Nation*, October 16, 1943; republished in *The Liberal Imagination*, 1950.

"Reality in America." Part 1 was in *Partisan Review*, January–February 1940, and Part 2 in *The Nation*, April 20, 1946; they appeared as one article in *The Liberal Imagination*, 1950.

"Art and Neurosis." First published in *Partisan Review*, Winter 1945. Some of the material added in this final version appeared in *The New Leader*, December 13, 1947. The entire essay was in *The Liberal Imagination*, 1950.

"Manners, Morals, and the Novel." A lecture at the Conference on the Heritage of the English-Speaking Peoples and Their Responsibilities, Kenyon College, September

1947. First published in *The Kenyon Review*, Winter 1948; republished in *The Liberal Imagination*, 1950.

"The Kinsey Report." A review of *Sexual Behavior in the Human Male* by Alfred C. Kinsey, Wardell B. Pomeroy, and Clyde E. Martin, in *Partisan Review*, April 1948; republished in *The Liberal Imagination*, 1950.

"Huckleberry Finn." An introduction to *The Adventures of Huckleberry Finn* by Mark Twain, New York: Rinehart, 1948; republished in *The Liberal Imagination*, 1950.

"*The Princess Casamassima*." An introduction to *The Princess Casamassima* by Henry James, New York: Macmillan, 1948; republished in *The Liberal Imagination*, 1950.

"Wordsworth and the Rabbis." A lecture given at the celebration of the centenary of Wordsworth's death held at Princeton University, April 21–22, 1950. It was published (under the title "Wordsworth and the Iron Time") in *The Kenyon Review*, Summer 1950, and in *Wordsworth: Centenary Studies Presented at Cornell and Princeton Universities*, edited by Gilbert T. Dunklin, Princeton: Princeton University Press, 1951; republished in *The Opposing Self*, New York: The Viking Press, 1955.

"William Dean Howells and the Roots of Modern Taste." A lecture given at Harvard University in 1951, first published in *Partisan Review*, September–October 1951; republished in *The Opposing Self*, 1955.

"The Poet as Hero: Keats in his Letters." An introduction to *The Selected Letters of John Keats* (The Great Letters series, edited by Louis Kronenberger), New York: Farrar, Straus and Young, 1951; republished in *The Opposing Self*, 1955.

"George Orwell and the Politics of Truth." An introduction to *Homage to Catalonia* by George Orwell, New York: Harcourt, Brace, 1952; reprinted in *Commentary*, March 1952, and republished in *The Opposing Self*, 1955.

"The Situation of the American Intellectual at the Present Time." First published (in a shorter version) in *Partisan Review*, 1952, and in *Perspectives*, 1953; republished in *A Gathering of Fugitives*, Boston: Beacon Press, 1956.

"*Mansfield Park*." The chapter on Jane Austen for the *Pelican Guide to English Literature*, Volume V, edited by Boris Ford, which also appeared in *Partisan Review*, September–October 1954; republished in *The Opposing Self*, 1955.

"Isaac Babel." An introduction to *The Collected Stories of Isaac Babel*, New York: Criterion Books, 1955; reprinted in *Commentary*, June 1955; republished in *Beyond Culture*, New York: The Viking Press, 1965.

"The Morality of Inertia." A lecture at the Institute for Religious and Social Studies, 1955, first published in *Great Moral Dilemmas*, New York: Harper & Bros., 1956; republished in *A Gathering of Fugitives*, 1956.

" 'That Smile of Parmenides Made Me Think.' " First published in *The Griffin* (bulletin of The Readers' Subscription), 1956; republished in *A Gathering of Fugitives*, 1956.

"The Last Lover." A review of *Lolita* by Vladimir Nabokov, in *The Griffin* (bulletin of The Readers' Subscription), August 1958; republished in *Encounter*, October 1958; republished posthumously, with the author's final revisions, in *Speaking of Literature and Society*, 1980.

"A Speech on Robert Frost: A Cultural Episode." Published in *Partisan Review*, Summer 1959.

"On the Teaching of Modern Literature." First published (under the title "On the Modern Element in Modern Literature") in *Partisan Review*, January–February 1961; republished in *Beyond Culture*, 1965.

"The Leavis-Snow Controversy." First published (under the title "A Comment on the Leavis-Snow Controversy") in *Commentary*, June 1962; republished in *Beyond Culture*, 1965.

"The Fate of Pleasure." First published in *Partisan Review*, Summer 1963; republished in *Beyond Culture*, 1965.

"James Joyce in His Letters." A review of the three-volume edition of *The Letters of James Joyce*, edited by Stuart Gilbert and Richard Ellmann, New York: The Viking Press, 1967; in *Commentary*, February 1968; republished posthumously in *The Last Decade*, New York: Harcourt Brace Jovanovitch, 1979.

"Mind in the Modern World." The first Thomas Jefferson Lecture in the Humanities sponsored by the National Endowment for the Humanities, Spring 1972; published as a small book by The Viking Press, 1973.

"Art, Will, and Necessity." A rewritten version of a lecture delivered at Cambridge University, 1973; published posthumously in *The Last Decade*, 1979.

"Why We Read Jane Austen." A lecture prepared for the Jane Austen Conference, University of Alberta, Canada, October 1975. It was left incomplete at Trilling's death on November 5, 1975, and published in *The Times Literary Supplement*, March 5, 1976; republished posthumously in *The Last Decade*, 1979.

"Under Forty." A contribution to a symposium on American Literature and the Younger Generation of American Jews, published in *Contemporary Jewish Record*, February 1944; republished posthumously in *Speaking of Literature and Society*, 1980.

Preface to *The Liberal Imagination*, 1950.

Preface to *Beyond Culture*, 1965.

Index